MAKING STRATEGY

MAKING STRATEGY

The Journey of Strategic Management

COLIN EDEN
AND
FRAN ACKERMANN

SAGE Publications
London • Thousand Oaks • New Delhi

SAGE Publications Ltd
6 Bonhill Street
London EC2A 4PU

SAGE Publications Inc.
2455 Teller Road
Thousand Oaks, California 91320

SAGE Publications India Pvt Ltd
32, M-Block Market
Greater Kailash – I
New Delhi 110 048

British Library Cataloguing in Publication data

A catalogue record for this book is available
from the British Library

ISBN 0 7619 5224 1
ISBN 0 7619 5225 X (pbk)

Library of Congress catalog record available

Typeset by Mayhew Typesetting, Rhayader, Powys
Printed in Great Britain by The Cromwell Press Ltd,
Trowbridge, Wiltshire

CONTENTS

Preface – Anne Huff   vii

Acknowledgements   ix

Using the cross referencing system   xi

PART 1: Theory and Concepts   1

Chapter C1
The JOURNEY of Strategy Making   1

Chapter C2
Strategy making as a JOURNEY   20

Chapter C3
The Political Feasibility of Strategy   45

Chapter C4
The Art of Good JOURNEY Making: working with strategy making *teams*   63

Chapter C5
Detecting Emergent Strategizing   79

Chapter C6
Developing Strategic Intent: exploring competencies and developing the business model   102

Chapter C7
Stakeholder Analysis *and* Management   113

Chapter C8
Managing Alternative Futures: strategic adaptability and opportunism   136

Chapter C9
Strategy Making Closure   158

Chapter C10
The JOURNEY Making Model: a summary   181

PART 2: Vignettes   189

PART 3: Practice: Methods, Techniques, and Tools   281

Introduction   281

Chapter P1
Detecting Emergent Strategizing: individual interviews and cognitive mapping   284

Chapter P2
Detecting Emergent Strategizing: working with strategy making teams – the Oval Mapping
Technique   303

Chapter P3
Strategy Making: working with teams – computer supported group workshops   321

Chapter P4
Strategy Making: working with teams – managing stakeholding and alternative futures 341

Chapter P5
Managing Process: designing interventions and facilitating groups   371

Chapter P6
Analysis: maps and models for workshops   399

Chapter P7
Delivering Strategy: closure – strategic programmes and strategy delivery support 424

Chapter P8
Delivering Strategy: communication, management, and review   452

Chapter P9
The Intervention: the facilitator and the client   475

References   485

Name Index   499

Subject Index   503

PREFACE

In the last few decades we have been led astray by airport books with sound-bite steps to strategic success, and elegant but equally unrealistic simplifications from theoreticians. In practice, strategy making is an ongoing, messy, incomplete process – as all who do sustained work in organizations know. I highly recommend *Making Strategy* because it provides both practical and theoretic insights into this complex reality.

Strategy is sometimes viewed as unnecessary, even harmful. Colin Eden and Fran Ackermann have the experience with public and private organizations to illustrate its utility. The theoretical discussion in the first third of the book develops a valuable view of contemporary strategy: an intermittent but ongoing effort, often driven by the need for change, responding to multiple stakeholders. The authors urge strategy makers to avoid the urge to 'blueprint', and even suggest that deliberate strategizing is not always wise. On the other hand, they recognize that many companies seek ways to change their current way of operating. Because these changes inevitably alter power relations, they give careful attention to the politics of strategy making. Consideration of this important topic alone sets *Making Strategy* apart from almost all other strategy texts.

In the second section of the book the authors illustrate their efforts to help clarify and possibly change strategy in a wide range of organizations. These vignettes clarify good theorizing in practice, and are thus of interest to both academics and managers. I believe the book makes a major contribution to the literature by respecting managerial intelligence, but suggesting what the outside academic can contribute to improving performance.

In addition to giving a feel for the way in which strategy can be jointly negotiated, the occasional mishaps and frequent uncertainties they are willing to describe actually create confidence in the methods outlined in the third part of the book. The authors use interactive, sometimes computer-supported, techniques to help top management teams and other stakeholders express and synthesize their knowledge and aspirations. A primary tool is the generation of a 'cognitive map' – visual causal connections that Eden and Ackermann organize in various ways to both improve understanding and connect operations with more general objectives.

The detailed discussions found in the tools section of the book are very useful even for those who are not committed to replicating the entire process outlined. For example, the section on setting up a workshop offers many practical tips of value to all who work with groups (for example, start with coffee to minimize the frustration caused by latecomers). Each chapter also has a 'yes, but' section which anticipates questions from those who are closely following the authors' agenda.

In short, *Making Strategy* provides a needed bridge between practice and theory. The steps it suggests are more complex than the average book written for a managerial audience; the theory it suggests is richer than the average book written for academics. It's a needed report from two individuals who are attending to the immediate needs of organizations, while satisfying a longer term objective to understand how these needs can be more effectively met.

Anne Huff
Professor of Strategic Management
University of Colorado at Boulder
and President of the Academy of Management

ACKNOWLEDGEMENTS

We would never have set out on this 'journey' without support from Tony Knight and Ashok Hegde in the early 1980s. They provided corporate settings in which to develop and test initial ideas. Our 'journey' of writing would never have been completed without continual nagging from John Bryson and Chuck Finn, who never ceased to have faith in our work. Both of us also thank our good friend Sue Jones for her encouragement and constructive criticism over a number of years. Steve Cropper started this 'journey' with us, and his initial thinking was an influence on the shape of the book; however, he moved to follow new interests which left him with little time to contribute further.

For us, an important part of this book is the contribution the vignettes make to illustrating both theory and practice. However, it is always difficult for the clients of strategic change processes to see their story in black and white. Nevertheless they have all appreciated our wish to make public their experiences and have, for the most part, been willing and able to 'sign off' their vignette without changes that would have sanitized the account. We thank them all.

Fran would particularly like to acknowledge support from Bob Bostrom and the University of Georgia for not only providing a wonderful place to write some of the book, but also loaning her a computer after the 'Great Fire' which completely destroyed the Terry School of Business in August 1995 and her computer! Colin is grateful for the opportunity of lengthy, and often heated, discussions with Kees van der Heijden as they have both sought to design and teach jointly an MBA programme in Strategic Management. Kees's book and ours were always intended to complement each other – reflecting a common orientation – however, the involvement of clients in the production schedule inevitably slowed publication of this book. We hope that readers of this book will feel persuaded to explore his book also.

Finally we offer our thanks to John Bryson, Ann Huff, Geraldine De Sanctis and Karl Weick, for being prepared to read the book in manuscript form, and for liking it.

Note

The single user software referred to throughout the book is Decision Explorer and the networked system is Group Explorer. Information about Decision Explorer can be found at hhtp://www.scolari.co.uk and for Group Explorer http://www.phrontis.com/.

USING THE CROSS REFERENCING SYSTEM

In order to help readers move around the three parts of the book we have developed a cross referencing system. This system acts as a 'hyper-text' like format, enabling readers to gain clues about 'what the techniques might look like in practice' (The Vignettes), 'how the techniques can be adopted' (Practice: Methods, Techniques and Tools) and 'why the techniques and methods have been devised' (Theory and Concepts).

Thus readers, for example researcher/academics, wanting to learn more about the JOURNEY Making methodology might concentrate on the *Theory and Concepts*; other readers, possibly practitioners, wishing to use some or all of the methodology might focus on the *Practical* part, with both of these types of reader dipping into the *Vignettes* when illustration is required. Finally MBA students who will be expected during their studies to learn about the various methods, theories, and approaches to strategy but who also will wish to know how to put what they have learnt into practice should find the integrated nature of the book helpful.

To use the cross referencing system identify the **word or phrase** that you are interested in (marked in bold in the text) and then move to the cross references at the end of the line in the text.

Select either the V/C/P cross reference (Vignettes, Concepts or Practice). For example, if you are reading about a particular topic in the Theory and Concepts section and you would like to see how it worked in an organizational setting then it is a simple matter of looking up the vignette page number. V34 given at the end of the paragraph indicates GO TO page 34 of Part 2: Vignettes.

Where more than one word or phrase is in bold on the same line, a colon separates the cross references.

THEORY AND CONCEPTS

CHAPTER C1

THE JOURNEY OF STRATEGY MAKING

'JOURNEY'
JOintly Understanding, Reflecting, and NEgotiating strategY

Introduction

This book presents an approach to strategy making designed to assist most organizations develop strategy appropriate to their size, purpose, and resources. The book seeks to:

1 outline the *concepts and theories* supporting this approach;
2 *illustrate*, through vignettes from real cases, the issues intrinsic to attending to the *process* of strategy making;
3 provide a *guide to methods, techniques and tools* that can help an organization make strategies which have some chance of being implemented.

These three aims are reflected in the three part structure of the book.
   Part 1 introduces the cycle, what we shall call the JOURNEY, of strategy making and sets out *the arguments* for recognizing strategy making as predominantly process oriented. Key themes are:

- the crucial significance of *political feasibility*;
- the role of *participation*;
- emphasis on *stakeholder management* as well as stakeholder analysis;
- thinking about *alternative futures* within the overall process of strategy making;
- the link between *strategy making and organizational change*;
- using computer assistance as *support to the strategy making team*, for organizational learning, and for strategy delivery.

Part 2 presents vignettes from a *range of organizations*, each of which involved the authors in engagements lasting from one day to several months to many years. The organizations differ in scale, culture, size, management styles, problems to be tackled, and ways of dealing with strategy making. They illustrate some of the most fascinating and difficult issues in strategy making. Two-thirds of the vignettes come from a range of public or quasi-public organizations, and the remainder are from the private sector, where the authors were constrained in their use of examples because of the demands of confidentiality. The vignettes are true (at least from the authors' perspective), have been validated by the clients within the organizations, and are presented as an unfolding story to give the reader a sense of the contingent nature of strategy making in practice. Although the vignettes presented are from UK organizations, they are excellent examples of similar work undertaken in North America.

Part 3 provides detailed *practical guidelines and procedures* for using the methods, techniques, and tools employed in the cases. Although most of these techniques have been developed by the authors, some of them draw on the practice of management scientists, management consultants, community leaders, organizational development facilitators, and of course strategic planners. This part of the book introduces the role of computer software to help manage the data of strategic thinking and manage group processes, although reading the book and applying the approach in practice is not dependent upon knowledge or use of the software.

Each part is cross referenced to the others through key phrases shown in bold type and accompanied by the relevant chapters and page numbers of the other parts. For example, throughout part 2, episodes within the vignettes cross refer to both the theories and concepts which supported the interventions, and to the tools and techniques that were employed. Using this system a reader can dip into any part of the book which is of interest and subsequently be drawn into the other parts. Managers may start reading the vignettes and then be drawn to the theory and concepts used to guide practice. Consultants may join the book in the methods and practice part and be led to the vignettes as examples of the methods in action. Academics and students may begin with the concepts underpinning our approach to the process of strategy making, and move from these to the vignettes and methods.

The reader is *not* expected to take away from the book a precisely replicable recipe for working, but rather to have reviewed ideas, techniques, and vicarious experiences that can assist their thinking and practice. In particular, the practitioner/manager should be able to apply the theory and practice contained in this book in a manner that addresses the contingencies of their own situation and organizational setting. Indeed, by following the tenets of this book the management team of an organization may create a practical and **deliverable strategy within the space of a single day**. A strategy so created will not be well refined or 'correct' but it will be a good start. Alternatively, and more typically, a management team might spend 10–15 days together over several weeks or

V224

months, and choose to involve actively other managers. These 'workshop' days may or may not involve an internal or external facilitator. Larger organizations with more resources at their disposal may wish to supplement many of the process oriented analyses we describe with more thoroughgoing 'backroom' analyses. These are not discussed here for there is no shortage of strategic management texts which provide help in how to set about such analyses.

The approach we take is suited to public, private, and not-for-profit organizations. Some might argue that this assertion discounts fundamental differences between these types of organizations. For example Nutt and Backoff (1992:24–30) suggest clear differences between public and private organizations. They focus on environmental, transactional, and organizational process differences and argue that the degree of *publicness* is an important differentiating factor leading to alternative approaches to strategy making. Our view is that these differences are less acute now than they were a decade ago. We do not ignore them, but rather allow the approach we use to encompass them. The approach has been used effectively many times in each of the three sectors within organizations in North America as well as the UK.

The rest of this chapter looks in more detail at what we mean by strategy and strategic management, going on to consider *contingencies* in the design of the most appropriate approach to take to strategic management in different organizations.

Strategy and Strategic Management

The term *strategy* is derived from the Greek 'strategos' meaning a general set of manoeuvres carried out to overcome an enemy. What is notable here is the focus upon a *general*, not specific, set of manoeuvres. Specific sets of manoeuvres are seen as within the local jurisdiction of those concerned with translating the strategy into operations. We go beyond this level of generality and examine strategy as something that is more obviously and clearly linked to operations, and, at the very least, provides a framework within which 'everyday' issues and problems are dealt with.

Strategic management is, for us, a way of regenerating an organization, through continuous attention to a vision of what the people who make up an organization wish to do. It is a pro-active process of *seeking to change the organization*, its stakeholders (in as much as they are different from the organization), and the context, or 'environment', within which it seeks to attain its aspirations. It is, particularly, about stretching the organization (see Hamel and Prahalad (1993)) to gain leverage from its individuality – its *distinctive competencies* and ability to change them. Strategic management involves creating and moulding the future, along with making sense of the past, constructing rather than simply predicting, and responding to, some predetermined future reality. It is also importantly about developing the capability for long term flexibility and *strategic opportunism* rather than making and sticking to long term plans.

V201   **Emergent strategizing** is a key concept for us. It addresses the way in which most organizations demonstrate patterns of decision making, thinking, and action, often 'taken for granted' ways of working and problem solving coming from the habits, history, and 'hand-me-downs' of the organization's culture. Whether the organization members are aware of this *or not*, even if they define themselves as 'muddling through' rather than acting strategically, such enacted patterns inevitably take the organization in one strategic direction rather than another. Organizations do not act randomly, without purpose. It is this process of going in one strategic direction rather than another, based on patterns or 'recipes' of perceiving and acting (Calori *et al*, 1998; Spender, 1989; 1998) that we call 'emergent strategizing'. Thus, we contend that any organization, big or small, *will* be acting strategically whether the emergent strategizing is quite unselfconscious, or rather more deliberate, as, for example, when there is a knowing reinforcement of the existing ways of working by key members of the organization in pursuit of particular outcomes or purpose. In either case the emergent strategic direction (Mintzberg, 1987), and its implicit or explicit goals and purpose, are detectable and, to a greater or lesser degree, amenable to change. For some organizations we can envisage this implicit or 'emergent' strategy to be best *for that particular organization*.

We thus relate the notion of strategy, and so strategic management, to a number of important statements about organizations:

'The crucial activities for decision-making are not separate episodes of analysis. Instead, they are actions, whose controlled execution *consolidates fragments of policy that are lying around*, gives them direction, and closes off other possible arrangements' (Weick, 1983:xix) (our emphasis).

'Policy making is typically a never ending process of successive steps in which continual nibbling is a substitute for a good bite' (Lindblom, 1980).

'Emergent strategy means, literally, *unintended order*'. 'Strategy [is] *pattern in action*' (Mintzberg, 1990a) (our emphases).

It follows that we see effective strategy as *a coherent set of individual discrete actions in support of a system of goals, and which are supported as a portfolio by a self-sustaining critical mass, or momentum, of opinion in the organization*.

A crucial outcome from strategic management, and so the journey of strategy making, is that of agreeing a *sense of strategic direction* – a mission, vision, strategic intent, or framework within which strategizing takes place. The expression of this strategic direction is a statement that explicitly states the basis on which the organization will do business (*its aspirations or goals*), *satisfy its key stakeholders*, and *co-exist with its environment*. For the private sector this is an expression of the 'business model' – the idea that will convert purposeful activity into revenue and profit – and in the public or not-for-profit sectors the 'livelihood scheme' – the *rightful* purpose of its existence as a public or charitable organization. Developing strategic direction will be informed by an exploration of the nature of the strategic issues which have, and can be anticipated to have, a long term and potentially irreversible impact on the well-being of the organization. This exploration will encompass an *analysis of the values and beliefs* of powerful members of the organization and of its key stakeholders, and an analysis of its *distinctive competencies*. The ability to link distinctive competencies and values creates the 'business model' or 'livelihood scheme'. The confirmation and (re)design of strategic direction will be also informed by the *strategic options* (surfaced through analyses of stakeholders, alternative futures, and the value/belief systems of managers in the organization) that are available to the organization. It is this analysis that provides the underpinning for realism in developing a sense of strategic direction.

Strategy making thus includes analysing and determining how core distinctive competencies are to be *exploited as a livelihood scheme or a business model* through the process of adding value. It leads to a negotiated agreement of a *network* of goals and valued outcomes, which may then be encapsulated within what may be called a *mission statement, or statement of strategic intent*. This analysis and negotiation will reveal core strategic beliefs about how the organization works – the *current organizational recipe*. The process will establish the *key strategic issues and strategic problems* faced by the organization: the basic *value system* relating to the wishes and aspirations of members of the organization. The process will facilitate the development of important *strategic assets* for the organization: portfolios of strategic options.

The above sets out the most significant language of strategic management that guides the journey making approach, phrases in italics signalling the set of concepts which inform our view of the nature of strategy and strategic management.

It is a view that leads to seeing the formulation of strategy as the making of an increasingly elaborated 'strategy map', as shown in figure C1.1. Here strategy is represented as a hierarchical network of elements, or layers, which can become confirmed or redesigned through the journey: an **aspirations, or goals, system**, supported in turn by the **strategies as a system** of interconnected statements about direction, supported in turn by *strategic programmes* as identifiable deliverables which in turn require the support of portfolios of *strategic actions*. The important characteristic of the strategy map is that it represents strategy as an hierarchical *systemic network of interconnected statements of strategic intent*. The hierarchy also indicates the priorities of strategy making, where negotiating and agreeing an aspirations system may be all that strategy making requires. In other cases an organization may reach agreement about the hierarchical network of aspirations and strategies (including consideration of the business model/livelihood scheme and so distinctive competencies). Yet other organizations may go on to agree a fully detailed set of action portfolios and the possible use of a 'strategy delivery support system' to track and

V248: V258

Figure C1.1   The strategy map. One set of linkages between 'tear drops' in the hierarchy is shown in full; there will be many other 'tear drops' as part of the overall network, and these are indicated in dotted and dashed repeats.

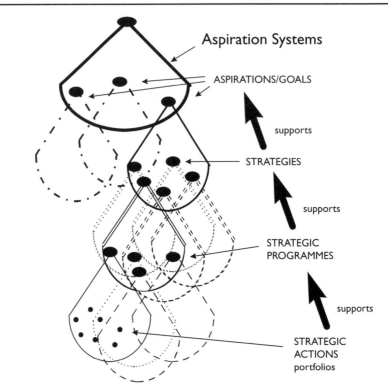

control their delivery. Thus, each layer 'downwards' is a further elaboration in the journey making process.

This 'strategy map' as a conceptualization, and practical output, of strategy making will inform discussion throughout the book. We shall suggest that detecting emergent strategizing is the best starting point for strategy making, and will accept that a *deliberate* agreement to let the organization continue 'muddling through' is a deliberate strategy. In this case we shall describe strategic management as *deliberate emergent strategizing* as opposed to non-deliberate emergent strategizing. This book is about developing a *deliberate and deliberated strategy* which is in the form of a more or less elaborated strategy map.

The Contingencies of Strategic Management?

The experience of most managers is that whilst there may be a debate about the best method of strategic planning, there is usually an expectation that there will be one single best way. This expectation fails to recognize that the most appropriate method of strategy making and delivery is *contingent* upon a large number of factors. For example, notwithstanding that one of the outcomes of strategic thinking is to reduce turbulence and uncertainty, an organization may suffer from such a high rate of change of events and unpredictability of opportunities and problems that it may not be helpful to have elaborately developed goals and processes. In this instance it may be more useful to work with a plan that is loose and easily adapted. Each organization will need a different approach to strategy making and to the delivery of the strategy.

For many organizations the nature of strategy will be most contingently influenced by the chief executive – their personality, skills, and personal aspirations. Indeed, some organizations are driven by the single-minded entrepreneurial capability of this one person. While the chief executive may be described as a 'man (or a woman) of vision', the vision will often not be articulated, but rather detected through their style and the pattern of entrepreneurial steps taken. In some ways this is the epitome of an emergent strategy. Patterns can be detected, but only just, opportunism rules, and 'muddling through with success' could be an appropriate description of the organization. To insist that such an organization should have a well-defined strategy may kill strategic success – as long as the chief executive remains in post. Similarly, a charismatic leader may drive an organization by creating entrepreneurial energies in others. This energy is channelled by following the merest of hints at strategic direction that emit from the leader as he or she stamps their personality on the organization. The chief executive also often has the power simply to say there will be no strategic management.

In the public sector, issues of accountability may be dominant contingencies in the determination of the right sort of strategic management. In many countries the attempts to, on the one hand put public servants through efficiency drives because of so-called market forces, and on the other to make them more accountable, have forced these organizations to produce strategic plans. All too often these plans have been created through the enforcement of 'blueprint' processes and formats taken as appropriate to all public organizations regardless of their role in society – for example, that the style of strategic planning for the police force is also sensible for health provision, refuse collection, city planning, and so on. The nonsense of this blueprint approach has often been driven by governments determined to centralize control and cut costs.

It is important to note that the very process of *reflecting upon the contingent nature of the organization in its context*, in order to determine the most appropriate approach to strategic management, *is itself a significant step in strategy making*. Managers ask us to help them develop strategy and this leads to a conversation with them about whether they are certain that developing a strategy will be good for them. For example, will the process of strategy making destroy those aspects of the organization that assure its future success? The question gets them thinking, and the thinking leads to questioning, and the questioning process and answers lead to the beginnings of strategic management! Nevertheless there have been several occasions when we and the managers concerned have together concluded that their apparent 'adhockery' and muddling through have extended their confidence and creativity, which in some instances, for example, was crucial for their keeping and attracting the best 'brains'.

Sometimes organizations are highly centralized, bureaucratic, and autocratic. Here strategy is a lever of social control and can be used to reinforce an autocracy. Strategy is likely to be in the form of a carefully contrived plan allowing little room for flexible thinking or action. If the strategy making involves high levels of participation then this will be with the purpose of manipulation. Effective strategy making should, of course, question whether this style of organization is appropriate given the choice made about purpose. Often, however, the management team is not as aware as they might be that strategic choices about purpose are available to them.

The approach to strategy making, introduced in this book, will be founded upon, at least, the management team understanding and reflecting upon their current ways of creating a strategic future and making choices about confirming or (re)designing it. Providing a *choice* about the strategic aspirations of the organization has been made, then the most effective way of working *may* be through a highly centralized bureaucracy or autocracy. If this is so, then strategic management is likely to be through strategic *planning*. In agreeing goals it may also be perfectly legitimate for one of the goals to be the 'satisfying of the ego, and need for control, of the chief executive', providing the chief executive has the power to implement such a choice.

Our point, illustrated by the above discussion, is that we can conceive of a continuum of different, and yet appropriate, ways of strategically managing an organization. *The nature of strategy and strategic management will properly vary from one organization to another.* There is no uniformly best form of strategy, or approach to strategic management, and in some instances deliberate and deliberated strategic management may not be a good thing at all. Thus, it is impossible to argue precisely which type of strategy might be most appropriate to a particular organizational type. Every organization will be positioned to exploit and develop its own individualism and chosen purpose, and a simple typology is therefore inappropriate. But there are some useful indicators that can prompt reflection about the role of contingencies affecting strategy. In figure C1.2 we point to some of the characteristics suggesting where to place an organization on a spectrum which moves from deliberate emergent strategizing to full strategic planning.

For our purposes pure *emergent strategizing* – that is, a process of letting the future emerge without appreciating that this is what is happening – is not strategy making, and so this form of strategic behaviour is off the left-hand end of the spectrum shown in figure C1.2. However, when a management team appreciates that embedded ways of working are determinants of a strategic future, and the organization *deliberately chooses*

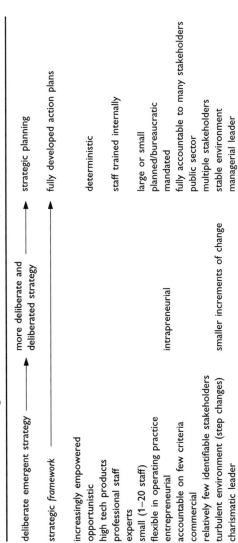

Figure C1.2 Some factors in the contingency spectrum.

deliberate emergent strategy ⟶ more deliberate and ⟵ strategic planning
deliberated strategy

strategic *framework* ⟶ fully developed action plans

increasingly empowered
opportunistic   deterministic
high tech products
professional staff   staff trained internally
experts
small (1–20 staff)   large or small
flexible in operating practice   planned/bureaucratic
entrepreneurial   intrapreneurial   mandated
accountable on few criteria   fully accountable to many stakeholders
commercial   public sector
relatively few identifiable stakeholders   multiple stakeholders
turbulent environment (step changes)   smaller increments of change stable environment
charismatic leader   managerial leader

not to understand and reflect upon these patterns, then the strategy of the organization lies at the left extreme end of the spectrum of strategy making. We shall call this a *deliberate emergent strategy*. The spectrum, in some senses, moves from – on the left, agreeing a strategic framework – to, on the right, developing all aspects of the strategy map, including fully detailed action plans (the full hierarchy shown in figure C1.1).

Strategic Management as a Process

The main thesis of this book is that the *process* of strategy making is the most important element in realizing strategic intent. It is our clear and convinced view that when strategic management fails to manage the real activities of an organization it is because of the inability of strategy to change the way in which key people in the organization both *think and act* as managers of its future. Thus, the issue of the political feasibility of strategic change will be central to our considerations. To argue that political feasibility is key is not new. What is new is that this book considers the issue in some depth – relating it to the theory and practice of managing power, politics, procedural rationality, procedural justice, the role of group processes in socially negotiating strategy, and the power of emotional as well as cognitive commitment in delivering strategy.

It is rare for strategy to promote the status quo. Strategy development will almost always imply changes in the organization – in its relationship with the environment and in its relationship with itself. Any organizational change that matters strategically will involve winners and losers, and so will involve some managers *seeing themselves* as potential winners and some as potential losers. It follows that any strategy development or thinking about strategy will, without deliberate intention, promote organizational politics. We discuss this phenomenon in more detail in following chapters and within the context of advancing a strategy which is politically feasible as a basis for achieving change.

The first, and obvious, point that must be made about strategic change is that the managers and management team in an organization are the most significant stakeholders. They usually have high levels of autonomy to determine the way the organization operates. They can withdraw their labour and move to another organization, and they can choose, to some extent, the character of the organization they work for. Although some argue that there is less job security and so greater uncertainty and less power for managers, it is nevertheless also true that good managers, who are key players in creating strategic futures, are still mobile because they are in demand. Managers, and staff, have enormous power to 'work to rule' – their rules – where their autonomy allows them to play up to the demands of senior management but deliberately fail to live up to them. It is relatively easy for middle to senior managers to argue that 'we tried our best but it just won't work'.

Our *process of strategy making* seeks to affect the way the key people in an organization both 'think and act'. We expect them to change their manner of 'thinking things through' and deciding what appropriate strategic action to take. Their emotional commitment to working together as an effective team capable of implementing their resolutions and agreements also shifts. The strategy making process leads to changed patterns of doing things – decision making processes, ways of seeing (including the role of management information), procedures, and reward systems.

We shall argue that it matters that key actors in an organization have a driving energy and wish to manage and control their future. Indeed this may matter more than that they have determined the analytically 'correct' future to create. It suggests doing *something* powerfully well, rather than doing nothing to achieve rationalistically correct intentions because there is no commitment. An energetic and committed management team can manage and control their world, whereas an analytically correct strategy will be useless without commitment. Too many books on strategic management concentrate almost solely on the strategic analysis and devote scarce attention to how the delivery of strategy is inextricably tied to the critical social process of strategy **negotiation**. Strategic management is   *V248* about people creating outcomes, not just about outcomes.

If strategy development does not change the way organizational members think, and so act, strategy can only have any real impact through coercion. Without changing ways of thinking, organizational members continue to see the same problems as they always did, and they continue to solve these problems using the same beliefs as before. Put more formally, their way of *construing* their occupational world has not changed. Furthermore, strategy can be embedded only when key actors have *emotional* as well as cognitive commitment to the strategy, and this commitment will always be higher when attention is paid to the process of strategy making rather than simply to the analysis of strategy.

All too often strategy starts from the top with a 'rational analysis' undertaken by support staff. The process is driven by the notion that the world outside is turbulent and the organization must respond to the imperatives set by the environment. The results are often powerful and logic driven attempts to change the organization. Then they come hard against the realities of the everyday organizationally embedded logic, a logic built over years by those who are expected to change. The result is little, or temporary, change, and a great deal of frustration on the part of those whose learning and wisdom have been ignored. This is not a plea for a participative approach to strategic management as if it were an end in its own right, it is a practical statement about how to create real strategic change that generates energy and commitment within the organization. Furthermore, participation is most likely to enable the fullest use of the organization's embedded distinctiveness while leaving behind that which does not sustain the organization into its future.

The need for a sense of cohesion among members of an organization is often underestimated. The motivation of a management team to stay together and the sense of attachment members have to the team – the extent to which they feel a sense of shared membership and want to work together – are important elements in strategy making. This raises the question of whether too much deliberate and deliberated strategy and too much commitment can make an organization blinkered to strategically important new opportunities, which can lead to a form of self-confirming 'group-think'. As we have suggested, most managers see strategy as giving their organization a sense of direction and purpose – one that might be helpful to all who work for the organization. It is also expected to help the organization better respond to, and manage its relationship with, both the expected and unexpected behaviour of the environment and other organizations who might wish to have an interest in supporting or sabotaging the intentions of the organization. It is therefore a way of helping all staff to act cooperatively with some alignment of action, or at least not in continual conflict with one another. While such acting in unison is often desirable, it does also carry the risk of encouraging a sort of systematic blindness to new alternatives. Sometimes strategies are made so that divergence of thinking is to be encouraged. Similarly, although continual and unintended conflict is not often thought to be helpful, some conflict generates the energy for creativity. The balancing act, between putting the well-being of the group as the primary consideration ('group-think') on the one hand and disorganized competing behaviour on the other, is an integral part of the strategy making process we discuss in this book.

Is Strategy Making and Strategic Management Worth It?

The case in favour of strategic management is not clear. There is a continuing debate about whether organizations are more or less successful if they employ strategic management principles and strategic planning. There appears to be supporting evidence in either direction, and also questions about the nature of whether the research can be trusted.

Measures of success of a strategy and of strategic management are elusive. In the end we need to know whether an organization is more or less successful *than it would have been without strategic management*. It is always notoriously difficult to make judgements about this *difference* between an actual and a hypothetical performance. As shown by the later fate of the organizational exemplars in Peters and Waterman's (1982) *In Search of Excellence*, the success of organizations can be temporary. For the evidence to be relevant it must relate to the role strategy has played in the long term *strategic* success of the organization.

Probably the most encouraging evidence of strategic management playing a useful role comes from research by Miller and Cardinal (1994) that has sought to evaluate and synthesize two decades of research on the topic. Their conclusions point to strategic planning being positively related to profitability when firms face high turbulence. The particular circumstance of high turbulence is an interesting outcome, for many other authors along with many senior managers argue that planning may *not* be appropriate for situations of high environmental turbulence (for example, Ansoff, 1991).

Nevertheless, we know of no *empirical research* that convincingly proves a relationship between strategic management and success. Indeed we think it is unlikely that there can ever be such research, and ultimately the most important reason why we think that research on this topic should be taken lightly is that the aim of strategic management is to exploit the unique competencies of an organization in order to better attain unique aspirations. This designed uniqueness makes comparisons, and so statistically based conclusions (of the sort many researchers are seeking to demonstrate) about the relationship between strategy and success, ill-founded. Each of the organizations who make up the sample is, by definition (or hope), different. In addition, as we shall argue below, the particular approach any organization takes to strategic management will, and should, be highly contingent. It will be contingent upon decisions the organization, and in particular the management team, can make (and will make, even if implicitly) about the nature of their organization and their own sense of vision (or not). Theoretical and empirical research into the sources of advantage is beginning to show that organizational capabilities, rather than product market positions or tactics, are the enduring source of advantage. It is organizational capabilities, and the resilience of the organization, that will be of particular interest in our consideration of the journey of strategy making.

In summary then, our view is that *the contribution, or not, of deliberate and deliberated strategic management is contingent on many factors*. We are not dogmatic, either intellectually or emotionally, about the importance of strategic management to the well-being of an organization. Strategy making and deliberate and deliberated strategic management is therefore not always a good thing, and the particular approach to, and degree of, strategy making and strategy delivery will, and should, vary from one organization to another.

Some Outcomes Managers Want from Strategic Management

V213

Over the years we have worked with many senior managers in large and small organizations and talked to them about what they want from embarking on strategic thinking and change. Some of the answers we hear most often are listed below. The list is not intended to be complete but it does give some indication of a range of outcomes that managers believe to be positively related to strategy making.

Resolution of a Strategic Crisis

A perceived crisis is often the spur to thinking about strategic futures. Sometimes an internal prompt comes from the arrival of a new senior manager (usually Chief Executive), or the need to satisfy the ambitious aspirations of one particular manager who has found, or created, a crisis which demonstrates 'the need for a rethink'. External prompts are common, and range from the demands of powerful external stakeholders, such as stockholders or funding agencies for public sector organizations, to the collapse of a profitable market or technological breakthrough. These may act as a driving force for revisiting current strategy or for 'starting again from scratch'.

The Demands of Powerful Stakeholders

One of the most often used arguments for developing and publishing a strategy is that it impresses external stakeholders. Indeed some writers argue that there is a requirement for an organization to declare a strategy, or else investors cannot be persuaded to financially support the future of the organization by providing the funds for organizational change and development. We do not believe that this is the case. Rather, it is a strategic *choice* that the management of the organization can make. It is a decision following stakeholder analysis, and the development of appropriate stakeholder management strategies. Nevertheless, whether or not a published strategy is demanded by external stakeholders, the relief that derives from a feeling of better management over powerful stakeholders is often felt to be an important positive outcome.

The Symbolism of Strategic Management

It is important not to ignore the symbolic role that strategy making plays in a top manager's life. It is very often taken as a symbol of good management, not necessarily by those who are being managed but invariably by the senior managers themselves. The notion of strategizing sounds as if it is an important activity that important people do. It is plausible to suggest that it is an act of good management. It is possible to elucidate a coherent and persuasive case for why developing strategy is an important activity for any organization.

However, it must be noted that there are highly successful organizations and CEOs who fervently believe that strategy making is unimportant and unhelpful. It is entirely possible to sustain a coherent argument that strategy making is unhelpful, irrelevant, and distracts managers' attention from the really difficult issues of management. The argument goes along the lines that the pace of environmental change makes demands on managers which cannot be satisfied by strategic management methods. Explicit deliberate and deliberated strategic management delivers too much consensual thinking, and discourages opportunism and aggressive entrepreneurial competition between managers. It is argued to be a waste of time in cost/benefit terms – particularly if done 'properly'.

In this book we shall, of course, seek to demonstrate that many of these well-rehearsed arguments against strategy making are based upon inappropriate understandings of strategy and the use of inappropriate methods. As we argued above, effective strategy making derives from doing it at a level, and in a manner, which is contingently appropriate to the organization within its own context. Thus, if opportunism and flexibility are strategic imperatives then the strategy making process and resultant strategic intent will reflect this outcome of a journey of strategic thinking.

Strategic Vision and Emotional Commitment   V223

Providing a sense of direction, through a strategic vision, encompasses a number of aspects that are important if the direction is to be followed. It can be important because it addresses the human need for something to strive for – a challenge – a reason for being. It can be related to Martin Luther King's 'I have a dream . . .' symbolism and rhetoric. A well-articulated vision and strategy can provide an image of the future that is attractive and worthwhile. More than an expression of the needs of external stakeholders it serves the purpose of encouraging employees to believe that the organization has a future, that their effort is worthwhile, and that their future is secure also as stakeholders. This is expected to enhance commitment of staff to the organization, such that when good staff are offered jobs elsewhere it will be their loyalty and sense of identity with the organization that will sway the balance towards not moving. 'If you want to move people it has to be toward a vision that's positive for them, that taps important values, that gets them something they desire, and it has to be presented in a compelling way that they feel inspired to follow' (Martin Luther King, Jr).

Furthermore, given the current, and likely future for, patterns of employment, the levels of stress that may surround job insecurity throughout an organization are likely to persist. The role that a powerful vision connected to a plausible success for the organization can play in stress reduction is often taken by managers to be important. Without a vision that is attractive to those who have to realize it, management becomes increasingly dependent upon coercion as the basis for organizational change and continued effectiveness.

Relatedly, for many managers it is important to feel that they play a role beyond that of ensuring continuing production or service provision at the operational level. They like to feel that their contributions link with the attainment of the vision and that they have the power and ability to play their part. Demonstrating the linking of strategic programmes and lower level responsibilities to grander organizational goals, linking changes in operations to strategic outcomes, and linking rewards for managerial thinking and action to the delivery of strategy is of course difficult. Yet it is only when this can be done that the individual manager can feel more than a 'cog in the wheel'. It is also this relationship between thinking and action which provides the necessary basis for individual, group, and organizational learning (considered in later chapters).

For this to work the strategy can't be a joke. This usually means that it can take as its focus stakeholders inside the organization by providing emotional commitment, or focus outside the organization by serving powerful stakeholders.

Managing Complexity – Strategic Thinking and Opportunism rather than Planning

Whether the world is indeed more complex, uncertain, and turbulent (in any objective manner) is less important than that managers increasingly believe they face more than enough complexity to make their job both challenging and difficult. The extent to which strategy can help managers better manage complexity is also seen as significant for the well-being of the organization. Having a framework to guide decisions helps relieve the stress of too many options, too many possible ways of acting and thinking. This idea of *managing* complexity contrasts with complexity *reduction*, where important and relevant aspects of a situation are ignored or not appreciated. Strategy is therefore expected to contribute to a manager's ability to 'act thinkingly' (Weick, 1983) – meaning that managers develop a capability to act quickly, without paralysis by analysis, and yet the actions are informed by a framework of previous thinking, actions which in turn inform future thinking and action.

Threatening environments, high uncertainty, and external control decrease rationality and so, we may surmise, reduce the ability to manage complexity. In addition, the perceived difficulty in absorbing and so using the plethora of data with which managers feel they are now bombarded makes planning an activity of limited rationality, and so makes 'long term' comprehensive planning very difficult if not impossible (Eisenhardt and Zbaracki, 1992; Mintzberg, 1994). Although managers often view themselves as operating in such high levels of external turbulence that strategy making is a waste of time, one of the fundamental positive out-comes from strategy making can be that of getting a 'grip on turbulence'. Thus an important outcome from the journey of strategy making should be to reduce the sense of threat, the feeling of high uncertainty, and degree to which a group believes it is at the mercy of external factors. A part of the journey will involve a management team learning about complexity and learning how to manage it. By so doing it can think, as well as plan, strategically and so act opportunistically with confidence.

So strategic management – strategy making – is likely to be more than strategic planning. Our own view is similar to that held by John Bryson when he says that 'strategic planning is not a substitute for strategic thinking and acting . . . And when used thoughtlessly, strategic planning can drive out precisely the kind of strategic thought and action it is supposed to promote' (1995:9).

Team Development
V194 V213 V231

Many of the senior managers we have worked with have wanted the strategy development process to be an indirect management and team development activity. Without using the term they have wanted to use strategy making as an organizational, group, and individual learning episode for the management team. Strategy and strategic management is very often used, in part, as a vehicle to create better managers and a more effective management *team*. This outcome is often not secondary to other outcomes, rather it is taken to be as important as creating a strategic future for the organization. In this context the strategy is expected to provide a manager with higher levels of self-awareness about what he, or she, is doing as a member of a team, and how what she, or he, is doing fits in with the strategy delivery of her, or his, colleagues.

Thinking and Doing Things Differently

A vision provides the motivation to do things but no help in deciding and behaving in relation to specific issues. An outcome of strategy making is to change the way in which decision makers make sense of their role and the things that are going on around about them. It will provide them with new ways of thinking about their world, new ways of doing things – a new 'recipe' or guidebook that can link the vision to action. In this sense the strategy provides a framework for 'acting thinkingly' rather than simply 'muddling through'. And so strategy is expected to be an instrument of social control by directing managers to act coherently with a degree of alignment between their actions and the actions of others, and also in a manner more in line with the desires of those who have power.

Thus strategy is an instrument of power, and so of change. Here, 'organizations must be seen as tools . . . for shaping the world as one wishes it to be shaped. They provide the means for imposing one's definition of the proper affairs of men upon other men' (sic) (Perrow, 1986:11).

A Conceptual Basis for Strategy Making . . .

The outcomes listed above focus largely on the role of strategic management in changing and sustaining the motivation and commitment to the organization by staff at all levels. The other impetus is that of managing external stakeholders. The managers who discussed these aspects of strategic management did not do so because other possible outcomes were unimportant to them but because they are rarely acknowledged as legitimate reasons for strategy making. Certainly these outcomes cannot be achieved without careful attention to the *process* of strategy making. In the next chapter we develop the notion of JOURNEY making as a process approach to strategy making. The rationale for this derives from recognizing strategy making as a human activity – one involving social negotiation and making choices about aspirations. It is also about making a choice about which stakeholders are important, and about managing and controlling the future rather than reacting to it.

The next chapter, chapter C2, provides an introductory overview of strategy making as a 'journey', a cycle moving from joint understanding amongst members of the management team and other participants, through reflection to negotiation and agreement. We take as a starting point the process of detecting emergent strategizing and JOintly Understanding and Reflecting on its implications for the strategic future of the organization. We move on through an *exploration of aspirations* as a system of interlinked goals, attention to *distinctive competencies*, and rehearsal of a tenable *business model or livelihood scheme*. Integral to the process of developing strategy are *stakeholder analysis and management*, and exploration of *alternative futures*. These help inform the confirming and (re)designing of strategy. Chapter C2 sets out the 'road-map' for the journey. It also relates our approach to strategy making within the context of the major schools of strategic management, and reflects upon their contribution to our process-oriented approach to strategy making in practice.

Chapter C3 examines in further detail the nature and significance of *political feasibility* in strategy making and strategic change which recognizes the need for commitment from the power-brokers and other key players in and around the organization. Chapter C4 explores strategy making as a process which demands negotiation – both psychological and emotional – amongst teams, particularly the management team. It addresses the ways in which the nature of group work needs to be *designed and facilitated* in order to encourage the sorts of conversations, agreements, and commitments that will encourage commitment to strategy and the delivery of strategy.

Chapters C5 to C9 enter the JOURNEY making cycle itself. Chapter C5 describes the process of detecting emergent strategizing. Reflecting on this is the starting point for the journey. Chapter C6 explores the importance of understanding distinctive competencies and their role in enabling an organization to meet, or not, their aspirations. It considers the generation of a coherent and powerful strategic intent for the organization to *develop a business model or livelihood scheme* through which the organization can deliver the sort of strategic future it wants. In chapters C7 and C8 we look respectively at stakeholder analysis and its role in developing *stakeholder management* strategies, and the consideration of alternative futures as a context for robust strategic making. In chapter C9 we discuss the importance of *closure to the strategy making process* and issues in the implementation of strategy. Finally, in chapter C10 we provide a brief outline of the 'stages' in JOURNEY making and show them in relation to our intentions outlined in chapter C2. This chapter provides the closest to a 'pull-out guide' to our approach, and illustrates consequences of the concepts of strategy making set out in part 1 for the methods, techniques, and tools set out in part 3. Thus, it is intended to act as the 'bridge' to other parts of the book.

Let us say again that it is our intention that any one part of this book can stand alone and contribute to ways of doing strategy making – this first part is expected to inform strategy making whatever methods or techniques and tools are used, part 2 is expected to provide vicarious experience of the attempts made by others so that mistakes can be avoided and good practice copied, and part 3 is expected to provide methods and techniques which may be used in many organizational situations from strategy making to strategic problem solving. However, the book has been written as an integrated whole and we hope that readers will be tempted to jump across the parts and contingently adapt and develop ideas to suit their situation and needs.

STRATEGY MAKING AS A JOURNEY

In this chapter we introduce the approach to strategy making discussed in this book. It is an approach informed by a number of key considerations.

There is a tendency for writing on strategic management to focus primarily on the external stakeholders (stockholders/competitors) rather than tapping the knowledge and wisdom of those inside the organization. Our approach, in contrast, advocates the involvement of those inside the organization – those with the power to act, to make decisions and therefore to create (or obstruct) organizational change. For small firms with owner-managers power lies clearly within the organization. For public or not-for-profit organizations managers also have ultimate power to determine the strategic future of their enterprise. It is, however, the case that most public sector managers hesitate to accept that they do have significant power to manage and control their strategic future. We shall return to this issue in a later chapter.

Whether we like it or not, there will be participation of kinds, even if in the form of sullen disavowal of change – and so it might be better if there were designed participation. It is managers – and staff – within an organization that have the knowledge and power to get things done. Attending to those accountable and responsible requires the recognition that, for the strategy making to be successful, the approach must address issues relating to power (regardless of the size of the organization), and at least carefully consider the extent of participation.

This is particularly so if we wish to secure the motivation of members of an organization to implement strategy, rather than rely on manipulation and control for compliance. As long as we acknowledge the considerable power of management and staff at many levels within an organization then we must also acknowledge the demands for participation in the strategy making process. Attending to the levels of participation ensures that important issues of implementation, usually regarded as a stage that follows strategy formulation, will be integrated into the strategy development process. When we consider problem solving in organizations we are aware that issues in the implementation of solutions arise in problem formulation rather than as a separate stage considered after solutions have been found (Eden, 1987). Indeed, problems are often implementation issues. In the same way, strategy development must involve integrally issues of strategic change and delivery. Those issues, which depend on the views of powerful internal players, need to be absorbed into the strategy making process where they can be addressed and *negotiated* by the participants.

Our model of the strategy making and delivery process, outlined in this chapter, is in these ways informed by the reality of dispersed power in organizations and by the role of emotional and reasoned commitment, and we shall return to this theme once more later in the chapter.

Approaches to Strategy

We propose that a method for helping an organization create a strategy must always recognize that the organization (however small) will, deliberately or not, be patterning a strategic future. This future is not random or accidental, but is rather a consequence of particular ways of working and ways of thinking that belong uniquely to that organization. The way in which we introduce our approach into an organization reflects this. Our starting point is to examine the cycle of pattern generation through which an organization will be creating its own strategic future by default. We then suggest an intervention into this cycle which will enable the organization to *confirm or redesign* this pattern and so shift to a position of *deliberate* strategizing. Our approach to the process of strategy making is one which is grown from, or knits into, the organization as it is. It is a process which thus pays due respect to the history and inhabitants of the organization seeking to '**honour the past** while estranging people from it'   *V257*
(Bryson *et al*, 1996:280), rather than presumptively suggesting that strategic change is inevitable or determined solely by considerations of the future. We say this notwithstanding the seductiveness of Pascale's view that the 'present is determined by the future not the past'.

Thirdly, and relatedly, the approach we suggest seeks to recognize the contingencies of appropriate strategy making where the form of strategy that results from this process will be highly contingent on a number of important characteristics relating to the organization, its powerful members, and its environment. The approach allows for different organizations with different needs to create a strategy which may, for example, be on the one hand a detailed strategic plan, or, on the other, an agreement to have no strategy at all. In either of these extremes the outcome will, however, be a deliberate strategic choice.

Emergent Strategizing   *V209 V216*

Figure C2.1 shows a *description* of the dynamics of organizational activity which represents the 'muddling through' (Lindblom, 1959) or 'logical incrementalism' (Quinn, 1980) of any organization without an effective strategy. The figure seeks to capture the essential features of 'emergent *strategizing*' (Eden and van der Heijden, 1995). By emergent strategizing we refer to a process (verb, rather than the noun used by Mintzberg and Waters (1985)), a stream of actions that are not random but form a pattern

Figure C2.1   Emergent strategizing.

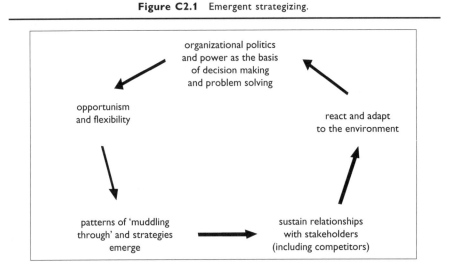

– a pattern which, as Mintzberg points out, usually becomes evident as such after the event rather than before. It is this detectable pattern in a stream of actions in the continuing cycle of sustaining relationships with those who have a stake in the organization, adapting and reacting to the environment, negotiating ways of doing this, and being opportunistic, that can be called emergent strategizing.

Emergent strategizing is, in effect, a deliberate strategy for organizations that have made no deliberate attempt to design a strategic future, and for organizations that have a strategy but one which has little real impact upon strategy delivery.

Figure C2.1 suggests that it is not possible for any organization to be without an emergent strategy. Very often the organization will not have made any effort to detect or confirm this strategy. It will be a pattern or stream of events that are the processes of the organization actually, if not willingly, 'muddling through'. The strategy will be embedded in the culture ('the way we do things around here') and in the heads of managers as they take courses of action in relation to their 'world-taken-for-granted'. This world taken for granted includes an implicit understanding of an appropriate direction for the organization and it will emanate through the problem solving and 'firefighting' activities undertaken on a day to day basis. We see tacit knowledge – knowledge which is implicit and embedded in action – being used in the way individuals and teams routinely work and manage projects (Wernerfelt, 1989). See Spender (1998) for a discussion of tacit knowledge.

V262   Let us consider each of the elements of **the cycle** displayed in figure C2.1 in more detail.

Within the 'everyday' process of emergent strategizing, managers talk and think about others who have a stake in the organization, in particular those who have the power to influence the future they are seeking to create. They attend to those who play a significant role in moulding the future of their own organization and to those who have an ability to satisfy the needs and ambitions of the managers. They think about how other 'actors' might support or sabotage their intent. They will also be doing lots of 'sense-making' aimed at discovering some of the possible futures within which they may have to work. In short, they will be seeking to manage and adapt their future rather than just to react to it, either supporting those possibilities which promote the direction advanced by them, or seeking to thwart those 'forecasts' of the future which do not.

Much emergent strategizing will be influenced by the way in which some events are defined as potential disasters and others are not. Emergent patterns will reflect as much what managers wish to avoid as what they see as desirable. Thus, for example, it is our experience that managers at all levels are frequently driven by the perceived requirement to address urgent issues – reactivity not pro-activity. The process of dealing with *strategic* issues that arise from attempts to sustain relationships and adapt and/or react to the environment generates tensions amongst the senior or top management team. These tensions derive from the extent to which adaptations to the environment and to stakeholders' expectations require resource shifts, possible restructuring – down-sizing, up-sizing, right-sizing etc. new products, new ways of working and so on. These shifts, in turn, inevitably mean there will be **winners and losers** in *V275* the organization. No change can be made without, at the very least, perceptions of potential loss and gain. Anticipating such outcomes, powerful managers in the organization play up some issues, play down others, and fight to retain their own power. Political negotiation, dependent upon the thinking, power, and information provision, will be a central feature of attempts to be opportunistic and flexible and agree upon strategic action. Indeed the 'need for flexibility' will often be used as a part of the rhetoric for maintaining logical incrementalism or sequential issue management rather than explicit strategic agreements. In this way managers retain the right to fight again – the fortunes of those currently losing battles are not sealed.

The outcomes of such processes will not be totally coherent or thought out as a pattern but rather be implicit in the behaviour, language, and action of the managers who will to some extent copy the underlying 'recipes' used by other managers (particularly those defined as successful), including those in other organizations. For example, as managers continually watch their competitors and react to them they will be seeking to 'maintain competitive positioning' to 'adapt to the environment' and 'exploit opportunities', which generates debate, argument and 'political negotiation', out of which 'strategies emerge' to 'maintain competitive positioning'. The 'logic' in logical incrementalism is the apparent logic of dealing with each strategic issue in turn.

The cycle is completed as external stakeholders attempt to 'make sense' of, and detect patterns from, the decision streams of the organization in which they have an interest. As this occurs, the stakeholders create an environment to which managers must react. Thus, for example, as a competitor tries to second guess the strategic intentions of a particular organization, these guesses will influence their own competitor positioning and so the environment of the monitored organization. Other organizations are also players, even if not deliberately so, as they too change the environment within which the organization must exist.

Managers used to sequential issue management, where if you lose one battle you might win the next, can be very resistant to strategic thinking and strategic management which can create long term losers and winners. Even those managers who expect to be the winners from serious strategy making can be suspicious of the extent of long term stability of their wins.

Schools of Thought about Strategic Management

Several authors have noted (Hampden-Turner, 1993; Mintzberg, 1990b; Whittington, 1993) that the last twenty years have seen the growth of a number of 'well-established' approaches to strategic planning and strategic management. These are each presented as if they are the correct way of setting about developing strategy for an organization. Some are overtly prescriptive and are usually only implicitly based upon a clear theoretical view of the nature of organizations. Others are supposedly descriptive but are, nevertheless, presented as prescription, often taking a highly normative stance which ignores the particular history, culture, and context of the organization.

The authors of the approaches have, for the most part, thought out their positions and presented attractive and plausible arguments for their correctness. Thus, they should not be dismissed lightly. Our view is that they each offer important help in understanding the process of strategy making where description and prescription need to weld themselves together.

Thus, where appropriate, we provide a context for our own approach by reference to some of these well-established approaches. In particular we shall use the well-known taxonomies of Mintzberg (1990b) and Hampden-Turner (1993) to inform the basis for comparison, focusing in particular on those elements which serve to illustrate aspects of the approach we introduce. We have no intention of offering a comprehensive literature review, or overview of the different schools, but rather intend to provide help to readers who might wish to understand better some of the ideas by reference to those of others.

Figure C2.2 is provided as a guide to the different schools and their proponents. The figure shows the different schools, their nature (descriptive or prescriptive), and our view of how they relate to each other (each school is numbered according to the order of its appearance below). The three schools in italics are not addressed in our discussion below.

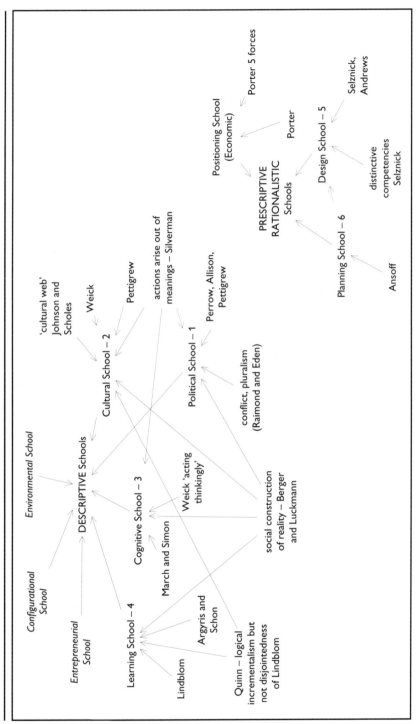

Figure C2.2 A guide to the different schools of strategy.

Figure C2.3   Emergent strategizing in context.

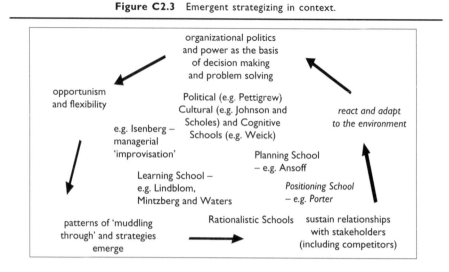

We represent a personal perspective, designed to meet our purpose, recognizing that this may not match that of other researchers and practitioners.

Figure C2.3 summarizes the way in which the different elements of figure C2.1, on logical incrementalism, relate to the primary schools of thought shown in figure C2.2. Here we explore further two important elements in the diagram – the role of politics and power, and the significance of opportunism – as they relate to the schools represented. We shall not devote space here to exploring the positioning, design, and planning schools. These are well known and well established, and are represented in most strategic management texts.

'Organizational politics and power as the basis of decision making and problem solving'

We start with the active business of agenda setting, problem formulation, problem solving, deciding, and acting which is patterned by the cognitive schemas, organizational scripts, bargaining processes and resource allocation procedures found within – indeed making – an organization. Our focus on organizational politics and power links most strongly with the *political* and *cultural* schools of strategic management. However, we also acknowledge the *cognitive* school, for our perspective emphasizing the role of 'making sense', of redefining, of tacit knowledge. Each of which suggests strategy making and organizational change opportunities as a mental process (Barr *et al*, 1992; Bartunek, 1984).

The political school emphasizes strategy formulation as a political process where strategic aspirations are disputed, conflict exists, and managers compete for scarce resources. In addition, we consider aspects of organizational politics that derive from the desire for power. Here what is thought of as the environment is seen as tractable, and the organization is an all powerful player which concentrates on positions and ploys within a strategic game. We are concerned with both (i) the internal political dynamic, and (ii) the dynamic between the organization and its stakeholders.

In the first instance, the organization is seen as 'the interaction of motivated people attempting to resolve their own problems [where] the environment in which an organization is located might usefully be regarded as a source of meanings through which members define their actions and make sense of the actions of others' (Silverman, 1970). Thus strategic action is largely determined as managers, or powerful actors in the organization, seek to manage the meanings (Pettigrew, 1977) that other actors will attribute to events. The focus of attention for understanding the patterns of emergent strategizing will be on those who have power in the organization, and analysis follows from this view (see Allison, 1971). That is to say, it becomes important to see the organization from a non-unitary perspective where pluralism is the appropriate way of understanding how strategic decisions emerge (Raimond and Eden, 1990). Critics of this school argue that it focuses too much attention on conflict and seems to imply that agreement and consensus cannot be reached. We accept that conflict is not only inevitable but also the energy source of an organization. Conflict and consensus co-exist, but the implication is that the process of *negotiating* action is central to organizational behaviour and so central to strategy making – a process of negotiation influenced by power of all sorts. However in all situations negotiation *of one sort or another* occurs. A designed strategy making process intervenes in that negotiation for the good of some staff and the ill of others.

Turning to the cultural and cognitive schools, these are related in a number of important ways. As Weick (1985) asserts, 'a corporation doesn't have a culture, a corporation is a culture . . . that's why it's difficult to change'. Thus strategy is ultimately expressed through **the culture of an** *V203* **organization** – 'if a strategy can make or break an organization, then a culture can make or break a strategy' (Salaman, 1979). Johnson and Scholes (1993) discuss the 'cultural web' where it is important to recognize the role of control systems, rituals and routines, symbols, stories, organizational structure, and power structures. That is the way in which shared beliefs develop into **'organizational recipes'** reinforced by tradition, habit, stories, symbols, and ideology to become the central analytical vehicle and so the *P415* central focus for change – strategy is about changing culture. Understanding shared meanings and then developing new shared meanings is at the core of the intervention. This implies in turn that incrementalism in strategic change is usually the most practical way of delivering strategy. It is through this notion of *meanings* – interpretive frameworks, a schema for construing – that the political school ('the management of meaning'), the cultural school (shared beliefs and traditions), and the cognitive school (mental processes) come together.

However, the cognitive school has a number of other important aspects to it. It focuses on individual action and the idea promoted by Weick (1979) that the implementation of strategy ultimately depends upon the extent to which managers are able to 'act thinkingly' given the limit to the amount of information human beings are able to process ('bounded rationality' – 'people act intentionally rational, but only limitedly so' (Simon, 1957:xxiv). The challenge becomes that of creating a *mental framework* or schema for strategic action. A framework that influences construal, and so issue definition, and so action.

Each of these three schools has both a descriptive and so prescriptive role to play, by addressing realities of behaviour in and around organizations, understandings of which then underpin the approach and methods to deliberative strategy making.

Thus, we are concerned with the role of culture, cognition, and politics in strategy making. We regard this triad of schools as probably the most fruitful perspectives to focus upon if we wish to understand the emerging strategizing of any organization. We also see them as the primary basis for intervention. If we cannot change the way in which strategic issues are construed, or the way in which they are dealt with, then it does not matter what a 'rational' analysis of the environment reveals or what a rational analysis of stakeholders (such as competitors) suggests.

'Opportunism and flexibility'

In addition the particular identification of opportunism and flexibility in our diagrams C2.1 and C2.3 addresses the descriptive reality of the operation of 'bounded rationality', leading to tendencies towards crisis management, 'firefighting', and sequential issue management by managers operating in turbulent and complex environments.

Such features of management behaviour lend some support to the ideas of Isenberg (1987):

- The rate of change of events and the unpredictability of opportunities and problems means that it is sensible for goals and processes not to be elaborately developed – it may be much better to have a plan that is loose and easily adapted.
- Keep many different issues and activities on the go at once, so that any chance encounters are likely to be relevant to at least one of them, and helpful interactions between them are exploited.
- Vast numbers of local small-scale improvisations are contained within a broad embedded longer term vision, which managers work incrementally towards.
- Since there is no time to gather more than a very small amount of the information on most issues, managers have to make use of 'intelligent guesswork' and hunches.

- There is a strong tendency for 'the urgent to drive out the important', and so many senior managers have to devise ways of tricking themselves into regularly thinking about the important rather than the urgent.
- Strategic opportunism is rational – a sensible way of working.

Strategy Development as JOURNEY Making

A central element of making strategy is the extent to which members of an organization can develop a balance of both emotional as well as cognitive commitment to the strategy. The need to capture both 'the heart and the mind' is dependent upon the *way* in which strategy is developed in addition to the appropriateness or otherwise of the outcome as a particular strategy. Effective strategy making will be related significantly to the *process* of strategy development and the *process* of strategy delivery in which the involvement of people is central to the development of the strategy. We shall develop the view that providing a process which is exciting and fun is as important to gaining commitment as is 'rational-analytic' activity.

However, gaining cognitive commitment is not taken to be routine or unimportant. The difficulties inherent in seeking to change the way in which members of an organization behave and decide is related to who they are and how they think within a particular organizational culture – a culture within which, to a greater or lesser extent, they have been able to presume ways of working, a world taken for granted, a sense of the future as they think it ought to be or not to be; a culture which is a part of a history that will need to be respected for what is good as well as for what needs to be changed. Thus strategy making will be seen to relate to what goes on now – to emergent strategizing which usually takes place within, and is influenced by, the context of a current published strategy.

Figure C2.4 now begins the move to a deliberate process where strategy making becomes a conscious and purposeful activity – what we refer to as JOURNEY making.

Here the process involves, first, reflecting upon the emergent strategizing of the organization, manifest in and through the patterns of decision making, problem definition, recipes, ways of working, formation of language, embedded goals – positive and negative (unwanted direction) – of the organization. Through designed conversational processes managers seek to confirm aspects of their emergent strategy and design new aspects to counter any dissatisfaction with the emergent patterns. The conversations ease the process of political negotiation as the beginnings of a sense of shared meaning relating to their organization and its purpose is *jointly* understood, *reflected* upon, and *negotiated* towards the agreement of a consensual strategy. The confirmation of existing strategy and the fashioning of new strategy is designed to facilitate the coherent exploitation of

Figure C2.4 The JOURNEY of strategy making and delivery.

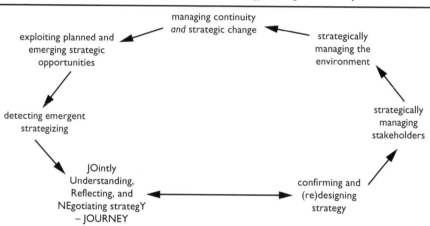

opportunities, continued adaptation to the environment, and appropriate competitive positioning.

A process for developing strategic direction involves a *journey* of strategy making which attempts to confirm and (re)design strategy. This is

P341 a *cycle* (the double headed arrow in figure C2.4). The conversational process – the journey of JOintly Understanding Reflecting and Negotiating strategY – produces the draft strategies, which in turn involves attempts to jointly understand and reflect upon their implications for managing stakeholders, the environment, and creating politically feasible organizational change as well as protecting the current operations – managing continuity and change.

We are arguing for a designed journey that releases deeper knowledge, beliefs, and expertise. By doing so we can exploit differences in beliefs as a creative tension and exploit the summation of deep knowledge as a systemic whole rather than as individual isolated chunks of expertise. On the surface, staff entertain apparently similar interpretations of situations. The lack of a design intended to surface deeper beliefs and knowledge, and an inherent lack of 'air time' for managers to express other than surface beliefs and knowledge means there can be little understanding of alternative perspectives or opportunity to reflect upon them. The political stance taken towards them is what then drives negotiation. Unless the design of strategy making recognizes the difficulties in exploiting wisdom and expertise then the dominant and surface (and mostly trivial) views remain foremost in conversation and in thinking and action.

Research on managerial judgement suggests that the need human beings have for imposing order on data through seeking causality in order to make sense of their world will make it less likely that they can entertain alternative problem formulations (Hogarth, 1987). In addition there is evidence that, without specific encouragement within designed processes,

P292 P333 P354 managers are unable to pay adequate attention to **feedback properties** in evaluating the dynamic behaviour of their own organization (Forrester,

1961; Richardson, 1991; Sterman, 1989). The sum of beliefs of each individual manager is rarely deliberately related to the beliefs of others. Each manager has a bounded view of the organizational world, both internal and external. It is only when these views are linked to those of others that it becomes possible to identify how one set of beliefs impact another set which impact yet another set and so create a closed loop which may encourage self-sustaining virtuous circles or unhelpful vicious circles of organizational behaviour. It is often the case that outcomes created by the policies and internal processes of their organization will be incorrectly attributed to the behaviour of the external world, be it the marketplace or other environmental variables. In this way the strategic opportunities for using internal policies are missed because they are seen as environmentally determined. Similarly the interaction of beliefs across several individuals can indicate negative feedback where undesirable, or desirable, internal stability is created. Here strategic change is inhibited by the forces of stability which might be easy to change if only they were appreciated. Strategy is all about recognizing a dynamic future, and so feedback dynamics need to be identified, understood, and reflected upon.

We have now introduced two new parts into the cycle of organizational strategizing depicted in figure C2.1 – that of a process (the journey) and that of confirming and (re)designing strategy. Each of these aspects both individually and together relate to three other schools of strategic management – *the learning, design, and planning schools.*

The most important aspect of these two new elements is that there is a cycle which shows the journey informing confirmation and (re)design which will, in turn, inform a further JOURNEY making episode. This is a cycle within the outer cycle of emergent strategizing. The new outer cycle in figure C2.4 shows a key feature of the learning school where strategy formulation and enaction are concurrent. This cycle shows a model of strategy making and its realization which is similar in form to the learning cycles suggested for individual learning by Kolb (1984), Argyris and Schon (1978), and to some extent by Kelly (1955) and Piaget (1971, 1972). In these cycles concrete experiences are the basis for observation and reflection, which enable the formation of abstract concepts and theory, and which create the ability to test the implications of the new theories in new situations. These in turn are the basis for observation and reflection. The model of strategy making and enaction is a model of an organizational learning cycle. The learning takes place at the interface of thought (the double headed arrow indicating the cycle of journey and design) and action (the outer cycle). The whole process is seen as a continuous cycle where strategy making *and* delivery is not long term planning where the plans are expected to remain constant. Instead, *strategy making and its realization together create a sequence of platforms for strategic change and organizational achievement.* Each cycle generates learning which informs a new journey of review and redesign which in turn creates a new platform for change. The cycle will be continuous and rapid (at the level of logical incrementalism described by Quinn but without the disjointedness implied by Lindblom).

Conversing about strategy through the use of a facilitated journey promotes confirmation and design in an incremental and cyclical manner (thus the double headed arrow between these two aspects of the overall cycle). The deliberate strategy in action grows rather than waits for completion. A management team engaged in an active journey about strategy is unable, in practice, to hold off from taking strategic action until the strategy making process is 'complete'. As strategic intent appears to be clear and robust, it will have become so because managers will have changed their thinking – new thinking and social relationships will have been negotiated, and so new action becomes obvious and feasible.

The idea of confirming and (re)designing strategy based upon the journey of strategy making introduces aspects of both the planning and design schools (see for example Andrews, 1980; Ansoff, 1965; Selznick, 1957; Tregoe and Zimmerman, 1980). As the label suggests, the planning school argues for developing explicit plans which are decomposed into sub-strategies and programmes (relating to our notion of the 'strategy map' – figure C1.1). It favours seeing organizations as bureaucracies where the central players in strategy development are the planners and so the emphasis is on the programme output as the message rather than on formulation or strategy making. The primary metaphor is that of organizations 'as machines', and so structural and technological concepts tend to dominate, and 'instrumentation' is one of the key design principles (Degeling and Colebatch, 1994). The design school follows the notion of seeking strategic fit through an external and internal appraisal which is central to a sequence of steps: clarification of organizational mandates, of organizational mission, situational strategic analysis, identification of strategic issues, strategy formulation, and implementation. Strategy, here, is also explicit but unique, working from the SWOT agenda of Strengths, Weaknesses, Opportunities, and Threats. Nevertheless, the design school sees strategy development as a controlled, conscious process of thought that must be kept simple and informal. The approach suggested in this chapter also sees strategy making as a designed and conscious process, but one which seeks to work with complexity rather than ignore it.

For us, the crucial contribution of these schools is to articulate a framework for closure to the strategy making process (see chapter C8) and to focus on delivery and realization. The leaning of the planning school towards understanding organizations as bureaucracies, and as 'machines', reinforces the role that programming, schedules, targets, and budgets plays in strategic change. As we shall suggest in chapter C4, these bureaucratic features that exist implicity, if not explicitly, in organizations, give some of the best clues to emergent strategizing. Similarly the assumption, held by some proponents of the planning school, that the environment can be forecast and should prescribe 'best fit' planning, should not be rejected completely but seen within the context of the need for a rhetoric of rationality. The focus, held by the design school, on strategy formulation as a process that explores mandates, mission, issues, distinctive competencies, and the interaction between the environment and

Figure C2.5   Hampden-Turner's twelve faces of strategy (Hampden-Turner, 1993:338).

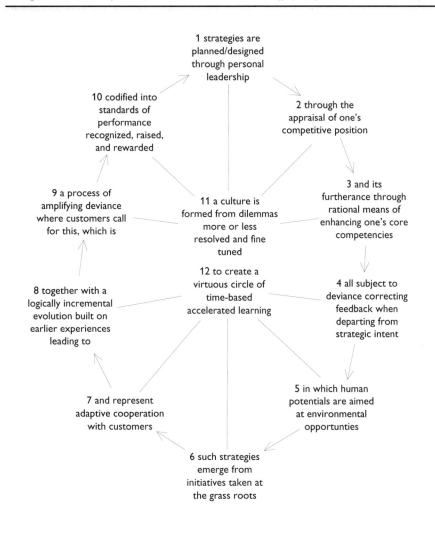

the organization from an 'open systems' perspective (where the organization, as a system, continually interacts with its environment), is the link between the JOURNEY making process and the negotiation which confirms and (re)designs strategy.

It should be clear that we are arguing that strategy making and delivery, in the real world (figure C2.1), manifests elements of a number of schools (figure C2.2). Rather than preferring one school of thought over another, it is more productive to see these as different aspects of the same complex journey to strategic achievement. The approach we take is similar, in some respects, to Hampden-Turners's attempt to lock together in a cycle the 'twelve faces of strategy' shown in figure C2.5 (Hampden-Turner, 1993:336–338).

Thus, as we outlined in chapter C1, we see effective strategy as '*a coherent set of individual discrete actions which are supported as a portfolio by a self-sustaining critical mass, or momentum, of opinion in the organization*'. This is regardless of whether these actions are, at one extreme, through a strategic plan, or at the other through opportunistic flexibility guided by a coherent strategic intent. They may also be somewhere else on the continuum represented by these two extremes (see chapter C1).

The coherence of strategy and strategic management is related to the extent to which: strategy statements do not contradict each other either singly or as meaningful 'chunks' of strategy; strategic action programmes do not contradict strategy statements or each other; systems and procedures – embedded routines – are not inconsistent with strategic intent; personal and organizational reward systems (costing, remuneration, transfer pricing) are not inconsistent with strategic intent; and actual behaviour (theories in use) does not contradict espoused behaviour (espoused theories). Strategy and strategic management is coherent when it can be recognized as a holistic phenomenon.

This perspective, however, represents a dilemma for management. **Coordinated and coherent thinking** and action are the basis for social organization and yet, at the same time are also forming a 'straight jacket' for the organization that reduces the likelihood of flexible action and continuous organizational change (see chapter C8). On the one hand organizational members must have shared beliefs, or a 'dominant logic' (Prahalad and Bettis, 1986; von Krogh *et al*, 1994), or 'strategic frames' (Huff, 1982) so that new events are interpreted in similar ways (Bougon *et al*, 1977; Gioia and Sims, 1986; March, 1991), but they must also retain individuality in their thinking so that new circumstances can entertain new interpretations and creative action. This tension between alignment and differentiation is an important strategic dilemma for all organizations. More alignment, and so coordinated action, derive from highly planned strategies, whereas flexibility and opportunism are more likely with a form of deliberate emergent strategy formulated as strategic intent.

Figure C2.6 seeks to demonstrate how an emphasis on designing processes of strategy making and delivery that involve multiple groups in jointly understanding, reflecting, and negotiating strategy deliver practical outcomes and intentions. The practical outcomes are:

P431

- Creating *political feasibility* for managing **continuity and strategic change** by developing better negotiated *agreements* and *emotional and reasoned (cognitive) commitment* which are not confounded by the lowest common denominator of compromise. Thus, group processes are expected to enable organizational members to contribute their expertise and ideas, to develop and reflect upon the synthesis of their ideas with those of others, to have been party to a procedure which is both just and rational (see chapter C3 on procedural justice and rationality). The journey is focused on small groups within both large and small

Figure C2.6 The JOURNEY of strategy making and delivery explained.

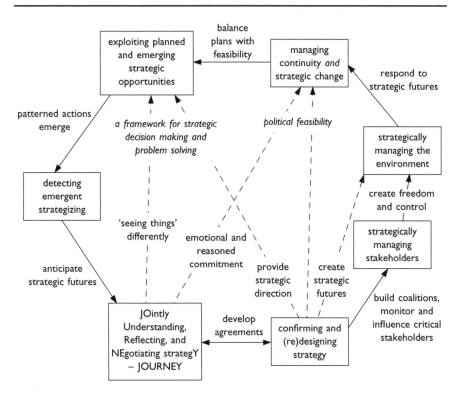

organizations – from top management teams to other **experts, opinion**   *P377*
leaders, creative people, saboteurs or blockers, winners and losers.
These groups work in a designed and structured manner to promote
individual and group learning.

- Helping people in the organization, the actors, to *see things differently*, to
  create new *frameworks*, and psychological schemas or construct systems,
  for strategic decision making and problem solving. The journey is
  expected to enable the *continual exploitation* of both planned and
  emerging (unexpected) opportunities. We expect managers to see issues
  and opportunities they would not have seen before, and no longer to
  notice issues that are less significant for determining strategic success.
  Thus, strategy making is about forgetting and ignoring as well as about
  seeing new and different opportunities. Colleagues will not be surprised or disappointed by the actions of others, rather they will see
  them as obviously congruent with an intended *strategic direction*. In this
  way there will not be a separation of thinking from action or vice versa.
  There is also no presumption that all can be known – that implementation follows choices which can have been made against certain
  and unambiguous data; rather strategic action will be framed not
  constrained.

Figure C2.7   The cyclical process of review and organizational learning.

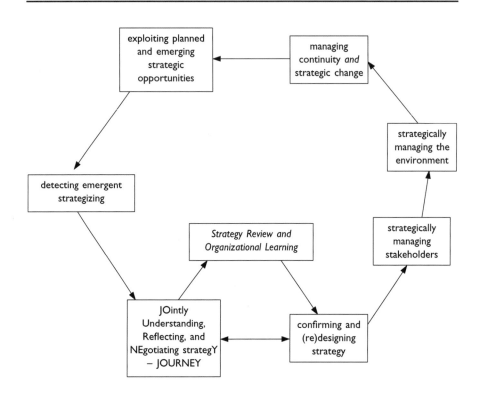

The process of confirming and (re)designing strategy (the result of developing agreements through the journey) leads to:

- Providing the *strategic direction* for the organization, the explicit (as opposed to cognitive) framework for action, by providing at the least a statement of strategic intent – vision, mission, goals, symbols.
- *Creating strategic futures* through strategically *managing* the environment, where the stakeholders are managed strategically by pro-actively building (and destroying) *coalitions and alliances* as well as seeking to directly *influence critical stakeholders*. This, in turn, will enable the organization to *interact with rather than react to different strategic futures* and so enable change to be balanced with continuity.

Figure C2.7 makes one very important addition to the picture we have been unfolding – that of strategy making and its realization as a continuous cycle of learning *through review*. Thus, strategy is re-launched from a new *platform*. The act of re-launching recognizes that progress has been made in strategically changing the organization. As strategic change occurs, expectations may be dashed as the organization learns about the success and failures of strategic change; equally success may be faster than anticipated. Distinctive, and core, competencies may turn out not to be sustainable after all. Most significantly the constraints on strategic change that currently persist and must be recognized in current strategies may disappear as the culture of the organization changes. From the platform of new competencies, a new culture, and new ways of thinking, new strategic opportunities, become realistic and politically feasible. These new directions are usually difficult to anticipate and plan for; rather the process of review – conducted as learning – offers the basis for redesign of strategy.

Building the Links

Concluding the overview in this chapter, we present four diagrams, each of which elaborates the logic of the activities that form the basis of the rest of this book, and in particular the third section describing methods, techniques, and tools.

Detecting Emergent Strategizing

Figure C2.8 elaborates the process of *detecting* emergent strategizing. The full description of this detection process occurs in chapter C5. However, here we note that a crucial task is to avoid believing that emergent strategizing has been captured when all that has been detected is the body of *espoused* statements from managers. These statements rarely fully or accurately describe the patterns of behaviour and decision making in the organization. That is to say, we should be aware of the difference between **'theories in use'** (how people think and act) and 'espoused theories' (how *P303 P353 P427* people account for how they think and act). Clearly official (espoused) statements are an important system of symbols that are used to justify action, and develop stories which influence the culture of the organization. However, there is no substitute for capturing 'theories in use' employed by managers as they deal with strategic issues, embed conscious assumptions and 'world-taken-for-granted' assumptions into bureaucratic procedures, or follow rituals dealing with routine developments that can profoundly affect the strategic future of the organization. As we argue in chapter C5, we are interested in surfacing patterns through (i) a study of strategic statements as they are expressed to stakeholders and to managers in the organization; (ii) examining assumptions embedded in procedures, such as the costing system, information system, budgeting system; and (iii) exploring the decision making processes – the bargaining methods used to resolve power and politics. But what is more important, is (iv) understanding the strategic assumptions – beliefs and values, which are declared through the way in which strategic issues are identified and dealt with – emergent patterns in what we know. Thus the exploration of (i) to (iii) follows the right-hand stream of figure C2.8 and (iv) the left-hand thread.

Figure C2.8   Anticipating strategic futures.

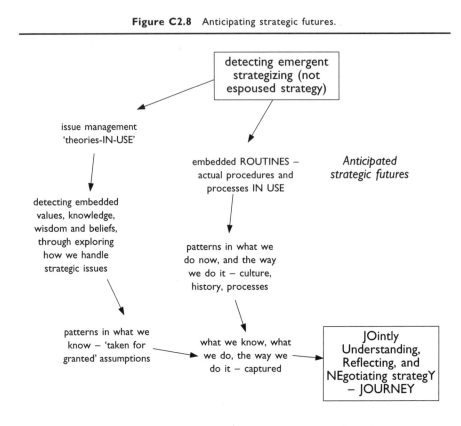

Developing Agreements

Figure C2.9 shows the important analyses that are the basis for developing agreements about strategic direction, from determining the business idea/livelihood scheme in the light of strategic aspirations and distinctive competencies, to stakeholder analysis, environmental analysis, the surfacing of strategic options, and so on.

Each analysis informs the other, and closure gradually arises as stability in conclusions becomes apparent. The crucial outcome from the journey is that of agreeing a *sense of strategic direction* – a mission, vision, **strategic intent**. The expression of this strategic direction is a statement that explicitly states the basis on which the organization *will do business* (its aspirations or goals) – what purposes enable the organization to satisfy its value system (e.g. be profitable, provide public service), *satisfy key stakeholders*, and *coexist with its environment*. For the private sector this is an expression of the 'business idea' – the idea that will convert purposeful activity into revenue and profit, or in our terms the 'livelihood scheme' – the right to exist as a public organization. Strategic direction is primarily informed by an *analysis of values and beliefs* of powerful members of the organization and of its key stakeholders, and by analysis of its *distinctive*

Figure C2.9 The framework for developing agreements.

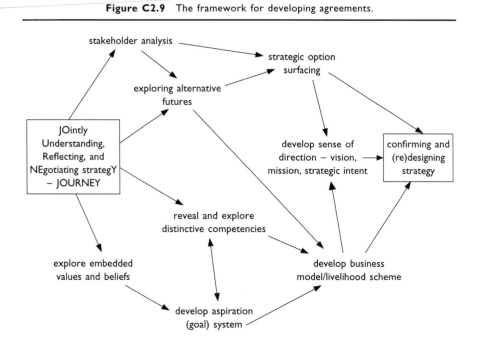

competencies. The ability to link distinctive competencies and values creates the *business idea or livelihood scheme.* It is the basis of the organization's rights to be in business. Strategic direction will be also be informed by the *strategic options* (surfaced through analyses of stakeholders, the environment or the value/belief systems) that are available to the organization – it is this which provides the underpinning realism in developing a sense of strategic direction.

The Outcomes of JOURNEY Making

Closure and the Delivery of Strategy

Figure C2.10 shows, in greater detail, the significant aspects of closure from the JOURNEY making.

Strategic direction is at the core and provides the framework for any, more detailed, strategic programmes. A statement of strategic direction, however, may be the full extent of strategy output – for example, where detailed planning, resource allocation, and strategic control are not essential for strategically managing stakeholders or providing the framework for exploiting planned and emergent strategic opportunities.

Output from the strategy making process must be appropriate for the nature of the organization (see chapter C1). Strategy is a framework of strategic intent designed to produce coherent action. Option surfacing

Figure C2.10   Closure and strategy delivery.

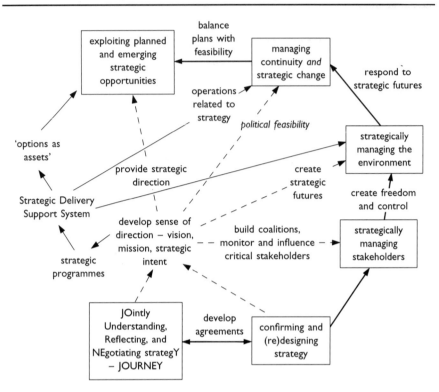

rather than action planning is emphasized – options are regarded as assets to be exploited if and when appropriate. The journey is designed to tune up thinking and arrive at shared meaning about strategic intent and strategic direction. Exploring strategic issues, undertaking stakeholder analysis, and scenario development are each related mental tools designed to facilitate the strategy conversation and to surface options. In this way the strategy making process is designed to influence *strategic thinking and strategic intent*. Organizational learning occurs around the journey, and it may be neither necessary nor appropriate to develop, for example, detailed action plans as commands to enact strategy in highly directed ways.

However, figure C2.10 also shows how the confirmed and (re)designed strategy can be developed into a detailed portfolio of strategic programmes complete with action packages that show the full linkage between operational activity, detailed strategic problem solving, and the mission of the organization. In chapter P8 we also go on to explore in more detail how the delivery of strategy can be aided by the use of a **strategy delivery support system (SDSS)**. This system is a computer based decision support system providing managers and implementation teams with a record of who is responsible and accountable for strategic actions and programmes, when these actions are to be delivered and the progress made towards their delivery, and the purpose of the actions along with

P334

other actions which support them. The system is used to ensure that options, as important strategic 'assets' of future value to the organization, are protected. The system also ensures that options which emerge during the strategy development process become a part of the '**organizational memory**' so that they may be considered and used when appropriate. Options are recorded in the system so that they are linked to the possible purposes for their enaction, and the system records the framework for choosing them against emerging opportunities.

P321 P437

Creating Strategic Change and Strategic Flexibility and Managing Continuity and Strategic Change

Our final figure in this sequence (figure C2.11) shows how the journey of strategy making is designed to promote both strategic flexibility and strategic change within the context of the need for continuity – 'managing the shop', and continuing to generate income from 'cash cows' *while* strategic change is resourced and managed. The significance of procedural rationality and procedural justice cannot be underestimated in preparing for strategic change through shifting the meanings staff attribute to strategic intent and purpose. The only change which can be delivered is that which is politically feasible.

The delivery of strategy is ultimately about being able to design a journey that will achieve every one of the linkages shown in figures C2.6 to C2.10, without any exceptions. Thus, the congruence across organizational members, of a cognitive framework that is derived from a journey involving *cognitive change*, supporting *coordination, cooperation, managing the complexity* of emergent tacit and deep knowledge, and ensuring a high degree of coherence in the exploitation of planned and emerging opportunities leads to effective social organization (Barnard, 1938).

To illustrate this requirement for social organization and the development of strategic direction, consider the list of factors below that block strategic change and were identified by senior managers working in one of the organizations we have been involved with (a public sector organization):

- apparent lack of sanctions or rewards for performance in relation to strategy
- lack of credibility of the initiative – seen as outside pressure
- lack of any driven change designed to impact directly on behaviour
- no control function from the top
- difficulties in evaluating strategic performance using quantitative measures
- initiative became power play between senior managers and with stakeholders
- reactive, rather than pro-active, nature of job done

Figure C2.11 The role of JOURNEY making for strategic change and strategic flexibility.

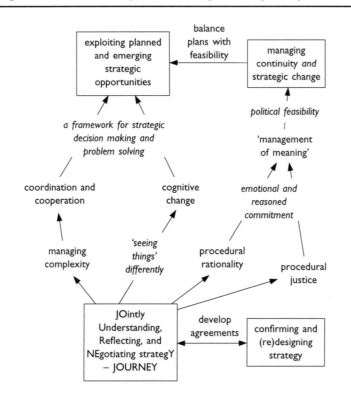

- lack of communication in explaining strategy ideas – what's in it for other staff
- no strategic slack for implementation – budget tightening, retrenchment
- bureaucracy already at critically high levels strategy delivery means more.

Each of these factors is typical of points made by managers in many types of organizations. The above model for a journey of strategy making and delivery is designed to address these issues as well as to allow a sensible direction for strategic change to emerge.

The Contribution of Our Approach

The theory and practice presented in this book, and outlined above, derive from a series of developments that have taken place over the last fifteen years. It is appropriate to provide a brief history of the developments so that readers can see something of the learning and experience which have guided the content of this book.

In the late 1970s effort was devoted to the task of helping groups understand the nature of problems they found themselves addressing. For some time, management scientists had been providing mathematical modelling support to industrial clients where the techniques were serviceable for relatively tractable problems involving little dispute about the nature of the problem. However, many management scientists wished to become more involved with complex and messy problems which inevitably had a political dimension, if only because there was a dispute about what the 'real' problem was. The use of qualitative modelling in the form of cognitive maps for understanding 'Thinking in Organizations' (Eden *et al*, 1979), taken alongside the effective facilitation of small groups, was developed and published under the title of 'Messing About in Problems' (Eden *et al*, 1983).

The work on messy problems inevitably led to consultancy and research with all sorts of organizations (including BT, ICL, Bath City Council) which began to shift the orientation towards the processes of addressing strategic problems. This experience, and the continual development of a theory of strategic problem solving, resulted in a combination of cognitive mapping techniques, group process methods, and computer software development for representing, manipulating, and analysing maps, acting together as a designed methodology (Strategic Options Development and Analysis – SODA) for providing Group Decision Support (Eden, 1990a; Eden and Ackermann, 1992). By the mid-1980s, the effectiveness of this methodology within the realm of strategic problem solving led senior managers in a number of organizations to suggest that the approach should be used as a process for strategy development. The approach was particularly attractive because it bypassed corporate planning groups and worked directly with the top management team as a powerful decision making group. In addition the ability of cognitive/cause mapping techniques and the associated computer software to analyse existing corporate strategy documents was taken to be an appropriate starting point for new strategy discussions. These analyses revealed weaknesses, in the form of inconsistencies, illogicality, and incoherence in a blunt and yet transparent manner that invited constructive change which was undertaken interactively with the group working in relation to a large public computer screen, often through multiple workstations. In addition, work with external stakeholder groups and examination of possible futures became a key part of the process as has the use of the resultant strategy map (or computerized model) for monitoring the progress of strategic change both at the macro and micro levels.

Gilmore and Camillas (1996) have suggested that many planning processes do not 'meet the reality test'. They identify a number of wicked characteristics to be addressed in strategy making:

- defining and solving the problem go together;
- the task is never done, solutions can always be improved;
- the problem is complex, composed of many interrelated problems;

symptoms cannot be distinguished from causes, hence deciding where and how to respond is difficult;
- the problem is substantially unique;
- there are diverse stakeholders with differing priorities and values;
- future hazards cannot all be identified; unknown contingencies will occur.

We would mostly agree with their characteristics and would argue that the approach we have developed seeks to recognize them and also to work within the context of the 'fundamental principles' they propose for dealing with them. These principles include: 'prototyping . . . planning is an on-going process'; 'exchange of information about concepts, needs, plans, decisions, assessments or opinions, but also the underlying assumptions'; 'inclusion of diverse, needed and affected people'; 'modularization and interconnection' . . . 'to deal with complexity'; 'win–win incentives' – design of effective reward systems. Our contribution, in part, is to provide the concepts that can guide effective practice that addresses these issues, and provide well-tried and tested methods, tools, and techniques which are the basis for effective practice and which meet the 'reality test'.

THE POLITICAL FEASIBILITY OF STRATEGY

'In the face of an obstacle which is impossible to overcome, stubbornness is stupid' (Simone de Beauvoir)

'There is nothing more difficult than to achieve a new order of things, with no support from those who will not benefit from the new order, and only lukewarm support from those who will' (Machiavelli, *The Prince*, 1514)

This chapter is a crucial part of the book. It discusses the single, most important, consideration in managing strategic change in organizations – that of political feasibility, achieved through (i) *determining the extent* of the political feasibility for change, and (ii) *making the likelihood* of change more politically feasible. By this we mean firstly becoming aware (explicitly enquiring) of the level of political feasibility surrounding particular strategic options, and secondly using this knowledge to design strategies in such a way that the likelihood of their implementation is high.

There is little in-depth attention in the strategy literature to issues of political feasibility. Somehow the rational processes of analysis are expected to carry the day. Thus, political feasibility, in so far as it is addressed, is expected to derive from the way in which a proposal can be demonstrated to be rational; a case can be made, reasons stated through attention to the facts, and to the relationship between the means and ends. This is what Simon (1976) called means/ends, or substantive, rationality. Even with this acknowledgement, the majority of attention remains focused upon the capture of the substantive material, or data, and the associated forms of analysis and data manipulation. It is attention to these processes that is taken to be the test of whether or not the strategy making outcomes are correct. Little, or no, attention is paid to the social processes of delivering, discovering, and negotiating the data, determining and manipulating its meaning, and agreeing the strategic direction.

This chapter seeks to highlight and discuss aspects that contribute towards acknowledging and incorporating political feasibility in strategy making. The discussion involves examining the politics of the organization, paying attention to procedural justice and procedural rationality, and exploring the impact and ramifications of group work and participation (see figure C3.1). Group decision support systems (underpinning the structure) provide a means of recognizing and managing the practical side and are addressed more extensively in the third part of the book.

Figure C3.1 Attention to political feasibility.

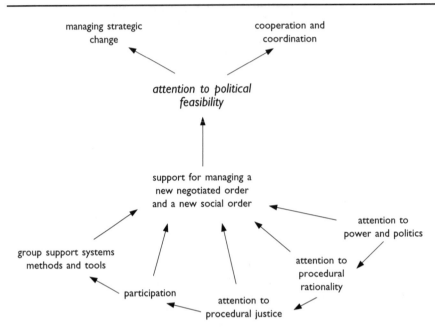

It is our contention that the content of strategic issues cannot be understood without an understanding of the issues of politics, power, personalities, and personal style. Likewise, design of appropriate process interventions cannot be done without understanding the nature of the substantive political issues faced by a management team. There is no separation between the **work of the rational analyst and the work of the social process facilitator**.

P380

Strategy making is usually expected to change, sometimes by large amounts, the way an organization works. As we have said, change of any sort will always be seen to have winners and losers by those who are the recipients of change. Indeed most of the key players in designing change will see themselves as potential winners or losers. As soon as strategy is believed to be influential then the process of developing strategy will generate significant **organizational politics**. For example, new coalitions will form and reform, key players will be seeking to position themselves for an uncertain future, and managers will be forced to live within the stressful environment of increased uncertainty and ambiguity. Indeed, if this is not so, then it can be assumed that strategy making is not going to change the organization. Our view is that organizational politics must be accepted as going hand in hand with successful strategy making.

P226

Issues relating to the implementation of strategic direction are as significantly related to attitudes, power, and managerial prerogative as they are to an appropriate consideration of the relations between means and activities and outcomes.

On the Politics of Organizational Change

A common experience for many managers is that the strategic planning process takes on the form of an 'annual rain dance'. The activity is taken to be important enough to devote some limited time to it because the intellectual arguments for doing so are difficult to argue with – 'of course an organization must have a strategy'. However, often the reality is that the activity will simply result in 'the usual annual budgeting battle' which is focused on short term issues and the retention of the status quo. Some managers will come off badly and others well, but this will be related more to their political clout and negotiating skills than any consideration of the longer term impact of the budgets on the strategic future of the organization. These budgeting rounds will have a real impact on the strategic future of the organization as a part of the emergent strategizing of the organization, but not in a thoughtful or designed way (Raimond and Eden, 1990). Statements about the strategic future of the organization will be used, when appropriate, as a part of the negotiation for resources but will not form part of a coherent whole, nor result in action.

When managers begin to realize that the strategy making process might be 'for real' and might actually have some consequences for the future of the organization then those participating in the process will begin to make judgements about whether they will **gain or lose** from the process. This *P377* assessment is influenced by their believing that strategic change will shift the balance of power, and will value some skills and resources more than others. The surfacing of strategic options carries the concomitant surfacing of anticipated social and political consequences. Indeed any organizational change is seen by many managers as an opportunity for **self aggrandise-** *PV226* **ment** and the acquisition of power (Frost, 1987; Mangham, 1978; Perrow, 1986). The politics that this process of anticipation creates will be the result of each participant's personal understanding of the impact of strategy. This understanding may, or may not, be accurate – what matters is that each participant anticipates and takes action to influence strategic thinking on the basis of these anticipations. 'If men define situations as real, they are real in their consequences' (Thomas and Thomas, 1928). The communication about strategy can then become dominated by each participant seeking to influence the definition of the situation in ways that anticipate possible changes in status, power, self image, and so on. Most senior managers are very skilled in the process of defining situations in a light favourable to their own aspirations and inclinations. Thus, the way in which situations are defined becomes crucial, as it determines the nature of the agendas to be addressed and the processes by which strategic issues are surfaced. The extent to which a management team is able to address the fundamental strategic issues, rather than address only the fears and aspirations of each member of the team, will be a measure of their likelihood for success. We are not suggesting that fears and aspirations of management, or other staff, may not be a legitimate strategic issue, rather we are making a distinction

P432 between those issues that directly affect the **core activity of the organiza-tion compared with those that facilitate** that activity.

These realities of effective strategy making mean that strategy making will be an emotionally charged process.

P425 **Coordination and Cooperation**

There is a need for coordinated and coherent problem-solving processes, which require some commonality of problem construal – of what matters for the future of the organization. This does *not* mean that the detailed construal of the problem(s) is similar, but rather that there is some agree-ment about what to see and not to see. The effective team will depend upon each team member offering different ways of understanding even though they may use the same problem label. It does, at the very least, mean a commitment to shared values (Peters and Waterman, 1982).

As noted in figure C3.1, addressing political feasibility is not only concerned with managing the process of strategic change but also with carrying out change that creates coordinated and cooperative action. Using methods that support and acknowledge a negotiation process is funda-mental – social and psychological negotiation is the bedrock of political feasibility. Strauss and Schatzman (1963) introduced the idea that organizations (hospitals, in their case) are a *negotiated order*. Negotiating a *new* order is the most crucial element of political feasibility. Here we extend the idea by suggesting that there are two aspects to the notion of organizations as a negotiated order. First, there is that aspect that arises from the attempt by members of the organization to change the nature of the organization so that it shifts its purpose and changes the means for achieving the purpose. As we have suggested earlier, this is always contested. Every person has their own ideas about what the organization is for and how it should get there. This means that any change will have to be determined through negotiation – the creation of a new negotiated order. This new negotiated order is determined independently of who is to deliver and maintain the new order. It is, instead, based upon principles of 'hard systems' where optimization is sought for problems such as logistics, production, marketing, business processes, and finance. It is possible for one person to determine the nature of the best new order by analysis of the 'facts'. But, in organizations, these facts are disputed, and so negotiation amongst powerful players is required to establish which facts are to be used in the analysis. This social negotiation aims to create a new order, new ways of doing things, determined by the needs of the organization as differently perceived by each player. Thus, this first aspect – creating a

P284 P305 P328 **new *'negotiated order'***, recognizes that resolution of the tensions between
P399 P478 what each of the powerful actors in the organization wants for the organ-ization demands a social process – JOURNEY making – that explores the different perspectives and negotiates an acceptable way forward.

However, the second aspect of the notion of organizations as a negotiated order attends to the extent to which organizations and groups exist within an established order of social relationships. Here people need to be able to work together acknowledging friendships, loyalties, dependencies, and most importantly established scripts and social roles (Mangham and Overington, 1987). There are major forces for maintaining the status quo of the current social relationships, and so any changes to social relationships need to be negotiated. The outcome of this process may be labelled the **new 'social order'**. Negotiated order and social order are two sides of the same coin, each emphasizing a different aspect of organizations as negotiated enterprises, with strategic management aiming to create a new negotiated order and new social order.

P305 P328 P478

The first aspect acknowledges that a social procedure of one sort or another is always used to make decisions. Decisions can rarely, if ever, be enacted without recourse to social negotiation and so a consideration of power and politics. The second acknowledges that any organizational change has an impact on **negotiated social relationships**. It is the second of these that means people have difficulty saying what they think ought to be done for the organization because to do so might have undesirable consequences for currently comfortable social relationships and existing informal trading agreements. At the very least, managers realize that future negotiations depend upon the conduct of current negotiations. The role of relationship building was a significant addition to the work of Roger Fisher (Fisher and Ury, 1982) on 'getting to yes' in negotiations by arguing for 'getting together: building a relationship that gets to yes' (Fisher and Brown, 1988). In organizations 'the bulk of our activity consists in "relating" itself . . . the most important aspect of activities, the ongoing maintenance of our ongoing activities and their ongoing satisfactions' (Vickers, 1983:33). Janis and Mann (1977) emphasize that the stress arising from concerns about personal and social losses that might be incurred following difficult decisions can lead to several dysfunctional coping patterns. Of relevance to reducing the probability of creating an effective new negotiated order or new social order are: (i) unconflicted adherence – where the complacent continuation of the current strategy is the easiest way out, (ii) unconflicted change – where there is uncritical adoption of a new strategy, (iii) defensive avoidance – where a group finds ways ignoring conflict, and (iv) hyper-vigilance – panic.

V227

As these two aspects of negotiated order are opposite sides of the same coin, neither can be ignored. Instead, they need to be carefully balanced as strategic change is designed and delivered. The strategy making must be designed to permit both aspects, so that a new negotiated order and a new social order can arise hand in hand. Acknowledging both aspects is contrary to the common view that problem solving in organizations is solely about the generation and evaluation of alternatives and choice from amongst them (Nutt, 1984). In addition, it suggests that decision *making* is influenced by the way in which issues are presented, the identification of their significance, their exploration as the group constructs

P304 P321 a **shared understanding** of them, and the point at which a negotiated settlement is likely. Coordination depends on developing, understanding and agreeing processes and procedures that are coherent with each other, analytically sound, objectively workable, and designed with respect to the realities of importance to the organization (the first aspect). Cooperation depends on good working social relationships as well as on procedures and bureaucracy (the second aspect). Cooperation is crucial to managing strategic futures, because strategic opportunism depends on the ability to work together on issues that cannot be dealt with by current procedures, but rather by team work and paying attention to multiple perspectives, within at least a reasonably common framework for construing the world.

Issues of *balance* are critical to effective strategy making. If there is too much that is influenced by the established social order then there is a risk of the 'realities' of the problem situation being ignored and 'group-think' (Janis, 1972) occurring, where the group negotiates a course of action that nobody wants and where nobody knew the others didn't want it. Jerry Harvey neatly describes an example of this phenomenon (known as the 'Abilene Paradox' (Harvey, 1988)) where a group finish up taking a bus ride to the town of Abilene, a ride that none of the group wanted. However, if the strategy making process is only dominated by the rhetoric of what is good for the organization (without participants considering their own role in the outcomes) then social relationships may become ambiguous. Participants then turn their attention fully to resolving this ambiguity in their social affairs. Consequently, there is a tendency for the organization to settle back to the old negotiated order as the easiest resolution of ambiguity – the old ways of doing things and the old social relationships. Here agreements are subsequently sabotaged because they are not politically feasible. At its worst, we can see this happening when a group of managers get together to consider a strategic problem and their deliberations are governed solely by the logic of a unitary perspective analytical model such as a decision tree or multiple criteria decision model. The logic of the model is powerful, the analysis of the facts is indisputable, apparent agreement to a course of action is reached, and yet after the managers leave the room the agreement is sabotaged. The analytical procedure ignored: (i) multiple perspectives on the facts, partly because the modelling technique only allowed for one view of the facts (albeit, sometimes with a recognition of uncertainty which can be taken as a range of views); (ii) the extent to which 'disagreeable' facts could not emerge because of its impact on social relationships, and so some of the group knew the 'answer' was wrong but could not negotiate because *P328 P385* the analytical procedures did not allow enough **equivocality** for balancing a process of discovering facts along with a gradual shifting of social relationships. It also ignored (iii) the need for the changes in social relationships, demanded by any new ways of doing things, to be negotiated with care. This is not to argue that analysis is unhelpful; on the contrary, it is to argue that it must sit within the realities of a social organization where facts are disputed; facts are determined as much by power as by knowledge, wisdom, and experience; and social relationships influence the practicalities of agreements being implemented.

The introduction of designed conflict as a dialectical device seems to be an obvious way forward, and one that has been promoted in many management books. However, situations like '**group think**', where groups *P298* show an excessive tendency to seek concurrence, are found to occur more frequently when the groups use normative methods for increasing conflict: for example, dialectical enquiry, devil's advocacy, and consensus approaches (Janis, 1989). The symbolic use of analysis to deflect attention away from issues, can give the impression of action. Adopting the symbolic analysis route may be the result of a group being unable to manage their social relationships and so failing to find ways of opening up the 'real' issues. The deflection is often something that no one wants and yet it is the only way the group can find of proceeding. The principle of JOURNEY making, which we encourage and design throughout this book, strives to increase the chances of productive dialectical enquiry by recognizing the importance of *facilitating both social and psychological negotiation* – where there is a greater opportunity for participants to genuinely change their mind as well as develop new rewarding relationships. 'Every negotiator has two kinds of interests: in the substance and in the relationship – in fact, with many long term clients, business partners, family members, fellow professionals, government officials, or foreign nations, the ongoing relationship is far more important than the outcome of any particular negotiation' (Fisher and Ury, 1982).

The need for balance between demands for the maintenance of the existing order and the creation of new order, supports the idea that organizational change relies upon incrementalism, upon many 'small wins', rather than the single 'big win' (Bryson, 1988). Major organizational change is more likely to arise from the systemic and strategic confluence of lots of small wins rather than through a single 'big bang' change programme. Sometimes, of course, incrementalism may not be possible, but we are suggesting that it will usually stand a better chance of success. We return to this debate in chapter C9 on closure.

On the Nature of Groups

Strategy making, as we propose it, can occur only in groups and teams. The **minimum expectation is that it will *involve* every member of the** *P376* **management team for the unit under consideration**, be this unit a department, a division, an operating company, or a large corporation. Earlier we referred to the balancing act between risking everyone thinking the same and disorganized haphazard behaviour – an important element of team working. Difficulties in attaining this balance often mean that a management team is unable to operate in a way that allows differences in perspective to surface. As a consequence, artificial agreement is reached. Where this occurs, members likely to disagree with the decisions made will believe that it is too risky to state their own views. They might be discouraged from doing so for a number of reasons or conditions:

- They may believe that their view is 'out on a limb' from the rest of the group.
- They may believe they will be subject to ridicule for expressing an alternative view.
- They may think that others have already said it, or thought about it, because it seems so obvious, and that the idea must have been rejected for 'good' reasons.
- They may have 'trading agreements' with others in the group that would be broken if they expressed a view which opposes that of their trading partners – to do so would have consequences for support on other issues.
- To dissent from the view of the group may put team cohesiveness at risk – threatening the established social order.
- It damages or destroys the camaraderie of being a team.
- They may be frightened of reprisals for expressing a particular view that is thought to be counter to the prevailing view of those in power.

Some of these reasons are influenced by the politics of organizational change. We have discussed earlier the rule of thumb that unless strategy making generates a political dynamic then it is unlikely to have much significance for the organization. But as this political dynamic unfolds it can be a major contributor to a team's being unable to address the fundamental issues and being diverted to internal coalition building designed to retain the relative security of the status quo.

When some of the above conditions persist in a group, it is likely that they will all finish up with the circumstances we discussed above, where there is agreement to a course of action, a strategy, which no one supports (the 'Abilene Paradox'). Social norms of a group can discourage the extent to which the thinking of each of the individuals in the group is used in the group decision making (Walsh, 1988; Walsh *et al*, 1988). Thus, while each individual has an idiosyncratic view of the situation their social processes and existing social relationships encourage only shallow thinking to surface – giving the impression to all of a common view of the problem they are addressing.

Ineffective group work can be the result of the strategy making process *placing too much emphasis on building* **emotional commitment** *without designing processes that reinforce high quality rationality* (Collins and Guetzkow, 1964). As we shall be emphasizing throughout this book, the relationship between these two aspects is complete and fundamental. *Without emotional commitment to delivering agreements the rationality of the reasoning becomes irrelevant and the balance has swung fully too far to cognitive* *commitment only.* The value of high quality thinking is close to zero without a willingness of managers to cooperate in implementation (Floyd and Wooldridge, 1992; Wooldridge and Floyd, 1990). Indeed there is a great danger of *deliberate sabotage of highly rational decisions that have not taken any account of the social needs of the group* (Guth and MacMillan, 1986). Choices made must recognize that *coordinated and cooperative effort is required to deliver strategy.* Strategy is not delivered by a system but by real people with social futures together. The social relationships of members of an organization are mostly expressed through the social order that exists in their ways of working together, their patterns of interaction, their dependencies. *Strategy development that is effective will, perforce, disturb these relationships.* Strategies that do so are at risk, regardless of their reasoned goodness, because sometimes *team members will sabotage them in subtle ways in order to retain social equilibrium.* And in delivering strategy *a lack of commitment to one part of the strategy will always have repercussions for other parts* (Eisenhardt, 1989).

We are here recognizing two opposing demands of organizational change. Firstly, there is a demand that change should be in aid of creating a new way of working on the core tasks of the organization and that for this new way of working to be the best possible it will need to account for the expertise of many people in the organization. However, organizational change must also allow for the second, opposing demand – the creation of new social relationships. New relationships between people who will implement the strategies are needed to create the new ways of working.

In the next two sections we consider two important elements of ensuring that teams can be party to an effective journey – procedural justice and procedural rationality.

Procedural Justice

V196 V244 P374 P477

The way of negotiating a new social order will, in part, depend upon designing 'procedural justice' (Thibaut and Walker, 1975) into the strategy making process. While there is an important relationship between procedural justice and the quality of the new negotiated order, ensuring procedural justice is an important consideration in its own right. For example, a particular decision may be unfavourable, and yet a team member will support it because the process of arriving at it was procedurally just. Procedural justice is concerned with attending to the fact that people are concerned about the fairness of the procedures used to arrive at a decision as well as the decision itself (Folger and Konovsky, 1989; McFarlin and Sweeney, 1992). It relates to an involvement in issue formulation, being listened to, and having a voice. However, it must be noted that being listened to, and involved in, are distinguished from having influence over outcomes. We are as much concerned by *perceptions of influence* as any reality of influence. As long as we expect to be able to design processes to address the perception of influence *and* involvement itself, then we expect to see some relationship between actual influence and the participant's perception of influence.

Recent research conducted with existing management teams suggests that 'leaders of strategic decision making teams can use procedures that improve the chances of gaining cooperation and commitment to decisions without sacrificing the quality of decisions in the process . . . when team *P284* leaders showed strong **consideration of team members' input**, team *P424* members saw the process as fairer, and consequently had greater **emotional commitment** to the decision, greater attachment to the team, and greater trust in the leader' (Korsgaard *et al*, 1995:76). More interesting from our point of view, they found a link suggesting that the extent to which leaders considered the input of team members, influenced positively the feelings of attachment and trust over time (which supports earlier studies not undertaken with 'real' teams (Leung and Li, 1990; Lind *et al*, 1990)). For strategy making, long term effects are particularly important if change is to be implemented.

Alongside this, Kim and Mauborgne (1995) explored the role of procedural justice in strategy formulation and implementation in global organizations. Their concern was specifically located in the problems of developing strategy for many strategic units in many countries (Kim and Mauborgne, 1991, 1993). However, there are some interesting aspects of the work that we believe apply equally to the methodology we are presenting in this book. We believe that the circumstances of the global organization may replicate, on a large scale, similar organizational relationships to those we meet in many other kinds of organization and so we can learn from the results of the study. The study sought to identify a small number of the characteristics of procedural justice which 63 'subsidiary presidents' regarded as significant when evaluating the annual strategic planning processes for being fair. Open-ended questionnaires were used to establish their views, and the results generated 63 statements which were then sorted, clustered, and subsequently checked with the participants. Their results suggested five dimensions that we list below in a form which we take to be relevant to most organizations:

- The extent to which a senior manager or top management team or chief executive gives middle managers 'an opportunity to voice their distinct perceptions, knowledge, and ideas but likewise are required to *V237* hear the opposite party out'. Kim and Mauborgne call this **'bilateral communication'**.
- The ability to refute and challenge the strategic views of the top management team; 'ability to refute'.
- The extent of seeking to determine a degree of local familiarity, on the part of senior management – examining issues from the coal face; 'local familiarity'.
V207 V236 - The extent to which middle managers 'are regularly **provided with a full account for the final decisions'** of the top management team –

for example, what steps were taken, why priorities were made; 'provision of account'.

- The extent to which the top management team does not discriminate but applies consistent decision making procedures across different parts of the organization; 'consistent decision making procedures'.

Kim and Mauborgne used these dimensions of procedural justice as the basis for exploring strategy implementation. Their findings support the view that procedural justice (as defined by these characteristics) does affect the likelihood of implementation of strategy across subsidiaries. If we see any medium-to-large organization as comprising competing 'subsidiaries' (departments and coalitions (Raimond and Eden, 1990)) then we may also expect these five dimensions of procedural justice to be important elements in the design of a strategy making methodology – each of the dimensions influences our attempts to design an effective strategy making journey.

Procedural Rationality

V244 V255 P329
P419 P477

Establishing that the procedure itself makes sense for the particular circumstances means managers are able to feel that they have embarked upon a process which is procedurally rational. That is, that the procedure itself is the outcome of a publicly stated reasoning and so can gather *cognitive commitment* from participants.

Procedural rationality is an extension of the notion of procedural justice as well as contributing to the negotiation process in its own right (see figure C3.1). Procedural rationality suggests that the procedures used for strategy making make sense in themselves – they are coherent, follow a series of steps where each step is itself understood (not opaque) and relates to the prior and future steps. 'Behaviour is procedurally rational when it is the outcome of appropriate deliberation' (Simon, 1976). Furthermore, it requires that it is not too time consuming nor too hurried, and that conclusions and agreements are closed off with an appropriate balance between **emotional and cognitive commitment** (that is, no paralysis by *P424* analysis, and yet the 'ground was covered'). Thus, the procedures of sorting out a strategic direction, considering alternative futures, capturing options, and undertaking stakeholder analysis identified in figure C2.8 are at least sensible and reasonably thoroughgoing.

This 'plan to plan' (Steiner, 1979) is referred to by John Bryson (1995:47) as gaining an 'initial agreement about the overall strategic planning effort and main planning steps'. It is designed to provide those who are setting out on the journey with an overall route plan – a plan that may be diverted from in order to reflect the realistic contingencies of blockages and fast progress (see chapter C1). It is about **setting some expectations** *P372* about what has to be done, why this is appropriate, how long it will take, and what the stages are on the way – process stages as well as content agreements (see figure C2.5 which shows both of these aspects as significant). The outcomes are expected to be more satisfactory if the procedure followed is rational rather than haphazard, *ad hoc*, or cannot be explained.

So far we have expressed the dilemmas of good strategy making in the following ways. The need to:

- balance cognitive commitment with emotional commitment,
- balance processes of negotiating new ways of working with negotiating new social relationships,
- balance reasoned (content) rationality with procedural (process) rationality and justice.

Each of these makes a similar point but in importantly different ways, because each implies attending to different aspects of the design of an effective strategy making process.

We do not expect all management team members to back fully the agreed-upon strategic change. The practical danger is pandering to the lowest common denominator to provide only the illusion of unity. The role of modelling to ensure that new options become the focus for negotiation, rather than argument about previously touted options, is crucial in moving away from the lowest common denominator (Fisher and Ury, 1982). However, it is, nevertheless, absolutely crucial that disagreements at the level of the management team are contained within that arena. Once a management team is seen to be bickering about the strategic future (rather than conversing during the process of strategy making) then others in the organization cannot be expected to respond to strategic direction. The opportunity for other staff to build coalitions around the different stances of their senior managers is enormous and any expectation of coherent action through either emotional or cognitive commitment can be dismissed.

V202 V225 V233
V238 V257 V284
Participation in Strategy Making

Embedded in much of the above is the demand for greater participation in the strategy making journey – more staff being involved in a meaningful manner. The primary benefit that derives from taking account of procedural justice, and its associated call for increased participation, is that of
P371 **greater ownership** by a wider group of staff to the strategy developed. Thus, as a minimum demand, we need to ensure that procedural justice is seen to have taken place amongst the most senior management team rather than to rely on the efforts of planning support staff.

The commitment of the senior team is absolutely essential. Without it the probability of anything happening is massively reduced (Hage and Dewar, 1973; Sabatier, 1991). At the other extreme we might argue for participation from all staff and from some external stakeholders.

Much of the early strategic management and organizational theory literature supports the belief that strategy is formulated by consensus among CEO and management team (for example, Ansoff, 1965). However, studies on organizational culture (Deal and Kennedy, 1982), the Japanese style of management (Ouchi, 1981), and incremental decision processes (Quinn, 1980) argue that it is often necessary to expand consensus on strategy beyond the management team.

John Harvey-Jones (1988) captured this issue rather well when he stated that:

'in deciding where you would like to be, as opposed to where you are probably going to end up, you need a great deal of discussion and a great deal of development of new thinking and new processes. The idea of doing this through the planning department, or through a paper on strategy presented to the board, seems to me to be quite inadequate. This process involves large amounts of time and constant discussion *with those involved lower down the line* who will actually execute the strategies on which the whole picture relies. This sort of circular debate, frequently widening out to involve others within and without the company, goes on until all are satisfied that the result is as good as they are going to get' (our emphasis).

The other side of this coin is represented by the tenable belief that staff should not be distracted by the wider picture. Rather staff should have clear and unambiguous instructions and procedures to follow. It follows that it is the job of the management team to think about strategy and the job of others to follow it within the context of a designed bureaucracy. For example, Campbell (1996) argues, on the basis of extensive research, that the police force should build strategy which is the basis of 'proactive reactivity'.

It is evident that some members of the organization need to be 'bought in' (an ugly phrase!) to the decisions and therefore careful consideration is necessary to determine the extent of involvement. By ensuring a 'buy-in' by participants – motivation through 'interest' – the probability of implementing strategy with a recognition of the interdependence on others for creating strategic order is increased. Furthermore, without gaining some buy-in or commitment from key managers (**opinion formers, power** *P377* **brokers, saboteurs**, etc.) early in the strategy making process, there is a high probability of 'counter effort' from staff (Guth and MacMillan, 1986). Nevertheless, gaining ownership suggests a manipulative activity involving *emotional* as well as cognitive management, and that may, therefore, be using groups to dupe its members into a false consciousness about the purpose of their participation. Here justice is, supposedly, seen to be done rather than has been done. Needless to say, success in duping such

V255 V227 V234 participants is rare – **staff in organizations are extremely good at guessing they are being duped** (even when intentions are otherwise!).

In addition, care must be taken when increasing participation, as it has been suggested that broad participation of decision makers may be seen to decrease the chances for collaboration, with narrower participation increasing it. Increased participation expands the range of perspectives that need to be accommodated, thus extending the difficulty and time required for the process of negotiation. As such, involving a wide and deep range of organizational members in the strategy making process requires developing the means for gaining commitment to the outcomes whilst denying decision making powers. Nevertheless, participants will always have a chance to influence others as well as influence strategy.

The argument for greater participation in order to attend to procedural rationality is that most managers have knowledge and experience that may be relevant to developing a good strategy. Thus, the argument is that greater participation is procedurally more rational. Participants are presumed to enhance substantive rationality in three ways. Firstly by offering multiple perspectives and by increasing the 'search' resource, and exposure to minority points of view, thus resulting in the deliberation of options that would otherwise not have surfaced (but see, for example, Hill, *P371* 1982) and secondly, from the **creativity** that comes from the synthesis and synergy produced by this increase in perspectives. Finally, substantive rationality will surface from the multiple expertise, which can make the evaluation of options more reliable.

We have suggested above that an increase in participation was desirable for the two reasons of a better decision and more commitment ('buy-in'). These outcomes offer mutual support to one another: a better decision is likely to gain more commitment (substantive rationality will be recognized and gain cognitive commitment); and an increase in participation in order to raise emotional commitment through a designed social process *P383* will, *providing social negotiation is designed to support **psychological negotiation**,* also increase substantive rationality. However, there is a third element, the need to consider the efficiency of the procedure. Higher levels *V202* of participation in strategy making take time. **Meeting productivity** is an important criterion of success. There is a concern for the client's attitude to the quality of problem solving in relation to time spent. Meeting efficiency is a recurrent concern of large organizations (see, for example, the recent study on NHS meetings (Brindle, 1991)).

'Half of every working day is spent in meetings, half of which are not worth having – and of those that are, half the time is wasted. Which means that more than a third of business life is spent in small rooms with people you don't like, doing things that don't matter. The only reason people have so many meetings is that they're the one time you can get away from your work, your phone and your customers. People say that the secret of a good meeting is preparation. But if people really prepared for meetings, the first thing they would realize is that most are completely unnecessary. In fact a tightly run meeting is one of the most frightening things in office life. These are meetings before which you have to prepare, in which you have to work and after which you have to take action' (Guy Browning on Office Politics in *The Guardian*, 9 December 1995).

However, involving as many staff as possible in the strategy making process is problematic. It is massively time consuming and can be very costly. In many of the cases reported in this book there was, what the management team regarded as, a very high level of involvement. High levels of involvement cannot be ventured without great care for the possible consequences. To involve staff and then to ignore the demands of procedural justice outlined above can leave senior management in a worse position than if there had been no involvement at all. It is also very dependent upon the long term commitment of the management team. The consequences of paying lip service to involvement, by not succeeding in creating a perception of being listened to, is much worse than no involvement.

Our own research, and that of others, suggests that some **staff do not** V201 **appreciate being asked to participate** in strategy making – they believe that it is management's job and they expect management to deliver on their responsibility for strategy. This does not mean that staff do not want to know how they fit in to the strategic future of the organization, but that they prefer to do what they take to be their job while others do their own job. This means that there will always be a cut off point for participation. This point will be contingent on the culturally bound expectations of staff, and on the balance between the needs of senior management to capture expertise and that of participation to increase 'buy-in'.

Other means for determining the cut off point focuses upon the amount of time that elapses during the process, and on the size of the organization. Where strategy making requires a lengthy period of time, possibly due to the need to involve stakeholders or carry out detailed analysis, then this may suggest that fewer members are involved; there can be disillusionment with the process if nothing appears to be happening following an input. Where the turnaround is relatively short (in one organization, we were involved in **developing a strategy within nine days** that involved V210 more than 45 people) it is easy to maintain enthusiasm and commitment. The other determinant, size of the organization, is a practical consideration, suggesting that resources and time constraints may result in only the management team being involved, or specific divisions/departments embarking upon the process.

Our view of the need for consideration of participation and empowerment must not be confused with the concerns of those for whom there is a moral crusade about democratizing the work place. Some of the process oriented approaches to strategic problem solving have been heartily criticized by commentators for being conservative and for supporting a managerial ideology (for example Rosenhead, 1989). The approaches they criticize may do this, but the proponents and designers of such approaches never declared that they set out to radicalize managerialism in organizations. Similarly, whilst in this book we argue for greater degrees of participation than usual, we do so for reasons which are to do with the nature of the difficulties in achieving strategic organizational change.

Procedural Justice and Participation

The *process* of strategy making creates important indirect, or invisible, outcomes. These are as important as the more obvious outcome – the published and publicized strategy. Less visible outcomes are important because they increase the chance of delivering strategic change (see figures C2.5 to C2.10) and also promote **team building**. To support the process, and to maximize the group's effectiveness, computer based systems have been developed to support group working – these are known as 'group decision support systems' (or GDSSs). Other terms are sometimes used to signify similar systems which are designed to use computers, often operating as a local network to give each participant input access to a large public screen, for example 'group support systems' (GSSs) and 'meeting support systems' (MSSs). We see GDSSs as systems for supporting the power brokers in the process of reaching agreements, and see GSSs as systems for supporting groups in surfacing multiple perspectives and individual wisdom, and collecting a range of relevant data from a group in a highly productive and participative fashion (Ackermann and Eden, 1998). Our use of such systems, as a single computer in support of group strategy analysis and **negotiation**, and as a **networked computer support system**, is addressed more fully in the third part of the book. However, it is important to note here some of the premises upon which these systems have been developed and their relevance to the business of JOURNEY making raised in this chapter.

V225 V238

P321: P336

One of the assumptions that has driven the design of many group decision support systems, similar to that which we employ, is that the free expression of ideas, and egalitarian participation is a desirable outcome of group work (Hoffman, 1965; Janis and Mann, 1977). Underlying this assumption are two notions. The first advances that fundamental to decision making is the exchange of information (DeSanctis and Gallupe, 1987). This aligns with statements above about sharing expertise and making good use of multiple perspectives, and is reinforced by research which suggests that 'communication in a successful group is open and full' (Harmon and Rohrbaugh, 1990; Shepherd, 1964). The second notion suggests that egalitarianism is, in itself, to be valued at some stages during strategy making – a dimension to be seen alongside the pragmatic requirement of both psychological and social manipulation to achieve 'buy-in' that we considered above.

It is certainly reasonable to presume that the value of a person's contribution to group work is not related to their social skills, or power, and thus a redistribution of 'air-time' with greater participation is likely to increase the quality of decision making. There is also a view that anonymity can help counter the destructive nature of role casting, where a person's previous performance in meetings provides a negative attribution to their ideas (Connolly *et al*, 1990). An efficient exchange of views is extremely difficult if each participant 'plays to the gallery'. Anonymity can also contribute towards a more open and honest exchange of views, cut down conformity, and reduce the impact of dominant members (Jessup and Tansik, 1991; Nunamaker *et al*, 1991). All of these contributions play an important part in diminishing the negative effects of the need to maintain the current social order.

Nonetheless, the individual characteristics of managers are taken to have the most impact on problem formulation, where the credibility of the person making the formulation has the most influence on determining whether it will be accepted or not. This is particularly important, as the strategic issue surfacing and formulation episodes of JOURNEY making are one of the most significant determinants of strategic intent. The need to recognize both the advantages of anonymity on some occasions and the advantages of identified contributions on other occasions is an important element of the practice of JOURNEY making. In contrast to many of the designs incorporated into some GDSSs we seek to **incorporate both** *P379* **aspects** into strategy making (Ackermann and Eden, 1998). By moving between modes, participants and facilitator are able to manage better the balance between negotiating new ways of delivering the aspirations of the organization and a new social order.

Each of these outcomes clearly creates a shift in power between participants. Designing more equality in the opportunity to contribute may make those contributions less dependent upon social skills, and **designing** *P298 P337* **anonymity** may make contributions less dependent upon links between the quality of an idea and its proposer (Valacich *et al*, 1992). The established social order is being unsettled temporarily. We have argued above that effective strategy making depends upon *negotiating* a new social order. Disturbing power relationships without having negotiated such changes, and the temporary nature of such changes, will make it difficult to sustain any substantive rationality that arises. As a result, commitment is often lost and the decisions made are 'rationalized' out in order to move relationships back to the status quo. Nevertheless, designing the process so as to provide an environment where there is a *perceived* balance of power (the chance to influence is a form of power) and positive encouragement towards collaboration, enables participants to gain the confidence to collaborate. However, the obverse is also true: where circumstances inhibit collaboration, then the group strategies identified by Janis and Mann (1977) to avoid decisions under stress may be adopted – stalemate, procrastination, shifting responsibility, and bolstering (the wishful rationalization of the least objectionable alternatives).

As noted at the beginning of this chapter, political feasibility is a critical element in the strategy making process as it contributes towards a successful strategic change process. It relies heavily upon different forms

THE ART OF GOOD JOURNEY MAKING: WORKING WITH STRATEGY MAKING TEAMS

'They are playing a game. They are playing at not playing a game. If I show them I see they are, I shall break the rules and they will punish me. I must play their game, of not seeing I see the game' (R.D. Laing, 1971)

Communication is central to organizational change. Whereas some would see communication as a device or tool that can be used to promote previously specified change, we see change as created and conceived through communication (Donnellon, 1986). Our view is that it is conversation that defines, develops and realizes the desired outcome. The forms of conversation may be conceived as symbols and theatre, as well as speech acts. Intended organizational change is typically presented as involving an *a priori* intention, a plan for change, and then realization – a beginning and an end. This can be seen in Lewin's (1951) notion of unfreezing and in the other classical models of organizational change which follow. When considering strategic organizational change, we see a continuing process where the JOURNEY making itself produces change as expectations and intentions are continually elaborated, plans are declared as a way of symbolizing closure, and temporary stability is created. Within the framework for strategy development introduced in chapter C2 we have placed the role of designed, structured, and supported conversation at the core of strategy development.

Without this dynamic view of strategic change we cannot take the actuality of, or commitment to, organizational learning seriously. The conversation process not only strongly relates to the notions of political feasibility and new negotiated order (as seen in chapter C3) but also to shared meaning (chapter C2) and, from this, individual and organizational learning (this chapter). In this chapter JOURNEY making through conversation, however, encompasses a number of key elements including a consideration of the cyclical nature of group work, difficulties for participants in contributing, the significance of synthesis, creativity and fun, and modelling through strategy maps.

As we shall argue in more detail in the next chapter, the most powerful conversation that can drive emergent strategic change is that focused on crisis, challenge, and 'firefighting' (Mintzberg *et al*, 1976). Managers attribute *cause and effect relationships* in their desperate attempt to *make sense* (Kelly, 1955) of the crisis. Their conversations are the starting points for 'issue selling' (Dutton and Ashford, 1993) where each manager seeks to influence their colleagues' view of what is important. In crisis, managers fight harder for their views, and the drive for action means they reveal – often implicitly – more of their embedded vision, surface more of their assumptions, and take one another more seriously than on 'special' occasions designated for strategy making (for example 'away-days'). However, the urgency involved in dealing with strategic crises can mean that whilst each manager surfaces more of their strategic assumptions, there is less time for other managers to check out their understanding of these assumptions. Consequently assumptions can be surfaced and missed, or can be severely misunderstood. These misunderstandings occur because the important stage of sharing meaning and making sense may have been bypassed, and each participant is forced to make untested assumptions about the implicit assumptions embedded in proposals for action coming from colleagues.

The speech act, and its realization through being listened to (others seeking to understand), is a part of the dynamic of each of us changing our position – our thinking – and so our actions. Verbal speaking is an action in language, as much an action as is the form of physical behaviour that we would usually call an action. Furthermore, the words we use express a part of our thinking, just as our thinking is influenced by the language and scripts we have available to use as speech acts (Mangham and Overington, 1987; Winograd and Flores, 1986). We do not dismiss the arguments that change requires top management commitment, ownership, shift in culture, and changes in the balance of power – as each of these factors is important. Rather we suggest that each of these is dependent upon the politics of the 'management of meanings' within an organization (Pettigrew, 1977).

In this chapter we explore the nature of designed conversation and debate that is likely to lead to successful and efficient JOURNEY making so that through it managers (i) will *change* their minds and so gain cognitive commitment to a strategic future, (ii) will *gain* emotional 'buy-in', (iii) will *discover* appropriate strategies which exploit distinctive wisdom and experience, and most importantly (iv) will *negotiate* agreements so that the expected change is politically feasible. Designing a journey where the outcomes depend upon the process as well as analysis is not easy. In the third part of this book we introduce the methods, techniques, and tools that can support the journey and are the elements of good design. Here we introduce the notion of providing, to teams undertaking the journey, appropriate group support (both computer based and manually constructed). We discuss some of the important phenomena which must be recognized if such support is to be productive. The issues we discuss apply whether only the top management team is involved or, alternatively, there are high levels of organizational participation.

Figure C4.1 The cycle of group problem solving (Eden, 1987).

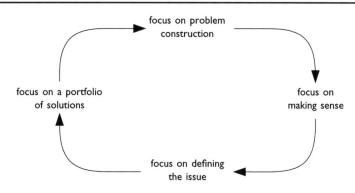

The Cyclical Process of Group Work

Decision makers typically cycle through the various stages of problem solving (Eden, 1987; Hickson *et al*, 1986; Mintzberg *et al*, 1976; Nutt, 1984) often repeating stages and going deeper into the substance of each stage. This phenomenon is, in part, a group naturally following a particular sort of journey of understanding, reflecting, and negotiating until they are comfortable about a way forward. Thus, in line with the general approach in this book, we seek to intervene in natural processes with a designed method that can improve rather than replace. Our presumption is (i) that 'natural' phenomena arise because they are, at least in some respects, effective, and (ii) that the probability of a group adopting designed (and so normative) interventions is higher when they do not completely deny current working practices.

The characteristics of the cyclical process (shown in figure C4.1) are important in determining how to effectively facilitate and so support a JOURNEY making group.

Our problem finishing cycle moves from problem construction to making sense, as the structuring process provides the building blocks for shared understanding. This shared understanding in turn helps participants define the issues relating to the problems – an effort that subsequently assists the generation and agreement upon options and further construction. The classical stages of problem solving – formulation, generating alternatives, evaluating alternatives and making choices – tend to ignore the role of cycles. Yet, the cycle is important because it *is* the conversational process, and it recognizes within the context of organizational change that the conversation continually moves onwards – strategic change is then incremental and made up of sequences of 'small wins' (Bryson, 1988). Thus 'muddling through' becomes organized incrementalism (see figure C2.2).

For strategy making we are concerned, in designing the journey, to recognize the stages each member of the group may reach in their own deliberations, and the state of negotiation.

Individuals in a group may change their mind about the nature and salience of a strategic issue in the following ways (developed from Ackoff and Emery (1972)).

- By *'dissolving' the issue through*:
  - a change in intentions or purpose or aspirations (where the valued outcome is no longer of interest)
  - change in the relationship between a person's value system and their belief system (where they no longer believe that particular actions will achieve the valued outcome)
  - change in the salience of particular aspirations for construing the situation (where the valued outcome becomes less highly valued)
  - downward change in expectations (a revision of what is possible as a valued outcome).
- By *'resolving' the issue through*:
  - arbitrary choice: the 'dice man' principle.
- By *'solving'/finishing/alleviating the issue through*:
  - replacing dissatisfaction with satisfaction: 'satisficing' (Simon, 1958)
  - each individual 'feeling that it is obvious what must be done': the proposed action is robust because, for example, by doing it few options for future actions are closed off
  - an unknown worry/anxiety disappearing, even if course of action is not defined, because, for example, the complex 'messy' issue is organized into a system of interacting tractable problems, because, for example, of a feeling that 'I don't know what I will do, but I know I will be able to decide when I need to'.
- But, *social considerations can affect the extent to which the group can negotiate a settlement*:
  - each individual in a team will become 'finished' with a problem at different times
  - the forming and reforming of coalitions mean that each person's expectation of what is possible/practical will often be changing
  - 'a problem is solved when the people involved find an actionable way of describing it': by finding the words used to describe the nature of a problem, that are explanations of why the problem persists; the explanations are, in effect, beliefs about how to intervene to change the situation
  - the politics of problem solving in teams can be viewed as the 'management of meaning'
  - and involves negotiation as a psychological as well as social process
  - there are dangers of 'working on the problem' being crowded out by the demand for 'maintaining or renegotiating the social fabric'.

Thus, our approach to the design of the facilitated support, and so the use of Group Decision Support Systems, must recognize *how* individuals will change their mind through a process of psychological *and* social negotiation – changing minds and changing relationships. Models used to record and encourage effective conversation must therefore be inter-active and changed in real time. The approach introduced in this book encompasses this need by using model building methods that: (i) actively involve participants in real time, and (ii) recognize that a model is a **'transitional object'** (de Geus, 1988). Furthermore, it must ensure that the   *P286* transitional object is deliberately amenable to continuous change and does not restrict the route of the journey at the outset, but rather allows for contingent looping, revising, restructuring, changing emphasis, and so on.

The Nature of Negotiation

The Role of Equivocality   *P385*

As we have said, in group decision making we expect to see a shift in the emotional attitude to the problem situation as well as a cognitive shift. Changes in emotional attitude reflect, in part, the role of intuition and hunch (Agor, 1989) which leads to a feeling of comfort about the way forward. Cognitive shifts are about someone 'changing their mind' – changed beliefs, changed values, and changes in the salience of particular values (see above). As we have argued in the previous chapter, it is more likely that the procedural rationality will influence emotional attitudes, and substantial rationality will influence shifts in cognition. However, each supports the other, because emotion and cognition are always linked.

Successful negotiation often depends upon participants being able to 'save face', as they change their mind and attitudes about possible out-comes and need to reconcile the stand they now take with their principles and past words and deeds. Effective negotiators make their contribution with a degree of equivocality. By using a communication mode open to several interpretations, social order is not destroyed *and* substantive information is proffered. *Equivocality* serves to maintain the balance of   *P385* order but also provides the fuzziness within which face saving can occur. An appropriate level of equivocality, balanced with transparency, is aimed at 'changing minds *and* emotions'; however, this might mean backing away from clarity as clarity begins to emerge.

Our approach to the design of the facilitated support must recognize the role of equivocality in models used to record and encourage effective conversation. The approach introduced in this book encompasses this need through the use of **'cognitive and cause maps' for understanding, reflect-**   *P286* **ing, negotiating and confirming strategy**. Cognitive maps permit an exploration of meaning, but do so within the context of enough equivocality to achieve psychological and social negotiation. A detailed explanation of cognitive maps (when working with individuals) and cause maps (group working) is provided in chapter C5.

Acknowledgement and Face Saving?

In chapter C3 we discussed the significance of social justice in attaining political feasibility. Associated with this is the relationship between a statement and the person who makes the statement. For the sake of justice a person needs to be assured that they have been listened to, which in turn implies that their particular contribution to the conversation must be associated with them. Giving generous credit for acknowledged contributions will also increase the contributor's stake in defending these ideas to others outside the group (Fisher and Ury, 1982). This is important for promulgation. It also, however, gives the person a stake in defending the idea within the group instead of entertaining the option of changing their mind. This might suggest that giving credit openly for ideas is more appropriate as a group moves towards consensus or agreement, but is not helpful earlier. However, credit to individuals will always reward some at the expense of others and so risk a step function disturbance to the social order. Furthermore, face saving can be made easier if statements can be made, noticed and possibly dismissed, without attribution of those statements to a particular individual. The proponent/originator can change their mind after hearing the debate about their ideas without needing to defend these as 'their own'. Similarly, it is a truism to note that good contributions are not necessarily correlated with either the social skills or the past attributions or the role of the individual making them. Thus, there can be significant benefits to be had from anonymity of contributors, at least at some stages of the JOURNEY making activity. At the very least it facilitates some staff in stating perspectives that they believe may result in punishment from those with power.

V256   **Shifts in power** from the introduction and use of GDSSs (and Decision Support Systems) have not been considered carefully (Eden *et al*, 1986). *V202 V244 P337*   Offering **anonymity** is a huge shift in power, and a shift that often displaces coalition forming and evaluation of input from the arena of the GDSS into other arenas, so making the GDSS irrelevant. However, there is a role for GDSSs in creating a 'safe place' in which discussions can take place that extend the boundaries of social order and so enable issues to do with negotiating a new order to surface.

Thus our approach to the design of the facilitated support must recognize the role of anonymity, or at least some level of it, in models used to record and encourage effective conversation. The approach introduced in this book encompasses this need through the use of a variety of manual and computer based methods for understanding, reflecting, negotiating, and confirming strategy. In particular we shall introduce, in the third part of the book (chapter P3), the roles which 'state of the art' computer based group support systems can play in enabling a facilitator to introduce anonymity, at appropriate junctures, for the elicitation of wisdom, for indicating preferences, and for giving a rating to outcomes and performance. We see this activity as significant in managing political feasibility.

The Role of Synthesis

Negotiation at the cognitive level is significantly enhanced by a good chairperson who is able to create a powerful synthesis of the contributions of all participants. This is further the case when such synthesis reveals a new way of looking at the problem. It is easier to create new social order when a group opens up new options that can be credited to the group rather than an individual. Not only is it likely that the new options represent progress with means/ends rationality but that they significantly provide room for negotiation to take place and lessen the role that designed anonymity needs to play.

Transparent models that represent the content of the arguments about what to change and why to make the changes are the 'transitional objects' (de Geus, 1988), or focus, around which negotiation can take place. In our case this is the cause map which is, by its form and structure, amenable to transparent analysis. Cause maps, as models for the group to work with, offer a form of synthesis and a new way of seeing the same data, because meaning is changed by being placed in new contexts with new linkages between the data – *new knowledge is created*. Effective modelling encourages synthesis in a way that is more positive than the somewhat negative dependency on anonymity.

These roles for a model can be seen as the key linkage between procedural rationality and means/ends (substantive) rationality. This is a major contribution that operational research and management science can make to the design of effective group support – the provision of support through transparent model building that is amenable to transparent analysis. Fisher and Ury (1982) argue that negotiation is more likely to be effective when participants don't attack the position of their colleagues, but rather seek to look behind it. Rather than asking about their position, the other person is encouraged to elaborate their interests, emphasizing the 'making sense' aspect of the cycle of problem solving. The debate is **supportive** rather than combative and is typified by 'that's interesting, *P385* why do you say that?' as a style of exchange (Churchill, 1990).

The direct implications of this type of exchange as a desired form of relating interpersonally are that the designed journey and the techniques/ tools associated with it must encourage elaboration rather than early convergence. The approach suggested in this book encourages the group continually to seek further elaboration in the early stages of the journey. However, one outcome is an increase in complexity. This increase brings with it concerns from the group about the debilitating nature of the complexity generated and so concerns about how the complexity will be managed without it being reduced as if it did not exist (Eden *et al*, 1981). It also raises the issue of effective time management – the continual elaboration required to facilitate both psychological and social negotiation, which will change minds, is expensive on the time required for the management of increased complexity.

Thus, our approach to the design of facilitated support must recognize the balance between debilitating complexity and the need to think broadly and deeply with proper management (rather than reduction) of complexity as the means to valuing simplicity.

V256 P371   ## Creativity

The synergy from the synthesis of the ideas of many participants opens up new options and is a form of group creativity. As we commented above, conflict is resolved not by dealing with the current options of members of the group but rather through the creative generation of new options by the group.

Whilst synthesis offers one form of creativity there are other ways for a group to become more creative. Clearly, the traditional forms of brainstorming (for example, Adams, 1979; Rawlinson, 1981) can offer some help but there are real difficulties in these approaches leading to participants changing their minds or gaining ownership of what emerges (Bouchard and Hare, 1970; Bouchard *et al*, 1974; Eden, 1983; Taylor *et al*, 1958). So called 'lateral thinking', almost by definition, does not allow for personal construct systems to be elaborated (Kelly, 1955) or 'scaffolded' (Vygotsky, 1962). As a consequence 'brainstormed' ideas tend to be rejected because, after the social event of the brainstorming session, they cannot connect with existing mental schemas and so do not persist as an actionable idea. Within the context of group strategy making, where the group is tasked with determining strategic direction and action, brainstorming can sometimes interfere with the flow of JOURNEY making. Brainstorming is often more appropriately used with groups who have expertise but no decision making prerogative. For strategy making groups some of the ideas promoted by de Bono (1982) may be more helpful but prescriptive: for example, the role of provocation to provide 'a whack on the side of the head' (von Oech, 1982) within the group may appropriately encourage lateral thinking which is within the flow of substantive work. Indeed, encouraging provocative ideas can help maintain social order and emotional commitment, because of its being fun. 'The more quickly you turn a stranger into someone you know, the easier a negotiation is likely to become' (Fisher and Ury, 1982) and a faster way for this to occur is to do something enjoyable together. Although provocation is not always fun!

Creativity is not only important for a group but also as an individual process. Emotional commitment to any course of action comes partly from having *played with* the ideas and alternatives.

Changing the Nature of the Conversation into a Designed 'Journey' – the role of maps as models in group decision support

The design of a structured strategic conversation must change the nature of the conversation as the strategy making journey progresses. There is a need for support to aid conversation about initiation (surfacing strategic issues) or propositions about action, construal, 'making sense', and closure in the cycling process discussed above. Throughout the strategy making, the use of cognitive maps as the basis of cause maps – which are 'strategic maps' – encourages conversation towards three objectives. The first is to 'make sense' of their own and others' views – by seeing each concept and argument within its context. The second is to explore propositions by seeing 'tear-drops' – hierarchical bundles of propositions supporting strategic options. The final and most important objective is to determine commitments by encouraging conversation which is action oriented, for example through the use of active verbs in the wording of concepts. This is the move to closure, involving conversations about agreements, commitments, and action.

In addition, conceiving of strategy as a map that can depict increasing abstraction as a group focuses on purpose, and yet can also depict increasing detail as a group focuses on action, facilitates the cyclical nature of conversation. The cycle encompasses both negotiation about substantive action (to shift Social Order) and social negotiation (to shift Negotiated Order). Thus, *the map, as a visual interactive model, acts as in the form of a changing artifact, a transitional object, that encourages dialogue, which in turn, demonstrates respect for the ideas of others and respect for others.* By the very nature of the two-dimensional contextualized network of propositions, with embedded equivocality, participants are encouraged to converse in a 'yes, and . . .' rather than 'yes, but . . .' format. Similarly the map as a transitional object can significantly reduce the energy participants devote to impression management. This is where they are inclined to devote so much effort to how they are perceived by others in the group that there is little energy left for attention to making sense of the strategic issue or psychologically locking in to agreements for action.

We adopt two important devices for changing the nature of the conversation. Firstly, as we have said, we use models as a negotiative device – as a 'transitional object'. The maps are devices that can encourage reflection by the group on something which is a representation available to all, amenable to analysis, capable of change by the group in real time, and available as an **organizational memory**. It can become that which belongs to the group rather than to any individual. Secondly, and relatedly, we use

V198 V273 P321 P462

models because they are visually interactive. That is, they can be seen by all and changed in front of all members of the group to more accurately reflect the conversation. To help with this, computers are used as a storage device so that the model's content can be seen by all involved, manipulated by all participants – not just the facilitators – and fast interaction can occur between group needs and modelling activities. Thus, often we use multiple workstations networked together so that all participants can communicate with the model, and with one another through the model, as well as through normal conversation.

All of this means that the modelling method used must recognize the need for the model to be transparent to participants as well as being appropriate to the task of strategic JOURNEY making. The modelling method must also be theoretically sound – for there is nothing so practical as good theory. The modelling method taken in our approach is cognitive mapping and its developed extensions – cause or strategy mapping. As we noted at the beginning of this chapter, it focuses upon the art of good JOURNEY making, specifically on the role of communication. Cause mapping is the negotiative device for group work, focusing upon relevant group processes discussed above including the cyclical process of group work, the importance of negotiation, and the significance of anonymity.

P303   These maps may be created directly by groups (using '**oval mapping**' techniques, or direct entry using computers) but they may also be created during and following interviews with individuals, where the output from
P298   the interview is a cognitive map. The **cognitive map** is intended to be a reasonable model of a particular person's thinking about strategic issues.
V196   The **collection of cognitive maps** is the source for the creation of a strategy
P329   map – **cause map** – which is the aggregation of the thinking of many people, including conflicting views, subtly different slants on the same issues, and different perspectives on similar views.

Thus, cognitive mapping is used predominantly when working with individuals and helps in the elicitation and structuring of each of the participants' distinctive perspectives – how he or she perceives the issue(s) being discussed. It provides a balance between providing the device for exploring meaning – through illustrating not just what the facts/issues are but how they fit together – and ensuring, through its qualitative fuzziness and imprecision, a sufficient degree of equivocality. When used in the context of strategic thinking, cognitive maps are typically used in capturing and exploring the thinking of each member of the senior management team, allowing tacit knowledge, assumptions, assertions, aspirations, and concerns to surface. These maps can then be woven together and analysed to form a group map or model that can support the process of developing agreement.

V254   The alternative approach to **producing group maps** is one that encourages group members to record and publicly display their views on large 'oval' cards. Unlike the use of cognitive maps that imply a more private environment (with only the interviewer/mapper and the participant) members are able to see one another's perspectives, add their own contributions to the map, and watch the strategy map unfold. During the process the ovals will be organized by a facilitator using many of the same guidelines as those used for building cognitive maps. A public analysis will be used to, for example, identify clusters within the context of a structured hierarchy, so allowing members the chance to identify and explore the emergent properties of the map.

Through this public procedure, group members are able to begin to change their minds as they examine the rationale of alternative viewpoints. They are not required to defend their own viewpoints as their own ideas might have changed as they are seen within the context of the views of others in the group. The process promotes synthesis by enabling linkages between and within clusters to be made. Group maps encourage creativity through the ability to see alternative points of view and from this position identify and develop new options and strategies. From encouraging **multiple perspectives**, providing an environment of *V202 V205 V227* equivocality and structuring the resultant knowledge and insights, the process demonstrates an attendance to procedural rationality – it makes sense – which in turn promotes emotional and cognitive commitment to the outcomes.

Whilst each form of mapping has its own specific purpose, each of the mapping techniques is grounded from the same theoretical standpoint – Personal Construct Theory (Kelly, 1955) – and is described in more depth in the following chapter (chapter C5). Regardless of whether they are individual or group oriented, the maps provide models that are designed to reflect the thinking, beliefs, and aspirations of those whose views have been incorporated. Consequently, they can provide a means for enabling group members to begin to jointly understand the perspectives of others, reflect on the emergent issues that are surfaced from them, and begin to negotiate an agreed strategic direction. The synthesis that comes from pulling together viewpoints, and the creativity that ensues both from synthesis and from multiple perspectives, helps this journey.

Group Support and 'Playfulness and Fun'   *P321 P387*

On many occasions the formality of interactive *modelling* can be tedious and lacking in humour. In the context of designing JOURNEY making we need to develop modelling techniques that encourage social activity and are entertaining. As Phillips (1984) has argued, 'this creative role of the model in problem solving would appear to differ from the descriptive role of models in science'. Computer supported group models have the capability of providing the group and each participant with the opportunity to experiment in a playful manner, providing a 'problem doodling' interface. Interactive 'real-time' modelling can provide an extension to mental simulation.

If problem solving should be fun then the use of computers might exploit game like characteristics (Smithin and Eden, 1986). However, fun is not intended to replace earnestness but rather support it. Describing children playing, Colin Ward (1990) suggests an 'intense curiosity about its [the problem situation's] ways and secrets. All are linked with pleasure and excitement in the activity itself and with an exploration of the nature of materials, structures and physical skills', for example the way throwing a ball against a surface 'gives the child an insight into the nature of a structure, its weight, solidity and texture'. The challenge for the design of a JOURNEY making system is to provide a group or individual with an opportunity to create *new knowledge* (the feeling of 'Aha, I hadn't thought of that before' – an *insight* relevant to the situation) through an exploration of the secrets of a strategic future.

V213 P305   **The Learning Organization and Organizational Learning**

Good JOURNEY making, the design of which has been informed by the issues addressed in this and the previous chapter, is probably the most significant contribution that can be made to developing a learning organization, and to directly facilitating organizational learning. Donald Michael argued, in 1973, for 'learning to plan – and planning to learn'. A sentiment close to the heart of this book.

This assertion is easy to make, for organizational learning is ill-defined and yet has become a current management fad. The benefits of becoming a learning organization have been well hyped: 'the ability to learn faster than your competitors may be your only sustainable competitive advantage' (de Geus, 1988). The ideas expressed by writers in this field are plausible and attractive, but often the views of organizational learning are confused by discussion which is about group or individual learning. Organizational learning, as we conceive of it, must be differentiated clearly from other learning if it is to bring the benefits suggested above.

Organizational learning must be such that it belongs to the collectivity, in the sense that it will be valuable only when taken in the strategic organizational context (Argyris and Schon, 1978:8–29). Thus, the knowledge will be relatively valueless in impact (as opposed to intellectual value) unless it is used in the context of the organization. If it is not relatively valueless to the individual outside the specific organizational setting then it is individual learning which travels with the individual, and so is less significant than organizational learning. The individual may, of course, contribute something very special to the organization, but it is special only when taken in context. Organizational learning cannot simply be just the sum of the parts (individual learning); if this were so then it would be group learning and the learning would travel with the group. It may be the sum of the parts when taken within the particular context of the organization. We can conclude that it is that which *sustains and develops distinctive competencies which belong to the organization* and to no individual or group within the organization.

This notion of organizational learning being something which has value in context is why JOURNEY making can be such an important vehicle for creating a learning organization. The activity of jointly understanding and reflecting takes place, perforce, within the strategic context of the organization. It is driven by the aim of drawing together the wisdom and expertise of individuals and setting them within the context of the culture, emergent strategizing, stakeholders, environment, and aspirations of the particular organization. As we shall see in the next chapter, a crucial task in the journey is that of exploring the interaction of all of these aspects, as a system of interrelated features, in order to identify a 'business model' or 'livelihood scheme' which represents the link between distinctive organizational competencies and the particular aspirations of this one organization.

The requirements of organizational learning are exactly those of good JOURNEY making. The journey is designed to facilitate learning processes that develop distinctive competencies which belong to the organization. They belong to the organization rather than to individuals in the organization because the learning is of relatively little value to the individual. However, for the journey to work effectively for strategy making, the learning which comes from the journey must also be of enough value to the individual for them to be motivated to join in the learning process – the journey is to the benefit of themselves as well as the organization. Clearly we expect that the individual may benefit personally from the learning process, but they cannot readily graft the organizational distinctive competence, derived from shared knowledge within a particular strategic context, elsewhere.

In sympathy with other normative approaches to organizational learning (Galer and van der Heijden, 1992; Garrett, 1990; Garvin, 1993; Hayes *et al*, 1988; McGill *et al*, 1992; Normann, 1985; Pedler *et al*, 1989; Senge, 1992) we shall identify six key characteristics of organizational learning. These characteristics are also key characteristics of good JOURNEY making. However, the primary focus for organizational learning must be that which is also at the core of the journey:

> *standing back* from the everyday life, detecting *emergent patterns* of behaviour, *reflecting* upon these, and *redesigning* ways of thinking and working.

In the next chapter we discuss the important first step in strategy making – that of detecting emergent strategizing. In chapter C2 we suggested that detecting emergent patterns to determine the strategic future of an organization (unless it chooses to redesign them) provides the starting point for the journey. The ability to stand back, take a 'helicopter view', 'see the wood from the trees', is the foundation of organizational learning. It is, however, dependent upon other characteristics:

1 A respect for *wisdom* – 'to be wise is not to know particular fads but *to know without excessive confidence or excessive cautiousness*. Wisdom is thus not a belief, a value, a set fact, a corpus of knowledge in some specialized area, or a set of special abilities or skills. Wisdom is an attitude taken by persons toward the beliefs, values, knowledge, information, abilities, and skills that are held, a tendency to doubt that these are necessarily true or valid and to doubt that they are an exhaustive set of those things that could be known' (Meacham, 1983). Recent research conducted by Warwick and Bath universities in the UK has shown how the recent trend towards leaner ways of working, which has resulted in downsizing through the loss of experienced staff, has had an adverse effect. The research concludes that the result has been to cut out muscle not fat, losing the 'corporate memory' and 'corporate experience'. In other words, organizations appear to have been throwing away that part of the corporate body which has owned the organizational learning. As we argued above, when the learning belongs to a group or individual and it has not become entrenched into the organization then it is unlikely to be *organizational* learning. In recent cases it has not been the loss of groups but rather the loss of whole cultures and corporate networks of individual and group learning and wisdom that has left organizations bereft of their 'taken-for-granted' organizational learning.

2 Appreciation of *systemic properties* in organizations – that systems impact upon each other in complex ways and that feedback loops exist within the system and across other systems. The appreciation that some patterns are self-sustaining, or reinforcing, through feedback loops – vicious and virtuous circles, and negative (controlling) feedback loops.

V202 V266   3 Respect for *multiple perspectives* on issues. This characteristic demands that organizations respect the actuality of differentiation in expertise, experience, and wisdom amongst individuals in an organization. Thus, there will be an expectation that there will be different views on the same problem. There is also a requirement that questioning dominant views is acceptable. These are not trivial, but very serious, demands on an organization. Encouraging multiple perspectives will increase the complexity surrounding any issue, and it will also generate more conflict. Indeed, the practice discussed in the third part of this book encompasses particular attention to managing complexity without losing different perspectives by 'averaging' out views. We suggested earlier in this chapter that increased complexity can be debilitating for groups, and that we have to find ways of managing the complexity rather than reducing it.

4 Recognition of the *dilemma of alignment versus differentiation* – strategy is partly about designing increased alignment of thinking and action,

but organizational learning requires some degree of differentiation through multiple perspectives. Part of the outcome from JOURNEY making will be the redesign of structures, procedures, and information systems as a source of meanings, reward systems, and so on. These are (re)designed to promote alignment of thinking and action in line with strategic intent. However, multiple perspectives depend on attention to individuality, open communication channels, preparedness to question views, and a management style shifting towards the 'manager as facilitator' and away from management as 'command and control'. The recognition of this dilemma is the important requirement, where balancing conflict with compromise, and creativity with standard procedures, characterizes the dilemma. We argued in chapter C1 that strategy was contingent – some organizations need a strategy that emphasizes and creates high levels of creative conflict whereas others may regard alignment as important for the attainment of their strategic intent. Usually choosing the appropriate balance between these two extremes is a serious strategic choice made during strategy making.

5   An ability to *detect key assumptions* and **'taken-for-granteds'** that are   *P284*
    driving the behaviour of the organization. This requirement simply supports the basic need to detect emergent strategizing. However, here we are highlighting the role of core assumptions about, for example, how the market works, what motivates the work force, whom to take notice of in the environment. These assumptions can often be based on a world taken for granted developed from assertions made 'years ago' by senior managers now retired. The ability to detect these assumptions, know their role in the emergent strategizing of the organization, and revisit their validity is a critical task for strategy making and for organizational learning. The use of cause maps to facilitate thinking about strategy provides at least an analytical device for establishing which assumptions are core to an organization's understanding of its strategic direction – but the assumption must find its way on to the map first.

6   A willingness to *experiment with ideas, thinking and action*. This demand
    simply follows from the **Learning Cycle** depicted by figure C4.2 (Kolb,   *P462*
    1984; Kolb and Rubin, 1991). Here the cycle moves from *acting* – testing implications of theories and concepts in new situations: to give concrete experiences: to give *reasoning* – observation to reflection: to formation of abstract concepts and theories to be used in *action*. The implication is that the organization must have a culture where mistakes are not inappropriately punished. An appropriate degree of psychological safety is required, where staff do not feel as though they must go 'out on a limb' to explore new ways of doing things. Typically this requires psychological *maturity* of the organization. Encouraging managers to reflect and question develops consciousness and self-knowledge, which is threatening to the power structure of organizations. In JOURNEY making we seek to promote this psychological safety through the use of computer based group support systems. As

Figure C4.2 The learning cycle (adapted from Kolb, 1984)

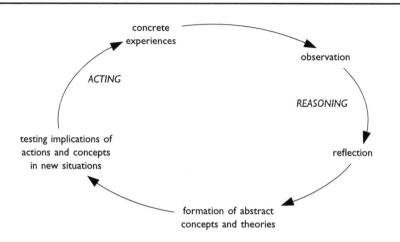

we commented above, it is important to sustain a balance between providing the opportunities to go 'out on a limb' when appropriate but take ownership as the journey proceeds.

7   Relating to the above, *playfulness* in exploration and reflection – 'play develops in an intermediate territory extending from the boundaries of the subjective to those of the objectively perceived or shared reality. This is the territory between fantasy and actuality, and is between the subjective and the objective, between the Art and the Science of Management' (Eden, 1993). This is the corollary of encouraging experimentation with ideas, thinking and action. For the experimentation to be effective it must open up the probability of discovery and creativity, and playfulness and fun can promote such outcomes.

Needless to say, these characteristics set out some of the requirements for effective JOURNEY making. However, although the existence of the characteristics above will undoubtedly make JOURNEY making more rewarding, the approach to JOURNEY making we present is designed to promote a learning organization when the characteristics are weak at the start. Nevertheless, unless an organization has some aspiration to become a learning organization then some of the approaches we discuss may be less effective and possibly unhelpful.

DETECTING EMERGENT STRATEGIZING

This chapter is about the aspect of the journey which seeks to establish the basic structure of the strategic direction that *will* emerge as long as the embedded procedures, structures, ways of working and thinking that currently persist within any organization are allowed to continue. It is concerned with detecting emergent strategizing (figure C2.7).

The importance of this stage of the journey is that it will reveal some of the strategic concerns which must be addressed as a part of building strategic direction. It will also reveal the aspirations of the organization as they currently exist, not those published or stated but those that drive strategic behaviour – detecting the emergent strategizing is the mirror to be held up to the management team. It allows them to reflect upon the strategic future that is expected to unfold if they choose to leave things as they are, and so confirm a deliberate emergent strategy. However, it will also be the base line for strategic organizational change if they choose a different strategic future and design strategic intent to guide the change (figure C2.3).

The process of jointly understanding, reflecting upon, and negotiating a new strategic future is structured by a consideration of the interaction between strategic aspirations, distinctive competencies, the demands of stakeholders, and the environment (figure C2.3). The outcome of this particular part of the journey will be a map of the interconnections between each of these related aspects of strategy making (see the lower portion of figure C2.9 – a focus on developing agreements). This map will show how core *distinctive competencies* are *exploited as a livelihood scheme or a business model* through the process of adding value. The picture also shows how to attain a *network of goals and valued outcomes*, all of which are encapsulated within a *mission statement or statement of strategic intent*. In addition this map will reveal *core strategic beliefs* about how the organization works – the current organizational recipe. Alongside this will be the *key strategic issues and problems* faced by the organization; the basic *value system* that reveals the wishes and aspirations of members of the organization; and finally a portfolio of *strategic options*. It is these data which are at the core of all JOURNEY making and which provide the context for exploring the multiple futures and the role of stakeholders (chapters C6 and C7).

Thus, the reflective process is expected to build a '**business model**' or '**livelihood scheme**' on distinctive strengths; identify where the model might be vulnerable or have the potential for expansion; develop strategies which will protect, sustain, and develop the livelihood scheme; and create a usable strategic vision for the organization.

V257 V266 P332
P425

Figure C5.1   Determining strategic direction – the cycle of coherence between distinctive competencies, livelihood, and aspirations.

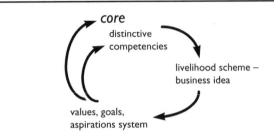

The Cycle of Developing the Business Model or Livelihood Scheme

The process is cyclical (shown in figure C5.1) and covers the following activities:

- Identify competencies, and so distinctive competencies (DCs).
- Determine a draft mission statement and goal system that clearly encompasses key values.
- Search for the way in which the distinctive competencies can be exploited – the Livelihood Scheme or Business Model.
- Provide added value, where value is measured by the attainment of goals.
- Redraft the mission statement to encompass fully the three elements of: competencies, the process of exploitation (which gives added value), and the goals/values to be attained.
- Revisit the competencies to establish those which are *core* to this process and reduce emphasis on those which do not play a role.
- Revise the Business Model or Livelihood Scheme to refine the linkage between core distinctive competencies and goals.
- Revise the Goal System and Mission Statement so that it truly reflects both core distinctive competencies and the Livelihood Scheme.
- Keep repeating the cycle until it is coherent across all three elements.

The final business model or livelihood scheme may act as the focus of a business restructuring project following agreement about the design and direction of the strategy. Similarly, competencies that are not distinctive may be candidates for outsourcing, although it is often the case that apparently peripheral competencies are absolutely essential to the sustenance of core competencies, and so need to be maintained with internal control. When a core distinctive competence is derived from the existence *P330* of a **self sustaining feedback loop** of non-distinctive competencies then these competencies, when taken together, are crucial, and so considering outsourcing of any one of them can be a recipe for failure. For example, in some instances competencies that appear unimportant at first sight, when seen in the context of what they sustain and how they are themselves supported, become a crucial link which, if outsourced, could spell disaster. Too many organizations are releasing these parts of their business without fully understanding their role within the overall context of success. However, more typically the search for a business model or livelihood scheme reveals a strategic need to search out new competencies that may ultimately become distinctive.

The processes we shall explore, that drive the organization's strategic future, address two linked streams of activity – procedures and structures within the organization, and the ways in which managers deal with strategic issues. Both will inform the mechanisms managers use for working on strategic concerns.

This chapter follows the format of figures C2.7 and the bottom half of figure C2.8 (concentrating on strategic intent). We shall consider the process of reflecting upon emergent strategizing in relation to competencies of the organization, and suggest the basis for determining core distinctive competencies and the business model or livelihood scheme.

Detecting Emergent Strategizing   *P289*

There are two important avenues for detecting emergent strategizing (shown in figure C2.7):

1   an examination of structural properties of embedded routines, actual procedures and processes in use – 'the way we do things round here' – and how they relate to formal and informal reporting and decision making structures of the organization; and
2   **capturing theories in use** – the *wisdom*, belief systems, around and *P303* about the organization that are the basis for action (both of which derive from and drive (1)).

Structural Properties and their Role in Determining Strategic   *P361*
Futures

Procedural and structural configurations ensure that managerial attention is limited and biased (Starbuck and Milliken, 1988). Although the interpretations of the data in original classical studies on managerial selective perception (Dearborn and Simon, 1958) have been questioned (Waller *et al*, 1995; Walsh, 1988), there remains the key assertion (which is almost trivially obvious) that data is not freely available to managers, and that information is selected out by the systems and procedures developed by the organization over time. The interpretation of the data is also influenced

V247

by the belief systems of the managers, but we shall consider this part of emergent strategizing in the next section. Here we are concerned with the **structural characteristics** of the organization that will significantly influence the strategic future of the organization. We include the influence, if it is significant, of the interpretations of the current published strategy.

Weick (1976) discussed problems confronted by an observer:

'our attention tends to be drawn to things that vary the most, and things that vary little thus have low visibility. The most obvious and visible coupling within organizations may not necessarily be the most critical to an understanding of organizational change, especially if the really important events occur infrequently. The remedy to this problem is a thorough immersion into the affairs of the organization, coupled with knowledge of the way things work in other organizations'.

In looking for the strategic impact of structural and procedural systems we need to be acutely aware of missing the obvious because it is often the most embedded part of our subconsciousness.

Some of the primary long term systems that will be of interest here are: the costing system, the transfer pricing system, the management information system, and the underlying assumptions about estimating processing time in the manufacture of products and services. We shall consider each of these in turn. However, in doing so we must recognize their relationship one to another and the powerful systemic property of coherence which will have grown accidentally or deliberately between them. The internal coherence of organizational systems acts to make each of them self-fulfilling and self-sustaining as determinants of the strategic future of the organization – they support and strengthen one another.

Understanding Costs

All organizations – from community groups seeking to offer a community hall for use by residents, to small consultancies or software houses, to large multinationals – will be making operational and strategic decisions significantly determined by the particular nature of their way of understanding their costs – often explicated as a costing 'system'. The costing system itself may be carefully constructed, possibly – but unusually – to reflect the strategic intent of the organization, or may simply be an informal set of 'obvious' assumptions believed to be 'matters of fact' which are taken to be the cost of undertaking activities. But this system, or set of assumptions, will be one of many ways of determining the cost of a service or product, each of which will importantly suggest very different strategic futures. Often such costing systems are designed with no regard to their strategic impact, but rather are designed by staff who have in mind the creation of a system which is closest to the 'truth' – a notion of the 'real cost'.

Let us take a couple of simple examples to illustrate the point. We shall deliberately simplify the situations discussed but not in such a way that the examples are unrepresentative. Consider a small printing firm with three printing machines and operators (one that is capable of undertaking specialist high quality work and the other two ordinary jobs) and a process planner who optimally prepares jobs so that they take the least amount of time and are printed to the best quality. The firm carries overheads for management, for selling, and for the cost of space, and it also worries about retaining access to funds when it is required to replace printing machines. If we take two plausible, but extreme, systems for costing jobs, for the purpose of illustration, then we see two different strategic futures unfold.

In the first case, overheads are spread across each of the four resources and profit margins are expected to provide a source of funding for replacement printing machinery when required. Jobs are costed according to the time each resource is used, and this cost is a consideration in pricing the job. In the second case, the overheads are distributed unevenly so that the machines carry a greater proportion because it is believed that the extent and type of space they occupy costs more than for the process planner. The cost of the higher quality machine is greater than for the other machines and so the depreciation costs are now included in the hourly cost rate and are higher for the more expensive machine.

Now, given that each of the systems is designed to reflect expected utilization of the resource, and that the aggregate cost recovery in either case will be the same, then the impact of each system will be different. In the second case, the higher quality jobs will carry a relatively higher cost, and jobs with a relatively lower proportion of process planning will cost relatively more. In the second case, the firm will find it easier to bid for jobs with a relatively higher proportion of process planning, indeed these jobs will probably begin to look more profitable than if the first system were used. If there are other firms using the first system then they will believe they make more profit from low proportion process planning and high quality jobs. The marketplace is likely to become differentiated, with each of the firms beginning to specialize by focusing their selling efforts and expanding accordingly. Each firm is likely to believe their strategic growth is successful and will ensure that their systems become self-fulfilling. Indeed, it is possible that for the first case the firm will emerge with a production oriented strategic future, where they are not oriented to product type but more concerned about selling production resource. Growth is more likely to be by expansion in accordance with bottleneck relief. In the second case, it is probable that the firm emerges with a product orientation, given that it has a greater capability of identifying costs by product.

To take an even simpler example, if a local community hall committee are deciding how they should charge out their large sports hall and their smaller meeting hall there are, once again, two plausible extremes. Firstly, they may split the costs based upon size according to the area of each hall.

In this instance customers will find the sports hall, when used for sports, to be attractive but those wishing to use it for non-sporting events unattractive. In deciding which hall to use, the non-sports customer will be concerned about the number of people they will be housing, the cost per person being the same if each were in optimal use. Alternatively, another community centre committee might argue that the cost should be related to customer use. If the badminton or football club use the sports hall then they should pay more than non-sports users because the extra capital cost and higher volume heating costs for the sports hall exist only because of their needs. This second scheme leads to pricing which may significantly reduce the demand from sports users and yet increase the demand from others who now see a lower priced large hall. As time passes this may lead the committee to consider closing the sports facility and adapting the sports hall to create two floors of halls, thereby increasing revenue or lowering costs and so prices to non-sports users. In the first system the demand from non-sports users may not be there and so the provision of sports facilities in the sports hall might be enhanced to encourage the apparently buoyant demand for the large hall by sports people. In either case, the strategic future of the hall will have been influenced by the costing system, and so pricing system, and so apparent demand from the community. The process of strategic development is very likely to have been emergent rather than explicitly designed or even recognized.

The impact of different ways of understanding cost cannot be underestimated, indeed the accountancy profession is now more generally recognizing that concepts of cost and profit should be accepted as social constructions rather than matters of fact (Hopwood and Miller, 1996).

In particular, it is important to recognize the strategic impact of apparently obvious decisions about distributing overheads. For example, we recall a new chief executive of a magazine publishing company who decided that central overheads needed to be fully distributed to the business units, in order to make the managers of these units more accountable. The basis for distribution was that of headcount, as this seemed to be a realistic reflection of the use of overheads since the business was people intensive. The managers concerned were awarded bonuses as a function of yearly profits. On reflection, it was not surprising that these managers looked for ways of reducing their headcount to reduce overheads relative to other units, and so make higher profits than their colleagues, and so be rewarded with a higher bonus. The simplest and fastest way of reducing headcount was to invite journalists to become freelance. The process was successful, the headcount was reduced, and the company total overheads were genuinely reduced as well as those for the particular unit concerned. However, some years later it emerged that freelance journalists had, quite reasonably, been servicing other organizations with the same expertise that had once belonged to the original company. This company gradually shared what had been a significant and distinctive competence. Journalists were doing well and were reticent to move back on to the payroll as normal employees. Meanwhile the strategic future of the company was, perforce, shifting from selling information to packaging information belonging to others. A procedure for keeping managers aware of costs had resulted in important emergent strategic consequences.

These are extremely simple examples that also simplify the dynamics of market forces and the gradual stabilization of costing systems. Nevertheless, they demonstrate how powerful reasonable notions of costs can be in determining a strategic future, even if the costing system was designed to have operational impacts only. Our experience suggests that it is often only an outsider who can detect these emergent consequences, for the systems tend to have become a part of the 'world taken for granted' of the management team.

The Role of Transfer Pricing

Second, consider the role of transfer pricing systems. These are common to many organizations, particularly those that have gone down the devolved 'independent' Strategic Business Unit route. It is obvious that the managers of these Units will want to demonstrate prowess in relation to their own unit. In order to do so, transfer pricing becomes a political football driving a considerable amount of manoeuvring and short term decision making. This form of decision making builds patterns of behaviour which can be difficult to break and can determine strategic futures in many unintended ways. For example, in many educational institutions the unit of trading is that of the number of full-time equivalent students that attend a class. Thus, transfer pricing is based upon a charge per student per class. Here many products (the degree programme spanning several years) become highly distorted because the providers focus upon those classes which attract maximum students rather than those which act as key elements within the context of the whole educational experience of the degree programme. The transfer pricing mechanism gradually reduces the quality of the product. This, in turn, determines a strategic future that is about servicing a particular market of degree awarding institution, rather than being an educational experience focused institution. The institution may choose either route, but the point here is that it is very likely that the chosen structure determines an emergent strategic future not a deliberate strategic intent.

Management Information Systems

Thirdly, and very obviously, management information systems (MISs) or executive information systems (EISs) deliberately exert a significant influence on the ways in which managers see their world, and do not see their world. They are often designed at great expense and regarded as a significant investment for the future. Although it is now possible to design MISs that are much more flexible (capable of continual redesign), in practice there are many reasons why organizations hesitate to use such flexibility. Consequently, the information systems act as a 'set of spectacles' through which to see or not to see, and can inevitably have a profound effect on the strategic future of the organization. Their potential as a control system and corporate governance system is well established. They encompass that which can be attributed numbers and ignore (so far) qualitative information. However, it is qualitative information that usually should dominate the thinking about the strategic direction of the organization. The response to management information as the basis for operational decisions produces patterns of decisions that only when taken together determine an emergent strategic pattern. These *patterns* are only sometimes intended, but they are always difficult to detect.

'Rules of Thumb'

Finally, and as a further example of procedures that are worth exploring for their emergent strategic properties, we mention the role that embedded 'rules of thumb' can play in the strategic future of an organization. Often these rules are used in organizations because there is not a more analytically sound substitute. Here we are particularly interested in those that are used to manage production or delivery of services. Examples of two rules of thumb which we have found to be important are: the use of 'learning curve indices' in manufacturing estimation, planning, and targeting; and the use of scheduling rules such as attending to the shortest throughput time of products as the first priority. The learning curve index is a rule of thumb based on 'Wright's Law'. It was developed in 1935 and has not been developed in a substantial way since this time. It suggests that the rate of learning to assemble products fits a logarithmic curve (to the base of 2), and that the index is a special characteristic of a particular plant, workforce, and product type. The index represents the rate of gradient of the curve – the lower the number (<1) then the faster the learning. Because these indices, that are generally determined through the analysis of historical data, have an impact on estimating for quotation, on production resource load planning, and on the way in which the workforce is targeted, they are fundamental to the character of the organization. They are often self-fulfilling, as history encompasses past targets and plans, and as managers fight to get standard times down to the targets set by learning curves based on the past, or alternatively feel satisfied by production fitting the expected curves.

Similarly, rules of thumb that are used to schedule production or service standards become self-fulfilling and can determine the character of market behaviour in relation to the organization. Thus, for example, banks which choose to schedule their tellers to take lunch breaks according to a given rule of thumb will influence customer behaviour that appears to support the rule of thumb used. If the bank chooses to let staff follow the same lunch break pattern as their customers' lunch then customers who are experiencing longer queues, either move to other times, or move their custom to another bank which has more teller staff available at lunchtime. If we hypothesize that customers who are constrained to visit their bank during their lunch break are those with less job autonomy and so lower incomes, then it is possible that the character of the market is unintentionally determined by the rule of thumb for scheduling the lunch breaks of the telling staff.

Ways of Making Sense – 'wisdom'

We introduced the significance of wisdom when discussing organizational learning; here we address its relevance to the processes of making sense, and take it to be:

> '. . . the "ability to think and act" – the ability to use knowledge, not simply store knowledge. It is the ability to define the "right" problem at the "right" time and determine an appropriate course of action. So wisdom is action oriented and is reflective (in the sense that action is guided by knowledge – that is a system of beliefs about the situation). Wisdom is also about *managing complexity not reducing it*' (Eden, 1993).

This recognizes the ability a person has to discover the nub of the issue – to account for all aspects of situations, *without simplifying* by pretending that some of it does not exist, and *choosing* that which is significant. Wisdom, therefore, is also the ability to choose.

> 'There may be a great many people with something to lose when somebody they love or depend on financially undergoes an operation. It is not a good reason to have them in the operating theatre' (Euan Baird, Chairman and Chief Executive, Schlumberger in *The Observer* – the Business, 10 December 1995, p. 13).

As a result, it is important to take care when deciding which people to involve in JOURNEY making. There are, as we have argued, good reasons for including as many staff as possible, but in practice **choices will have to** *P376* **be made** – some will participate and others will not. And the extent of wisdom that can be brought to the table is one of the criteria for choice.

> 'The ability of a director to help the management be successful has nothing to do with the particular market or technical challenges of the period, but a great deal to do with his or her proven ability to handle change successfully in the past . . . there is no textbook which replaces having been there' (ibid.).

Espoused Theories versus Theories in Action

This book focuses on strategy development as the discovery of how to *manage and control the future*. It is concerned with capturing the *experience and wisdom* of organizational members about how they believe an attractive vision of the future can be attained. Strategic thinking is thus action oriented and concerned with identifying how to intervene in the incrementalism of the organization itself and its relationship with its environment. The data gathered is the outcome of managers thinking about the future, and thinking about the future involves creating *new theories* (Spender, 1989) about the relationship between the organization and its environment. These theories are based on experience and wisdom rather than precise forecasts or quantitative analyses. *Judgements* are made about how the market and the organization *will* be working, rather than how it is currently working. Experience and wisdom are embedded in ways of thinking in action, they are another part of a world taken for granted – 'nothing evades our attention so persistently as that which is taken for granted' (Ichheiser, 1949:1). Strategic decisions do not arise from nowhere but rather from cognitions which are shared across the organization (Burgelman, 1983). Most significantly they are the consequence of 'sensemaking' (Weick, 1995) where shared meaning and shared action and experience are created, and so collective intuitions facilitate enaction rather than reaction. The cognitions which are shared represent a part of the emergent strategizing, and the inter-subjectivity from different experience, wisdom, and deep knowledge represents the source of new ways of thinking about the strategic future of the organization.

The data of strategic thinking will, therefore, be largely qualitative *belief systems* that represent 'theories' about how the world works and thus how it can be changed. These belief systems develop as managers seek to make sense of their world and resolve ambiguity. Resolving *ambiguity* is crucial to sensemaking and involves looking for plausible explanations for events – it is different from resolving uncertainty where the search is for the rules which exist but are not remembered or accessible. Making sense is not an act of reference but rather an act of intellectual discovery. The need to recognize the complex interaction between the multiple beliefs of organizational members reflects the reality and necessity of every goal being qualified by others and every strategy being potentially constrained or enhanced by a network of other strategies. Our task in detecting emergent strategizing is to access these ways of thinking as they *affect* judgement and action, not as they are *espoused* to do so. It is no use simply asking managers what they believe, or what their aspirations are. In order to ascertain the role of beliefs and values in emergent strategizing, we need to be as certain as possible that we access the belief system which actually affects thinking and action, rather than that which is claimed to do so. This is not to suggest that we tell each other lies about our beliefs, but rather that what we say is not always the same as what we do.

Furthermore, what we know and do cannot always be explained to others. Language, thinking, and action are related but are not necessarily the same. What we say affects what we think, and what we think affects how we act, and how we act affects what we think, and what we think affects what we say.

Good managers do not always deliberate before they act – they are able to use tacit knowledge, and provide habitualized responses that are the result of 'taken for granted' beliefs and aspirations. Experienced managers can use 'theories of action' without taking the time to consciously know about them. In detecting emergent strategizing we are seeking to detect and understand these theories of action, understand the patterns which are not simply individual episodes but the source of overriding strategic threads. These threads are patterns that are coherent and evidenced across many members of the organization. They ultimately represent the culture, or ways of thinking and working of the organization, that go beyond any individual. These patterns are not dependent upon single managers; rather, if any one manager were to leave the organization then the patterns would be little disturbed. Detecting culture and its role in strategic futures is absolutely crucial. 'Culture pervades and radiates meanings into every aspect of the enterprise . . . culture patterns the whole field of business relationships' (Trompenaars, 1994:17).

At the core of the method we use to capture emergent strategizing of organizational actors, is the technique of 'cognitive mapping'. Although 'cognitive mapping' has a variety of interpretations in practice (Axelrod, 1976; Huff, 1990), this particular form of cognitive mapping is uniquely based on personal construct theory (Kelly, 1955), which pays attention to the way individuals make sense of their world through anticipating and differentiating events and seeking out ways of managing and controlling their future. Personal construct theory sees 'man [or woman] as a scientist', constantly trying to make sense of his world through anticipating and differentiating events, and seeking out ways of managing and controlling his future. It is designed to be a model of thinking in action. Thus it is a model which is ideally constructed through careful attention to **'theories in use'** not 'espoused theories' (Argyris, 1982; Argyris and   *P353*
Schon, 1974; Eden and van der Heijden, 1995). The process of capturing cognitive maps is akin to undertaking 'action research' (Eden and Huxham, 1996) where the aim is to find out what actually happens during organizational change.

Capturing 'Thinking in Action' *P284 P286*

As we said earlier, the best way of getting cognitive maps that are close to thinking in action is to be a part of the process of a management team dealing with urgent 'firefighting' strategic issues, where the managers are attempting to deal with crisis. In these circumstances espoused theories tend to lose their place alongside the need to decide how to act. The beliefs and aspirations that surface, either directly or indirectly, are the basis for understanding emergent strategizing. What is particularly valuable about *P289 P314 P429* these circumstances is that we see '**negative-goals**' being discussed – that is 'aspirations to avoid' type outcomes. 'Negative-goals' tend to give strong clues about the emergent strategic direction of the organization.

One way of understanding how significant negative-goals can be is to consider them at the personal level. We gain a clearer sense of ourselves, by reflecting upon what we seek to avoid doing and what causes a feeling of great anxiety as we anticipate the future – studying the thinking which produces sleepless nights! Similarly, in organizational settings we gain a clearer understanding of emergent strategizing by studying the **nature of** *V197 V223 P329* **strategic issues** – how they are defined (yielding the belief system) and why they are defined as issues (extracting goals and negative-goals: the current aspirations system).

Using the management of strategic issues as the basis for constructing cognitive maps is more reliable as a way of getting at theories in use. However, the data will be restrictive, but rich, if only one or two strategic issues are the data source. The maps will be, inevitably, dominated by beliefs which are specific to the particular issue being dealt with, and many beliefs will be concerned with operational rather than strategic issues. Nevertheless, it is important to note that the *patterns of beliefs* about operational issues, and the aspirations that emerge, will often give valuable indications of emergent strategic thinking.

This approach to surfacing 'theories in use' is not always practical, because an involvement with a management team as they deal with strategic issues may be difficult to arrange. However, those involved in facilitating the journey of strategy making have often been involved in strategic issue resolution with teams of managers and have adequate notes which enable them to reconstruct the cognitive maps of managers involved – that is, determine the nature of the belief system and map it. For example, we have been involved as facilitators, using cognitive maps and group decision support, with a number of organizations as the groups have worked through strategic issues such as product development, reorganization of central services, competitive positioning (Ackermann, 1992; Eden, 1985; Eden and Huxham, 1988; Eden and Jones, 1980). In these instances the cognitive maps and subsequent group cause maps have been a natural and powerful starting point for a journey of strategy development. But, these opportunities do not occur always. Thus, we have to devise alternative approaches, which are, nevertheless, guided by the same considerations of seeking out theories in use.

V242 P284 With this in mind, the most common way of **collecting experience and wisdom is through a series of interviews** with members of the executive team, in each case using some of the techniques discussed below to get as close as possible to the theories in use. Each interview (or two) generates a cognitive map that belongs to a particular manager. These maps are verified by each manager to be a reasonable representation of the thinking

that the manager is prepared to declare about **emergent strategic issues**   *P329*
that are relevant to the development of strategy.

We accept that cognitive maps that rely upon an interview with an individual are mediated by considerations other than that of a theory of cognition. An interview is also a social and political act (Eden, 1992a; Eden *et al*, 1992) focusing the thinking in particular directions, considering the implications of options, etc. Furthermore, during the interview **the cogni-**   *P286*
tive structure of the individual is likely to change as ideas are explored
and better understood (Weick, 1979) – 'how do I know what I think until I see how I act', which translated to the domain of this chapter would be taken as *how do I know what I think until I see what I say*. With similar implications Nisbett and Wilson (1977) discuss the role of verbal reports of mental processes.

In order to get as close as possible to theories in use, the interviewer may use a number of techniques to encourage their explication. We introduce them here and discuss them in detail in the third section.

1.   Invite the interviewee to **explore the** *strategic issues they see*   *P298*
facing the organization over the next 'n' years. This attempts to lock the interviewee into a focus on the future but with a crisis, or firefighting, frame of reference. The issues need not be disaster oriented, they could be issues that arise from problems in attaining positive outcomes, but as we noted above, they provide a mandate for the interviewee to express concerns about negative outcomes. Unfortunately much management training has tended to punish such thinking – 'problems must be seen as opportunities', 'think positively', and so on. In addition, some of the well-known approaches to dealing with strategic issues start with an assumption that managers know what their objectives are, or that problems are to be formulated against an idealized conception of where the organization wants to be (Ackoff, 1974; Checkland, 1981; Kepner and Tregoe, 1965; Ozbekhan, 1974). Thus, managers are used to the idea that unless they know what their goals are and can clearly articulate them then they are lousy managers. In exploring emergent strategizing our experience is that often a management team is more confused about the clarity or otherwise of their goal system – strategic intent – than about almost any other aspect of strategy development. As we shall see below, the relationship between their beliefs about competencies and their aspirations is a journey that is often very significant for a management team, and yet it is also a journey which, when structured, need not take an inordinate amount of time.

2.   *Critical Incidents and 'Laddering'*. In social science research the   *P288 P389 P426*
critical incidents methodology has a long history (Campbell *et al*, 1970; Flanagan, 1954). Recently, it has been used to gather and analyse information about ethics, attitudes, and other topics (Bryson *et al*, 1996; Clawson, 1992).

Critical incidents are events that are particularly consequential. For our purposes, we use the following guide to what might constitute critical incidents for the interviewee:

- a turning point, or 'flip-flop';
- a particularly memorable episode or distinct piece of action that stood out from the flow;
- a 'fan' or 'junction point' offering multiple possible choices in which a decision about which choice to make was made with confidence;
- a point at which alternative futures became apparent;
- a point at which something 'fundamental' happened, or an important milestone was reached;
- something that stopped the interviewee 'in their tracks';
- a decision the interviewee was glad to have got 'right', or something they were exceedingly glad they didn't get wrong;
- something the interviewee was distressed to find they 'screwed up' or got 'wrong'.

From van der Heijden (1996:148) we add the following possibilities (that he uses for scenario development, but which are as relevant for these interviews):

- inheritances from the past: pivotal events that the interviewee believes should remain in everyone's memory;
- major constraints that are stopping urgent strategic action.

Each of these is designed to surface responses that will help the interviewee explain their world in relation to issues in their occupational life. As the issues are explored the interviewer takes care to 'ladder' upward (see the subsection below) to reveal goals and negative-goals.

P288 P389   3.   Shell Group Planning have favoured what they call *the 'Oracle Question'*. This question invites the interviewee to consider visiting an oracle who knows the future and to think of questions they would wish to ask. The invitation, once again, focuses on the resolution of expected future strategic issues through knowing about them in advance. Thus, for the interviewer they reveal something about the key uncertainties that are important. From this information it becomes possible to understand something of the nature of their beliefs (the data requested from the oracle is *believed* to influence outcomes for the organization) and aspirations (the outcomes can be assumed to matter and so be valued by the interviewee).

P288   ### Eliciting a Personal Aspirations System in an Occupational Role-setting

(This subsection is adapted from Appendix 1, 'Eliciting the value system in an occupational role-setting', in Eden *et al* (1979).)

With the account that follows, steps in the procedure which are statements made to the participant are inset from the description of the process.

1. Describing the purpose and process. The purpose of this session is to provide me with a picture of the setting within which your decision making takes place and to identify some of what you believe to be the important outcomes of the decisions you have become involved in. I want to try to do this in a fairly formal way so that I can avoid arriving at erroneous conclusions and making false assumptions about the special context within which you make your decisions. It is therefore likely that you will think I am asking some stupid questions – I hope you will feel able to excuse this and understand that I believe it to be necessary.

   > I would like to use some representative decisions that are a part of your job, as the starting point for getting at important outcomes, goals, or aspirations. I realize that quite a lot of the decisions you make are related to the needs of the organization itself, such as managing the people working for you, providing a proper working environment, and general departmental administration. I would like you to include this type of decision during this exercise but also think about the sort of decisions you take (or persuade others to take) which you believe have an impact on the business.

2. Identification of about ten representative decision elements which are recorded as D_i, $i = 1$–10.

   > Please think very carefully about the decisions you have made, or issues you have dealt with, during the last few weeks or so, including those where you responded to others. Can you describe to me a few of these which you believe to be representative and which resulted in something subsequently happening which made you feel pleased or disappointed with your decision and which is likely to have long term consequences?

   It will be useful if some decisions identified produced outcomes which were undesirable; in this way it is possible to identify 'negative-goals' which are often not discussed in organizations and yet may be driving emergent strategizing. Typically the participant will find it difficult to remember ten decisions in the last few weeks. As the participant 'dries up'; the time period should be progressively increased however, data from recent decisions is less subject to 'rewriting of history'.

3. A triad of these decisions, D_i, D_j, and D_k, are selected and noted. The decisions should be, ideally, of a similar type so that the participant is not presented with a solvable but difficult comparison problem. The process may be aided by using cards with the key words associated with each decision written on the card as a reminder.

   > Consider the two decisions I have grouped together and think of the outcomes (attitudes, behaviour, people, environment, etc.) which are common to these two decisions. Now consider these outcomes with respect to the third decision and tell me about an outcome which is common to the first two decisions but not common to the third. If these two decisions had not been made, what outcome (common to both decisions) would have resulted?

P290
    This establishes an outcome construct C_i and its **contrast, or opposite pole** $C_{\bar{i}}$; at the same time the pole which is the preferred outcome should be elicited and underlined (the preferred outcome will be C_i). Often the dissimilar construct outcome associated with D_k will, alternatively or in addition, be preferred. This need not be rejected. The constructs C_i, and $C_{\bar{i}}$ should be noted and the process repeated until about ten constructs and their contrasts are noted. A triad is chosen so that a higher order outcome is forced by the comparison of two decisions and yet is covered by the need for comparing with the third decision.

4.   Each outcome construct C_i and its contrasting construct are written, in turn, on separate sheets of paper so that the superordinate outcome

P310
    constructs may be elicited. The extent of the '**laddering**' upwards to higher order outcomes is determined by the participant preferring a goal (or 'negative-goal') which is a 'good (or bad) thing in its own right'. Sometimes it may be helpful to ladder up from a 'negative-goal' by asking whether a desired outcome might have alternatively occurred if the undesirable negative outcome had not. This may help elicit goals which are 'taken for granted'. The sequence stops as soon as the participant hesitates and has to search for a reply, and this goal (or negative-goal) is taken as the most superordinate for the ladder being explored.

> Why do you consider the outcome (C_{ij}) as a preferred outcome? What would you reckon the alternative outcome to be if outcome (C_{ij}) did not occur? What might you hope to achieve or avoid by attaining this outcome? And what would that help achieve or avoid?

And so on . . .

5.   The outcome from the 'laddering' exercise (based, as it is, on recent decisions) will produce several hierarchical chains of goals and negative-goals. The participant will, typically, have mentioned the same outcomes in more than one ladder. As the ladders are interconnected, a 'goal system' as a hierarchical network of interconnected goals and negative goals will begin to emerge. This goal system will have been elicited from recent decisions and so should facilitate the elicitation of goals which relate to 'theories in use'.

The Basis of Cognitive Mapping

Cognitive mapping has been developed, following extensions to the use of 'Repertory Grids' (Fransella and Bannister, 1977), for the purpose of capturing a 'personal construct system' (Eden 1988; Eden and Jones, 1984; Eden *et al*, 1979). The map seeks to represent the beliefs, values, and so embedded expertise and wisdom of managers. These are captured as a model of a part of the person's construct system, and the model is a *cognitive map*. The cognitive map is made up of constructs (nodes) linked to form chains (shown by arrows) of *action oriented* argumentation (see chapter P1 for detailed guidelines).

In sympathy with personal construct theory this action-orientation means that argumentation about issues is coded to reveal, or highlight, the implications for 'managing and controlling the future' through the way the issues are 'anticipated' (examples of mapping argumentation in this way are given in figure C5.2a). Arrows (illustrating chains of argument) show the implied possible actions and possible outcomes as suggested by the 'theories' a person uses to explain the world as they see it. *Thus meaning is given to a construct not only by its content, but also from the consequences attributed to it (forming the chains of consequences to the **value/goal/*** **P425** ***aspirations system**) and from the explanatory constructs that support it (the belief chain).* In gathering data and in building the model, the central questions guiding the coding of the map are 'what are the implications of *using* the "theory or belief about the world" as a basis for intervening in the world so as to protect or support values?' and 'what might explain or support the assertion?'. Consequently the map is made up of 'constructs' (or concepts) and arrows (relationships) indicating the direction of implication assumed by the belief system (see chapter P1).

Assertions, or 'facts', about the nature of the world are taken to have significance. Rather than an assertion being a simple, isolated, statement of 'what is', a cognitive map demands that assertions have consequences or implications. Thus, an assertion is elaborated by considering why the person is making it – 'what does the manager expect someone to do as a result of knowing the assertion?'. For example, if the manager asserts that 'customer loyalty is the result of developing long term personal relationships with particular individuals' and that 'helping the customer solve problems is one important aspect of getting the right relationship instead of always treating the customer to a sales pitch, as some of our less intelligent sales staff do', then we might code this part of the cognitive map as in figure C5.2a. In the same manner, when a manager makes an assertion such as 'most of our customers are well qualified', then it becomes important to review the context of the assertion, within the holistic sense of the manager's view, to discover, and so state, the way in which this statement is regarded as significant. Clues derive from other statements such as those made above and others such as 'many of our salesmen can only discuss football – the last thing they might do is hold together a conversation about what's going on with the technology our customers deal with'. These contextual assertions might lead to an extension of figure C5.2a to create the part of the map in figure C5.2b.

The most fundamental property of a cognitive map is the value system embedded within it. Providing the interview, or other elicitation technique, has been used properly, and coding of the interview data has been thorough, then analysis of the map should reveal the value *system* of the

interviewee (the network of values – where each value informs others and is, in turn, informed by others). Values will be defined both by the property of the words making up the construct and by the position of the construct within the hierarchy of a map. Thus, analysing the map to find those constructs that are most superordinate ('heads' of the map) is an important task. These constructs are the primary candidates as values. If the content of the construct suggests that it is not a 'valued outcome' for the interviewee, then the interviewer should seek an opportunity to conduct a further interview that will explore consequential outcomes using a 'laddering' process discussed above and so reveal values which will then be coded as hierarchically superordinate to the previous 'head'. Alternatively it may require only additional links to other existing material, thus weaving the 'head' into the model more thoroughly.

It is important to be clear about the distinction that can be made about the status of different types of cognitive maps. Our particular form of cognitive mapping is aimed at being a reasonable way of formalizing a body of cognitive theory (personal construct theory). It is designed to be so, and the coding guidelines discussed in part 3 of the book (also see Ackermann *et al*, 1990) have been developed so as to be faithful to Kelly, and the process of elicitation as a development of the Repertory Grid method. A cognitive map is not supposed to be a model of cognition but rather a thoughtful interpretation of Personal Construct Theory.

A cognitive map is taken to be a device that translates Kelly's theoretical framework into a practical tool by representing that part of a person's construct system which they are able and willing to make explicit. Therefore, whilst Kelly is clear that a construct is not the same as a verbal tag, it is nevertheless *useful* to collect verbal tags as if they were constructs. As a result, a cognitive map, in practice, is dependent upon the notion that language is a common currency of organizational life and so can be used as the dominant medium for accessing a construct system.

For many perfectly good reasons a person will not make explicit many beliefs to another person, let alone a strategy consultant. This is the case even if the manager believes that the interview is totally confidential. Thus, the cognitive map, developed in strategy development, is significantly biased by the necessary **social interaction**, that is the basis of elicitation through the interview. *P290*

Furthermore, the manager will not necessarily be prepared to validate a cognitive map so that it can be used as a contribution to joint understanding, reflection, and negotiation. Therefore, the so-called cognitive map that a strategy consultant can work with is always likely to be significantly different from cognition, but at least it will be in the spirit of Kelly and in the spirit of working with a manager's own theories about their world. More significantly it can be a tool to *facilitate* negotiation about different possible strategic futures for the organization – a *negotiation* that can take place between those managers who have the power to act, that starts from the individual subjective worlds of the participants, and that elaborates those subjective worlds (Vygotsky, 1981).

P285 P325 P329

Strategy Maps – using cognitive maps to support JOint Understanding and Reflection

The combination of detecting the emergent patterns from an aggregation of the individual cognitive maps, along with the indications of emergent strategizing detected by the study of procedures, usually forms the basis for the first part of joint understanding and reflection. This composite map is structured as a hierarchy where possible goals are at the top; these derive *V256 V257* from **strategic issues**, which in turn are impacted by strategic problems and possible strategic options (see figure C5.3). The categorization of each of the statements, that make up the map, into each of these levels within the strategy map is a rough one at this stage. It will gradually be refined as (i) the group works with the map, and (ii) an analysis of the structure suggests possible statements that can act as the labels encompassing a 'tear-drop' of argument and explanation. The group map (formed from the merging together of the cognitive maps) will contain the core belief statements that explain other statements, and imply an emergent aspirations system. This is the data to be used by the management team as the first steps in exploring strategic intent through the analysis of emergent competencies and their coherence in relation to aspirations.

At this early stage of the journey our approach focuses on the emergent aspirations system and aims to identify the core beliefs that may represent distinctive competencies. After the process of aggregating the cognitive maps from the interviews with management team members, or alterna-

V197 V248 V257 tively the generation of a group cause map (through oval mapping – see

P329 below), the most hierarchically superordinate concepts will be a first **draft of the aspirations or goal system**. The process of establishing this draft goal system is discussed in chapter P3. However, in principle the most hierarchically superordinate constructs are assumed to be goals. Following this, each level below is considered in turn on the basis of whether the concept expresses a desired outcome that at least one member of the management team sees as good 'in its own right'. To be a goal, the concept will not be treated as an option by the individual but rather assumed to be a clear aspiration for the group and organization. As we noted above, these aspirations may be expressed, at this time, as 'negative-goals' – that is 'we should not allow this outcome to occur, to do so is as important as attaining other positive goals'. Following on from this is an analysis of the group map focusing on identifying a first draft of emergent competencies and distinctive competencies. Chapter C6 discusses in more detail how these are identified.

Having established a representation of beliefs about distinctive competencies and goals/negative-goals, the first part of the journey is about jointly understanding and reflecting upon these characteristics. But which is to be explored first? In figure C5.1 we have shown in detail a part of the cycle of JOURNEY making (in itself a cycle), thus further reflecting the ongoing conversational process. Our experience suggests that starting

Figure C5.3 The strategy map as part of the strategy making process.

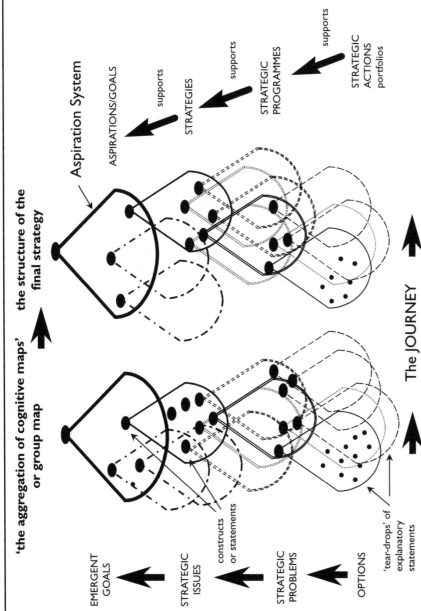

the discussion by concentrating upon the draft aspirations/goal system can be lacking in focus and too abstract for many management teams. In addition, it will not always be grounded in the practicalities of the organization. Therefore, the first episode of the journey is usually more successful and rewarding if it focuses on an examination and exploration of the distinctive competencies, and then moves to the goal system. Discussion which is conducted in the light of the draft goal system and the debate about competencies is presented the next chapter.

Working with Group Maps as a Starting Point

In some cases it is impracticable to conduct interviews. The reasons may be that there is not, at the start of the journey, enough commitment to carrying out interviews with all of the management team, or there may not be time or the opportunity. However, a group session using a group version of the cognitive mapping technique may be possible. The group mapping process will be guided by the same considerations as for interviews, but with a full recognition that it will not be possible to collect the richness of individualism that can be so helpful in creating ownership and creativity. Nevertheless, the specific processes for developing group maps, discussed in the third part of the book, seek to attend to increasing the probability of individualism in group work through specific group techniques and the use of computer based group work.

An alternative reason for using the group mapping process follows from the first series of strategy workshops conducted with the management team. These workshops will have started the process of jointly understanding and reflecting on the emergent aspirations system, possible competencies, and strategic issues. They will have been based on the initial round of one or two interviews with the members of the management team. The process may now shift to working with other groups, in a workshop setting, and so aim to incorporate more members of the organization to increase both procedural and substantive rationality. Usually these workshops involve between 6 and 24 people who will be invited to influence the strategy of the organization through the further identification and elaboration of strategic issues and emerging goals.

This group work, which will produce 'cause maps' (strategy maps), generally uses a combination of 'nominal group techniques' (Delbecq *et al*, 1975), the use of oval 'sno-cards' (Backoff and Nutt, 1988; Bryson *et al*, 1996; Eden *et al*, 1983), and often the use of the special purpose mapping software for recording, analysis, and display purposes. Participants work in groups of 10–15 people (sometimes requiring two sub-groups to work in parallel) and are encouraged to use the 'oval' cards to record and publicly display their own views of the strategic issues facing the organization within the context of the views of other members of the group. The process of using the **'oval mapping technique' (OMT)** is presented in full in part 3.

P303

The group may be provided with 'triggers' that are labels for the issues emerging from the analysis of the composite cognitive map of the management team – the initial draft of the *strategy map*. To aid this identification of the strategic issues, computer software is often used as it has a number of analysis methods that detect clusters of constructs, central constructs, organizational values, core beliefs, etc. (Cropper *et al*, 1990; Eden *et al*, 1992). The emerging issues form the agenda for, and so frame, workshops for the other members of the organization. They are designed to focus the group on further elaboration of issues of importance to the management team. It is not usually, however, intended to constrain the group from the identification of new strategic issues. An alternative mechanism when starting with an 'oval mapping' workshop is to use a carefully constructed starter question to promote discussion.

Focusing on **strategic issues** rather than the development of idealized scenarios or preferred goals is deliberately designed to match the focus in interviews on getting as close as possible to 'theories-in-use' (Bartunek and Moch, 1987). Doing so also helps reduces the possibility of participants discussing 'espoused theories' derived from attendance at management courses! This helps avoid strategy being constructed as 'motherhood and apple pie'. The clusters of ovals are specific theories that apply to the world of the participants' specific organization rather than any organization. *V228*

When **prompting group members to record their views** the same questions used for individual interviews are used – 'what might explain or support that assertion?', 'what are the implications of this particular belief?'. Here the group map constructed will not be a cognitive map but rather will be a cause map that acts as a model of some of the aspects of both individual beliefs, individual beliefs set in relation to the beliefs of others, and group beliefs. *P309 P310*

As participants display their ovals on the wall in front of them, they are **continuously organized** by a facilitator, with help from participants, into clusters (draft maps without links) of related statements. In addition, they are implicitly arranged by the facilitator into hierarchical 'teardrops' following the cognitive mapping guidelines so that the most superordinate outcome is at the top and the most detailed means or option at the bottom of the cluster. Each *cluster* of statements represents a possible *emerging 'strategic issue'* identified by the group. The group members are encouraged to elaborate and contradict the emerging view of issues being displayed on the wall. The process promotes synthesis through enabling linkages between and within clusters to be made. Group maps also encourage creativity through the ability to see alternative points of view and from this position identify and develop new options and strategies. *P308*

The clusters, their content, and the interrelationships between the content within clusters (inter-cluster linkages), and between clusters (intra-cluster linkages) are added to the existing composite map (if one exists). Thus the organizational strategy map, which is the focus of the journey for the management team, is continuously elaborated as each workshop unfolds.

DEVELOPING STRATEGIC INTENT: EXPLORING COMPETENCIES AND DEVELOPING THE BUSINESS MODEL

'Nothing recedes like success' (Anon)

'All organizations have the weaknesses of their strengths' 'and all organizations have the strengths of their weaknesses if they are recognised' (Pugh's Paradox, Derek Pugh)

Attention to distinctive competencies (Selznick, 1957) or core competencies (Hamel, 1994; Prahalad and Hamel, 1990; Schoemaker, 1992) has often been taken as significant in the success of Japanese industry. Organizations with strategies based on core competencies are argued to survive recession better than others and to emerge stronger as economic recovery develops (Bogner and Thomas, 1994). The success of Honda has been attributed to its recognition of having a distinctive competence in the building of engines and the subsequent appreciation that this was also core to its business success. The recognition of the strategic significance of this competence prompted them to succeed in many apparently disconnected markets from generators to motor cycles, and motor cars to lawn mowers. The notion is very powerful. Our experience suggests that a necessary part of the journey of strategy making is for any management team in any type of organization to jointly reflect upon the organization's competencies which are distinctive. However, the crucial activity is to go on and discover the *patterns* of distinctive competencies so that *core* competencies can be identified (see figure C5.1). Discovering, and working with, patterns – the systemic properties, not lists – of competencies and distinctive competencies is absolutely essential to this part of the journey. Rarely are the systemic properties revealed by the interrelationships between competencies and distinctive competencies analysed, and yet it is these properties that can be the strongest determinants of core competencies. In other words, the synergistic linking of competencies – the whole rather than the parts – is what makes distinctiveness.

The basic starting question that must be answered by an organization is, 'What do, or can, we do exceptionally well that our customers perceive adds more value than alternative providers?'. An organization stays alive by providing 'value' to a stakeholder-base. These stakeholders of interest are most often 'customers' for private organizations, and some parts of the public sector who gain *services as public goods* (Downs, 1967). This value is derived from a combination of stakeholder demand and the distinctive competencies of the supplying organization. 'Distinctiveness' here means some measure of difference, of being able to offer to the 'customers' something that no other competitor can. For an organization to be able to claim a position of sustainable profitability it has to be able to satisfy a 'customer' market in a manner which resists easy emulation.

If time is short and a team is determined to agree upon a strategic direction (a mission statement, a strategic goal system, and some important strategies) then tackling the task from a starting point of exploring distinctive competencies is usually the most effective. The process focuses attention on the aspects of emergent strategizing most critical for locating (a) those properties differentiating the organization from others, and (b) the links between these and desired outcomes, which enable desired outcomes to be levered in a way unique to the organization. Identifying these two is the essence of the *'business model'/'livelihood scheme'*. On many occasions a management team, using **appropriate group support systems,** V194 P329 P382 **has developed a strategic intent, in this way, in 5–7 hours of concentrated work.** The designed process has also ensured high levels of both cognitive and emotional commitment. Thus, attention to distinctive competencies is a powerful means of creating a strategic direction that can be sustained, is politically feasible because it is based on existing patterns of emergent strategizing, and which, even though developed within a short time (and so the outcome is likely to need further validation), will not produce future discomfort.

Distinctive Competencies

V266 P304 P330
P410

Distinctive competencies are those particular strengths within an organization that are very difficult to emulate and which can be utilized in a way that generates sustainable profits (private sector) or marks out why the service should not be provided elsewhere or not provided at all (public sector). The competencies often exist regardless of the industry or market. It is their exploitation *within a particular market* that makes them of particular importance. Distinctive competencies are the features of the organization that underpin long term success. They usually, but not always, have an external orientation, such that stakeholders are aware of, and are attracted to, the results of an organization's exploitation of the competencies.

Barney (1991) suggests that distinctive competencies must have four characteristics: that they are unique (difficult to substitute), rare among a firm's competition, imperfectly inimitable, and valuable (exploit opportunities or neutralize threats). Miles and Snow's (1978) typology of competencies notes that they provide some form of competitive advantage and suggests four different forms. The first form is that of 'defenders' –

suggesting a narrow market focus combined with production efficiency. The second, 'prospectors', refers to a broad market definition with product innovation. 'Analysers' whose interest is in production efficiency in stable markets and who track product innovations developed by competitors in other more dynamic markets is the third form. Finally, there are the 'reactors' who are doomed to failure. Porter (1980) argues that competencies must be capable either of differentiating the organization's products from those of others, or producing them at low cost – but not both, although research now suggests that there can be a mix of these.

Competencies within an organization should feed on each other to create synergies, or patterns, that give *distinctive strength*. Such distinctiveness can rarely be bought. It is built up over time and that is what makes emulation difficult. Drucker said over 30 years ago that future corporate success is based on existing strengths rather than those the organization has yet to acquire. This concept is the basis of strategic management within the organization: success is based on the exploitation of *existing* distinctive competencies and the protection of their ability to be self-sustaining, *as well as* the development of new distinctive competencies. As we shall argue later, the cycle of exploring existing distinctive competencies in relation to aspirations will enable the realization of the business model through the identification of strategies to develop new competencies as well as the exploitation of existing competencies. Thus, strategic vision must not ignore knowledge of distinctive competencies and the focused utilization of them. Within the context of developing strategic vision, core distinctive competencies are those that primarily drive the aspirations system – thus there are direct and powerful links between the competence and many of the goals (figure C5.1). Core competencies also have the power to self-sustain a strategic future. Consequently these competencies are very potent and so too are the links between them and the business model or livelihood scheme.

Some examples of possible distinctive competence types

These types are not presented as if they were in any way a complete list, and not all of them are relevant to all organizations. There is a great danger in developing typologies of distinctive competencies because, by definition, the best distinctive competencies may well be those which distinctively fall outside those that are typically within a typology! However, the examples provide clues about the type of property to look for.

Some of the items often proudly presented as distinctive competencies include large scale production, high market share, successful diversification, or sole organization in the marketplace. These are not distinctive competencies but rather are usually the *consequence* of the exploitation, either deliberate or emergent, of distinctive competencies. Indeed they are most often the successful exploitation of a system of interlocking distinctive competencies. Thus, it is important, in any discussion about competencies, to separate outcomes from the competencies which drive the outcomes. The outcomes may, or may not, be desirable in relation to aspirations and goals but must be distinguished from characteristics that are exploitable emergent properties. The distinction is often difficult to make, but discussion aimed at drawing out the distinction is usually helpful in good strategy making.

Reputation and trust   The decision making of customers is often importantly influenced by something *built up over time*. This is powerful when the good reputation is difficult and costly to create, particularly when, as is often the case, the cost of entry is precisely that of gaining reputation and trust. It is also, of course, often easy to lose reputation and trust.

Some examples are:

- successful branding which is based (usually amongst other factors) on *having been in the market for longer than anyone else;*
- reputation for technical excellence, quality and reliability (for example, that exploited by German car manufacturers) – a competence *that takes a long time to attain* but little time to lose;
- reputation for honesty and trustworthiness;
- reputation for dependability of delivery where the complexity of delivery is known to be high – thus for some organizations project management capability might be a distinctive competence, and delivery dependability the *outcome* noticed by the stakeholder.

However, whilst reputation and trust are often used as distinctive competencies, again in reality they tend to be outcomes rather than competencies. For example, trust may be acquired through an organization dealing fairly with customers, providing good after-sales service. Reputation and trust can be strategically exploited, but it is the identification of the distinctive or important competencies underlying the creation of these outcomes that is the key to understanding the business model or livelihood scheme.

Assets   This type of distinctive competence is usually manifest where an organization is strategically different, but not necessarily unique. The differences are noticed by customers and other stakeholders who have a choice about whether or not to form a relationship. To them the nature of the assets may provide reason for a preferential relationship. It is important to note that these assets can be hard or soft – physical resources and reserves, or the skill of the work force, and other such resources that do not normally appear on the balance sheet.

Some examples are:

- Access to resources (financial and human) across many cultures through local networking and special relationships in many countries, for example family connections to senior government officials in some developing countries. This can sometimes be bought through acquisition, but can also easily be lost after acquisition through the dominant culture of the acquirer being contrary to that of the acquired.
- Legitimacy with governing authorities and effective lobbying abilities. Whilst this is usually based on the longevity of trusting two-way relationships, it is possibly too dependent upon specific individuals to be a distinctive sustainable competence.
- Exceptional motivation, loyalty, and morale of staff that depends upon the staff as a group rather than one or two individuals. This reflects a situation where any single member leaving does not affect the group spirit.
- Embedded and taken for granted commitment to customer service.
- Specialist know-how in terms of technology, market, or operations that belongs to the organization as a working network rather to any small number of specific individuals.
- Ability to create strategic alliances and joint ventures which give all partners a feeling of '1+1=3'.
- Ability to make collaboratives work. It is becoming increasingly important for organizations to develop strategic futures through collaborations that can link distinctive competencies, and yet research shows that success in collaboration is immensely difficult. Thus, the ability to capitalize on the potential for **'collaborative advantage'** (Huxham, 1996) can be very distinctive.

V248

Uniqueness of products or services   A distinctive or unique position can come from ownership of a product/service, or process (for example, in the public sector, the ability to carry out a sophisticated and complex bureaucratic procedure which cannot be executed by others), that cannot be easily emulated. Usually this means that the product or process has high levels of embedded complexity within it which has been managed through many years of development and application. This distinctive competence can be particularly powerful when the owner finds it difficult to understand why, or how, it works – it is truly an emergent systemic property of the organization, where the whole is significantly different from the sum of the parts. It is powerful because it will be difficult if not impossible for competitors to emulate, and the owner is unlikely to lose it easily through, for example, the loss of individual employees.

Finally, distinctive competencies must be retained when they relate or contribute towards the continuing need to manage the shop and retain income from cash cows. There is a danger of forgetting to support existing distinctive competencies while new markets and services are being developed through strategies designed to create new distinctive competencies.

Distinctive Competencies as a Distinctive *Pattern* of Competencies

The above discussion takes the traditional view of distinctive competencies, but misses what is probably the most powerful aspect of a distinctive competence. This is that it is the result of a *pattern of relationships* between competencies and distinctive competencies that can often yield the most significant distinctive competencies. Indeed *a pivotal, core, distinctive competence is often the combination of a particular unique **pattern of interrelated** competencies*, where it is the pattern that is distinctive.   P330

Many organizations discover that, as they list possible distinctive competencies, they find great difficulty in distinguishing the list from a similar list they imagine their competitors might construct. And yet they feel certain that they have strength in these areas because there is something distinctive about their organization. In these circumstances we find that an exploration of the links between each potential competence gives a clue to distinctiveness. That is, it is the way in which one competence supports or sustains another, and that, in turn, supports another, that is distinctive.

When competencies are explored through a group cause map these characteristics are easily identifiable, for the relationships between them are already noted in the map. Thus, the exploration is relatively easy: the group cause map is searched for concepts which fit any of the above definitions, and these are categorized accordingly (as competencies, distinctive competencies, or even by category of competence). Although these concepts may be scattered about the cause map, rather than directly related, the detailed argumentation which links them together can be suppressed to give summary direct linkages (computer analysis makes this process simple).

As patterns are made explicit and displayed, the patterns that are most powerful as a potential distinctive competence are the following.

- A *loop of competencies* might make the feedback *loop* a distinctive competence rather than its components.
- Similarly a feedback *loop with at least one distinctive competence* in it is important because it sustains the distinctive competence:
  - loops with *ability to resource the distinctive competencies* makes the distinctive competencies more powerful.
- A *patterning of competencies* might be particularly important (the pattern is the distinctive competence because nobody else could achieve the pattern even if they could get the competencies).

Feedback loops of distinctive competencies are particularly important because they explicate their self-sustaining nature. Thus, an outstanding distinctive competence incorporates the sustaining *relationships* as well as the distinctive competencies themselves. As we shall note below, if these feedback loops of distinctiveness are positive (that is they support the organization's aspirations) then they must be prime candidates to become a *core* distinctive competence simply because of their power to self-sustain a strategic future. Figure P3.3 shows an example of a pattern of distinctive competencies which potentially forms two feedback loops.

In practice, many public sector or voluntary groups have extraordinary difficulty in identifying their distinctive competencies. In a number of cases this is simply because they do not have any, and must develop some. At other times it is because they have not considered that the uniqueness of their competencies might be the relationship between them – they have developed unique ways of working. In the UK the process of 'market testing' has sharpened the process of *thinking* about distinctiveness; however, unfortunately the outcomes of market testing have not involved a proper consideration of distinctiveness but rather have focused almost exclusively on that of cost. Often this has led to the demise of the service, as the competencies were not discovered until their loss was noticed.

Distinctive Competencies and their Relationship to Aspirations – the 'business model' or 'livelihood scheme'

Basic knowledge and awareness of distinctive competencies must start with an appreciation of what strengths an organization has and how its current success originated, before any attempt can be made to consider the future. This is the first part of the journey – jointly reflecting upon the belief system and aspirations system underpinning emergent strategy before considering change. As we have said, the strategic future of an organization, or division, or business unit, or department, whether private, public or third sector, depends totally upon its ability to exploit competencies in relation to its aspirations. The security and stability of that future depends upon the distinctiveness of the competencies and their sustainability. The ability to *link competencies to aspirations* is the business model or livelihood scheme (for the public and not-for-profit sectors). Even for the third sector, where the livelihood may be a mix of voluntary energy and effort combined with the ability to raise income, the extent of the distinctiveness of competencies that support aspirations provides the basis for a strategic future.

The journey that explores this linkage between competencies and aspirations initially seeks to (i) validate the competencies, (ii) validate the distinctiveness of those marked as such, (iii) validate the distinctiveness of patterns of competencies and distinctive competencies, and most importantly, (iv) validate the links on the cause map between competencies and goals. Typically each of these discussions leads to their redefinition:

- Some competencies, that managers are proud of, are noted as isolated from others, and so play no role in the support of those which are distinctive.

- Some patterns of competencies, or distinctive competencies, are noted as disconnected from aspirations.
- Some aspirations are revealed as having no support from any competencies, and so new competencies must be developed.

The crux of the journey then is the following.

- The aspirations system is rebuilt so that it better exploits distinctive competencies.
- Distinctive competencies are identified that need to exist so that the aspirations system can be attained, and thus some aspects of a business model are created.
- A cluster of competencies is noted as having the potential for self-sustaining feedback – but only if a strategy can be executed that creates a new supporting link on the map. This becomes an important strategic option.

Typically this process tends to lead to new goals being encompassed into the aspirations system, goals that are a rewritten form of a distinctive competence or cluster of competencies making up a distinctive competence. Thus, for example, a feedback loop that represents a cluster of sustainable competencies and which is a distinctive pattern, remains on the map in its detailed expression but also becomes restated as a goal. Here the goal, in itself, is a statement of the business model, and its wording should be made to read so that it clearly expresses the basis of livelihood.

As figure C5.1 indicated, the process is cyclical – *aspirations are modified, as distinctive competencies are identified and changed, distinctive competencies are identified as being necessary given the desire to retain particular goals, and gradually new competencies are created through the possibility of delivering strategic options.* In addition, other distinctive competencies are seen to be irrelevant or unhelpful resulting in a possible shift of energy and resources. This cyclical journey gradually reveals those distinctive competencies which are core.

'Core' Distinctive Competencies?

Core distinctive competencies are those that primarily drive the aspirations system – thus there are direct and powerful links between the competence and many of the goals. Consequently these competencies are very potent and so too are the links between them and the business model or livelihood scheme. As we noted above, when the distinctive competence is a loop then it will inevitably show up as core because the probability of links to many goals or many links to a single goal will be higher (**potency** *P411* of a competence). Each node on the loop can be tracked to at least one goal/aspiration in its own right but also through every other node on the loop.

However, we need to be aware that sustained success can very rarely emanate only from completely new or yet to be acquired competencies.

Distinctive competencies must be maintained and, preferably, sustained otherwise they can dissolve away, gradually be duplicated or no longer be fully relevant to a particular market. Thus, distinctive competencies must be explicitly understood and appreciated so that as necessary they can be protected (often via legal barriers), enhanced (by adding or strengthening), changed (by dropping those that no longer help to create customer value) or refreshed. None of this is easy; awareness of the potential failure of distinctive competencies comes not so much from a study of strengths and weaknesses, but from being aware of the competencies in the first place, how they relate to one another and how they support the aspirations system and the business model. It comes from determining whether a long-standing distinctive competence has inadvertently been allowed to decline and must be re-invigorated, or whether a dormant distinctive competence's time has now come and thus it needs careful nurture, or whether a previously upheld distinctive competence is no longer relevant to the organization's business. In any case, strengthening of distinctive competencies comes from internal renewal. It is difficult to achieve sustainability by buying in something unless this strategy is taken as the device for locking that which is 'bought in' into the organization *in such a manner that it cannot be bought by another organization*. To do this requires recognizing that the strategy explicitly seeks to link the acquired competence to a network of other competencies.

P332 *An Emergent Mission Statement*

P424   This early stage of the journey will have established a **first draft of strategic intent** by clarifying the realistic *aspirations system*, supported by a *business model* that in turn is linked to *core distinctive competencies*. One final test of this draft goal system comes from the dialectical device of drafting a mission, vision, or strategic intent statement. We do not find it theoretically helpful, or pragmatically useful, to debate the definition of a
V197 P431   mission statement. Throughout this text we shall use the term **mission to refer to that statement which expresses, with some drama**, the intention of the organization in terms of delivered outcomes, the manner in which they are to be delivered, and the character of the organization expected to deliver them. For some organizations this statement will be brief (a few lines of text), for others it will be longer (maybe up to a few pages of text). Our definition of this statement is encompassed by figure C6.1 which has been mostly influenced by the work of Campbell (1989).

Figure C6.1 (a) The basis for the mission statement; (b) Relating the four aspects of the mission statement.

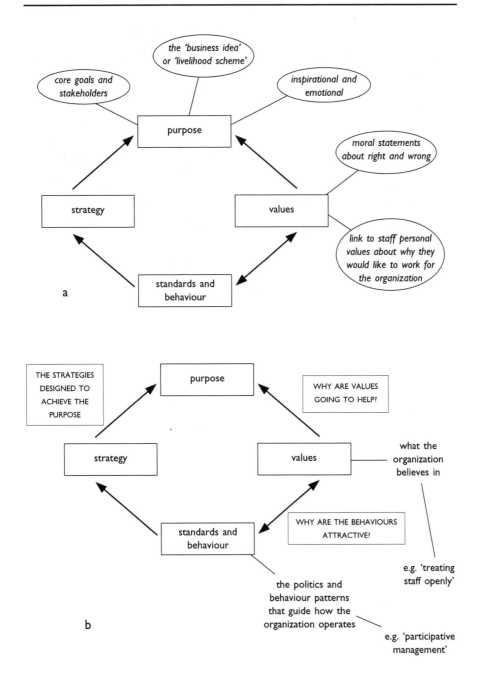

The purpose of the statement is to express – through the traditional mechanics of sentences, phrases, and paragraphs – an emotionally attractive and coherent statement of what the organization is all about. To some extent the draft goal system does most of this; however, it often tends to be too logical and reasoned and misses the call for emotional commitment. Nevertheless, at this stage of the process, the precision and refinement of the statement is not as critical as is developing something that the members of the management team are able to live with (politically feasible) and that represents the aspirations and competencies of the organization. The final drafting of the mission statement usually occurs during the closure (or agreement) stage. At this point, issues such as exploring the rationale of having a mission statement, determining the elements to be included, and ensuring that the result acknowledges the organization's strategic intent are considered. As represented in figure C6.1 the process of drafting a mission statement may result in the distinctive competencies and aspirations being revisited – thus returning to the strategic intent cycle.

STAKEHOLDER ANALYSIS *AND* MANAGEMENT

'To have a good enemy, choose a friend; he knows where to strike'
(Diane de Poitiers, 1499–1566, Mistress of King Henri II of France)

Probably one of the most important outcomes of a strategy making journey, for any organization, public or private, is that of developing a way of better managing the interface between the competing demands of different stakeholders. To a greater extent than probably any other factor to be considered on the journey, stakeholders determine the ability of an organization to achieve its aspirations. Understanding and appreciating the significance of stakeholders comes through an assessment of the stakeholders' interpretation of the strategic behaviour, of the strategic future, of the past performance of the organization, and of their own influence on the organization. These assessments are crucial to the implementation of future strategic options.

In a small company, the attitude of the bank, as stakeholder, can be more important than anything which is happening in the market. In a public agency, the attitude of the media towards specific strategic thrusts can be a stronger determinant of the political feasibility of strategies than the rational analysis which led to their adoption.

In the public sector it is our experience that many managers do not believe they have a capability for strategic management. This belief is largely founded on experience that stakeholders have so much power over their strategic future that the organization can only *react* to them. In this sense managers see many stakeholders as if they were a part of the environment that cannot be influenced. Thus, nearly all of the stakeholders are seen as what we shall label 'context setters'. The conceptualization of stakeholder analysis that we introduce in this chapter is designed to help public sector managers empower themselves by discovering that it is often possible to develop strategies for managing those stakeholders who can influence their strategic future.

Contrastingly, in the private sector, there is a stronger inherent belief that stakeholders can be managed – indeed that managers are, as a matter of course, intuitively doing this well. Our task in this case is to find appropriate forms of analysis that will, perforce, suggest yet more effective ways of managing stakeholders. We aim to carry out this analysis in ways that are coherent with agreed strategic direction, but, as we shall see, the process of reflecting upon stakeholders usually plays a significant role in *determining* strategic direction rather than simply *testing* it. As with all aspects of the strategy making journey, the designed processes are cyclical in their importance for one another.

A Background to the Analysis of Stakeholders

One influential model of organizational processes is the *input–output* view of organizations as transformers (see Checkland, 1981, for his mnemonic CATWOE that explicitly requires groups to examine the *Transformations* that take place). This sees the life of an organization as involving interactions with others at the boundary of the organization. Inputs are seen as coming from investors and suppliers, employees add value with the help and guidance of managers in transforming inputs to produce output, and this output is valued by customers. The value customers place on the transformation provides in turn a return to investors, and compensation to employees and managers. Such a model gives credence to management's view that it is important to attend not only to shareholders and competitors as stakeholders, but also to the needs of customers and employees. Braumhart's (1968) survey of managers showed how much managers subscribe to this view, and more recent surveys (Clarkson, 1991; Halal, 1990) have supported this observation.

Considerations about stakeholders are thus often focused upon a market view of the primary interactions of a business. In part this follows from the input–output model mentioned above. A market view of stakeholders clearly simplifies the complexity of business, and ignores stakeholder issues for public organizations. For example, the relationships an organization has with its accountants/auditors, consultants, and lawyers are very different from those with competitors and customers, and yet they are particularly important in understanding feasibility in strategy making practices.

The market view of the world sees 'customers' as the important beneficiaries. The financial view sees 'shareholders/owners' as the primary beneficiaries. The extended stakeholder model breaks out from these marketing and finance views by arguing that *all* persons, groups, or organizations who have a legitimate interest, and participation, in ensuring the well-being of the organization will do so to seek benefits. Following the work of Freeman (1984), the analyst is encouraged to think about the strategic future of the organization by considering, as equally important stakeholders, political groups, communities, trade associations and governments as well as customers, suppliers, investors, and employees. In essence, organizations are seen as having to *negotiate a balance of pluralist needs* (something akin to agency theory and transaction cost analyses (Williamson, 1985)). Whether this negotiation is explicitly undertaken or not, for our purposes we are interested in the negotiation being *managed strategically*, so as to support the achievement of the aspirations of an organization. We are interested in a process of *analytically sustained manipulation*.

It is also worth noting that a perspective emphasizing a broader view of stakeholders is increasingly reinforced by national and transnational laws. For example, the Companies Act in the UK asks that company directors include the interests of employees in their decision making. The intention of EU legislation is to permit organizations to take account of the interests of employees, creditors, customers, as well as investors in the justification of their decisions (Orts, 1992). Most of the above encouragements to organizations are encompassed by contemporary debate about corporate governance. However, this legislative and societal shift only defines a framework within which strategic thinking must take place. *It does not determine the choices that an organization must make in relation to these stakeholder interests.* It is important to see these developments as a part of exploring strategies to manage the environment at large, rather than as the main focus for stakeholder analysis and management.

The privatization of utilities in the UK has shown how the stakeholder balance can change in striking ways. As senior managers have been given share options, the 'rigours' of the stock market have become paramount in the strategic management of these organizations (BBC *Panorama*, 27 March 1995). The rhetoric of servicing the shareholders as the primary, and as some have argued, the only, stakeholders, has been used to legitimize massive payoffs to individual directors of each of the privatized organizations. Consumers, who are acknowledged publicly as stakeholders, have seen their power significantly reduced and consequently suffered high price rises in some cases, within the monopolistic markets. Paradoxically it appears that these organizations, which used to be public services, and have now become monopolies, have moved backwards to the old view, that it is the shareholder who is singularly important, whereas other organizations operating within a competitive market have moved towards recognition of the power of a broader set of stakeholders.

A Stakeholder Theory View

Most literature that discusses stakeholders introduces this theme as a stakeholder *theory of organizations*. The basic thrust of the theory is that better understanding of what actually goes on in organizations derives from considering the interactions between the organization and those with whom it has to deal. It suggests that organizations can survive only if they attend to the interests of *multiple* parties, rather than simply those of shareholders. We too have included attention to stakeholders as central to emergent strategizing (see figure C2.10). Typically, however, stakeholder theories focus on those who have an interest in the success, rather than demise, of the focal organization. They generally ignore those who are intent on controlling the destiny of the organization but do so without a legitimate (in the eyes of the controlled organization) role so to do. Many of those who have a stake in the focal organization are interested in sabotaging the strategy of the organization if it threatens their own strategic future. Most obviously, in the private sector, competitors are very significant stakeholders who have a stake sometimes in the success of the organization as the 'good competitor', and sometimes in its failure. In the public sector those of different political hues have an obvious stake in the failure of others. In both examples the stakeholders are amenable to stakeholder *management*.

Freeman (1984:31) argues that the term 'stakeholder' originates from the work of the Stanford Research Institute and meant 'stockholder' – 'those groups without whose support the organization would cease to exist'. Note, once again, the focus on support rather than sabotage and to some extent a financially oriented view. This approach sought to develop 'measures of satisfaction' for stakeholders within the context of environmental scanning. Others rejected this notion and preferred to see stakeholders as constraints. The difference between the two approaches is that one sees stakeholders as interfering, and the other as responsible for the organization's welfare.

However, both these approaches were oriented to understanding stakeholders in order to produce better forecasts. There was little concern with *changing* stakeholder behaviour, rather they sought to forecast it. For this reason there was little interest in the level of aggregation or dis-aggregation of stakeholder categories. When the need is to forecast behaviour, there is less interest in the motivation behind the behaviour. But when the aim is strategically to manage stakeholders, it is imperative to think of them as goal seeking within the context of a locus of power determining their strategies for achieving their goals. Thus, determining the loci of power within any generic category of stakeholder is import-ant. Simply naming a stakeholder organization is not enough, it is of the essence to think about how this named organization could be managed strategically. In doing so, it is typical for managers to realize that their sphere of influence of the stakeholder is at a level lower than that originally suggested. For example, it is common for 'the government' to be named, and yet when asked to envisage how 'the government' could be managed strategically, it becomes clear that what is meant is govern-ment as a particularly powerful politician or powerful government department. In general, thinking about stakeholder *management* generally leads to extensive and particular dis-aggregation of the stakeholders expressed by the broad categories suggested by Freeman and others.

Most of the early influential writing about stakeholders does not see the identification of stakeholders (for any particular organization) as problematic. There seems to be an implicit view that a standard list can be used and that the organizations or groups on the list can be dis-aggregated to an appropriate level. The notion that negotiations must generally take place with someone, or at least a negotiating party, rather than a reified entity, was ignored. Of course, in many instances, the negotiation will take place with a categorized mass of people – as with categories of consumers – but often the stakeholders who can most powerfully, and deliberately, influence the strategic future of the focal organization are specific individuals and groups.

However, this stakeholder theory approach is in contrast with our view that sees stakeholders as potential *actors* – people or small groups with the power to respond to, negotiate with, and change, the strategic future of the organization. Stakeholders need to be recognized for being associated with interactions that are dynamic and possibly unstable. There is a potential for conflict of a 'win/lose' sort, which might, in turn, suggest specific interest groups who see a role for negotiation and getting involved.

Not surprisingly, many of the discussions on stakeholders put the organization at the centre of a series of two-way interactions between the organization and a particular stakeholder group (see for example Bryson, 1995:72; Freeman, 1984:55). Stakeholders are not seen as part of a *system* of interactions that can occur in relation to the organization. While we are not concerned necessarily to understand all, or many, of the interactions between stakeholders, we *are* concerned to understand those interactions which are designed to influence attitudes of various stakeholders towards the focal organization itself. Typically there are influence networks amongst stakeholders, including amongst competitors (for example, recall the collaboration of the major airlines in their response to Jim Laker and Laker Airways in the 1970s as precursor to recent similar episodes designed to threaten new airlines). These come into play when the organization seeks to implement particular strategies. There are approaches that consider competition. Porter (1985), for example, argues that the achievement of *'competitive advantage'* is dependent upon such factors as ability to produce a differentiated product, having wide and coordinated geographical competitive scope, and so on, and describes a 'good competitor' in terms of such attributes as 'understands the rules' and 'has realistic assumptions'. Such factors are undoubtedly crucial to competitive success, and by explicitly drawing attention to them, Porter made a significant contribution to the discussion of competitive strategy in organizations. This sort of approach, however, does not pay attention to the *dynamics* of inter-company competition that may stop an organization achieving its advantage even though it is technically sound in other respects.

Senior managers in highly competitive industries frequently focus on the actions of their competitors. What seems to be important to them is that they put their efforts into 'winners', and this is, to a large extent, determined by what others do. For example, it may be important to avoid putting resources into developing a new product if another organization is developing something similar, only better or more quickly. It is important not to decide to standardize on a particular model if a number of your major competitors agree, in a coalition, to standardize on a different version, and so on. In addition, managers are often concerned about the actions of other parties. For example, they are often mindful to keep ahead of relevant new government legislation, to keep abreast of government support for, or subsidies to, their competitors in different countries, to predict the likely moves of their customers, and so on. Within the public sector there are well-established influence networks between other agencies, voluntary groups, and so on that can be used by stakeholders to form coalitions that may sabotage strategies (or if strategically managed, formed to promote strategies of the organization).

Stakeholders Influence Other Stakeholders

'Systems/OR' people (particularly Ackoff (1974)) have argued for a systems view of stakeholder management where there is recognition of the extent to which stakeholders are a community who work together in a patterned interaction. Ackoff specifically argued that many societal problems could be solved by the redesign of fundamental institutions in conjunction with the support of the stakeholders *in the system*. However, in this case, the notion of 'stakeholders in the system' differed from the approach set out in much of the strategy literature. In essence it argued for more of a cooperative activity and assumed common value systems (in particular between for example the 'poor' and 'capitalists'). This view was particularly represented in Ackoff's book 'Redesigning the Future' (1974) which encompassed some radical proposals for participative organizations. This liberal stance on stakeholders relies on a normative approach that asserts that each stakeholder has rights (see for example Evan and Freeman, 1988). The proper treatment of stakeholders is assumed to be a strategic aspiration, an end in itself, where the *purpose* of an organization is taken to serve as a vehicle for coordinating stakeholder interests. This is in contrast to our approach where stakeholders are managed only as a means to pursuing strategic ends. *Stakeholders are not treated as having rights, only having power and interest.* To treat any stakeholder as having rights is a strategic *choice* which may then be reflected in the aspirational system of the organization.

The liberal stance also sidesteps the utility of a multi-stakeholder view in the successful strategic management of many of these relatively powerless stakeholders. The market as a stakeholder can then be blamed for profits that are seen as too high by the customer as stakeholder. The deficient standards of safety as seen by society as a stakeholder can be blamed on the customer (as a 'powerful' stakeholder) who refuses to pay the price for safety, after all it is not the role of the organization to make judgements but rather to accept the judgement of the consumer. Each of these interactions must be properly thought through to achieve a degree of strategic *management* of multiple, and interacting, stakeholders in the interests of the strategic future of the organization. Stakeholders have different interests that will, often, place them in conflict with one another and with the organization itself. It is the strategic management task of the organization to manage successfully these conflicts and if necessary actively manipulate them.

Thus, while we will not be advocating the approach taken by Ackoff, we do recognize the potential for *managing* stakeholders in a pro-active and highly focused manner. This is not to suggest that it is inappropriate to take a liberal stance that calls for greater participation, and so empowerment, of a wider set of stakeholders than capitalism would suggest. Rather, it is to recognize that to do so must be a deliberate strategic choice. Nor do we argue against the view that organizations may be too narrow in their attention to stakeholders, in fact this is often the case. The episode, in 1995, between Shell UK and Greenpeace about the destination of the Brent Spar oil platform demonstrates that pressure groups are serious contenders as significant stakeholders. If it is argued that Shell mismanaged the episode, then it must be seen as a failure of stakeholder analysis and/or management. In addition, it can be argued that stakeholder analysis often fails to recognize the power that small or medium sized companies can have in stopping large organizations from abusing market power. These companies are often a significant source of innovation. For example, many large organizations who have 'downsized' innovators out of their organization are now struggling to regain contact with, and possibly formally collaborate with, the very small organizations which have subsequently been formed by their innovators. These small organizations are, in their own right, forming themselves into **networked** *V248* **collaboratives** or virtual organizations. These collaboratives are formed in order to gain the power of a coalition with respect to the larger organization, and, in the oil industry in particular, the collaboratives are becoming increasingly powerful as the oil companies depend on them for research and development.

Stakeholder Analysis   *V198 V261 V273*

This section of the chapter seeks to translate the above discussion about the nature of stakeholders and incorporate it into a journey of analysis. In particular, the analysis seeks to avoid the trap of presuming strategy in advance of the analysis, for example assuming that shareholders are important. Where an organization makes an aspirational statement that identifies a stakeholder, such as 'our aim is to provide shareholders with high growth and dividends', then this must be treated analytically: as a choice, first, made amongst other competing aspirations; and second, as an *a priori* assumption that stakeholder analysis will reveal shareholders to be both powerful *and* primarily interested in the organization meeting this aspiration. The second of these must be proved by the stakeholder analysis and then, and only then, converted into a stakeholder management strategy. One *option* to support this strategy is to deliberately incorporate shareholders into the publicly stated aspirations, even though the statement is not expected to drive strategy as it is enacted. Thus, it is not a 'real' aspiration but rather a stakeholder management strategy that must be thought of as such. It is, for example, usual for the annual report of an organization to be used as a deliberate stakeholder management vehicle. This may occur in such a manner that the statements contained within the report, and the emphases given to those statements, are at variance with the 'internal' strategy.

In undertaking a stakeholder analysis, it is usual to focus attention upon a large array of actors who have an interest (stake) in the strategic future of the organization, whether or not they have significant power in relation to the organization. Indeed, as we discussed above, stakeholder analysts often make a plea for the specific inclusion of disadvantaged and powerless groups – the analysis being driven by a value-laden, rather than utilitarian, view of the role of stakeholder analysis.

In contrast, our own concern with stakeholder analysis has a strictly utilitarian aim of identifying stakeholders who will, or can be persuaded to, *support* actively the strategic intent of the organization. An important aspect of the analysis we discuss below is that of prioritizing stakeholders in relation to strategic management possibilities. We shall use two dimensions – the power of stakeholders to influence the strategic future of the focal organization, and their interest in the strategic future of the organization – as the basis for prioritizing. In addition we shall use a more detailed analysis of the bases of power and interest, for those prioritized, to help determine the appropriate level of dis-aggregation for stakeholders. In this way we shall focus attention on the strategic management of the power and interest of stakeholders who can most significantly support or sabotage the strategic future of the organization. Thus, we are concerned with those who will seek to, and have or can develop the power to, *sabotage* the successful management of strategic intent, as well as provide *support*. In particular the analysis considers the possibility of enacting a particular strategic intent that would have the consequence of encouraging the formation of *coalitions* amongst those stakeholders. The stakeholders may have little individual power to begin with, but by

V248 forming into a **collaborative grouping** they acquire significant power. Where the stakeholders are already powerful, this resultant coalition may have disastrous results on the strategy being implemented. In this sense, stakeholder analysis is focused on identifying strategic and tactical options that arise for the organization itself by anticipating the dynamics of stakeholder attitudes and actions. Consequently it acts as a process of review to ensure that the options under consideration are both robust and coherent.

For example, in our work with government in Northern Ireland, we were concerned specifically with exploring the ways in which apparently powerless groups (such as prison visitors and the families of prisoners)

V232 may build themselves into **coalitions** with the media and others. By doing so we were concerned that they could increase their power to sabotage the strategic intent of the Northern Ireland Prison Service.

Thinking about Stakeholders – the stakeholder grid

V255 P314 P341 P344

It is clear that an important task in developing a robust strategy for an organization is that of testing the emergent strategic intent against the responses and aspirations of powerful stakeholders. This implies that we must identify stakeholders in terms of the extent of their power and the nature of their interests.

In this context then:

> '. . . the point about stakeholders is that (contrary to shareholders) they cannot put their interests in companies up for sale. The workforce, the local community and also banks and even suppliers and buyers are, as it were, stuck with the companies to which they are committed. This can be regarded as an undesirable rigidity only in an inhuman world in which it does not matter whether firms are bought or sold, taken over, merged, extended, reduced, or closed as long as the shareholders get a maximum yield for their investment. In truth, it does matter. What is more, competitiveness is not increased by lack of commitment, especially if companies choose to go down the high skill rather than low pay route. Reliability and predictability have their own value in business relations across the globe. Recognition and involvement of stakeholders is the practical answer' (Ralph Dahrendorf, *The New Statesman and Society*, 15/29 December 1995).

Thus to help conceptualize the relationship between different types of stakeholders, and so think productively about stakeholders, it is helpful to categorize possible stakeholders according to the two dimensions we identified above:

- Their *interest* in the strategic activity of the specific strategy making organization.
- Their *power* to influence the achievement of the strategic intent of the organization. Here, deliberately, we do not define power except to say that it is a subjective not objective measure that is important. As long as the focal organization believes a stakeholder to be powerful then it is this which is significant at this stage of the analysis. Beliefs about the bases of power are developed as a second stage of analysis.

These two dimensions seek to distinguish actors (those with enough power to influence strategic futures) and stakeholders (those who are interested and want to influence the future of the organization – negatively or positively). The overlap of these two groups represents the most significant 'players' in strategy making (see figure C7.1).

Figure C7.1 Stakeholder analysis – the power/interest grid.

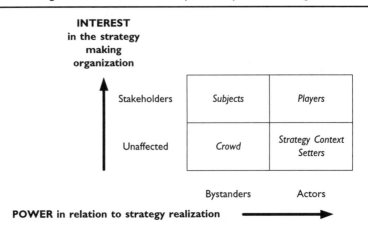

Actors, who have the power to act in a way that has an impact on the
future of the strategy making organization, are both ***players*** and inde-
pendents or *context setters*. Without other considerations an organization
must, at least, pay attention to all *actors*. Those actors who are also
stakeholders are those who respond to the strategies declared even if the
response is supportive, destructive or simply observation. To this extent
they can be manipulated by the organization but also may, on their part,
seek to manipulate the organization.

Leaders are treated as a part of the environment – they can significantly
influence the organization but do not do so with intent; similarly they will
not see, hear, care about, or respond to strategies implemented by the focal
organization. 'Context setters' are 'independent' actors who can fundamentally affect the context within which the strategy must work and yet have
no stake in the organization. Moreover, they are largely uncontrollable by
the strategy making organization and so need to be treated as a part of
possible alternative futures (see chapter C8). In exploring the potential for
stakeholder management strategies to support collaboration or alliances it
is the players and subjects who are of interest. For the most part the
unaffected bystanders – '*crowd*' – are unimportant for stakeholder analysis, unless they can be encouraged to become interested and powerful.

Subjects are those who feel as though they are subjected to the
consequences of the strategies of the focal organization. They have a high
interest in what the organization is doing and seeks to do, and so they
would like to influence the behaviour of the focal organization. However,
they do not have the power base to have substantial influence. Nevertheless, they represent an important part of the stakeholder analysis for
their interest, if positively disposed, may be exploited by strategically
influencing their power base – primarily through encouraging the
formation of coalitions and alliances.

The significance of the power/interest grid (figure C7.1) lies in the
extent to which categorizing organizations and people:

V201

1 Narrows a very large number of possible organizations, groups and people down to those of significance to strategy making. In practice, once stakeholder analysis goes beyond the small list of broad categories that are expected to be applicable to all organizations and seeks to identify those that might matter for the specific organization, then strategy analysts, and a management team, usually generate a list of potential stakeholders and actors that is too long to be helpful. Focusing effort in developing stakeholder management strategies is an important part of effective and efficient stakeholder management deliberations. While 'subjects', 'players' and 'context setters' are all important for considering stakeholder management, it is absolutely crucial that those players at the top right of the grid are considered in some detail. However, it may sometimes be possible for a management team to consider a sub-set of players; in this case it is essential to take first the 'natural' cluster of players with most power and interest (usually this means addressing at least 5–6 players).

2 Separates those who have the power to take a central *acting* role in potentially sabotaging or supporting the intent of the strategy making organization (actors – players and context setters) from those who have a *stake* in the organization (stakeholders – subjects and players). We expect **'players'** to act deliberately to sabotage or support the strategies the organization seeks to play out, whereas we expect the success or failure of the strategies to be significantly influenced by the behaviour of 'context setters'.   *V205 V273 P345*

3 Identifies those *actors who are susceptible to stakeholder management* as distinct from those who need to be encompassed in a scenario analysis (context setters) and treated as a part of thinking about the possible futures within which strategy must work.

4 Creates a framework for *understanding the changing nature over time* of those in each of the categories; thus suggesting, in its own right, a developing scenario. Thus, while some of those positioned on the grid can be placed easily in one position, others will be expected to move position over time (unless strategically managed otherwise), and yet others will move between several positions according to the strategy the organization is seeking to implement. The dynamics of changing stakeholder attitudes are often ignored and too much emphasis placed on analysis of the situation as it is currently.

5 Encourages a debate about *the nature of the power and interest of each organization*, group or individual being placed on the grid. Thus JOURNEY making takes place naturally as a team argues about the position of names on the grid. In addition it generates organizational learning and serious strategic thinking which facilitates members of the team changing their mind and their view of the strategic context of their organization.

We discussed, above, the problematic nature of deciding on the appropriate level of dis-aggregation of any particular entry on the grid.

V230 P345   In addressing the issue of where to place a potential stakeholder on the power/interest grid it is very important to **find the appropriate level of dis-aggregation**. Our experience suggests that management teams initially work at too high a level of aggregation. When this is the case, the JOURNEY making is negligible and the possibility of using the analysis for meaningful strategy development is low. Indeed, the analysis itself becomes trivial where the grid reveals nothing more than truisms. However, it is also important not to dis-aggregate too far and so miss the level of *strategic concern and power,* thus risking placing the potential stakeholder at a position of less power on the grid than is appropriate.

The attempt here is, in the first instance, to form a general view of the power and interest of possible stakeholders in relation to the focal organization. However, as noted earlier when considering the benefits of using the power/interest grid (iv), for many of the entries it will be difficult to characterize them in a general manner. Their position on the grid will vary significantly depending upon the strategy being addressed. As a result the positions on the grid will, therefore, be an average, but possibly with a high variance. High variance can occur when the response of one stakeholder to a strategic initiative is very different from that of another – for example, they are a player in one case and a subject in another. In particular, power is often issue specific. When the grid becomes overly 'fuzzy' due to a general level of indeterminacy about the general positions, it is imperative to avoid the inclination to tidy the picture. It is much more important to recognize that the uncertainty reflected in the grid is an important strategy making message, where strategy with respect to stakeholders will necessarily need to be more contingent than where there is certainty and stability about power and interest. For some organizations the grid is tidy and the number of entries low (10–20). In this case some aspects of stakeholder management will be easier and more predictable. However, when the grid contains a large number of entries and the positions of these entries are mostly fuzzy, stakeholder management will be very difficult with the stakeholder environment being of a highly turbulent nature. In this case the overall strategy of the organization will need to recognize this circumstance with strategies deliberately contrived to manage stakeholder variability.

V200 P345   As the analysis unfolds, it will not only become clear that there is variability in power and interest, or not, but also the debate will reveal the **disposition of potential stakeholders** to the organization. There will be a recognition that some of the potential stakeholders are usually positively, some usually negatively, and others variably, disposed to the strategic intent and strategies of the organization. Thus, we identify three types of entries on the grid – potentially hostile (coloured red), potentially collaborative (coloured green), and those whose attitude is dependent upon the strategy the focal organization expects to deploy, or the strategic issue being addressed by the stakeholder and the focal organization (coloured blue).

As we noted above, most of the stakeholder literature sees **stakeholders**   *P356*
as belonging to broad categories – consumers, suppliers, trade associations, employees, etc. While we have argued against the use of these
categories for the generation of the entries in the grid, it is helpful, after the
grid is drafted, to look for possible categories and use signifiers (colours,
typefaces, etc.) to identify them. These categories tend to be organization
specific rather than general categories, and it is important that they are
allowed to emerge, so that the categories themselves can inform strategic
thinking rather than the other way around. Thus 'employees' is not a
useful general category. It is helpful to look for emergent categories within
the general heading of 'internal stakeholders'. Likewise, external groups
may naturally emerge as media, environmental pressure groups, etc.

The overall picture and colours within the grid informs a general
evaluation of the strategic positioning of the organization in relation to
stakeholders. Thus, a grid that is dominantly red in the top left, showing
players dominated by those negatively disposed towards the organization,
is of strategic import, relative to equivocal players dominating or positive
players dominating. If the powerful and interested players are predominantly green, showing positive disposition to the organization, then
stakeholder management will be influenced by the need to maintain such
support. Similarly if the players' category is dominated by internal
stakeholder categories then there will be a clear message that higher levels
of participation in the strategy making process may be required. Alternatively this might signal a recognition of the issues relating to political
feasibility – particularly if these internal groups are also negatively
disposed to the currently drafted strategic intent of the organization.

Other strategy writers suggest the use of similar matrices or grids – for
example Johnson and Scholes (1993:177) and Freeman (1984:60) develop
the matrix from a different perspective to that used here. Johnson and
Scholes are interested in the grid as a basis for understanding the environment (the linking arrow between stakeholder analysis and environmental
analysis in figure C2.3) rather than the use of the matrix to focus upon pro-
active stakeholder *management*. Our own approach has been developing
over the last fifteen years as a result of a deliberate attempt to link
stakeholder analysis with conflict analysis and hyper-game analysis with a
clear intention to develop strategic options (Bennett, 1980; Eden and
Huxham, 1988; Eden *et al*, 1993). Our early approaches to stakeholder
management focused on coalition building, for example a project with ICL
in the early 1980s suggested, as a result of the analysis, the strategy of
coalition building amongst European computer companies to combat the
IBM communication standards. Similarly, and later, in the Northern
Ireland case there was a focus on exploring the dynamics of coalition
building and 'game playing' (Eden, 1996). Each of these demonstrated the
analytical leverage to be gained from the power/interest grid and from the
explicit analytical focus on exploring the bases of power and interest
(below) as the foundation for considering the dynamics of strategic moves
amongst stakeholders.

V200 V231 P341   **Modelling the Bases of Power and Interest – the 'power/interest' star diagram**

The next step in stakeholder analysis follows on from the outcome of the power/interest grid by simply asking – 'what is the basis of power?' and 'what is the basis of interest?' which determined the positioning of elements on the grid. Some of the data relating to the assumptions about power and the nature of interest will always surface during the process of *P345* debating the position of stakeholders on the grid. Here we **consider carefully these assumptions for those stakeholders that matter most for the future of the organization – the players**. This step is essential to the development of stakeholder management strategies. In addition, the JOURNEY making achieved throughout the conversations required to construct the star diagrams typically changes and develops team members' views of the stakeholders from general attitudes to specific embedded knowledge that can be used in strategic action. This enhanced under-standing is likely to influence their everyday treatment of the stakeholders. The 'star diagram' models generated through examining the two dimen-sions validate, or not, the position of stakeholders on the power/interest grid. It is very unusual for this model building process not to produce important changes in the position of entries on the grid.

The needs of stakeholders will vary enormously, and some stake-holders will make quite contradictory demands of the focal organization. The process of thinking about each *player* in turn facilitates a recognition of the variety of demands and the variety of bases of power. In addition, because power is always issue specific, then the analysis checks the assumptions in the power/interest grid for variability in the disposition of interest and of power. When the basis of interest is not locked into issue information – the selective perception of the stakeholder focuses on output such as annual performance rather than activity such as strategic moves – then it is unlikely that power will be used in unpredictable or highly variable ways.

P344   The **journey towards building a** *power/interest model* involves considering each player, in turn, starting with that player closest to the top right of the power/interest grid – the most powerful *and* most interested. Each player being considered is examined in terms of the specific nature of the support mechanisms and available sanctions which are the bases of the player's power, and secondly the input stimulus framework which prompts the use of the power – the *outputs*. Figure C7.2 shows the general character of the 'star diagram'. The *input* shows the nature of the 'spectacles' through which the player views the organization – what information they collect, what activities they notice, how they make sense of the information. Often the basis of power comes from the ability a player has to influence others with power on the grid (including 'context setters'). This should be included but also noted with respect to the development of the *'influence network'* model below.

Figure C7.2 Stakeholder analysis – the 'star diagram'.

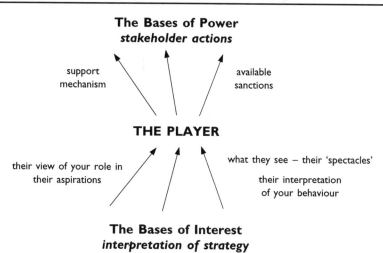

Strategy analysis is a practical activity and so can be oriented only to a single stakeholder, or quite specific *hierarchy* of stakeholders, not to all stakeholders. The hierarchy reflects the significant differences in the power to act in relation to the interests of the focal organization and reflects the specific strategic aspirations of the focal organization. That is, who the 'stakeholders' and 'actors' are, and what part of their perspective is of interest and is dependent upon the specific interests of the focal organization. This will be different for different organizations (even those in the same industry).

The process of thinking about sanctions will alert the management team to the amount of unrealized power held by some of the 'subjects'. For example, the healthy role of some small to medium sized enterprises (SMEs) derives from their potential capacity to prevent large organizations abusing their market power – they do this through their ability to innovate and their ability to provide a source of employees. However, this power base is unlikely to be realized by SMEs and is also a power that probably cannot be delivered by them because of their inability to form an effective coalition. The role of coalitions of organizations is most often seen by those in the same business who get together to protect themselves from the 'bad competitor' (Porter, 1980) – who does not understand the **'industry recipe'** *V274 P356* (Spender, 1989) – and act in a manner which enables all to be profitable. This happens through the creation of trade associations and joint training programmes. Consequently, the focal organization needs to strategically manage this group of organizations and take care to monitor the possible ramifications ensuing from the formation of a coalition through, for example, business associations. It is tempting to leave them as 'subjects', or more likely 'context setters', rather than deliberately and strategically make them into 'players' who can then be managed strategically. It is both possible and sometimes highly desirable to strategically manage the creation of a coalition among stakeholders who would otherwise not have realized their potential power.

V200 V230 P342   ## Actor Influence Network Maps

As organizations, groups, and individuals take their place on the power/ interest grid and the bases of the power and interest are mapped out, it becomes clear that many of the sanctions which actors can apply depend upon their ability to influence others on the grid. Thus the power, for example, of a Member of Parliament in relation to a lobby group lies not in their own personal power but rather their power to influence a Minister of the government. The power of a particular competitor may lie in their leadership of a trade association. It is worth noting that this ability to influence other stakeholders is generated through the links or relationships that exist between stakeholders and that these links may be either formal or informal. Formal links occur where there are contractual agreements or well-established rules of conduct. Informal links are those between individuals on the basis of mutual aspirations and perspectives.

P349   However, typically, most of these bilateral power or influence relationships are relatively obvious. What is less obvious is the ***network of influence relationships***, within which some players (and possibly context setters) turn out to be central 'conduits' of influence. In these instances the latent power of these actors can be underestimated unless the network of influences is considered. Through antagonizing one particularly well-positioned stakeholder an entire strategy may fail as the 'knock on' effect ripples through to other stakeholders being convinced – through being subjected to the negatively disposed stakeholder's perspective – and supporting the central stakeholder. Thus, for example, one small and apparently powerless community group may be crucially important to the development of a large shopping centre and so be powerful with respect to the civil engineering contractor wishing to manage the construction of the centre without trouble. In turn the contractor may have as its Chairman a person who is also on the Board of Directors of a major competitor of the focal organization, and who may be prepared to fund the community group in their battle with the focal organization. One significant element of stakeholder management is to facilitate strategically the empowerment of some players, and so it becomes important to analyse the network of such actors.

Once again the analysis introduces questions about the appropriate level of dis-aggregation. In considering influences between actors it will often become clear that the power base lies with personal, and informal, relationships between key people within an organization, rather than in the organization itself. Well-known networks such as Masonic Lodges can be obvious routes for information exchange and strategy formulation. The aim of the analysis is to discover whether some entries on the power/ interest grid act as 'hubs of influence' because many will seek to influence them and they in turn can influence many other powerful players. Very often the analysis shows that a 'subject' or 'context setter' may be able to play a significant potential role in supporting or sabotaging strategy simply because of their *indirect* impact as a hub or 'conduit' through which all important 'network' information passes. The map gives, probably, the best indication of the **potential for coalitions and collaboratives** and the frequency and likelihood with which they might come about (Eden, 1996; Finn, 1997).

V230

Stakeholder Analysis to Stakeholder Management

V198 V230 V262
P430

The foundation of stakeholder management is to consider how power bases can be changed and how interest can be shifted. In other words how can entries on the power/interest grid be shifted around the grid to suit the strategic aspirations of the focal organization. The strategy making organization may consider strategic action to shift subjects to become players (and vice-versa), and to shift context setters to become players. The simplest example of managing the perceptions of shareholders, as players, is through the annual report. It is precisely for this reason that the annual report is regarded not as a reporting mechanism but as something to be managed through public relations consultants. Thus, we would see the annual report as one of the information sources used by shareholders, but also the stakeholder star map would show the interpretative framework used by shareholders as they read the annual report. From the perspective of stakeholder management, influencing this interpretative framework is usually more productive than manipulating raw data. Indeed, a post-modernist view of business may argue that this process of image management is the essence of business life!

If we consider the possibility that organizations, groups, or people may change their position both within and between each quadrant then the modelling requirements become more complex. As a consequence, organizations may shift their own interests in the direction of our interests and so may become a part of the 'stakeholder' analysis by becoming a player. Their own cognitive activities either through the organization's strategic intent or due to some other purpose, have led to a change in the value system or a change in the belief system (and so a change in values) in a way that is now significant. The opposite may also occur when stakeholders move from consideration in stakeholder analysis to significance within scenario planning. In other words, we can conceive of actors moving from context setter to player and player to context setter – from one quadrant to another in the power/interest grid. Figure C7.3 shows the directions of movement that will be of most interest to the strategy analyst.

Figure C7.3   Stakeholder management.

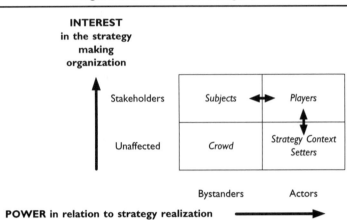

A possible act by the focal organization might be to move, for example, the media from being a 'context setter' to 'player' when they can be convinced that those defined as 'subjects' (who have a stake in the organization) are media consumers. If the media are defined as a context setter, then they have been taken to have the power to significantly, but unintentionally, influence the strategic success of the organization.

When the power/interest grid reveals that the disposition of most of the 'players' is a mix of positive and negative then it is helpful to continue the analysis in greater depth. This may be achieved by developing a further grid which plots importance (their closeness to the top right of the power/interest grid) against support or opposition. Nutt and Backoff (1992:191) then provide the labels of 'advocate' for important/support; 'antagonistic' for important/opposition; 'problematic' for less important/opposition; and 'low priority' for less important/supporting. The labels indicate the focus for stakeholder management and give an indication of potential coalitions that might be built by players or facilitated by the organization. In particular it helps identify 'neutral' or undecided stakeholders who could be targeted for special lobbying by the organization.

In principle, thinking about possibilities for stakeholder management follows simply and naturally from modelling using the power/interest grid, the power/interest star diagram, and the influence network diagram. They provide the means of JOURNEY making from a number of different stances and through this provide opportunities for information to surface that would not have been possible with only one of the models. Furthermore, as the process unfolds, each step of the analysis helps confirm those previously visited, thus resulting in a more robust perspective and one that is embedded in the management team's mind. To suggest a sequence from stakeholder analysis to management is misleading, for it denies the principles of JOURNEY making with its locus in cycling between understanding, reflecting, negotiating, and agreeing. Many of the options for managing stakeholders will have fallen out from the analysis stage.

There are, nevertheless, some obvious checks. Strategies must be explored and developed for all players close to the top right of the power/interest grid. Strategies must reflect attempts to change the power base (output of the star map), for example, by developing negotiating strategies that can affect the use of power, and building coalitions with others to increase the organization's power relative to that of **key players**. Similarly,   *V230* manipulating the interpretative frameworks of key players as well as attending to the channels of information to them may contribute towards increasing the success of stakeholder management strategies. The influence network indicates places where influence patterns can be changed.

In many more instances than management teams anticipate, they are able to find ways of managing potentially supportive context setters so that they become interested and so move to become positively disposed players (as, for example, through the use of lobby groups). In the same way, thorough analysis reveals ways of shifting negatively disposed players to a position of disinterest, or, through breaking coalitions amongst stakeholders, moving them to become subjects.

In the public sector, particularly, the opportunity for developing fully blown strategies for moving entries in the grid from subject to player are usually greater than expected. Thus, the potential exists to strategically facilitate the formation of coalitions and collaboratives in order to build the power base of subjects positively disposed to the strategy of the organization. The power of a coalition is usually much greater than the sum of the parts.

Collaboration, Joint Ventures, and Strategic Alliances

One of the important aims of stakeholder analyses and management is that of improving the position of the focal organization within a particular coalition. That is, an organization may be dependent upon its position within a network that promotes conversation about topics of interest to the organization. For example, many large organizations will seek to retain their position in the network by sharing information that a market view would suggest should be retained. This is true in the field of academic research where an organization may seek to publish, through academic journals, the results of its own research programmes in order to gain a position within the network of researchers in the field and so gain the rights to participate in their conversations. The frequency of interaction and the extent to which members of the network give as well as take is important in retaining a position in the network or coalition.

An important element in stakeholder analysis is the realization that it is not a zero-sum game: strategically promoting the power base of one stakeholder does not necessarily reduce the power of another. Similarly, creating or destroying coalitions can increase or decrease the overall power to influence the implementation of strategies. It is interesting to note that there is even some evidence from analysis of Fortune corporate reputation surveys to support this non-zero sum assertion. Nevertheless, it does not need such a survey to arrive at this conclusion.

Stakeholder analysis provides the basis for identifying potential networks as well as more formal coalitions. Indeed some have argued that there are now examples of networking where barriers between the firm, its customers, and its suppliers have almost disappeared – examples often cited include Nike and Harley-Davidson. The stakeholder management drive is to improve the position of the organization in the network or, if creating a new network, to move into a central position by reducing its own dependency on the network and increasing its indispensability to others in the network. A network that is overtly acknowledged by its participants is relational and so implies a minimum frequency of interaction to sustain it – the maintenance of the network is one of the costs of strategically managing stakeholders in this way.

The strategy makers may also deliberately attempt to gain *collaborative advantage* (Huxham, 1996) by encouraging subjects to form themselves into a coalition, and so gain enough power to be defined as collaborating players. The aim might be to create a viable collaborative structure within which all the stakeholders can, with varying degrees of success, pursue their aspirations. Sometimes an appropriate strategic action can be to find ways of reducing the power of a coalition, currently placed in the 'player' quadrant of the grid, so that it is broken into a number of 'subjects' – successfully managing a 'divide and rule' policy.

Collaboration that achieves something of significance depends on many factors. However, in the approach discussed above, the process of bringing together a selection of 'subjects' and increasing their power and influence so that they become positively disposed 'players' depends significantly on understanding the aspirations of each collaborator. It is the process of analysing the possible congruence of aspects of the goals of each individual collaborator at the level of the organization and the level of the individual representing that organization that can reveal the potential for a realization of **meta-goals**. These are goals that none of the organizations could attain on their own (Eden *et al*, 1994). Only when meta-goals can be identified is it possible to conceive of the means for supplying a potential collaborative advantage for the members of the collaborative. The trick for the 'sponsor' of the collaborative is to anticipate the potential for collaborative advantage and to manipulate a sharing of perspectives in such a way as to enable the collaborators to see meta-goals that will coincide with the strategic intent of the sponsor.

We mentioned above the possibility that a *deliberate choice* can be made to service the needs of one particular stakeholder group, for example shareholders. Within the public sector, stakeholder analysis and management may be almost totally concerned with the task of empowering some groups within the community – for example, racially disadvantaged groups – where the core strategic intent is to shift subjects to players.

V250

Stakeholder Role-think *V231 V273 P342*

As any strategies are drafted it becomes crucial to simulate their effect on stakeholders. Understanding the varying possibilities for significant dynamics that can seriously affect the successful implementation of strategies is difficult, particularly when it is the JOURNEY making rather than the analysis that is important. Game theoretic approaches should provide some analytical help. However, they are largely of a 'back-room' nature and so cannot involve easily the understanding and reflection processes that are so crucial to committed strategic thinking and action. In addition, **game theory analysis**, including 'hypergame theory' (Bennett, *P435* 1995), which better replicates the strategic behaviour we are interested in here, is difficult to use when there are more than a handful of actors. When such analysis can be conducted in a visually interactive way (using group support software such as 'INTERACT' (Bennett *et al*, 1994) and with a skilled game theory facilitator), then JOURNEY making with respect to understanding strategic moves amongst a small number of key actors becomes possible.

Nevertheless, the hypergame framework may be seen as a 'theory of the world' – that is, it describes the way in which a part of the world works (Bennett and Huxham, 1982). While game theoretic approaches are narrow in their view of interaction, they do capture, in some sense, the essence of conflict, and therefore competitive, situations. Analysis of *post hoc* and live case studies, using the framework suggested by the theory, has shown that at least some situations can be reasonably modelled in this way (Bennett *et al*, 1980, 1981). Although reviewing case studies is a retrospective activity, it is nevertheless useful for detecting previous stakeholder actions, providing the means for reflection and aiding organizational learning.

Key elements of the game theoretic approaches might also be used as a framework for thinking about the implementation of a particular strategy. Thus, game theory suggests determining *who is involved in a particular situation, what they can do, what are their aims* and hence *their preferences* for various outcomes – elaborating the 'star diagram'. The hypergame framework leads to questioning whether those involved might have a different understanding of the 'game' from the focal organization or from each other. Other aspects of the theory lead to asking about the effect of other situations that actors are involved in, and so on.

In the context of stakeholder analysis, we have gone one stage further than this and devised a process of JOURNEY making that effectively can use the **embedded knowledge** that each of the management team has *V275* about stakeholders. Furthermore, it can capitalize, in a practical way, upon the outcomes of the analysis already conducted above (the grid, the power/interest star diagram, and the influence network map). The journey is based on role play, or more accurately **role-think**, that not only asks the *P350* management team key questions, but also helps to elicit answers from them (Eden, 1986). The process is very similar, in many respects, to that used by Radford (1984).

The intention is to analyse, through role-think, the following:

- What does any particular strategy look like from the perspective of a stakeholder? That is, what would be their immediate response given their values and interests?
- Given this response, what might be the underlying assumed aim? Furthermore, do these aims explain the response as a whole or just some part of it? If a series of strategies or strategic options is being examined, do the resultant responses highlight a consistent set of aims?
- Would the response seek to involve other stakeholders and if so who might these be?
- Does the response produce a stable interaction which supports or sabotages the strategy, or is the dynamic of the interaction between the organization and the stakeholder or the interaction with other stakeholders likely to be unstable?

One danger is that we do not consider the ways in which important stakeholders may have fundamentally different ways of thinking about business. For example, family and kinship relations can be the driving motivation for retaining particular sorts of control and not extending ownership in South East Asian countries. The market metaphor is often assumed to be dominant in countries where this is not the case.

The Coherence of Strategy Making – the interaction between aspirations, distinctive competencies, strategies, and stakeholder management

V251 P358   The key to successful strategic change is the *coherence* **of strategy**. This coherence comes from continuously cycling between JOURNEY making and confirming/designing strategy (see figure C2.4 – the double headed *V276* arrow) as well as ensuring the strategic direction's **robustness** through examining the stakeholder interactions and possible futures (chapter C8).

Thus, the work we undertake to determine stakeholder management strategies is expected to be fully informed by the aspirations system, which was developed to be coherent with distinctive competencies and the business idea. Stakeholder issues may suggest elaboration and changes in the aspirations of the organization – to make them more realistic and yet still aspirational, and to encompass important stakeholders' positions into the goal statements. In rare circumstances there may be a need to encompass stakeholders into the goal statements simply as a mechanism for stakeholder management when stakeholders are overwhelmingly powerful. More usually, however, stakeholders are recognized as significant constraints rather than goals, and so specific strategies are developed to manage the restrictions of the constraints. Stakeholder power and accompanying interests will rarely act as more than constraints. Thus, the strategy is about meeting and managing the limit of the constraint and no more. As we noted above, it is also common to use public statements of aspiration weighted in favour of key stakeholders, but allowing them a less significant role in the determination of strategic decisions and solution to strategic issues.

The draft strategies that emerge from the journey, and which are based on those strategic issues, and competencies detected and the emergent business model, will have been tested through a consideration of stakeholders' responses. These analyses and the role-think approach will have led to the modification of strategies so that they are more likely to be effective. Similarly, they will now be supported by stakeholder management strategies that are specifically aimed at ensuring success.

The 'context setter' will be carried forward as input into our consideration of the environment and so will be included in scenario thinking. The form of figures C2.1 and C2.3 indicates that stakeholder analysis and scenario development are interdependent and should be conducted as a cycle of analysis, rather than as if they were separate procedures. In this book we have separated the analyses into two chapters – this implies a separation that cannot exist in practice. Unfortunately the current fad for scenario planning does not help integration. Rather, it reinforces separation.

The journey through stakeholder analysis models will have led to ideas about new strategic issues and so new strategic options will have been surfaced. It is important to remember that each time we bring forth, and negotiate, beliefs about how the strategic future of the organization will be influenced, then we implicitly surface strategic options.

In the spirit of JOURNEY making it is very important to be reminded that *the journey itself is as important as the above outcomes*. The JOURNEY making experience is expected to result in a form of mental preparation for appropriate and coherent opportunistic behaviour in relation to stakeholders. The management team will better be able to devote time and effort to stakeholders that matter and less time to those that do not. In addition they will have reached a sense of shared meaning about who the stakeholders are, which are significant, and what are the possible avenues for stakeholder management. Emotional and cognitive commitment to appropriate strategic change comes from involvement in the analysis and strategy making rather than simply agreement to its rationality.

MANAGING ALTERNATIVE FUTURES: STRATEGIC ADAPTABILITY AND OPPORTUNISM

'Predictions are always unreliable and particularly so when they are about the future' (E.F. Schumacher, *Small is Beautiful*, 1973)

'Time present and time past
Are both perhaps present in time future
And time future contained in time past.'
(T.S. Eliot, *Burnt Norton*, 1935)

'Scenarios are hypothetical sequences of events constructed for the purpose of focussing attention on causal processes and decision-points. They answer two kinds of questions:

- precisely how might some hypothetical situation come about, step by step,
- what alternatives exist for each actor, at each step, for preventing, diverting or facilitating the process' (Herman Kahn, 1967)

Strategy has often been argued to be about responding effectively to changes in the environment. As we noted in chapter C2, a dominant approach to strategic management has been that derived from economists. In particular, Porter and Ansoff emphasize *positioning* an organization in relation to its environment, and committing the organization to a management style and model that will be *responsive* to that environment. Admittedly they would not reject a pro-active view but nevertheless the emphasis is on reactivity. Ackoff (1974) rejects either pro-active or reactive and prefers to use the term interactive.

As figure C2.3 has shown, our view is governed by the belief that the future is to be controlled and managed rather than forecast. Thus, our task is to imagine that part of the future, or multiple futures (chapter P4), that affects our aspirations and, once identified, seek to manage it to our own strategic ends as best we can. It is not just a 'clever' statement to argue that 'any forecast of direct relevance to the organization which comes true is a bad forecast', it is also true. To put it another way, a good forecast is not necessarily the accurate forecast (Ikle, 1967). Potentially bad forecasts that are identified, negotiated, and managed may achieve, through the specifically tailored strategic actions, good results for the organization.

Consequently, the future is something to interact with and to shape rather than to accept passively.

Thirty years ago, Warren Bennis (1968) stated that for him:

> '*The future* is a portmanteau word. It embraces several notions. It is an exercise of the imagination which allows us to compete with and try to outwit future events. Controlling the anticipated future is, in addition, a social invention that legitimizes the process of forward planning . . . most importantly, the future is a conscious dream, a set of imaginative hypotheses groping towards whatever vivid utopias lie at the heart of our consciousness.'

The first point that Bennis appears to be making is that the future cannot be forecast with a high enough degree of certainty for precise strategic plans to be constructed that will not be knocked off course. A management team needs, therefore, to understand the structure and character of possible futures rather than predictions. By understanding the nature of multiple possible futures, the team will be in a position to act opportunistically within a strategy framework. More importantly, it will be able to do so faster than its competitors, or fast enough to avert disasters, or fast enough to lever aspirations more efficiently.

Bennis's second point suggests that strategically managing the environment requires recognizing that the future is largely the result of purposeful 'players' and 'context setters' (identified during stakeholder analysis) seeking to create their own future, in the same way as the management team is seeking to create theirs. The primary purpose of strategy is to influence the affairs of the organization *and its environment* in such a way that aspirations can be attained. If this is the case for one organization then that organization's strategy will affect the environment of other organizations, and vice-versa. The corollary of one organization having the freedom to implement strategy is that it creates forecasting uncertainty for other organizations. Thus, the future will be largely about understanding the impact of the behaviour of other organizations.

It follows that any information about the future is politically loaded. When we are told about facts, we are told about those facts *rather than other facts* – to know is also not to know. A particular set of facts are selected to portray one version of the future rather than an alternative, and possibly equally plausible, version. Equally, a management team can devise strategies for presenting the future to others in such a way that their behaviour is modified towards creating a future which is acceptable to that team. This is one aspect of stakeholder management, and represents some stakeholders as part of the environment – in the sense that negotiation with strategy context setters is not possible, but management of them may be.

Research supports the view that an organization which changes its strategy in response to changes in the environment will outperform those that maintain their current stance in the face of new conditions (Haveman, 1992; Smith and Grimm, 1987). Indeed it appears that those who fail to adjust their strategy at the appropriate time lock themselves into a downward spiral (Cameron *et al*, 1988; Hambrick and d'Aveni, 1988). What this means is that the mental models that drive an organization are resistant to change.

In this chapter we shall not present a view of the usual approaches to analysing the environment. These approaches have been fully represented in many strategic management texts and we shall take them as a necessary but not sufficient basis for strategy making. In most instances they are an essential part of a continuing research and analysis programme to be undertaken in the 'back-room' by expert analysts. When an organization cannot provide itself with such analysis then it may be made available through industry wide services or through government statistics. Here we shall consider only that part of considering the environment which is likely to directly involve input from the management team – their wisdom and intuition. We consider also that part of thinking about the environment which is critical to JOURNEY making because it depends upon social processes, negotiation, creativity and a direct interaction with other aspects of strategy making we have considered in this book. Most importantly we shall argue that the consideration of multiple futures by the strategy making team is critical to a preparation for strategy implementation. Seeing the future as a series of multiple scenarios makes a major contribution to strategic opportunism and strategic adaptability. The primary purpose of the process is as an aid to strategy *making* now, and adaptability in the future, rather than forecasting the future.

Forecasting the 'Environment'?

Forecasting, except at the micro level, has a poor record. For example, doomsters warned that supplies of minerals were fast running out (in fact recoverable reserves have increased), while optimists promised that the price of oil would fall for the foreseeable future! The second of these forecasts was based upon trends in technological advances making the process more efficient. However, as has been seen, the changes in oil prices have been dominated by non-technological factors – the politics of oil production and the shifts in the balance of power between consumers, retailers, those who own the rights to extract oil, and those who own the land. In this case the strategic resolve on the part of key players was as important as the initial resource dispositions. (This suggests that a game theoretic analysis of the sort discussed in the previous chapter might have helped thinking about the possible ways in which the situation might unfold).

The experience most managers have of forecasting is that of graphs which plot some variable of interest against time. Thus, in industry we see sales plotted against time, and we experience the use of mathematically sophisticated methods to use past data better to extrapolate forward into the future. For short term forecasting, plotting a variable against time can be helpful, as it clearly states that the variable is a function of time. For the purposes of strategic thinking though, there can be nothing more dangerous in its implications. As long as strategic outcomes are indicated as if they were a function of time then they are also, by implication, unmanageable, unless the organization has access to a 'Time Lord'! The task of strategic management is to ensure that they are not a function of time but rather of purposeful management.

In the public sector we have seen major planning episodes dominated by attempts to forecast the population of an urban area. Moreover, in some urban planning approaches these forecasts of population have been bereft of any consideration of changing birth and death rates, let alone contemplating the determinants of urban mobility (although attempts by Forrester (1969) and subsequent modelling sought to change this approach). Even though these forecasts have been clearly recognized as failures, there is still a belief that to forecast a single future is an appropriate and helpful activity when building strategic plans. As a sop to the inadequate record of forecasting, there is now a greater acceptance of the need to treat such forecasts with a band of uncertainty – but the notion of a single, but uncertain, future remains.

Most notably, forecasts, and we include econometric methods and system dynamics simulation modelling (Forrester, 1961), have not accounted for the possibility and role of 'flip-flop' events, crises, catastrophes. Here we are not focusing on events in the natural environment but political events – the sort of events that could be characterized in the same way as a Kuhnian crisis in science is characterized.

Traditional forecasting methods, such as trend extrapolation and regression, are seen to be too dependent upon a projection of the past into the future to be useful for anticipating changes. Similarly they suggest a single view of the future (albeit with attached uncertainties). In contrast, **scenario planning** suggests a number of distinctly different alternative *V266* futures, each of which is possible. Scenarios focus 'less on predicting outcomes and more on *understanding the forces* that would eventually compel an outcome; less on figures and more on insight' (Wack, 1985:84 – our emphasis). They are more concerned with understanding the discontinuities surfaced when creating alternative futures, by recognizing that the *structure* of the environment may change, than single projections into the future.

We consider the process of thinking about multiple futures by examining event-based scenarios. We should make it clear that we do not dismiss the help that can be provided by some 'business policy' analyses. In particular, the approaches offered for analysing competitive positioning (such as those introduced by Porter (1980)) and the Delphi approach (Dalkey and Helmer, 1963) are not to be discarded. However, their role within the context of a journey taken by the management team and other organizational participants is less clear. As we stated earlier, they are strategy analyses that are often best conducted by experts (in the 'back-room') and used to *inform* the journey. In this way, these other approaches can be treated as complementary approaches rather than alternatives.

Multiple Alternative Futures

Figures C8.1 and C8.2 depict the trumpet of uncertainty. For some organizations the trumpet will be narrow, and classical planning approaches involving step by step moves that are well designed and resourced can be appropriate. However, for most organizations the trumpet will open rapidly, and fulfilling aspirations will involve the organization 'keeping options open'. Scenario analysis is aimed at helping to determine how strategy can be *robust* and, at the same time, appropriately flexible and opportunistic.

It is popular to assert that the world is more turbulent and more complex than it ever has been before. One organization's turbulence can be another's stability. Turbulence is a subjective not an objective phenomenon. It is also a variable, in that it can be strategically managed. One of the tasks of strategic thinking is to reduce the turbulence faced by an organization by successfully managing it. A set of events, which describe a possible future, can for one organization be absolutely critical, and yet another organization will be rightly indifferent to them. The environment we wish to understand is infinite and so we must ensure that the part which the management team jointly seeks to understand and reflect upon is that which is relevant to the strategic future of their organization. Thus, generic forecasts which are offered by industry 'think-tanks' can be helpful but also misleading if not taken as only informing an organization's *V206 P363* specific view of possible futures. The task of **deciding that part of the environment to be considered** is a conundrum. The part of the environment being analysed must be relevant, but also, for the purpose of strategic thinking, it must stretch thinking and encourage the consideration of new opportunities. In principle, a particular future matters because the impact on the organization is expected to be very high. Nevertheless there will be many futures which fit this category, but they are so unlikely that when we compute the 'expected value' (probability multiplied by impact) of that possible future, it is relatively much lower than the expected value for other alternative futures. Needless to say, these calculations of expected value cannot be accurately quantified – a qualitative feel on a relative scale is required. For example, in the work with the Northern Ireland Prison Service, the so called 'peace scenario' (see figure C8.4 below) where the possibility of the government agreeing a ceasefire with the paramilitaries was, at the time, regarded as a very low probability by the management team. However, they did regard the impact on the strategic future of the Service as extremely high, and so it was used as a part of the strategy journey. The process of assessing the probability and impact of possible futures also serves as part of the JOURNEY making

Figure C8.1 The trumpet of uncertainty – classical planning methods (Rosenhead, 1989).

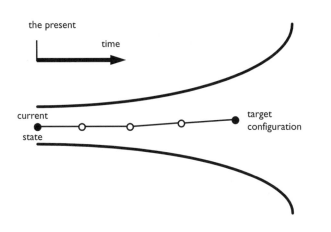

Figure C8.2 The trumpet of uncertainty – robustness in strategy (Rosenhead, 1989).

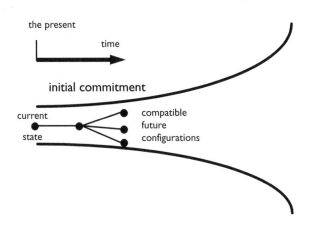

process through its role as a dialectic. By encouraging group members to offer alternative perspectives and examine the resultant futures, a more complete, and therefore robust, understanding is gained – one that is shared by the management team.

Involving the Management Team in Exploring Alternative Futures

The process of thinking about alternative futures has been made out to be a complicated task that demands the use of mathematical and statistical expertise. In addition, many have indicated that expertise in the particular field of interest is crucial. There is no evidence to suppose this is the case. Indeed studies have shown that the difference in the forecasting ability of experts over non-experts is small. Also forecasts by experts were wrong more often than they were right! The conclusion drawn from these studies was that it is better to do environmental analysis in-house. This conclusion is particularly convenient for us, since it fits in with our plea that thinking about the future is so crucial to a journey of strategic change that it must be an integral part of that journey. In addition, it is the management team who should be directly involved in creating alternative futures, for they must devise and be responsible for implementing and adapting the strategic management of the environment and being pro-active about opportunities. They must also integrate thinking about the environmental futures with stakeholder analysis and management, and vice-versa.

It is worth noting, however, that this is in many ways contrary to the well-known scenario building approach developed by Shell (Schwartz, 1991; van der Heijden, 1996; Wack, 1985, 1987). They valued the use of 'unusual people' who became a part of a well-resourced scenario planning group within the Shell Group Planning department. Undoubtedly Shell has had some significant success in the development and uses of scenarios. However, they are a large organization with a professional planning team. In this book we concentrate on the sort of efforts in which 'ordinary' organizations can engage. We have also argued above that exploring alternative environmental futures is absolutely integral to all the aspects of strategy making. If it is not, then the strategy will be neither coherent nor well informed.

Strategic thinking, and the journey into the future, is concerned with the future as a means of illuminating the present. Therefore it is about informing strategic thinking and the design of strategy so that the chances of an organization getting its strategy right are higher. It is not about prediction.

Godet (1987:17) identifies seven key aims which are applicable for the journey into the future:

- 'to clarify present actions in the light of the future,
- to explore multiple and uncertain futures,
- to adopt a global and systemic approach,
- to take qualitative factors and the strategic actors into account,
- to always remember that information and forecasts are not neutral,
- to opt for a plurality and complementarity of approaches, and
- to question preconceived ideas on forecasts and forecasters'.

Each of these we also would regard as important. 'The power of "scenario analysis" lies in the potential to help us develop an understanding of situations that appear to be unstructured and threatening. Scenario analysis forces us to consider the horizon, to extend our mental models, to consider cause and effect, and to identify levers that we can use to establish a degree of control over a situation' (van der Heijden, 1996). It therefore helps identify those futures that are both likely and important – those that have the greatest expected value for considering strategy, rather than those most likely.

A Journey into the Future

We have established above that the first principle for thinking about the future involves accepting that there are multiple futures to attend to, rather than a single future to forecast. We have also made it clear that the 'futures journey' is unique to each organization. This uniqueness is determined by the importance future happenings have for the aspirations of the organization and the delivery of the business model/livelihood scheme. As a result, the first part of the journey must be about determining an initial list of environmental variables that are significant. At the beginning of this process it is helpful to focus upon those that appear to be outside the strategic control of the organization.

As the management team think about the future, they will need to determine the time horizon over which their thinking must stretch. We commented above that the ease with which multiple, well-differentiated scenarios can be generated is one indication of the level of turbulence facing an organization. Similarly, if scenarios produce a wide trumpet of uncertainty over a short time horizon then the degree to which this uncertainty can be strategically managed or exploited, and the trumpet so narrowed, will determine the appropriate time horizon. We start by thinking about the uncontrollable variables or constants, and then try to get a feel for the shape of the trumpet. This means we must stop the management team thinking farther ahead than is necessary for the purpose of effective strategy making. We need go no further than where the future is no longer important to the organization – this could be because aspirations are expected to change (for example from new ownership, or an anticipated change in government mandates), or the probability of the future occurring multiplied by its utility diminishes as the time horizon is increased. Inevitably the number of alternative futures to be considered as the time horizon is extended is greater. There will be point where the number of possible futures being considered is unmanageable and is debilitating to the strategy making process.

Identifying Key Scenario Events   *V206 V267*

The grid in figure C8.3 provides a useful device for facilitating the part of the journey concerned with identifying important events. The entries placed in the grid are *events of significance in determining, or influencing the character of the strategic future* of the organization. These must include events associated with each of the 'strategy context setters' identified in the

Figure C8.3   Scenario events.

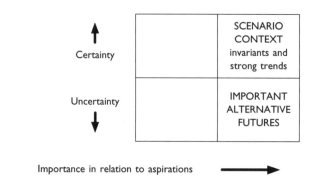

stakeholder analysis (chapter C7). When considering stakeholder management, we focused on 'players' whom the organization could influence
through exploring their bases of power *and interest*. However, for exploring
alternative futures it is the 'strategy context setters' whose power we are
seeking to examine and validate by explicating the events they can create
that will have a powerful impact on the organization's environment.
Entries therefore, should all be located in the right-hand quadrants of the
grid showing a focus on the importance axis.

Events that matter are those that will trigger many other related events
which in turn have an impact on the aspirations of the organization.
Events noted will usually include:

- *Invariants* (see also Godet, 1987:20) – variables assumed to be constant
  or permanent up to the time horizon and yet are very important
  contextual features within which other changes will lie. In some sense
  they are an event – the event of constancy. An example might be
  Microsoft's continued dominance in the operating system market.
- *Strong trends* – these are similar in the sense that they are continuing
  change of a predictable nature. Where trends may or may not reach a
  critical point, they are treated as uncertain events. So, for example,
  advance in technology is a trend – one that may result in a significant
  breakthrough or alteration of the ways of working for some
  organizations and can therefore affect their strategic future.

These entries will be events because they are variables which are,
surprisingly, expected to remain locked into a predictable pattern – thus
the event is that this particular part of the world is *not* turbulent. Such
events may be relatively certain or uncertain, and so placed in the top or
bottom of the grid. Variables that are expected to remain constant or
continue along an expected pattern of behaviour are usually multi-
tudinous. So it is vital that the grid does not become swamped. The entries
must be important for the strategic future of the organization.

V206 V267 P362

'Flip-flop events' – these are events that are like switches – they will either happen or not happen. Each 'flip-flop' can act as a trigger to two futures – the one where the event occurs, and the one where it does not occur. In identifying flip-flop events we also need to think about trends which reach a critical mass and so cause a serious event, or 'flip-flop' to happen. For example, a market might reach the critical point of being 'swamped', or the trend in growth of the population of a village may reach the critical point where the school cannot cope and new building may be an option, or a trend in global warming may reach a critical point for the construction industry with a recognized need for fundamentally different housing. Thus, although the variable being considered is following the same, and relatively certain, trend, the point of criticality of a flip-flop may be uncertain, and so the event may be uncertain. Other, more obvious, examples of past flip-flops of importance to some organizations include 'a nuclear accident such as that at Chernobyl', or 'the fall of the Berlin wall', or the 'commitment to build the Channel Tunnel between the UK and France', or the 'introduction of fundamentally different ways of managing social welfare in the USA'.

The notion of flip-flop events is, in our experience, sometimes difficult to grasp. Many books introduce categories of events, such as PEST (Political, Environmental, Social, Technological), as a way of prompting the thinking of the team. We are uncomfortable with this approach, although it sometimes can be used as a checklist (see below) once the flow of events placed on the grid has slowed down. It is more important to see categories as an output rather than as an input to exploring futures. Thus it *may* be relevant and helpful to categorize events into the four categories above after a group has identified the events of importance to their strategic thinking. To do so before, as an input to thinking, is to constrain thinking in a manner which turns out to be highly inappropriate for the nature of futures to be considered by the group.

A recent research project conducted by Brightman *et al* (1997) set out to establish a set of guiding principles for the identification of scenario events. These principles were, in part, influenced by our own work and that of van der Heijden (1996) and we include them here in a modified form because they represent, to a large extent, our current view of the best way of helping a management team create scenarios which will most effectively guide their strategic thinking. The overriding, and obvious, consideration is that 'events should have repercussions over a number of years'. However, another more interesting general principle is to identify 'puzzles' for the industry or sector. A puzzle flip-flop occurs when the 'data does not stack up' – for example one 'usually reliable' indicator suggests one outcome and another suggests a contradictory outcome. For example, government economic forecasts suggest growth whereas OECD forecasts suggest economic stagnation – here the flip-flop event becomes 'economic growth (Govt view), rather than stagnation (OECD view)'. Sometimes such flip-flops occur as a result of contradictory views from internal experts, and sometimes they arise from a single source where an 'expert' who feels they can usually predict the nature of an outcome has become uncertain about which way things will unfold. Other more specific principles suggest:

- external changes that will lead to step changes in demand characteristics: for example, an industry body or government are planning the introduction of a new regulatory system, or the creation of, or action by, a powerful lobby group or coalition.
- a significant shift in client and/or user attitudes: for example, students believe themselves to be customers of the education system, rather than being told that they are.
- technological breakthroughs:
  - the emergence of new or advanced technology;
  - the emergence of a new way of doing things (processes and procedures): for example, the IBM experience of the PC entries.
  - previous technology failure comes to light, or previous technology fails.
- changes in the *structure* of a market, or public service system:
  - for example, a step change in international trading conditions, or a change in relationship between small and major players (including restructuring – e.g. reorganization of local or regional government, the possibility of a British Airways/American Airlines link);
  - a step function implication of a trend reaching a particular level.
- a major 'strategy context setter' undergoing major strategic change:
  - their changing the 'core strategy' or policies;
  - their introducing a new 'recipe' or new way of working;
  - their 'shaking themselves about': for example, major organizational restructuring such as the creation of strategic business units after highly centralized control.
- the resolution or complication of current strategic issues facing the industry or sector: for example, the agreement to industry wide training or apprenticeship schemes, or the release of critical information hitherto withheld (e.g. by government or research body).
- previously anticipated events now not going to happen but originally taken for granted as occurring. The identification of these can offer major strategic advantage in scenario terms because competitors may be locked into a 'taken for granted' view of the future – a view which may no longer be as certain as it is taken for granted to be.

As we noted above, the events of interest when constructing scenarios are those on the right side of the grid. Those in the top right quadrant provide the context for scenarios. They may not be included in them but they might provide significant contextual validity to the events in the bottom right quadrant. For example, in the run up to the UK general election of 1996/7, the uncertainty about who was to be the winner of the election was reducing significantly, and so the event – Labour wins – gradually moved to the top right quadrant by mid-1996. Nevertheless the event, as a flip-flop of great importance to some organizations, was taken to be the more certain context to possible events noted in the bottom right of the grid, such as changes in taxation.

The **dimension of uncertainty** which separates the two quadrants is *P363* conceptually problematic. An event may be regarded as relatively certain to happen, but there might be huge uncertainty about the timing of the event. For example, in considering scenarios with Scottish Natural Heritage, the event – a major oil spill on the west coast of Scotland – was taken to be relatively certain and yet the time it would occur was 'in the next 4–10 years'. In this case the *uncertainty of timing* was crucial to strategic thinking and so the event appeared in the bottom right quadrant indicating high uncertainty and high importance.

As with previous elements of the journey, the coherence of one set of data in relation to data surfacing from other elements of the journey matters. In this case we find that entries appear on the grid because the management team are clear that they are important, and yet the logic of their importance, as related to the aspirations, is not clear. In these instances there are two possible explanations. The first is that the event is important, and is, in effect, the indication of an emergent strategic issue not previously identified during issue identification episodes. If it is a new strategic issue for the organization, then it is possible that it, in turn, implies an unidentified new aspiration that needs to be encompassed within the draft aspirations system. The second explanation is that although the event is important, and it has appeared for that reason, within the context of the current draft strategy it is no longer important. In this case it is a response to thinking appropriate to the past emergent strategy rather than to the newly identified strategy. Each explanation has its own implications for the JOURNEY making team. In the first case, the aspirations system will need to be revisited. In the second case, the event must be removed from the grid, and the team need to signal the shift in strategic thinking which has resulted in its deletion. Attaching some sort of ceremony to the removal of proposed important events may help when the thinking of, at least, one member of the team has not been changed in the manner that the JOURNEY making process might have expected.

Actors as Event Drivers – the role of 'strategy context setters'

Let us reinforce the comments made above, and in the last chapter, as we believe examining the role of strategy context setters in the JOURNEY making process to be crucial. Significant elements of the structure of the environment are other organizations, individuals, groups, or governments. Although different actors (strategy context setters) in the environment are defined as important 'driving forces' within multiple futures, they are not seen to be interested in the strategy that the focal organization is attempting to execute. Organizations or governments, as actors within a scenario, generally do not act as parties interested in the strategic issues facing the organization. Nevertheless they do have significant power to influence the context within which the strategic issues are resolved and therefore must be considered.

Within scenarios, actors must be seen as thinking decision makers who have, at the very least, preferences and options open to them (to deliberately use a game theoretic view of them). To establish preferences and options requires modelling at least some aspects of their thinking. However, there may be occasions when it is helpful to go beyond this simple view of explaining actions and proceed to model the value systems and belief systems that determine their preferences and options. At the simplest level this implies the equivalent of a role-think, by the management team. This involves exploring the thinking of the 'strategy context setters' regarding some of the events on the grid which would be of specific interest to them. At the more complex level it may be important to explore the unfolding dynamics of the interactions between strategy context setters, using either game theory methods (Khalifa, 1996) or formal cognitive modelling (Bossel, 1977; Eden, 1977) where there is an attempt to model the way in which an important strategy context setter thinks, and so how they might act, in relation to a range of situations of interest to the organization.

A focus on preferences and options allows analyses to be carried out that explore the dynamics of the potential interactions between 'strategy context setters' as players in a game. These interactions are examined to determine which of them impact on the strategy making organization – although it is recognized that they are not deliberately intended so to do. As a result the orientation of the strategy context setters is towards one another and to the issues they jointly face *which are also of concern to the strategy makers*. This can be achieved by some form of game theory-based analysis – the most apt being 'hyper-game' analysis (Bennett, 1980, 1995). This form of game theory analysis allows for each player to have differing perceptions of the nature of the 'game', whereas traditional game theory assumes that the game is seen as the same by each player. The process of analysis allows scenarios to unfold over time as the interactions run their course towards a stable outcome and considers 'strategic moves' that could be made by players in order to arrive at their own preferred outcomes. Nowadays the analyses can be explored using computer software (for example, 'INTERACT' – Bennett *et al*, 1994). Our own experience nevertheless suggests that the conceptual framework of 'hyper-game analysis' is more powerful than the analysis itself – that is, the notion of strategic stability which is often contrary to win/lose strategies is powerful, as is the notion of deliberately exploring the different perceptions of actors. Generally the number of 'strategy context setters' that need to be considered makes the formal analysis too unwieldy. As we discussed in the last chapter, we have found instead that 'role-play' and 'role-think' exercises discussed in the last chapter are powerful for both stakeholder and scenario analysis where the exercise is informed by, in particular, the notion of stability as it is used in hyper-game analysis.

·

It is interesting to note that the futures modelling activity supported by the Club of Rome in the 1970s was concerned with the issues of locking together models of the behaviour of decision makers within models of environmental forces. Notably **System Dynamics modelling** which formed the basis for *Limits to Growth* (Meadows and Meadows, 1972) excluded consideration of stakeholders altogether. 'Practically all system models of societal systems developed to date concentrate on the representation of the material processes of these systems and all too often entirely neglect the cognitive/normative components of the real processes which dominate decision-making and action' (Bossel, 1977). In a similar vein Eden and Harris (1976) argued that less ambitious modelling should be more attuned to the need to model the decision makers' desire to control their environment. To do so requires **a better way of understanding the act of construal – the process of *managerial cognition***. 'A selectively perceptive social being capable of producing conflict and struggles for the power to become a reality definer' (Eden, 1978) is more often than not seen as a problem to builders of scenarios.

V206 P366

V274

A fundamental assumption about the future is that it will, to a large extent, be a product of human activities. In creating future scenarios we should therefore be interested in answering the following question: 'What is involved, when we say what people are doing and why they are doing it?' (Burke, 1969). The stakeholder analysis was the first step in acknowledging this need and provided some of the answers although, in stakeholder analysis, there was the danger in presuming that too many are 'players' rather than 'strategy context setters'.

When considering scenarios we also find it helpful to refer to Kenneth Burke's answer to his own question above:

> '. . . you must have some word that names the act (names what took place, in thought or deed), and another that names the scene (the background of the act, the situation in which it occurred); also you must indicate what person or kind of person (agent) performed the act, what means or instrument he used (agency), and the purpose'.

This answer represents a dramaturgical perspective for understanding 'players' – one which matches closely the dictionary definition of a scenario as: 'A summary of the plot of a play, etc., including information about its characters, scenes, etc.' – *New Collins Concise English Dictionary*. As with many of the words in the manager's vocabulary the meaning has expanded, but it does nonetheless suggest the idea of an unfolding story where one event prompts another and where the story involves characters who do things. In a similar manner, our array of events as entries on the grid become stories. **Each story, or scenario, is importantly different from another**, in that it communicates some different strategic considerations. Each story will have a moral to it, the moral being directly related to the aspirations of the organization – so events have consequences that matter.

V270

In short, Burke suggests the following pentad:

- what will happen? (act)
- when and where will it happen? (scene)
- who is going to make it happen? (agent)
- what will make it happen? (agency)
- why will it happen? (purpose).

To be of any relevance in a scenario planning exercise, we must consider the transformation that occurs between the time to which these answers relate and the time horizon of the scenario. To do this we must consider the current configuration of act, scene, agent, agency, and purpose, thus building on Burke's pentad.

What this means is checking the entries in the stakeholder power/ interest grid for all 'context setters' and providing answers to the above five questions. This process ensures that we can begin to 'tell the story' about their role in the future. This check typically revisits the stakeholder management possibilities because it becomes clear that some of the context setters are really players who can be managed directly. If they turn out to be players, then stakeholder management strategies can be developed. The process, with respect to the strategy context setters, will show an:

- identification of their individual motivations, and the constraints and resources for action (potential or present);
- understanding of the possible strategies of strategy context setters, and their alliances and conflicts;
- exploration of the seeds of change in the context setters' strategies (Godet, 1987).

However, be careful; strategy analysis is a practical activity and so cannot be 'complete' but rather must consider a specific *hierarchy* of context setters. The extent to which strategic thinking and scenario exploration moves down the hierarchy is encompassed by the same considerations as for other parts of strategy making – the potential impact of context setters on the business model (and so aspirations), and the likelihood of the story unfolding. Thus, the hierarchy reflects the significant differences in the power and resolution to act in relation to the interests of the strategy making group. It will be different for different organizations (even those in the same industry). Strategy analysts' concern to construct scenario models that are supposedly statements about reality rather than about that which is relevant to the strategy makers can be a significant explanation for the sort of disillusionment with overambitious forecasting models that seems to persist. This is because the analysts do not adhere to the need for the sort of 'requisite modelling' (Phillips, 1984) we suggest here.

There are as many approaches to constructing scenarios as there are scenario planning experts. At the present time scenario analysis is popular, and like most management fads it produces experts out of thin air! Here we make a plea that the fad is ignored. The arguments that support the need to consider multiple futures as a part of strategic thinking are powerful. When the fad for 'scenario planning' is gone, these arguments will persist and continue to be persuasive.

As we stated above, the approach discussed here is presented in a manner we take to be conceptually sound in its own right. However, it is intended as a part of a *complete* journey *with the management team* rather than an isolated activity. Thus, in some respects, it may be described as 'quick and dirty', but deliberately so because it is designed to be set within the theory of JOURNEY making. For a thoroughgoing approach to scenario planning, but with the same focus on 'conversation' about futures and their impact on strategy, we would commend Kees van der Heijden's book (1996) that elaborates and develops the approach used by Shell Group Planning (of which van der Heijden was a key member). It is an approach that sees scenarios as the centre piece of strategic thinking.

We have focused on examining alternative futures partly because of our wish to distinguish ourselves from both the comprehensive approach advocated by afficionados such as van der Heijden, and from the current heightened interest in scenario planning. Nevertheless the term scenario does aptly fit the analyses we are suggesting.

Constructing Scenarios of Multiple Futures

The first step in working with the array of events is to link them together where appropriate so as to build up a network – a potential story with a moral. Events are linked together when one is dependent upon the other. Causal chains appear on the grid and during the process some of the events become identified as **major triggers through their relationships to** *V267 V271* **many other events whereas others form a part of a single chain**. In effect, the grid is becoming a graphical representation of a 'cross-impact matrix' approach (Helmer, 1981, 1983) to scenarios where the links are causal or temporal.

The process of linking typically generates more events than those initially identified by the group. As participants offer connections the link sometimes needs to be explained through intermediate events; in this way the stories begin to build. Some bundles of events will finish up being linked together to form a distinct cluster which is completely, or almost completely, disconnected from other clusters of events. When there is complete disconnectivity then we treat each cluster as a possible scenario which is distinguishable from others (in the sense of not being dependent upon them). If all of n events are completely disconnected then we have, in principle, 2^n scenarios because each of the events may, or may not, occur with each of the other events which may, or may not, occur. Similarly each cluster as an independent scenario may, or may not, occur alongside other scenarios. In each case we need to be clear that the scenario has an impact on the organization's aspirations – otherwise it is of no importance and need not be considered. Events in the 'scenario planning region' (bottom right quadrant) can each link to other events elsewhere on the grid depending upon which side of the flip-flop is being used as the trigger. Thus, with respect to the general election result (discussed above) there might have been two scenarios – one for a Tory victory and another for a Labour victory (even though these were opposite sides of the same flip-flop). In the 'peace scenario' (in figure C8.4) there might have been an alternative scenario following from the trigger 'Government refuses to acknowledge cease-fire'. In the event, this was not taken as an important scenario *relative to others being considered in exploring strategic adaptability and opportunism.*

Each scenario, or scenario portfolio, develops as the story unfolds towards events that impinge directly on the strategy of the organization – in the sense of requiring strategies of adaptability or allowing opportunism. Figure C8.4 below shows an initial draft of the 'peace' scenario (modified for reasons of confidentiality) for the Northern Ireland Prison Service. The scenario is triggered by 'agreement of a cease-fire with Republican paramilitaries' and several elements of the story begin to unfold until they impact upon the strategic consideration of the Service (shown in italics). Thus, the scenario combines both 'developmental' (sequences of events that lead to a future situation) and 'situational' (the final outcome) scenarios into one scenario.

P365   As a scenario becomes refined, it is helpful to convert the picture into a memorable written story. An important aspect of **making it memorable comes from giving it a notable title** (see Schwartz, 1991:234). For example, each of the set of five scenarios constructed by the management team of a local community-based organization carried the title of a recent film – with 'Braveheart' being the exciting battle unfolding against crime and economic decline!

The ease with which a management team can create different scenarios is one measure of the degree of turbulence faced by the organization. Ease of creation suggests high turbulence, while difficulty in generating different scenarios suggests a more equable environment. However, a *P366*   practical 'rule of thumb' suggests that a **management team should draw their strategic thinking attention to about 5–7 possible futures**. To use at least five alternative futures removes the temptation of developing three obvious categories of future – expected, pessimistic, and optimistic. There is no particular logic in favour of these three categories – it can be just as relevant to strategic thinking to work with, for example, five optimistic scenarios each of which suggest developing strategies for exploiting potential opportunities. However, those to be used should emerge from the data and be representative of the overall set of events unearthed. To use more than seven generally overloads the JOURNEY making benefits.

While we have just discussed one quick method for exploring several futures, and intimated a couple of others, there are additional approaches we explore in the third part of the book (Chapter P4). As we suggested above, the theory of scenario building is not well developed, and many of

Figure C8.4 The first draft of the 'Peace Scenario' – an event based scenario (modified for confidentiality).

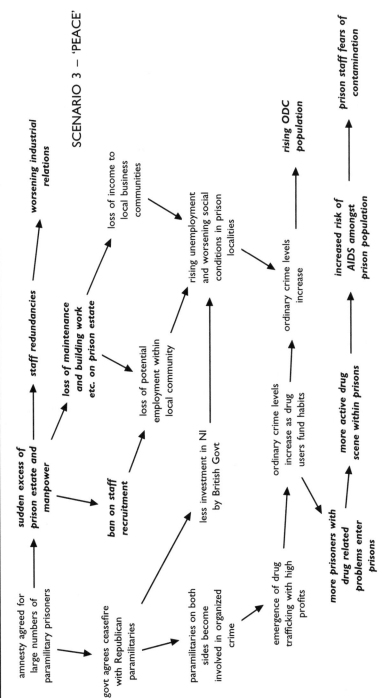

SCENARIO 3 – 'PEACE'

Source: NIO/SU 1991–2

the approaches have been the result of trying it in practice. Those included within this book have been designed so as to fit within the theory of JOURNEY making and provide benefits (as seen through various examples) to management teams.

V205 V267

Finally, although we stated earlier that the use of experts is not necessary, it is sometimes helpful to **use a group of outsiders to bring an alternative view of the future** to the table. This is particularly helpful when the management team believe that their own way of looking at the environment might be too narrow. For example, Scottish Natural Heritage felt that their own understanding of future environmental events was bound to be limited. The CEO invited a group of twelve experts across many fields, from sea life to industrial development, to spend a day building scenarios. The approach discussed above was used with the help of computer support to the group (a process discussed more fully in the third part).

V271 P368

Van der Heijden argues that one of the most important features of successful scenario building is the use of what he calls '**remarkable people**' – people who bring a distinct and original view of the future to the organization. These people are typically, although not necessarily, out-siders. Our experience supports the important role such people may play, however it is not easy to identify such people or inexpensive to obtain their relevant input. As a result, the processes we have developed depend on using the merging of different perspectives from each individual in a group so that the process of developing interconnections between these perspectives can create the equivalent of the input from an 'unusual

P337

person'. Thus, the designed group processes (using '**Oval Mapping Techniques' and the Networked Computer System with associated degrees of anonymity**) encourage individuality and originality of expression in the events identified. When using this process there is, of course, significantly greater ownership of the futures identified than when they are overly influenced by outsiders.

Managing the Alternative Futures

Monitoring

One of the most important outcomes of a JOURNEY making approach to considering alternative futures comes from the mental tuning of the management team. Their involvement in thinking about alternative futures means that key members of the organization are able to spot different scenarios unfolding before they have unfolded. These scenarios may not necessarily be those immediately identified but other combinations of the crucial events that may be perceived as new events unfold. Thus, everyday monitoring takes place without special effort, and will ensure that the management team are able to act strategically in advance of events tumbling into crisis. It is important to remember that each of the 5–7 futures that are the concrete outcome of the journey is unlikely to occur. *The future is a system of interacting improbabilities* (Beer, 1966:56). Each alternative future represents a mental prompt to other alternative futures and a reminder of the need to think of the future as alternative futures, rather than as a forecast or predicted single future.

Nevertheless, a management team will always want to make choices between the futures they have identified on the basis of some being more likely than others. This must be resisted for the reasons presented earlier in this chapter – what matters is their role in *making strategic choices now about how to be, or not to be, strategically adaptable and opportunistic*. If there are many important alternative futures which can easily be identified (high levels of turbulence) then it will be important to design the organization for strategic adaptability, whereas if the futures identified vary little in their impact on the organization then strategies can be longer term and recognize greater stability. Of particular importance is the extent to which the organization needs, or does not need, to establish procedures (both mental tuning of managers and proper monitoring routines) to enable the identification that some futures are becoming increasingly likely and others less so.

A management team must manage the present from the futures (make choices now – strategic pro-activity, or at least what Ackoff (1974) calls strategic 'inter-activity'), not the future from the present (by allowing futures to force strategic re-activity). Consequently it must be possible to **determine some of the key triggers associated with the alternative** *V270 V271 P366* **futures and monitor them**. The model constructed during the analysis, made up of event maps, is amenable to some analysis for this purpose. Some of the events will drive many paths of unfolding events, some will be entry points into feedback loops (which depict self-generating dynamics), and so on. With the use of computer software (Brightman *et al*, 1997) it is possible to analyse the overall model for these features (the process of analysis matches the 'MICMAC method' suggested by Godet (1987:38) and, in effect computes the 'reachability matrices' – the extent to which one event impacts upon others). The events identified become those which are routinely monitored by the organization.

The Coherence of Strategy

In most organizations the success of a strategy depends partly on its fit with the planning context – the scenario planning region. One way of ensuring that a strategy is robust is by testing the strategy against a number of possible futures which represent the context within which the organization is likely to operate. Scenario planning is an approach that tries to reduce the uncertainties about the future by attempting an understanding of the environment through the use of mainly qualitative and holistic forecasting and modelling methods (Schnaars, 1986; Schwarz, 1991). Thus scenario planning, in some senses, seeks to bring uncertainty back into the strategy making discussion whereas traditional forecasting approaches tend to encourage the development of increasing certainty about the future. As we noted in the stakeholder chapter (chapter C7) the key to successful strategic change is the *coherence* of strategy as well as ensuring that the options are robust. Coherence comes from continuously cycling between JOURNEY making and confirming/designing strategy whereas robustness is achieved through examining the stakeholder interactions and possible futures.

Formal robustness analysis methods can be helpful (see Rosenhead, 1980), and can be related specifically to the outcome of scenario analysis exercises. These forms of analysis seek to ensure that strategic options are not closed off – thus any strategies delivered now still enable a robust future to be protected (see figures C8.1 and C8.2).

Revisiting Stakeholder Analysis

Scenarios will have included the most powerful strategy context setters. As we suggested above, the process of deliberately including them in scenario development often will have changed their position in the stakeholder power/interest grid. Some strategy context setters will have disappeared from the scene altogether (and become 'crowd') and others will have lost their salience and power in the future, even though historically they may have been strategy context setters. Conversely, some new strategy context setters will have surfaced. As we identified in the stakeholder management chapter, one of the most creative tasks that the management team can undertake is that of finding ways of turning strategy context setters into players. If a strategy context setter is overwhelmingly significant in a scenario then it is rare that some strategy for negotiating with them cannot be found – for example through the use of formal lobbying experts in order to influence government.

In some cases, negotiation is not the best approach. Rather, seeing the leader as a target for indirect lobbying becomes the best approach. Thus, when, as a result of the role play/think exercise applied to 'strategy context setters', it becomes obvious that it is desirable to consider influencing the behaviour of one of the strategy context setters, a detailed form of cognitive modelling is required. This greater detail is required because, in effect, the strategy makers are considering manipulating (through, for example, the use of propaganda) the belief system and/or value system of the context setter.

Sometimes internal stakeholders or stakeholders who are 'players' (and so amenable to stakeholder management) are central flip-flops or triggers in scenarios. For example, the prospect of one member of staff leaving the organization might have been identified as a trigger to an important scenario, but not identified during stakeholder analysis. In these instances it is crucial to return to stakeholder management possibilities.

Revisiting Aspirations

We have already suggested above that it is of paramount importance to make sure that the alternative futures considered in relation to strategy making are those of relevance to the business model and so to aspirations. However, it is equally important to recognize that sometimes it becomes clear to a management team that a particular possible future is crucial to the strategic future of the organization but that the current drafted aspirations system would not have suggested its importance. In these circumstances the coherence of strategy will depend upon revisiting the aspirations so that they truly reflect the emergent strategic issue implied by the extent to which the identified future is crucial. Either the aspirations system is modified, or the identified future is downgraded in its importance to the organization. Otherwise the strategy is incoherent.

CHAPTER C9

STRATEGY MAKING CLOSURE

'We trained hard . . . but it seemed that every time we were beginning to form up into teams, we would be reorganized. I was to learn later in life, that we tend to meet any new situation by reorganization; and a wonderful method it can be for creating the illusion of progress while producing confusion, inefficiency and demoralization' (Petronius Arbiter, 210 BC)

We argue throughout this book for strategic management to be seen as a continuous process where organizations continue to learn, continue to change and improve, and continue to re-evaluate their strategic future (see figures C2.3 and C2.4). This is unrealistic in many respects. For example, we discussed, in chapter C2, the tension between continuity and change, and in chapter C3 we discussed the stress of strategic change on managers and the associated organizational politics which must ensue. This stress on managers is also a stress on the organization which can have a profound effect on the operational effectiveness of the organization.

Managers cannot be stopped from acting to solve immediate problems as a result of their continuously changing their mind about strategy as they think about strategy. Strategy *will be* implemented incrementally before any more formal closure has taken place. If the involvement of managers in the strategy development process is designed to influence their thinking, then we must not be surprised when this happens. Moreover, when it happens at all it will happen incrementally, not at one perfectly timed end point.

We also have argued that serious strategy making will often occur when the organization is facing some sort of crisis, and when the crisis is averted then the organization loses interest in strategy making. Therefore, given these admissions, why are we suggesting that it should be a continuous process?

As with so many aspects of strategic management we are struggling to attain an appropriate balance between one end of a spectrum and another. *P461* In this chapter we acknowledge the real need for **closure** and stability with the equally real need for continuous organizational learning and strategic change. Thus, we must devise processes that enable us to monitor, review, and confirm a sense of strategic control, processes which in themselves promote organizational learning. We must also ensure that these processes do not stultify strategy by its becoming associated with tedious administration. We must also ensure that through the JOURNEY making process there is respect for a carefully developed strategy and that operational effectiveness and efficiency can develop.

Too often conversations about strategic change never go beyond verbal rhetoric or nice sounding strategy statements which have little meaning in terms of action implications. The statements allow managers to do almost anything and be able to justify it within the framework of the statements in strategy documents. We have argued before that strategy making is about strategic change, and the formation of strategy cannot be divorced from issues of implementation (Simons, 1995). As we have seen from our attempts to model the meaning statements have to an individual using cognitive maps, it is both the purposeful outcomes expected *and the actions to be taken* that give meaning. Thus, *without clear closure involving conversations about* **action plans**, *all concerned can be left with the impression that reaching shared understandings is tantamount to making things happen* (Beer *et al*, 1990).

Thinking and Acting Differently

It is worth stressing that, in many respects, shared understanding – JOURNEY making – about strategic intent will make things happen differently in the organization. This has been the essence of our case, that the most successful strategic change will come from managers construing their world differently *and so acting differently*. However, alongside this, it is important to note that this approach to change denies the need for successful change to be related to 'performance conversations' (Ford and Ford, 1995) – action oriented communication, as well as understanding. Regardless of how realistic this approach to organizational change may be, it does not satisfy the need a person and an organization has for an artifact. People have a need for something concrete that signifies that the task of strategy development has been completed (Bridges, 1980) and, later, that progress in strategic change has been made. As we stated in chapter C4, 'for strategic organizational change we see a continuing process where the conversation itself produces change – expectations and intentions are continually elaborated, and plans are declared as a way of symbolizing closure but in fact create temporary stability'. In part 3 (chapter P5) we emphasize the role of 'milestones' and stages as a deliberate part of planning the facilitation of strategy making teams, so that they are encouraged to close particular episodes of the journey by agreeing and committing to strategy intentions which have action implications. Thus, we discuss (in chapter P3) the need to design interventions in such a way that they can be closed at almost any time without having to go through a strategy making process that has the prospect of never being completed (for the reasons outlined above). JOURNEY making has been deliberately contrived as a process that can be closed after a **'quick and dirty' one-day workshop** which has clear action *P324* implications, and yet can also be continued as the strategy making cycles around further episodes of elaboration and refining. This also implies that the process of closure must involve explicit attention to **evaluating strategic** *V260 P441* **programmes and strategic options** in a more or less detailed manner. Thus, even if the evaluation does not involve detailed consideration using formal methods (such as cost/benefit analysis, multiple criteria decision modelling, resource allocation models, etc.) because the team take the strategy to be obvious, it is still important to acknowledge option evaluation as having been undertaken, so that it is a part of a closure ceremony.

V278   One important way in which we can find out whether an organization has changed is by listening for the **changes in the scripts** used as a part of the conversation of organizational problem solving. In chapter C5, we argued that one important aspect of detecting emergent strategizing comes from understanding the language of strategic issue management, and from understanding organizational processes. Thus, it follows that any evaluation of strategic change should explore changes in the language of strategic issue management. However, while a 'researcher' may see fundamental changes in the strategic issues being addressed, it will be less easy for the organizational members to detect these changes themselves. The researcher, for example, will be able to observe the way that strategic issues are defined, the ways of working (culture), and so on, whereas, if the change is to be long lasting, it will have become so well embedded both cognitively and behaviourally that for the members of the organization this can become almost imperceptible.

A difficulty in this debate is the need to be clear about what constitutes an actionable statement. In a strategy map the actions are those statements that are taken to cause a given outcome. However, each action in turn is informed by actions that support them (explanations) placing the former action *as an outcome*. Therefore, each node on the map is both an action and an outcome depending upon the *level* of abstraction required. (We have seen how cognitive maps and subsequently strategy, or cause, maps are deliberately coded with an active verb so that each of the ideas/constructs *P290*   constitutes a **call for action**. The call for action also provides an example of personal constructs as contributors to the process of 'manage and control'.)

For senior managers and the top management team it can be clear what actions need to be taken in relation to a strategic declaration. However, apparent resistance at lower levels in the organization may occur. This may be as much to do with a lack of clarity about what is expected and when, as with an outright disagreement with the course of action. Thus, what is an actionable statement for one person may remain ambiguous or meaningless for another. The confusion can be further exacerbated when senior managers, who believe they are acting consistently within a world of complex multiple goals, are perceived to be acting inconsistently by others who are more singularly focused in their tasks. Double messages seem to abound, particularly where a senior manager demands one thing from his subordinates but appears to pay lip service to it himself by doing the opposite.

Nevertheless, one of the reasons that change will have been successful will be because the new ways of doing things appear obvious and the old ways forgotten. Thus, as we said above, the more successful the change process, the less easy it is to recognize it. It is similar to the dilemma for the facilitator who manages successfully the process of a team of managers genuinely changing their mind (rather than being compromised into agreement). A genuine change of mind will have been largely imperceptible for the person who has changed their mind, and so the role of the facilitator in the process will be difficult to acknowledge. As a consequence the facilitator is not rewarded and so not used again! The facilitator who is acknowledged as successful is often forced to use performance measures that can be counterproductive to the reality of success where hidden and subtle objectives may be paramount (and only sometimes known to the single client rather than to the management team as a whole). In the same way an organization and its managers needs to create success measures for strategy which can be, in many ways, counterproductive to successful strategic change.

Below we discuss two important aspects of closure: (i) the need (or not) for the **routine symbol of strategy** – the 'mission statement' – (ii) the need   *V263* for action plans (and their potential for reducing flexibility).

The Mission or Vision Statement   *V277 P332 P429*

Very few organizations in the Western world believe that they can get away without a statement which starts 'our mission is . . .'. To some extent this is a pity. The mission statement has become disreputable, and organizational cynics about strategy will use mission statements as an example of strategy nonsense. Their case is that the statement is meaningless, unrealistic, not related to what the organization is really doing, has no impact on the behaviour of senior management, and so on. They are often absolutely right. There are frequent examples of double messages evident in an organization's strategy, where a statement that is made public is not taken seriously by the management team. Sometimes there is confusion on the part of all in the organization, senior managers and other staff, about the **role of a mission statement in stakeholder management** compared   *P431* with its force as a statement intended to effect strategic change. While the logic of a mission statement for stakeholder management can be sound, the subsequent potential confusion about its role within the strategy must be taken seriously. The rhetoric of strategy is to dismiss the confusion by stating that the two purposes are the same – and for a fully coherent strategy they should be. Nevertheless, as we have seen in our discussion about stakeholder management and multiple futures, there can often be a need for different statements internally and externally.

A **mission statement**, as a 'call to arms' or 'battalion flag', can be a   *P430* motivator for strategic change. As a consequence we should use this symbol of closure purposefully and take great care over its content. As we have said, a mission statement can be, at one extreme, a short and pithy statement (a couple of sentences) which must nevertheless differentiate the organizational aspirations from those of other organizations. At the other extreme it can be a full page of contentful material that clearly sets out a realistic strategic intent and which is designed for internal consumption. Our own preference is towards the longer version – a version which expresses a full account of strategic intent and encompasses the business model or livelihood scheme. To do so within the confines of two sentences is difficult, if not impossible. However, sometimes designed ambiguity in strategy, and in particular mission statements, is important: 'Strategic ambiguity fosters the existence of multiple viewpoints in organizations. The use of ambiguity is commonly found in organizational mission, goals and plans. . . . It is a political necessity to engage in strategic ambiguity so that different constituent groups may apply different interpretations to the symbol' (Eisenberg, 1984:231).

Fortunately there is good research material indicating how an effective mission statement should be constructed (Campbell and Tawadey, 1990). Our own version of this work is represented in figure C6.1, and the figure shows how purpose, values, strategy, and standards and behaviour must be linked together. The arrows on the diagrams show the manner in which the statement should be constructed. A statement of purpose is at the core of the document and is supported by the priority strategies encompassed by core values of the organization. The language used needs to make structural sense of the network of goals and the supporting network of strategies, so that the document projects coherence as well as rhetoric and drama. Unfortunately, too often the copywriters lose the carefully embedded logic and attend only to the good turn of phrase. This is not to underestimate the use of drama and rhetoric and good graphic design. On the contrary, these are absolutely necessary but nowhere near sufficient requirements. The style and presentation of the mission statement constitute, in themselves, a statement about the organization and so must be suited for the purpose.

We are often asked to provide examples of good mission statements. We refuse to do so – the answer is riddled with contingencies. A mission statement cannot be generally good, only specifically good for a particular organization, strategy, and business model, with a relative degree of sophistication with respect to the strategy. The context of a mission statement cannot be set out alongside an example. It is easier to provide bad examples, but they are bad because they simply break the guidelines set out in figure C6.1. For example, there are many mission statements that are neither aspirational nor inspirational. We consider the procedures for developing a mission statement in part 3 of the book – procedures that start from creating a dramatic and appropriately stylistic text version of the aspirations/goal system, and adding inspiration.

Action Planning

One aspect of closure that dominates many journeys is the need to provide an answer to the question 'but so what are we actually going to do, and when?'. In chapter C1 we set out a continuum showing the full spectrum from deliberate emergent strategies (where an organization makes a strategic choice to provide only a strategic framework for action) to full blown strategic planning (where an organization produces detailed strategic programmes encompassing deliverables, time scales, budgets, etc.), and argued that organizations need to determine where they should be on this spectrum. We argued that this was an important strategic choice in its own right. The JOURNEY making process will help make this choice, and the decision about when to go for closure is the reality of the choice. For example, late closure generally means that the organization has chosen a route that embarks upon increasingly more detailed planning. Alternatively, deliberate early closure around a statement of strategic intent, and a belief in the JOURNEY making approach itself as an important outcome, puts the strategy making process at the 'deliberate emergent' end of the spectrum. However, as closure towards strategic intent is realized, a mission statement as an artifact is appropriate whereas action plans may not be. Nevertheless, there will still be pressures from all involved for 'action plans'. In these circumstances it may be important to resist them.

The structure of strategy as a hierarchy (see figure C9.1) deliberately positions increasingly subordinate statements as increasingly detailed actions. The structure is expressed as a set of goals supported by strategies, strategies supported by portfolios of strategic programmes, and strategic programmes supported by portfolios of actions. The depth of action planning will have been determined by the choice of positioning on the contingency spectrum (chapter C1). This choice in turn will have been informed, in part, by stakeholder pressures and a view about the *robustness* of strategies (Rosenhead, 1980) and therefore, also, about the required flexibility. Of course some aspects of strategy may be amenable to detailed action plans and other parts demand high levels of flexibility. (As we argued in chapter C1, the continuum is a generalized scheme designed to introduce the idea of contingencies in strategy output.)

The Relationship between Action and Strategic Intent – strategy as a map

Each strategy is supported by a tear-drop of strategic programmes (figure C5.3 – the strategy map), where any strategic programme may act in support of more than one strategy, and so be potentially more potent. Each of the strategic programmes represents a 'tear-drop' of actions, and some of the actions will be particularly potent because they impact several programmes. The strategy map as a network provides the basis for serious analysis of action plans through the exploration of the following.

- The **potency of actions** in relation to programme delivery and so, in   *P411*
  relation to aspirations, indicates rough priorities. This is a first stab at
  option evaluation which must then be tempered by good judgement.

Figure C9.1   The strategy map as part of the strategy making process.

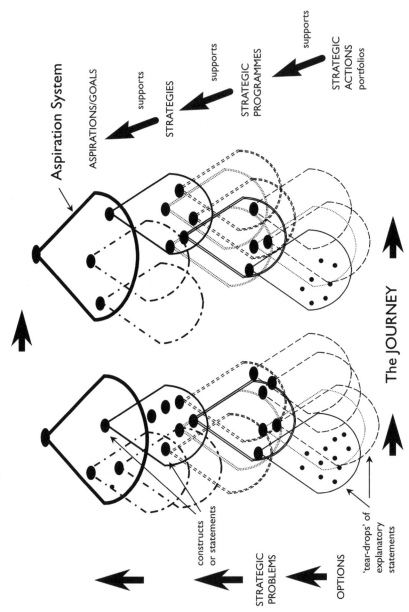

- The degree to which a set of actions work together as a portfolio can be used to cluster together responsibilities for delivery. For example, the management team may create interdisciplinary teams so as to involve staff from several divisions or departments or disciplines. Alternatively, responsibility may be kept together in one part of the organization. In some cases organizations have been redesigned to reflect the structure of the strategy map, so that, for example, particular tear-drops become the responsibility of a single division or department.
- The structure of actions within the network allows the resource demands of each strategy (as if the strategy levels in the strategy map were **'resource gates'** (Eden and Cropper, 1992)) to be checked by *P441* tracking *down* the hierarchy to explore all actions and their requirements that support the strategy.
- The loads on individual managers can be assessed. As **responsi-** *V260 P441* **bilities are assigned and delivery dates agreed** (for start, progress, or completion), then the structure provides ways of analysing the implementation loads on individual staff, departments, or divisions.

The use of the special computer software that facilitates the above analyses also provides the most effective basis for a **computer based** *V222* **Strategy Delivery Support System (SDSS)**. This is a system that can be routinely locked into strategy reviews with individual managers, teams, or the senior management team (Ackermann *et al*, 1992, 1993). The system can also be used with great effect as a Decision Support System (DSS) in the **annual performance reviews for staff**, so explicitly locking reward *P437 P464* systems into strategy delivery. Finally, the system acts as an organizational memory (a 'transitional object' – de Geus (1988)) allowing regular reference checks to be made as well as informing new members of the organization of the strategic direction – as a coherent system of action oriented intentions. Many of the 'vignettes' presented in part 2 of the book provide examples of the use of such a SDSS, and part 3 of the book expands the processes that are involved in option evaluation using the above analysis approaches.

Aspects of Strategy Implementation

Studies undertaken at the University of Warwick, in the UK, by Pettigrew and colleagues (Pettigrew and Whipp, 1992; Pettigrew *et al*, 1992) suggest that strategic change has been most successful when the interaction between five activities occurs (figure C9.2). These activities, which should be seen as an interacting system, are: environmental assessment, recognition of human resources as assets and liabilities, linking of strategic and operational change, leadership of change, and coherence.

Within our model these aspects are recognized. Environmental assessment is recognized through the identification of multiple futures as well as

Figure C9.2 Five elements of effective strategic change (based on studies by Pettigrew and Whipp).

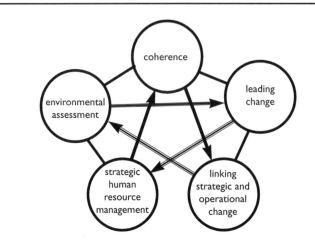

through identifying and managing stakeholders. Distinctive competencies are seen to be as much about the wisdom and special skills of human resources as about the technology of process. In addition, the emphasis upon participation in strategy making to create political feasibility emphasizes human resources as crucial. The focus on JOURNEY making is all about cognitive and emotional commitment – a human orientation. Linking operations with strategy comes through a recognition of the balance between continuity and change, and the delivery of strategy through the 'strategy map' that shows the links between actions, strategic programmes, strategies, and goals. Involving a top management team in a journey of strategy making and delivery is the basis for increasing the probability of leadership from key managers. The commitment to emotional as well as reasoned approaches (procedural rationality), that in turn leads to change, is more likely to generate energy as a primary leadership resource. Finally, the emphasis on coherence between the aspirations system, distinctive competencies, business model or livelihood scheme, stakeholder analysis and management, and attention to multiple futures ensures that coherence is continually audited and developed. The use of a computer based strategy map reinforces continual checking of coherence of detail, as each strategy statement as a node on the map is always seen within the context of its role as a means to an end, and also the context of the intentions which support it as an end in its own right. The map can be seen in overview or in detail enabling the detail and the whole to be checked for coherence (Eden and Cropper, 1992).

We have emphasized 'coherence' of strategy over and over again in this first part of the book. This is not an accident; we take it to be central to strategy making and to the probability of implementation (as suggested by Pettigrew's work). Our adherence to Kelly's personal construct theory is to acknowledge that people seek to make sense of their world by developing an internally consistent set of beliefs (within limits). Even though arguments exist about the role of cognitive consistency, by showing that elements of novelty and inconsistency are important parts of our mental life, nevertheless the theme of seeking consistency prevails. At the level of debate in decision making arenas, the charges of internal inconsistency and poor internal logic are the most damaging interventions that can be made. Even though this book has emphasized the social processes in organizations, our emphasis on coherence is intended to balance this orientation by suggesting that strategy should make a 'good case'. In practical terms, our experience suggests that participants in an organization can easily spot incoherent strategy – one where there are contradictions, double messages, soggy argument, where it does not come together as a 'piece', there is too much meaningless 'motherhood'. Often participants are not able to be specific about why they are unable to 'believe in it', but as they are helped in talking around and about it they gradually identify some, or all, of these characteristics. We have argued earlier that culture is partly a system of meanings which provide for the need to make sense of an ambiguous environment. Without attention to the coherence of strategy it is possible that organizations become characterized by the stress of espoused theories, which do not make sense conflicting with personal theories in use. This tension may then become one of the strongest forces for social change (Geertz, 1974), and new emergent strategizing, *which is set against* the (re)designed, or confirmed, or deliberate emergent, strategies occurs.

Being Realistic – priorities

Any thoroughgoing journey produces ambitious requirements for the organization. In addition, a proper recognition of the complexity of what is needed can throw an organization into confusion. These two facets are particularly true when the strategy is properly mapped out as an holistic interlocked system showing all of the complexity rather than reducing it by turning it into lists. A strategy map reflects statements of intent set fully within their context, and consequently the strategy actually looks as complex as it actually is! Members of the organization may be faced with too many demands, particularly given the need to 'keep the show on the road' as well as create a strategic future – the tension between continuity and change. Thus one aspect of closure is the need to establish priorities and recognize the additional demands on staff.

Being Realistic – creating organizational 'slack' for strategy delivery

Unless there are high levels of strategic slack, strategic change is almost impossible without consensus building through a strategy making journey.

The slack for radical change without consensus or incrementalism, big wins rather than small wins, only comes rarely. Strategic slack at this level often arises through crisis. Crises that may occur when territory, budget, reputation, and autonomy have been shifted through a step-wise deterioration in the well-being of the organization. Often a self-evident outside threat, or a massive growth opportunity allows new resources to be distributed where there will be no losers, only those who gain.

The need for organizational slack – in terms of the resources of cash and time – is one of the significant limitations on strategic change being implemented (Chakravarthy, 1982). However, often more important than cash and time is the need for resource slack in relation to employee energy that is driven by motivation. Slack can be bought in a number of ways. One means is through the use of external consultants to release the *routine* loads on managers, not to undertake the strategic change. Nevertheless, it must be appreciated that established commitments are difficult to shift (Monteverde and Teece, 1982). Moreover, when new commitments have been made as the result of well-designed JOURNEY making, they then become a routine addition to a manager's everyday task and can produce a massive overload. Given the recent move towards 'lean organizations' there is likely to be much less obvious slack for strategic change in the organizations of today.

Pettigrew (1985) argued that 'when strategic change does occur it tends to occur in radical packages – revolutionary periods interspersed with long periods of absorbing the impact of the radical changes, of further periods of incremental adjustment and then a period of education, persuasion and conditioning leading to the next revolutionary break'. This suggests that priorities may need to be bundled, where each bundle represents a particular cycle of strategic effort, rather than expecting continual delivery of the whole of the strategy. In practice, we find that a focus on more than five major strategic programmes at one time can cause confusion of effort and reduce effectiveness. However, it is important, when possible, to select programmes that lock together as a system of small wins creating a big win outcome. In addition, consideration can also be given to selecting action portfolios that not only support the five prioritized strategies but also go some way to supporting those strategies currently put on the 'back burner'. Similarly it is important to consider, *P441* when thinking about priorities, means of **ensuring that the overall programme for the given time period includes within it some 'quick wins'**. Quick wins are those which:

- do not require significant culture change;
- are probably already well under way because they fell out of the JOURNEY making as robust strategic changes in advance of closure;
- are linked to input provided from participants 'down the line', and so reinforce procedural justice;
- can 'kick start' a strategic programme.

These quick win actions not only provide spurts of progress and demonstrate commitment to the strategy project, but they make the future feel as though it might be manageable (Boal and Bryson, 1987).

Being Realistic – political feasibility through small wins

'Because strategic planning leads organizations to focus on what is fundamental, it may also lead them into the trap of pursuing 'big win' strategies when doing so may be quite unwise' (Bryson, 1988:13). By 'big win' strategies Bryson means something where big risks are taken and gigantic payoffs are achieved. Where big wins are achieved, the person in charge is a hero, but the opposite can also be true. Many managers skilfully move themselves into the top job after a sequence of small wins has created the impression of a big win, and then lay claim to it. For strategy makers 'changes in degree lead to changes in kind' (Karl Marx).

The initial thesis, expressed in chapter C2, for JOURNEY making was that strategic change can rarely be created through a big win strategy. Simply too much has to be done in concert for it to be realizable. In addition, the journey itself is a creator of change. When strategy making is successful, managers are *continuously changing their mind and making small adjustments, small wins*. These small wins gradually come together because they, step by step, move into concert. They occur less through some grand plan than because they are each coherent sets of action and are products of coherent thinking within the context of a growing strategic intent. The changes use coalitions of thought and of power and of continuous leadership. Successful strategic change, therefore, relates to the extent that the management team have translated a common and coherent construct system to other managers within the organization, and designed controls that permit creative and dynamic change to occur within the organization. Success at this level is rare, but the likelihood of strategic change is increased when these aspects of strategy making have been attended to. In chapter C1 we alluded to the dilemma of the need for strategic control systems versus flexibility and managerial autonomy. We suggested that 'it is important to note that the very process of *reflecting upon the contingent nature of the organization*, in order to determine the most appropriate approach to strategic management, *is itself a significant step in strategy making*'.

To some extent the successful imposition of strategic control makes it more likely that the only way a major strategic shift or 'big win' can be achieved is by finding new leaders with fundamentally different cognitive frameworks (Boland *et al*, 1990). We discuss this issue further below, but would argue here that the business of converting agreements into delivered and coherent strategic action across the organization is perhaps the most difficult problem facing strategy making.

JOURNEY making, as the basis of strategic change, is designed to create gradual, incremental change. There are many occasions when the nature of the strategic crisis facing an organization is such that 'big win' change is the only conceivable way forward. In these circumstances JOURNEY making is inappropriate.

Leadership

It is a matter of almost trivial comment that strategic change rarely takes place without strong and consistent leadership that is informed by the JOURNEY making process. We have seen excellent strategies, that have gained high levels of both cognitive and emotional commitment from large numbers of managers, not be delivered. This is because, in the end, the senior team did not provide leadership or even worse bickered amongst themselves. We are not suggesting that there is a need for a single charismatic leader, although that can help. Rather we are suggesting that the key members of the organization, including 'opinion formers', are seen to be 'putting their money where their mouth is'. For the most part strategic change is a collective activity, which is why we favour participation from many people in the journey. This means that a sense of collective leadership needs to be fostered. The use of teams to deliver parts of the strategy welds the strategy across an organization and ensures that strategy making is not seen as something different from strategy delivery, or 'running the shop'. The attitude of 'leaders' to this possible differentiation can be critical. If the organization's leaders continually demonstrate through their own actions (scripts, behaviour, problem identification, firefighting inclinations, decisions) a separation between considerations of strategy and considerations of day to day management then it is not surprising that others do the same. This often happens with those at that level of management who span a boundary between the requirement to join in strategic conversation 'at head office' on some days and 'manage the shop' on others (for example, divisional commanders in the police force) – they can easily develop complete mental separation between each of these activities.

Creating Strategic Intent and Structural Change

The way in which we understand the emergent strategizing of an organization, gives us a clue as to what needs to be changed in order to see this transformed. In chapter C5 we identified structural characteristics such as learning curves, costing systems, management information systems, and reward systems as a part of the emergent strategizing. We used these as clues as to what was and what wasn't being used to *filter out* aspects of the strategic environment (both internal and external) and to suggest one particular strategic direction rather than another. If we want to create newly emergent patterns of behaviour which are deliberate then these **structural characteristics of the organization** must be changed to reflect the new strategies. It is no use expecting cognitive change in the way strategic problems are construed as long as the data which provides the source of issue definition is not also changed. *It is important to consider that procedures, reward systems, and bureaucracies are aspects of an organization that are explored when trying to detect emergent strategizing. The corollary is that they must also be levers for strategic change.* For example, if scenarios are expected to be an important part of the strategic decision making routines, then it is important to embed them into the control mechanisms.

V247 P466

The development of standard operating procedures which map on to the strategic direction and associated vision statement are crucial to facilitating strategic change (Hannan and Freeman, 1984). As noted earlier, one of the important ways of detecting emergent strategizing is to investigate the implications of **standard operating procedures** for the strategic future of the organization. If this is so, then the procedures themselves must be contributors to change.

V261

'The practice of strategic control is much more complex than most writers on the subject have acknowledged. Problems include:

1. Devising strategic controls that can accommodate uncertainty and flexibility in the implementation of strategy.
2. Defining strategic goals that are suitable for motivating managers.
3. Ensuring that strategic control systems assist, rather than attempt to replace, management judgment.
4. Building a strategic control system that enhances, rather than destroys, mutual confidence between management levels.

While the benefits of strategic control remain theoretically attractive, there are evidently considerable difficulties in devising a practically useful strategic control system.'

This quotation is from 'The *Paradox* of Strategic Controls' by Michael Goold and John Quinn (1990) – our emphasis. Their view aptly summarizes our experience of creating adequate strategic control systems.

Strategic control is, perhaps, a particularly unhelpful label for ensuring that strategic actions are to be achieved. Van der Heijden (1991) has argued forcibly that 'short of coming to a much better shared understanding of the company's corporate strategic vision it is probably better to de-emphasize the accountability aspect of appraisal, and stress the joint learning and problem solving aspect'. Although the context for his assertion was that of appraising the performance of subsidiaries, we see joint learning within the context of strategy adjustment as the primary form of strategic control. Diagnostic control systems are designed to monitor and control performance by correcting deviations from plan. They depend on appropriate, and usually quantitative measures, so that exception reporting can be relied on. But *more often than not such measures are incomplete, inappropriate, and inaccurate and produce dysfunctional outcomes.* Controlling sales staff by calls made per week, for example, may increase sales calls but do nothing for sales closed. The search for quantitative measures in strategic control can destroy a strategy.

'The folly of rewarding A, while hoping for B' is the title of a classic article on reward systems (Kerr, 1995). The point of the article is 'that the types of behaviour rewarded are those which the rewarder is trying to discourage, while the behaviour desired is not being rewarded at all'. Often strategies reinforce the 'double-bind' implied in the quote from R.D. Laing at the beginning of chapter C5 – 'to play the game of not playing the game'. Examples of reward systems in organizations that attend to quantified short term performance indicators and yet expect longer term strategic behaviour abound – 'cooperate' versus 'compete', 'let's learn from mistakes' versus 'you will be punished if you make a mistake', 'take the initiative' versus 'don't break the rules'.

Kerr's article was first published in 1975 and yet is still very relevant today. Using their own 'advisory panel' the editors of the journal (in which it was published) asked the panel what the obstacles were to dealing with the 'folly'. They said:

- 'The inability to break out of the old ways of thinking about reward and recognition practices'
- 'Lack of holistic or overall system view of performance factors and results'
- 'Continuing focus on short term results by management and shareholders' (1995:15).

Each of these applies particularly to the role of reward systems in making strategy happen.

Project Management using the Strategy Delivery Support System (SDSS)

An SDSS can play an important supporting role in strategy delivery, and this is discussed in detail in part 3 of the book. Its role can be more profound than simply being a model of the strategy and associated actions. As we suggested above, it can provide a decision support system (DSS) on managers' desks, **a system that can ensure that those delivering actions are certain of the context within which their actions are to take place.** In addition the system can inform members as to what the rationale is for the

P463

actions they are to take, and what actions are needed to support them. In this way the system is akin to a project management system where it reflects dependencies and so can explore the reasons for blockages.

The most important role the SDSS can play is that of **focusing attention on to the *reasons* why actions are to take place**. Implementation blockages sometimes occur because while actions are taken, they are taken for the wrong reasons. For example, designing a new product with the strategic aim of demonstrating attention to quality and so building a reputation for quality (three statements linked up the strategy map) will need to be an important part of strategy review if the quality strategy is to met. Without a clear sense of the linkage it is possible that the strategic aims for the new product development get forgotten but the product is still developed. In a strategy map implementation can focus as much on the *connections between* the action nodes as the nodes themselves. Thus every action is to be done *in such a way* that it will achieve its expected purpose. Thus, the question, in our example, will always be 'are you developing the product in such a manner that it is demonstrating quality and will enable us to gain a reputation for quality?'. Each of these requirements of '*demonstrating*' and '*enabling* reputation' makes demands which may be ignored as 'new product development' becomes the focus isolated from its specific strategic aims. There are usually multiple ways of delivering an action, some of which are the reasons it is a part of the strategy while others simply enable the manager to 'tick off' the action as completed and yet do not contribute to strategy. It is these latter reasons that unnecessarily absorb the managers' time and become a part of the 'overload' which is seen to result from strategy making. Consequently, it is important to remember that *an action is not defined by the words but by the reasons – why it is to be done – and the supporting actions that help make it happen.*

The SDSS can also act as an interactive model for recording progress. Often strategic change depends upon a portfolio of several strategic programmes being delivered – that is, a systemic attack. If any of these programmes fall away then the whole strategy can fail. The symbolism of making progress and *the SDSS recording that progress* keeps energy levels up as staff remain motivated and engaged.

P464

Reviewing the Success of Strategy

Our starting point for the journey was to detect emergent strategizing. The purpose of doing this was to gain a feel for the unfolding strategic future of the organization. To achieve this, we considered both the structural and cultural/cognitive aspects of organizational behaviour. If this activity is appropriate for discovering the emergent strategic future the organization would create for itself, then it must also be an appropriate way of determining the success of strategy making. We expect success to be indicated by comparing strategic intent with the new emergent strategizing, and we expect the new emergent strategizing as a result of deliberate strategy making ('confirming and (re)designing strategy' – figure C2.4) to be different from that detected at the start of the journey.

Thus, success may be best determined by detecting, once again, the emergent strategizing. How is the organization working – procedurally and cognitively? What are the new emergent patterns of behaviour of the organization? What distinctive competencies now stand out and are they self-sustaining?

Distinguishing Strategic Performance from the Performance of Strategy

The evaluation of strategy has two very different aspects. The obvious measure of performance is that which derives from an evaluation of the extent to which the organization has met its aspirations – this is strategic performance. We argued in chapter C1 that such an activity is riddled with problems. The other aspect is that of evaluating whether the strategy contributed to the strategic performance of the organization – this is the performance of strategy. An organization may meet its aspirations without the strategy having made any contribution to this performance. Given the difficulty of strategy delivery and managing strategic change it is possible that an organization can continue to 'muddle through' and luckily meet its aspirations, at least to some extent, through an accident of the market or the economy. It is important to make some assessment of whether there is a relationship between strategic performance and strategy delivery.

One of the common pitfalls in the evaluation of strategic performance is to pay attention only to outputs, the traditional measures of success of an organization. These outputs should clearly be influenced by strategy, but not usually directly or in a way that is likely to be capable of correlation. Strategy is, after all, intended to be about putting into place a way of *managing the future* and allowing the organization to be coherently opportunistic – able to pounce on opportunities with the protection of the 'warm coat' of coherent strategic context. Thus, the proper evaluation of performance itself is dependent upon the process of strategy development

V261 P445   having **established 'success or performance indicators'** that can be easily recognized for being more directly related to particular strategies.

In addition, performance needs to be evaluated with respect to expectations of success, rather than against some absolute criteria. Such a process of evaluation inevitably risks self-congratulation, as success is viewed through 'rose-tinted' glasses. The likelihood of self-congratulation is higher when the management team have a high level of commitment and ownership of the strategy (which is what we have been seeking to attain). However, it is less likely when the team are confident in the coherence of the overall strategy and so prepared to learn about how it might be improved. Evaluation is also likely to be more productive when the management team do not feel threatened by punishment for failure.

> 'Scrutiny can be just as effective if it is made with a touch of gentleness, good humour and understanding' (Queen Elizabeth II of England, 1992)

To repeat van der Heijden (1991), strategy review should be characterized by a number of facets. These include drawing lessons from experience, promoting openness and free communications, ensuring no punishment for mistakes, welcoming challenges, and guarding against the organization feeling too competent.

Review and learning are crucial parts of the journey. Consequently, the direct involvement of the team in the evaluation of the journey is obviously crucial to any ownership of subsequent changes or outcomes of the evaluation. Thus the *process* of evaluation must be designed with the same objectives as other parts of the journey – to reduce the likelihood of 'bounded vision' and 'group-think' (Janis, 1972).

The purpose of undertaking the exercise with the management team is to continue ownership and encourage reflection. This purpose is not dependent upon the output of the evaluation but upon the effectiveness of the process design. Secondly, the purpose is to establish the degree of consensus in the evaluation. Finally, the process assists in the identification of key strategic issues that need to be addressed further during the coming period. Typically strategy review is most effective when it is a regular part of management team meetings – each meeting devoting some time to review of a part of the overall strategy (for example, one 'strategic programme'). However, it is helpful to undertake a **major review with respect to performance indicators established in relation to strategies and goals** at least once every year. *P468*

Strategic Performance *V213 P469*

Strategic performance must be related to:

- expected achievement given the environmental circumstances, and what would have happened using competing strategies, or at least the old strategy (which may have been emergent only) so as to acquire a relative measure of performance, and
- a network of aspirations, that are multiple criteria.

Given these demands, it is unrealistic to expect a process that can be any more than indicative, rather than absolutely accurate. A conversation focused on learning about the difficulties in delivery provides the highest payoff for the future because it provides a constructive approach to realizing implementation or adapting strategy to make it more 'realistic'. Thus an *exploration* of each individual goal, and the related strategies, with respect to expectations is the only realistic approach. We do not, of course, ignore the more routine managerial review of progress against agreed action programmes (using the SDSS as a DSS).

P436

P445

V261

The evaluation of strategy is traditionally dependent upon **establishing a set of performance indicators** that are clear cut, quantitative, and measurable – a process that may require an iterative approach as suggestions for the indicators are considered against strategies and adapted where necessary. It is both possible and helpful also to gather views about performance against **qualitative indicators**. A systemic approach to mapping a number of qualitative indicators, where no one indicator is an accurate or easily measured factor, can assure a more reliable understanding of performance than inappropriate adherence to measurable factors. Thus, we would not expect to measure the performance of a teacher by examination results alone, although these measurable outcomes might constitute one aspect of a performance indicator. We might want to explore the extent of learning, interest levels of students, ability to apply in practice, and so on (the quantitative versus qualitative debate discussed above).

For example, Govan Initiative sought to measure performance on the strategy 'improve the quality of living' using as one performance indicator: 'improve the visual quality of the environment through increasing the number of high quality local areas'. As a means to test the appropriateness of the indicator, participants in the process of evaluation attempted to show where on a scale of 0–100% achievement they currently felt the organization was positioned. Here the anchor points on the scale were related to their expectation of reasonable achievement over the given time period, thus 100% was the best they might have expected from a fully successful delivery of the strategy over the given time period. Not only did this help them assess whether the indicator was appropriate – could be used in practice – but it also provided a benchmark against which a review could be examined. This approach (described in chapter P7) used a social process to elicit views about performance and thus ensured the members' commitment to, and understanding of, the measures.

The outcome is intended to encourage discussion and subsequent modification of the strategy. Alongside this process is a process that categorizes the strategies and/or strategic programmes into four quadrants of performance (see figure C9.3). The performance of strategy becomes categorized as 'magic' – where 'we got there but don't know how', 'brilliant' – where 'we got there and it seems to be because we knew what we were doing to make us get there', 'try harder' – where 'we seem to know what we ought to do, but it's not having the desired effect', and 'disaster' – where 'nobody knows what to do or how to do it, and we aren't meeting our aspirations'. By so doing, the strategy can be modified to reflect the realities of strategy implementation as seen by those who

Figure C9.3 Evaluating strategic performance.

IMPLEMENTATION

100%

Achievement

MAGIC:
unknowing
progress

BRILLIANT:
strategy and
outcome related

0%   Understanding   100%
                      and commitment

GOALS AND
STRATEGY

DISASTER:
no understanding
and no implementation

TRY HARDER:
difficulty
'making it happen'

0%

must have an ownership and emotional commitment to the logic of the strategy and its continuing impact. Where strategies appear in the 'disaster' quadrant this suggests that additional effort (both in terms of energy and understanding) must be employed. The use of the quadrants, or others that get at the issues of linkage between delivery of strategy and strategic outcomes, is useful. In part this is because it enables 'Post-its' to be placed and moved around a chart 'on-the-wall' and in part because the clusters then can be explored to see whether there is linkage and commonality between the strategies that appear in each of the quadrants.

Having got a measure of the performance of individual strategies it is useful to add a second dimension to the analysis and evaluate whether implementation success (or not) is the result of an understanding of strategy existing across the managers of the organization. In chapter C4 we considered the issues that determine the degree of participation in strategy. Participation was aimed at building increased alignment through cognitive and emotional commitment, and cognitive commitment is derived from creating and managing shared meaning and understanding (Pettigrew, 1977). In this analysis we revisit these issues by plotting understanding and commitment against the degree of achievement of each goal and strategy. The outcome of the analysis may suggest that short cuts, by lower participation, were mistaken.

The figures C9.3 to C9.5 show the stages in the analysis. Figure C9.3 categorizes the strategies into a school report of 'brilliant', 'try harder', 'disaster', and 'magic'. Figure C9.4 offers simple explanations and figure C9.5 describes the nature of the organizational learning opportunities for three of the outcomes.

Figure C9.4   Evaluating possible implementation difficulties.

Figure C9.5   Focusing on learning.

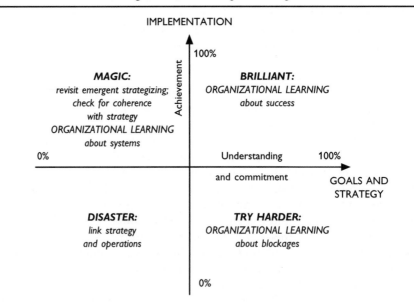

The Performance of Strategy and the Performance of Strategy Making Assumptions

Strategy is of any value only if it is built on firm founding assumptions about how to manage the strategic future of the organization. If the assumptions are wrong, then there is no basis for strategic *management*. 'There can be no intervention without a theory of intervention, and a strategy is about making theories of strategic intervention explicit and known throughout an organization'. As others have argued (Lorange *et al*, 1986; Schreyogg and Steinmann, 1987), changes in the assumptions that underlie strategy need to be monitored both for shifts in the 'world-taken-for-granted' and in relation to the robustness of the assumptions. Strategic assumptions are retrospective theories about how the world is going to be, in the sense of how the world will work. In part 3 we consider in detail the process of evaluating strategic assumptions – determining whether the 'arrows' in the strategy map are still taken to be valid and considering the consequences of them not being so.

The validity of the assumptions made during the strategy development process and in particular during the negotiation of the strategy are central to the future success of the strategy. These assumptions are the arrows on the strategy map. Exploring these assumptions is the core organizational learning outcome from strategy review. Whilst assessing strategies against achievement and understanding (above) provides a useful interim progress report, review is also necessary of the goals, strategies, and links between them. Examining the aspirations of the organization to determine whether they are still appropriate, and then examining each link that supports the strategy, enables the management team to review their choice of strategies and, if necessary, redesign the strategic intent accordingly.

Strategy is therefore expressed as a network of theories or assumptions about what strategic objectives are expected to be achieved (the strategy map). An analysis of the structure of these statements (that is the way in which they are related one to another) divides the network into 'natural' clusters, with these being the basis for identifying the core strategies. Each cluster usually represents one strategy, with subordinate strategic programmes relating not only to one cluster but sometimes to several clusters. Analysis of the structure of the strategy map reveals those strategic assumptions that are most significant to the achievement of the overall strategy. The assumption (link) is significant when, if the assumption were untrue, a substantial part of the strategy as a whole would become untenable. It is these assumptions that must be reviewed regularly – typically once a year.

Earlier, we introduced the key concepts that determine effective organizational learning (chapter C4). Closure and strategy review contribute extensively to the learning process. The major concern for any process design that facilitates organizational learning about the assumptions built into the strategy must be to encourage 'standing back' from the

Figure C9.6 The dilemma of alignment versus differentiation.

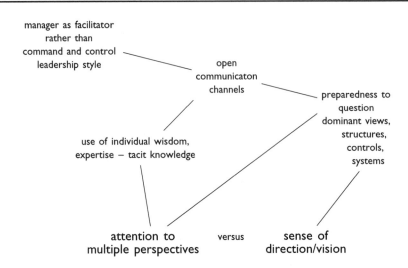

strategy itself. There is inevitably a danger that the continuing need for commitment to the strategy gets in the way of exploration and questioning. The dilemma is, once again, that of balancing a retention of alignment with the need for differentiation of view about what is and is not working in creating strategic change (figure C9.6) – structures and control systems can reinforce the sense of direction/vision but reduce the need for attention to multiple perspectives.

Despite the view that strategy assumptions must be reviewed, many recent research papers suggest that most organizations find it extremely difficult to do so (for example, Zajac and Shortell, 1989). This is particularly so for those that have chosen to develop strategies at the extreme end of the planning element of the contingency spectrum – where plans are detailed for many years with budgets set (see figure C1.1). Indeed, we see many public organizations who have been forced into the detailed planning approach by central government as a means of ensuring public accountability. These organizations often find they are within a straight-jacket and that the pain of strategic change is great, as procedures, and culture, act as negative forces and those actions not achieved are held up as failures – **strategy becomes a 'hostage to fortune'**. To some extent an incorrect positioning of the strategy outcome on the contingency continuum can be blamed for the inadequacy to change.

P456

THE JOURNEY MAKING MODEL: A SUMMARY

'Experience – a comb, life gives you after you lose your hair' (Judith Stern)

This brief chapter provides a summary of the JOURNEY making model. It begins with determining 'Who is the client?', the first point in any intervention. Four key figures are presented as summaries of (i) this part of the book about the underlying concepts (figures C10.1–10.3), and (ii) the practice part of the book (figure C10.4). Figure C10.1 presents the overall conceptual model for JOURNEY making, and figures C10.2 and C10.3 summarize, respectively, the first substantive part of JOURNEY making – that of 'Detect Emergent Strategizing' – and then a depiction of the major tasks discussed in chapters C5–C9. The summary, as text, focuses on the tasks as if they were stages; however, they should *not* be treated in this way – the final section reinforces the point that the entire process is cyclical.

The JOURNEY is a *process*
and so has process outcomes – building political feasibility
and
the JOURNEY is *cyclical*
not sequential (as represented below)

Who is the client?

- Identify *who* is the *client* and *sponsor* for JOURNEY making (it will not be the organization, but rather an individual manager, stakeholder, or possibly small team).
  – Chapter P9
- Determine, with the client, who is to make up the 'management team' – who are to be the focus for the JOURNEY making and the power brokers in terms of final agreements about strategic management.
  – Chapters C4, P5, P9

Figure C10.1   The JOURNEY of strategy making and delivery explained.

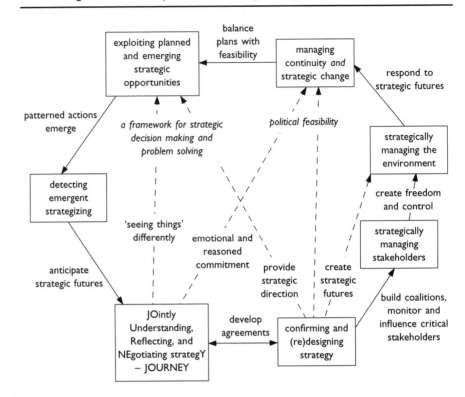

Detect Emergent Strategizing

- What do the procedures and systems (costing, reward, information, etc.) say about the nature of an unfolding strategic future? Explore the embedded routines, 'recipes', the way resources are allocated, the way information frames problems and the way they are addressed.
  - Chapter C5
- What does the management team see as the important strategic issues and strategic problems facing the organization, and how do they think about these issues (their perceived causes and consequences)? What are the fears and hopes of members of the management team? What strategic options are implied by the explanations for these issues and problems? Interview managers – to derive 'cognitive maps' or use 'oval mapping technique' workshops, and so develop a team 'cause map' as a hierarchy of embedded aspirations, strategic issues, strategic problems and strategic options.
  - Chapters C5, P1, P2
- What do these procedures, systems, and strategic issues imply about the embedded aspirations system of the organization? What is

Figure C10.2 Anticipating strategic futures.

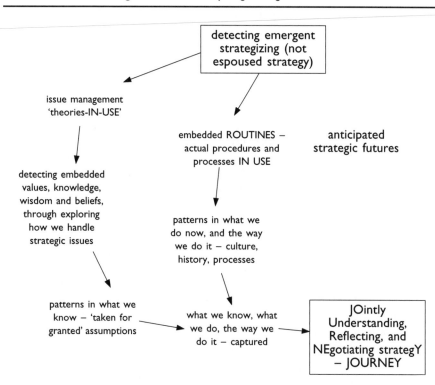

expected to be achieved by addressing the issues? Infer the driving forces of organizational behaviour and so issue identification. Ladder upwards from issues towards 'goals' and 'negative-goals'.
- Chapters C5, P1, P2, P7

JOint Understanding

- How does the management team respond to the unfolding strategic future implied by the emergent strategizing (embedded aspirations, issues, problems) which has been uncovered? Is it attractive? Depressing? Worrying? What is believed to be happening in the organization and outside world to generate the issues? If the initial strategy map is thin on elaboration (options, explanations) then, with individuals or the group, ladder down from issue and problem labels to elaborate emergent beliefs? Try the 'Oracle' question.
  - Chapter C5
- How might this response modify the emergent aspirations system?
- How comfortable is the team with the modified aspirations system which has emerged from considering strategic issues and the strategic

impact of procedures and systems? Try formulating a vision or mission statement from the draft aspirations system – how does it feel?
    – Chapter P3

Reflection

- Can the distinctive competencies of the organization support the aspirations? Does the organization have any distinctive competencies (unique patterns of competencies)? Reflect upon competencies, and explore the patterning in their relationship one to another. Patterns, particularly self-sustaining loops, suggest distinctiveness.
    – Chapters C6, P6
- Explore the logic of the links that suggest that distinctive competencies can support aspirations – consider whether these links are the basis for the 'business model' or 'livelihood scheme'.
- Reflect upon the link between distinctive competencies and aspirations. Is it strong enough to sustain a livelihood? What new, or modified, competencies need to be acquired in order to attain the aspirations system? What modifications to the aspirations system are required so that the business model or livelihood scheme is realistic?
    – Chapters C6, P3
- Formulate, in draft form, strategies for the development and modification of competencies and distinctive competencies so that the business model or livelihood scheme is viable strategically.
- *Consider extended participation beyond the management team* – consideration of 'anticipated winners and losers' as participants?
    – Chapter P5
- *Cycle around the above stages with other participant teams*
    – Chapters C3, C4, P2
- *Consolidate the emerging strategy map* as an embedded aspirations system, strategic issues, strategic problems, strategic options.

NEgotiate strategY

- Negotiate and agree the aspirations system, so that it is realistic, practical and yet still aspirational. *and/or*
- Negotiate and agree strategies for developing new distinctive competencies, and maintaining those which are core to the business model or livelihood scheme.
- Build a draft vision or mission statement based on a combination of the aspirations system and the business model/livelihood scheme.
    – Chapter P3

Figure C10.3 The framework for developing agreements.

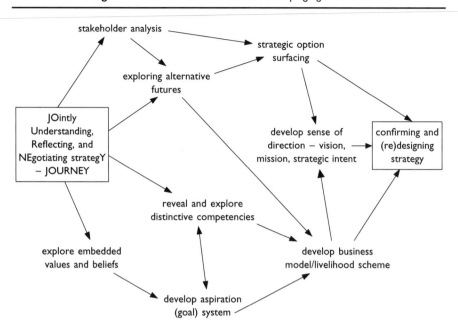

- Monitor/check the political feasibility of delivering these strategies. Use data from participant workshops.
- Determine the appropriate nature of strategic management – providing a strategic framework only through to fully developed strategic plans. Consider the nature of the business model/livelihood scheme as the basis for this Reflection and NEgotiation.
  - Chapter C1
- Agree the first draft of strategic direction/strategic intent (a draft which has not formally accounted for stakeholders or multiple futures). The first draft of the strategy map as an aspirations system (goals and negative-goals linked together as a network), draft strategies, strategic programmes, action portfolios.

JOint Understanding and Reflection

- Build an understanding of the relative power and interest of potential stakeholders. Which of these are the most significant for the strategic future of the organization (high power/high interest)? Construct the 'power/interest grid' with management teams.
- Reflect upon the bases of the power and the basis of interest of 'players' (and note the other 'actors' – that is 'strategy context setters') as actors in environmental scenarios. Construct 'star diagrams'.
  - Chapters C7, P4

- Build an understanding of the important alternative futures the organization may have to face. Include powerful context setters.
  - Chapters C8, P4
- In the light of these futures, should the nature of strategic management be modified to be less elaborated and be more flexible and opportunistic?
  - Chapters C1, P4

NEgotiate strategY

- Effect strategic management of stakeholders by considering coalitions, shifting the power base of 'players' so they become 'strategy context setters' or 'subjects', shifting the basis of interest of subjects so they become players (or vice-versa).
  - Chapters C7, P4
- Effect strategic management of the environment in the light of reflecting on multiple futures.
  - Chapters C8, P4
- Negotiate a new draft strategy based upon possible futures and the necessities of stakeholder management.
- Begin the process of closure of strategy making.
  - Chapters C9, P7, P8
- Develop commitments, action programmes.
  - Chapter P7
- Agree resourcing, control systems, procedures, reward systems.
  - Chapter C8, P7
- Agree performance indicators for goals and strategies.
  - Chapter P7
- Build and sustain cognitive and emotional commitment. Check political feasibility. Who are the anticipated winners and losers? Have they been a part of the strategic thinking of the management team?
  - Chapters P5, P6
- Build a Strategy Delivery Support System (SDSS) encompassing performance indicators.
  - Chapters C9, P7

Design Organizational Learning through Strategy Review

- Redetect emergent strategy – compare and contrast.
- Review the performance of strategy and strategic performance of the organization against performance indicators.
  - Chapters C7, P8

Figure C10.4   JOURNEY making – a brief summary of methods, techniques and tools.

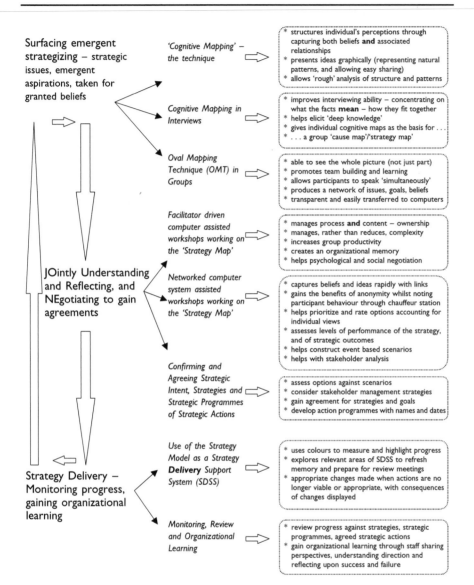

Surfacing emergent strategizing – strategic issues, emergent aspirations, taken for granted beliefs

'Cognitive Mapping' – the technique

* structures individual's perceptions through capturing both beliefs **and** associated relationships
* presents ideas graphically (representing natural patterns, and allowing easy sharing)
* allows 'rough' analysis of structure and patterns

Cognitive Mapping in Interviews

* improves interviewing ability – concentrating on what the facts **mean** – how they fit together
* helps elicit 'deep knowledge'
* gives individual cognitive maps as the basis for . . .
* . . . a group 'cause map'/'strategy map'

Oval Mapping Technique (OMT) in Groups

* able to see the whole picture (not just part)
* promotes team building and learning
* allows participants to speak 'simultaneously'
* produces a network of issues, goals, beliefs
* transparent and easily transferred to computers

Facilitator driven computer assisted workshops working on the 'Strategy Map'

* manages process **and** content – ownership
* manages, rather than reduces, complexity
* increases group productivity
* creates an organizational memory
* helps psychological and social negotiation

JOintly Understanding and Reflecting, and NEgotiating to gain agreements

Networked computer system assisted workshops working on the 'Strategy Map'

* captures beliefs and ideas rapidly with links
* gains the benefits of anonymity whilst noting participant behaviour through chauffeur station
* helps prioritize and rate options accounting for individual views
* assesses levels of performance of the strategy, and of strategic outcomes
* helps construct event based scenarios
* helps with stakeholder analysis

Confirming and Agreeing Strategic Intent, Strategies and Strategic Programmes of Strategic Actions

* assess options against scenarios
* consider stakeholder management strategies
* gain agreement for strategies and goals
* develop action programmes with names and dates

Strategy Delivery – Monitoring progress, gaining organizational learning

Use of the Strategy Model as a Strategy **Delivery** Support System (SDSS)

* uses colours to measure and highlight progress
* explores relevant areas of SDSS to refresh memory and prepare for review meetings
* appropriate changes made when actions are no longer viable or appropriate, with consequences of changes displayed

Monitoring, Review and Organizational Learning

* review progress against strategies, strategic programmes, agreed strategic actions
* gain organizational learning through staff sharing perspectives, understanding direction and reflecting upon success and failure

PART 2

VIGNETTES

The Vignettes – Introduction

This part of the book is designed to help readers gain a feel for how JOURNEY making occurs in practice. To this end, we decided to use a series of vignettes describing a variety of episodes taken from a range of organizations. Each vignette describes either a different approach to the same part of the journey, or a different part of the journey. However, for a number of reasons, discussed below, it is not possible to cover all possible ways of JOURNEY making or provide a complete story.

For example, we use more vignettes taken from public or not-for-profit organizations than from others. It is easier to for us to publish material from these organizations because much of this material is, in any event, in the public domain. Work on strategy making for commercial organizations inevitably depends upon confidentiality, indeed it is unlikely to be of strategic significance if it were available for publication (unless such publication were a part of stakeholder management!). For similar reasons there are no examples of work which illustrate the development of a 'livelihood scheme', because for all types of organization it would be inappropriate to publish distinctive competencies. Although we introduced briefly the organizations featured here in Chapter C1, as the vignettes unfold it will be possible to develop a more intimate understanding of these organizations, the client, key actors and other participants.

It is obvious that these vignettes describe events from our own perspective. However, they have each been ratified by the client. Inevitably others within each of the organizations would have other stories to tell. It is, of course, important to note that a client's perspective will always be different from that of other participants. The client is likely to want many outcomes from the journey which are not declared to others. Thus, the client's, and so facilitators', criteria of success will be complex and often at odds with the criteria used by other key actors. Strategic change usually involves winners and losers – the client will usually be a winner!

The vignettes are also, for the most part, episodes within success stories. Needless to say, although the sample size is relatively large, there are few failures. This is not necessarily because the approach we have developed, and described in this book, is faultless. Rather it reflects the extent to which clients choose us and the approach to strategic change because they believe it might work and we believe it might work. If we, or the potential client, suspect it might not work then we would be unlikely to continue with the intervention. In this way the potential for failure is inevitably relatively low, and the population of projects undertaken is biased in favour of success. In this book we have attempted to set out the theoretical and conceptual reasons why JOURNEY making makes sense (part 1 – chapters C1 to C10) and present the methods, techniques, and tools which turn this theory into practice (part 3 – chapters P1 to P9). We trust that the contents of the book persuade the reader that success in strategic change is more likely when these theories and methods are employed. However, we also trust that the reader will discover the important contingencies that influence judgement about the likelihood of success in any particular setting.

All of the stories involve the authors as facilitators. To use the stories of others who have employed the JOURNEY making approach would be problematic because (i) we were not there, (ii) we would be unable to validate the stories with the clients, and (iii) we would be uncertain that the JOURNEY making theories would have been employed in a coherent and consistent manner. We argue that one of the significant issues for successful strategic change is attention to process issues, in particular power and politics. These issues can be known intimately only by those directly involved in facilitating the approach. We have tried to provide, within the vignettes, a level of intimacy which would not be possible through the stories of others.

Some of the most 'juicy' bits relating to the politics of strategic change cannot be published without insult or embarrassment. However, we have been able to illustrate some of the important issues of process by changing the names and specific detail of the episodes. Thus, in some instances, the stories have been modified to protect people and organizations. Where this has been done both the client and ourselves believe that the essential features of the story remain. For many of the vignettes the name of the client is their own (and is signalled by the surname being noted), and in all cases the client has agreed that our version of events matches their own (but not necessarily that of other participants, who were often not fully aware of the objectives of the journey, and anyway were not the 'client'). In all cases the client has written the 'postscript'.

How to read the vignettes

The reader is invited to read the book by starting with any of the three parts. We expect practising managers to start with the vignettes, become interested in either (i) why the particular part of the journey being presented was undertaken – and so cross refer to the relevant paragraphs, or range of paragraphs, of the 'theory and concepts' chapters, or (ii) the detail of the methods, tools, and techniques being used – and so cross refer to the relevant paragraphs, or range of paragraphs, of the 'practice' part of the book. We expect academics to enter the book through the first part. This part describes the rationale and conceptual framework that drives the JOURNEY making approach to strategic change. While reading about the conceptual foundation it is likely that they become interested in (i) how it works in practice – and so cross refer to the relevant paragraphs of a number of vignettes which illustrate that specific part of the framework, or (ii) the methods used to apply the part of the journey discussed conceptually. We expect consultants and facilitators to start by reading some aspect of part 3 as a result of a specific personal interest in the practice of working with a group on a particular part of a journey. It is anticipated that they then will become interested in (i) how it works in practice – and so cross refer to the relevant paragraphs of a number of vignettes illustrating that specific part of the framework, or (ii) why the particular part of the journey being presented was undertaken – and so cross refer to the relevant paragraphs, or paragraph range, of the 'theory and concepts' chapters. We hope that all readers will move around the three parts of the book in a manner reflecting their own interests, and will not feel constrained to read the book in sequence.

As with elsewhere in the book, the cross referencing system is based on phrases set in **bold** in the text. Each of the phrases signals a cross reference to a particular paragraph elsewhere in the other two parts of the book.

Figure V1 shows each of the vignettes set out on the continuum of deliberate emergent strategy to planned strategy (see chapter C1). Those towards the left end of the continuum are organizations whose strategies were developed to provide strategic direction and intent only, whereas those towards the right end involved more detailed planning. The primary topics discussed within each vignette are discussed in the short summary provided at the beginning of each vignette along with details of the company and cast list. In this way readers can locate topics of specific interest and so a vignette that illustrates the chosen topic.

Figure VI The vignettes – an overview related to the deliberate-emergent to planned strategy continuum.

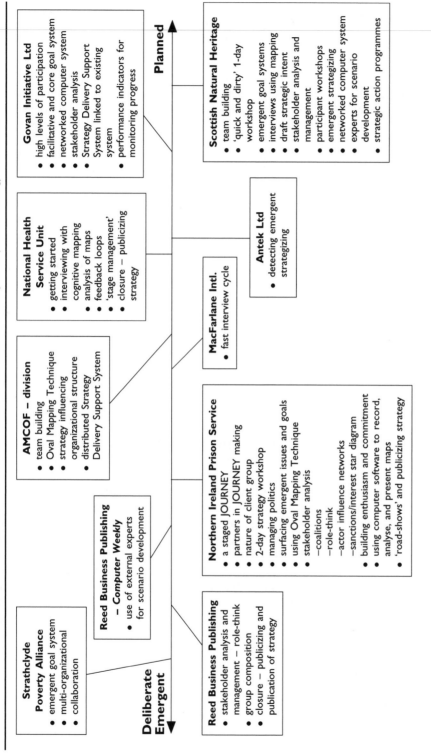

Scottish Natural Heritage – a conservation organization formed from merging two organizations

The Organization: Scottish Natural Heritage. A Non-Departmental Public Body (NDPB) which has a role in the process of national government but is not a government department or a part of one. The organization is therefore independent of government but nevertheless accountable to it. It was set up to both conserve and enhance the environment whilst facilitating enjoyment and understanding of it. It was formed in 1992 through the merging of two separate conservation organizations.

The Vignette: Team building. 'Quick and dirty' 1-day strategy workshop. Emergent goal system. Interviews using cognitive mapping. Developing draft strategic intent. Stakeholder analysis and management. Participant workshops. Emergent strategizing. Networked computer assisted workshops. Using 'experts' for scenario development. Strategic action programmes.

The Cast List: The client and sponsor – Roger Crofts, the Chief Executive. The Management Team: Angus, Geoff, Bob, Barbara, Sandra, Kim, Samantha, and Kevin. Two facilitators – Colin and Fran.

Roger was seeking help as to how he was going to find a way of producing (in his words) 'a strategy for the management team, focusing on its role of *managing* SNH which we [the team] have collective ownership for, rather than the many "planning" documents which we have *not* collectively created'? One of his biggest challenges was that he was trying to bring together two previously separate organizations into a merged new single one. There was a significant culture difference, and also many of the management team had come from a central government background. The expression management 'team' was probably a misnomer.

In addition he wanted something practical. Something that would provide tangible output, but not so practical as their last effort towards **team building**! This had involved them going on an outdoor team building exercise (including rafting – or was it sinking – on a large, deep lake) with disastrous results! Many of the team (especially Roger) found the event individually threatening, but it did indicate to all of them the scale of the task of leadership. Roger wanted something that would provide him with **process *and* content**; however, he and his team were extremely wary of embarking on any such event again . . .

Consequently, he had no intention of launching upon some grand plan. Nevertheless, after meeting with Colin and discussing options he was prepared to dab a wary toe in the water again (not a lake though) and try out Colin's suggestion. This was to start with a **'quick and dirty' one-day** strategy workshop using 'oval mapping' and with the primary aim of jointly understanding each other's view about the strategic issues facing

C17 P374

P380

C103

the organization. The management team had planned to get together soon anyway, so why not add an extra day to this event and see what unfolded. While making it clear in his briefing letter that '**no commitments beyond the day** have been agreed with the consultants', Roger noted that the objectives of the workshop would be to: *P375*

- surface strategic issues (we) face as a management team;
- consider a wide range of external environmental factors, some of which we seek to manipulate;
- consider the reaction of the different stakeholders inside and outside of SNH;
- identify an emergent goal system and mission statement.

This set of tasks was one Colin and Fran had used before (in various permutations) and one they felt happy with.

Time passed . . . The workshop was held and the team were left pondering what next . . .

Riding high on the success of the first 'quick-and-dirty' workshop Colin and Fran discussed next steps with Roger. Reflecting on the day, they noted that at the end of the workshop the participants had been very exuberant. Comments like 'this was magical – we made so much progress without the usual tensions' were typical. In addition, when reviewing the workshop the management team had indicated they wanted the exercise to continue. Colin was keen on finding a means of elaborating the emergent key issues. Due to the workshop's time constraints a broad raft of issues had surfaced but with little depth and conflicting views. They needed fuller exploration. Roger, Fran, and Colin also were not convinced that all of the issues had surfaced. There was a danger that, because the management team was not really a team, the underlying tensions may have resulted in **various issues not being aired**. If these issues could be *P374* surfaced and/or further developed then it would provide a focus for a more intensive and thorough workshop, possibly leading to the **negoti-** *P424* **ation of a strategic intent**. In addition, Roger was concerned that Angus, a key member of his team, who due to illness had not been able to attend the 1-day event, should have a **chance to contribute**. Time management was *P400* also an issue – Roger was keen to keep up the momentum. Fran suggested a round of interviews using cognitive mapping.

They could use the issues from the one-day event as an agenda and also collect reflections on the workshop – after the euphoria of the day had worn off. If they prepared a set of maps from the **Oval Mapping** part of *P303* the 1-day workshop and then explored these with each of the management team members they could add material as the interview unfolded. Interviewees could fill in the detail of the issues, and at the same time become more familiar with the mapping way of working. They also decided to do Angus's interview first. This would allow any new issues that surfaced to

C53   be introduced to others in their interviews – a form of **procedural justice**. To make the plan more robust they also included the option of doing two interviews with him, once at the beginning and once at the end of the

P297   series. Doing **two interviews** would give Angus extra air time but also provide a means of getting beyond the set script that often unfolds on the first interview (after all he didn't know either Fran or Colin). Once the interviews were carried out, the material could be entered into the

C72   computer model **merging of all the maps to create a 'strategy map'**. This would be the basis for a second workshop – what did Roger think?

'Yes, that would be good – but would I be interviewed too?', responded Roger. 'Of course – it's absolutely essential to get the Chief Executive's

P475   view, as **client**, throughout', Colin emphasized. A quick review of participants' diaries, alongside Fran and Colin's revealed that it would be possible to manage to complete the round of interviews in a relatively short period of time. Both Fran and Colin were keen to ensure that the interviews were scheduled within a fortnight of the workshop – what they referred to

P302   as a **'psychological week'**. Fran would interview Angus, Geoff, Bob, Barbara, and Sandra whereas Colin would speak to Kim, Samantha, Kevin, and of course Roger. Roger agreed to make the necessary arrangements.

Interviewing Angus was a challenge (not just because it was difficult to find his office) because he simply wouldn't stop talking! The only chances

P293   Fran did have, to **keep up with her mapping**, were when his staff interrupted them. Although normally Fran would have worked hard to discourage these constant interruptions as it broke the flow of thought and possibly inhibited the interviewee, Angus appeared to have no such concerns – he was apparently not worried about letting others know what he thought. 'Given his confidence', Fran thought, 'he is probably outspoken about his views and isn't concerned about others hearing him.' No fundamentally new issues emerged from his interview – reassuring to both Fran and Colin – they could build on the material surfaced during the 'quick and dirty' 1-day workshop.

The other interviews went according to plan with deeper views being expressed and considerable elaboration added to the workshop material. During the interviews some of the management team tempered their initial enthusiasm for the exercise with comments such as 'one day is OK but can we make this work have any real effect on the organization or on our effectiveness as a management team?' – a view noted by Fran and Colin. Once the interviews were completed Colin and Fran then pulled together the individual's maps into an aggregated strategy map using the computer software. They began to prepare for a 2-day workshop using a number of the analyses of maps available to them [see chapter P6] . . .

Time passed . . . Work on the aggregated map continued with particular areas being examined . . .

While working on the design of the workshop [chapter P5], which in this

P429   case was for 2 days, Fran and Colin went back to the **draft mission**

statement they had created at the 'quick and dirty' 1-day event. At the time the group had been very committed to it, but would that continue given that Angus had not provided input to its construction and further material had been surfaced through the follow-up interviews? Whilst discussing this, Roger intervened. He wanted to be clear about 'how the mission statement was produced and how it fitted in with the **mandate** *P428* provided by Act of Parliament related to the existing mission statement that had been approved by the Board, and with the rest of the workshop'.

Colin explained that the draft mission statement was simply a normal text statement of the map of the **goal system** they had developed together. *C98* 'Got it,' said Roger, 'I had become attached to the goal system as a map and had not really paid much attention to the link with the "sentence" based version.' Colin and Fran reflected that they had, up to this point, not spent much time describing the logic of the first workshop. They had said nothing about why they had taken a **strategic issue management** per- *C90 P314* spective and worked the goals up from them. As was often the case when starting work with a client, they had reckoned that it was more important to simply do something effective. To give Roger a better feel for the fairly routine procedure of drafting a mission statement from a goal system, and to continue to build a good client relationship [chapter P9], they decided to go back over the first workshop. The 'quick and dirty' workshop had comprised a session using the Oval Mapping Technique (OMT) in the morning. This session had surfaced a number of issues along with detailed comment which made the cluster of Ovals a map of an issue. These issues had acted as a stepping off point for identifying possible emergent goals. Each cluster had been examined and the group asked 'Why is this an issue? What aspiration is it protecting or driving?'. The group had laddered upwards from one possible goal to the next until the last to be identified seemed to get close to realizing the mandate. Through this procedure possible goals, for example, 'develop an effective board/staff relationship to expedite decision making' and 'establish effective partner- ships' had emerged. Each goal had then been examined to ensure that it was a good outcome, or aspiration, in its own right. Also they had been explored in relation to all the others identified to determine whether it supported other goals (or resulted from them), and to clarify meaning. The result of this effort was a goal system consisting of 11 interrelated goals.

Constructing a mission statement from this goal system had then been a mechanical process of adding text to the hierarchical structure to improve the flow but retaining the hierarchy by starting with the most superordinate goal and then weaving in the remainder of the system. Roger was reminded that the statement, in this form, was not like a final mission statement because it missed the **drama and style** that would make *C110* it attention grabbing, but it was the draft basis for working up a mission statement.

Roger reflected that he rather preferred the map of goals because it showed the way each goal sustained higher order goals and was sup- ported by others. He reflected that he would prefer Colin and Fran to keep the map as the working picture for the next workshop and ignore the text version . . .

Time passed . . . The Management Team 2-day workshop had been completed, now they needed to reflect on the workshop and consider the results . . .

It seemed to Roger, Fran, and Colin that the two-day workshop had been a success. They had reviewed and revised substantially the goal system – that had taken almost a morning in itself. Alongside this they had

P290
P338
explored each of the **key issues**, prioritized them (providing the group with some potential strategies) using the computer networked **preferencing system**, and finally worked up these prioritized strategies with viable options. The group had become engaged by the process and didn't want to stop now – there were so many things to do. The next step was for Colin

P420
and Fran to produce some **hard copy feedback** so that the team could begin working on some of the agreements made at the end of the 2-day workshop.

'What sort of information will you include?' asked Roger. 'I thought I would put together a pack of material covering all of the stages of the workshop', replied Fran. 'I usually include (a) a small diagram represent-

P409
ing symbolically the overall **'tear-drop'** of **hierarchical categories** (figure V2 [and figure C5.3]), (b) a map representing the goal system, (c) maps showing how the strategies and key issues relate to the goals, (d) a set of maps depicting the strategies with their associated option portfolios [the ones completed during the workshop], (e) the issues requiring further development and elaboration [these were the maps a sub-group would focus upon], and (f) the results of the computer based preferencing exercise. To help participants recall what happened I will print out the maps in colour – it makes it easier to link between what was seen on the

P420 P421
screen and the maps.' The diagram (figure V2) simply acts as a **'road map'** for the rest of the material, with the maps depicting slices of the model – allowing those working on specific tasks to focus on the material.

The feedback would also serve as a record noting the progress made, and rationale for decisions. Alongside this hard copy material, the com-

C71 P321
puter model would act as an **electronic organizational memory**. To manage the outputs from the workshop, the management team split itself into two sub-groups – each sub-group being responsible for the completion of a task. One sub-group was to focus on completing the option generation process for those key issues that had not been addressed in the workshop.

C119: C129
The other would carry out some **stakeholder analysis** leading to **stakeholder management strategies**. This second task stemmed from the discussion (at the workshop) of the goal of 'influence others to care for the natural heritage'.

The 'purples sub-group' (as they called themselves – key issues having been coloured purple) met together for the first time with Colin and Fran and then continued to work on their own. To help them they used the

Figure V2   Feedback 'road map'.

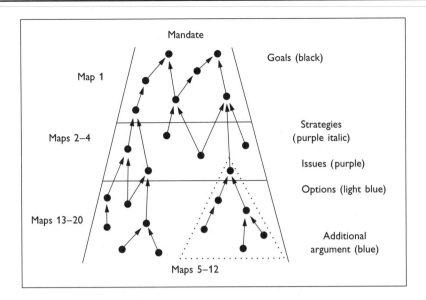

maps from the feedback pack. Their intention was to work directly on the maps and then get Fran to update the model. Their main task was to agree priorities among the key issues, and to reflect upon the clusters of issues that should be worked on further. Roger deliberately did not attend these sessions so that the group could discuss priorities without his direct influence and then subsequently report back to him. He decided this would give them a greater chance of negotiating agreement amongst themselves and creating a higher level of group ownership.

The stakeholder analysis and management sub-group decided that they would like more extensive help from Colin and Fran – what was the best way to surface and then examine the stakeholders? An initial half day was agreed upon. The session started with Colin asking the group to suggest all of the stakeholders that came to mind. Each stakeholder's name was captured on the public computer screen, and positioned on a grid according to their relative power and interest in SNH's activities. Thus, the Scottish Office [the Central Government department providing the funding for SNH], an early contribution, was positioned in the top right hand corner of the **power/interest grid** (large amount of interest and power). *P344* The Ramblers Association, however, were towards the top left (lots of interest and relatively little power), and the Department of the Environment (based in London) towards the bottom right. The sub-group quickly got involved in the process. Within 45 minutes they had over 50 stakeholders up on the screen [for public sector organizations this is typical]. As they began to discuss the relative position of each, Fran encouraged them to think about what was the appropriate level of **dis-aggregation** – that is, *P345* was it the office, the department, or the individual that could be managed strategically? A lively debate soon got under way as some members of the sub-group were convinced that in some cases the position taken was influenced by the particular personality involved rather than the office, with others arguing the opposite. In addition to surfacing knowledge about the stakeholders under discussion, this process also saw new stakeholders emerging, thus further enriching the picture. By the time a break was called there were over 100 stakeholders on the map!

P345 After the tea break and building on their earlier efforts, Colin suggested that the participants begin to **categorize the stakeholders** in terms of their stance (was it positive, negative, or issue specific). The group surged forward with a new lease of energy – negative stakeholders were easy (and were marked red). However, the differentiation between positive and issue specific stakeholders was more problematic. In some cases it depended on the strategic action being taken by SNH, in other cases it was due to the position taken by other stakeholders. This highlighted the fact that most of the stakeholders in some way or another communicated and influenced one another. One of the participants wanted to know 'was there some way that the relationships between stakeholders could be draw in?'. 'Yes', said

C124 P349 Colin, 'we can capture the **formal and informal relationships** in the form of a network. We could also explore some of each stakeholder's sanctions

C126 P346 and monitoring activities using what we call a **sanctions/interests star diagram**. But, I am not sure we would be able to do it in the remaining time.' After a quick discussion, the sub-group requested a further meeting with Fran and Colin. As almost a parting shot (once the others had left) Geoff noted, 'I wasn't really sure about the use of this exercise when I arrived, but now I can begin to see how it will help us. I shall be interested to see how we get on next week'.

The second session began with the sub-group raising further stakeholders. During the time back in the office, they had been making a note of anyone/group that came to mind – the grid continued to grow. They then surfaced, and with Colin and Fran's help, developed an actor influence network map. This would display the perceived relationships between the stakeholders. Before work could begin, however, Richard wanted to re-categorize the stakeholders according to different groups. A number of categories were quickly identified (environmental pressure groups, media, governmental bodies, landowners). Using different colours to represent the categories, the group identified which category of stakeholder was the most numerous, which were most interested and who had the power – a

C128 useful basis for extending the **actor influence** map.

As the group participants suggested influences between stakeholders they also began to surface information about their various forms or procedures for monitoring activities, as well as their sanctions (means of blocking or controlling a particular action). Thus, in the same way as the influence network naturally grew out of the grid, the star diagram grew out of completing the influence network. In some cases the relationships between stakeholders, especially informal ones, were purely 'informational' – thus highlighting a form of monitoring. Due to the large number of stakeholders and limited time available, the sub-group agreed to work on producing sanctions/interest star diagrams for those stakeholders (the **'players'**) in the top right quadrant – they were the most significant. *C122* Sanctions emerged as participants began to discuss the various coalitions stakeholders might build to protect their interests. The session therefore began to take on a cyclical nature, with periods of activity being focused upon capturing the relationships/influences between players and then considering their sanctions and monitoring activities. As this was captured, the sub-group began to identify recurring patterns where particular strategies might trigger a reaction from a whole range of stakeholders. By the end of the morning the group were animated. Not only had they generated a wealth of stakeholder material but also, and more importantly, they had began to identify means of managing strategically some of the stakeholders through the potential influences and sanctions that could have a multiple payoff . . .

Time passed . . . both sub-groups had completed their tasks; Roger now had his management team convinced that generating strategy using a JOURNEY making approach was a good idea. Now he wanted to **involve** *P444* **more of the organization**, particularly the senior managers. These would be the main force in putting the action into place, however . . .

. . . Staff, including most managers, prided themselves as specialist scientists and considered that 'management was for others'. Because of this, Colin, Fran, and Roger had been aware from the beginning that getting managers to **take an interest in a 'strategy** that demanded attention *C59* to managerial effectiveness' was going to be difficult. Roger, in one of his early explanations of the organization, had noted that the majority of the organization's managers were scientists by profession, including himself. For many of these managers their job was their passion. They had joined the organization, or one of its predecessors, to be scientists not managers. 'Interesting', Colin had remarked, 'until now we have never worked in an organization with so many highly qualified scientists as managers'. Fran and Colin began to think that this aspect of the organization was likely to establish a significant framework within which the strategic future of the organization would be formed. It would have an effect on any **emergent** *C4* **strategizing** and the long term future. In addition it seemed unlikely to them that Roger or the management team had thought through the impact this characteristic of the organization would have on their everyday way of solving strategic problems. After all, as they later commented, they had not been trained to address these types of management issues.

Whilst thinking about the managers, Fran commented that she and Colin had presumed that the managers, would be just like those in other organizations. That is, they would have some interest in all of the strategic issues facing the organization, not just those which impacted their own scientific kingdom. As a consequence of this meeting and the 2-day workshop, Roger and the management team agreed that having the involvement of these managers in making strategy was both necessary and desirable. Thus the JOURNEY making process was extended to include the

C56   **participation** of 52 of the senior managers.

Having agreed to extend the participation, they now needed to discuss how to involve them. Fran and Colin had already done some thinking about a possible design, and asked Roger if he would be interested in their current ideas. 'Sure', replied Roger. Colin began, 'The organization currently has around 50 senior managers, each of which has considerable knowledge about the organization. Each of them is important to the implementation and therefore must understand and own the resultant product. Why not ask them what they think about the strategies that you and the management team are working on – we would benefit from

C73 C76   **collecting and modelling alternative views**'. 'Okay', said Roger, 'this will also help begin to weld the organization together. Many still work as though they belong to one of the two original organizations, or even for the organization from which we recruited them. How do you think we should do this?'

Fran replied 'if we ran 5 workshops of around 10 people, involving a mixture of people from headquarters and the field we could start using the Oval Mapping Technique (OMT). However, instead of it being entirely open, we would use the developing strategy labels and possibly the

P306   remaining issues as **triggers**. This way the groups would focus on areas already agreed by the management team. Following this, probably after lunch, we could then work on those areas where there are different views,

P336   particularly those that they think are important. We could use the "**networked computer system**"'. 'What would that do for them?' asked Roger. 'It enables participants to add their ideas directly on to a map displayed on

C68 P337   a public computer screen. It ensures that each contribution is **anonymous**, providing participants with an environment conducive to presenting

C58   alternative perspectives. We can also **rapidly capture** information, which might be important with more participants in each workshop', replied Colin. 'We could then end the day using the preferencing module. This would allow us to identify which of the emergent strategic options are most favoured.' Something nagged at Roger. 'The strategic options that they come up with – what if they turn out to be impractical? Or just too many? Won't participants expect to see them being put into action?'

'We would deal with that by making it clear to the managers that this is a chance for them to influence the direction, not make decisions', Fran answered. 'In our experience, most managers don't expect organizations to be cooperatives, but are pleased to be asked for their contributions'. 'We will make it clear in the introduction and conclusions that their views will be put to the management team for their final decision', Colin added. 'Capturing and taking into account their views will demonstrate that procedural justice has been done'.

'It might be nice to get members of the management team to be at these workshops, to act as sponsors – people to report back to the entire management team', suggested Roger. 'Great idea', both Fran and Colin said in unison (he was suggesting a process similar to that used to great effect with the Northern Ireland Prison Service). 'This way they could support the effort, provide clarity if the issues/strategies were not immediately clear or if there were questions, but otherwise take a back seat'. 'Hmm, and how exactly do we get Angus to take a back seat? – gag him!', muttered Fran, thinking of how Angus tended to dominate conversations. 'I guess we will use the usual facilitation techniques – talk to him beforehand to explain the situation and then try to restrain him if he tries to take over'.

Time passed . . . the series of Oval Mapping workshops held with the senior managers was completed . . .

Full of good news Roger called Fran and Colin. The managers had seemed pleased with their opportunity to have their say. In some cases this had been the first time they had got together after the start of the new organization. Fran and Colin were less pleased; the workshops had appeared to be a bit of a moaning session. However, they both agreed, the moaning appeared to signal something about the current state of the organization's **culture** and so was probably an important cathartic experience. Roger   C27 continued: he had been visiting one of the area offices and a manager had told him how much he had enjoyed the workshop. In particular, he had found being able to structure all of the statements on the main wall useful. He could begin to see how other people viewed the organization and what their problems were. As for using the computers – these seemed to make the whole event more productive than other meetings about strategy that he had experienced in his career. He had really enjoyed entering his ideas into the map. 'But,' Roger interrupted, 'did you have any new ideas after the morning session?'. 'Oh yes, seeing all the material related to the issue helped prompt me, as did the request to focus on actions; it was really good fun. The preferencing was good too; having the options linked up on the main screen, helped me understand the impact that voting for one would have on another. I also really liked being able to prioritize against two criteria'. Roger was pleased – and Fran and Colin were pleased that he was pleased. They were also accustomed to participants reporting to their managers what they hoped he/she would want to hear.

Following up on this discussion, Colin, Fran, and Roger along with the management team reflected upon the unfolding nature of the senior managers' participation. The concern regarding the managers' level of interest in contributing to developing strategy resurfaced. During the discussion, Fran noted that 'when exploring emergent strategizing we usually pay considerable attention to the nature of informal, as well as formal, reward systems and their role in establishing ways of working. However, if you review the workshops, it was almost blatantly obvious that all the modes of mutual rewards were related to scientific tasks, even though we had got the managers together in mixed groups (by geography and discipline) to discuss managerial strategies'. 'Yes', Roger replied, 'I noticed that in the workshop where I was a sponsor. Often, masterly managerial skills were derided, and time devoted to managerial issues regarded as time wasted. The language used to debate strategy seemed to suggest that anything related to management was an unnecessary bureaucratic overhead, a constraint or weakness'. 'I also noticed signs of that', Colin added. 'Those members of the management team who were clearly and unambiguously associated with science were lauded. This was often done very subtly. However, those associated with management were derided through recourse to statements such as "they're necessary evils acting on behalf of an unsympathetic government"'. 'Yes', commented another of the management team, 'the statements about science, which were often superbly indirect, were usually rewarded by the body language of their colleagues. Even those who were not scientists and administrators played the game of "science is king"'. Outside the meeting Roger noted that, 'it is obvious these reward systems, embedded in the culture of SNH, are supported by many on the management team, and are crucially affecting our future . . . We had identified this as an important strategic issue at the first workshop. It was a central bundle of "oval" things'. 'Remember, though, opinion was split as to its importance or even existence', Colin commented. They each reminded themselves that the management team had, during the first workshop, easily agreed that professional and quality standards were important for all scientific work.

Roger and the management team next returned to their concerns about too much participation, and what to do with so much material. It was all very well involving all of the senior managers, but how did the management team allow participants to have a say whilst not taking away their managerial prerogatives. Each of the management team felt that their own managers had, for the most part, been impressed with their chance to contribute. However, some had felt that it was not their job but that of the management team. (As a postscript, it was interesting to note that many senior managers had, during follow-up interviews conducted after the strategy had been agreed, expressed a view that their involvement in strategy making was unnecessary. They considered strategy making to be the job of the management team – their job was to do what they were good at: being good scientists. This appeared to reinforce the significance of informal reward systems within the culture of the organization in emergent strategizing.) In addition, they were aware that some managers had begun to assume that their statements would be adopted regardless of the political ramifications. This situation, if not managed carefully, could begin to be an issue in the organization, as many managers were unaccustomed to being asked for their views and were unsure of its consequences. This worry arose even though Roger (as a part of his introduction to the workshops), and Fran and Colin (during the workshops), had emphasized that the senior managers' role was to influence strategic direction rather than decide it.

This discussion led them to review a forthcoming workshop to explore alternative futures [chapters C8 and P4] – one of the outcomes that had emerged from sub-group working on stakeholder analysis and management. It was to involve a number of the key stakeholders in a pro-active but, potentially as far as Roger was concerned, risky way. If they got it wrong then their stakeholder management could result in exactly the opposite outcome to that desired. The purpose was two-fold: firstly to surface a number of scenarios from an external perspective rather than just from internal knowledge, and more importantly, to continue to make these stakeholders aware that the organization was working hard to ensure best practice, and to gain their help and contribution.

Roger also knew that he had another sticky issue to resolve: the size of the management team. Nine members geographically scattered across the country was not an effective way of working – the management team agreed he needed to slim it down to 6 or 7. He knew that if he tried asking them to discuss the issue, lots of posturing and politicking would mean little productive work being done – not that he blamed them. Using the networked computer system was in order! The anonymity of the system combined with the ability to structure comments on a public screen seemed likely to open up the discussion in a realistic manner.

Time passed . . . the scenario workshop drew closer . . .

Ten key stakeholders identified in the stakeholder analysis had been invited to attend a workshop to help the organization consider possible alternative futures. When the workshop had been suggested, it had sounded like a great idea, but now they were actually coming and it was important to ensure that the organization sponsored an effective day. Roger was wondering how the participants might react. How would they get on with each other? What would be the substantive outcome? The choice of stakeholders had been carefully made, acknowledging not only the results of the stakeholder analysis but also addressing a number of other concerns. Consequently, it was to involve stakeholders that the management team felt: (i) were significant **players** (lots of power and at least some interest in SNH's strategy), and (ii) had **different perspectives** and so could contribute widely, and (iii) were prepared to spend a day helping the organization think about possible futures. To this end, the list included a European Member of Parliament (to get a politician's view and, in particular, a European view), a member of the World Wide Fund for Nature, a marine expert (to provide environmental information), an influential business man, and a senior employee of the British Broadcasting Corporation (to get a perspective from the media).

The workshop design incorporated two objectives. The first was to generate a number of scenarios. These would be used (i) to test out some of the strategic options being considered, and (ii) to compare these scenarios with those that had been created internally. The second objective was to use it as a stakeholder management exercise. By bringing the stakeholders together and focusing upon alternative futures, Roger and his team expected they would be able to demonstrate their attention to

C154 P355

C123
C73

strategy, and also 'buy in' some of the stakeholders so that they would be more supportive of the organization. Through working together on *C140* **possible futures, within the context of the mandate** of the organization, Roger felt that they could provoke key stakeholders into becoming more attuned to the difficulties and responsibilities of SNH.

The day was to begin with an introduction to the aims of the workshop *C143* before asking the participants to surface **key events** outside the strategic *C145 P362* control of SNH. These events were to be either **'flip-flops'** (for example, an oil spill) or the point on a continuum where a significant change would be experienced. These would then be further explored, with the group working to identify how they could trigger possible scenarios for the organization. It was hoped that by the end of the workshop four or five scenarios focusing upon different aspects of the environment would be developed.

This was realized. The resultant scenarios were interesting for two reasons. They were firstly different from those produced internally, and, secondly, one of the scenarios contained a number of positive feedback loops suggesting that the scenario was likely to be self-sustaining. Follow- *C149 P368* ing this observation a **system dynamics computer simulation** model was built to explore these feedback loops in more detail.

Time passed . . . and . . .

Roger was keen to begin putting the emerging strategy into place. Having (i) run the series of Oval Mapping and computer assisted workshops allowing the participation of his senior managers in influencing strategic direction, (ii) made progress on stakeholder analysis, (iii) completed an internal scenario exploration, and (iv) involved a number of stakeholders in a scenario workshop, he wanted to get things moving. In addition, he wanted to involve his senior managers in developing the more detailed *P436* **strategic action programmes**. He agreed with Fran and Colin that a series of workshops which would involve all senior managers and the management team in sub-groups to agree on the actions would encourage further commitment to the strategy. Therefore, the 52 senior managers were assigned to one of eight workshops (each workshop focusing on a specific, prioritized strategy) and mandated to develop a skeleton strategic action programme.

Each workshop would also involve at least one of the management team who would act as 'mentor' to the sub-group, and, from then onwards, be accountable to the rest of the management team for progress on the agreed action programme. Participants would be asked to consider the resources required – cash required, time and energy. They were also to consider existing tasks and loads (addressing the realism/practicalities of *P445* implementing the action), as well as responsibilities, timescales, and **performance indicators**. In addition, each sub-group was expected to suggest possible actions for the following workshop involving other managers working on another strategy. This 'rough and ready' package of suggestions would be used by the next sub-group as a contribution to their thinking. The main purpose was to enable each sub-group to work on one strategy at the substantive level and to create awareness of a second strategy. The order in which the strategies were dealt with (and so the order of the workshops) was determined by the relationships between strategies depicted on the strategy map and was designed so that the implications of decisions made by one group could be carried forward to the next group. By doing this there was more chance of the action programmes properly informing each other. The resultant skeletal action programmes would then act as the framework for more detailed proposals, developed after the workshop by two participants of each sub-group. These two managers were selected from separate parts of the organization, usually one manager from HQ and the other from the field, and were helped by their management team member. They were expected to be constrained by the framework and yet check the coherence of agreements, resource requirements, and complete their proposals in consultation with their management team 'mentor'.   *P139*

Postscript

The workshops were completed and the journey continued over the next 3 years, resulting in major structural changes to the organization as well as the delivery of the majority of the strategies. As Roger commented three years after the start of the journey . . .

'We started the exercise following a negative experience and born out of a strong desire as a management team to work collectively. Our previous experience did not fit our collective characteristics – macho team playing and emotional searching at an individual level were not for us. From the outset, we felt comfortable individually and collectively with the facilitative approach and were able to contribute thoughts and views within a managed environment, which otherwise were unlikely to be aired. Our first efforts were tentative, but as we built up confidence in the techniques and the facilitators, and began to understand each more, then our confidence grew and the outputs which we achieved also grew. Being prepared to work in small groups, rather than the whole management team, and also engaging our middle managers, were major breakthroughs. Also **feedback to the latter group** on their efforts, including explicit criticism of our lack of direction and leadership, was particularly important. Over time, we also made the shift from the analytical approach to the action oriented approach. Development of an action plan and individual tasks also gave us great comfort that we were responding to our own and our managers' concerns.   *C36*

When I reflect back on the process, I believe that it was the right thing at the right time. On the positive side, was the opportunity to get away from the phone, fax, etc. (although that took a little time) and to think collectively and openly, to produce output over which we had total ownership, to articulate what we were doing to our middle managers, and to reassure our Board [the Board was non-executive and made up of the 'great and the good'] that this was a worthwhile exercise. It satisfied us because of its analytical approach. On the downside, the exercise was complex, and even with the software which some of us mastered, we had difficulty in handling all of the material. However, building the material into models showing interactions proved to be valuable. Finding the time sometimes proved to be extraordinarily difficult and has led to focusing the new, and smaller, management team on a more strategic role. This smaller team came out of discussions during the strategy making. The process had given us sufficient self-confidence, however, that when we came to review our operations and our structure, we decided to take this forward ourselves, although I did get some private advice from Colin and Fran. Overall, the time investment was invaluable, and, due to the continuity of personnel in the new management team, the individual and collective memory of the process is very valuable. And last, but by no means least, the value statement which the new management team now has, stemmed from the analysis we and our middle managers did during the strategy making process. Middle managers have now taken over ownership and the delivery of the strategy'.

Antek – an international consultancy company

The Organization: Antek – an international consultancy company employing 65 experienced and specialist staff.

The Vignette: Detecting emergent strategizing.

The Cast List: Jim – the Chief Executive; one facilitator – Colin.

Before starting on a JOURNEY making project with the organization Colin was keen to explore some of the existing bases of **emergent strategizing**. *C21* Jim, the Chief Executive, was a long time business colleague of Colin's, and had always been committed to the extensive use of computer networks to provide the company with an information system. His organization, a specialist consultancy company, had now been operating for around ten years. From the beginning, his aim had been to develop an information system that would capture all of the expertise gained by his 65 staff, as well as details of the projects completed. Colin had observed frequently that Jim was aggressive in his insistence that staff not only use the data within the system but also provide qualitative and judgemental input. To achieve this, the system had been designed specially so that it used hypertext principles for linking both quantitative *and qualitative* data. It was a system that Colin considered was likely to be a significant determinant of the emergent strategizing of the organization.

'The use of the system is "taken for granted" – it is a regular part of staff's working lives', Jim noted. New staff seemed to be absorbed into the system and its use with ease – the culture makes sure its use is unquestioned. As a result, Jim continued, 'it is something that differentiates the organization from competitors'. 'Staff have been entering qualitative information about clients into the system and cross linking it to market data (qualitative and quantitative) since we started'. 'The information is also linked to models of possible market scenarios and the library-based data provided by our own librarians'. 'Thus', he added, 'although my consultants are mathematicians and scientists by background, and their job is to construct sophisticated computer models, their ways of thinking and defining the nature of their models naturally works within a qualitative modelling context'. Colin was impressed, and said so, commenting that 'being able to see actions along with their associated rationale and outcomes, must really frame their way of thinking. It must influence the work they do for clients and have a profound impact on their way of working with clients'. 'In principle, and, I believe, in practice' replied Jim . . .

Colin used these reflections, and others, about emergent strategizing as a part of the discussions within the initial round of interviews. Interviewees were asked about their own views of the impact of the information system on the way they thought about getting future work and developing their own professional practice . . .

MacFarlane International – small engineering company

The Organization: MacFarlane International – a small engineering organization made up of specialists, many of whom were based in different parts of the world.

The Vignette: The 'fast interview cycle'.

The Cast List: Bruce – vice president; 18 interviewees; 2 interviewers – Fran and Colin.

P302   Fran and Colin knew it was important that, in order to keep momentum going, they should try to ensure that the **time intervals between interview rounds and workshops were kept to minimum (as they liked to think of it – within a 'psychological week'** incorporating the beginning of one week to the end of the next). But, they were now to get involved in a

C59   **strategy process that was to be completed within a week**! This form of the process was to prove an alternative mode of working – and one to be embarked upon only if urgency is required (or a heart attack!). Bruce, a vice president of an international engineering company (who had known Colin for years and so was familiar with the process), had two aims. His first aim was to ensure the process incorporated interviews with his senior team to allow a deep coverage of the statements whilst at the same time involving all of the other members. The second, and overall aim was to produce a strategy within a very short timescale. Well, Fran and Colin had always argued that the faster the turnaround the greater the ownership – here was a chance to try it out!

To ensure that Bruce felt comfortable with the outcome, the three of them came up with a design that was to meet both of Bruce's aims –

P380   addressing **process *and* content**. The process would start with both Fran and Colin carrying out a round of interviews with the management team over a 2-day period. This would then be followed by a day back in the

P400   office, sorting and tidying the resultant model, or **aggregated map**, of what had been said. Once the model's structure had been sorted they would then use the analysis to highlight a number of issues or labels which

P303   would act as prompts for 2 separate days using the **Oval Mapping Technique (OMT)** with the rest of the senior managers. The results from these workshops would then be added into the model, the resultant map

P383   analysed [chapter P6] and would form the basis for a **2-day** computer supported **workshop** involving the management team again. At the end of these 2 days they would have their strategy! 'Just as well we haven't got too much on at present', thought Fran, 'this is 7 days non-stop – what a roller coaster ride!'.

P293   The interviews started well. Colin and Fran had **scheduled interviews** so that there was time to allow the interviewees to overrun their time allocation if it seemed appropriate whilst still giving the two of them time to build the model as they went. On both days, lunch was a process of one person eating a sandwich and talking at the same time (!) whilst the other typed the statements into the computer model – then a quick swap over so that the other could get a bite! In this way, Colin and Fran not only saw 18 people for an hour to an hour and a half but also shared insights, and constructed the computer map – they were exhausted at the end of the first 2 days . . .

National Health Service – a unit of five hospitals

The Organization: A National Health Service (NHS) Unit – a consortium of five hospitals. It has become common practice in the public sector of the UK for strategy development to closely follow that which is employed in private sector settings. Here the story started with the General Manager needing to develop an organization wide Quality Assurance strategy – a requirement resulting from a prescribed initiative from central government. Gradually this strategy transformed from a focus on Quality Assurance to one that encompassed most of the activities of the organization. The process of JOURNEY making had the consequence of successfully developing the management team, providing a sense of strategic direction, and, through its success, initiating an individual performance review process.

The Vignette: Getting started. Interviewing with cognitive mapping. Analysis of maps. Feedback loops. 'Stage management'. Closure and publicizing the strategy.

The Cast List: Peter – the General Manager of the Unit; Katherine – a 'partner' to the facilitators; Members of the Management Team, including Derek, Margaret, Simon, Susan, and Celeste; 2 facilitators – Fran and Steve.

Peter felt he was faced with too many strategic and tactical problems. Which of these problems should he expend the Unit's energy on. He continually commented, 'Too much change is being expected of one unit'! However, the political ramifications of an externally imposed directive ('something perilous to ignore') and his own curiosity led him in the direction of developing a strategy for quality. Rather unfairly, he thought, his Unit was perceived as a backwater by the local Health Authority (funding body) and treated as such in terms of resource allocation, reward, and status. Could developing something new and exciting be an opportunity to change the image? But how . . .?

Whilst pondering this, he met Steve (a colleague of Fran's) at an event hosted by a research group interested in developing information requirement systems for health service units. Steve was doing a presentation of previous strategy work undertaken by Colin, Fran, and himself. Peter suddenly had an idea – here was a new and innovative approach that would tie in with his state of the art computer based manpower planning system and could involve fully his management team. This might be a way *P372* of **getting started** on developing a strategy for quality assurance. Just to add icing to the cake, the Unit had recently completed a Patient Quality questionnaire and could use this information, and the recently agreed upon 'organizational values' (which at the time no one could work out a way of using), to help design a way forward. Peter thought he had, at last, found a way of cementing the top down organizational values with the bottom up questionnaire results. Finally if the process worked he could then extend the strategy from its focus on quality to the entire organization.

Peter, with this rough idea in mind, approached Steve. He wasn't too sure what he was letting himself in for and wanted to test the ideas with Steve. At the meeting Steve began to build a 'computer based cognitive map' [chapter P1] of some of the key issues that Peter was raising. As the computer model unfolded in front of his eyes, showing him how the issues interacted, Peter became excited and a little more reassured. He would take the plunge.

The next step was agreeing the programme of work. What was it that Peter wanted? Whilst one of his central **reasons for embarking on** *C13* **strategic thinking** was to prove to the funding authority that the Unit was *not* a backwater, the other, equally important, reasons were to:

- help middle and senior managers make decisions about quality in a **coordinated** and coherent manner; *C34*
- pull the various existing quality initiatives together to form a coherent whole;
- provide a management process to address and help monitor the quality of service.

In addition to these public aims, Peter was really keen to do some serious **team building**. He felt that the senior managers needed to work *C17* together more effectively, learn more about what one another did, and increase the **organizational learning**. Moreover, if he and Steve could find *C74* a way of designing the strategy making process so as to produce a document (something tangible for the funding authority) and an action plan, he would have markers to **assess progress**. *C175*

This was all very well but the managers were not used to being con- sulted – **participation in strategic thinking** had never occurred before! *P299* Also, many of the 'new managers' in the NHS had never been involved in a strategy, and Peter suspected they would probably find the whole process a bit unnerving. How could they be persuaded to open up? What did Steve think would be a good way of starting the journey? Steve suggested doing some individual interviews [chapter P1] – in this way the managers could be more open than if they were in a group where they would worry about who was listening. Peter liked it – firstly he was aware that the **culture of the organization** was not one of openness, and *P374* secondly, managers would have the opportunity to think the issues through more thoroughly if they had to explicate the ideas to Steve. At this stage Steve suggested bringing in Fran to help him. Now they needed to decide whom to interview . . .

Time passed . . . and Steve, Fran, and Peter prepared for the interviews . . .

A schedule needed to be agreed – whom to see, when, and where. Fran argued that it was **useful to start with the most powerful people** first – *P301*

P477   the **'key actors'**. This way she hoped to elicit the broader, more visionary, strategic issues early on. These issues then could be gently inserted into the subsequent interviews in a way that meant everyone would have had their say on these strategic issues. Steve, somewhat surprised, commented 'isn't this a bit manipulative?'. 'Yes . . . but this way not only do they widen their viewpoint, and so don't come to the workshop totally surprised, but also they begin to feel these issues are also their issues. In that way we can begin the important process of negotiation and building a group map', Fran replied.

Whilst designing the schedule, they also built in enough time between interviews for Fran and Steve to tidy their maps of the interview and catch up with one another to share emerging issues. To help with this scheduling Peter suggested that they ask Katherine to arrange things.

P479   Katherine was a godsend! She quickly became a potential **partner** to Fran and Steve. She understood the organization, understood the client, had a good idea about current gossip relating to what Peter was up to, as well as arranging the interviews, rooms, coffee and sandwiches! Somehow, in a busy hospital, she found private offices for both Fran and Steve – a help when encouraging those being interviewed to be more open. Finally, details sorted out, Peter sent out a memo inviting all those to be interviewed to participate. The memo provided the reasons for the interview, made it clear that the content of each individual interview would remain confidential to Steve and Fran, and that the material, in aggregated form, would be the basis for a group workshop.

The first interview started well – for the first minute or so. Fran and

P302   Steve had prepared a short introduction to the process – to **set expectations** and reduce, as best they could, any nerves or apprehension. The introduction included some commentary about the context for developing a quality strategy and its importance to the organization, and the nature of the interview (it would last for about an hour, and was not 'questionnaire' based). They did not comment on their taking notes as maps. To do so often distracted the interviewee and reduced the later pay-off from

P299   interviewees' **curiosity about 'spider diagrams'**. During the introduction, just when Fran was stating that the interviews were a chance to be open and that the notes were confidential, Derek burst in to say 'I don't have any worries about anything . . . how can you possibly think that!'. Backtracking rapidly, Fran commented that not everyone felt as confident about the issue as he did, and so it might help others if he could say something about why he was comfortable with the future. Derek sat back and began to talk – firstly about his confidence and then gradually about his worries. Towards the end of the interview, and as predicted, Derek commented on Fran's weird style of taking notes – 'spider webs'! Not waiting for a second chance, she began to explain the reason for mapping. She showed

P289: P289   him chains of argument, 'busy' **clusters**, important outcomes, **goals, or**

P289   **aspirations** and so provided herself with a check as to whether she had understood what he meant. He commented, 'goodness me you have been listening to what I've been saying'. Fran hoped this meant he was beginning to **trust** her and that he believed she intended to take him seriously. If so, she reckoned the interview would have been an important **cathartic experience** for him.

The second of her interviewees, Margaret, was fascinated as the map unfolded before her eyes – she began to make corrections by writing directly on to the map and added to the areas she felt needed more elaboration. Back in Steve's interview room Simon was now really beginning to get into his stride – he declared that his own thinking had begun to make sense to him! By having to explain to Steve his worries and ambitions, he said he could begin to understand how they related – helped by the map. Indeed he argued that he had, through the interview map, sorted out what to do about a couple of local issues. This positive outcome reminded Steve of how important it was for him to **record a map of what the interviewee meant** (not necessarily the same as what they said . . .) rather than fitting it in to his preconceptions of what he thought was important. He had some strong views about the National Health Service and hospitals (his wife was a nurse) and needed to keep his own views in check if he was to get ownership from his interviewees.

As it turned out, Steve and Fran were both having difficulties in finding the time to do a little tidying of the maps, as none of the participants had a shortage of things to say. The non-verbals of the interviewees seemed to suggest that this was the first time anyone had listened to them – consequently they used their opportunity to express their views to the full. To some extent this 'magic' had been helped by the mapping technique as it became obvious (to both the interviewer and interviewee) which were the 'busy' points – the main issues – and which were the aims – heads. The rough analysis proved very useful. To finish up each interview Fran and Steve sought to provide a clear **explanation of the next steps**. It was apparent that there was a considerable amount of curiosity relating to what other participants might have said, and this meant that everyone was keen to see their map aggregated with those of others – the next step towards a group workshop. Fran and Steve were confident they would all turn up to the strategy workshop. Peter had never been certain they were all committed to the process he was 'pushing on them' (as Katherine reported it).

Meanwhile, the time between the interviews became chaotic. Fran and Steve used the corridor to swap notes, exchange ideas, catch up on any issues to be interjected and get a hastily swallowed cup of coffee. They also caught tempting scraps of conversations where participants who had been interviewed compared notes with each other! Unlike other times when Fran had used interviews, they did not have enough time to actually begin building the **aggregated map** as the interviews were conducted, although they had set up a computer to enable them to do this at the breaks between interviews. Using **the computer software** meant they could keep adding, changing, and analysing the current state of the model as they went along. But in this case, there was no time. The problem was fitting all of the interviews into one day and working on, what turned out to be, a highly emotive issue where virtually every interviewee over-ran their hour.

P293

P298

P293

P302

P400

P298

Fran and Steve had not forgotten Peter in all their rushing around the corridors. They wanted to make sure that he was happy with the way things were going and provide him with a sense of control over the process. This was important because it would help build up a good *P480* **'facilitator–client' relationship**. Peter himself was keen to know what issues were emerging. However, this *did not* mean reneging on the deal with staff and telling him who said what, rather just what the issues were. Fran and Steve needed to know whether there were any issues that Peter really felt uncomfortable about addressing in a group setting. This was tricky because, if there were, then some means of managing their concealment would have to be found. Fran, when working with previous clients, had found herself very carefully negotiating a means of avoiding some very difficult interpersonal issues during the workshops without risking the process losing credibility; she was not in a hurry to repeat these experiences. Luckily for Fran and Steve, Peter was completely relaxed. Both wondered 'did this mean that there were no new or "crunchy issues" – had they missed some key issues and so missed getting a handle on the *C21* **emergent strategizing** in the organization?'.

Although Fran and Steve had not been able to build the model during the interview round they did have 5 hours on the train! So they put this time to good use. In beginning to capture it in a computer model they found additional material surfacing as the maps acted as prompts (for remembering bits of the interview not captured in the hand-drawn maps). Doing it jointly forced them both to explain to the other exactly what was meant by the various statements and chains of argument, thus making the model clearer. This process did get a bit fraught – it had been a long day and sometimes it felt the other was being provocatively thick! To *P400* ease the process of **building an aggregated model**, Steve and Fran decided to start by focusing on the emergent issues each of them thought had arisen from all of their interviews, rather than on the individual maps. Using common issue labels, for example 'provide a more efficient service', enabled them to get started. Entering all of the material supporting/opposing an issue statement meant that the material became woven together in an efficient manner. On previous occasions Fran had *P297* tried to get **two interviews** with each individual as this meant that each interviewee had an opportunity to check the map and to add elaboration. However, this meant that individual models had to be built before aggregating maps. This approach was both harder and easier. Harder in so far as the chunks remained stubbornly individualistic and a lot more analysis was required before the model was properly woven. On the other hand, building issues up one at a time helped the process of drawing comments from each participant into an issue map, and two interviews made sure each issue was addressed. As each issue with all its attendant material was entered, cross links between the issues were checked as well as end points (heads).

As the train drew into the station two exhausted but satisfied individuals got out. They had done the interviews and had a good first draft of the model; the next step was to begin to analyse it – but that was another day . . .

Time passed . . . and back at base Fran and Steve now had the job of tidying up the model created from the interviews . . .

'How different is analysing models built using interview data from models arising from Oval Mapping sessions?' Steve asked. 'Not massively, you still use most of the analysis techniques', replied Fran; 'however, you find usually that interviews result in a deeper, more elaborated model incorporating more individual knowledge than would oval mapping workshops. As you have found, you can spend more time exploring individuals' views'. However, before they could analyse the model they had created from the interviews, both wanted to do some more tidying up. This involved ensuring that there weren't any improper **orphans** left lying   *P402*
around and also trying to cut down duplication of statements. Finding the orphans was easy – the software command listed those statements currently unlinked, and it was a relatively straightforward job to link them, when appropriate, into the rest of the model. This was helped by the fact that Fran and Steve were able to remember what had been said in the interviews and therefore find the relevant related statements on their interview maps. 'This would be much harder if we left it a couple of weeks, by which time I, for one, would have forgotten a lot of the material', noted Steve. Reducing any duplication was much harder. Firstly they had to find instances where there were near identical concepts and then they had to check whether they really were **identical in meaning**. It   *P403*
produced some energetic debates about the extent to which the statements were the same or just related to one another. Having the context of each statement (in-arrows and out-arrows) helped. In many circumstances subtle variations reduced the amount of merging. Both Fran and Steve were also concerned that they took care in **considering the language** and   *P291*
expression used by the individuals – if they were going to merge the statements, then as much as possible, language from both statements needed to be incorporated into the newly formed statement. After all, they could test out similarity during the workshop, a better option than risk losing ownership through someone's statements being lost!

Now they needed to check for inadmissible **feedback loops**. Both were   *P410*
aware that, at this stage, it was likely that incorrect loops might have been formed by mistaken coding. As it turned out, they found five loops which were the consequence of building the model very quickly. They were not surprised; this was typical. The next step was to see if they could find a potential **group goal/aspiration system** – one that every member of the   *P403*
group would have some sympathy with. Technically these would be those statements towards the top of the model that indicated an outcome 'good in its own right'. Fran and Steve had considerable difficulty in working out this draft goal system – mostly because many of the statements at the top of the model seemed to be good labels for clusters of statements that might

represent strategic issues rather than goal labels. [This situation was not to be resolved until much later, (during the workshop) when they discovered that a set of what had been called 'organizational values' had been agreed recently and that participants had been taking these for granted.]

P405

P405

P427

Nevertheless they continued to try to establish a draft goal system. They started by using a number of the analysis methods, available within the software, to explore the structure of the computer based model. Firstly they attempted to discover the most **'busy' statements**. They did this in two ways: (i) identifying those that had the most context immediately around each statement, and (ii) identifying those with the highest density of statements within the broader context (exploring several levels away from the statement of interest) thus gaining a measure of **centrality**. Each of these analyses provided an indication of which statements were of critical importance to the overall structure of the model. For example, the analyses suggested the two issues of: 'build staff motivation' and 'improve understanding about each other's roles and departments'. Fran and Steve were interested to note that they were both concerned with the internal working of the organization **(facilitative) rather than core** goals. Once all of these statements were identified they were then coloured with a new font in the computer model, to make identification easier.

P403

P407

At this point Steve was still not convinced that they had identified all of the **key strategic issues**. As a way of checking, Fran decided to use the **clustering** algorithm in the software to slice the model into groups. Not entirely reassured, Steve agreed with the plan. It would at least allow them to display smaller bundles of statements on the computer screen. (It is never helpful to try to make sense of over 250 statements at once!) Through clustering statements according to their link similarity, Steve noticed that one or two of the clusters appeared to be strongly related to others. In addition Fran identified two clusters not containing any strategic issue labels (identified as 'nubs' of the model). However, each cluster did have links to at least one other cluster rather than being independent of the others. If there had have been an isolated cluster then it might have been necessary to address it independently. The results of the analysis proved a good starting point for checking the key issues. As a further test, the clusters were printed out, revealing some links that had been overlooked.

P380

P413

It was at this stage of working that Fran and Steve began to notice a difference in their **working style**. Steve was particularly concerned that **the model was perfect** (well, as much as he could make it) whereas Fran simply wanted it to be a device to facilitate reflection and negotiation at the workshop. Her view was that the model had to be faithful to a degree, but that regardless of how much work she and Steve did, it would never be perfect. Both of them were to continue finding working together a help (they could manage the process better) and a hindrance (they had to agree).

Having made a number of changes to the model, all the analyses were rerun to examine the impact before carrying out another type of clustering analysis – creating hierarchical clusters. These hierarchical clusters were thankfully all about the same size as each other, with no outliers (big or small) creating problems. The analyses also provided a means for testing which of the current statements were *potent* **strategic options** – those having consequences for many key strategic issues. Usually Fran and Steve would do this in relation to goals, but in this case they were so uncertain about the nature of the goal system they felt the analysis would not be reliable. *P411*

Finally Fran and Steve performed the analysis to find feedback loops again. The purpose this time was to discover 'real' loops rather than mistaken loops. There weren't any, but if some had been discovered then they would have been of great importance for strategy development.

Now they were able to **prepare the strategy model for the workshop**. Both were aware that they needed to ensure that the participants could understand the model as a whole and so **navigate** their way around it. An **overview map** was created by collapsing upon the key issues labels. This was drawn up on a flip-chart so that the participants could refer to it continuously during the workshop. Before it was written up, a quick check was carried out to determine whether each group member would recognize at least some of the labels. They also needed to remember that the first thing that interviewees do when viewing the aggregated model on the public computer screen was look for their own statements. Having been reassured that their proposals were captured appropriately they would then begin to explore the other statements on the screen. In addition to the overview a number of prepared views were created. This preparation was a political act, as much as it was dependent upon content analysis. The model was to facilitate negotiation. These views of sub-sections of the model would allow Fran and Steve to help the participants become familiar with the model's content, satisfying their **curiosity about the other participants' points of view**. The scene was now set for the first workshop . . . *P414* *P415* *P415* *P418*

Time passed . . . and the pair began to think about the **stage management** of the workshops . . . *P378*

Although Fran and Steve now had their model sorted and ready for the group, they still were not certain about the **venue for the workshop**. As far as Fran was concerned it was very important to get it right. They wanted somewhere where the participants could be away from their offices and concentrate on the task at hand (Fran had had enough of participants demonstrating their importance to each other by continually being interrupted by phone calls). However, NHS working practices and facilities did not suggest a conducive environment. This was partly because the participants were part of a culture where continual interruptions were usual. They felt that they had to make themselves available to deal with emergencies. The second problem was that Fran's usual option of using a local hotel was not viable; the NHS did not have the cash, and Peter was not prepared to spend taxpayers' money in this way. It was not only the location that concerned them, it was also the room itself. *P378*

Steve suggested they use the function room in the main administrative centre of the Unit. This would at least provide participants with a familiar environment, and would go some way towards stopping participants having the outside world intrude upon them. Fran agreed, only on the grounds that she could check it out. She wanted lots of room for hanging flip-chart sheets (to write on and display progress), plenty of light and yet suitable conditions for computer projection (participants had to see the projected computer screen!). Steve and Peter both saw Fran's concerns as a little excessive. How did she manage with other organizations? What did they do? 'Well', Fran replied 'I can remember a colleague of mine actually imported furniture to one hotel!': Peter was amazed – 'what were the benefits?'. Fran explained: 'the chairs at the hotel were really uncomfortable for long periods and they were heavy and static. As a result, he "borrowed" comfortable chairs that, on the one hand were not so comfortable so as to facilitate sleep, whilst on the other were not so uncomfortable to produce fidgeting and distress'. 'In addition', she added, 'he wanted to have chairs on castors so that the group could move around several work spaces in the room with ease, and the social dynamics could be varied easily'. Peter was amazed: 'Didn't it cost a lot?'. 'Actually very little compared with the cost of the managers' time, and the importance of the issue they were addressing. The potential loss of benefit far outweighed any hire costs', replied Fran. 'It is unfortunately the case that all too often the best thought-out meetings in organizations can fail through a lack of consideration of apparently trivial issues of stage management'. Peter was not wholly convinced. Fran found herself trying to ensure that a balance was retained between not offending Peter (after all Peter was very proud of his function room) and getting things right for the workshop.

As a result of all of this debate, and inspecting the function room (which led to its rejection), Fran and Steve decided to run the first workshop away from the main hospital. They decided to use a room usually used as the education centre. However, as time was getting short they were not able to view this alternative (something both had hoped to do) and were to rue this. The room was problematic. It was cramped, narrow, and long, with the seating arrangements providing a challenge (how could they get everyone to see the material?). The unfaced brick walls with their glossy paint caused the flip-charts to slide gracefully down to the floor, rather than remaining on the wall in full sight. They were also almost impossible to write upon because of the uneven surface. Something had to be done for future events!

Time passed . . . a series of further workshops were undertaken, building up the management team, increasing their understanding of the issues and developing a set of actions. It was time to manage closure [chapter C9] and publicize the strategy . . .

Peter already had been successful in presenting his strategy to others within the NHS. As part of this exercise, he had involved the management team in these presentations and this had helped cement ownership at that level of his organization. However, he had become anxious about **com- *P452 P457* municating the final strategy** to other departmental heads and other staff. He therefore arranged for another presentation to be made to the Heads of Departments at their next meeting. This was much more polished – the group now had the experience of the one made 'up-the-line', they also felt less intimidated by the audience.

The apparently whole-hearted endorsement received from his Heads of Department meant that Peter was not to be stopped. Peter felt that **a document was needed to signify closure**. It would provide an artifact – a *P460* visible demonstration of the commitment of the Unit to a clear strategic direction. The document needed careful consideration and needed to be done soon. Unfortunately, whilst Peter wanted to get the production of a strategy document under way, work pressures increased and time passed.

Finally Peter, Fran, and Steve got together with Susan and Celeste (two key members of the management team) to discuss what to include. Peter had strong views on what he wanted to see included, but so did Susan and Celeste. As a result there was considerable debate about what form it should take. Peter's key aim was to include portions of the computer based strategy model. However, he acknowledged that it was important to match or augment this with 'normal' text. Fran and Steve agreed. The majority of recipients had not experienced the process and therefore would not understand the 'map' format, and Peter wanted everyone to be able to feel comfortable with and understand the document. Susan agreed and added that the culture of the Health Service was very much geared towards normal text format. A mix of maps and text was agreed upon. Deciding what content to include also added to the debate. Peter wanted to include material from the model but he also wanted to publish a strategic action plan that would not become 'too much of a **hostage to fortune**'. For *P456* example, one of the strategic actions was to reduce waiting lists to a specified level. Although this was a reasonable strategic aim, the political cost of underachievement was likely to be large. Nevertheless he did want to give staff a clear idea of what was to be achieved.

Fran supported Peter's concern. Through previous work with other organizations, she could appreciate the balance of indicating a desirable future with having limited resources and therefore avoiding overcommitting and not meeting expectations through non-achievement. Fran and Steve therefore agreed to work through the model and provide Peter with a *list* of all of the Goals, with the Strategies indented below each of the goals they supported. This became the outline of the document. Peter, with the help of Celeste and Susan, began to flesh out the document. After a short period of trying to pull the material together they decided to bring more material in from the model. In this way they could ensure that the richness and detail was encompassed within the document. In addition, whilst working on the structure they also began to review the language or wording of the statements in the model. Susan noted that whilst the meaning of various actions was clear for the management team, it was likely to be

P455 **cryptic to those outside of their group**. They needed to elaborate some of the actions and make the meaning of the strategies more obvious. At this point Celeste suggested that Steve and Fran join in – after all they knew the model well and could provide useful help in structuring the document.

With Fran and Steve's help an introduction was drafted. It provided a brief background to the process, a list of those involved, and how the strategy related to other initiatives that were ongoing. A list of the organizational goals followed, leading into the combination of maps and text. As the Organizational values/goals were considered to be the most significant aspects of the model, Fran and Steve suggested that the maps be focused around them. To this end the goal system of six goals was divided into two pairs and two singletons. The rationale behind this was that two of the Organizational values/goals focused on staff and two focused on patients; therefore, keeping them together made good sense. The other two values were addressed separately. As a means of illustrating how they fitted together an overview or route map of the organizational values and their

P444 relationships was included before the detailed maps. Some **simplification of the strategy maps** was also necessary, as two of them comprised 30–50 statements. A balance was needed, keeping the overall sense of the map without providing so much detail that it might confuse readers.

The document concluded with a list of key strategic actions, including

P441 **'quick wins'**. Fran had suggested incorporating these into the document so as to be able to demonstrate early progress as the strategy was delivered. Throughout the document production process there had been a continual battle between adding information and keeping the document short enough to encourage staff to read it. The final document, which comprised 18 pages, was in Peter and Fran's opinion about right; however, Susan would have liked to add at least 3 more pages!

Postscript

P459 Following the production of the document, a series of **'road shows'** were used to publicize the final version of the strategy to all members of the organization, and providing them with a copy of the document meant that all staff were aware of its content. With this presentation round, and Peter's insistence that resources be argued in the light of the strategy, they ensured that the strategy was seen as a big success. However, three months later, following a move towards Trust status, the Unit was merged with another. Peter, determined not to lose the benefits of the strategy work involved new members of the management team in an exercise that reviewed and revised the strategic intent of the organization. This agreed

C165 P437 P472 strategic direction then acted as the focus for a **SDSS encompassing individual performance objectives** supporting the strategic direction. A new journey had begun.

Northern Ireland Prison Service

The Organization: The Northern Ireland Prison Service (NIPS). Northern Ireland has a number of state prisons. However, the crime rate in Northern Ireland is low. The majority of prisoners are 'politically' motivated and are associated with either Protestant or Catholic terrorist organizations such as the Provisional Irish Republican Army (PIRA). Managing the Prison Service in a strategically sound manner is crucial to the prospect of peace in Northern Ireland.

The Vignette: A staged journey. Partners in JOURNEY making. The nature of the client group. Two-day strategy workshop. Managing politics. Surfacing emergent strategic issues and goals using the Oval Mapping Technique. Stakeholder analysis – coalitions, role-think, actor influence networks, power/interest star diagrams. Building on enthusiasm and commitment. Using computer software to record, analyse and present maps. 'Road shows' and publicizing strategy.

The Cast List: The Chief Executive – Richard; 16 senior managers (including the Chief Executive) who made up the 'Senior Policy Group' (the senior management team); Terry – one of the senior managers; Paul – Richard's lieutenant and a member of the management team; involvement of 120 staff across the organization; Christopher, Rhoda, Patrick and Alistair – staff within NIPS; 2 facilitators – Fran and Colin.

As a result of previous experience Richard was suspicious of using outsiders to help them develop a strategic direction. Nevertheless, part of his support team were persuading him that involving a lot of staff in the exercise was a sensible way of tapping their expertise and providing them with a **sense of ownership** in the future of the organization. Still wary, he *C15* sent a couple of his staff to visit a number of outfits who helped organizations think through their strategic future. One of these visits was to Colin and Fran. The support team had heard positive comments about their approach and decided to meet them 'in the flesh' and see 'how they tick'.

After the visits the support team reported back to Richard with a recommendation that they engage Colin and Fran. Richard invited the pair to Belfast and, after chatting with them and asking a few probing questions, decided to proceed on a **staged basis** so that he could get a feel for *P482* how the approach might work. This basis suited Fran and Colin, who often commended it to clients as a sensible and robust way for clients and consultants to establish whether a **good working relationship could be** *P480* **created**. The first stage or test was to be a **2-day strategy workshop** with *P383* the senior management team – a workshop that was to be commonsensical rather than sophisticated – no jargon, no mystique. Its aims were to **uncover the major strategic issues** facing the organization and *C90* (covertly) gain commitment from the management team to strategy development. However, whilst there were various possible ways to go forward after the workshop, no agreement about next steps had been made at this point. Richard wanted to see what would unfold. It was up to Colin and Fran to demonstrate that their approach could work and that they could manage a difficult bunch of people in a sensible and constructive manner. Nevertheless Richard wanted the workshop to be of direct use in its own right, even if nothing else was to follow.

Time passed . . . Colin and Fran began to think about the design of the workshop and their relationship with the support team . . .

P479 One of their concerns was centred around identifying a **partner**. This was not as straightforward as usual. Each of the three members of the support team who had visited Glasgow wanted to assume the role – each with a valid reason. Christopher wanted to be a prime mover in generating the strategy; Rhoda, recently seconded to the 'centre', was keen to find a role; and Alistair was keen to make himself noticed – he wanted promotion. To make things more complicated – well at first anyway – the most senior of the three (Alistair) added a colleague of his (Patrick) to the support group. Patrick had been involved in a financial evaluation of major strategic importance. Taking account of Patrick's previous involvement and Fran and Colin's personal preferences, it was agreed that Colin and Alistair would partner and liaise with Richard and Fran, and Patrick would partner and liaise with the others in the management team.

While building the partnerships, Fran and Colin were also pondering how to modify their normal working approach to meet the requirements set by Richard. These included (i) keeping computers out of the event, and (ii) reaching a significant stage after only 2 days and without any back-

C2 P382 room work. Whilst they were aware that Richard was hoping for a **draft strategy at the end of the 2 days** (something not too sophisticated), they suspected that his expectations were fairly low and that what they needed to do was ensure that the 2 days were seen as productive by the management team.

P372 This was all very well but what were the **expectations** of the management team? If Richard had low expectations then did that suggest something? Although Richard had been prepared to discuss his senior managers, he had not described them in any terms other than glowing . . .

V224 His **relationship** with Colin and Fran was not sufficiently established at this stage for him to be completely open with them.

So it was back to the partners to get a 'run down' on each member of the management team. This was certainly a revelation! Their views were in stark contrast to the polite descriptions provided by Richard, and it became apparent that, according to them, at least a couple of the manage-

P377 ment team were **cynics**, one a **potential saboteur**, one a 'wait and see' (he
P377 was about to retire), and two who could be **potential winners**. And these were the people to impress! However, there was some good news: a

significant and apparently widely held view was that the last strategy had been developed in private and presented as a 'fait accompli' to the senior managers. Any attempt to consult was likely to be seen as a step forward albeit with some degree of suspicion – **participation** being seen as paying   C56 'lip service' to involvement. This was further complicated by the size and composition of the team. There were 16, with half being career civil servants and half having lifelong careers in the organization.

Time passed . . . and the 2-day strategy workshop was about to unfold . . .

Colin and Fran had now agreed upon a design for the 2-day workshop – one they hoped would be workable given their increasing concerns about the possible **negative attitudes of many participants**. The first challenge   C58 as far as the two facilitators were concerned was to provide a clear explanation of the workshop. This was especially important given their overwhelming sense that the first question most attending would ask was 'what the hell is a workshop?'. The culture of the organization suggested that, for most of the participants, the design Fran and Colin proposed would be a very different way of working from that with which they were familiar. Some would expect to deliver their own input as and when they could get some air-time, and some would expect to get a lot of air-time because they were more socially skilled at managing meetings. Others would expect to remain quiet. How would **realistic expectations**   P323 be established? Should they be framed by an advance notice, or introduced at the beginning of the workshop, or both? With Richard's aid (once again ensuring that the client felt comfortable with the design) the three decided that the best plan was to issue a modified '**standard calling**   P380 **note'**.

but . . .

Fran and Colin still had to resolve the issues surrounding the management team workshop's room design and **stage management**. Whilst Richard and   P378 others appreciated that managers in the private sector were accustomed to working off site so that the event could be used for social intercourse as well as concentrated work, there wasn't a budget for such events. They were concerned that using public money for 'extravagant luxuries' would seem inappropriate. The current culture suggested that social intercourse was not regarded as important in its own right. However, Richard did recognize that having the session off site would help with **team building** –   C60 something that he saw as a significant invisible objective.

In addition, Fran and Colin's requirements of two adjacent and preferably identical work rooms with connecting doors, no fixed furniture, and wall space capable of accepting flip-chart sheets attached with Blu-Tack certainly ruled out local facilities. These requirements were not particularly extravagant, supporting the technical aspects of group work rather than providing any 'perks'. Patrick came up trumps – a country hotel with good modern facilities was found. It was almost ideal for the workshop (as far as Fran and Colin were concerned they wished that they could always work in rooms like this). Two rooms were formed by dividing a single large room with a plastic coated concertina dividing wall that could be used from top to bottom and wall to wall as a work area. Thus, each room had the same large work space, making it ideal for working with two sub-groups. Communication between the rooms could be easily achieved through not using the last two panels of the dividing wall. Fran and Colin could easily move between the rooms to check the relative level of progress of the sub-groups and update one another. Finally, a third room nearby provided a break out area for coffee and tea. It was perfect.

Time passed . . . Colin and Fran arrived early to allow them to set up the room, nervous about what the day would bring and discussing strategies for managing the participants . . .

Often they would know at least some of the participants (through carrying out one to one interviews with them), but this time they had only a brief chance to chat with them over coffee immediately before the workshop – a somewhat forced conversation. This apprehension was further increased by neither Fran nor Colin having detailed knowledge about, and experience of, the culture of the organization. However, as is usually the case, they were not the only ones feeling apprehensive. As the participants began to arrive they too exhibited signs of uncertainty. Why had Richard asked these facilitators to help them? Were they going to be able to manage to make their contribution to their satisfaction? What was the right way to behave in this new setting? The rules seemed very unclear. The only ones who seemed unconcerned about the whole event were those who were clearly convinced nothing would come of it! On top of all of this it seemed that many of them were asking themselves, 'Had Richard a

C46   hidden agenda? What was the **politics** driving the event?'

The tension increased even further as the participants finished coffee and moved into the room – which was not *normally* laid out! There weren't any tables. Instead there was lots of flip-chart paper on the walls, and the

P378   seats were scattered around! The event was being **stage managed**. What is more, one of the important senior managers, Terry, had not yet arrived. While this had to some extent been predicted by the partners, Colin and Fran had felt that providing a period for coffee at the beginning of the day might act as a buffer. They were wrong! Not only did the delay waiting for Terry unsettle people but Richard was obviously angry and frustrated – a bad way to start the day! As Fran whispered to Colin, 'we have to turn this around quick – getting a bad start can take hours to recover from', both of them heard two of the other participants commenting that 'Terry is

C47 P477 **playing politics** by being late deliberately – he doesn't want to be seen at Richard's beck and call'. This worried them more, as they had put Richard and Terry in the same sub-group – would this work? Both also noted that the participants sat according to their predefined roles – those who expected to have something significant to say sat at the front whilst those more **cynical sat at the back**. Richard began his introduction. A stony silence and expressionless faces met him. An air of suspicion filled the room, and Fran and Colin wondered if they should run for it while they had a chance.   *C58*

Colin and Fran had, to some extent, expected *some* of this, and had designed the day to begin with an active event – focusing the group's attention on the task rather than on the intra-**group dynamics**. To further help with this expected problem, the group of 16 was divided into two sub-groups of 8 – with Fran and Colin facilitating one each. The task – using the **Oval Mapping Technique** – required all the participants to vigorously write their views on to the ovals, move about the room, be seen to contribute and have enough air-time to do so. They both felt that the first event should act as a signal as to the nature of the workshop. Thus, they aimed to incorporate high levels of participation, little confrontation (through the semi-anonymous mode of working), relatively low personal risk, and some fun! As they set off to work with the groups Colin quietly commented to Fran, 'how much fun do you think this will be – for us or them?'. After a very slow start the two groups became engaged in the process of presenting their views about the key issues facing them as the next few years unfolded. Normally it takes about 10 minutes for the group to warm up; however, in this case it took around 25 minutes, resulting in Colin and Fran working harder than usual to provide lots of encouragement. In addition, Fran and Colin were used to using 'friendly participants' to get things moving. Richard did an excellent job of putting up provocative statements (always a good way of getting others to contribute) and generally encouraging other participants to contribute.   *C49*   *P303*

The groups were asked to respond to the **simple 'trigger' question** – 'what important strategic issues are you likely to be facing in the next 3–5 years?'. Statements finally began to flow and within an hour around a hundred had been collected by each group. As they were placed on the flip-chart sheets in front of the group, they were moved into **clusters** by Fran or Colin – with each cluster representing views about a single substantive strategic issue. Having two groups allowed Fran and Colin to get as much diversity as possible (without doing interviews, that is) and whilst there was some similarity between the issues (one group generated nine issues and the other eleven) much of the supporting material reflected the **different perspectives**. Each issue was then organized in a rough **hierarchical map** with detailed statements at the bottom moving up to broad issues or general worries at the top. Fran and Colin did not explain this as a set of rules. Rather, they simply did it as if it was the obvious thing to do with the statements. Participants were invited to question, contradict, or correct the shifting layout of their data. Sometimes as they did this the resultant discussion led to more views appearing or, where multiple interpretations of the consequences of the original idea existed, links to the related material in other clusters were captured.   *P306*   *P308*   *C73*   *P311*

P311   Just as headlines for the clusters/issues were being agreed, Terry slipped into Colin's group. Richard did well – he suppressed his anger and tried to set the scene by explaining what had been going on. Colin continued to try to test out a summary of the developing picture and invited Terry to add his own commentary as the 'structuring' of the data was attempted. Both Colin and Fran always encourage new data to emerge on a continuous basis so that **structuring and data gathering are cyclical**, and Colin saw no reason to change this. Terry did not say or do much for at least 30 minutes, then suddenly he stood up and moved to the wall. His intervention was an outburst aimed to rubbish the emerging sense of one cluster. Colin let him 'vent his views', writing his arguments down on Ovals so that they could be captured on the wall. At the end of the outburst, Colin added Terry's views to the cluster and invited Terry to confirm that he had captured and structured them correctly. This process of merging his views to those already there, and more importantly of recording his views in a neutral manner seemed to reassure Terry and make him feel part of the proceedings. Terry seemed impressed with his contribution, and from then onwards joined the workshop as a participant

P481   (albeit a **difficult participant** with singular views on most topics). The other participants also seemed pleased with his contribution. It had added to and not subtracted from the cluster.

Time was running on, and the participants wanted a break. Fran and Colin therefore decided it was time to provide them with a chance to prioritize the emergent issues/clusters with respect to their relative importance for the strategic future of the organization. By doing so, participants would be able to feel that they had made some progress –

P313   achieved a stage in the workshop programme – and the **preferencing** would provide a form of closure. Each participant therefore was given a number of self-adhesive sticky spots and told that they could allocate their spots across the different issues. If they felt strongly about a particular issue, they could put more than one of their spots on an issue. In addition, two different colours were chosen – red spots for those issues important and needing immediate attention and green spots for those important and more long term issues. The participants enjoyed watching where one another put their spots, although the results risked being driven by

P338   opinion formers (something the **networked computer system** corrected). Fran and Colin, however, warned the groups about not taking the preferencing too seriously, but rather to treat it as indicative. Nevertheless,

P338   it was a helpful way of providing **closure** to the morning session.

C101   *Time passed* . . . Having surfaced a number of **emergent strategic issues** and prioritized them, Fran and Colin now focused on eliciting an emergent goal system . . .

As the participants went off to lunch, Fran and Colin grabbed five minutes for a quick updating on progress but didn't dare spend too much time away from the participants, as they wanted to listen to comments on the morning's work. Needless to say their host of aspirant 'partners' also demanded to stay back and review the morning's progress. All felt that the group was warming up – well, in relation to how it had started the day, and in relation to their behaviour at other events. During the discussion, it was agreed that after lunch they would follow their original plan and the sub-groups would start by considering the **emergent goals/aspirations** of *P314* the organization as suggested by the issues 'on the wall', and then move to explore more external issues. This design would enable them to surface the underlying goals by examining each of the clusters and asking the 'so what?' question. For example, why is this particular issue important?, what is driving it? From this they could get the participants to surface material further up the hierarchy. Fran and Colin also decided to follow their original plan of swapping the groups so that Colin would work with Fran's group and vice versa – not Fran's favourite outcome as she would now get Terry!! However, swapping the groups would force participants to read the other group's material, and therefore a degree of convergence, or at least mutual understanding, would be gained. Having agreed on this plan of action they joined the others for lunch – ears tuned for comments – would the participants be positive? Yes, there were some enthusiastic remarks *but* on the whole there still seemed to be a high degree of wariness, with the participants wondering where is this all leading to?

Lunch over, Colin began to explain the afternoon's activities. He and Fran were both keen to make the task reasonably active, as they were concerned that the 'after lunch sleepies' might affect performance. They need not have worried – as participants began to discuss goals, energetic debate about whether a particular issue was legitimate or not broke out. During the debate Fran and Colin frantically wrote up possible goals on to 'Post-its' (so that they were clearly distinguishable from the rest of the material) and placed them at the top of the issue clusters. They also began to capture any links between goals – a possible goal system began to surface – each goal supporting others. Two draft goal systems gradually were agreed.

Time passed . . . the goal systems were refined and agreed upon, and now it was time to focus on one part of the external environment – stakeholders . . .

Some work on this had already begun, albeit implicitly, as they had **identified various stakeholders** during the Oval Mapping issue surfacing *P314* session. These stakeholders ranged from those who had a direct interest in the future of the organization, to those who could have a significant impact upon the success of any strategy of the organization (e.g. the media). They included other organizations, individuals, coalitions of people or those with direct power to provide mandates (for example, particular Governmental bodies dictating directions for public organizations). Although Fran and Colin had marked the Ovals that mentioned stakeholders, they had not attempted explicitly to categorize them.

When they had been describing this stage to Richard, Colin had remarked that 'managers instinctively think about the dynamics of the interactions between their own decisions and the various responses it would create – what we aim to do is begin to surface and make explicit some of that knowledge. This is easier for commercial organizations because they quickly focus in on competitors and shareholders. For the public sector it is more difficult because there are usually so many of them'. In line with Fran and Colin's belief, Richard commented that whilst his managers subconsciously did think about stakeholder dynamics the actions tended to be, not surprisingly, focused on responses to operational decisions not strategies. What Fran and Colin had to do was design a process that would concentrate on the emergent strategies whilst enabling participants to surface their knowledge of the various stakeholders who would respond to these strategies. This was something that the managers had rarely done before.

However, in the manner of many workshops, the reality was different from the design. Colin found his group wishing to spend more time on *C129* **coalitions**, whereas Fran's group concentrated upon exploring in detail the *C131 P345* profile of a small number of the **key players**. Diverging from the plan was fairly typical – both knew it was important to respond to the particular interests and knowledge of the group rather than be overly constrained by the agenda. They had started with the participants highlighting those stakeholders implicitly or explicitly mentioned in the Oval maps and then moved to stakeholders that were missing. The names of stakeholders were written on to new Ovals and spread around blank flip-charts covered with a sheet of clear acetate. The participants then reviewed the material to check *C124 P345* for omissions and also to **dis-aggregate the stakeholders** where necessary. It is common for groups to start off with a broad category. For example, public sector groups often identify 'the Government' and then, upon reflection, focus on those within Government who can be managed strategically. Each sub-group ended up with 30–40 actors. These were organized into a grid against the axes of power and interest. Those who were both powerful and interested (the top right of the power/interest grid) amounted to 10–15 and they were the centre of attraction for further debate.

Colin's group, using the acetate and coloured water-based OHP pens, then began to explore the links between stakeholders (representing the different sorts of relationships between the actors). Using the acetate and pens allowed them to easily draw in, remove, edit, and refine the links. *C128 P349* This produced an **actor influence network map**. To aid the process of exploring the networks, a number of the potential strategies identified in the morning were used as a vehicle for identifying the way in which coalitions might form. The group was both fascinated and also a little worried about the knock-on effects the implementation of a strategy could have on various stakeholder groups. This concern grew as they began to identify the way potential coalitions might build. They began to realize that, as stakeholders responded to a particular strategy, some stakeholders would naturally seek out coalitions in order to increase their power base.

They realized that stakeholders moved around the grid in response to strategy implementation!

Meanwhile Fran's sub-group had been considering the implicit goal systems of four of the most significant stakeholders (well, significant according to the participants; there had been some heated argument about which were the most powerful!). As the participants had begun to surface what they perceived as the core values and beliefs of each of the stakeholders, and examine the relationships between the goals as an integrated system, they had begun to develop a clearer understanding about what motivated each stakeholder. Also, they had begun to note similarities and differences between some of the goal systems. This analysis concerned them because it implied, in some instances, a potential for the stakeholders to work together to sabotage the implementation of the emergent draft strategies. Although they were not yet complete, Fran's sub-group was moving towards a set of more formal **power/interest 'star diagrams'**.   *C126 P346* Regardless of their different approaches, both sub-groups finished the day having produced the data to support a 'role-think' exercise to take place early the next morning. Before joining the group for dinner, however, Fran, Colin and the others set about consolidating the two experiences . . .

Time passed . . . Colin and Fran (with the partners) worked on merging the goal systems, and preparing the material for the 'role-think' exercise that would start the second day of the 2-day workshop . . .

The preparation had involved creating four groups of four participants as syndicates for the **role-think exercise**. Having four would ensure that there   *C133 P350* was sufficient experience in each sub-group, whilst at the same time enough groups to explore stakeholder dynamics. Fran and Colin pondered 'which strategies would be useful to trigger these dynamics? And which stakeholders would be best to use for the role-think?'. During the evening they had identified a list of nine obvious stakeholders and 40 possible strategies. However, Fran's group, when working on stakeholders, had produced goal systems for four of the stakeholders. Reference to the actor influence network map suggested that all of these were central players. As they considered the strategies, four began to appear as obvious contenders. These four strategies would be bound to create major responses from the stakeholders as well as being obvious candidates in the final strategy. Others were included partly to add to the mix, and partly to ensure that the strategies considered came from each of the two sub-groups.

The next morning Fran and Colin found themselves introducing the exercise to half-awake people. Although both facilitators saw workshops as a bonding process – **building teams** – they wondered whether the group   *C17* had perhaps bonded a little too late into the night! However, they both knew that role-think exercises are enjoyable as well as enlightening and so weren't too worried. The first step was to provide an effective briefing – especially important because few senior managers have ever been part of a structured role-think exercise. To do this Fran and Colin used examples from other work with both private and public sector organizations, where each had resulted in very effective stakeholder management strategies.

P354
Each sub-group was asked to try to think themselves into behaving in the manner of the stakeholders they were playing. The supplied goal system (a part of the 'star diagram') was to act as **an aid to this process**. They were briefed that it was important to think about how the particular stakeholder group would respond to each of the proposed strategies – what was likely to be their 'knee-jerk' reaction? Some of the questions the sub-groups were asked to consider were:

- Where and how would the stakeholder learn about the strategy?
- Which strategy was the most noticeable? Either because it impacted positively or negatively on the stakeholder's particular aspirations.
- What was the reaction of the stakeholder to attempts to implement the strategy?
- What was the rationale to the reactions? Participants were asked to go beyond the 'agree/disagree' reaction.
- And, most importantly, how should the strategy be modified so that it could be more successfully implemented?

P354
The answers were to be noted on **flip-chart sheets headed 'Response' and 'Reasons for response'**. As Colin and Fran had decided upon evaluating 10 strategies the sub-groups were given an hour and three quarters to work on their role-think.

The report back was fascinating – producing many counter-intuitive results that appropriately challenged commonly held assumptions. The sub-groups had made good use of the actor influence network map and the goal systems. In some cases the responses were not so much fascinating as frightening – highlighting the impossibility of some of the strategies in their current formulation. It became clear that the mix of responses from all four stakeholders could generate a potent form of unmanageable chaos. As

P354
a result everyone decided that a **second round of role-think** would be beneficial. Here the sub-groups now reviewed their responses in the light of the responses of other stakeholders. The results were even more fright-

C120
ening as **unforeseen coalitions** with tremendous destructive power began to emerge.

The workshop continued with a session devoted to refining the draft goal system and subsequently revisiting the drafting of a package of potential strategies necessary for driving forward each of the goals . . .

Time passed . . . The workshop concluded with Richard thanking everyone and promising to get back to them with details of the 'next steps'. Fran, Colin, and the partners finished the workshop with a 'post-mortem' on the 2-day strategy workshop noting that . . .

The workshop with the management team appeared to have ended well with Richard pleased and surprised with the progress that had been made.

Particularly, he was pleased that his senior managers seemed to be gaining commitment to a way forward that he also felt comfortable about. Richard believed he had gained a mandate from his managers to push on with the detailed development of a new strategy – one that was, he thought, becoming politically feasible. His first experience of involving his management team in a social process that had not involved tabling a paper in advance had worked better than he had expected.

Fran and Colin were also pleased, firstly that they had escaped unscathed, but more importantly that the process had produced the type of result that Richard, as *client*, had been looking for. It seemed to both of them that Richard had developed some confidence in the JOURNEY making approach. This was also the feedback that came from Alistair, Patrick, and Rhoda over a drink at the end of the workshop. More significantly Paul, Richard's lieutenant, appeared at the post mortem/ wash up. His presence was apparently a good sign. Patrick whispered to Fran, 'if Paul is here then it means Richard wants to take things further'. This view seemed to be supported by Paul asking Colin and Fran what they thought the next steps should be. Colin and Fran at this time had no firm view about their wish to be involved further. They were not entirely sure how they would take things further, except at a broad level. Their suggestions about a way forward were tempered by the need to ensure that the proposals were independent of their own skills and guidance. However, they were keen to point out the need to build on the enthusiasm and commitment that seemed to be apparent at the end of the workshop. Colin noted that, in any event, it was important to provide participants with some 'hard-copy' *feedback material as soon as possible* and preferably by the end of the next week. 'So soon?' asked Paul. 'Yes, if you want to keep their motivation levels high'.

Fran went on to suggest that it might be worth thinking about seeking the **participation** of other key staff in the strategy development process. A *C56* significant element of the material surfaced in the workshop had been concerned with problems of morale and motivation coupled with an air of cynicism about the role of strategy. Involvement of at least a selected cross section of the staff could help, particularly if this cross section was made up of the **opinion formers** in the organization. Colin added to this by noting that designing the groups so that they included staff from both *P377* 'headquarters and field' to work together on the future of their organization, might have its own rewards. Both took care to emphasize that such an undertaking could not be taken lightly for it often led to the surfacing of issues that could be difficult to resolve and uncomfortable to acknowledge. If they were to consider involving key staff, Richard and his team must be aware that doing it and ignoring the output from it was worse than not doing it at all!

Paul (and the rest of the group) listened carefully to these suggestions, before Paul said that he felt that they were ideas that would be taken seriously. He would need to talk to Richard about them. Colin and Fran were perturbed by the possibility that Paul had entered the arena as another possible partner or maybe even a client! A large part of their journey home centred on discussing Paul's role and its implicit implications. Would it mean that each time they wanted to meet with Richard to discuss next steps they had to go through Paul?

P420

Before leaving, however, Fran reiterated that if nothing else was to be done, then it was important to provide the participants with some form of **feedback**. Paul quickly stated that producing feedback was the role of his department and that one of the reasons Patrick and Alistair were allowed at the workshop was so that they could produce such a report. Colin, however, suggested that rather than producing just a traditional report, he

P391

and Fran had found that **incorporating photographs** showing different stages of the workshop would help to remind participants of what had occurred during the workshop. He added that it was helpful to create a brochure reflecting the multiple aspects of the two days, that the event was not just a case of rationally analysing the strategic future but also building on the social cohesion of, and emotional commitment within, the group. Paul was agreeable, and suggested that Alistair and Patrick work with Colin and Fran to pull together a 'brochure'.

Patrick and Alistair arrived at their meeting with Colin and Fran in great spirits. They had 'walked the corridors' and listened to the views of all of those involved in the workshop. In Fran and Colin's terms they were becoming good partners, providing the inside picture. Both reported that

C58

whilst there was still some **cynicism** around, and a feeling that the event had been a stunt to allow Richard to do whatever he was going to do anyway, there were generally positive reports. Some wanted to build on the workshop and push things forward as fast as possible. As a result of this Alistair had been asked to negotiate for the continued involvement of Colin and Fran and to ask them if they could propose a method and timescale for the involvement of more staff. As Fran and Colin had by this stage decided that it would be interesting to continue work with the organization, they agreed to put some thoughts down on paper and send it to Richard.

This development suggested that the brochure should allow for building upon the initial work. Therefore using the software to record, analyse [chapter P6] and present the information would be a worthwhile exercise. The first step was to use the software to enter all of the Oval Mapping data into a model to create a computer based cause map, linking statements formally to give a large means–ends hierarchy. This fascinated Patrick who was engaged by the ability to structure the data and so better make sense of it all. Recorded along with the statements on the Ovals were the

P407

preferencing scores. **Styles (fonts) were created to differentiate clearly the different categories of data** – goals, strategies, and options. As much as possible the team kept to the original wording to ensure that the participants could easily recognize their own contributions within the greater whole. However, as Colin pointed out, because the statements will no longer be handwritten, participants will begin to assume that some of the statements were their own, even if they didn't generate them on the day.

This, he continued, was the beginning of **negotiating a group ownership** P320
of the strategic issues.

The brochure began to take form. First, was the draft goal system as a map with its associated draft mission statement. This was followed by maps showing each of the strategic issues. The issue maps did not show the links (these maps were deliberately printed without them to replicate the appearance of the issues at the workshop). However, the goal map, actor influence network map, and presumed stakeholder goal maps were printed out with their links, as these links had been generated during the workshop. In addition, photographs were woven throughout the document showing the group progressing the material. Fran and Colin made sure that there was at least one picture including each participant.

Time passed . . . Richard agreed the design of the workshop series and Colin and Fran ran five workshops involving about 120 staff from a cross section from each of the area offices and from Headquarters . . .

With Fran and Colin's help attention had also been paid to developing alternative futures [chapter C8 and P4] and testing the emergent strategic actions against these scenarios. In addition, Richard had agreed to a final 'closure' workshop with the management team to negotiate an agreed strategy. This workshop, he felt, had gone surprisingly well. Sub-groups of the management team had examined all of the material supporting the strategies and had made changes that were appropriate and necessary. They had found the material, presented as a set of colour maps formed into a booklet representing a draft strategy, an easy way to explore the strategies and test their coherence. Following this work, each sub-group made a presentation to the whole group suggesting the changes that needed to be made to make the strategy workable. These changes were made in the computer model as they were suggested. In this way the ramifications of changes could be explored on a public screen. Colin and Fran were also pleased with the results, especially the way the management team members had maintained the coding practice [chapter P1], often arguing amongst themselves about the direction of a link. To help maintain a consistent coding practice, a series of flip-charts with the coding rules were displayed around the walls (figure V3). Richard now had a strategy

As a result of this workshop they now had a strategy that they were committed to **publicizing** throughout the organization. Richard, however, P452
was concerned about publishing a document. There were lots of stakeholders determined to sabotage the strategy, and if he published the strategy in its entirety then these stakeholders could use the material to their advantage.

In addition, Richard did not want the strategy document to provide too much detail about the definite actions – there were too many stakeholders watching the organization's performance. As the discussion continued, Fran commented that what they were doing was in essence considering the strategy presentation as a form of strategic option and considering the

Figure V3 Coding practice guidelines.

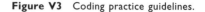

Developing 'Cause Maps'
– re-organize the cluster

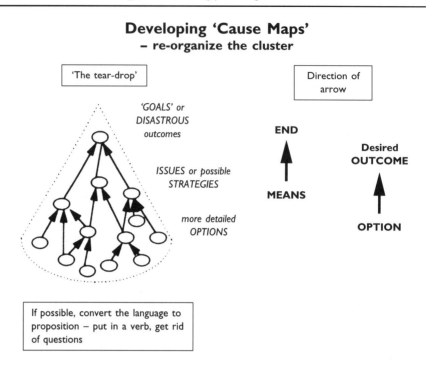

'The tear-drop'

Direction of
arrow

'GOALS' or
DISASTROUS
outcomes

END

MEANS

Desired
OUTCOME

OPTION

ISSUES or possible
STRATEGIES

more detailed
OPTIONS

If possible, convert the language to
proposition – put in a verb, get rid
of questions

stakeholder reactions to it. It was just as they had done for any other strategic option. Consequently, the trio formalized their decision making P455 activity and considered carefully the **stakeholders' responses to different options for presenting their strategy**. There was, for example, a lengthy debate and analysis of whether to produce (i) an internal document only, (ii) external and internal documents, or (iii) one document for internal and external consumption. In the end they reckoned that an internal document would become external and so they must be the same. Richard also wanted to involve members from the management team in the production of the strategy document. This would help keep their interest and enthusiasm. To that end he suggested that they draft the strategy as it would appear in the published format.

Three months later, and after several drafts, the strategy document was agreed, not just by the management team but also by the appropriate Government Minister. However, an integral part of the bargain with the participants in the workshops was that they should be able to comment on it before it was publicly announced. Fran and Colin were very keen on fulfilling this promise, and Richard was also enthusiastic. Consequently, a C54 P459 series of **'road shows'** was planned that would allow Richard and members of the management team to present the final version of the strategy 'that had been substantially influenced by members of the organization and by representatives of potential collaborating organizations'.

Richard was delighted by the management team's reception of the idea of road shows. This turned out to be a surprise to him, and Colin and Fran. Any cynicism felt earlier by the management team seemed to have disappeared, and all wanted to demonstrate their commitment by a direct involvement in the planned road shows. The only effective way for this to be done was for each of them to be involved in two presentations on a rolling basis and for Richard to be involved in them all. They genuinely felt that they had done justice to the input from the participant workshops that they had sponsored and wanted to show this. Even so, Richard and a couple of the management team were convinced that there would still be vocal outbursts from some participants who felt their worries and thoughts had not been given enough attention. To try to alleviate these fears the road shows were carefully scripted and Patrick and Alistair developed a rehearsal schedule intended to help identify appropriate responses to difficult questions.

As a result of Richard's concerns about the details of the strategy being made public in advance of the proper release date the road shows occurred in rapid succession. Due perhaps to their careful preparation, their anxieties were unfounded. The reception was uniformly good, and in some cases remarkable and memorable. On one occasion a trade union leader took to the floor and seemed poised to launch a vitriolic attack on the presentation. She was known to be outspoken in her condemnation of senior management and was a charismatic opinion leader. Richard and the two sponsors waited with bated breath . . . she stridently congratulated Richard and the management team for their work in involving staff, in **taking them seriously**, and in creating a high quality strategy for the   C54 whole organization . . .

Postscript

Richard was promoted and **replaced by a new Chief Executive**. So what   P472 of the strategy?

Richard reports that the strategy is soundly in place, to the extent that it has changed attitudes of those within and outside the organization. The strategy as a holistic system of goals and programmes has been significant in defending the service against *ad hoc* policies imposed by politicians. It has enabled senior managers to undertake change that would not otherwise have been possible.

As time passed, the new man has become convinced of the strategy, partly because the management team had such a strong commitment to it. It would have been difficult for the new Chief Executive to have dismissed the strategy without major repercussions amongst staff as well as the management team. Over 4 years on, the strategy remains the 'bible for managing every aspect of the organization'.

AMCOF – a traditional engineering company

The Organization: AMCOF – a division. A traditional engineering company in the oil and gas field operations business, with over 500 employees. The work was undertaken 6 years ago.

The Vignette: Team building. Oval Mapping Technique. Computer assisted workshops. Using the networked computer system. Strategy influencing organizational structure. Distributed Strategy Delivery Support System (SDSS).

The Cast List: The Client, the Managing Director of the division – Phil; Barry – a newly appointed internal staff member and trainee facilitator; Phil's senior managers, other directors from the company, and senior managers from a customer organization; 2 facilitators – Fran and Barry.

Phil contacted Fran. He had just been appointed to run a Services Contract and had great plans for **team building** as part of a strategy development process. Therefore, he wanted to ensure that the journey involved as much **participation** as possible. He believed that if he could involve all the managers in the process then they would have an increased understanding of the contract/project, and also be able to take more responsibility. In addition, he wanted, at some stage, to involve a few members of the customer group to ensure that the direction taken by his team would be in alignment with that of their significant customers. However, he added whilst providing Fran with the background, 'the organization's culture is still a little conservative – could we start JOURNEY making using manual techniques but quickly move into using the computer based approaches?'.

'Sure', Fran said, 'we could spend the morning surfacing the issues and their context using the **Oval Mapping Technique** (OMT) and spend the afternoon working on the prioritized issues using the computer based version of the resultant OMT map. However, we would need someone to help in the morning to put all of the material from the Ovals into the computer'. 'No problem', said Phil, 'Barry can help us'. Barry had recently been recruited by the company and he already knew how to use the software. As the discussion continued, Fran and Phil began to **negotiate the design**. There would be five workshops to ensure everyone who should attend could attend. Each morning would be spent using the Oval Mapping Technique, with Fran facilitating the **clustering and structuring**, and Barry capturing it all in the model. When explaining this to Barry his immediate comment was, 'Hang on, if you are going to be moving the Ovals around the wall so as to cluster them, how am I going to avoid entering the material in twice or missing things?'. 'Because I shall also be numbering the ovals, all you need to do is type them in in any order that seems convenient. Just type the number and then the content. Periodically

Margin references: C60, C56, P303, P479, P308

it is useful to list all the input to identify missing numbers', Fran replied. Following this, the entire Oval Map would be reviewed, and extended to capture linkages and additional elaboration. The group would then break for lunch. This, it was hoped, would give both Fran and Barry time to ensure that the statements on Ovals, links, and clusters were in the computer model and to prepare for the afternoon session. Working in this fashion would enable the link between the computerized model and the wall picture to be simple and transparent.

Time passed . . . and the five **'standard' 1-day strategy workshops** unfolded   *P382*
. . .

Phil and Fran's design worked, although the **'stage management'** of the   *P378*
workshop did mean the participants, who were not used to being without chairs and tables in the room, did take a little time to settle! Fran found herself learning more about their particular business than she had ever expected. Ovals came thick and fast from the 15 participants – prompting Barry to comment, 'I don't know how you manage to cluster them, it all seems to happen so fast'. 'Practice, and I guess a little luck', Fran joked, 'however, there is a set of OMT guidelines you might like to look at' [chapter P2]. As with other OMT sessions, the participants spent a little over an hour generating material (over 120 Ovals) before beginning to wind down. As a means of re-energizing them and extending their thinking Fran had suggested that they (a) identify ways of achieving some of the statements on the wall, (b) consider possible practical problems, and (c) put more argument up about why particular issues seemed to be important. Following this burst of activity the group broke for coffee. Ostensibly this was to give the participants a reward for their hard work, but in reality it was to provide Fran with a chance of sorting out the clusters. After coffee Fran carried out a quick review of the clusters before beginning to work on each cluster in more detail. Here, the **structure of the**   *P311*
cluster was examined, with Fran, with the group's help, moving super-ordinate statements to the top of the cluster and the more detailed options to the bottom. Consequently the clusters began to appear 'teardrop' shaped. Throughout the process of linking the statements with arrows (to show influences, presumed causality, and implications) more material surfaced. For an example of a cluster see figure V4. This occurred as the participants began to notice that they had different interpretations of a particular statement and therefore new material was needed to elaborate their meaning. To help this Fran often asked **challenging or 'obvious'**   *P308 P387*
questions about what specific phrases meant (particularly when one of the participants was looking confused). In a brief aside to Barry, she noted that often participants didn't understand the material themselves but didn't dare ask in case they lost face. No one would expect her to know, and so she could help out others by asking 'innocent' questions! At the end of each morning (there were five workshops) they had on average around two hundred statements with links between them captured in the computer.

Figure V4   One cluster from an OMT session.

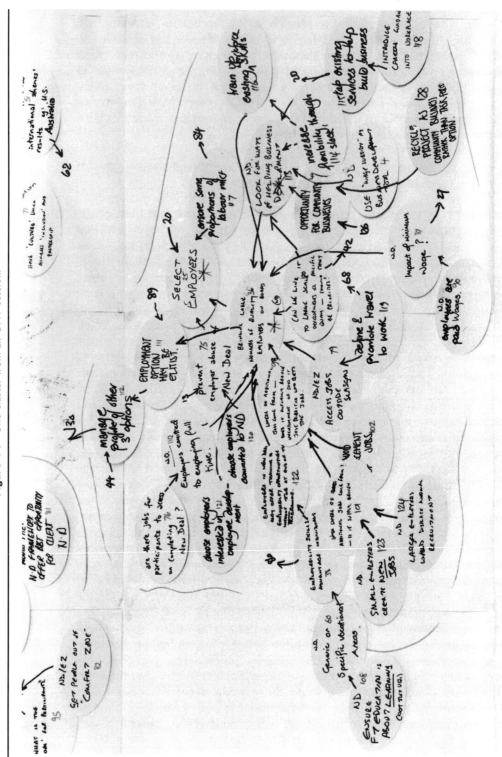

While the participants were enjoying lunch, Fran and Barry worked hard to ensure all of the material from the Oval Mapping session was in the model. 'Its not fair', muttered Barry, 'we did all the work and they get the lunch!'. 'Real facilitators don't each lunch!' Fran joked back, 'but don't worry there will be time for a quick sandwich; besides we ought to go and listen to discover how people are finding the process'. This time, however, it was a very hasty sandwich. Before starting after lunch, Fran had set up a number of mini maps in the computer so that the material for each issue/cluster was presented in an identical manner to that on the wall. By doing so, she explained to Barry, it helped participants transfer attention from the wall to the model and trust in the computer based version of the work they had done in the morning. She had concentrated on the issues that had emerged from the results of participants expressing their **preferences** – the final part of the morning's session. They had P313 considered preferences from two angles – which issues were (a) the most important, and (b) the most appropriate to work on that afternoon. However, it still took time to produce just the most preferred issue clusters, and the participants, enthusiastic with their progress, were keen to start early.

The first step after lunch was to explore how all of the key issue clusters and the emergent goals, implied by the identification of the issues, fitted together. Focusing upon them on a projected computer screen helped with this process. It also provided Fran with the ideal opportunity to explain what she and Barry had been doing during the break. They wanted to show participants how the **computer model was simply a copy of the wall** P327 **picture**. They also wanted to demonstrate that it could display the numerous relationships (between and within clusters) more easily because only the statements and links of interest were shown on the screen, with the remainder accessible when required. As participants began to gain confidence in the computer model, trusting that Barry had captured their material accurately, they began to refer less and less to the wall picture. It was interesting to note, though, that when they wanted to create a cross cluster link they returned to the wall picture to check it. They could remember exactly where on the wall the statements were located, and they were initially suspicious about everything being accessible from the computer model. Starting with the **overview** picture (with all of the key P415 issues and emergent goals, and their interlinking) was helpful because it was relatively uncluttered. The groups typically had identified around 11–12 issues/clusters and the same number of goals. With 25 statements to view, it was easy for them to see the whole of the summary picture displayed by computer model. It was also an ideal way of showing how easy it was to move statements around the screen, make links, edit statements, and change categories by using different colours and fonts. It was in this way that goals identified in the morning session could be re-assigned as key issue statements and vice-versa. The summary picture was introduced as a first draft of a strategy map – showing goals and the key strategic issues that might later be converted into strategies. Another reason

P415   for working on the summary map first was because it helped the group 'navigate' around the model.

Once the group felt comfortable with the overview strategy map, they then moved to considering in more depth the issues they had prioritized before lunch. It had been of interest to Barry that, although each of the five groups had undertaken the same process, there was variation in the issues raised (and even those with the same issue label had different material defining them). Fran had commented, 'You can maybe understand why

C90 P298   we like **doing an interview round when possible** – then differences of perspective across individuals can be attended to, as well as across groups'. The first stage of working on a key issue (that had started life as a cluster of Ovals and was now a computer picture showing statements linked together by arrows) was a quick review of the material already surfaced through the OMT. Once the group understood the ease with which statements could be changed, new statements added, and others elaborated they began to develop the map itself and suggest cross links to material in other clusters. Barry, operating the computer, was less adept at manipulating the software than he was to become with practice. To help

P336   him, Fran **captured the new material on the flip-charts they had positioned handily around the screen**. She did this while participants were talking and every now and again would stop the group and review her mapping of the discussion with participants. Her intention was to be able to reassure the group that their views were being heard, whilst giving Barry extra time to edit the screen in alignment with her flip-chart maps. This was different from working solo, where Fran captured the discussion directly on to the computer screen instead of mapping on paper, thus keeping the computer model up to date in real time. This way of working, however, can have its own drawbacks. It is harder to manage the process and pay attention to recording and structuring content. Working in tandem makes it easier to ensure that an appropriate balance between

P380   **process management and content management** can be made. Besides, in AMCOF's case, as with so many strategic change projects, it was important that someone within the client's company became an expert in using the

P436   software, particularly if later on they were going to **use the computer model to monitor progress (Strategy Delivery Support System)**.

As each issue was worked on it appeared to go through a cyclical process. The group would begin by considering the material on the screen, before launching into an animated discussion about the issue, raising new ideas, amending existing ones, and adding new links. It was easy to see participants checking that their own material was faithfully recorded as part of an issue, before they began to consider this material in the context of others. All of the new material was captured in the model and cross links made to other parts of the model when appropriate. The participants appeared to revel in the process of discussion being captured rather than

P325   forgotten, as in other meetings. They could see the **changes being made in real time** and correct any mistakes that either Fran or Barry made. The process of correcting/editing was critical because it was not usually the case that Fran or Barry had been wrong, but rather that others in the group wanted to present alternative interpretations. Because the computer system was deliberately focusing attention on a restricted amount of material, sometimes it took the participants a little while to realize one of the advantages of using the computer system over Oval Mapping. The fact that a single statement could appear on several of the multiple maps being used at the same time aided cross linking, especially as editing a statement on one map/screen would automatically revise the wording on another. Barry gradually got used to pulling material from other stored maps on to the current screen, realizing that it would remain in the original prepared issue map. As the group slowed down, Fran reviewed the structure and implications of the material generated. This process of review served to act as a form of closure to a stage – providing the group with a **sense of** *P388* **progress**. Sometimes it also provided the signal for a 'comfort break' – a chance for participants to recharge their batteries over a cup of tea.

During each of the discussion periods, Fran worked hard to try to ensure all participants were able to contribute by **bringing quieter par-** *P386* **ticipants** into the conversation and ensuring all of the **key actors** could be *P477* heard. A quick 'round robin', giving each participant a chance to express their views about a particular topic, was sometimes appropriate. In addition, she continually monitored the reaction of Phil, the client, just in case the group moved into an area he did not want discussed. Whilst this proved not to be a problem she continually had to stop him from dominating the discussion. Phil had strong views on many of the issues and was keen to express them. This, combined with the fact that he was relatively new to the organization, meant that some of the other participants who had not yet determined how open to alternative ideas he was, were tempted to say less. The only time this was not an issue was during the workshop with the senior managers. Phil, in considering the group membership of the five workshops, had wanted to involve a number of the directors of the organization so that he could (i) demonstrate the rationality of the outcomes, and also (ii) gain their knowledge and insights. It was, as expected, this workshop that saw him at his quietest!

The final stage of the workshop reviewed each issue cluster and identified which of the potential strategic options embedded in the cluster were most preferred. Fran used this process to give the group a sense of progress and of closure to the workshop. She was also very aware that there were more options within each cluster than resources available and so some rough prioritization was essential. The first step was for the group to explore the map of the cluster displayed on the public screen and determine which of the statements represented potential strategic options. Some of the statements were explanations of the linking between a proposed option and its consequences. Each participant was then invited to use the **preferencing module of the networked computer system** to *P338* distribute 'resources' to the four best options. The results were then reviewed by the group and those gaining the highest resources were placed in a new category labelled *key* strategic options. In addition, Fran

P358   was able to use the computer system to **check the level of agreement** amongst the group. There appeared to be a high degree of consensus with

C68 P337   no obvious outliers in the group. The **anonymity** of the process (as far as participants were concerned) gave Fran some confidence in this conclusion compared with the use of the manually applied self-adhesive spots. As a way of closing the workshop, Fran provided a brief explanation of what

P390   was to follow – **setting clear expectations** about the next part of the journey. Phil thanked participants for attending, and contributing to the overall effort.

Most of the participants left with a sense of achievement, coming up and thanking Fran and Barry for 'a much more productive day than was usually the case'. As they left the room, many commented that the process was interesting because Fran had not been evaluative, rather 'every contribution was taken seriously, even if it then gradually got modified as others in the group worked with the statement as if it were theirs'. One participant suggested, 'I don't think I've ever paid so much attention to what my colleagues said before – I think it's because others built on my arguments and I built on theirs in a constructive way, instead of the usual point scoring'. These comments helped Phil and Barry understand better

C53   the points Fran had been seeking to make about the role of '**procedural**

C54   **justice** *and* **procedural rationality**' in JOURNEY making.

When designing the workshop, Fran had built in time for her, Barry,

P481   and Phil to undertake a **review of the event**. Their observations revealed that participants Phil had expected to cause trouble didn't, whilst those signalled as quiet had been quite vociferous – once again careful stage management had paid off. This vindicated some of the time spent before the workshop reviewing the participants' expected behaviour. While reflecting, Fran commented that it might have been useful to get the participants to do the mapping of the clusters using the standard guide-lines (see figure V3). This might have helped with ownership. However, she concluded, it would have taken longer and, on balance, prevented other important activities. Reviewing the day also helped Barry understand how careful design of process could significantly change normal behaviour patterns of participants. Nevertheless, he did comment that pulling all of the material together and then deciding what was to be done was going to be quite a task . . .

Time passed . . . and Barry and Fran got engrossed in some of the essential 'backstage' work . . .

Having linked the models from each of the workshops together – a process Barry had found fascinating – Fran, Phil, and Barry began to think about how they could take the process the next step forward. Given the required time scale for the whole journey, Phil and Fran needed to plan how to get firm and committed agreement to actions and priorities. There were far too many key options from the workshops for them all to be

P434   implemented. Alongside this, Phil was still keen to **involve some of the**

senior managers from one of their major customers. He reasoned that if they could involve a couple of significant players from a customer in the strategy process, then his team would gain. Not only would they get a clear idea of the customer's priorities, but they would also get to know the customer better. The other people he would like to involve included his senior managers – resulting in around eight attending the workshop. Fran could see this was going to be another of 'those group size discussions!'. Ever since she had started working with Phil she found herself continuously having to persuade Phil that the **best group size** for decision making was around 8–10 participants. Phil appreciated that whilst it was possible to work with larger groups when participants were attending as a source of expertise and to increase involvement, decision making groups had to be smaller. However, he frequently seemed to sneak extra managers into decision making groups. He always did this just before the workshop and always with very good reasons! If Phil was to involve the senior managers from the customer, it was important that the workshop was clearly successful, and having too many people would reduce that probability.

P376

Phil agreed it was important to ensure the workshop went according to plan, and promised that there would be only two members of the customer's organization along with his six managers. Although that added up to nine participants once she had added Phil to the group, Fran agreed. Barry would be helping her after all. The next question was 'how long should the workshop be?' At this stage Barry chipped in, asking whether it was possible to run a two-stage process. The first day could be with the customer's senior managers to show them the process and get their contributions, and then the following day would be just with Phil's senior managers – deciding what should be done. 'Yes', Fran agreed, 'that would be a good way of working. Furthermore, given the number of issues we have, maybe the second stage should be a 2-day event; that way we can ensure that all of the issues are addressed'. Phil agreed and promised to arrange things. Meanwhile Fran and Barry continued to design the two workshops. For the start of the workshop, when the customers were present, Fran decided to produce a clear overview of the key issues already surfaced and how they related to each other as part of the introduction. 'What will you say?' questioned Barry. 'Well, to ensure that the customers get an understanding of the **purpose of the workshop**, I would probably explain how the material had been gathered, how it is linked, and how the day is to unfold. This will provide them with some context to the workshop and demonstrate how serious you are about building the right strategies for them. After all, the first five minutes or so are crucial'. Barry muttered, 'Hmm, won't harm the senior managers either'. 'What would be the next step? How would we use the overview?'.

P385

'Well, it will provide us with a means of navigating around the computer model, but will also allow us to get people to express preferences about those issues they see as the most important both in the long and short term. The computer system will record how the customer's preferences compare with those of Phil's senior managers. If there is a difference between preferences, then depending on what the customer's senior managers are like, the group could perhaps discuss why there is a difference. Watching how the customer expresses preferences on the facilitator monitor will give us some valuable clues as to which issues to address for the remains of the workshop'. 'Sneaky, but I like it', commented Barry. 'Nothing of the sort,' retorted Fran, 'just an efficient use of the system and good facilitation! Good facilitation is always manipulative. It cannot be anything else. It needs to be so as to get the best out of a group – careful and contingent design is everything!'.

Time passed . . . Barry and Fran finished tidying up the model and agreeing the design. The first stage of the workshop was run and the three were reviewing its effect . . .

'Wow!' commented Phil, 'that was quite a workshop, what did you guys think?'. 'Well, one of the customers [Peter] seemed to get more from it than the other. All Tom [the other customer] could do was continuously raise concerns and requirements', commented Barry. 'However, they both seemed pleased to be there, and thought that the day was worthwhile from their point of view. They both also seemed impressed with what we were trying to do through the workshops'. 'That's my impression also', Phil noted, 'however, Tom is the one we really need to build a good relationship with, and, as you said, he kept raising concerns'. 'I don't see making lots of comments as a bad sign', Fran interjected, 'my guess is that Tom was quite engaged by the process of seeing his statements captured within the whole of the model, and saw it as an opportunity to express his point of view'. 'OK, fair point. I can't say I am surprised by their overall focus though – that is concentrating on cost effectiveness and safety, I guess that is what they would say. However, they did suggest some good ideas about how we could work more effectively on new projects, and certainly helped me get to see how it looked from their side. We now need to work with the senior managers to begin to sort out what we are going to do and how to put it into practice' . . .

Time passed . . . The second stage workshop was undertaken with the senior managers, with the strategic intent and action programmes being agreed upon and responsibilities assigned to those most appropriate . . .

Phil was now keen to set up a means of checking progress on the actions that had been agreed. As his staff were scattered around the country, having regular meetings on progress was very difficult. He was conscious that managers were unable to have casual chats in the corridor and so there was no informal mechanism for updating one another on their progress in implementing strategic actions. Moreover, the results of the strategy workshops had suggested that some review of the current structure and job tasks was required – changes needed to be made. He therefore decided that he would **restructure** the division to follow, in principle, the structure of the strategy map expressing the **strategic intent**. His aim was to set up a series of one to one meetings where he would use the strategy model as a means of providing each of his senior managers with job descriptions. In addition, any new material in terms of tasks or responsibilities that surfaced through these meetings could be added into the model, and changes made. He would also be able to use the model to show them how their tasks and targets related to those of his other senior managers. Following the restructuring of the organization, each senior manager would be given the task of putting into place the part of the strategy that related to their own function. They would use the model to remind them of their responsibilities and flag progress.

C82 C171 P463
P467
C171

Although Fran had agreed that this process would help ensure delivery of the strategy, she anticipated problems with the managers working with the model's material as a **Strategy Delivery Support System (SDSS)**. If they simply worked on hard copy then it would be difficult to reflect the dynamic nature of implementation (not just in terms of the progress but also in the inability to record any changes that were made due to changing environmental circumstances and problems encountered during attempts at implementation). Phil agreed and mused upon whether it was possible to allow all of the senior managers to have access to the strategy model using the computer network in the organization – that way they could keep their part up to date and yet continually review the progress and decisions made in related parts. Furthermore, he noted, having some means of securing access, providing a notice board and having shared work space would be essential. All of this is possible, noted Fran, 'Why don't we put it into place?'.

P436

Postscript

As a result of involving a number of other Directors in the Division's journey, the Managing Director promoted the JOURNEY making approach to the next level of the organization to develop a company wide strategy and an IT strategy. In addition, many of the tools and techniques have been used extensively within the organization for strategic problem solving.

Strathclyde Poverty Alliance – a multi-organization charitable company

The Organization: Strathclyde Poverty Alliance (SPA) – a multi-organization charitable company limited by guarantee. Funded from many sources and set up to deal with poverty in the largest Region of the UK. (The organization is now called The Poverty Alliance following the reorganization of local government in the UK.)

The Vignette: Single 1½-day workshop. Uncovering an emergent goal system in a multi-organizational setting. Collaboration.

The Cast List: The Chief Executive – Damian Killeen; 10 members of the Board of Directors; 13 staff; 2 facilitators.

Damian (the Chief Executive) was concerned about how he could develop a **coherent set of goals** for the organization. He wanted the goals to reasonably reflect the multiple interests of all the organizations who were represented on the Board of Directors. These representatives came from large charities such as Barnardo's [focusing on children], small charities living on a 'shoe string', and local government officers representing funding agencies. For some time he had been reflecting whether the approach that Colin and Fran had written about might help his group. If he sought to address the aims of the organization as an interlinked system of goals, as suggested by them, might that be the basis for the successful **negotiation** of a set of goals for SPA? Furthermore, if this was possible it could generate some energy from each member of the Board, and take them beyond simply acting as representatives of their own organizations. He called Colin and arranged a meeting to talk about developing a goal system and some associated strategies.

As they began talking about the possibility, Damian mentioned that at previous meetings when Alliance members had talked about goals, they usually became bogged down. Long lists of wonderful sounding aims were discussed but, he continued, these were mostly unrealistic and did not represent the real responsibilities and interests of the people at the meeting or of their organizations. To provide some context, Colin began to explain his and Fran's orientation – that they liked to start by getting participants to relate to what they actually did rather than what they said they did. As Colin spoke, Damian's interest increased. Damian was attracted to the idea of working up the goals from the issues the representatives sought to address. Fran and Colin's 'standard' JOURNEY making approach of using interviews or the **Oval Mapping Technique** (OMT) to surface issues and so get at an **emergent goal system** seemed to make particular sense for a **multi-organizational setting**.

Damian commented to Colin that SPA had always had difficulty in getting all of the members of the Board of Directors together for more than

Margin references: C5, C11, P303, C98 P426, C106 C119 C120

a couple of hours at a time. This was because they each had other jobs and responsibilities. However, he was hopeful that if they could be persuaded of the usefulness of the outcome and, more importantly, the likelihood of achieving it, then they might attend a full day off-site workshop. He promised Colin he would try to get their commitment and then get back to him. Damian was successful. When he floated the idea of a workshop there seemed to be enthusiasm for having another go at something they all thought was important. He and Colin then began to design the workshop, working together so as to develop something Damian felt comfortable with and building the **consultant/client relationship**. One day became two *P480* days, and expanded into a bigger task – to get the issues on the table, get at goals, and attempt to resolve some of the most important strategic issues. However, Damian noted to Colin, if this was now to be the aim then others should be involved. Colin could see the **group size** increasing! *P376* Damian explained that he managed a relatively small organization of full time staff (at that time 13 project workers and administrative support staff). He wanted to include them as well as the directors. He soon persuaded Colin that it would make sense to include all 22 **key actors**. *P477* After all, involving all of these actors would increase the likelihood of ownership of the outcomes by all who were expected to deliver the agreed strategies. Colin, agreeing, warned him that this would mean two facilitators working, for some of the time, and splitting the group into two sub-groups. Damian did not feel that was a problem. By now he was warming to the idea of mixing the two groups for 2 days. In his and Colin's opinion there were a number of benefits from this social mixing. One benefit came from working off site and participants being able to pay more attention to each other's views, the other from the strategic issues being surfaced from two, sometimes competing, perspectives (those involved on an everyday basis and those who were part time).

As with many of the public sector bodies that Colin and Fran had worked with, **accommodation for the workshop** was an issue. The organ- *P378* ization was about resolving poverty, so it was clear that it could not spend any more money than absolutely necessary on meeting facilities or accommodation. After some debate Damian and Colin agreed on a location. The workshop was to be held at a mediocre quality hotel. It was 100 miles from the offices of participants, and accessible by cheap public transport. When Colin arrived at the hotel, he was dismayed by the workshop rooms, which were far from ideal. Not only were they unattractive, but they had uncomfortable seats, and no decent daylight. Working in them was not going to be easy! Nevertheless, the rooms did have the main requirement of decent wall space for 'oval mapping'.

Colin and Damian had agreed that the first day should start after lunch with issue generation using oval mapping undertaken by two equal sized sub-groups. Each sub-group would have a mix of staff and directors and would be asked to suggest 'the major strategic issues that SPA should address in the next few years'. To facilitate this, Colin and a colleague he had asked to help followed the 'standard' approach for OMT. They worked

on getting participants to dump statements on to ovals before moving on to
P311 **clustering, cluster labelling**, and capturing some of the links both within
and across clusters. As usual, each group changed rooms at the break. Their
task now was to build a goal system through determining the goals implicit
in the strategic issue clusters that had been defined by the other sub-group.
This not only meant that both groups had to read the other's material but
that a degree of negotiated convergence could occur.

As the goals were produced, they were placed into one of three
P427 categories. The first category comprised **facilitative goals** – goals that did
not express the main aspirations of the organization but which were seen
as fundamental to facilitating their achievement. The second category
focused on the goals of SPA that were also goals of member organizations.
C132 The third category was '**meta-goals**' – goals that could *only* be achieved by
successful multi-organizational collaboration. Damian was keen to separate those goals which could represent 'collaborative advantage' from those
which meant SPA was supporting the activities of member organizations.
'After all', he commented, 'if we are an alliance and we can't identify some
meta-goals, do we have a right to exist?'.

The afternoon session finished with the whole group together, packed
tightly into one of the rooms. Colin had picked the goals off from the oval
maps in each room and set them out separately on one wall, in a very
rough hierarchy. With his encouragement, the group made some attempt
to organize the structure of the top of the hierarchy. New goals were
added as original goals needed more explanation. By the time the workshop stopped for dinner, 37 goals had been noted and about half had been
roughly linked.

After dinner the work started with a vengeance for Colin and the other
facilitator, with intermittent help from Damian. Damian's part attendance
was the result of a conflict between his wanting to engage with the
important after-dinner socializing and also gaining a better feel for where
the group had got to. He reported that most people seemed pleased with
their work and with the progress made. The participants, according to
him, felt that structuring the issues to encompass the views of staff and
directors seemed to have been informative and constructive. They also
believed that the explication of goals from issues seemed to have got closer
to real, and realistic, aspirations.

Before they could finish up for the evening, Colin and his colleague had
six tasks ahead of them. The first task was to move all the 'ovals' into one
room and merge similar issues generated by each group into a single map.
Colin's colleague agreed to have a go at this. Concurrently Colin worked at
P423 **rewriting the goal system** so that each goal could be more easily read.
Following this he cross checked each of the goals with each of the issues so
that each goal could be related to at least one issue and vice-versa. The
combined issue clusters were laid out on the biggest wall so that they were
placed in the same relative position as the goal to which they were most
linked (following the goal system map). Both of the facilitators then tried
P428 some draft **merging of goals to reduce the number** to something more

workable. Finally, with their remaining energy, they attempted a draft summary goal system (see figure V5). The goals were roughly clustered into bundles – the dotted lines – to match the issue material. From this initial system they drafted a 'mission statement'. Just as they were leaving for bed Damian popped in and reminded Colin that SPA members did not like the idea of having a mission statement. He and his team felt 'they are for big business'. A quick change of terms and the mission statement became a statement of strategic intent.

The first task for the next morning was to ratify the 'tidied' **goal map**   *P314* with the participant group. They then focused upon checking the logic and coherence between the issue maps, issue cluster relationships, and the related goals or goal clusters. One of the goals, 'survival of SPA', had been left hanging as a 'head' during the last group session on the previous day and needed attention. As Colin and Damian had hoped, it did not take long for the group to demand that it had some consequences, and so it was linked into the goal hierarchy. As the group refined the goal system, it was interesting for all to note, understand, and reflect upon the apparent two-sided nature of the system. One side showed the goals relating to influencing policy, and the other showed the goals relating directly to those in poverty.

By starting at 9 a.m., the entire goal system had been agreed by 10.20 a.m. and so, before a coffee break, the whole group did a 'quick and dirty' **exploration of alternative futures**. The 'important events' raised by this   *P361* analysis were then checked for **coherence** with the goal system. Questions   *C134* like 'If the event is important, why is it important?' were asked. In each case, the answer was checked to ensure it related to a goal on the draft goal system. If not, the group asked themselves, 'Is there a goal missing? Or, is the event not important?'. As the day unfolded, the strategic issues were rated in importance (bearing in mind the goals) using the self-adhesive spots to highlight **preferences**. The important strategic issues   *P313* were then worked on in sub-groups.

Postscript

After three years, the resultant goal system built during this workshop is still a driving framework for the organization. Whilst 'survival' continues to be a key issue it did not become an end in itself without reference to other objectives. The principal goals identified at the event have been written into the Alliance's formal statement of Aims and Objectives, and later revisions of strategic objectives are produced in the context of these goals. One key outcome of the event was a clearer understanding of the different roles of staff and voluntary Board members. This has assisted the Alliance to be more confident in allocating and delegating responsibilities within a complex organization. Alliance building between member organizations has now developed significantly since the event.

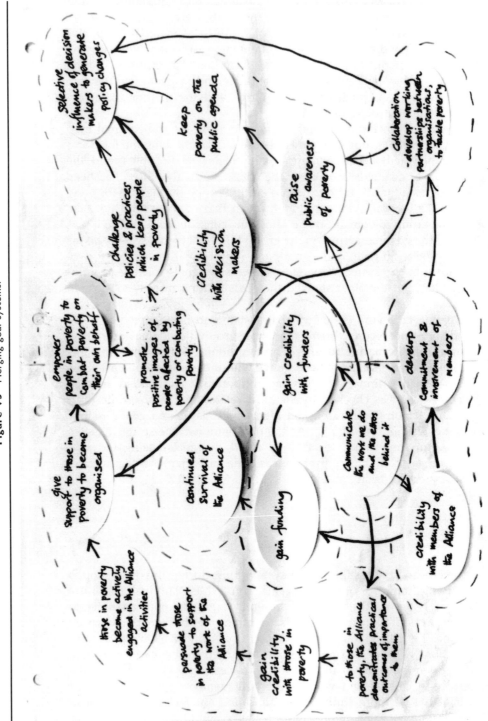

Figure V5   Merging goal systems.

One of the 'hot' strategic issues which emerged at the event was the possibility of shifting status from a regional (local) to national orientation. The Alliance is now making this move and this has engendered a review of the goal system identified at the event, while at the same time the goals informed the thinking about making this step.

Govan Initiative Ltd – quasi-public – 150 staff

The Organization: Govan Initiative Ltd – Govan Initiative is a public sector organization set up by National, Regional, and City authorities in order to address the severe economic problems stemming from the serious decline in ship building and heavy engineering in the area. The company currently employs 150 members of staff.

The Vignette: High levels of participation. Facilitative and core goal systems. Networked computer system. Stakeholder analysis. Strategy Delivery Support System (SDSS) linked to an existing Quarterly Monitoring System. Performance indicators for monitoring progress.

The Cast List: Ron Culley – Chief Executive and client. He has been in that position almost since the inception of the company 10 years ago. He views management and leadership as plural words which imply the participation of a great number of people in the process. Damien – an Assistant Chief Executive who acted as a partner/facilitator and champion; 1 external facilitator – Fran; 9 members of the Management Team (including Ron and Damien), other members of staff, and some external stakeholders.

Damien, an Assistant Chief Executive of the company, had just completed a part time MBA. This experience had led him to become convinced about the significance of a JOURNEY making approach to strategic change. His organization had just received the results of an external appraisal suggesting that it was time for a strategic review of the company – and here was the means to achieve it. After a contacting Fran to see if she was interested – she was – he then set up a meeting with Ron (his boss and the Chief Executive) and Fran to talk things through. From the beginning it was clear that Ron was very keen on getting as many, if not all, of the then

P303   110 staff involved. To do this, it would mean that at least six **Oval Mapping** and computer supported workshops [chapter P3] were likely to

C72   be necessary. Moreover, **workshops rather than interviews** were chosen because both Ron and Damien believed the organization to have an open and participative nature. They also liked the idea of having a **workshop**

P434   **involving their key stakeholders** – it would add to the internal focus. The project was rapidly increasing in size and Fran was beginning to get a little concerned.

She was worried that, after the first workshop, Ron might decide that he didn't want to continue, or for that matter she might decide she wanted to drop out of any further involvement. What they needed was something that allowed for these possibilities and yet still produced a worthwhile outcome in its own right. One that did not restrict the options for the

P482   future. After some discussion the three designed a **staged process** where at the end of each stage clear tangible outputs could be delivered and used by the organization, whilst at the same time also ensuring that each stage capitalized upon the previous one(s). In addition, it would also allow Damien to facilitate some of the workshops – something he was keen to do as Ron wanted to transfer the JOURNEY making skills into his organization.

Time passed . . . A series of internal strategy workshops was arranged, took place . . . and now they moved towards Involving Stakeholders in Strategy Development . . .

Ron and Damien, as a result of the JOURNEY making they had already done, had become aware that strategy development and strategy delivery could not be separated. They realized that if some of their key stakeholders became involved in the process of strategy development, they could impress them with the process of strategy making they were undertaking, and so 'buy' them further into the organization. This would be achieved through three routes. Firstly they hoped that their ability to surface, structure, evaluate and agree a strategic future in a thoughtful and rational manner would add credence to the outcome – they could demonstrate **procedural rationality**. They also believed that through their involvement   *C55* of senior, middle and junior staff they could demonstrate to the stake- holders that they were serious about the exercise. Finally, by tapping external views they could ensure that the resultant strategy paid attention to the strategies of other key stakeholders. They had to decide whom to involve. As they were a local economic development organization and therefore dependent on funding from a number of sources, they wanted to involve those who had a clear interest in the strategic behaviour of their company and were powerful enough to take action to block or support the company in achieving its mission. They were uncertain which of the stakeholders were the most significant, and in any event were unable to involve all of them. Consequently they used Damien and Ron's knowledge of the funding bodies and other key influential players to complete a **power/interest grid**. This acted as the basis for choosing whom to invite.   *C121 P344* In addition, as Fran was going to facilitate the 1-day workshop she needed to get an idea of the personalities of those attending. Ron briefed her, and agreed that he, as Chief Executive, would send out the invitations personally.

    Just before the workshop, a number of people rang to say that they could not attend, although some sent substitutes. This was a real disappointment to both Damien and Ron, as two of these were key players and would be sorely missed. However, as Damien commented, both were very senior people in their own organizations and so it was not surprising that they had to cancel. The day began with Ron providing a welcoming introduction to the group, thanking them for their time, and hoping that the day would be as useful to them as to Govan Initiative. Fran then took over as facilitator and went on to describe the process, drawing upon the previous work with Govan Initiative as background. The briefing included some examples of

P307 how each participant could contribute to help **set expectations**, and reassured each of them that they were important to the day. As with the

C98 previous internal workshops, the group were asked to suggest **emergent strategic issues** that Govan Initiative should address using the Oval Mapping Technique. However, to Damien's amazement, by the end of the morning session the wall picture was not as well fleshed out as some of the previous workshops. Reflecting on this, Ron and Damien surmised that this was probably due to the diversity of perspectives between members, and their lack of familiarity with one another, the topic, as well as the process. Fran's experience with multi-organizational groups led her to agree, noting that 'mixed groups always tend to be slower in warming up at the start of the day especially when using a strange technique'. This is because the participants are trying to 'suss' one another out. However, as they become more familiar with the technique the process takes off.

During the structuring of the Ovals, Fran began to notice a problem. One of the participants, the Chairman of the Board, whose position gave him a greater knowledge of Govan Initiative, was more interested in exploring visionary issues than some of the more immediate concerns that others were focusing upon. He continually stated that these concerns were 'detail and don't matter – look to the future!'. This contrasted strongly with some of the other participants' views who felt that getting the 'housekeeping' right was the basis of the future. To try to resolve this

P388 **conflicting approach within the group**, Fran once again stressed that all of the perspectives were valid and useful and encouraged participants to capture the ideas on the Ovals. Once these Ovals appeared on the wall, the tension seemed to abate. Nevertheless, managing this balance was to continue during the afternoon session where the computer supported mode of working [chapter P3] was used. The 'visionary' had been used to swaying others' views through the sheer power of his rhetoric and charisma. He found himself unable to control the computer mediated debate, as others were able to enter their statements into the system and

C68 argue for them – **social power** had shifted. This loss of power forced him to be disruptive. Fran sought to exploit his sense of fairness and commitment to Govan Initiative as a way of encouraging him to appreciate the synergy that could come from his statements being structured together with those of others. His strong commitment to Ron and his organization helped in persuading him to 'play the game'.

Damien and Ron were pleased with the outcome – a large number of the stakeholders seemed to have bought in to what Govan Initiative was trying to do. They also appeared to support the process. They could now see how the different aspects of strategy related to one another, how a strategic direction could be formed, and, more importantly, be put into practice. They also began to appreciate how the welding of views from

C70 several people through the Oval Map enhanced **creativity** and produced new perspectives that went beyond that of any of them.

Moreover, two of the stakeholders began expressing an interest in using the JOURNEY making process in their own organization (and subsequently did so). Ron felt he had achieved all of his objectives with respect to some of the key stakeholders . . .

Time passed . . . and with the internal and external workshops complete, strategy delivery became the focus of attention . . . along with Delivering Action programmes . . .

With the stakeholder workshop completed, Ron was keen to start thinking about strategy delivery. How were they to set about doing this? The previous workshops had received such 'good press' that many others in the organization wanted to be involved. How could he involve more of his staff in the exercise of determining more detailed action plans? Ron had, from the very start, been keen on **increasing the participation** levels. *C56* Fran's suggestion was that the management team provide the strategic framework for the organization, by agreeing the goal system and core strategies. Once this had been done, the next step would be to agree the means of achieving the strategies. This might be an opportunity for other members of the organization to contribute. Fran, however, was also aware of another objective – that Damien should gain experience in facilitating and managing the process. This was partly so that he could help complete this part of the journey as an **internal facilitator** and partly to allow him to *P381* facilitate future JOURNEY making in the organization. Her idea was to run a series of **action workshops**. The first two she would facilitate (pro- *P440* viding Damien with a chance to see how it was done) and Damien would complete the series. This plan of action was agreed by Ron.

The workshop to establish the strategic framework began with an examination of the **draft goal system**. Ron was concerned that this goal *C98 P425* system was mostly externally focused. It concentrated on their core **busi-** *C79* **ness model** without expressing any goals relating to how they might achieve it. He therefore proposed that they add a goal 'establish and maintain Govan Initiative as a leader in economic development *through its excellence, innovation, and collaboration*' – a more process oriented or **facili-** *P427* **tative goal**. It was also the case that, without this goal, a number of the key strategic issues could not be converted into a strategy that linked to a goal, leaving the **strategy map** incomplete. The rest of the management team *C98* agreed. Finally, after an hour they agreed to an interrelated set of five goals that they felt would be able to support a previously agreed mission statement. This mission statement had been agreed the previous year, and they felt comfortable with it, and did not want another change. Normally the **mission** is developed after the goal system has been agreed and is *P429 P430* based upon an understanding of the emergent strategic issues. In this instance the goal system needed to reflect the emergent issues but also be coherent with the already established mission statement and so **honour** *C21* **the past**.

Deciding on the strategies was to be more lengthy. Using the analysis within the computer software, Fran had sorted the material into four areas. This clustering of material was designed to avoid the management team being overwhelmed by the mass of statements from the previous six workshops which had involved the management team, many staff members, and some of the key stakeholders (see chapter P3.3). The first step was a quick review to re-acquaint the group with the material and

P338 then, using the **networked computer system, express preferences** about which of the key issues should be converted to strategies (see figure V6). With Damien's help, Fran had chosen two criteria for the participants to express their preferences. First (distributing red spots, as if resources) prioritize those key issues that were critical and must be addressed in the short term. Second (using green spots in the same way) identify those that were important but could be dealt with in the long term. This was designed to help participants differentiate between short and long term strategies. The team needed no prompting on how to use the software – they were now experienced users. Following the electronic preferencing, the results were examined and the top ten or twelve (of both red and green spots) were selected as potential strategies (see figure V6).

C5   After further reflection and negotiation the workshop concluded with an agreed **system of strategies**, relating to the goal system. Through seeing these strategies as an 'overview' that explored them as a system, slight amendments to the wording were needed for the system to make sense and be coherent as a whole. They now felt able to agree the design of the action workshops. Each of these would last half a day, would involve around 8–10 participants, and would be facilitated by either Fran or Damien. Ron and another member of the management team promised to identify the appropriate participants for each of the workshops, making sure that those involved would be able to generate and agree relevant actions – some of which might then be allocated to them.

Each of the four action planning workshops focused on between three and four strategies. Each half day began with either Fran or Damien providing a comprehensive explanation of the process that had so far been undertaken. They also presented the resultant strategic intent expressed as a system of goals and strategies – which they stated 'were not up for grabs'! This information would not only allow participants to focus on the appropriate areas but also provide them with an overall view of the journey so far and its current outcomes. Participants were encouraged to ask questions. Following this introduction, the material currently support-ing each of the three or four strategies they were addressing was examined so as to further provide context. Hard copy maps were supplied to each participant to help. Although for each of the strategies a body of support-ing material existed, both Ron and Damien wanted the staff members to have a chance to contribute new statements.

P338   Working on each of the three or four strategies in turn, participants used the **networked computer system to gather** their statements about specific ways to make the strategy happen. They were asked to be practical

P450 and to include blockages to success. They were also given the **facility to enter links** between their own input and the existing statements. Fran warned participants that if potential actions or blockages appeared

Figure V6 Screen shots of client preferencing: top, client/console view; bottom, public view.

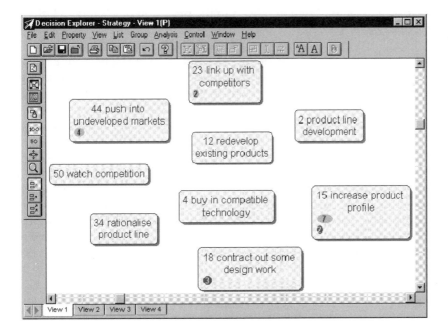

without being linked then they would be deleted. Each action had to have at least one specific purpose (that is, at least one arrow out of it). Statements flowed quickly and the screen filled up until they had run out of ideas. To ensure that everyone had become familiar with the various options now captured, Fran (or Damien) reviewed the material with participants, checking for missing links and amending statements where they were too cryptic because of shorthand such as abbreviations or jargon.

Copies of the screen were printed off during the coffee break (also useful for some quick tidying up). Fran and Damien noted that the participants had generated many more potential actions than they thought could be implemented – they needed to reduce the number. To help focus the next part of the workshop, participants were asked to identify, in relation to each strategy, their top five actions (using the maps as data sources) and rank them, using the ranking part of the networked system. Finally, a review of each of the agreed actions (with the caveat that not all of them could be implemented in the immediate future) concluded the workshop. The action planning workshops along with those earlier meant

P444   that the level of **staff participation** was around 70% of the total staff in the organization. This level of involvement was expected to ensure that staff not only had a greater understanding of the emerging strategy and were able to question their understanding of the strategies but also were committed to delivering them . . .

Time passed . . . and attention moved to the provision of a Strategy Delivery Support System (SDSS) . . .

Having run the action planning workshops, Fran and Damien then
C159   reviewed the number of preferred actions. They needed to get the **actions reviewed by the management team to ensure that they were feasible** – for example, resources (cash and staff time). Secondly they needed to
C165   check the **allocation of responsibilities** for each of the actions. The participants involved in the action workshops had been asked to suggest members of the management team and other staff members they thought would be the most appropriate to be held accountable for the actions. In order for each of the management team to be committed to them they also needed to agree the suggestions. In addition, they needed to check whether any one of them had too many responsibilities – were they overloaded? How should they go about doing this? It was time for Fran and Damien to have a progress meeting with Ron, as client. Ron had been very clear from early on that he wanted a system that would help the organization measure progress. Moreover, the system should match the way they had worked on developing and agreeing the strategic direction and actions. Because of the nature of the organization's funding (from the public purse) he had to have a mechanism that clearly showed how the
P481   money was being spent on strategy and **how much progress was being achieved**. Many of the fund holding stakeholders had been impressed

with a presentation of the goal system and associated strategies but they also wanted to monitor its effect on the performance of the organization.

At the progress meeting Fran mentioned a scheme she had used for other organizations that could be adapted. Once the actions had been agreed and time-scales added, the same software could be used as a decision support system to show progress. A colour scheme denoting the level of progress could be adopted. In addition, by identifying a mix of both **qualitative and quantitative performance indicators** for each of the strategies their progress could be measured at both micro and macro levels. Ron was enthusiastic but commented that it would be really helpful to the organization if there was some way to link the strategic direction with the on-going operational tasks. The **organization currently had a Quarterly Monitoring System (QMS)** which comprised a large number of very detailed tasks. If Fran and Damien could link the two systems together, then not only could they improve their effectiveness in monitoring progress, but they could also potentially get greater synergy from the tasks supporting the strategic actions. Fran agreed to give it a try. She suggested that she print out maps with each management team member's currently allocated actions as they related to strategies. She would ask them to review these actions and to add to the map their QMS tasks. Once this was done the management team would then meet in sub-groups (there were a number of natural sub-groups) and review the maps, checking the progress of the tasks and ensuring that they were linked to the most appropriate strategic actions. Using sub-groups would help with scheduling and also shorten the length of meetings whilst allowing a degree of integration. Ron agreed, but also suggested that in addition to this means of agreeing actions, it would be useful to use the management team annual off-site review meeting to bring the whole of the team up to date. This event would be an obvious opportunity to undertake some serious **stakeholder analysis** and also identify performance indicators for each of the strategies. The three of them decided to have the review meeting first – it had been a while since the management team had been involved in the strategy and this would be a way of revisiting the material and rebuilding commitment.

The review (a form of 'retreat' or 'away-day') began by reviewing the agreed goals and strategies and then asking the participants to begin to **identify potential performance indicators**. These were surfaced initially by the participants saying them verbally and Fran entering them into the computer system so that they were displayed on the public screen. However, once the participants had identified a number of possible performance indicators for one strategy, they felt comfortable completing the rest using the networked computer system to speed up the process. By the end of the session each strategy had around four to six potential performance indicators. Fran and Ron were pleased that the management team had needed little reminder of the way the process worked. Fran was now keen to try to get them to assess their current position on the agreed performance indicators. This exercise could provide the organization with

C176 P446

C171

C119 P341

C174

a benchmark. It would also ensure that the performance indicators were usable – some of those suggested appeared to Fran to be fairly unworkable. That evening she drew up flip-chart sheets with the strategy written at the top of the sheet and the performance indicators listed below. For each of the performance indicators a continuum from 0% to 100% was drawn. Her aim was to allow the participants to show their personal views of where, in terms of their anticipated objectives, they felt they were currently placed. 0% represented no progress and 100% represented total expected achievement when the strategy was complete. In addition, space was reserved at the bottom of each sheet for any further comment. Each participant was given self-adhesive spots and asked to put one at the point on each performance indicator continuum matching their view of perform-ance. Fran explained that 'the process is not designed to be deadly accurate, rather it provides an *indication* of the degree of agreement within the team, as well as a feel for their current position, which could later act as a reference point. Often there is lots of variance or lots of agreement highlighting issues that we can then discuss so that possible misunder-standings can be uncovered and explored'. The reason for doing this manually, rather than using the networked computer system, was to introduce variety into the process.

As participants began to try to place their self-adhesive spots it became obvious that a number of the performance indicators were unworkable. Firstly, for many it was virtually impossible to be able to place their spots, and secondly some of the performance indicators seemed to relate to measures that were not solely within their remit and seemed instead to be dependent upon the behaviour of other organizations. This observation *C129 P355* reminded the participants that they needed to refine their **stakeholder management** strategies. Fran reminded the team that 'here is another *C22* example of our needing to **cycle around the different strategy making tasks**, and make sure that each part is coherent with the others'. The ensuing discussion resulted in the group agreeing that having a set of 'tracking indicators' in addition to the performance indicators would be useful. These tracking indicators would relate to improvements in the geographical area in general, and would be contributed to by their own organization and others. They would help them measure their area's performance in relation to other geographical areas. As the group discussed each strategy's indicators new performance indicators were identified and others reworded to avoid ambiguities. At the end of the session, the group had a set of measures for both strategies and goals and were keen to work on assessing the allocation and viability of the actions. Having a means to measure not only the performance against the strategies and the goal system, but also progress with actions, would provide them with an integ-rated strategic delivery support system.

Fran, with Damien's help (for linking), then spent time 'off-line' entering the QMS tasks into the system. She marked them out from the other material by creating a new style and colour. During this process both decided that for the sake of clarity a means of simplifying the process would be to keep the QMS (see figure V7) but to augment it by including within that system the strategic actions from the strategy model as titles for the tasks. Thus, the strategic actions would appear in both models and act as an overlap or **bridge between the strategic direction and the operational necessities**. Because of the relatively large number of QMS tasks, they decided early on that these tasks could be linked only to actions rather than into strategies directly. In this way the model could be shrunk using the collapse command in the software on to the strategic direction with the QMS tasks hidden. This would make the model simpler to use and more focused on the agreed strategic direction – a necessity, as both Ron and Damien wanted to be able to use the model on a regular basis at their monthly review meetings.

P466

Each of the sub-group meetings commenced with an explanation of the new colouring system to indicate progress, and of the coding rules. This was followed by each individual reviewing their allocated actions and tasks, with omissions being captured. Initially allocated tasks not suiting current roles were re-distributed and checked so that the QMS tasks were linked to appropriate actions. Once participants understood the process, Fran suggested that instead of her manipulating the software, they each have a chance to become familiar with the working of the software. Some team members jumped at the chance while others were more hesitant; nevertheless, the process was effective at introducing them to an activity which was to become commonplace as the system translated itself to their desk-top computers.

A number of the participants had arrived feeling a little sceptical that so much could be achieved in a morning. They were surprised at how much was possible – each sub-group was able to realize the meeting objectives in a short space of time. After completing these workshops, Fran and the organization now had a pair of connected models. The first was the higher level strategic intent, showing the goals, strategies, and strategic actions. The second contained the strategic actions and the QMS tasks. These were to be the basis of further **dissemination across the whole organization** and also signalled **closure**.

P452 P456
C161 P452

Postscript

Since the **publication of the strategy** brochure to staff, external stake-holders and Board Members, the management team has received an astonishingly positive reaction to the process. This has been evidenced in the results of the staff attitude survey, and various stakeholder bodies embarking upon the JOURNEY making process themselves. The organization uses the SDSS at its monthly strategy meetings, updating one another on progress, agreeing changes and reviewing priorities. It is about to embark upon a major progress review and is involving both senior and middle management. As Ron Culley the Chief Executive comments:

P452

Figure V7   A selection from the Quarterly Monitoring System, showing progress.

Action Progress

Strategy	6	**Develop and secure employment opportunities for local people**

Strategy Performance   18 %

Action Action	Lead Person		
66 Support a greater match between job opportunities created and the skills base of the local community	Richie Damien	**Progress %**	0
1041 Listen carefully to companies so that GI brings forward relevant support mechanisms	Damien	**Progress %**	28
1144 Operate a sponsored program to assist unemployed client placement	Jim Richie	**Progress %**	3
1145 Operate a dedicated team to address the requirements of client who are approaching job readiness	Jim	**Progress %**	27
1146 Provide a co-ordinated service to assist people to progress to employment	Jim Jean	**Progress %**	31

(Progress bars shown on scale 0 – 50 – 100 – 150: action 66 = 0, 1041 = 28, 1144 = 3, 1145 = 27, 1146 = 31)

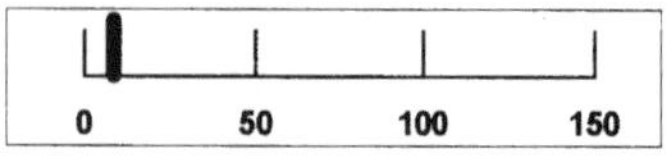

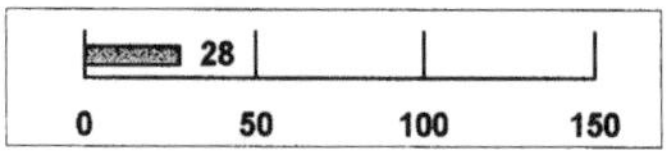

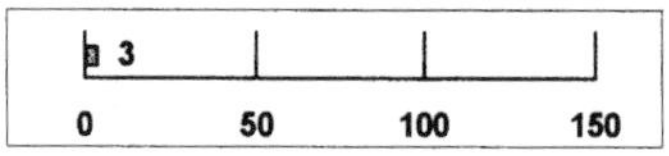

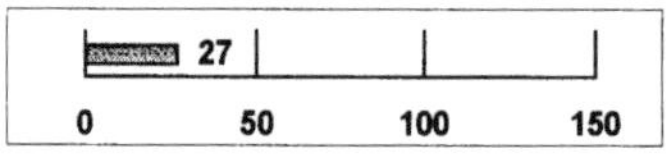

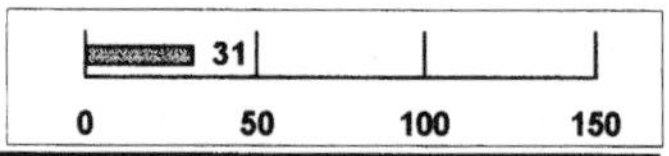

Strategy	52	**Pursue Quality and excellence relentlessly and at all levels**

Strategy Performance   40 %

Action Action	Lead Person		
51 Develop Customer care practice	Jean Pam	**Progress %**	60
54 Improve organisations ability to evaluate effectiveness at all levels	Ron Jim Mgmt tea	**Progress %**	0

(Progress bars shown on scale 0 – 50 – 100 – 150: action 51 = 60/60, 54 = 0)

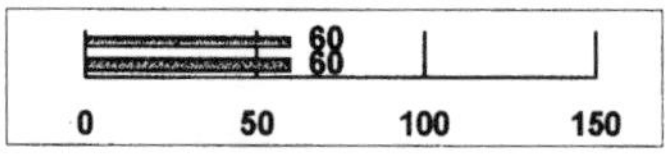

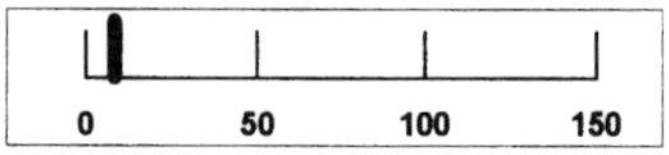

'JOURNEY making has been a revelation to our company. It's not just that we now have a strategic orientation which makes sense for us, our customers, and our stakeholders, but we have managed to engage all of our 150 strong workforce in its design. It is difficult to put a price on the value of individual ownership but we can put a price against the efficient use of staff time and the opportunity costs of getting our strategy wrong and having to return to the issue time and time again.

However, the real saving is in our implementation phase. Everyone has been involved in shaping the strategy and knows how they fit into the big picture. The synergy this offers is obvious and the feeling of us being "in control" most reassuring. JOURNEY making has added value to our collective ability to capture ideas and points of view and meld them into coherence. It has infected all of us with a rational and consensual approach to decision making within the company'.

Reed Business Publishing – scenarios for computing

The Organization: Reed Business Publishing: *Computer Weekly*.

C139 *The Vignette*: Use of external experts for a workshop to **explore alternative futures**.

The Cast List: Gavin Howe – a director of the organization (currently President and Chief Executive Officer of Reed-Elsevier Technology Group). 14 'experts' from the computer industry. 1 facilitator – Colin.

Gavin and his management team, while working on the development of their strategy, began to realize that their own views, from within the organization, about the future environment might be restrictive. Although Gavin had often commissioned forecasting work from his own staff, and had also done some preliminary scenario workshop activity, he felt that this might not be enough. This was not only because it was dependent upon the particular thinking and culture within the organization, but also

C76 because the internal work suggested that they may be missing **alternative perspectives**. Here was an occasion for the management team to begin to consider calling for the views of 'friends' of the organization. These friends might offer a range of alternative perspectives on the future. But how were they best to involve the friends? Having worked with Colin before, Gavin suggested they met to discuss the proposal.

To provide some background, Gavin explained to Colin that this requirement had surfaced as a result of their focusing attention on the strategic future of one of their major products – *Computer Weekly*, a controlled circulation newspaper. Their strategy development had led to a strong strategic commitment to 'business to business' publishing in the computer industry. Moreover, he continued, the organization (and this

C103 product in particular) had a **distinctive competence** in providing a recruitment service to any organization wishing to recruit staff for their computer and IT departments. This service generated revenue. Journalism also represented a competence which was close to distinctive but not quite – it was all linked together. What was more, Gavin continued, his team were concerned about getting their strategy as near perfect as possible. As they had been considering possible futures for the computer industry, and particularly for the nature of jobs and recruitment, they felt they might be missing something of significance. For them, something of significance could render their distinctive competence out of step with their aspirations

C79 – even to the point of attacking their **business model**.

Colin agreed with Gavin. By getting together a group of external people, and asking them to begin to flesh out possible futures from their point of view, a number of objectives could be realized. It would provide Gavin's team with some potentially critical material but it could also act as a good

PR exercise. As a first stab at exploring other futures they decided to invite a range of **industry 'experts'** to attend a 1-day workshop in the centre of London. These experts were a range of 'friends' who they thought would be interested in the outcome of a day thinking about the future of the industry with others likely to attend. After considerable debate, a list was finally agreed. Those invited included respected journalists from the national press, the CEO of the British Computer Society, an Information Systems professor, IT directors from several industry sectors, representation from mainframe computing and from the PC industry, software developers and vendors (large and small), and hardware R&D managers. Both Colin and Gavin were struck by the difficulty in getting the group down to a size that would result in about 12 people attending with different perspectives! Only one senior member of the management team (the editor) was to attend as an observer and **sponsor**. Finally a date was established, from the selection offered, that ensured agreement from 14 experts. The gradual process of encouragement combined with diary negotiations demanded many telephone calls on Gavin's part (or rather his secretary's!).

C154 P369

P476

The design of the workshop was slightly different from the 'standard' **event-based focus for scenario building**. Gavin had a sense that the significant trends identified by each expert, when brought together, would describe events that would not be identified by any single expert. 'Okay', said Colin, 'why not focus on the linkages between important **"flip-flop" events?**'. The workshop would then be billed as 'in search of key flip-flops and their relationships' rather than explicitly focused on the business model. 'In this way', he continued, 'events remain industry related, so retaining, as much as possible, a broad interest for all those attending. We can refocus the material, if necessary, after the event'. Gavin agreed.

C143 P361

C145 P362

The next decision was where to hold the workshop. Two factors governed the final choice of a hotel near the centre of London. The first factor was to ensure that the location was one suitable for the travelling ease of the experts and the second was to provide those attending with an exceptional lunch (bribery). However, as Colin had found to his cost before, a **good workshop room** was difficult to find, and this proved no exception. As they had decided to use the **'Oval Mapping Technique'** **(OMT)** as the means to capture and arrange the expertise presented by participants, lots of appropriate wall space was required. This was further exacerbated as the main objective was to 'discover' key flip-flops. To achieve this, it was essential that the material could easily be rearranged to explore a variety of possible clusters linked to specific **driver events** or flip-flops. More wall space was needed than usual, requiring a large flat wall that could be seen easily by 12 participants. Finally as the links between 'Ovals' would need to be redrawn possibly several times during the workshop, they would need some means of being able to draw in and then remove them. Colin planned to use large acetate sheets. These sheets would be laid over the Ovals so that links could be drawn, deleted, and

P378
P303

C151

V268
redrawn using water based OHP pens. This process of repeated experimentation with the shape of Oval clusters and links between Ovals and between clusters also meant that a **photographic record** would be needed on a regular basis. Therefore, the basic tools were expected to be: a good supply of Ovals, flip-chart paper to cover the whole wall, plenty of 'Blu-Tack', coloured pens for each participant, OHP pens, flip-chart pens and the rolls of flip-chart width acetate.

As Colin had noted to Gavin when they were originally designing the event, one difficulty with 'expert' scenario workshops is that the experts are so pleased with the opportunity to chat to one another that it is difficult to get the workshop started! So it was at this workshop. As expected, two potential participants cancelled at the last moment, leaving the workshop with the designed number of experts. Getting the right

P376
number of participants in a workshop is always a delicate balance. In the case of expert workshops Colin had found it best to oversubscribe, then more people would feel pleased that they were asked to contribute, whilst the group size would not increase too much, as there were always cancellations. As part of his introduction, Gavin took considerable care to focus the aims of the workshop in such a way that the futures considered related to the needs of business to business publishing and the distinctive competencies supporting the business model but without losing the industry focus. However, he and Colin had decided to encourage a focus on business to business publishing by indirectly framing responses with

P306
trigger Ovals already on the wall. They reckoned they had identified a dozen triggers which were likely to be of interest to all participants. The workshop objective was pre-written and hung at the top of the flip-chart paper covered wall.

Although some of the participants had met before, they did not know other participants as working colleagues. Most knew of each other by repute. This situation suggested a 'warm up' process that would give each of them individual air-time with a guaranteed audience. This was achieved by carrying out a round-robin of introductions which also requested an initial statement from each about their own 'bee-in-your-bonnet' significant trend for the future. Unfortunately the expert who started the 'round robin' was long-winded and set an inappropriate standard. As a result the process took longer than expected, with each expert justifying their statement for more time than had been anticipated. Next time, thought Colin, I will make sure we make a better guess of who will be concise! Due to the long-windedness, the introductory statements ended up taking until the morning coffee-break and left Colin and Gavin with only about twenty Ovals, all written up by Colin. Although time had been lost against the plan, the coffee-break suggested that the perspectives offered had gained interest from all.

There was enthusiasm to move on, and participants were ushered back to the workshop with ease. But, the workshop design was awry, and already looking as if it was too ambitious. Following his usual practice, Colin had not declared the expected timetable; instead he had given the group a rough outline of stages using 'everyday' language. His idea of using the acetate to help create different perspectives on the linkage between trends was abandoned – there wasn't time. Once back in the room, Colin urged the participants to extend the 'picture on the wall' by adding other significant trends. Not only did a fair amount of new material surface, but participants were also keen to contradict each other's 'opening statements'.

As the new Ovals appeared on the wall, now written by the participants and therefore at a very fast rate, Colin was having a difficult time structuring them. He was looking for both similar topics and for possible causal links. He had hoped to use the computer system [chapter P3] to support the workshop, but Gavin had been keen to keep technology out of the day. At this stage he was regretting that he'd given in. At the back of his mind he was aware that linkages between statements from managers in the same organization, and made about strategic issues, would remain more constant than causal links for scenario data. After all, one of the most enthralling and important tasks for scenario building is that of getting the participants to argue for links. However, in this case Colin was resigned to very rough **clustering of the Ovals**. This was mostly done with the *P308* objective of creating space around each Oval so as to make sure that new contributions were not discouraged because of an impression that space was limited.

It was within half an hour of lunch that the group stopped making contributions. Discussion between participants had remained high, and Colin had some difficulty in making certain that important events that had cropped up **in heated debate were captured on the wall**. Rather than get *P310* engaged in the debates, Gavin was forced to help by writing Ovals of others' statements. Extra flip-chart paper had to be added to the wall, and many of the bundles (hardly clusters in any formal sense!) had to be moved to release space. Rather than start linking the data, Colin thought it best to break for lunch and then start linking after lunch with enough time to make decent progress in one go. However, both he and Gavin were really pleased that the selection of participants was working so well. There were many different perspectives on the future which were, nevertheless, not independent of each other. Even if the workshop stopped at this point it had been worth it.

General discussion at lunch suggested that most of the participants were also getting something useful to themselves out of the event. Unfortunately there was one exception who was definitely in the 'difficult participant' category. The software publishing expert was of the clear and certain view that most of what had been contributed was a waste of time and space. In his opinion it was simply wrong! His certainty about his own position worried Colin. It seemed likely that he would want considerable air-time after lunch to 'put everyone right'. By the end of the lunch he was even more frustrated as other participants became increasingly intolerant of him and stopped paying any attention to his diatribe. After lunch he disappeared, never to return. In some respects this was a great pity because his views had been interesting and it would have been very helpful to have his contributions to the afternoon session. On the other hand, Colin felt a sense of relief, one he suspected was shared by many others as nobody mentioned his disappearance on returning to work.

The afternoon started on time with the difficult task of managing 11 vocal participants suggesting causal links. Colin now wished he not only had the computer system but the networked computer system. When it is used, this stage is easy, as each participant can 'throw' their own statements of links at the screen at the same time. While this initially produces a considerable mess of arrows it is not a problem as everyone who has contributed is happy to help remap the mess into clusters and produce separate maps on each of many computer views. Even with a single computer projected image, participants could have shouted out links. For example '43 to 67', '75 to 117', and so on. All Colin would have done is type in the links as 43+67, 75+117. In this case the task was manual and took that much longer – but, as Gavin had argued, they were not distracted by the technology, and given their interest in IT they may well have been more interested in the system than the content.

To help with the task, the large sheets of acetate had been overlaid on to the wall during the lunch break. It was just as well that the acetate was available (even if not used at the planned time), for links regularly got added and subtracted and reversed. If the links had been made directly on to the flip-chart paper, changes would have been more difficult. 'On the other hand', Colin wryly whispered to Gavin, 'without the acetate, it would have been possible to move Ovals around to reduce the length of arrows across the wall'.

It did not take long for two particular events about the future – noted on the Ovals – to emerge as important (**'potent'**) **drivers** for considerable parts of the picture. The most significant of these generated, in effect, two very **distinct scenarios**. That is, the consequences of each side of the flip-flop led to different events. Given the year this workshop took place, these two driver flip-flops were fascinating to all in the group. In the mid-1990s it seems more obvious! One flip-flop focused on software developers. One side argued for software being developed by a small number of very large players that mopped up small players as they emerged. The other side focused on software developed by a very large number of small and specialist players. This flip-flop was seen as having important consequences for standards, for hardware design, for margins, and ultimately for different rates of growth of the industry. The second flip-flop focused on the nature of IS delivery in the workplace. One side suggested that this would be dominated by extremely powerful personal computers, each of which could deliver the power of a mainframe computer. These computers would exchange information through networks. The other side of the flip-flop argued that managers would have a keyboard and flat screen with all the power coming from central computers. (Hints of the Java (Oracle) versus PC (Microsoft) battle of the mid-1990s?)

C155

C149 P366

By the time the tea-break arrived there was a consensus about the importance of the two flip-flops and the four scenarios emerging from them. In addition, there were seven other clusters which represented alternative scenarios. After tea the group explored the proposal that the pairs of scenarios actually represented four scenarios that could occur together – flip1/flip2 (0,0); flip1/flop2 (0,1); flop1/flip2 (1,0); and flop1/flop2 (1,1) versions of the two flip-flops. The latter three were seen as possible joint events.

As they discussed the afternoon during the tea-break, both Gavin and Colin were pleased with the outcomes although Colin was beginning to feel somewhat exhausted keeping up with the material. The aim of coming up with something '**remarkable**' that would match what is sometimes hoped for when introducing a 'remarkable person' had been met. C154 However, the most important (at least for Gavin) part of the day was yet to come. Earlier, with Colin's help he had asked whether the group could say something useful about the **signals that would indicate triggering the flip** C151 **or flop, in each case**. He needed to know something about how, and when, to make a judgement about which 'horse to back'. The group, whilst developing the scenarios, had provided some indicators by showing causal links, from trend based Ovals, into the central flip-flops. Over the tea-break Gavin was keen to check with Colin that he was intending to spend the rest of the time getting participants to concentrate their efforts on the task of identifying causes of the key flip-flops so that the best trends to monitor could be identified.

Colin was amenable but was aware that three of the participants had to leave to meet transport constraints. While discussing the final part of the workshop, each of them had checked with Colin to find out what was planned next. Two of them decided to take later trains because they were also curious about the 'triggers', but the third had to leave. There was only about 45 minutes left against planned closing time. Colin decided that to get things moving fast, he would use the self-adhesive spots for '**prefer-** P313 **encing**'. This way he could get each participant to choose, from the events/trends leading into the key flip-flops, which were the best to monitor. From the results, it became clear that, while there was some consensus, many of the events/trends chosen were impractical to monitor. With twenty minutes to go, Colin thrust them back to writing on Ovals. The task set was that of suggesting more **practical variables to monitor** for C155 those with the most spots. The outcome was reasonably successful, but many participants thought that more time would have been needed to develop the picture into something directly and easily usable.

Gavin honoured the agreements made and closed the workshop on time. He thanked everyone for their participation. However, to his and Colin's delight, five of the participants stayed behind. Together they worked on structuring the last set of Ovals. It was worth it, the outcome gradually became more useful.

Following the workshop, Gavin and Colin spent some time together putting the material into the computer mapping software, carefully

Reed Business Publishing – role-think in stakeholder management

The Organization: A division of Reed Business Publishing in the mid-1980s.

The Vignette: Stakeholder analysis and management – **extended 'role-think'**. Group composition issues.

C133 P345 P354
P435

The Cast List: Simon Timm – the Managing Director of the Division; 20 senior managers; 1 facilitator – Colin.

Simon was contemplating a complete relaunch of one of his division's most profitable products. This consideration had come about as part of the division's strategic change efforts. However, even though Simon was sure that the strategy was right, he was nervous. The relaunch would involve committing a high level of human and cash investment alongside the strategic risks of getting it wrong. As he had worked with Colin and Fran before, he called Colin for a chat, focusing upon the nature of the risk. As a first step Colin suggested they explore all the negative commentary and outcomes that were captured in the **organizational memory** – the pre- *C71 P321* viously created strategy computer model. This model reflected the thinking of staff across the company – the optimists and the pessimists. Revisiting the model reassured Simon that the relaunch was undoubtedly the right idea, but it also highlighted concerns that competitor responses could possibly lead to a lose–lose outcome. Both Colin and Simon reflected that they had not had enough time, during the strategy development, to explore fully competitor dynamics. The **stakeholder analysis** had revealed some *C119 P341* very powerful competitors who were most certainly interested in monitoring their strategies. There was a danger that if the division simply prompted a series of changes within the industry it could cost all of the *C123* **players** more for few market gains. 'Adding to this', Simon noted, 'there is one competitor in particular who is generally thought to have the "clout" to sabotage the planned strategy'.

As a means of deciding how to manage the relaunch risks, Simon and Colin reconsidered what had already been achieved from the stakeholder management efforts. The management team had earlier tested out some elements of the strategy through using a relatively simple 'role-think' exercise encompassed within 'standard' workshops and with mixed groups of staff. These had, as always, resulted in extensive modifications to the strategy so that competitive responses were more likely to become 'win–wins'. However, as Simon noted to Colin, 'because of the enormity of the strategy, particularly given its impact on the "bottom-line", we need to be more reassured'. It was clear to Simon and his team that any market research and market testing done needed to be supported by a much clearer idea of competitor responses.

Colin and Simon began to consider options. Just replaying the 'role-think' exercises already undertaken was not likely to be helpful unless much more data about the **managerial thinking of competitors** was available. Simon then hit upon a possible way to augment this information. Two Business School students were around the company and needed projects to complete as a part of their degree requirements. He and Colin quickly enrolled them in investigating, from any angle the students chose, the strategy and strategic decision making processes of the key competitors. They were asked to pay particular attention to the personalities and personal styles of the Chief Executives and to the speed of response (in terms of thinking and deciding as well as implementation) of each competitor. As a final touch, Colin and Simon asked them to also consider in some detail the strategy **'recipe'** for the industry and the intake of new senior managers to each company. Where had these managers come from? What 'recipe' had they brought with them that might lead them to suggest particular types of strategic response? and so on. As a means of helping them consider the major competitor, the students used the Myers-Brigg Type Indicator as a guiding framework for surfacing the personality and styles of senior decision makers and also the way they worked as a team.

On reviewing the project results, Colin and Simon noted that the students reckoned that the major competitor (with the 'clout') had no guiding strategy to inform response. The response would be *'ad hoc'* and largely stemming from the Chief Executive. The research could identify no process for thinking through a strategic response nor identify how senior managers advised the Chief Executive. Both Colin and Simon were surprised and concerned about this view. They were both habituated to thinking about competitors as strategically sophisticated. Here was a setting where it was more, rather than less, difficult to anticipate the possible responses of a stakeholder because of the possibility of it at least appearing random! They were both keen to try to find some way to manage this.

Together they designed a workshop to refine competitor **stakeholder management**. It was to be held in a local hotel and was to involve all members of the management team and the senior staff who would be responsible for implementing the strategic change. Simon felt that unless these staff believed that the changes could be successful in their own right as well as within the overall strategy that had been formulated for the division, then it was unlikely to succeed. Their ownership of, and commitment to, the strategy was crucial. Colin agreed, although he was somewhat concerned that this meant that the workshop was to involve twenty senior staff! To help manage both the numbers of participants and facilitate the activity, they agreed to base the workshop around 'syndicate rooms' rather than the usual plenary room. Each syndicate room would be fully equipped as a base for one of the competitors. The rooms would contain all the data available, including product, market, financial, personality, style, and culture profiles.

To help manage the dynamics, two members of the management team were identified as syndicate leaders with the other senior managers spread

C149

C127

C129 P355

between the rooms. This Colin and Simon felt might help ensure that the potential '**saboteurs**' of the strategy were distributed evenly. When they *C23 P377* had discussed the design with the senior executive responsible for the product, she, however, had argued for the opposite. She was so bullish about the strategy that she was keen to put all the potential saboteurs into one team so that they could establish for themselves that the strategy was good. Simon, however, was concerned that one of the possible consequences of this activity might be that it resulted in the managers believing themselves to be '**anticipated losers**' from the strategy's implementation. *C23 P377* He regarded each of these staff members as crucial to the success of the strategy. Both he and Colin felt the managers were likely to be '**anticipated** *C23 P377* **winners**' but needed to be persuaded that this was probably the outcome. Therefore, they stuck to the original plan with the leaders of the syndicates having an important role in influencing expectations. Simon decided his role should be to watch from the 'sidelines' and work with Colin on running the simulation. As it turned out, Colin was relieved to have his help; the simulation did not run to design . . .

Their initial design had called for each syndicate to have 90 minutes to absorb the data in their room and move into the role. In some cases the data available enabled each member of the syndicate to take on the role of a particular manager in the organization. Not surprisingly, there was strong contention for some of the roles . . .! Following this, the product's planned strategy was carefully presented by Colin. It was presented as a sequence of events that would be visible to the outside world but with no interpretation of the purpose behind the events. Moreover, Colin rather than Simon presented the events, so that it would have less personal loading. A mock up of the product was also introduced as a part of the presentation. When designing the workshop, Simon and Colin had spent some considerable time thinking about the timing of the responses delivered by syndicates. They had discussed whether it was more appropriate to focus on days, weeks or months of simulated time. Eventually, they decided that for this exercise it seemed appropriate to vary timing according to the stage of implementation. Initial responses, particularly to the financial and trade press, were able to be made within days, and product responses over weeks. The syndicates were subsequently sent away to provide responses, if any, to the first tranche of events and given 2 hours to do so. Colin and Simon's intention was to have them complete the presentations before lunch. As part of the rules the syndicates were required to respect all the data they were given. Although Colin allowed them the freedom to disagree with, and so change, the data, they were asked not to do so without due respect to it in its original form. This allowed syndicates to use their own '**deep knowledge**' about the competitors and to interpret the data *C133 P359* available, an aspect Simon had been keen on.

The original plan was that the whole of the day would be devoted to a continuous simulation over 6 months. However, after the first report back it became clear that some aspects of the strategy were faulty. This was a useful, although time consuming, outcome. The use of competitors' public relations machines and control of the trade press was believed to enable one competitor to gain too much power over the interpretation of the strategy. Lunch was therefore late as twenty staff worked hard in **'fine tuning' the strategy** so that it was robust to such PR efforts. Although some of the changes were quite detailed, **the second run of the simulation** gave everyone more confidence. Not only was the strategy **robust** to several scenarios of initial responses, it was also possible that some responses would act to reinforce the strategy.

P352

P354

C134 P350

The day ended up being much longer than had been anticipated, and arrangements with the hotel had to be renegotiated. Dinner was very late in the evening and followed two other detailed redesigns of the strategy. Four months of simulated time were completed, and had there been more time available to managers, the simulation would have continued into the next day – just to be sure. But by the end of the day everyone agreed that the efforts of the day had not only been worthwhile but essential. Some staff thought that some of the problems should have been spotted in earlier role-think exercises, but most thought this was only 'with the benefit of hindsight'. Simon left with a much clearer idea about the relaunch.

Postscript . . . by Simon

Addressing the relaunch from the standpoints of both our principal competitor, and of a potentially dangerous new entrant, showed up our lack of awareness of what we might trigger them to do. The fundamentals of our planned relaunch were right, but this further examination shifted the whole team's thinking from 'Is this the right thing for the market?' to 'Is this the right thing for a market full of competitors?'.

We realized that we knew our principal competitor only from their public face. We had previously failed to address the damage to our profitability which a cornered competitor – and especially a major new entrant – would have brought. In hindsight I believe the relaunch would still have won in the market, but the spoils would have been much reduced.

Thinking in advance about what we would do when faced with competitors' likely responses gave the whole team a 'warm coat' of strategic comfort. Of itself this boosted confidence that we would win. Of course we didn't anticipate everything, but the principal competitor didn't introduce nearly as many responses as we had first anticipated. Vitally, we were able to help dissuade the potential new entrant from coming in.

The publication had, for internal investment reasons, previously been hobbled and prior to its relaunch was a distant No. 2 in the market. Free to develop its own strategy for the first time, its relaunch was highly successful and resulted in the competitor being overtaken. The publication went on to become the most profitable in Reed Business Publishing. More than a decade later its profits are very significantly higher and it remains the market's No. 1.

Reed Business Publishing – launching a division's strategy

The Organization: A division of Reed Business Publishing in the mid 1980s.

The Vignette: Closure – publicizing and publication of strategy.

The Cast List: Simon Timm – the Managing Director of the Division; Clive Foskett – the deputy Managing Director; 1 facilitator – Colin.

Simon was also considering how to **present the strategy**. He had involved   *P456*
all his line managers in a series of workshops to ascertain what they felt
was important and to tap their creativity. Likewise he and his management team had reviewed, refined, and agreed upon the way forward
building upon this material. Now, however, he needed to present it back
to them. Colin suggested that one way, given that the organization was
known for its professional presentations, was to produce a brochure. After
all, if a publishing company couldn't achieve this then there wasn't much
hope for other organizations. In addition, they would accompany this with
a live presentation. Clive, Simon's second in command, agreed, suggesting
that they not only produce a booklet but include two inserts: one detailing
the **mission statement** and the other the **goal system as a map**. This way   *C161: P456*
staff could pin them up on their office wall or easily refer to them without
having to read the entire document. Both Simon and Colin liked the idea.
     Clive moved on to consider the nature of the live presentation. He
commented that, 'this is all serious stuff, but can we not get a bit of
humour into it somehow?'. 'Good idea,' commented Colin, 'how about   *P456*
also capitalizing on your two different styles – you, Clive, are known to
have a natural jokey style whereas Simon's is more serious. If we could
build that into the presentation then it would add to it'. 'During the
strategy making workshops, you were always giving us funny, but
exaggerated, examples of how staff do things now compared with what
you want them to do when the strategy has been delivered; could we use
some of these in the presentation?' Simon suggested. 'Sure', noted Clive,
'we can work on that. Why don't we get one of our cartoonists to show
"now" and also show "how it's going to be" – if we get it right everyone
will know exactly what we're getting at. We could do a pair of cartoons for
each strategy and I could work from them in my part of the presentation.
They'll connect much better if they can laugh at themselves . . .'. 'That
sounds a bit like another organization we've worked with, where they
used a video of actors showing how things happened now, and then how
they were expected to happen with the strategy implemented', Colin
replied. 'It also relied on humour in the situations to get the message
across. In their case they used it as a way of reaching staff across the
globe'. Simon built on the suggestions – 'How about also having some
form of memorable image for the statement of strategic intent. The strategy

map is a bit like a jigsaw, with all the pieces connected together – why not build a cardboard or plastic model with the mission statement in the centre and surrounding goals and strategies linked in around it. We could build it up in front of the audience. I could use computer projection of the summary maps for each strategy and talk them through'. 'OK', said Colin, 'we've got Clive on one side of the stage working off projected cartoons, Simon on the other side doing the serious stuff, and a jigsaw image gradually being built up in stage centre?'.

Just to add a final level of detail Simon also suggested that the computer model be available on a number of workstations so that participants could explore the detail, see the chains of argument, and also see that their input had influenced the strategy.

Postscript . . . by Simon

Just doing the feedback and revealing the input – and indeed the specific language – of the line managers into its content was a powerful way of fixing the strategy in their minds. The dual mechanism of the presentation and the printed record proved very effective. The division's ownership and knowledge of the strategy was high.

Two pieces of evidence support this, one empirical and one from an independent survey:

1. The strategy was designed to deliver growth and profit in markets and in an economy where opportunity abounded (this was the boom of the mid/late 80s). A part of the strategy addressed the need to retain the key staff and, in a memorable phrase, 'to take risks on good people early'. The idea was that a high performer should be pushed up to the limit of their ability and beyond the limit of their experience in order to reward them with career growth and so retain their skills to allow expansion and performance in the market.

    When counselling individual managers on their career aspirations this phrase was frequently quoted back to me. It made for some uncomfortable – is this person in fact 'good'? – but honest sessions which benefited both parties.

2. Some time later, the whole company undertook a staff feedback exercise in the form of a survey carried out by the Industrial Society, an independent and highly reputable body experienced in such things. Their report on the division highlighted their surprise at finding an unusually high level of awareness of strategic goals and actions through **the way they described their working life**.

C160

Figure V8 A page from the strategy brochure.

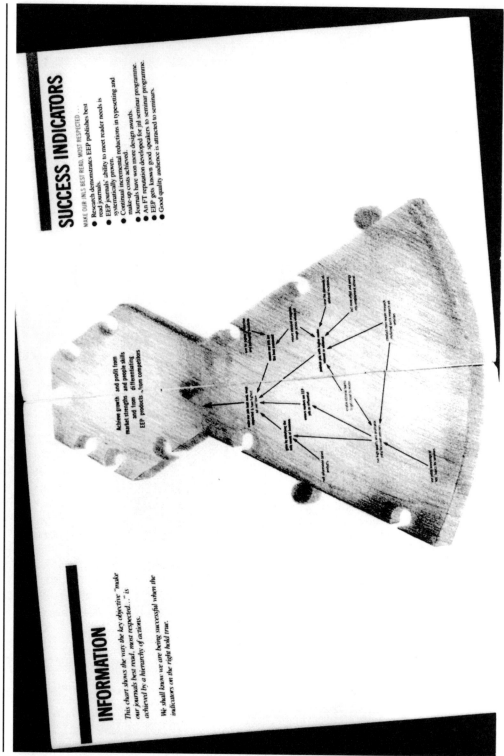

PART 3

PRACTICE: METHODS, TECHNIQUES, AND TOOLS

INTRODUCTION

This part of the book concentrates on providing detailed *practical guidelines, procedures, and 'handy tips'* for using the methods, techniques, and tools employed in the vignettes and developed from the theory and concepts discussed in part 1. The part of JOURNEY making addressed in the following chapters is that of developing agreements – the link between JOintly Understanding, Reflecting, and NEgotiating StrategY and its design and (re)confirmation (figure C2.6). Thus, this part begins by detailing guidelines and procedures for increasing participation amongst members of the management team, as well as amongst significant numbers of staff. This participation is designed to pay attention to multiple perspectives, and detect key assumptions and deep knowledge at many levels in the organization. To help manage this wealth of material we set out guidelines to assist in the capturing and structuring of the material. These guidelines in turn enable participants to appreciate the systemic properties of the material, detect patterns, surface and understand emergent strategies, and move towards developing a sense of strategic direction and vision. We also give attention to the design of appropriate procedures for designing interventions, managing groups, and helping the management team agree upon a strategic direction. The final set of guidelines deal with assisting organizations in the implementation of strategy and monitoring its progress.

Embarking upon JOURNEY making for the first time may appear as a daunting venture for the manager/facilitator. This is partly due to the publicness of the process as we describe it – it is not done in the 'back-room' but in front of the power-brokers and other staff. Also JOURNEY making seeks to use an inter-disciplinary body of theory and concepts, which implies the use of a range of methods demanding analytical competence, facilitation skills, computer skills, and a clear understanding of the nature of organizations. Nevertheless, as we noted in chapter C1, significant added value can be gained by working with just one of the methods or techniques for aiding strategy making. Having worked with a number of organizations and trained, and worked with, managers and consultants as JOURNEY makers, we suggest that, rather than embark on a fully fledged intervention, it is helpful to start with the use of one or two of the techniques and build competence and confidence gradually. We have tried to reflect this approach into the design of these chapters, each adopting the following format:

- An *introduction* to the content of the chapter, providing background information. This section of each chapter links to the Theory and Concepts part of the book (part 1).
- A series of *guidelines*: noting actions as an imperative, in a step by step manner. To aid with the reader's visualization of the procedures, there are many cross links to and from the Vignettes part of the book and links to the Theory and Concepts part where this may help.
- A question and answer session entitled *'yes but . . .'* drawn from questions the authors have been asked when training managers and consultants.
- *Further commentary* where relevant. This section discusses the network computer system.

Chapter C2 proposed that JOURNEY making commences with the management team reflecting upon the emergent strategizing of the organization through designed conversational processes. The Theory and Concepts, and Vignettes, parts of this book show that the nature of capturing and developing assumptions can take many forms. As such, the first four chapters in this part of the book deal with different methods available, encompassing not only how to use the different techniques but also providing clues about when they might be used. They are:

- Individual Interviews Using Cognitive Mapping – chapter P1
- The Oval Mapping Technique – a manual way to support groups – chapter P2
- Computer Supported Group Workshops – chapter P3
- Exploring Stakeholder Analysis and Alternative Futures – chapter P4

All four chapters discuss the capture and development of assumptions – seen at the top of figure P0.1. Following these four chapters we introduce two chapters dealing with *managing* this information:

- The Management of Process, the Design of Interventions, and the Facilitation of Groups – chapter P5. This chapter informs and is informed by chapter P6 (the double headed arrow between the elements in figure P0.1)
- Analysing Interview Maps and Analysing Maps / Computer Models for Managing Workshops – chapter P6. Here attention is directed towards helping manage the complexity of the strategy material rather than reducing it.

These two aspects come together through the workshop model – the Group Decision Support System – enabling issues relating to political feasibility to be addressed as the management team negotiates towards a strategic direction. The double headed arrows between chapters P5 and P6 and the capturing chapters (P1–P4) illustrate the necessity of taking a cyclical approach to design. We continue by addressing the final stages of JOURNEY making, dealing with implementation and review:

- Delivering Strategy – Agreeing Strategic Intent and Strategic Programmes – Developing Strategic Programmes, Actions, and a Strategy Delivery Support System (SDSS) – chapter P7

Figure P0.1   Developing agreements.

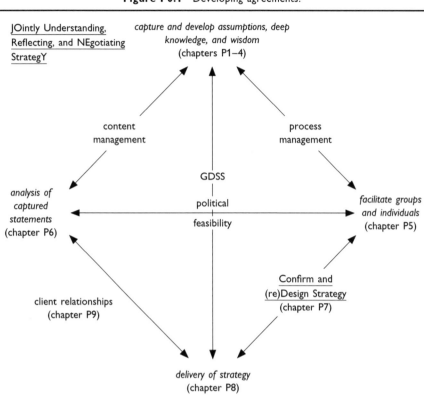

JOintly Understanding, Reflecting, and NEgotiating StrategY

capture and develop assumptions, deep knowledge, and wisdom
(chapters P1–4)

content management

process management

GDSS

political

feasibility

analysis of captured statements
(chapter P6)

facilitate groups and individuals
(chapter P5)

Confirm and (re)Design Strategy
(chapter P7)

client relationships
(chapter P9)

delivery of strategy
(chapter P8)

- Delivering Strategy – Communication, Project Management, Strategy Review – chapter P8.

Finally the practical part of the book concludes with discussion about:

- The Relationship between Facilitator, the Organization, and its Managers – chapter P9. In some respects this is an appendix. But we regard the subject matter of the chapter as so important that it is included as a chapter within the main body of the book. The 'client', as a single person or small group of people (rather than the organization), is involved through the process of JOURNEY making, and their ownership and commitment is critical to a successful outcome.

This part of the book also introduces the role of computer software to help manage the data of strategic thinking and to help manage group processes. As we have stated clearly elsewhere, this part of the book, and applying JOURNEY making in practice, is not dependent upon knowledge or use of the software.

Note: The single user software referred to throughout the book is Decision Explorer and the networked system is Group Explorer. Information about Decision Explorer can be found at http://www.scolari.co.uk and for Group Explorer http://www.phrontis.com/.

DETECTING EMERGENT STRATEGIZING: INDIVIDUAL INTERVIEWS AND COGNITIVE MAPPING

Introduction

This first practical chapter focuses on (i) what cognitive mapping is, and how to do it, and (ii) how/why it can be used in an individual interview setting to understand strategic issues. Whilst the second focus includes issues relating to interviews in general, it is not our intention to provide a comprehensive account of interviewing practice, other than to note that in the context of strategy making the interviews are generally of 'elites'. The particular issues of dealing with elites and other aspects of interviewing are dealt with by others (for example, Campion *et al*, 1994; Cannel and Kahn, 1968; Healey and Rawlinson, 1993; Lofland, 1976; Whyte, 1957). However, we shall highlight those issues particularly relevant to JOURNEY making. Good interviewing and listening skills are very important; without them the quality of the interview material is likely to suffer regardless of the technique adopted for capturing and managing the interview content. Chapter C5 indicates the approaches that can be taken during an interview to provide *C77 C89 C90* appropriate prompts to elicit **embedded assumptions and wisdom** about strategic direction.

The use of one-to-one interviews and the adoption of cognitive mapping to capture and structure the issues relating to 'what we know, what we do, and the way we do it' may depend on (i) the particular type of task being addressed, (ii) the nature of the organization, or (iii) the client objectives. Therefore the choice of which technique to use when capturing assumptions, deep knowledge, and wisdom involves the consultant/facilitator and the client designing the intervention *together* to ensure that the technique used is the most appropriate. This choice includes using either individual interviews as addressed in this chapter, oval mapping (chapter P2), computer assisted workshops (chapter P3), or stakeholder and alternative futures analysis (chapter P4). There are a number of reasons for using interviews and cognitive mapping, each of which is examined in further detail in the second half of this chapter. These reasons include the use of interviews *C48* when (i) interpersonal or internal issues are prevalent (**new negotiated order**), (ii) working in an organizational culture that is not familiar or comfortable with *C54 C56* **participative methods**, and (iii) working with a client who wishes to get a very deep and rich understanding of the issues from the standpoint of individual managers.

What Is Cognitive Mapping?

Cognitive mapping (Eden, 1988; Eden *et al*, 1979, 1983) – explained in chapter C5 – is a technique designed to capture the thinking of an individual about a particular issue or problem in a diagrammatic, rather than linear, format. The map is designed to focus on the values, beliefs, and assumptions an individual has about a particular issue – in our case, strategic issues. The theoretical basis of the technique owes its origins to Kelly's (1955) Theory of Personal Constructs. He asserted that 'man as a scientist continually checks the sense he makes of his world by using his current understanding (construct system) to anticipate and reach out for the future', and so suggested a means of identifying this construct system and the construct's relationships to each other – the 'Repertory Grid'. Building upon this work, cognitive mapping has been designed to provide a process through which (i) additional richness could be ascertained, (ii) the map is immediately useful to both mapper and interviewee, and (iii) the process is not constrained by a formal structure but can follow a 'natural' conversation (Brown, 1992).

To work with messy, complex strategic issues it is not only important to know what each statement means (through its content *and* context) but also why they fit together as they do. These structural properties can determine the basis for pulling a 'mess' into a system of interacting issues. By capturing statements/ideas and relationships in the form of a causal or implication network of argumentation – using cognitive mapping – it is possible to make sense of large amounts of information regarded as relevant by the interviewee. This network not only demonstrates the causal or implication links between statements, but does so in a hierarchical manner. In addition, the map permits an exploration of both detailed and holistic properties using various forms of analysis. For example, the exploration of hierarchy helps identify and explore option packages at a detailed or micro level and at a macro level to identify potential strategies. The map also reveals how the issues relate to each other and how changes in the *character* of one issue may have repercussions for another. Each construct (which may be taken as an option, assertion, fact, goal, belief) is linked to others through the use of arrows indicating 'may lead to', 'has implications for', or 'supports' moving up the arrow; or 'may be explained by', 'is implied by', or is 'supported by' when moving down the arrow.

Those statements (or constructs) at the top of the map may be taken as values, aspirations, or goals with possible strategies supporting them, and more detailed options and assertions occurring further down the hierarchy (see figure C5.3). This conceptual scheme, as applied to cognitive mapping in an individual interview, is expected to replicate the structure of the **'strategy map'** used in group work. Thus, the technique, through its ability to show multiple explanations and consequences, is able to represent dilemmas, feedback loops, multiple options, and the anticipated positive and negative ramifications of options. For the interviewee the map acts as a 'mirror' that seeks to provide an accurate representation of how they wish the interviewer to understand *their* world. The structuring of the interviewee's arguments and reasoning enables analyses to be undertaken, increasing the understanding of the interview. The *detail* of the material captured in the map is not usually new to the interviewee. Nevertheless, having the ability, through the map, to see the *structuring* of their statements along with their implications, typically facilitates individual JOURNEY making and the development of new insights. For example, when generating a cognitive map, the interviewee is often surprised at the extent and significance of his or her knowledge. A cognitive map acts as the

C98

C67 'transitional object' through which the interviewee and interviewer can jointly understand and reflect upon the significance of the interviewee's knowledge and wisdom within the context of strategy making. It is not unusual for the map to act
C89 C91 as the basis for helping an interviewee gather their thoughts together, **change their own mind** through the reflective power of the map, and find the ways to explicate knowledge hitherto remaining as deep assumptions. The experience is often cathartic. A good interviewer, who is also a good mapper, can provide an important start to JOURNEY making.

C67 The main purpose of mapping goes beyond the interview itself. The map is the basis for sharing knowledge and views, and will act as the vehicle for **negotiation** in groups as maps are merged to represent the aggregated views of a group. Clearly a cognitive map belongs to an individual; after cognitive maps have been merged, or aggregated, they are no longer a representation of aspects of thinking (cognition) they become a device to facilitate negotiation and become referred to as a 'group map' or 'strategy map'.

Guidelines for Individual Interviews Using Cognitive Mapping

Before You Do It

1.1 *Meet with the client to understand whether there are issues she or he believes must be explored by the group.* This will allow these items to be gently introduced and discussed during an interview. The process of allowing interviewees to present their own views on the selected issues provides the basis for negotiating a group view of strategic issues. As maps are aggregated, all participants are more likely to feel they have contributed to determining the meaning of the issue to the
C53 C55 organization – **procedural justice and procedural rationality**. It will also help initiate a good consultant–client relationship

1.2 *Use unlined paper and a self-propelling or automatic pencil, with a 0.5 mm lead and built-in erasure.*

    1.2.1 Having blank paper allows for a more flexible use of space.
    1.2.2 Use a self-propelling or automatic pencil to avoid bluntness and so the likelihood of writing too large.

1.3 *Keep the map to one page only (A4/letter size or A3/twice letter size) if possible.* By writing in small lowercase it is possible to get 50–60 constructs on one page of A4 size paper. This promotes the creation of a 'tight' map as the relationships can be recognized and drawn in easily, and material is less likely to be forgotten; also, and perhaps more importantly, the structural characteristics will show through. Some mappers like to start with a large sheet of folded paper and allow the map to expand by unfolding the paper as the interview progresses. This approach helps draw the interviewee into the mapping process as the map becomes visible as 'a peculiar style of note-taking!'. Involving the interviewee in the map (however crude and messy it looks) acts as a powerful interviewing method and creates quick ownership of the model being created.

1.4 *Start the map about two-thirds up the page and in the centre.* This assumes that most interviewees respond to the prompt about the nature of issues, rather than offering detail. It will leave space for goals to be entered at the top of the map, and

Figure P1.1   An example illustrating the beginnings of a cognitive map. Already one goal and two key issues have been identified. More information can be added to both key issues along with fleshing out the goal further.

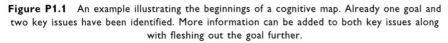

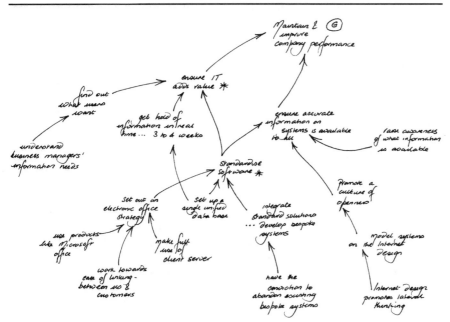

elaboration of detailed explanation, and so possible options, underneath. Issue labels turn out, in practice, to be about two-thirds up the hierarchy of reasoning.

1.5   *Write down statements as rectangular blocks of text rather than a single line.* These blocks of text typically measure approximately 3 cm by 2 cm (¾ in wide by ½ in high). Thus, a block of text typically contains up to a maximum of about 80 characters, or 8–15 words. Noting constructs as blocks of text helps manage the information on the map. Blocks of text can be inserted more easily at the appropriate place and relationships drawn as curved flowing arrows around the text rather than angular (similar to electrical circuit diagrams) and disjointed links. See figure P1.1 for an example of a map during the early stages of an interview.

1.6   *When possible, sit at right angles to the interviewee rather than opposite or along-side.* Sitting opposite the interviewee tends to create an atmosphere of competition, whereas sitting at right angles creates cooperation (see Argyle, 1988). This position also allows the map to be shared more easily between the interviewee and interviewer. This will not only validate the map but it will also reassure the interviewee that his or her statements and beliefs have been captured, thus building confidence and trust. It may also highlight areas that have been overlooked (also see 1.3 above).

How to Do It – building a cognitive map

Building the map

Once seated, and having set expectations through an introduction, start the interview with a broad inquiry to lead the interviewee into the discussion. Thus an interview may start by the interviewer inviting the interviewee to 'discuss some of the strategic issues facing the organization', or to comment on some of the 'issues mentioned by others' (including those suggested by the client). Other important prompts are the **'oracle question'**, recall of **'critical issues', and 'laddering'**. The oracle question focuses on emergent issues through data shortage, whereas the critical issues approach focuses on eliciting emergent goals, and laddering is designed to help elicitation of an emergent **goal system**.

C92: C91

C92

Rather than have lots of questions in advance – a tight agenda – the emerging map itself takes on the role of an agenda. The agenda is formed through the map prompting the interviewer to ask questions such as 'how might that be done?' moving down the network and 'why might that be important?' or 'what outcomes would you expect from . . .?' or 'so what . . .?' to ladder up the network. Other questions will become apparent as constructs seem unlinked to others, and the intonation in the delivery of statements suggests some themes are more important and therefore might be elaborated further. Typically, as the map unfolds, the mapper will discover difficulties in linking (making sense of) constructs and so will need to follow up with statements such as 'I noted . . . but don't think I understand what you meant by it . . . as you can see from my network of notes, I'm not certain how it relates to other things you've told me . . .'. The process helps the interviewer understand *what the interviewee meant*, rather than what the interviewer wants a statement to mean.

2.1 *Separate presented statements into distinct phrases.* This process seeks to identify each construct (block of text). It will enable a greater degree of depth or subtlety to be gained as well as making the process of linking the constructs more meaningful.

2.1.1 *Ensure each construct contains only one phrase.* For example an interviewee may state 'we need to set out an electronic office strategy using products like Microsoft Office so that we can standardize our software'. Here three constructs can be identified – (i) 'set out an electronic office strategy', (ii) 'use products like Microsoft Office', and (iii) 'standardize our software'.

2.1.2 *Split statements up where there are two or more possible actions implied.* For example an interviewee may state 'we need to increase and improve our product range'. This suggests two different constructs. The first deals with the necessity to increase the product range, whilst the other focuses on improvement. Options for 'increasing our product range' may be different from those focused on 'improving' it. They may even be in conflict. However, it is also important to recognize that sometimes the interviewee specifically means that more than one thing must be done together – in this case the statement remains as one construct.

2.2 *Build up the hierarchy.* By listening carefully to a series of constructs, try to identify which is the *option* and which is the *valued outcome*, which is the *means* and which is the *end* (as seen by the interviewee).

2.2.1 *If in doubt ask the interviewee* what the preferred outcome is, rather than blindly following the order of the chain of argument as presented. Taking the above example: the chain of argument when mapped may look like 'use products like Microsoft Office' so that the organization can 'set out an electronic office strategy' in order to 'standardize our software'. However, this was not the order the interviewee used when mentioning it.

It is important to understand what is meant (rather than said) by the interviewee.

2.2.2   *When appropriate, use opportunities to gain confirmation of the emerging map.* When a natural break (not just a pause for breath!) occurs, play back the material using the map as the basis for the feedback. For example, the interviewer might say 'if I understand correctly, a key issue is to standardize your software and one way of doing this might be to set out an electronic office strategy using products like Microsoft Office'. This will enable the hierarchy to be validated (or changed if necessary). The play-back would be a direct presentation of the map as drawn in draft form rather than seeking to repeat what was said. In addition, the feedback should seek to provide added value derived from visual analysis of the map in its current form. For example, stating that 'there seems to be **cluster or theme** about . . . which seems central to your thinking' invites   *V214* confirmation or elaboration such as, 'actually no, I've said a lot about the topic, but it is not really central, I should have said more about . . .'. The map is intended to be a model of what the interviewee *means*, not what was said. An interviewee can state their views only in a sequential manner, sometimes jumping from one topic to another, whereas the map can hold many arguments together.

2.2.3   *Use the time playing back the material for down-loading material not yet captured.* Consider both constructs and relationships. Interviewees, when engaged in a topic, often speak faster than the interviewer can write and so it is important to find means for capturing the material without stopping the flow. By playing back to the interviewee the chain(s) of argument being captured, additional material can be written in. In addition, the individual will feel reassured that the information is being captured and will move on. Repetition of argument is often a sign that the interviewee is uncertain whether it has been captured correctly, and is seeking reassurance. Reviewing the map may alleviate this concern and allow them to address further concerns/issues.

2.3   *Watch for values, aspirations, final outcomes, **goals**.* Goals are those outcomes   *V214* that are 'good (or bad) in their own right'. Those that are bad represent '**negative**   *C90* **goals**' – disastrous outcomes which are as important as goals in driving action. Negative goals are important aspects of a person's **emergent strategizing**, for they   *C81* more often drive a manager's thinking and behaviour than do positive goals. These constructs will be at the top part of the hierarchy (see above).

2.3.1   *Recognize that often an interviewee starts by surfacing issues that are of key concern to them rather than goals.* One way of eliciting the goals, therefore, is to ask questions such as 'why is this an important issue?', 'what are the consequences of this issue occurring?', etc. These questions seek to 'ladder' up the map until the interviewee has discussed outcomes which are good in their own right. This process may have to be repeated several times before goals are detected. However, do not force the laddering, otherwise the interviewee may start making up answers in order to satisfy the interviewer rather than providing answers that are indicative of thinking and action.

2.3.2   *Mark the goals on the map in some way so that they can be readily distinguished.* We use an asterisk.

V198   2.4   *Watch for those constructs that act as labels for strategic* **key issues**. These are phrases that describe an issue which is broad based, costly (in terms of time, energy, and money), often irreversible, and takes a long time to achieve. They often emerge early on in the discussion and may be the cause of 'pain' and worry, or are emotionally key, or the primary focus of attention. Strategic issue labels may also emerge from a rough *analysis* of the map's structure.

2.4.1   *Examine the extent of the elaboration presented*, that is, the number of explanations (options and beliefs provided to support the potential issue) and consequences (reasons for carrying out the issue). If the construct appears 'busy', with lots of explanations and consequences, then it may be an issue to the interviewee.

C97   2.4.2   *Monitor the interviewee's* **non-verbals** and general sense of concern. In these instances there might not be as much elaboration as in those issues identified in the above manner, but the issue is emotionally significant for the individual. About two-thirds of the data in an interview can come from non-verbals (Argyle, 1984). Use these data to validate and adjust the meaning derived from the verbal tags used by the interviewee.

2.4.3   *Mark key issues* (using a different notation from goals) – we circle them. It may be worth noting the form the key issue takes – whether it was analytically determined or flagged by emotion. We use a 'wiggly' circle for what we take to be emotionally driven issues.

C94   2.5   *Hold on to 'contrasting poles'.* **Contrasting, or opposite, poles** are those instances where a 'rather than . . .' is, *implicitly or explicitly*, expressed. For example, a senior manager, when discussing finance for the organization, argued that they should seek to 'sustain grants-in-aid rather than suffer government cuts'. In this case a clear contrast was stated through the use of the expression 'rather than'.

2.5.1   *Listen for opposite poles* – instances where the interviewee explicitly mentions *this* 'rather than' *that* – and capture them on the map.

2.5.2   *Use the abbreviation of three dots* (an ellipsis) to represent the expression 'rather than', for example, 'sustain grants-in-aid . . . government cuts'. (This convention matches the display of the computer software if it is used.)

2.5.3   *Watch for instances where the interviewee begins with the first part of a bipolar construct, elaborates it, and then discusses the contrast.* For example, during a discussion about the structure of the organization, the interviewee was arguing to 'develop a local focus so as to devolve management and help develop an effective organizational structure rather than end up with an over centralized administration which centralizes management' (see figure P1.2).

2.5.4   *Use the expression 'rather than? . . .' to clarify instances where you are not sure what a construct means.* Do not hesitate to ask when uncertain about something which appears to be important: 'I'm not sure I understand . . . can you say some more about. . . . What might this contrast with . . .?'.

C169   2.6   *Write each construct in an imperative form to give the map an* **action orientation**. For example, if someone talks about 'level of staffing', it is difficult without a verb, or an evaluation, to determine what is meant. If the construct had been 'increase the level of staffing', 'examine the level of staffing', or 'too little

Figure P1.2 An illustration of opposite poles.

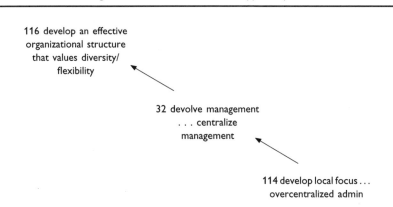

116 develop an effective
organizational structure
that values diversity/
flexibility

32 devolve management
. . . centralize
management

114 develop local focus . . .
overcentralized admin

staffing', additional clarity would be obtained through the action implication. Where something like 'too little' is uttered, then an action may be to 'correct the level of staffing'. However, it is important to retain the meaning as intended – if too much violence is done to the original phrase then ownership may be lost.

2.6.1 *Develop an action orientation* to a construct – make it read like an 'option'. Use a verb to imply action, and use a format which includes, when possible, answers to who? what? where? and when? (The other part of the pentad – why? – is established by the consequences – arrows out of the construct.) For example, the 'management team [actor/who] provide [verb] clear leadership [what] urgently [when]'. It is unusual for all elements to be stated. Often a full statement is not necessary, as there is an obvious consensus about meaning, but sometimes assumed actors or timing can be mistaken. Additions to the map to provide this data can be made after the interview is complete.

2.6.2 *Avoid incorporating words such as 'should', 'need', 'must', 'ought' in the map.* For example, where an interviewee says 'we must make more of our marketing staff' or 'we need to turn around customers' orders more quickly', capture them as 'make more of the marketing staff' or 'turn around customers' orders more quickly'.

2.7 *Retain the **interviewee's ownership** of the statement by using his or her language or intended language.* The participant should easily recognize the construct on a merged strategy map or during the feedback of the map. Securing maximum ownership of the map is important for beginning effective JOURNEY making. Thus, capture the exact words used by the interviewee, rather than paraphrasing them, unless confident that new words will result in the interviewee feeling 'that's exactly what I meant'.

2.8 *Identify options and outcomes.* When attempting to link the statements forming the chain of argument, the process of determining which of the pair is the option, and which the outcome expected from that option, is absolutely crucial. The meaningfulness of analysis of maps depends upon the use of consistent coding rules within and across interviews.

V217

2.8.1   *Examine which of the pair of constructs the interviewee regards as the desired outcome.* For example, the statement 'one of the ways we might reduce work pressure is to minimize bureaucracy'. Consider which of the pair of constructs is the *more* desired outcome, and the direction of the link can be identified. In this case the option and the outcome are clear: consider minimizing bureaucracy to create the outcome of reduced work pressure.

2.8.2   *Ensure that the more generic concept (broader-based concept) is superordinate* to the specific items that contribute to it. For example when exploring the 'privatization of prisons', one option was to 'privatize laundry' and another was 'privatize catering'. Both of these were seen as more specific forms of privatization and so each of them had the output of privatization, even though each of them may also have highly specific other outcomes. Future discussion may reveal consequences of privatization which are, for example, very different from the consequences of privatizing catering. Coding in this way allows for the specific to contribute to the generic and so possibly help create consequences of the generic, and yet also show consequences of the specific without implications for the generic outcomes.

2.9   *Retain the first 'pole' of the statement* – regardless of whether it is taken to be a negative description. By recording the construct in this manner, the map portrays the strategic issues as the interviewee sees them. This in turn gives the interviewer some clues as to the potential difficulties/problems which may exist when developing strategy. For example an overworked member of a marketing department might say that 'we [the marketing department] are experiencing too much rush and panic . . . rather than having the time to do more in-depth work'. Coding or mapping the concept as 'experience too much rush and panic. . .have the time to do in-depth work' will indicate clearly the current preoccupation of the interviewee. Another staff member may talk of the 'time to work in-depth, rather than being in a state of panic'. In the first instance we may suspect a negative construction of the situation whereas in the second a more aspirational view.

Tidying and refining the map

3.1   *Provide some 'rough' analysis of the map* by using the analysis techniques that are typically applied in the 'back-room'. The interviewer can not only validate the material, but also feed back emergent properties. The most often used analyses are:

- identifying the 'busy' points as possible key issue labels;
- checking whether there are any isolated statements and, if there are, asking the interviewee for clarification. The additional statements may begin to be linked into the main body of the map and prompt further elaboration;
- exploring 'heads' (statements with no consequences) to see whether the interviewee might 'ladder' further upwards towards more superordinate goals or aspirations;
- roughly identifying clusters and 'islands' of linked statements as possible strategic issues. Typically each cluster will have at least one 'busy' statement within it;

C30   • identifying and checking possible **feedback loops**.

Value-added feedback produces confidence and **trust** from the interviewee and   *V215*
demonstrates that the interviewer has listened well. Often during this review
process, the interviewee notices something that they consider key has not been
mentioned and so further elaboration/extension is provided.

3.2   *Prompt 'off the record' comments.* By deliberately providing sufficient time at
the end of an interview for a general review the interviewee may say things 'off the
record'; the map can act as an artifact separate from the interviewer, and so
encourage such comments. These often provide an important source of data about
organizational politics.

3.3   *Ensure there is time set aside during the interview for closure.* Allocating about
10% of the interview time to this activity will result in a number of benefits.

3.3.1   *Provide the interviewee with a sense of closure by explaining the **next steps** in*   *V215*
the process. For example, whether a workshop will follow, what will
happen to the cognitive map next, whether there will be an opportunity
for the map to be reviewed carefully after it has been 'tidied' after the
interview.

3.3.2   *Avoid interviewees having to suddenly get up and rush to other meetings.*
Providing a sense of good time management suggests a professional
attitude. By clearly informing the interviewee that there are only five
minutes left, they are given the choice of winding up and voicing any final
concerns or cancelling/delaying a subsequent meeting so as to continue
with the discussion and further work on the map. A good, well-run interview is difficult and is therefore usually appreciated by the interviewee.
Managers are rarely properly listened to, and so for an interviewer to do
so is a notable occasion that will reap rewards later in the process.

3.4   **Schedule the interviews** *so that there is time between interviews to further tidy*   *V210*
the map. This will allow the interviewer to note down any remaining statements or
linkages that have not yet been added to the map. The process is more accurate
when it is conducted immediately following the interview. To create a map
capturing deep knowledge and wisdom, the map must reflect all aspects of the
interview, not just notes but images and social interaction. If too much time is left
between an interview and working on the map then too much is forgotten,
particularly if the task is delayed until after another interview.

Yes But . . .

How can I adhere to all these mapping guidelines and still hear what is said, maintain eye contact,
and provide appropriate non-verbal encouragements?

Nearly everyone, when trying to learn cognitive mapping, or any other formalized
note taking method, has found learning the **technique very demanding and**   *V196*
interviews more difficult. Novice mappers feel overwhelmed, believing that they
cannot remember and implement all of the above guidelines whilst at the same
time capturing an accurate record. One way of dealing with this is to gain experience in low risk environments such as mapping the news on TV, mapping a
colleague during an informal meeting, and practising in meetings. At first only
a few of the mapping guidelines should be adhered to, but as the process becomes

more familiar then more of the guidelines can be adopted. In the first instance try mapping without links, and practise breaking up what is being said into concepts as blocks of text. Secondly, practice making the concepts action oriented. Thirdly, try rough linking by lines without arrows. Finally, try mapping with arrows. In any event, an interview map tends to be sketchy with some concepts well noted and others not, some links well established and others left as lines with question marks. It is always important to remember that if the formalism of the technique is getting in the way of a good record of the interview then it is not being used properly. All the guidelines are formulated so that they force important questions of the interview and the data.

Learning to map is no more complex than learning to drive a car, and in the same way it initially appears that there are just too many actions required but gradually (and often imperceptibly) the process becomes internalized.

The technique, however, does require substantial effort – cognitive mapping demands that the mapper *listens intensively*, and captures not only the statements and knowledge being generated but also the relationships, thus understanding the structure and meaning behind them. Whereas, with linear notes, statements can be jotted down without consideration for their ramifications, maps demand a better and fuller understanding. As a mapper becomes well practised, their listening ability improves because the map, as a model, and the formalisms become an active aid in the interview.

Why not tape record the interview?

It is tempting to make the interview recording and mapping easier by tape recording and listening to it afterwards so that mapping can be done at your own pace. Notwithstanding the risks associated with tape recordings failing and the reaction of the interviewee to a tape recorder, to do so denies many of the significant JOURNEY making benefits. As we have discussed above, important visual non-verbal cues are lost through a tape recording. Most significantly, a developing map constructed during the interview is one of the best methods for managing an effective interview – it helps construct appropriate questions, and provides the basis for good summaries which contain added value.

Tape recording interviews tends to encourage the interviewer to become lazy and so miss many of the more subtle but important parts of an interview. It also results in maps with missing links as this lack has not been identified during the interview and questioned.

I find it difficult to know which way an arrow goes

Don't worry. This is the most frequent concern when first learning to map. If the outcome is unclear then ask the interviewee for help. When questions arise because of the mapping conventions they are usually helpful questions for both interviewee and interviewer. Often the interviewee is pleased at the opportunity to think through what they meant.

In many circumstances, arguments seem to be presented 'backwards', resulting in an 'upside down' map. For example, during a health service interview about 'improving the planning of care', the interviewee said:

Figure P1.3 Determining optimum outcome direction.

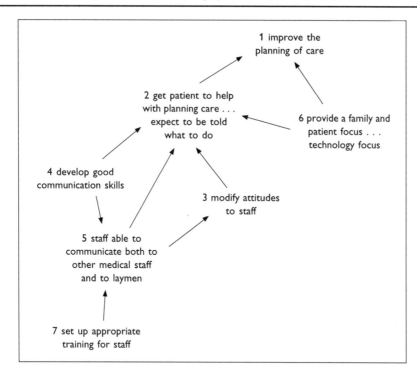

'I want to improve the planning of care, which means I need to get the patient to help with planning care, rather than being told what to do . . . and we need to provide a family and patient focus instead of a technology focus. If we are going to get the patient to help plan the care then we must modify the attitudes of our staff and develop their communication skills, which means setting up appropriate training and enabling staff to communicate to both medical staff and laymen.'

If we map the above point of view in the manner in which it is presented then the *outcomes* of the chain of argument show as 'set up appropriate training' and 'enable staff to communicate to both medical staff and laymen' – both unlikely outcomes given their specificity and purpose. The outcomes intended by the interviewee are seen in the figure P1.3.

How do I make statements into action oriented concepts?

Reformulating statements often causes difficulties, especially when attempting to adhere to step 2.8 above – 'using the interviewee's own language'. Two tips help:

- Ask the interviewee what *action* is required. For example, if the interviewee during a discussion on the redirection of resources has said 'and of course there are catering standards', then asking how these catering standards affect the redirection of resources may provide the answer. The interviewee may respond 'we have to agree on catering standards so as to determine how much resource we need to allocate before redirecting resources'. Interjecting a verb and monitoring the response not only clarifies the situation but also adds more meaning to the construct.

- Try an active verb added to the 'playback' of the map. If the action implied by the active verb introduced is not what was meant then the interviewee will usually say so, and in doing so provide the correct one. For example, she might say 'no that's wrong; it's not about maintaining catering standards, its about agreeing them – we can't maintain them until we have a set of standards although we will have to then'.

What do I do if the interviewee is continually restating the same thing?

If the interviewee continually restates an issue or statement, it may mean that either she does not think it has been heard and/or that it is very significant (2.2.3). Sometimes, when interviewing a number of people, there is a danger of not visibly capturing a statement because it has already been voiced by previous interviewees. This is particularly likely if the maps are to be 'merged' together and used to support a workshop. However, the interviewee does not know that this information has already been said and captured, and so keeps reiterating the statement. In addition there is a possibility of missing some of the subtlety. When the statement has already been said and captured in a previous map, further detail may be missed by not discovering a different meaning for the apparently identical statement. Demonstrating that the statement has been captured often stops the repetition and frees the interviewee to go on to other issues.

When repetition is because the statement is central or important, then allowing the interviewee to explain it fully and clearly *marking* it as a key issue (see step 2.4 – look for key issues) will reassure the interviewee and ensure the map shows a centrality which could not be detected using structural analysis only.

My map is a mess!

Do not worry about the messiness of a map – particularly if the individual believes that her data is being captured fully. See figure P1.1 for an example of a 'real' map. Whilst it is understandable to want to tidy up the map, before sharing it with the individual, there often isn't the time or opportunity to do so. Also if the map *does* capture the thinking of the interviewee, then they will be impressed by its faithfulness and not perturbed by its messiness. When an interviewee is disturbed by messiness, or by mapping, it usually indicates that the map has recorded the thinking of the interviewer rather than that of the interviewee.

What if the link only works for one pole of the statement?

This usually means that the opposite pole may be a second concept – try separating the two poles into two constructs and detect opposite poles for each of them.

Help, I have three poles!

As with the above problem, three poles usually suggest that there are three options. For example, one member of a marketing department was discussing how the department should be re-structured in the light of a suggested strategy. In the course of the conversation the interviewee mentioned that the group needed to 'become a profit centre rather than a central service' but later on mentioned that the group should be 'a profit centre rather than a cost centre'. Here there are three options and so three constructs – become a profit centre, become a cost centre, or remain as a central service (in each case, the expressed 'rather than' may still be used as a part of the construct). Subsequently each was presented with its own unique line of argumentation supporting the option, and with some different and some similar consequences.

I seem to have too many links

Check whether they are all legitimate. Often when building maps (either through cognitive mapping in interviews or using group techniques) superfluous links are captured. If two chains of argument exist between two points, for example, A→B→C→D and A→D, ask whether the second chain illustrates a different argument and, if not, delete it. Where it does suggest a second path then try to insert an additional statement between the two, highlighting the different paths. Typically a strategy interview gives a map with a ratio of 1.15–1.25 links to concepts (aggregated strategy maps, and maps developed using the 'oval mapping technique', usually have a higher ratio).

Further Commentary on Individual Interviews Using Cognitive Mapping

Producing a printed version of the map soon after an interview enables the interviewer to (i) provide a tidy copy to the individual for their retention and also (ii) use the map as a focus for following up an interview. Using the special mapping software makes the process easier and enables subsequent merging of several maps, although mappers may use standard drawing packages, or hand draw maps. Using different styles of font or colour to represent different properties of the map – goals, key issue labels, strategic options, etc. – indicates clearly an important part of the interviewer's interpretation of the interview. A printed map not only provides the interviewee with a concrete record from the interview but also shows the structured representation of their thinking. The map may be used as a focus for a **second interview** – allowing further development and modification of *V196 V216* the map. This may also provide better data, encourage elaboration of those areas not yet well defined, and allow checking of relationships between constructs. Whilst second interviews are often costly in terms of time and money, they can increase substantially the depth of material captured. This is because interviewees further explore their understanding and move away from the 'scripts' that they often roll out during the first, relationship building, interview. Perhaps most importantly, it provides a chance to reflect and develop thinking – an integral part of JOURNEY making and a potential for 'double loop' learning (Argyris and Schon, 1978).

V215

In addition to using the cognitive map to structure graphically an *individual's* thinking and so be able to carry out some rough analysis, the maps are the basic support for *group* work. Here maps of several individuals are usually merged into a single map (see chapter P6, Analysis). While it is possible to create a merged map manually, the process is greatly facilitated through the **use of the special purpose software**. The software not only allows the individual map to be entered as a computer model, analysed, and printed, but also allows the aggregation of a series of individual cognitive maps.

Merging individual maps will, at a future workshop, enable those participants who have been 'mapped' to begin to explore each other's thinking and from this position begin to increase their understanding of the strategic issues and possible solutions. Computer supported workshops are the vehicle for doing this – where the merged computer model is used to jointly understand, reflect, and negotiate a group view of the strategic issues facing an organization. The merged computer model is initially presented so that each construct cannot be identified with any specific participant, although each construct will be known to belong to at least one

C61

participant present for the workshop. **Anonymity**, during the early stages of such a workshop, facilitates the process of joint understanding by enabling all participants to pay attention to the views of all others.

C72 V242

Further Commentary – Some Particular Reasons for Using Interviews, Cognitive Maps, and Group Maps

Working on interpersonal or internal issues of political feasibility

As we mentioned earlier in this chapter, the strategic issues being addressed may take one of two forms. First, the current situation is such that participants are concerned with extracting themselves from what they see as an uncomfortable/difficult situation, *but* are not clear about what would make the situation better beyond being certain that it would *not* be the current situation. Second, a clear understanding of a better situation is known *but* participants are unsure about the means of achieving it. For the former of these, where the strategic future appears to

C91

be disastrous, the **nature of the strategic issue**(s) is often such that it is internally focused, dealing with interpersonal problems, disagreements, and tensions. In these instances, using individual interviews particularly helps because the relative anonymity provides an environment where the interviewee is able to discuss the problem without fear of direct recrimination. The outlier views can be encom-

C51

passed within the group, helping to avoid '**group-think**'. An external interviewer can act as a sounding board, being seen as relatively unbiased.

V215

The interview can act as a **cathartic device**, releasing tensions and enabling participants to begin to determine what can be changed and how to change it. By acting as a type of release mechanism, the issues can be separated from the individuals involved and a more reflective approach adopted – a movement away from physiological tension and emotion to a more reasoned stance.

The good interview can provide the interviewee with an opportunity to open up and express views about other managers. These views about why the organization is unable to change may or may not be right, but as long as they are held they can be significant constraints on creating desired strategic change – 'if men define situations as real, they are real in their consequences' (Thomas and Thomas, 1928). Mapping the individual views and enabling the interviewee to reflect on them, within the context of the overall strategic situation depicted by the map, tempers the views and defuses potential dysfunctional confrontation. Using a group map permits alternative views to be knitted together and presented in a less confrontational manner. For example, in one organization, it became apparent, through the interviews, that one of the major blockages to strategic change was a particular manager's style. The manager supported favourites and continually reacted emotionally to any suggestions for change. During the interviews it was possible to explore the best mechanism for dealing with this. As the interview cycle progressed, the interview agenda was able to be influenced by analysis of the developing merged map being constructed by the interviewer in between each interview. By using the interview situation and individual maps as the basis for negotiation, gradually most participants moved to supporting the suggestion that outright confrontation was not the best mechanism to resolve the problem (as they had hitherto thought). They were content to determine a more reasoned approach once having been able to 'blow off steam' and understand the situation from a number of perspectives.

Working within an organization unfamiliar with participative/consultative methods

In many organizations where the use of facilitators, or external consultants, is unusual, it may be necessary to find a means of reassuring and encouraging participants to contribute. In the NHS vignette (part 2), many of the **interviewees** *V213* **were exceptionally nervous** about their contributions. Asking them to contribute to a group discussion, even if well facilitated, would have resulted in the participants feeling threatened and being less likely to surface all of the important issues. By providing a low key, low threat environment managers found they could begin to discuss their own aspirations for the organization, their beliefs and options for moving forward. Many of them were surprised at the extent of their knowledge and how easily the process unfolded.

Hesitancy on the part of participants, about being open, particularly in a group setting, is more common than any single manager supposes. Participants not only want to avoid 'rocking the boat' but also fear reprisals. Contradicting a superior or suggesting alternative options is often perceived as politically unwise and so statements do not get surfaced. Interviews also help assure a less socially skilled manager that dominant or extrovert individuals cannot grab all of the air-time for themselves.

One means of opening up interviews and increasing the chances of capturing more of the relevant material is to provide a clear explanation as to the purpose of the interview, the form it will take, and what will happen to the information. Noting, in passing, that the notes will be taken in a '**type of spider-diagram** *V214* approach' will help avoid too much unnecessary curiosity. It is important to avoid describing the process in a manner which itself restricts conversation as interviewees may become more concerned about the mapping than the issues discussed.

Nevertheless, some level of curiosity can be helpful because it provides an excuse to share the map, at a later stage in the interview.

Reassuring participants that any information they generate will be treated confidentially (if this is to be the case), allows options and issues to be surfaced without as much fear of recrimination or blame. This reassurance is worth repeating at the end of the interview when the next steps are discussed. Many managers have poor experiences of consultants acting as a conduit from one person to another, indeed some managers expect to be able to use consultants as a conduit for their own political ends.

The mapping process itself typically helps some managers gain more confidence in their own view about strategic issues – a recognition that they do have embedded wisdom that is worth contributing. Often interviewees arrive with an agenda of concerns – some bring prepared notes. When interviewees leave the interview with an increased sense of self-worth it aids effective JOURNEY making. The outcomes of social negotiation are more lasting when they occur within a situation of self-confidence (Fisher and Ury, 1982). In our experience, senior staff have as many concerns of this sort as do more junior colleagues.

Disadvantages of using interviews

Whilst interviews are beneficial in terms of building confidence, opening up issues, and expanding individual understanding of the material, they can have drawbacks. The first and most obvious concerns costs – interview time for managers and interviewer, time to complete a cycle of interviews, cash for travel when interviews involve extensive travel. Each initial interview needs to run between 1 and 1½ hours, about 1–2 hours to make sense of the interview, and the equivalent of about 1 hour per interview for merging of maps.

In addition, the time lapse involved when carrying out the interviews can be a serious drawback. If a management team has decided to start a journey of strategy making they often want to start as a team from the outset and start immediately. On many occasions strategy making arises as an urgent issue to be dealt with over a short time horizon and with only a few days of time available. These circumstances can often occur just after a firm has been subject to a change in ownership and the new owners 'want a new strategy tomorrow'. On other occasions a change in chief executive can prompt a different approach to strategy development, or a strategic approach when none has been in place before. The problem of scheduling interviews around other work tasks, and dealing with the problems of absence through sickness or vacation, can destroy the best intentions of a fast interview turnaround. Using a group workshop method, such as the Oval Mapping Technique, may yield faster and less expensive results but without the level of detail or the possibility of discovering important multiple perspectives. Unless the interviewee is going to be involved in a subsequent group workshop, the interview process does not allow him or her to see any of the alternative perspectives. One of the benefits of working in a group is being able to explore other points of view and through this acquire a greater understanding of the organization (for further detail see McGrath's (1984) comparisons on electronic versus group working).

Notwithstanding these problems, it is possible for two facilitators to conduct 20 interviews with senior managers, run two 1-day oval mapping workshops with other participants, construct individual and group maps, analyse the maps with the chief executive, and run a 2-day strategy making workshop over a 9-day cycle (Eden, 1985). The cycle is tiring for the facilitators, but can be extraordinarily effective in meeting the demands of balancing a new social order with new negotiated order.

Managing the Interview as an Intervention

Scheduling interviews to gain maximum benefit

When designing the order of interviews, it may be helpful to **begin with the more powerful participants**, who are often more senior managers. Senior participants often have a more strategic or holistic view of the organization, covering a wider range of issues but concomitantly not usually in the same depth or detail as more junior members. Once these broader or strategic issues have been identified, they can then, at an appropriate time, be carefully fed into subsequent interviews as triggers. The process achieves three particular advantages: V213

1 Interviews usually commence with the interviewee beginning with a flurry of statements before gradually building the case. It is at this point of the interview that any of the strategic issues emerging from the more senior managers can be used as triggers – which may produce no response, and if so need not be pushed. The process is deliberately manipulative, but reflects the realistically different power bases of different members of the client group.
2 The second benefit focuses on the process after the series of interviews has been carried out. The process of weaving or merging individual maps together to form one group map is simplified when there are clear overlaps forced by the triggers. The overlap is unlikely to be in meaning but rather in a common core construct for the issue. The strategic issues raised by one powerful decision maker will now be elaborated with contributions from other participants.
3 Finally, the triggers from previous interviews provide interviewees with a stimulus to consider the issue during the intervening time between the interview and the group workshop. Having this opportunity means that participants can perform better at the workshop and not be confronted with issues that are completely new to them. As a consequence they feel more comfortable at the workshop, as well as able to raise new statements and comment on existing ones. In this way a form of psychological negotiation is beginning to occur across the group so that group ownership of the issues to be addressed is increased.

Scene setting

This subsection deals with issues concerning the actual process of interviewing using cognitive mapping. Whilst the issues are not hugely significant in themselves, paying attention to them helps to increase the chances of a successful intervention.

Interviews are often held in the interviewee's office or in a conference room. Take account of the best seating relationship in an interview – guideline 1.6.

V214 V215   It is important to attend to time management of the interview. Take care to provide time to set **clear expectations** of the process and to ensure that there is time at the end of the interview to review the map and check its accuracy. Carefully plan the length of an interview, breaks between interviews, and the duration between interview and subsequent group workshops. It has been noted in many texts on facilitation (Ackermann, 1996; Bostrom *et al*, 1993; Phillips and Phillips, 1993) that clearly setting the scene is important. Experience suggests that scheduling first interviews for an hour to an hour and a half is optimum. It provides sufficient time to explore detail without becoming oppressive in terms of effort for either the interviewee or interviewer. A minimum of half an hour between interviews provides time to be used for (i) tidying up the map and preparing for the next interview, and (ii) having some slack if the interviewee is generating important material and wants to continue past the agreed time. Finally, designing the intervention to avoid too much time elapsing between the interviews and subsequent work on the group map will ensure that participants have not forgotten what they had talked about and that the organizational context has not changed too drastically. This requirement is also true when using group methods for statement generation and from extensive work with groups. A period of 10 working days from Monday of one week to Friday of the next week should be taken as a maximum time gap – a

V196 V210   *'psychological week'*.

Carrying out interviews with care aids in building relationships with the participants. Interviews often result in interviewees not only sharing thoughts about the issues being discussed but also sharing other topics. If an interviewer is good then the interviewee will leave the meeting with a sense of satisfaction that they have been able to 'have their say', that it has been captured competently, and that they are clear about the next steps of the process. From this position, subsequent working with the group as a whole is easier because there is a degree of trust to build on.

DETECTING EMERGENT STRATEGIZING: WORKING WITH STRATEGY MAKING TEAMS – THE OVAL MAPPING TECHNIQUE

Introduction

The **Oval Mapping Technique** (OMT) is designed to enable *a map of aspirations, beliefs, and assertions* to be created by a group. This map will resemble a 'cognitive map' in that it will represent group and individual assumptions about relationships between beliefs and assertions. It may also act as a substitute for a map derived from aggregating cognitive maps from interviewing each participant. Although the technique was originally designed to enable groups to create maps directly, it has also been designed to increase the group's productivity and to provide a very *efficient* way of capturing the views of participants. The technique enables the capture of a *large* number of ideas, assumptions, beliefs, and 'facts' from 4–14 participants in a relaxed environment and in a relatively short period of time (around 200 ideas in 30–90 minutes). These assumptions can then be structured, with participants, into a cause map, providing a synthesis of each participant's knowledge and enabling the map to be reclassified as a strategic map (a further 30–90 minutes). Consequently, the *structure of the map* so produced provides the group with added value which may be derived from a model that can be analysed by the group. *(C72 C100 V195 V210 V227 V238 V248 V254 V267)*

The OMT provides *groups* with the ability to surface issues simply using a manual technique, although it is often used in conjunction with computer assisted forms of group workshops. As with the approach to cognitive mapping of interviews, the technique is used to elicit the '**theories-in-use**', and also to allow a wide range of participants across an organization to experience a part of the journey together. *(C37 C81)*

Oval mapping is not designed to stop conversation, but rather aid the capture, structuring, and understanding of it. Participants are able to 'speak' simultaneously, think about issues, talk with colleagues, reflect on others' perceptions as they are appearing on the oval map, and take the occasional nap! All of these activities can take place without losing track of the emerging group view.

Because the technique reduces some of the difficulties commonly associated with multi-status or multi-disciplinary teams, participants can be polled from a variety of different hierarchical levels within an organization and/or from different departments. OMT provides a forum for people with different knowledge and skills to be able to work together in a constructive manner. By engaging groups of differently minded people in the journey the technique provides an opportunity for creative new solutions to be generated, especially as more introvert or reticent participants are drawn into the process. Views can be elicited from members of the organization at all levels, allowing, for example, senior managers to gain some insight into those issues concerning members of the organization 'at the coal face' and line managers to begin to appreciate a more holistic view of the organization.

C50 Participants begin to develop a **shared understanding** of the material. The technique's ability to capture both general, rather broad statements, and also detailed options, means that, if necessary, it is possible to develop action plans, and commitment to them, during a short workshop.

The Oval Mapping Technique (OMT) was developed by Eden during the 1970s and was originally based on the use of 80-column computer cards rather than the currently used oval cards. As time passed, these cards had their corners trimmed and the shape transformed to ovals. Coincidentally, and independently, the similar Metaplanning process was being developed (Schnelle, 1979) which resulted in the use of ovals of almost identical size and colour (a yellow ellipse 7½ in × 4⅜ in or 185 mm × 110 mm made from thin card)! The current version of OMT can be compared with the 'Snow-card' approach (Spencer, 1989) and the magnetic 'Hexagon' tool kit. It is also now often used with 'Post-its' to act as a substitute for ovals. Our view, after 20 years of exploration and use, is that ovals are both theoretically sound and practically more effective. The use of 'Post-its' suffers from 'rectangular thinking' where structures are inclined to rows and columns, and the use of hexagons encourages 'six-sided thinking'. Neither are effective for generating free form *cause map* structures.

OMT was developed for, and has been used extensively with, the Strategic Options Development and Analysis (SODA) approach (Ackermann 1992; Eden, 1989; Eden and Ackermann, 1992) to aid in rapid idea generation and structuring. Unlike other 'brainstorming' techniques the emergent strategizing, that is 'what we know, what we do, the way we do it', is captured as a structured map (a model), thus facilitating its use within the context of JOURNEY making. It is not a brainstorming, or lateral thinking, technique (although it can be used in this way), it is a mapping technique where participants' attention is focused on strategic issues and their action oriented resolution. Brainstorming data rarely generates high levels of

C52 **cognitive and emotional commitment** to a group view. The intention with OMT is to create *JO*int *U*nderstanding, *R*eflection, and *NE*gotiation. The structuring ability of oval mapping helps reduce the messiness and ambiguity by providing groups with an ability to (i) manage the resultant complexity through the identification of emergent themes, (ii) prioritize the emergent themes for subsequent development, (iii) understand the nuances and ramifications of the material as each oval is viewed in the context of other ovals, and (iv) begin the process of stakeholder identification.

The technique is typically used with groups ranging from 4 to 14 participants, but can allow even larger groups (up to 200 participants) to be involved through the use of sub-groups. The task of a group can range from: detecting emergent

C103 strategic issues and so emergent aspirations, identifying **distinctive competencies** as patterns, option surfacing, action planning, or deliberately exploring divergent perspectives. Sub-group working can also provide a means of addressing different aspects of the company's strategy. It is one of the most useful techniques for increasing participation in strategic thinking across all levels of the organization. Participants may be from different areas of the organization, different levels of management, and different disciplines, resulting in a wide coverage of assumptions, deep knowledge, and wisdom. Senior managers in multinational organizations are able to join such events, as well as more junior managers who are more likely 'to do what they are told'. Indeed after being involved in a number of OMT workshops senior managers will often continue using the same technique amongst their own local teams with the manager as facilitator.

When used as a device to increase participation, the resulting material is usually used to *influence* the direction of the strategy that will be agreed by the management team, rather than for supporting decision making by the group itself. Because OMT produces a map connecting together the views of all participants, it also facilitates participants to learning from one another about the interaction of issues in one part of an organization with those of other parts. The mapping process enables participants to see their own statements and perspectives in the context of those of other participants. Typically, using the OMT with participants from different parts of the organization enables participants to begin to experience the difficulties and skills of other departments and professions and, from this, begin to understand how the organization functions as a whole. In addition to this **organizational learning**, the mix of social *and* cognitive elements of the technique encourages participants to learn more about each other as thinking and social beings. Although OMT specifically aims to facilitate a **new negotiated order**, the impact on generating **new social order** through team building can be very significant for successfully creating strategic change. Through this ability to learn and appreciate each other, participants will be more likely to work together as a team in implementing agreed strategies and strategic programmes. The effectiveness of OMT for learning and team building depends on choices made about the composition of the groups and the facilitation techniques employed (see chapter P5).   *C74*   *C48: C49*

Guidelines to the Oval Mapping Technique (OMT) – a manual way to support groups

These guidelines should be read in conjunction with the further detail contained in the facilitation section (chapter P5).

Before You Do It

The customary setup for oval mapping workshops requires the following preparation:

1.1   *Arrange the room.* Select a large room with comfortable chairs, preferably on castors, encouraging participants to move amongst themselves and to the wall. Moving chairs discourages fixed social grouping and fixed coalitions among members of the group. Remove tables so that the physical relationship of participants to each other is fluid, and each person can gain easy access to the wall. Ensure the availability of plenty of wall space for flip-charts to be placed using Blu-Tack. Check the surface of the walls for flip-chart work – often walls are wood panelled or carpet covered making writing on them difficult. Sometimes the hotel/conference centre may not permit the use of Blu-Tack – check in advance.

1.2   *Place flip-charts on to the wall.* Fully cover a large flat wall space with flip-chart paper upon which the ovals or Post-its will be attached (typically a 2 × 6 or 2 × 7 flip-chart layout is used).

1.3   *Distribute ovals.* Provide at least 40 ovals per participant (or large size 'Post-its', which are more easily available but much less effective, see above).

1.4   *Distribute one pen to each participant.* Use a set of one colour (preferably black) felt tip pens. These pens *must* be the same colour and provide line widths of about 2 mm (1/16 in). This ensures that colour does not identify participants, and the line width constrains the size of lettering. If smaller widths are used then too many words are written on ovals and cannot be read easily from a distance.

1.5   *Have a range of coloured flip-chart pens accessible.* These are water based pens for the facilitator to label clusters of ovals, number each oval, and draw in the lines and arrows showing the relationships between ovals.

1.6   *Supply participants with a lump of 'Blu-Tack'.* Provide each participant with 'Blu-Tack' or other form of self-adhesive putty (to permit ovals to be attached to, and moved around, the flip-chart paper).

1.7   *For preferencing (see 'How to Do It' section below) prepare self-adhesive coloured spots.* Cut up strips of five or seven 3/8 in (10 mm) diameter coloured spots in at least two different colours (usually red and green).

V227   1.8   *Write up **trigger question**(s).* The trigger, or starter, question or set of questions needs to be pre-written on to a section of flip-chart paper large enough to be clearly visible to all those seated around the wall. Getting the question(s) right is important as it can make a substantial difference to the amount and breadth of material generated. Questions that are reasonably broad without being ambiguous are often best for getting at emergent strategic issues. Starting with 'How . . .?' or 'What . . .?' and inviting an action orientation provides useful responses. An example is 'How can Spiders Inc perform best over the next 2–3 years' or 'What are the key strategic issues which are likely to face the organization over the next 5 years?'. The second of these will usually require some hints about what is meant by the term 'strategic issue'. We use the following phrases: broad based, long term in nature, resource intensive (both in terms of finance and people time) and often irreversible. Questions that invite yes/no answers do not work and should be avoided. The intention is to encourage participants to make explicit their deep knowledge about how their world works and how they expect it to work in the future. Sometimes it is helpful to use Kelly's notion of contrast and similarities to help participants get at their knowledge – for example, comparing past with present, future with past, or present with future. Thus, 'How will the next 5 years of strategic development contrast with the last 5 years?' may capture learning which might not otherwise surface.

V202 V268   1.9   *Identify and write up **trigger ovals**.* Often it is not appropriate for participants to be given an open agenda (blank wall). Key issues surfaced by the management team, or other participant groups, may act as a predetermined focus, where the intention is to derive new perspectives on these issues from other staff in the organization. This process not only focuses participants on areas of interest to the management team (a way of communicating the nature of strategic issues down the organization), but also bounds discussion when time is short. Where there is a clear need for procedural justice, the facilitator can make it clear that these ovals are simply intended to act as triggers and not constraints – 'if they are not developed, then they will be discarded (taken off the wall)'.

How to Do It

Provide an introduction to the process

This is important – covering the following steps will give participants a clear idea of what is expected of them, what the technique is aiming to achieve, and how it works.

2.1 Set expectations. For *participants*, who are not the decision making team, be clear that the meeting/workshop is 'their' chance to influence (not decide) the direction of the organization. All the material generated will be captured and used *to inform* the decision making process of others. The technique has been developed to help participants surface issues as they see and experience them – they are themselves the 'experts'. V255

2.2 Contributions are written up, even if first spoken. Stress that it is important to write the issues, assumptions, assertions, statements, and beliefs that occur to them on to the ovals – 'it is impossible for the facilitator to remember everything they say, and so if they want to influence strategy then they have to write on to the ovals'. 'There will be no post-workshop chance to state that a particular issue or concern was not addressed – this is their chance! If it's not 'on the wall', in the map, then it will not be carried forward and will not influence the structure or content of the developing group map'.

2.3 Consensus is not necessary. Explain that the technique is not seeking consensus and does not need to resolve conflict as views are surfaced. Rather it aims to get a feel of how participants view the organization and its environment. Disagreement is not ruled out.

2.4 List the rules

2.4.1 *Stress that disagreeing with statements is okay.* However, 'it is the rationale behind the disagreement that is important so write down *why* the disagreement occurs'. Likewise, 'where there is agreement and further reasons for supporting an option, write down why the option should be supported rather than just "yes" or "I agree"'.

2.4.2 *Participants are not allowed to remove others' ovals or edit them.* If a participant wants an oval to be in an alternative place then a second copy can be made. If a participant wants to edit the view expressed then they can write an alternative oval and place it alongside the existing one.

2.4.3 *Put statements up on the wall as soon as they have been written.* Discourage stockpiling so that it is easier for others to 'piggy-back'.

2.4.4 *Use 'Blu-Tack' sparingly.* Recommend that only a very small amount of 'Blu-Tack' is required on the back of the ovals to stick them to the wall (half the size of a pea) – this allows the ovals to be moved around easily.

2.5 Explain the role of the facilitator. While the participants are there to generate the material, the facilitator's role is to help with the structuring of it (management of content). The facilitator will also seek to manage process issues: for example, encouraging participants to write down their statements, encouraging full participation, managing time, and so on. Therefore she or he will be 'doing their best' to put the statements into natural clusters or groups. However, later review of the clusters and 'tidying them up' will be done as a group. Any help from participants as to which cluster they think their oval fits best is to be encouraged, but if participants don't know where to put their statement then they can place it either to one side or on its own.

2.6 Ask for brief but pointed statements on the ovals. Encourage participants to keep the wording of the statement to around 8–10 words; 1–3 word statements are usually unhelpful. This not only makes it easier for the statements on the ovals to be read by other participants but also helps keep to one statement on each oval. It is helpful if the wording makes a clear point, and even better if it contains a verb (thus making it action oriented). The number of words will be constrained by the pens.

2.7   *Encourage participants to 'piggy back' on one another's statements.* In this way new, creative, and innovative options may be raised, increasing the range of alternatives available.

Facilitating the process

Some participants grasp the technique quite quickly and start writing up and displaying their statements, while other participants take longer before they begin to feel comfortable and become engaged with the process. Typically, a group who are new to OMT will take 10–15 minutes to get going. If the group has already experienced the technique then statements will quickly start appearing on the public wall. Where there are different levels of familiarity – for example, some are accustomed to the OMT while others are fresh to it – then experienced users must be briefed to allow extra time and new users given special encouragement.

C101 V227 V238
V269

3.1   *Begin to* **cluster ovals**. While the first 5–10 ovals may appear slowly, once participants get the idea ovals will appear at a more rapid pace – don't panic. Typically it takes a group 10–20 minutes to get under way.

3.1.1   *Start by separating the ovals* into very tentative potential clusters. This promotes seeding of many more potential clusters than will finally be identified – there is plenty of space around the initial themes, enabling subsequent ovals to be placed nearby. Determining which ovals are possible seed ovals and how to cope with them arriving at any time is not difficult. Different topics or themes are more obvious than might be expected and the group can be invited to help in this exercise.

3.1.2   *Don't be afraid to break up apparent clusters.* Where new material appears to suggest new groups or the creation of sub-groups, reflect it in the structure. Move a group of ovals to a new position to indicate a new cluster. As further ovals surface, additional insight will be gained, resulting in more appropriate clusters.

3.1.3   *Move clusters around.* By placing clusters near to other clusters of related material, cross links between clusters, and sub-clusters are easier for participants to identify. This may mean moving the cluster more than once.

3.1.4   *Ask participants for elaboration where the meaning of the text on the oval is unclear.* Often abbreviations or specific company related terms have been used and it is worth clarifying these. Capture the elaboration either on the oval in question (if the explanation is brief) or on additional ovals if it is lengthy. Often participants themselves are unfamiliar with terms used by

V239

their colleagues, and having the facilitator **ask apparently obvious questions** helps them also to comprehend the statement in question.

3.1.5   *Identify statements that are broad based and general.* Place these towards the top of the clusters, with those more specific lower down and those most detailed at the bottom of the cluster. This process will be refined during the second half of the oval mapping workshop where the draft clusters are validated, reconstructed, and further elaborated by the participants. It is useful to remember that the clusters will gradually become hierarchically organized cause maps and so organize the ovals *as if* they were being connected with cause arrows.

3.1.6   *Place outcomes towards the top of a cluster and options beneath them.* Thus means lead upwards to ends, options lead upwards to outcomes. The facilitator may get some of the hierarchical positioning wrong and so must treat positioning as a draft, in the same way as the clustering must be a draft for the group to confirm and develop and change. At this stage it is important not to use arrows, so that changes made by the group are easy to make.

3.2   *Number each oval.* This helps identify, and capture, links without having to traverse the entire wall with an arrow (thus a small arrow in or out can be noted with the number showing the oval to which the arrow is to go). Also if the map is being recorded using the mapping software, the numbers on the wall will match those used in the computer model.

3.3   *Encourage participants to **elaborate the issues** emerging.* One means for   C101
doing this is through asking direct questions, for example 'this cluster seems thin on material but I get the sense that it is important, could you add some more . . .'. Participants may, of course, suggest that it is thin and important, and that it is partly important because of its thinness! Questions prompt not only the proponents but also other participants to add alternative perspectives as they discover that their interpretation of the statement was different from the view of the creator. Do *not* seek to establish which view is correct, rather collect all views. So, if one person claims that they placed the oval and that it meant x and another person suggests they thought it meant y then both views can be collected.

3.4   *Try to reword the statements in the imperative* to get an action orientation but *without doing violence to the intent of the oval.* Doing this in collusion with the participant may often encourage her to formulate other statements in this manner. The process demands ensuring that a future oriented verb is contained in the text. Full detail would encompass 'who, what, where, and when', with the 'why' appearing as another oval that will be linked using an arrow of causality. For example, 'good people should be kept in the organization' could be changed to 'keep good people in the organization', even though it still misses the 'who' (which is presumed), and the 'where and when' which are probably not necessary until analysis of the map has been completed and this part of the map is taken to be significant.

When the statement written on the oval is short (see 2.6) further elaboration is usually sought. For example, an oval with only the word 'costs' may be posted on the wall. By seeking an action orientation, not only does the querying prompt a verb (the action orientation) but usually the 'who' and 'what' as well. For example 'get finance department to "manage costs" better' or 'reduce the "costs of product" A' are elaborations of the part in double quotes. From this, not only will participants gain a clearer idea of what is meant but the extra detail may again prompt further statements.

3.5   *Encourage participants to write their statements down,* especially those less vocal or dominant.

3.5.1   *Gently familiarize participants with the process.* Where participants seem uncomfortable with contributing to the 'picture on the wall' get them to talk about their views and then the facilitator writes these statements on to ovals and puts them on the wall. As they become more forthcoming, get them to write the statements directly on to the oval and position them, and so gradually get them involved in the workshop. By making sure that the particular participant's statement is up on the wall, their confidence is increased as they see that their statements are a part of the material from others.

3.5.2   *Encourage participants who are in debate, argument, or discussion to make sure*

V269

they **capture their statements on to the ovals** during the conversation so as not to lose the material. Remind them that agreement is not necessary at this stage. Often participants get caught up in the discussion and fail to capture the new material surfacing.

3.6   *Split ovals containing two issues or statements* by capturing each on new ovals. This will enable participants to elaborate both statements separately rather than trying to respond to them as a pair. For example, 'agree upon a single word processing package so we can stop having difficulties when working on reports' – would break down into 'agree upon a single WP package' and 'stop having difficulties when working on reports'. Here agreeing on a package is only one of many possible options for stopping difficulties.

3.7   *Watch for when the group begins to slow down.* When participants run out of statements either:

3.7.1   *Get them going again by asking them to consider how they would achieve some of the statements* written up and posted on the walls, or why would they wish

C94 C101

to implement some. This process **'ladders'** down or up the map, respectively. Going down the map tries to get statements about more detailed options, and going up the map seeks to uncover implicit goals and aspirations.

3.7.2   *Break for refreshment, both mental and physical* (Eden, 1990b).

Further structuring and added value

During the refreshment break it is useful for the facilitator (and possibly client) to review the clusters created. The review will check that all the material is either in a draft cluster or set to one side ready to be dealt with by the group on their return. Doing this with the client will help build the relationship and yield valuable clues about placing the statements. The client might take the opportunity to indicate some areas of the map which could usefully be developed and others they would prefer to be downplayed. During this period participants may also spend time (i) reviewing material on the wall, (ii) talking amongst themselves about the process, and (iii) asking about the process. Paying some attention to the conversations being held will provide useful clues to the facilitation of the second half of the workshop. At the end of the break, do the following.

4.1   *Carry out a quick walk through the draft clusters* that have been generated. This review cues participants back into the material as well as familiarizing them with the various clusters so they can work more effectively.

4.2   *Examine each draft cluster in depth.*

4.2.1   *Check each cluster's material to ensure it is relevant to the cluster.* When creating the clusters, especially if the facilitator is not familiar with the industry or specific part of the business, it is easy for them to have put ovals into the wrong cluster. With the group's aid they can be moved to the appropriate cluster. This may, however, mean writing a repeat version of the oval because the oval's statement has two distinct meanings; the first relating to the cluster being considered and a second meaning when in a different context. Arrange the wording on each oval so that the text helps clarify the differences. On other occasions where both instances have the same meaning, putting a lengthy link on the wall is too messy to be helpful, thus the oval is repeated with the same reference number.

4.2.2 *Confirm the structure of the clusters.* Ask participants whether the oval at the top of the cluster is the most superordinate (closest to a desired or disastrous outcome) and whether those at the bottom are the most subordinate (detailed options). This will help in the structuring process. *V227 V239*

4.2.3 *As ovals are being repositioned, tentatively draw links* between the ovals, displaying the chains of argument as they unfold (see figure P2.1). This will ensure that the ovals are positioned correctly. Finding a position which results in the shortest arrow will suggest the best location. Remember that arrows are best pointing up the map to keep the map as a hierarchy. The process of exploring the relationships will generate new material as the relationships between ovals are made apparent (through the explanation of the chain of argument), or participants discover they have attributed a different meaning to the content of an oval.

4.2.4 *Capture new material by prompting participants to write down the new material on to blank ovals.* This enriching of the context and content during the group's reflecting on, and structuring, their map often increases the wall picture by around 50–60% as well as increasing participant's under-standing *and developing a sense of shared meaning.* From this new material further structuring can take place reinforcing the **cyclical nature** of the process. This period of group work is crucial to the group's taking on a group ownership of the material, moving away from their own con-tributions as the only centre of their attention. *V228*

4.2.5 *Note inter-cluster relationships as well as intra-cluster relationships between ovals.* This can be done either by drawing a link between the ovals in the two clusters or, if the related cluster is too far away, then drawing a small link (arrow) from, or to, the oval and attaching the related oval's number to it. Intra-cluster relationships are often identified when participants cannot agree or decide upon which cluster an oval fits, as it relates to a number of clusters. The linking will also demonstrate the 'holistic properties' of the picture, providing a synthesis of the material. Sometimes it is possible to show only a general link between clusters rather than links between ovals within clusters. In these cases a different type of arrow may be used to indicate a broad relationship between clusters.

4.3 **Label the emergent theme** *identified by the content of the cluster* once a cluster has been refined and the relationships drawn in. Examining the content of the cluster may suggest a label that can act as a title. The label may be one of the existing ovals. Labels form the basis of identifying the key strategic issues that either the current group or management team will address. *V250*

4.4 *Revisit ovals earlier placed on one side* because their meaning or context was unclear. In some cases participants may request that an oval currently on the side be moved to the cluster being examined and in the process provide additional content and context. However, this process will not occur for each of the un-clustered ovals and time must be spent determining the meaning and position for

Figure P2.1 A single cluster of ovals from an OMT session.

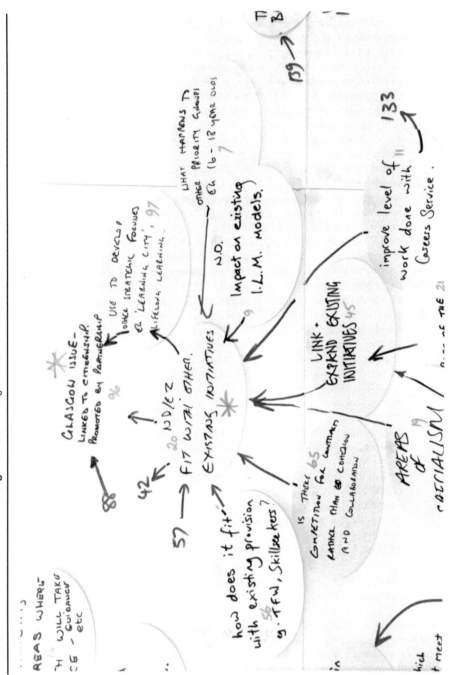

all 'floaters' or orphans. Often, participants will be able to provide valuable assistance through the structuring and elaboration of clusters. Sometimes the oval remains as an 'orphan' and may be labelled as a cluster of one.

4.5   *Encourage the group to reward itself* for completing the examination and for tidying up the wall picture. It is worth everyone clearly acknowledging that an important 'stage' has been completed in an efficient and participative manner. If a group are invited to comment on the depth, breadth, and amount of material generated and structured in the time used, they will usually be pleased and amazed at their productivity.

Additional Stages of the Oval Mapping Technique

While the above stages of the OMT provide the group with a structured picture of all of the material they have generated, there are a number of further steps that may be useful during a single workshop event. All of them can usually be attained in a half-day workshop. They involve prioritizing either issues (clusters) or options, identifying stakeholders, and identifying explicit and implicit goals.

5.1   **Preferencing** *either the issues (identified by the labels) or options* (see next   *V228 V241 V251* section 6.1 for the identification of options). Both forms of preferencing provide   *V271* only a 'rough' means of prioritization. Nevertheless they are usefully indicative and can be particularly useful if participants have only a small amount of time of the workshop remaining. Consequently, they may wish to identify which issues to work on during the remaining time or provide some indication to their senior managers as to the issues or options they consider critical.

5.1.1   *Provide participants with a number of prepared self-adhesive spots.* The spots act as preferences. A rule of thumb that appears to provide a good balance between ensuring that for each participant at least one of their preferences is selected, and not providing so many preferencing opportunities as to reduce the prioritization process, is to allocate a 2:3 ratio of preferencing spots to number of issues/options. For example, if there are 12 issues then allocating 8 spots to each person.

5.1.2   *Explain to participants that they can place all of their preferencing spots on one single issue/option or spread them across a number.* However, do remind them that they are not allowed to move or remove others' preferences.

5.1.3   *Consider using two colours of preferences.* This allows participants to determine, for example, which are the most important issues/options in the short term (those that are critical to hit now) and which are the important but more long term issues/options. Using red and green spots works well, as red signifies immediacy and green is used for longer term prioritization.

If political feasibility is important, it is helpful to provide green and red spots, where green indicates 'I would put some personal/departmental energy into this strategy area – it is important' and red indicates 'I'd probably find excuses not to do anything with this – it is unimportant as I see it'. All green spots indicates high feasibility, whereas mixed or all red indicate potential political infeasibility. (The use of computer assisted preferencing where anonymity can be assured may be advisable – see chapter P3.)

5.1.4 *Review the results and identify those issues/options with the most preferences.* This process is another helpful 'stage' by providing a sense of completion/achievement to the group.

6.1 *If preferencing options then identify which options are available for preferencing.* Options are those statements that contribute towards resolving the issue identified by the cluster. Therefore they are statements which are relatively easily actionable: for example, 'produce a skills directory of all members of staff' rather than assertions or statements of fact.

6.1.1 *Mark potential candidates with an asterisk for clear identification.* The asterisked statements may then be considered candidates for the preferencing exercise.

6.1.2 *Aim to identify at least one option per cluster so as to get an even spread.*

6.1.3 *Review the list of identified options in relation to the handwriting of participants.* Where possible ensure that there is an option selected from each participant as this will increase their ownership and 'buy in' to the process.

7.1 *Identify stakeholders* during review of the material by underlining any possible, or potential, stakeholders mentioned on an oval. This process may be an input to stakeholder analysis undertaken later in the workshop or at other *C121 V229* workshops. From this, either a list of the stakeholders can be elicited or the **Power/ Interest Grid** mentioned in chapter P4.

8.1 *Identify goals/aspirations* – those objectives/values that are good in their own right. For example 'increase profit and growth', 'maintain and improve company performance', 'maintain motivation and morale of staff', 'grow market share', 'relieve the plight of homeless people'.

8.1.1 *Ask 'so what?' questions of the clusters, particularly focusing on the label/issue.* By asking 'Why is what is contained by the cluster an issue to the *V197* organization?', the answer begins to **ladder up the hierarchy to goals**. *C90* Many of the answers to the question will appear as **'negative-goals'**. A negative-goal reflects an aspiration to avoid an outcome of significance to the organization. Sometimes it is possible, and helpful, to turn these statements around so that they reflect a positive outcome. However, this is not always possible since the outcome is only relevant as an aspiration of avoidance. (The general category of 'negative-goals' is discussed in chapter C5.) As mentioned above, strategic issues are broad based but are not ends in their own right and so are the basis for discovering aspirations but are not aspirations themselves. By ascertaining what it is that the group hopes to achieve through them, emergent goals can be identified.

8.1.2 *Write down goals identified, on ovals of a different colour.* We use yellow as the standard colour, and white for goals. This way the wall picture can be expanded upwards and goals seen clearly.

8.1.3 *Prompt participants to continue up the chain of argument.* Sometimes the first responses result in further strategic issues being identified rather than goals. (If the issues generated prompt further discussion, it may be worth tabling them for further discussion.)

V229 V251 8.2 *Construct a **goal system** map.* Separate the emergent goals and negative-goals from the general body of material, or rewrite their content on to new ovals,

Figure P2.2 A complete wall 'map' showing the results of an OMT session.

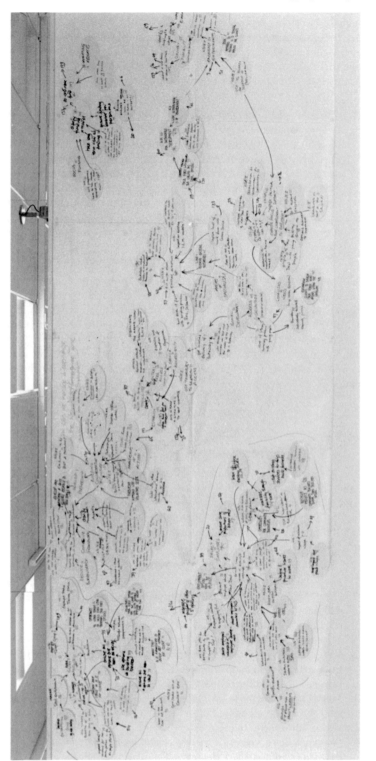

Note: The purpose of this diagram, taken from actual material, is not that it should be readable, but provide an indication of form rather than content.

and begin to build them into a goal map (see figure V8). By identifying the linkages between the goals and determining which goals are sub- and superordinate, a draft aspiration/goal system can be produced providing an overview of the emergent strategic direction of the organization. When working with large groups use the sub-groups (see chapter P5) for the following steps.

8.2.1 *Create several draft goal maps.* By asking each group to develop a goal system for the wall picture generated by *another* group, each group will then be forced to 'listen to', understand and reflect upon other material. The process powerfully begins the process of sub-groups gradually developing a shared view based upon careful listening to others. As material is merged into a whole group map, participants will be increasingly convinced that they generated the material of other sub-groups, and group ownership will be increased.

8.2.2 *Bring all of the sub-group goal maps together and refine the structure with the group.*

8.3 *Prioritize goals.* Use the preferencing procedure mentioned above to indicate roughly which of the goals are considered crucial by participants – 'if you were forced to identify with only a small number of goals which would they be?'. It may also be useful to indicate different rating categories by, for example, a star rating – giving 3-star, 2-star, and 1-star goals (when the computer software is used each rating might appear in a different size font and colour). The outcome represents a draft aspiration system and provides the facilitator with the opportunity for closure.

Post-work

9.1 *Take photographs of all the material* on the wall. By using a standard 35 mm fully automatic flash camera or digital camera, a record of the workshop's effort can be produced. This record not only informs participants of what was achieved but does so in a way they can relate to. It pictorially represents the workshop's activities. The material provides an artifact reinforcing participant's ownership and signalling closure.

9.1.1 *Photograph each flip-chart sheet in portrait mode.* This works best as each sheet fits a single exposure allowing the material to be easily read. 400 ASA colour film is easiest to use, and developing can often be obtained within an hour so that participants can leave the workshop with a record of their work.

9.1.2 *Take photographs of the group working.* Providing the group with a record of their actions will help them recall not only the content of the workshop but also the social process.

9.1.3 *Mount the photographs (including of their working as a group) on A4 (or letter size) paper* (4 to a page). Add a list of those who attended, a date and a title at the bottom for reference.

9.1.4 *Photocopy (monochrome copies of colour photographs works well enough) and distribute within a short time period* – a psychological week.

Figure P2.3   Photograph template for displaying results of OMT sessions.

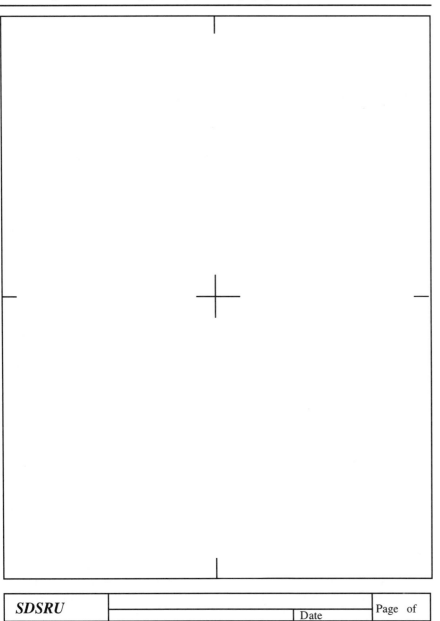

SDSRU			
		Date	Page of

Yes But . . .

What if I don't see clusters, or I can't make sense of them?

Regardless of how well (or not) you know the material, it is likely that initially the clusters will not be easily evident. If possible, start working on one 'easy' cluster and wait until more material has been generated, as it may provide clues. Moving ovals with similar phrases or expressions on them into clusters is usually a start. Another technique is to place those ovals that appear to be about issues external to the organization on one side of the wall and those more internally focused on the other. *Do not fail to elicit the help of the group and so get them involved in the structuring process. The role of the facilitator is to help the group, not to do the work for them and so cause them to lose ownership of the outcome.*

There are frequently occasions where ovals do not appear to fit obviously into clusters and these can be positioned as a separate single-oval cluster. Be careful about putting them to one side, as this may suggest to their contributor that they have less significance.

Why not get the group to do the clustering?

This alternative approach to using OMT is one we use quite regularly, and it can be very effective with some groups – those who 'like the idea of maps or charts'. Here we request that the participants themselves structure the OMT material. Whilst this takes additional time and will therefore need to be built into the workshop design, as participants become familiar with both the material and the technique it does add substantially to their ownership and understanding of the resultant themes/ key issues. This is as a result of (i) participants agreeing their own patterns/ clusters, rather than the facilitator, and (ii) participants beginning to absorb and apply the coding rules.

To undertake this method it is necessary for the facilitator to ensure that a clear explanation is provided, detailing both the coding rules and the task itself. Having flip-chart sheets written up in advance with both the steps to be taken and the coding rules (see figure V4) is helpful as it is an easy reminder and reference to participants. It is worth stressing that frequent changes to the clusters' content and structure is not only OK but recommended, as different patterns emerge from the material and new insights are gained. As discussions about positioning and meaning ensue, participants should be encouraged to continue to capture the substance of these discussions, both in terms of new material and links between existing material. During the process, however, it is worth ensuring that all participants are able to contribute and do not feel left out from the exercise.

As a further extension, divide the participants into sub-groups and ask them to work on particular areas of the wall picture (where some rough clustering may have taken place) – according to their skills and interests. Using this method reduces the amount of time required for the exercise, as the sub-groups work on only one part of the material; however, it also limits participants' ability to see the whole picture, and therefore they may miss links between the different parts of the wall picture. To counteract this, a feedback/presentation session can take place where participants are encouraged to begin to link their sub-group's efforts to those of others.

What if the statements come too quickly?

Don't worry about this. During the first 15–35 minutes, after the group has got started, a lot of information can be generated; however, this will slow down. Work on building up easily identifiable clusters until the 'rush' of material lessens and there is more time to reflect on how clusters may be formed. Use the refreshment break to further tidy up the wall and if necessary ask the client for help. Not only will this help in clustering but it will also make the client feel more in control.

What if the group won't cooperate and refuses to put statements up on the wall?!!

This situation usually arises because participants are new to the process and uncertain: about what to write, about whether what they write is good enough, about how much to write, about whether their writing will be good enough, and so on. Ways of addressing the situation depend upon assumptions about its cause. However, when the above reasons are dominant, building experience of the working of the OMT *through the facilitator* may help. Begin to explore issues verbally with the group, capturing the material as they discuss it and placing it on the wall. Once this has become a precedent, move towards getting participants to write their own ovals (saying either that you are not able to capture it all accurately or prompting them to begin to take a more active role). From here the move to actually placing the ovals on the wall picture is relatively straightforward. Working with a participant who appears more open or responsive may also help. Getting participants out of their chair and up to the wall helps get the process going.

When there is less certainty about the underlying blockages, it may be appropriate to ask the group why it is that they are uncomfortable. Confronting the group in this manner (Phillips and Phillips, 1993) may lead to a clearer idea as to the problem (not clear enough explanation, uncertainty as to what is expected of them, etc.). The problem is often with the facilitation rather than the group. However, where the technique has not been used before by the facilitator or there is a sense that this reluctance may be politically motivated, the first approach may be more appropriate. Do not underestimate the significance of the political hesitancy and general cynicism. OMT is, however, one of the best techniques available for gaining participation when cynicism is high.

Our experience suggests that the use of OMT is very unlikely to fail with any type of group within a Western culture.

Further Commentary on the Oval Mapping Technique (OMT)

As we suggest above, there are many occasions when it is very helpful to record and further develop the material or capture multiple oval mapping sessions using the computer software. Each oval is entered into the software as a statement/ assumption/fact and displayed in a similar format to the statements on the walls. The numbering of the ovals (see above) helps entry of the content of ovals into the computer model. Links between statements (inter-cluster) and clusters (intra-cluster) can be entered. Content and links can be entered in any order. It is usual to enter material as it is generated, using a battery-run lap top computer and an extra facilitator so that material is recorded in 'real-time'. The group can then be supported by the 'picture-on-the-wall' and computer projection in parallel. The resultant computer model is amenable to a variety of analyses which can be undertaken interactively with the group, and the computer record is a simple organizational memory which can be added to and changed as the strategy making progresses.

As a workshop using oval mapping typically takes 3–4 hours (a morning's work) the computer model can then be used in the afternoon to: elaborate 2–3 of the prioritized issues, work on the goal system, and/or generate new options. Participants are able to refer easily from the OMT to the computer assisted mode of working (Chapter P3) – the links between the two models are transparent – statements on the wall can be matched directly to those in the computer model. Whilst the OMT allows participants to be able to see the 'whole picture' rather than a small section of it on the computer projection, the OMT cannot easily represent the relationships (the arrows) adequately. Intra-cluster relationships which span the entire picture are usually abbreviated, resulting in participants searching for the referenced numbered oval. The computer is able to work in 'relational space' and convert those links and concepts into 2 dimensions as required. Working with both modes means the transfer between oval mapping and computer supported mapping appears natural. The group can check that the statements are captured correctly and then begin to expand the computer model – the principles of structuring being the same. Importantly, the facility to edit concepts easily on the computer will ensure that every statement moves increasingly from individual ownership to **ownership by several participants**. Our research shows that several individual participants will claim they contributed the same material, and most of this 'cognitive commitment' will occur during clustering, and as the group shifts from the oval map to computer recorded map.

V235

Whereas the OMT can easily be run by one person, the use of the computer software means that an assistant or second facilitator may be needed. As well as entering concepts and links the assistant or second facilitator is also able to create 'sets' which match the emerging clusters. Using 'styles' to denote categories, issue labels, goals, options is also easy. The same computer model can be extended to contain the output from a series of oval mapping workshops.

As we suggested in the opening discussion, it is sometimes appropriate to encourage divergence of views at the beginning of an OMT workshop. When this is important, participants should be asked to spend the first 10–20 minutes working individually and keeping their ovals with them. Once the participants have generated their own individual thoughts the ovals can then be placed on the wall, initial clusters formed. From this point the elaboration and discussion, through the picture-on-the-wall, can seek to merge alternative views (even if they remain in conflict).

STRATEGY MAKING: WORKING WITH TEAMS – COMPUTER SUPPORTED GROUP WORKSHOPS

Introduction

In addition to the use of interviews and oval mapping – both manual techniques – an alternative method for capturing assumptions, deep knowledge, and wisdom is through a computer supported, visual interactive modelling workshop. These workshops may be seen as a form of electronic 'oval mapping', as the statements and relationships are captured in a similar manner. Computer supported workshops (CSW) capitalize on the benefits gained through using computer technology, for example fast retrieval of information, real-time editing, the use of colour to categorize in many different ways, and additional and more accurate analysis. Moreover, the process continues to maintain an environment conducive to **negotiation** and group interaction. The computer and associated software allows participants' material to be captured in a 'cause mapping' like form. Consequently it enables the group to '**play**' with ideas, explore their different perspectives on the strategic issues, and begin to arrive at a **shared understanding**. The computer support is designed to facilitate a more productive journey and also to create an **organizational memory**.

C60

C73
C50

C41 C71 V198 V273

Working in a computer supported mode has been the most common form adopted when using the SODA methodology for strategic issue resolution and strategy development. It has been used with management teams extensively since 1980 (Ackermann, 1992; Eden, 1990a; Eden and Ackermann, 1992; Sims and Eden, 1984). The nature of the technology and the software has been continuously changing over this period. Early approaches involved the use of cumbersome projection facilities and DOS based software, whereas current approaches involve portable high intensity projection facilities that can be used in daylight, and multiple notebook computers so that each participant has 'access' to the public screen.

Workshops using the direct entry form of computer support involve the facilitator driving the public display and designing opportunities for participants to interact directly with the system. However, it is not necessary to use the networked computer system, and many facilitators simply transport a single computer and projector to the workshop site. Therefore, this chapter will assume that the networked computer system is not being used, as it considers that form of working a simple elaboration of single user group support (Ackermann and Eden, 1998). Nevertheless, a fuller description of the networked computer system is provided in the elaboration section at the end of this chapter. Single user group support sees the facilitator manipulate the keyboard rather than the participants, allowing participants to concentrate on the issue at hand without being distracted by the technology. When working on complex, messy tasks, particularly strategy development, participants find focusing on the issue, its context, and ramifications demanding enough, and do not always wish to interact directly with the computer model. They are content to leave the computer manipulation to the facilitator.

The software's graphical interface allows the map to be explored from a number of different angles, and enables new material to be entered into the computer model (an electronic group map) in real time. Additionally it provides participants with the opportunity to begin to move from a set of individual views to a position of *shared* understanding and group ownership.

After computer supported workshops, many participants leaving the workshops/meetings comment on their feeling 'drained', or 'exhausted'. This is taken to be the consequence of the amount achieved: (i) examining the wealth of material captured in the computer model as a systemic whole, (ii) negotiating with their colleagues towards a shared understanding, and subsequently (iii) agreeing a way forward. While this partly suggests a negative view of the workshops, the significantly *increased productivity* results in participants' viewing the workshops as effective, but demanding, events. The computer support permits participants to *attend to greater complexity* and so become more *confident of their conclusions* (Eden, 1992b, 1993).

Computer supported workshops (CSW) may be used for a number of purposes:

- to enable participants to develop the material generated during either cognitive mapping interviews or oval mapping workshops,
- to allow other participants to explore and build upon a computer based map created by others,
- to support decision making groups,
- to tap experts (often external to the organization) for their wisdom and insight, and finally
- to support groups just getting started.

Whilst each of the above purposes requires many of the same stages and procedures, they do have differences in operation that will be explained in the 'how to' sections below. Each specific mode of working will be addressed as well as the common practices.

As with the considerations made when choosing to use either oval mapping or individual interviews, there are a number of important considerations relating to the use of computer supported workshops. For example, using either oval mapping or individual interviews provides participants with a chance to become accustomed to the methodology and working as a group before being exposed to computer support. More detail regarding these concerns is provided in the facilitation chapter (P5). In addition, before running a computer supported workshop, it is, as always, worth resolving the practical issues relating to the setup of the workshop, for example, group composition, venue, room design, and processes to be used.

Guidelines for Computer Supported Group Workshops

Before You Do It

We list below, some of the guidelines that are specific to CSW; more general facilitation issues are explored in chapters P2 and P5.

1.1 *Have access to colour computer projection.* This may be a powerful (high lumens) portable or ceiling mounted projector or an overhead projector panel. The first is better because it enables the group to work in daylight rather than in a darkened room which can be very tiring. Projectors which have zoom and focus facilities mean they can be placed out of the way of participants and yet produce large images that are in focus. LCD overhead projector panels distractingly spill light from the projector.

1.2 *Set up one or two portable computers running the computer software.* The first portable drives the public screen through the projection device. The second allows screens to be previewed before they are presented to the group, and also enables analysis of the computer model. Copies of the most up to date computer model will need to be transferred regularly from the public view computer to the second computer.

1.3 *Have easy access to a printer and photocopier.* This enables participants to have copies of particularly important screens whenever necessary and enables the facilitator to provide participants with a record of what has been achieved before they leave the workshop.

1.4 *Lay out the room in advance.* Although generally important, for CSW this task is particularly crucial. Deciding where to place the public display screen and the facilitator tables in relation to sources of daylight and the entrance door often requires experimentation.

How to Do It – general considerations

The steps, set out below, are those relevant to the reasons cited above for using CSW. They are divided into three sections: an introduction, main focus, and conclusions (Ackermann, 1996; Bostrom *et al*, 1993).

Introduction to the workshop

The workshop introduction section along with the two succeeding sections are strongly related to facilitation issues and should be read in conjunction with that chapter.

2.1 *Provide an explanation of the workshop.* Computer supported workshops, like any form of workshop or meeting, benefit from the facilitator providing an explanation to the day and establishing **realistic expectation**s. This may take the form of a list of objectives and/or an agenda, and also a brief summary of the process design for the workshop (see figure P3.1).

V225

2.1.1 *Manage expectations and role uncertainty.* Providing a list of objectives alongside process design helps participants determine what is expected of them, and what outcomes, or deliverables, will result. This is important here, as many participants will be unaccustomed to computer supported facilitation and will be uncertain about how the workshop will unfold. Providing a brief and humorous example of a map, the use of colour categorization, and the ease of editing and moving material about the screen will demonstrate some of the expected benefits from using computer support.

Figure P3.1   Flip-chart sheets showing Govan Initiative's objectives and associated colour coding.

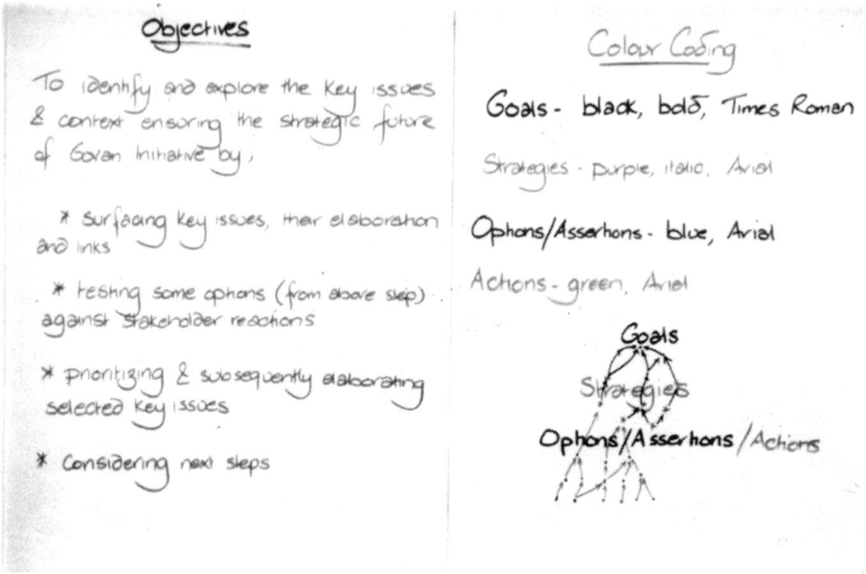

2.1.2   *Avoid the agenda indicating a precise timetable.* Computer support can accelerate some of the usual aspects of a workshop but slow down others because of the increased ability to handle large amounts of material. As CSWs provide for greater opportunism and flexibility, rigid timing can lose developmental opportunities available to facilitator, client, and group. However, some indication of timescale can provide a means of motivation for a group, and a clear marker for start, finish, and breaks is important.

2.1.3   *Review the background to the workshop.* Often the material used during a CSW will have been generated on other occasions and stored in the computer model as organizational memory. Thus, it is helpful to provide some context: how the material being worked on was produced, who was involved – ownership – and what categorizing and analysis have already been done. Also commentary on why a CSW is to be used will 'cue' participants into the agenda.

2.2   *Explain the conventions of the software.* Whether the group has used the software before will provide clues as to the required detail of the explanation. So will identifying whether participants have been involved in either cognitive mapping interviews, or an oval mapping workshop. Below are some issues worth considering regardless of participants' familiarity.

2.2.1   *Explain the meaning of the arrows* on a map. Indicate that they represent causal and implicative type relationships and may be interpreted as 'may lead to/may have implications for' or 'may be explained by/may be implied by'. 'Negative' links are used to show that the option leads to the second or contrasting pole of the outcome. If a second pole has not been entered then it is worth reading the second pole to be the same as the first, only in this case preceded with a [not]. For example 'decide publicly not to report the state of the natural heritage' may lead to '[not] have effective flows of information with external bodies' and so show a negative sign on the end of the arrow.

2.2.2 *Explain the overall structure and attendant styles.* The computer modelling software maps out statements and links as an hierarchical structure matching the manual approach. This helps the group manage the complexity of the information better as well as navigate around the model more easily. It is often worth drawing up the structure of a '**strategy map**',   *C98* with attendant colours used to indicate the different categories of data so that participants can continually refer to it.

2.2.3 *Clarify the use of an ellipsis (three dots) to indicate 'rather than' – the separator between contrasting poles.*

The 'general' workshop

These comments apply to most CSWs, although as each intervention is unique, some care will have to be taken when designing the process. Details of specific CSW workshops are considered later in this chapter. The general presumption is made that the workshop will follow on from interviews or the use of OMT, and so there will be existing material in the computer model. Typically the use of the computer might follow from using the OMT in the morning of a 1-day workshop.

3.1 *Provide an overview* of whatever material already exists in the computer model (see chapter P6). It can be unnerving for participants if they cannot sense what type of material might turn up on a map, particularly when statements stored in the computer model and linked to material already on the public screen are gradually brought into public view. Similarly, they need to be able to call up existing content that may be related to new material and be reassured it is stored in the model database.

3.2 *Focus participants' attention on specific strategic issues, in turn.* Results of any analysis done on existing material and/or conversations with the clients or participants may help when choosing which issue to focus upon first.

3.3 *Capture in '**real time**' the discussion – arguments as statements and relation-*   *V242* *ships – of the participants.* This includes suggested editions or alterations of statements or links. When capturing this material, follow the cause mapping guidelines, paying particular attention to the direction of the linkages and capturing the statements in the fullest manner possible.

3.4 *Use new and existing material to prompt further elaboration.* As new material is entered into the computer model, greater understanding and new insights can be gained by the *participants*. This in turn often generates further new material.

3.4.1 *Use debate about linkages to stimulate further elaboration.* When entering and linking the statements into the computer model's structure, participants often discuss the meaning of the statement, its relationship to other statements, and in the process generate further new material. This additional material either adds explanatory text or, through explication, prompts other participants into realizing that their statements are different in meaning, if not in words.

3.4.2 *Cross link areas of apparent similarity*. This demands that the facilitator is knowledgeable about the material in the computer model, and can locate the relevant concepts quickly and easily. This is made possible by the search routines available within the software and the use of a second computer as mentioned above. Once the statements are identified on the second – slave – computer and validated as being useful, the *facilitator* can then display the material on the public screen in front of the group (using the multiple view facility) to examine the content.

3.4.3 *Ask for elaboration of 'cryptic' concepts*. These are statements that may (i) be in a form of shorthand, (ii) use jargon, (iii) incorporate abbreviations, and (iv) not explicitly state either the actors or the intended actions. By asking the individual who proposed them to comment further the map can be enriched and made more transparent. Do not get into issues of the semantics of a statement – the 'definition' of any statement derives from its context of contrasting pole, explanation, and consequences rather than just from the words in the statement. Focus always on the action orientation to derive meaning – what might be done (explanation) and what might be achieved (consequences). This will avoid wasteful debate about definitions.

3.5 *Encourage quieter participants to contribute*. By managing the group processes towards a more equal contribution, quieter, more introverted participants can add their contribution.

3.6 *Review progress every 20–30 minutes*. A cycle time of about 25 minutes where the facilitator listens to discussion, changes and elaborates the computer model, and then draws the attention of participants to the emerging model, seems to work well. Pausing to examine both the new and existing material, encourages participants to discuss whether there are any obvious gaps and begin to jointly understand and reflect on their work. Consequently, participants can determine whether there are any other views to be put forward in conjunction with an issue or whether it is appropriate to move on to the next issue, given the balance of time available. As noted earlier, it is sometimes possible for a group to become highly creative and wish to continue working on an issue beyond original plans. When a group is working well and the cycle of debate and reflection is moving towards successful negotiation of strategy it is not helpful for the facilitator to stop the process simply to keep to a rigid timetable.

3.7 *Use refreshment breaks effectively*. These can be used for determining how participants feel the workshop is progressing, and more importantly building client relationships through regular contact. They also provide time for model analysis, determining whether there are any new and interesting emergent properties, e.g. feedback loops, emergent clusters.

Conclusions

4.1 *Carry out final review of material covered*. Although there is always pressure to use all the available time in a workshop working on the material, it is important that the facilitator provides participants with the chance to reflect jointly on all the material they have generated and refined.

Figure P3.2 A group using the computer assisted mode of working.

4.1.1 *Check whether anything important has been missed*. Through a final review, participants can check that they have covered all of the issues relevant to them, and elaborated them as fully as they wish.

4.1.2 *Focus on next steps*. This process will capture participants' knowledge concerning implementation or next steps. It will not only help them understand where the process is going but also provide information as to the most likely options or most important issues.

Each of the 'how to do it' examples below will assume that the above general notes have been read and so they will be repeated only when a different emphasis is required.

How to Do It – groups working on a computer model created from interviews or oval mapping workshops

Where **CSW follows on from an oval mapping workshop**, participants will be *V241* familiar with cause mapping, and may have had some introduction to the use of the computer software for recording the data. Similarly, if it follows a series of interviews using cognitive mapping, participants will have been provided with some idea of the structuring and presentational form adopted as a note taking device (chapter P1). When participants in the workshop are the interviewees, they will arrive at the workshop with a heightened sense of curiosity about what other participants have said and how their maps fit into this other material – the facilitator can exploit this curiosity in gaining commitment to attendance at a workshop.

5.1 *Review existing material*. These workshops require care in reviewing the material already captured. For subsequent workshops the review will seek to remind participants of the material they have already generated, avoid repetition, and also help cue them into the process.

Following interviews, much of the material will be new and so the purpose of the review is to encourage psychological negotiation between participants. Review screens need prior preparation to ensure that they reflect both the analysis of the computer model and that the early review screens show statements from all, or most, of the participants. Detailed research shows that as a review screen appears, participants look first for their own material and are reassured as they see it. They then begin to look around the context of their own material for its linkage with the views of others and for differences in perspective, and finally they absorb the overall map shown on the screen. All of this exploration occurs without anyone needing to respond to the content, and so instant physiological and emotional responses become tempered by a more thoughtful response to the whole of the

C50   screen. The natural **equivocality** and yet action orientation of the maps facilitates psychological and social negotiation. The process of bringing together several views as a map on the screen changes the views of participants by expanding and tempering their own view.

This psychological negotiation which occurs during a carefully designed review of the computer model, where each participant changes their mind towards a group view, is absolutely crucial in JOURNEY making. During the review each participant will come to believe that their interview or their contribution in the OMT workshop was significantly

C48   *greater than it actually was. This is fundamental to creating* **new negotiated order**.

5.1.1   *Use a flip-chart picture as an overview or route map of the computer model*, as it will enable the clusters, strategic issues, key options, and their inter-relationships to be followed as detail is considered – combining holism and reductionism. It will also act as an overall picture to aid navigation around the content of the model.

5.1.2   *Seek general confirmation* that interview data has been captured correctly, or that the organizational memory of the last workshop has remained intact. Make no attempt to argue for its absolute correctness. As with checking interview maps with an interviewee during a feedback interview, the map belongs to the participants not the facilitator. Participants may have changed their mind. They may be balancing political considerations in the

C49   process of negotiating a **new social order**. Use the process of correcting the computer model as a device for facilitating negotiation of order and social relationships.

How to Do It – groups working on a computer model created by others

When aiming for high levels of participation across an organization (for increased ownership and commitment), and/or to elaborate the strategic issues as fully as possible, participants may be asked to elaborate and work on a computer model that was developed by others. This model may have been created using any of the different capturing methods – the oval mapping technique, interviews, or a previous computer supported workshop.

6.1   *Review the existing material*. In this situation an overview picture is particularly important. Each aspect will need to be summarized on the screen without

going into all of the subtle detail. Much of the data shown will appear cryptic or be misunderstood because it was not generated by any of the participants. This stage in the workshop will be seen as a chore because there will be little, if any, ownership of the computer model. The only basis for interest in the computer model will be curiosity and a belief in the **procedural rationality** *of the overall*   C55
process and so the need to 'listen' to other groups involved in the journey.

6.2   *Encourage participants to think outside the existing issues.* There is a danger for participants working on material not generated by themselves of feeling too bounded by it. They may be too tempted to elaborate it rather than contribute new issues or alternative perspectives. Unless the workshop has the purpose of specifically developing the material of other groups, it will be important to legitimize criticism and their rights to increase and widen the strategic perspective being offered.

How to Do It – 'the quick and dirty – 5-hour – strategic intent'   C103 C159

Here we are considering the production of a draft strategic intent for an organization that includes consideration of strategic issues, the embedded aspiration system, distinctive competencies, and designing the business model/livelihood scheme into a draft mission statement. *This outcome cannot easily be attained successfully on a tight timescale without computer support.*

7.1   *Gather strategic issues (about 40 minutes).* Ask each participant to produce a list of the strategic issues faced by the organization over the agreed strategic timescale. Use a round-robin to gather these **emergent strategic issues** so that they   C90 C91
are scattered around the public screen, but loosely place apparently related issues close to each other. After completing the round-robin gathering, check for any extra issues prompted by the screen content. With a group of 6–8 people a 45-minute round-robin often creates a screen containing 30–70 issues. Careful positioning based upon the facilitator producing draft clusters of similar or related material means that the screen can absorb this number of issues without confusion. This procedure follows the first 'ideation' stage of a Nominal Group Technique (NGT) (Delbecq *et al*, 1975).

7.2   *Link issues (about 40 minutes).* Using the public screen invite participants to link issues so that a cause map is constructed. The issues will form *clusters of linked material.* However, links suggested by participants may not match coding guidelines, and so the facilitator will need to gradually introduce the group to the guidelines through examples that arise.

7.3   *Draft* **emergent goals/aspirations** *(about 40 minutes).* For each cluster of   C98
issues in turn get participants to propose the implied goals (or negative-goals) that arise from the issues within the cluster. Link the goal statements out of one of the statements in the issue cluster. If time permits, return to each cluster and check each issue in the cluster to validate that the proposed goals relate to the cluster.

7.4   *Construct a draft goal/aspiration system (about 30 minutes).* Establish linkages between each of the emergent goals, highlighting goals supporting other goals and/or being supported by goals or the resolution of strategic issues. Completion of this stage will produce a fairly comprehensive and interconnected **cause map** of   C72
the top part of a **strategy map**. Identify goals in a distinctive style (colour and font)   C98
differentiating them from the issues. Use the software to map just the goal system on a separate screen view in the software.

7.5 *Check the draft goal system (about 15 minutes).* Ask the group to respond to this goal system map as if it were a complete (albeit first draft) description of the goals that *will actually* drive their organization into the future. Edit and elaborate until it is a fair reflection of strategic goals *in use*, not espoused.

C103   7.6 *Elicit and explore possible **distinctive competencies** (40 minutes).* It is our experience that the discovery of distinctive competencies and core distinctive competencies in organizations is profoundly difficult (particularly in the public sector) but absolutely essential.

> 7.6.1 *Provide participants with guidance about the nature of a distinctive competence.* Distinctive competencies often contain the following characteristics. They are difficult for others who might wish to deliver the goals to emulate. Thus, in a government department it may be necessary to consider the extent to which other specialist departments may be able to take the goals conceived and easily deliver them. Alternatively, they are what distinguishes the focal organization from others elsewhere with the same goals. The competencies cannot be bought; the cost of entry is high, and they would take a considerable amount of time to acquire. Often the important distinctive competencies for not-for-profit organizations are uncodified. They have been developed over decades of working practice. The cultural knowledge is often totally underestimated, and the purpose of a strategy journey is partly to force these out into the open so that they can be reflected upon and confirmed or (re)designed.

C80   > 7.6.2 *Note that distinctive competencies may be a pattern, particularly a **self-sustaining feedback loop**.*
    > 7.6.3 *Capture distinctive competencies on public screen.* Return to the round-robin process, first stage of a Nominal Group Technique approach, and ask each participant to write down their own views of potential distinctive competencies or notable competencies. Collect these on to an empty screen (the third screen view within the software – view 1 giving the issue goal map, and view 2 the goal system). Develop a cause map of these interrelationships between the competencies. Evaluate them to determine whether patterns are distinctive, or some are clearly distinctive in their own right. Use a new style/font/colour for distinctive competencies, including using another style for each of the statements that make up a distinctive pattern.

C107   Figure P3.3 shows an example of a **pattern of competencies** discovered during a workshop with the management team of a medium sized private organization (the data has been disguised but the pattern of relationships remains). The nodes that comprise the distinctive pattern have been distinguished from other nodes. Some of the nodes were originally categorized as competencies and some as distinctive competencies. However, the management team were keen to note that while other competing organizations could replicate, either currently or in the near future, many of these, they could not replicate the pattern. It is important to note the dotted arrows. These represent links that they could not claim currently, but which they felt they could create through strategic change. In addition they could make the pattern self-sustaining through the creation of two positive feedback loops. Thus, they had discovered two important potential new strategies. It is also worth noting that they believed that there were key competencies and distinctive competencies which supported the pattern as a potential core distinctive competence.

Figure P3.3 An example of a pattern of competencies, and the potential for a loop. (Nodes that make up the pattern which is a potential core distinctive competence are shown in a serif, roman font; other distinctive competencies which support the pattern are shown in a serif, italic font; other competencies are shown in a sans-serif, roman font.)

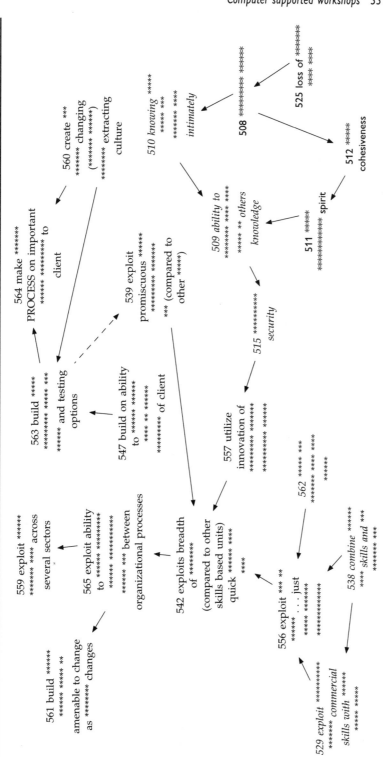

Often public sector organizations experience difficulty in listing any distinctive competencies. Management teams can become very depressed at this stage! Using a triad approach may help. Ask participants to consider three other providers, or organizations with the same sort of goals, and then explore similarities and differences in competencies. If they are working on a strategy for a department within a public organization they should think of other departments who may compete for their role, and of other similar departments in other similar organizations.

Our experience suggests that public sector organizations do have important distinctive competencies, and can develop them; however they have rarely been thought about, let alone made explicit. This part of the workshop can provide significant added value to the management team.

Beware of assuming that distinctive competencies are necessarily worth exploiting. Unless they link to aspirations, they may be wasting resources and need to be down-valued. Similarly some distinctive competencies can be very unglamorous and yet critical – it is important to elicit these, particularly when they might provide the link between others which shows a self-sustaining feedback loop.

7.7 Investigate possible distinctiveness that could be developed (about 20 minutes). Typically the exploration of linkages between competencies shows important, and sometimes obvious, potential for strategically creating a new link. This will then enable the formation of a self-sustaining positive feedback loop. Do not yet explore these in depth, but rather note the possibility.

7.8 Determine the basis for a business model / livelihood scheme (about 30 minutes). Ask participants to validate that the distinctive competencies, if there are any, can support the goal system. This process demands that participants clearly demonstrate to themselves that each distinctive competence clearly and unambiguously supports at least one goal, and that each goal is supported by a distinctive competence. This task is usually difficult, and participants become tempted to enter links when the link is very weak. Each link (arrow) must be carefully checked – the facilitator will need to discipline the group firmly.

7.9 Attempt to create the business model / livelihood scheme (about 20 minutes). Participants are rarely satisfied with the linkages established. Some distinctive competencies will be shown to be redundant, and some goals will not be supported. Unless a goal is supported directly then it may need to be revised, or a new distinctive competence developed. Similarly some distinctive competencies will emerge as unused, and may be dropped. In any of these cases a strategy to promote the changes will need to be developed at a later workshop. The final draft version of the **business model or livelihood scheme** is represented by existing *and proposed* linkages between existing or new distinctive competencies and the goal system. The business model is not the content only, but more importantly the links (as they are the means for generating outcomes). This means that the business model must be seen as a map not a list.

C79

Completing this stage in 20 minutes is possible but unlikely – it is this stage that requires the most care and most creativity.

Remember that this workshop is, in miniature, a full journey and so the workshop will involve clear cycles around goal system, distinctive competence development, and business model drafting (see figure C5.1).

7.10 Draft a mission statement based on the business model / livelihood scheme (about 20 minutes). See figure C6.1. This part of the workshop should use only the material produced during the event. Any careful copywriting to fulfil the complete demands of a **mission statement** should take place later. The workshop may close with a draft agenda for a future workshop to develop strategies to deal with the

C110 C161

issues which remain important, strategies to develop distinctive competencies, and strategies to remove resource effort on unwanted competencies. However, the workshop should have a first draft of strategic intent.

How to Do It – using the computer supported workshop to reach agreements about action

Computer supported workshops are not only used to generate material to influence and develop strategic intent, and widen perspectives, but also to agree strategic programmes or portfolios of actions. This particular form of working relates closely to the more detailed material presented in the chapter on the development of 'Strategic Thinking and Strategic Intent' and 'Strategic Action Planning' (chapter P7).

8.1   *Review existing material.* This review of existing material focuses specifically on the hierarchical structure since decisions will need to be made within the context of analysis (see Chapter P6) of, for example, potent options. Hierarchical sets ('tear-drops') indicating the structure of the computer model in relation to goals and possible strategic programmes will act as the guiding framework for discussion during the workshop. Navigation around the model is through the hierarchy of core or potent options/actions, to possible key strategies, to the goal system.

8.1.1   *Examine an overview.* In order to focus attention on goals, it is valuable to produce a flip-chart of the goal system. Also a flip-chart showing the hierarchical strategy map (figure P3.1) with the colours and styles used by the software to indicate each type of concept.

8.2   *Explore and validate any **feedback loops**.* We have noted elsewhere that feedback loops are particularly significant when developing strategy – particularly for the understanding of distinctive competencies.   C30

8.3   *Explore possible interventions in feedback loops.* There are two types of feedback loop – negative and positive. Interventions that may be considered are:

8.3.1   *Break negative feedback loops.* Where the degree of control is undesirable, break the loop by a change in policy, or change the nature of causation so that the loop behaves as a virtuous circle. For a vicious circle: 'rub out' one of the arrows by a change in policy or by changing the nature of one of the beliefs. For example make the loop into a controlling loop, a negative circle, by changing the direction of causation, or destroying the causation. Alternatively, find a number of influences on nodes that can shift the direction of behaviour so that a vicious circle becomes a virtuous circle.

8.3.2   *Support positive feedback loops.* For a virtuous circle: reinforce one or more of the nodes by exploring influences on each node in turn.

8.3.3   *Watch for the possibility of major strategic change.* This occurs when the *structure* of the situation may be changed. For example, new loops become dominant, or the 'central' core of the 'cause map' shifts by the deletion of some beliefs (that become insignificant) and others move to prominence. It also may occur when the desired outcomes (goals – those variables with no arrows out of them) change.

8.4 *Explore issues or themes* to help participants gain an understanding of the material in the computer model, rather than to address the issues. Working on specific issues comes later in the workshop, usually following a process designed to allow participants to choose their own agenda of priorities for using the workshop.

8.5 *Identify deliverable actions to create strategies from strategic issues.* Regardless of whether the computer model has been created by the workshop participants or by others, there are usually more options available than there are resources to deliver them. Therefore, the most significant part of this type of workshop, is deciding which of the options available gain most *leverage* for the delivery of strategies and goals. Typically, a workshop based on earlier issues surfacing through interviews or group workshops will have generated options expressed in general terms. These options, particularly if they are *potent* (capable of levering many strategies and/or goals), need to be elaborated to create a portfolio of detailed options that can be clearly understood and practically delivered. The process of determining which issues to focus upon should be informed by a mix of group judgement, formal analysis of the map using the software, and group consensus. Electronic preferencing, or the use of self-adhesive spots, will help determine the priorities in relation to the total list of issues to be addressed. Typically, only three or four issues with attendant actions will be able to be addressed during a 1-day workshop. Participants should be encouraged to address feedback loops before strategic issues, given their particular significance.

8.5.1 *Watch for 'gung-ho greening'*. It is usual to change options to actions by changing their style from light blue (to signify option) to green (to signify 'go'). Once participants understand the principles and begin to make progress towards developing a portfolio of actions there is a tendency to agree to more actions than can possibly be delivered – we call it 'gung-ho greening'. It is always important to build time into the workshop agenda to re-examine the agreed actions, as this often induces an air of reality and participants go on to prune and prioritize them.

8.6 *Agree upon timescales and responsibilities.* Agreement about the date on which the action will be implemented or progress assessed, and who will have overall responsibility for delivery, helps in considering resource demands. The *C40* process is also the beginning of creating a **Strategy Delivery Support System** allowing actions to be monitored. Once the person responsible and a date for completion have been identified, this information can be entered into the computer model by annotating the particular action. This facilitates searches on dates and names of persons responsible for actions.

8.7 *Clarify wording.* This is particularly necessary if the person being given responsibility for the action is not present at the workshop. Often statements are clear to those at the workshop but cryptic to those who have not attended. Spending time clarifying wording will ensure that the action is not only carried out but carried out according to plan. This is where the full pentad of 'who, what, where, why, and when' are essential. However, remember that all actions will be presented with respect to their purpose (statements at the end of arrows out of the action) and to their associated actions or context (statements leading into the agreed action). Thus, all actions will be read as a part of a map not as a list. By doing so, the pentad will be encompassed not only through the wording of the action statement, but also through associated context on the map.

8.8 *Examine resource demands.* Listing the actions at the end of the workshop not only allows some degree of reality check to be carried out, but also allows participants to examine the number of actions they have tagged to particular individuals to check personal loading. Sensible consideration of financial, energy, and time resources of the organization against the portfolio will increase the likelihood that those actions finally agreed upon will be put into practice. Evaluating resources required for each 'resource-gate' – strategic programme or strategy or goal (Eden and Cropper, 1992) – and comparing resource demands against pay-off provides a further check on expected leverage per resource. These processes help provide participants with a sense of closure and progress achieved. When options need to be more carefully examined, the structure provided by the software enables multiple criteria analysis to be used – the goal system becomes the criteria tree against which options will be evaluated (Bana e Costa *et al*, 1997; Belton *et al*, 1997).

How to Do It – tapping the knowledge and wisdom of experts

Tapping the knowledge and wisdom of experts often involves bringing people in from outside the part of the organization developing strategy, as well as using internal staff as domain experts. Most of the material related to 'groups working on a computer model created by others' will be relevant to this task. Similarly, discussion in the chapter dealing with stakeholder analysis and alternative futures analysis (Chapter P4) should be consulted. As with the design of any intervention, issues relating to group composition, and particularly to client relationships are important.

9.1 *Pay particular attention to explaining the workshop process.* The introduction to the workshop not only has to deal with the processes of running the workshop but also provide context about the overall purpose and possibly the organization. What is wanted from them, as experts, will need to be clarified.

9.2 *Ensure that the workshop has a clear purpose but is also enjoyable.* When involving experts, one of the most significant factors that will influence their energy and commitment to offering deep views comes from their understanding of the purpose of the workshop and from their personal enjoyment of the process. Their own enjoyment may come from the nature of the event itself, but more often it derives from their gaining something of value to their own expertise and role outside the workshop. Offering to provide copies of the outcome can be an important reward for their efforts.

Yes But . . .

How do I manage both process and content?

Managing the group and capturing content and using the computer software is an intensive process and demands a considerable amount of mental energy from the facilitator. This is particularly the case if the facilitator is not familiar with the software. One obvious solution is to involve two facilitators – one to manage primarily the software and the other to manage primarily the process (Ackermann,

1990). However, process and content management are tied to each other (Eden, 1990c). Whilst this does require additional resources, dividing the work makes both aspects more manageable. The use of two facilitators works well when each facilitator is competent at both aspects of the role and so can exchange roles during the workshop. Changing roles (Andersen and Richardson, 1997) provides mental refreshment for each facilitator and a change for participants. In addition, it allows each facilitator to take a primary role and yet also be effective in contributing to a secondary role. For example, working one-third as process facilitator and two-thirds (the primary role) as content facilitator, and vice-versa.

If it is not possible to involve two facilitators, an alternative approach is to become familiar with each aspect of the workshop as separate skill development episodes. For example, first become familiar with the software in the 'backroom'; then use the software with a group, but only for presentational purposes; and then run a low risk interactive workshop with a small group (4–6 participants). As with all other skills, there is a learning curve where initial episodes are very demanding, but there is exponential acceleration towards competence. We have found that good process facilitators who later begin to use computer support find the extra demands easier to cope with than analysts who are software literate but then move to process facilitation.

Use the review periods to check that all has been captured correctly and catch up on the process. Participants, during these periods, will be able to check whether their views are all represented in the computer model and that the linkages are
V242   appropriate. Writing **statements into a map up on flip-chart sheets** will also ensure that none of the material is lost. This material can then be added to the computer model during a break and the linkages added as part of the review after the break.

What if the computer hardware or software fails during a workshop?

Portable computer hardware is relatively fast and reliable nowadays. We discussed, above, the use of a second computer to help review material without the review appearing on the public screen. This computer acts as a backup if the main computer fails. However, for this to be effective it is important to make copies of the model to the second computer on a regular basis. The software creates its own backup files on a regular basis (at time intervals set by the user), and it is wise to use the save command regularly.

C60 V202   **Further Commentary – the use of the networked computer system to support groups**

CSWs frequently rely on the facilitator to manage the capture and structuring of data. However, by using the networked computer system, it is also possible to allow participants to enter their statements directly and anonymously, make preferences regarding the potential strategic issues they want to focus upon, and rate options against strategies. This mode of working requires each participant, or, in some circumstances, pair of participants to have access to a dedicated computer so as to be able to directly interact with the computer model. There are three different tools available to the participants: (a) gathering and linking, (b) preferencing, and (c) ranking. Each allows the participants to contribute towards the process of surfacing issues and detecting emergent themes. Typically it is used intermittently throughout the workshop rather than exclusively; it will be used alongside single user work by the facilitator and alongside oval mapping. Intermittent use provides participants with a change which in turn acts as a sense of 'mental refreshment'. Using the networked system alongside the single user system ensures a balance which recognizes the importance of 'socioemotional' communication in the successful functioning of groups, as well as using computers to provide maximum 'air-time' for participants (DeSanctis, 1993).

A significant advantage in using the 'networked computer' system is that it provides the facilitator with a 'chauffeur' machine enabling an examination of, amongst other things, who is and is not contributing to the process, and specifically what they are contributing (Ackermann, 1996). Consequently it helps the facilitator ensure that the outcomes are politically feasible. The networked computer system is designed to replicate the OMT as well as provide additional facilities for the workshops discussed above. For example, the 5-hour strategic intent workshop is easier and more effective using the networked system, because of productivity gains. The main features are discussed below (see figure P3.2).

Gathering and linking

This tool provides participants with the ability to enter statements (and links) into the computer model very quickly. By being able to directly type in their views, participants no longer have to wait until another has finished talking – they can talk 'simultaneously' as with the OMT. This replicates the manual OMT insofar as statements are typed in using the workstations and posted on the screen where everyone is able to view them. However, they are also stored in the computer model as they are displayed. Participants not only see all the contributions on the public screen but also see their own contributions as a list on their own private screen. Material can be entered in as quickly as the participant thinks of them and can type them. This gathering tool is particularly helpful when wanting to elaborate an option or strategy in a very short time.

Two other important reasons for adopting this mode of working are: firstly, when an issue is contentious or controversial with significant political ramifications, and secondly, where there are dangers that dominant/extrovert participants (or more senior participants) may prevent quieter participants from being able to contribute. An example of when the system was particularly useful was when an executive team had decided to reduce their size. They obviously found it difficult to discuss how to proceed, given that some of them were to be removed from the team! While the politics remained, the **anonymity** of the system for gathering data *C61 C68 C154 V202* enabled participants to, at least, raise issues that would have been difficult to raise *V244* in normal discussion. In fact the 'gathering' stage was a breakthrough in the debate. The issues gathered were realistic considerations that, when structured into a map, enabled participants to discuss sensibly and considerately how to move forward.

Enabling participants to enter links into the computer model at the same time as gathering content, or as a separate activity, enables them to propose a chain of argument rather than just single statements. The process depends upon a consistent understanding, on the part of participants, of the coding rules for linking, and so is best used when the group already has experience from other workshop events of mapping. For example when considering actions for a particular strategy, participants were asked to find ways of achieving potential options already on *V258* the screen and in doing so **link the action** to the appropriate option. This process ensured that the material generated served to achieve the strategy displayed as well as providing sufficient structure to enable the participants to carry out the process with less effort.

As noted above, the chauffeur facility provides information about the process. When using the gathering tool, it is useful to identify the level at which participants are participating. A quick chat with the low level participants might reveal a lack of understanding in the process, or a desire not to contribute because of a lack of knowledge. In addition, it is possible to examine an emerging cluster to determine whether it comprises statements made by one participant or reflects a widespread view.

V243 *Preferencing*

The form of electronic preferencing employed using the networked system replicates that which is used during an 'oval mapping' workshop. By replicating the manual process in all respects the system provides continuity as well as increasing flexibility and the ability to retain the information in the organizational memory. As with the OMT, participants are provided with a number of electronic coloured spots. These can be used for prioritizing which key issues or options or any other category are most important. The public screen, showing the graphical representation of the results of the preferencing (either in map or list form) may be turned on or off during the process. Turning off the results adds flexibility to the process, *V228* as it avoids **participants adopting tactics when carrying out the preferencing**. Sometimes the system is simply used as a quick method for gaining a consensus about agenda options for the remaining part of a workshop – for example, which issues to work on in more detail.

V198 V258   In addition to being able to **show preferences** on issues or options, there is also the facility to use, again in a manner similar to the OMT, different colours to represent different preferencing criteria. For example, it may be important for the group to determine which of the key issues/strategies are both important and immediately critical and distinguish them from those issues/strategies that are also important but more long term. An alternative form is to ask participants to determine which of the options are the most likely to happen (red spots) and which might provide the greatest leverage (green spots). Many different colours can be used during one preferencing session.

As with the gathering tool, information on preferencing patterns can be gained through the chauffeur machine. For example, the facilitator is able to see which participants have not started or finished – information useful when managing the process of the group. In addition, for each item being preferenced, the facilitator is able to determine whether the resultant score for an item is due to one participant placing all of their resources (spots) on the item or whether a range of participants *V244* have placed their resources on it – a **means of measuring the level of agreement**. Furthermore, it is easy to identify the client's preferences, ensuring that the facilitator can determine whether the results are politically feasible.

Figure P3.4 Using the preferencing system: top, console; bottom, public.

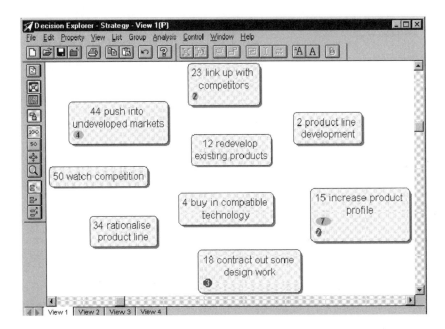

Rating

The final tool – rating – allows participants to be able to explore both individually, and in a group, their assessment of how particular items perform in relation to a specific item. For example, in the Govan Initiative case, the rating tool was used to confirm and benchmark performance indicators for strategies and later to determine whether progress had been made. Where there seemed to be divergence in views, participants were able to explore the rationale behind the positions taken, and then, in the light of the resultant further information, carry out the analysis again to see if views had changed. An alternative use for the tool is assessing how much leverage, for example, an issue has for achieving a goal. Once again the results can be used as a dialectic, prompting participants to examine their different viewpoints, surfacing further information and resulting in organizational learning as they reflect upon this information. As with both the preferencing and gathering tools, the chauffeur provides on-line information as to the progress and spread of views.

STRATEGY MAKING: WORKING WITH TEAMS – MANAGING STAKEHOLDING AND ALTERNATIVE FUTURES

Introduction

This chapter focuses on capturing assumptions, deep knowledge and wisdom about the external world of stakeholders and events – although, as we shall see, some part of the stakeholder analysis will involve consideration of internal stakeholders. There are two main purposes for undertaking each of these analyses. The first purpose is to develop strategies for effectively managing key stakeholders and the environment, and the second purpose is to enable the organization to be mentally prepared for a variety of different futures and so be capable of strategic opportunism. Alongside these main purposes these analyses are also expected to test draft strategies and options to increase the robustness, effectiveness, and viability of the strategy. This chapter will commence with stakeholder analysis *and* management before moving on to exploring alternative futures and the development of multiple scenarios.

One means of managing stakeholders is to involve them, as experts, in an alternative futures analysis exercise. Involving stakeholders as experts can be undertaken as a deliberate part of stakeholder management and may be an appropriate way of 'buying them into the strategy of the organization', particularly in the public sector. This is why we shall consider stakeholders first, although it is important to remember the **cyclical nature of strategy making** and not be rigidly devoted to one order rather than another. Both of the analyses can also be used to surface emergent strategic issues and so may be part of the process of detecting emergent strategizing. The relationship between the two externally focused analyses can be seen in Figure C2.9. Both forms of analysis will be discussed within the context of manual and computer supported group working. *C30*

Stakeholder Analysis *V261 V273*

There are four JOURNEY making techniques commonly used for stakeholder analysis and as the basis for stakeholder management, each of which can be carried out manually or with computer support. The first technique is the development of a **'power/interest' grid** that enables participants to distinguish actors (those with enough power to influence strategic futures) and stakeholders (those who *want* to influence the future of the organization – negatively or positively). The overlap of these two groups – stakeholders who are also actors – represents the most significant 'players' in strategy making. The second technique is the use of the **'power/** *C126* *C121*

interests' star diagram which is designed to validate the position of stakeholders on the power/interest grid. It is also primarily designed to determine the possible mechanisms for stakeholder management based upon an exploration of the bases of power and the focus of interest of each of the key stakeholders identified from the grid. Third, **actor influence network maps** explore the network of influence relationships. Within these maps some players (and possibly strategy context setters) turn out to be central 'conduits' and are therefore particularly important for developing and implementing stakeholder management strategies. The final technique is **stakeholder role-think** which, along with important benefits for testing and 'tuning up' stakeholder management strategies, offers significant process benefits. This technique is often employed when seeking to unfold a complete draft strategy in a 1-day workshop. It provides an enjoyable, active, and useful after-lunch activity, helpful when participants are at a physiological low.

C128

C133

One of the benefits of using multiple techniques for stakeholder analysis is that they provide flexibility, allowing the intervention to be easily tailored to suit the task, organizational culture, and client. In most instances all of the techniques are employed within the same organization and in some considerable depth, but in others the techniques may be used selectively and for 'quick and dirty' analyses. For example, one technique might be used for raising awareness and enabling a large number of people to contribute, with another being used to concentrate on more focused, and detailed, exploration. Thus, the techniques should be seen as applicable to large and small organizations, and to those able to devote anywhere from half a day to several days on the exercise.

Another benefit from these stakeholder analyses is eliciting valuable stakeholder information in such a manner that those involved consider it as a legitimate activity. Most staff know, to some extent, staff from the various stakeholder groups as a result of attending the same functions, sales conferences, trade associations, and professional society meetings. However, many managers do not see the knowledge they elicit from casual conversations and other forms of information gathering as particularly important as input to strategy making. This may be because they feel it is an isolated piece of information, a one-off, and something that cannot be assumed to occur again. Additionally, it is often seen as though the process of carefully thinking about stakeholders is illegitimate 'manipulation'. However, when this information is pulled together, small pieces of a 'jigsaw' often fit together to enable a complete picture to unfold – a picture that indicates important strategic options. Additionally, data taken from isolated events for one manager often becomes validated and substantiated when it is compared with data from many different staff members.

Guidelines for Exploring Stakeholder Analysis and Alternative Futures

Before You Do It

1.1 Consider the workshop method to be used – i.e. full group or sub-groups. When using a manual approach, particularly with a large group, consider creating sub-groups of 3–5 participants. The power/interest star diagram and role-think techniques benefit from small group work, allowing concentrated efforts and more air-time for each participant. A round-robin sub-group feedback to all participants will validate and elaborate the work of the sub-group and bring ownership across the whole group. However, when computer support, particularly the networked computer system, is employed it is possible to make good use of the whole group without loss of individual input.

1.2 *Set up flip-chart paper*

1.2.1 *For the power/interest grid.* Place four sheets of flip-chart paper in a rectangular formation with the axes of power and interest written in. If the technique is being used following an oval mapping session, place the flip-charts near to the wall picture to enable participants to check the material already generated. This activity is best conducted using all participants, even if the group size is up to 20 participants.

1.2.2 *For the power/interest star diagram.* Single sheets of flip-chart paper can be set out on the wall in front of each sub-group and used sequentially – typically one stakeholder for each flip-chart.

1.2.3 *For actor influence network maps.* All participants should be involved in addressing the same output material. Directly use the power/interest grid output. This is best managed using large sheets of clear acetate so that possible influences can be drawn in using water-based OHP pens, and so permitting continual modification of the map as the group debate and change their mind. After photographing the outcome at the end, the acetate can be removed so that the power/interest grid can be seen without the complication of the network links. The acetate can be replaced when needed.

1.2.4 *For role-think.* For each sub-group, who may be in separate syndicate rooms for this task, place at least two flip-chart sheets (portrait) on the wall and next to each other horizontally. Label the left sheet 'response' and the other 'implied goals'.

1.3 *Supply each sub-group with coloured flip-chart pens, OMT pens, and Post-its*

1.3.1 *For the power/interest grid.* Have four different colours of flip-chart pens available – preferably red, green, and blue, as well as black soft tip pens (as used in OMT) for each participant to write stakeholders' names on Post-its.

1.3.2 *For the power/interest star diagram.* Each sub-group uses one flip-chart pen.

1.3.3 *For actor influence network maps.* The facilitator uses coloured *water-based* OHP pens to write on the acetate.

1.3.4 *For role-think.* Provide each sub-group with one flip-chart pen.

1.4 *Role-think – produce lists of stakeholders and potential or draft strategies to act as triggers and to be 'tuned'.* Each sub-group will take on the role of one or two stakeholders and will consider the response of these stakeholders to the list of strategies. The stakeholders need to be selected with great care. In considering which to choose, the following issues should be considered:

- Start by considering stakeholders who have been positioned in the top right quadrant of the power/interest grid.
- Choose stakeholders about whom the participants will be able to use their own knowledge and analytical skills; others may be analysed better through back-room work.

- Consider the possibility for multiple perspectives on stakeholder responses. If this is likely, several sub-groups might role-think the same stakeholder, or the roles might be explored by several different sub-groups at different workshops.
- If external stakeholders are involved in the task, then exploit their presence by letting them role-think other stakeholders in the same workshop.

Strategies to be explored are those that are likely to produce the most subtle and complex responses from stakeholders. Also critical strategies that will be of considerable interest to stakeholders will be worth exploring in depth. About 8–10 strategies can be addressed in a 'quick and dirty' 45-minute session. They need to be expressed in relatively unambiguous terms even if they have not yet been fully developed – the role-think is designed to help with their development. If the exercise is being used as an after-lunch exercise, it is important to consider strategies that are likely to generate the most interest from sub-group members and
C74   those that will create maximum **organizational learning**.

How to Do It – manually

C121 C126 V199   *Power/interest grid*
V255

The technique is based upon the view that the most important organizations, groups, and individuals that need to be addressed in strategy making and delivery are those that have substantial power to affect the strategic future *and* an interest in so doing. It is the preface to the other techniques for stakeholder management. For example, the manual approach is the most appropriate way of identifying quickly a list of stakeholders for a role-think exercise.

2.1 *Identify and place each identified stakeholder in relation to their power and interest.* If emergent issues have already been identified using the OMT, then, as a first step, transfer stakeholders mentioned in issues on to the grid. Encourage all participants to write the names of stakeholders on Post-its and *roughly* position them *relative* to those already on the grid.

Power represents an ability to affect what happens whereas interest reflects a stake in the strategy of the organization, suggesting some strategies will be preferred to others. We deliberately do not define power carefully – it is helpful to allow participants to use their own definitions – by doing so, more useful data is likely to emerge and the 'star diagram' will check the bases of power used by participants. To assist in differentiating the entries, the grid is divided into a 2 × 2 matrix. For further clarification the grid may be extended to include titles for each of the four quadrants (crowd, subjects, players, and leaders) and/or labels for the pairs of quadrants on each axis (bystanders, actors, stakeholders, unaffected). See figure C7.1.

2.2 *Position each stakeholder relative to others already positioned.* After participants have completed a first tranche of entries, begin the process of detailed positioning. In practice it is usually easiest to start with one dimension while ignoring the other. Thus, for example, arrange all the entries relative to each other across the horizontal axis of power. Start by moving the most powerful to the right edge of the paper and then work by identifying those with increasingly less power, using the dimension as a continuous variable. Often more flip-chart paper will be needed at the left to permit relative power to be expressed. After working on power, start with those on the extreme right (with most power) and arrange them along the vertical axis of interest. It is important to retain a discipline in this process. Without discipline the activity tends towards individuals making assertions about the 2-dimensional position without enough discussion, and valuable JOURNEY making is lost. Completing the grid in two steps keeps discussion about power separate from that about interest. The first version of the grid is based on considering power and interest as they are perceived at the present time and without the application of any new stakeholder management strategies, although accounting for any routine stakeholder management strategies currently in place.

2.3 *Note discussion which might be useful for developing the star diagram.* As each potential stakeholder is evaluated along the two dimensions, the discussion (and often heated argument) about their attributes provides data that is relevant to developing the power/interest star diagram. We noted above that the development of star diagrams is often best undertaken by sub-groups whereas the grid is developed by the whole group. This means that the group will need to be reminded that the discussion is relevant to the next stage, and that the facilitator may make notes on side flip-charts which can be used later. With small management team workshops it can be helpful to start elaborating the star diagrams for obviously powerful 'players' (the top 5–6 players) as debate about the grid continues.

2.4 *Revisit elements and check for an appropriate level of **dis-aggregation**.* We have noted, in chapter C7, that participants usually submit potential stakeholders at too high a level of dis-aggregation. It is important that all of the actors are dis-aggregated to a level which is appropriate for stakeholder management in the case of players, and a decision making unit for strategy context setters. Thus, it is unusual for 'the government' to be an acceptable context setter or player. Participants will need to consider who, in government, is doing the acting. Who would need to be influenced if their policies were to be influenced as a part of a stakeholder management strategy? Who is determining the policy, if they are to be treated as a part of the uncontrollable environment? Therefore, a government department, individual senior civil servant, politician, or political lobby group may be a more appropriate level of dis-aggregation.   *C124 V199 V230*

2.5 *Note general **disposition of players** towards the organization.* Starting with the players at the top right of the grid, identify whether a player is generally positively, negatively, or 'it depends on the issue' disposed to the organization. Mark positively disposed players with a green asterisk, negatively disposed with red solid blob, and 'it depends' with an open blob. (The different shapes ensure that monochrome photographic records retain the disposition data.) The colours offer a quick way of gaining an overview of the state of players – green suggesting 'status-quo' stakeholder management strategies, and red suggesting the need for careful thinking about how to strategically manipulate players. When the overall top right of the grid shows red then stakeholder management will be particularly important in strategy making, and so it is likely that considerable 'back-room' analyses and **extended role-think** will be appropriate..   *C124 V200*

V273

2.6 *Note the first draft output.* The top right quadrant (players) represents the current focus for stakeholder management. However, where there are a considerable number of players in the quadrant, selecting those in the top right corner of the quadrant will provide an indication of **key players** – on whom it is worth focusing most effort. This ignores, at this stage in the analysis, the extent to which it may be strategically appropriate to manage the movement of subjects to become   *C123 C126 V230* players, or strategy context setters to become players. The bottom right represents those actors who are likely to be a part of thinking about alternative futures. The development of effective stakeholder management strategies follows from analysis of the *bases* of power and interest – the power/interest star diagram – and from analysis of influence networks. As a further step it is often helpful to distinguish internal from external players. One of the most effective stakeholder management strategies for internal stakeholders is to ensure that they are designed into the process, and so these players may need attention immediately.

Figure P4.1 shows an example of a power/interest grid after 45 minutes of debate.

V200 V231   *The power/interest star diagram*

The analysis of stakeholders using the power/interest grid will have indicated those stakeholders for whom star diagrams should be developed – the most significant or key players. However, the process of developing star diagrams for internal players is usually highly sensitive politically and so may not be a part of sub-group or main group activity.

3.1   *Start the diagram.* Each sub-group writes the name of a stakeholder on to a flip-chart sheet – the names positioned in the middle.

3.2   *Identify the power bases and performance indicators of key stakeholders.* Depending on the group, its progress, and the facilitator's design, this stage can either start with examining the power bases available or identifying the monitoring procedures, or allow groups to work at both together. It is helpful to display large – flip-chart size – copies of figure C7.2 around the room to act as guidance for the groups.

3.2.1   *Determine what strategies/actions are monitored and the way in which they are construed.* The aim is to elicit the nature of the interest the player shows in the organization. This interest may be reflected through monitoring routine information promulgated by the organization, or through rumour and gossip, or through regular reporting channels, etc. Any player will selectively interpret these data according to their own interests. Thus, one player may be interested in financial indicators whereas another may be interested only in what new products are being developed. Funding bodies may interpret financial data differently from, for example, clients.

3.2.2   *Identify the power bases available to stakeholders.* This focuses on the power of a player to either support or counteract particular actions. For example, a power basis for a controlling stakeholder may be the withdrawal or withholding of funds. Other groups may be able to lobby government or build alliances to undercut or undermine the action (see network analysis below for potential alliances); thus the power base is the ability to influence the views of other specific players. These power bases have strategic consequences for the organization. Not all have negative implications; there are positive power bases that may be used by a player to support strategies. Figure P4.2 shows an example of the first draft of a star diagram.

3.2.3   *Categorize power bases and interest monitors.* This process is easier using computer support as once both the bases and monitors are identified they

Figure P4.1 An initial effort identifying stakeholders and positioning them on the power/interest grid.

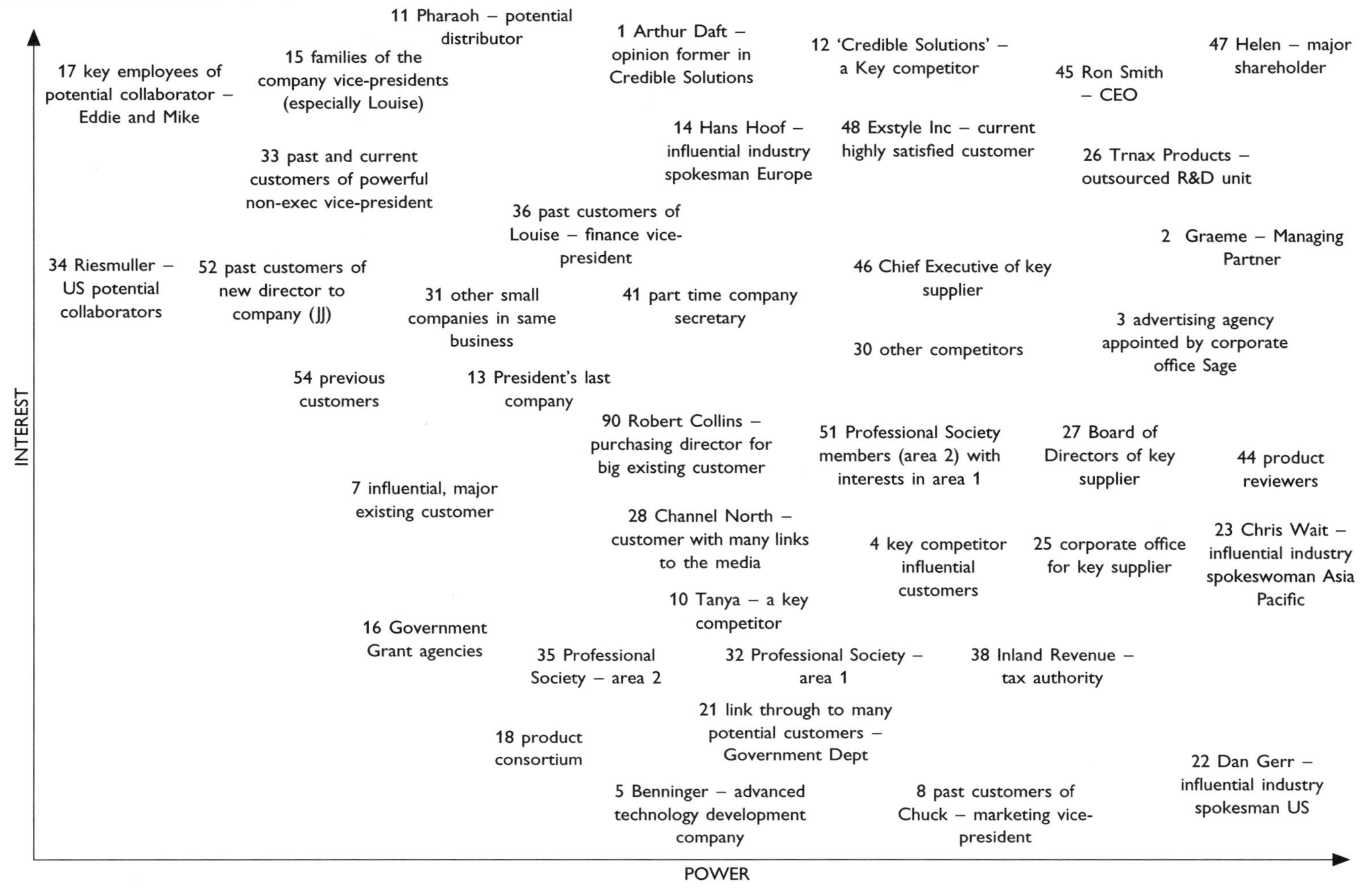

INTEREST

POWER

47 Helen – major shareholder

2 Graeme – Managing Partner

45 Ron Smith – CEO

26 Trmax Products – outsourced R&D unit

3 advertising agency appointed by corporate office Sage

44 product reviewers

23 Chris Wait – influential industry spokeswoman Asia Pacific

22 Dan Gerr – influential industry spokesman US

1 Arthur Daft – opinion former in Credible Solutions

12 'Credible Solutions' – a Key competitor

48 Exstyle Inc – current highly satisfied customer

14 Hans Hoof – influential industry spokesman Europe

46 Chief Executive of key supplier

30 other competitors

27 Board of Directors of key supplier

25 corporate office for key supplier

38 Inland Revenue – tax authority

8 past customers of Chuck – marketing vice-president

11 Pharaoh – potential distributor

15 families of the company vice-presidents (especially Louise)

33 past and current customers of powerful non-exec vice-president

36 past customers of Louise – finance vice-president

41 part time company secretary

51 Professional Society members (area 2) with interests in area 1

4 key competitor influential customers

32 Professional Society – area 1

21 link through to many potential customers – Government Dept

5 Benninger – advanced technology development company

34 Riesmuller – US potential collaborators

52 past customers of new director to company (JJ)

31 other small companies in same business

13 President's last company

90 Robert Collins – purchasing director for big existing customer

28 Channel North – customer with many links to the media

10 Tanya – a key competitor

35 Professional Society – area 2

18 product consortium

17 key employees of potential collaborator – Eddie and Mike

54 previous customers

7 influential, major existing customer

16 Government Grant agencies

Figure P4.2   An example of a star diagram.

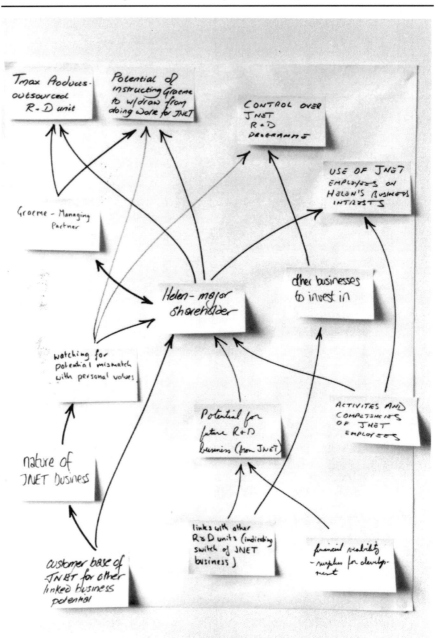

can be allocated a specific font to indicate their status. Using different coloured pens or Post-its achieves the same effect if working manually.

3.2.4   *Examine power bases and interest monitors in relation to the other stakeholders.* Where the stakeholder in question is linked to other stakeholder(s) then determining whether the power bases and monitors employed by one stakeholder overlap with those used by another or whether they conflict, can provide useful information. For example, if one of the power bases requires the support of another stakeholder, then addressing the two together may ensure that the stakeholder management strategy is robust.

Actor influence network maps   *V230*

Actor influence network maps capture any **formal or informal influence links**   *C128 V200* that exist between subjects, players, and strategy context setters on the power/ interest grid. The aim is to discover whether any entries on the grid are particularly central as 'conduits' able to influence many players. Sometimes an entry on the grid is incorrectly positioned as a subject because of the discovery that they have significant influencing power that had not been noticed in the first draft. The map will be important in determining stakeholder management strategies, where, for example, stakeholders who are a central conduit may be used as a vehicle to reach others.

4.1   *Start with key players and work out from them to explore influences with subjects and context setters.* We suggested above that this activity is best undertaken with all participants and using the power/interest grid output with large sheets of transparent acetate placed over the flip-chart sheets. (We shall see later in this chapter that, as with the grid itself, the process can be quicker and easier when using the networked computer system.) For this exercise we are interested in the power to control the actions of others and the ability to influence the views of others in a manner that is likely to be significant for the strategies of the organization. We therefore include social networks such as 'playing golf together', belonging to the same club or dining circuit, and being a part of the same 'old boy' network.

4.2   *Identify influences between entries on the grid.* Draw formal and informal links between stakeholders on the grid using the water-based OHP pens (so that they can be changed easily). It is sometimes useful to distinguish different types of links using solid lines with arrow heads to indicate formal links, dashed lines with arrow heads for informal influences, and lines (solid or dashed) without arrow heads to indicate influences in both directions through regular conversation. Links may be bidirectional to show potential and significant use of power and influence in both directions dependent upon the issue, or to indicate that the relationship is generally on an equal footing. As with most of the 'modelling' techniques employed in JOURNEY making, too much formality can destroy the process of negotiation and agreement because the technique gets in the way of jointly understanding and can frustrate the group.

4.3   *Examine and analyse resulting networks.* The analysis of networks can be conducted easily using the computer software. Even if the network has been constructed as a 'picture on the wall' it may be worth transferring the data into a portable computer for the purpose of analysis (if time is short, the names of the entries need not be used, the network can be recorded using numbers and links only). There are three particularly important features of such networks. First, there are those entries that can influence the greatest number of other entries, either directly or indirectly. If they are players, they might not only have power in their own right but that power is enhanced by their ability to influence others. Second, there are those entries which are a social junction or conduit (they have a high number of in-arrows and out-arrows). Third, there are important bridges between conduits where if the bridge did not exist then either of the conduits would lose substantial influence over the network (thus an entry with one in-arrow or one out-arrow which joins together two conduits may be significant). Stakeholders that are relatively isolated may be more prepared to cooperate or collaborate.

4.4 *Generate separate actor networks for specific issues.* If the technique is used manually, it may be helpful to simplify maps by considering stakeholders by category. Manually working with a map of more than about 20–30 entries can become overcomplicated. To simplify, consider, for example, a map for all competitors, or for all financial stakeholders. Such simplification can, however, be dangerous as it can easily miss some of the most interesting and counterintuitive links. It is more reliable, when a subset of stakeholders are being considered, to focus on those interested in a particular strategic move under consideration. In any event, there is benefit to be gained from developing separate actor networks for strategies being considered. Figure P4.3 shows an example of a part of an influence network developed using the computer software.

The network might also be used to inform the role-think exercise through providing additional information in relation to possible sanctions or support mechanisms.

C133 V231   Role-think

The purpose of this technique is twofold. One is extracting valuable knowledge about stakeholders which is 'in the heads' of staff – knowledge they often are not aware they have until accessed through the demands of role-thinking a stakeholder. The second is using this knowledge as the basis for testing the

V276   **robustness of strategic options**. Careful use of the technique provides more insight into the political feasibility of strategies and strategic options than any other. Role-think may be used to explore internal as well as external stakeholders.

This technique has been used following thorough preparation and research and at other times as a 90-minute exploration using data derived from earlier parts of the workshop. It not only provides important insights but does so in a way that engages and stimulates participants (Eden and Huxham, 1988). Participants carrying out a role-think exercise usually find it to be a particularly enjoyable activity. The exercise is specifically designed to help surface 'taken for granted' knowledge about stakeholders. Indeed, many participants often suggest, at the outset, that they do not have enough knowledge to sensibly and reliably become involved in the exercise in a meaningful manner. They are usually concerned that their knowledge is not validated, or well researched, and that it will be incomplete. After the exercise they are more confident that their contribution was useful – even when, on some occasions, the main conclusion is that they now 'know what they don't know, and now know what they most certainly should find out!'.

The main purpose of the exercise is the collection and collation of qualitative and subtle data about stakeholders and about the *dynamics* of their response to any

Figure P4.3 An early effort at identifying formal and informal relationships.

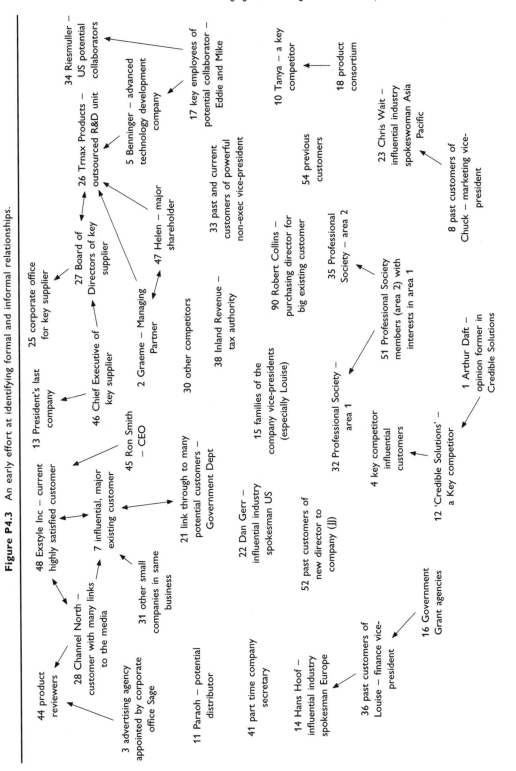

strategic moves being considered. As with much of JOURNEY making, the organizational learning and individual learning from the exercise can be as important for the strategic future of the organization as the output that is to contribute to the making of the strategy. Sometimes effective strategic stakeholder management can take place through everyday contact with stakeholders made by managers at all levels. This contact must, however, be set within a framework of strategic direction. A series of role-think exercises with different groups, when well designed, can help do this.

In option surfacing workshops, where participants are requested to be as creative and innovative as possible, little consideration is given to the practicality of options in relation to possible stakeholders' responses to their implementation. If the options are to be considered further, then not only do they need to be evaluated according to their resource requirements but also their impact on players. If an option, when implemented, causes a stakeholder to feel threatened or to react in a negative manner, then the consequences could be that the organization loses a valuable partner, pushes the stakeholder into a coalition with others, or even moves a stakeholder from benign indifference to active competition, *and* these moves may further prompt other dynamics among stakeholders. Thus entries on the power/interest grid become dynamic. It is this

V276   process of testing out the options, determining reactions, and then **'fine tuning' the strategy** by tailoring the options to either diminish the negative outcomes or reinforce the positive outcomes that results in the identification of a more robust set of options.

Because the technique is enjoyable it is usefully time-tabled after lunch, during a 1-day workshop, when the physiology of the body wants to slow down.

5.1   *Choose stakeholders for the role-think.* These notes extend those listed above as a part of the 'Before You Do It' preparation (guideline 1.4) and require a number of stakeholders to be identified before the start. This choice is usually made jointly by the facilitator and client. The client will also provide valuable views about the make-up of sub-groups. Typically, the background work informing this selection comes from the output of the grid, influence map, and star diagram. When this pre-work has not been undertaken, and yet a role-think exercise seems appropriate (for example, as an after-lunch activity), then the following brief preparation possibilities may be used:

5.1.1   *Use the final 10–15 minutes before lunch* to get participants to list the stakeholders they believe may respond aggressively to some of the options they have been identifying.

5.1.2   *Use a fast (30 minutes) development of the power/interest grid.* This will help prompt for stakeholders and does so in a way that facilitates a more informed choice for the role-play.

5.1.3   *Consider carefully the choice of internal or external stakeholders* or mixture of both. It is sometimes helpful for managers to discover the possible responses of internal stakeholders (such as trade unions, or particular operating companies in a large multinational organization). This exercise is good at helping particular stakeholder groups in an organization to begin to understand the legitimate interests of alternative stakeholder groups and so consider refining options so that they become more workable. It helps develop a degree of empathy and a switch from stubborn implementation of impractical options to modifying them to politically feasible outcomes.

5.1.4 *Choose stakeholders that participants can relate to.* Participants must have a working knowledge of stakeholders to be able to take on the roles. Getting less senior managers to take on the role of the senior managers can be very powerful in enabling junior managers to become aware of the multiple and conflicting pressures on senior managers. The process can also act as a cathartic device. When the role-think exercise is used as a part of an external stakeholder workshop (see guideline 1.4), it is often useful to ask one stakeholder to role-think one of the other stakeholders in the same workshop. In such circumstances we have found consistently that the role-thinking has been more perceptive, in that the stakeholder who is the subject of the thinking reports that the outcome is closer to **'theories in use'**, whereas they would have reported themselves in terms of **espoused theories**.   *C37* *C89*

5.2 *Identify the 'strategic options' to be used during the role-think.* When the technique is used as a part of an OMT (or a computer supported) workshop, then strategic options can be selected from those displayed on the map. With a more extensive and elaborate role-think exercise it is likely that the strategic options to be explored will be selected carefully from the draft strategy. There are usually many more options that can be usefully considered than can be dealt with during a short role-think exercise, and so some discrimination is necessary.

5.2.1 *Pick those strategic options that are specific and well elaborated* rather than those which are, as yet, ambiguous and underdeveloped. If they are underdeveloped and yet of strategic significance, it is important to draft a more specific version for use in the exercise. It does not matter that they are not yet firm proposals; experimental versions of a strategy can be just as helpful as more firm proposals; what matters is that they permit serious exploration from the perspective of stakeholders. The outputs from the role-think will inform the redrafting designed to provide a carefully crafted version of the option. Choosing well-specified strategic options ensures sub-groups are clear about what is intended and are able to devote their energies to thinking about stakeholder responses rather than trying to understand what the option means. Broadly stated options are more difficult to pin down, and may require substantial time as the sub-group argues about the nature of the option rather than undertaking a role-think.

5.2.2 *Select strategic options that promote reactions from the chosen stakeholders.* Ensuring the options chosen are those that stakeholders are able to react to makes the exercise more enjoyable and will also produce richer stakeholder information. Many important strategic options will not lead to important stakeholder responses.

5.3 *Break the large group into sub-groups.* We have found that breaking participants into sub-groups of around 3–4 persons produces the best results. The number of sub-groups will influence the number of stakeholders required as each sub-group is required to role-think at least one stakeholder. Where there are a lot of key stakeholders or gaining an internal view is useful, it is possible to assign two stakeholders (one internal and one external) to each sub-group. The best sub-groups contain participants who have some experience with the stakeholders.

5.4   Give each sub-group up to 10 strategic options and 2 stakeholders. Depending on the available time, and whether each sub-group is covering one or two stakeholders, a range of around 10 options provides an appropriate breadth of exploration. It is best that these be identified before starting this exercise (see 'Before You Do It' notes). It is not necessary for each sub-group to have identical lists of options – options that may be appropriate for one stakeholder may be inappropriate for another. However, some commonality between the lists of options helps retain interest during the feedback from each sub-group to the large group and provides a wider range of response with some test of reliability of responses. Sub-groups are able to compare and comment on their reactions relative to those of other groups. When the role-think is being used following

V273   carefully prepared research, and involves selected managers in a **1–2-day role-think workshop**, it is usual for the workshop to explore, in detail, just 1–2 options in relation to a set of stakeholders who respond strategically to each other's moves.

V232   *5.5   **Provide each sub-group with some background data.*** The most useful data is that available from the star diagrams. This should be set out in front of the sub-group, preferably on a flip-chart, so that all members of the group can see it. The amount of data made available can expand towards that provided for the full 2-day role-think workshop, where all known stakeholder information is provided, including, possibly, psychological profiles. However, for most versions of the exercise, the aim is to elicit assumptions and wisdom embedded in the minds of the participants. Thus, it is often more help to encourage groups to start with no data other than that generated by the group itself during other parts of the workshop.

V232   *5.6   Provide each group with paper to **record their responses**.* See 'Before You Do It' notes. As sub-groups tackle each of the options in their assigned roles, their responses to the option should be written on the 'response' sheet immediately as a 'knee jerk response'. After this response has been noted, participants reflect on *why* they believe the stakeholder would respond in that manner. The second step is an attempt to uncover the assumptions made by participants as they determined the response. If the initial response is too well thought through it is likely that the sub-group will miss the discovery of important 'taken for granted' knowledge about stakeholders. The task is to identify the action of a stakeholder and then work back to discover the *theories*-in-action. After reflection about the theories-in-action, the sub-group may wish to modify their first draft response. To avoid the first response being lost as data, it is important to put a line through it in such a way that it remains readable, and so the *sequence* of changes is recorded.

5.7   Ask the participants to present back their findings. Requesting that each sub-group feed back to the whole group ensures organizational as well as individual learning and provides a natural conclusion to the exercise. It is worth the facilitator's choosing the order of feedback carefully so as to start off with a sub-group that is likely to do a good job and therefore encourage others. Also finishing with a good group helps round off the process.

5.8   Encourage discussion after each presentation. This seeks clarification of differences in view about the outcomes reported and aims to explore potential coalitions and conflicts across stakeholders.

V232 V276   *5.9   **Run the role-think twice.*** Encouraging sub-groups to extend the role-think by taking into account the first iteration ensures that the dynamics which result from coalitions are explored. As with the fuller 2-day role-think workshop, it is

C30   important to consider the likelihood of **'stable' dynamics** where each stakeholder settles to a position in relation to other stakeholders and in relation to the success or failure of the strategic option being considered.

Stakeholder Management   *V262 V274*

Each of the four analyses discussed above surfaces potential strategies for managing stakeholders – both implicitly and explicitly. However, it is important to extend the analysis into the specific consideration of stakeholder *management* strategies.

The *grid* determines which players must be considered. It also provides the 'chess board' for seeking to move, for strategic benefit, entries from one quadrant to another. Strategies may be developed which aim to move subjects to become players by encouraging coalitions, and vice-versa by breaking coalitions and reducing power. For example, **involving a number of their key stakeholders in a**   *V205* **workshop designed to help with developing alternative futures** may be a stakeholder management option. Such an event provides stakeholders with an opportunity to formulate strategies that would help each of them attain their goals but at the same time promote the organization's strategies, and so create the potential for 'collaborative advantage' (Huxham, 1996). Thus, one possible task is to develop a set of strategies addressed to stakeholders interested in the organization but who currently have no or little power (Eden, 1996). These workshops are often also designed to get the stakeholders more acquainted with the organization's purpose and intent. As such it may be possible to encourage *strategy context setters to become players* by gaining their interest in the strategic future of the organization. Other possible options include targeting these stakeholders for special services, developing joint projects, and trying to 'bring them into the organization'. Finally, strategies may be developed so that *players are persuaded to become strategy context setters* by convincing them that they have no interest in the organization. By working to reduce the profile of the organization in their eyes and avoiding or terminating certain behaviours, it is anticipated that those stakeholders who are powerful and interested but negatively disposed may become disinterested. These approaches to stakeholder management are particularly appropriate for public and not-for-profit organizations.

The *star diagram* provides the data needed to determine how to manage specific stakeholders. Strategic management of the impression stakeholders gain of the organization is often used – utilizing the bottom part of the star which specifies 'ways of seeing'. However, the strategic management of negative power bases through attempts to change the power base of stakeholders can be more significant. Every item on a star diagram should be explored as if it was a variable to be strategically manipulated.

The *influence network map* provides the data for considering strategies for promulgation of selective information through multiple conduits. Social influence networks, particularly informal networks, can shift information fast – share price changes are sometimes contrived through the exploitation of such networks. Building special relationships with selected stakeholders who are central to the network (as determined by the analyses discussed above) is particularly important. However, it is also sometimes possible to develop strategies designed to change the nature of the network. Changing the speed of delivering particular types of information to central players in the network can ensure that one type of message

C127

is promulgated before another less advantageous view develops. In these ways it can be possible to break free of the power of an out-of-date **'industry recipe'** ahead of others.

How To Do It – using computer support

The grid and influence network, particularly, can be developed more effectively with computer support. It is faster, more productive, and routinely creates an organizational memory which can be accessed by any manager if required, and allows material to be modified. It is also helpful to ensure that the output from the star diagram exercise is stored alongside other stakeholder data so that it can be recalled at any time during any strategy workshop.

Power/interest grid

Follow the same steps as for the manual process. When the networked computer system is employed, each participant can 'throw' their own contributions about potential stakeholders from their workstation to the public screen. With the single user system, participants shout out their suggestions. The public screen is used so that the x-axis is taken as the power axis and the y-axis as the interest axis. Using the software allows the axes to grow or contract to suit the data.

C125

The software facilitates the taking of background notes (using the 'mem(ory)' cards) about each stakeholder. It also enables colouring and different fonts to code disposition, and additionally can enable other **categories to be created** (using 'sets') collecting, for example, media, government, competitors, and so on. It is also easier to work with many stakeholders (typically 100–150).

Star diagrams

Each of the players (top right quadrant) can be copied ('bring') on to a new 'views' and the power bases and interests developed. When a power base derives from an ability to influence another stakeholder, this link will show on the star diagram but also be translated to the grid as a part of the influence network. As with the grid it is possible to use the networked computer system or the single user system.

Influence network maps

The power/interest grid data is easily used to develop the influence network – all that is required is to link the entries. The software permits the links to be displayed or not, and so it is easy to switch between a focus on position on the grid to influence network and analysis display. Different types of links can be generated to illustrate formal and informal links, as well as bi-directionality, and strength. As we suggested above, the analysis of the network is fast, reliable, and easy using the software.

Yes But . . .

It is difficult to fix stakeholders in one position on the grid!

As participants begin to fine-tune the grid and carefully examine and debate the positions taken by potential stakeholders (guideline 2.2) they will often, quite rightly, decide that entries cannot be placed in a single position on the grid. For example, entries could be in many different positions depending upon the strategy of the organization. One instance of this is pharmaceutical companies who would have a significant *interest* in, and reasonable *power* to influence the strategy of, a National Health Service Unit to shift from the use of generic drugs to branded drugs; however, they would have no interest in, or power to influence, the implementation of a strategic expansion of the hospital into hip replacement operations. Thus in one case the element would be a 'player' and in the other a part of the crowd. This is an instance where the stakeholder can be located in different places depending on the issue being addressed. Depending on the degree of variation between the different positions and the frequency of the occurrences, it may be helpful to annotate the Post-it/computer entry with the issue it relates to. When using computer support, background data can be noted in the 'memo'. When a stakeholder can move between several positions on the grid it may be helpful, and important, to reflect this by putting the entry on a line of variability or within a prescribed area of possibility (for example, circle, ellipse, rectangle). Because this process can make the grid confusing to read, it is sometimes better that this detail be captured only for those who with respect to some strategies become players. For general purposes stakeholders may be placed in an average or modal position, or placed within an indicated boundary of expected movement. The use of shapes within which a stakeholder might move works well with a small grid but is unworkable with larger grids, and when using the software the degree of movement might be noted in the 'memo' card.

When stakeholders appear for only a small number of strategic issues it is possible that these issues, if they are strategically significant, will need their own stakeholder grid. In any case, for a full role-think workshop, preparation will usually involve constructing special purpose grids that relate specifically to the strategies to be tested.

It is difficult to be certain about the appropriate level of dis-aggregation of stakeholders!

The first clue about too little dis-aggregation comes when the grid reveals little that is new to participants. In these circumstances the grid may be expressing too general a model of stakeholders and could be applicable to most organizations in the same industry. Until the grid declares a pattern that is unique to the particular organization, it is unlikely that all stakeholders have been identified, or that they have been dis-aggregated to the level of strategic management focus. Discussion about the appropriate level of dis-aggregation should not be seen as a requirement of the technique but rather a requirement of good JOURNEY making about stakeholder management. The discussion is an important output of the technique.

As noted earlier, when dealing with 'the government' or a large organization not all parts of the stakeholder organization are interested or powerful but rather one or maybe two specific parts of it. In these cases the particular departments, groups or individuals, rather than the entire stakeholder, must be entered in the grid. Another helpful tactic is considering whether the position on the grid is dictated by the policies and procedures of an organization or the particular individual currently in a position of power in the organization. This distinction may help in identifying whether the position is likely to remain static for some time, as well as indicating whether the entry should be the organization, an individual in the organization, or both. For example, for a conservation organization, landowners as a group may have a view, but also one or two individuals may be particularly vociferous and powerful and should be entered in their own right.

Work on stakeholders is changing the work on other parts of the journey!

C134

All parts of the journey interact with one another. This is an intended part of JOURNEY making, where each episode informs and validates both previous and future parts. The strategy must be absolutely **coherent** for it to be deliverable. Each part must be cross checked with previous parts so that the cycle from one part to another ensures coherence. For stakeholder analysis and management, important coherence checks involve:

- potential stakeholders raised during issue generation being considered in stakeholder analysis, and vice-versa, where players are usually only powerful and interested because they generate strategic issues for the organization;
- leaders being considered as a part of thinking about alternative futures;
- strategies for managing stakeholders, as they are an integral part of the strategy for the organization and must be embedded with action programmes and resources related to other strategies; they are not an added extra;
- internal stakeholder analysis that is fundamental to attaining politically feasible strategies. Consequently, all strategies must, at one time or another, be subject to all four forms of stakeholder analysis. Indeed the analysis is very helpful in deciding who should be participants in the strategy journey.

Stakeholder analysis seems to take more time than that available to the management team?

As with everything discussed in this book there will always be a balance between full and thorough analysis and the pay-off from the time spent. All of the stakeholder analyses can be undertaken within a tight timescale, but also they can be undertaken over extended time and with considerable thoroughness. As we have consistently suggested, a first draft approach to each part of the journey is helpful, where a 'quick and dirty' first draft run through of all parts of the journey is taken before choosing which to concentrate further effort on. This 'cascading' approach ensures that effort is devoted to those areas which require the most work and will produce the best pay-off.

Further Commentary on Exploring Stakeholder Analysis

The Extended Role-think

On many occasions we have found that a more extensive version of the role-think exercise is necessary for exploring particularly important and new strategies. These strategies are usually those expected to cause considerable upset to competitors, establish new standards, or interfere with the 'industry recipe'. In other words, they are often the sort of events that competitors might be including in their own strategic thinking about possible alternative futures. The strategies worth exploring in this degree of depth will tend to be those that will produce complex dynamics of responses from stakeholders rather than strategy A produces response B. Thus the expectation is that a strategy 'game' may unfold where A produces response B from stakeholder X which, in turn, promotes response C from stakeholder Y which promotes a necessary modification to strategy A, etc. For example, in 1996 the move by British Airways and American Airlines to form a strategic alliance would obviously have benefited from an extended stakeholder role-think.

For an extended role-think it is likely that there will have been considerable background research to establish which actors are likely to respond – be a part of the unfolding 'strategic game'. The strategies of these actors will have been researched and all available documentation for each of them collated into role-think packs. On a number of occasions this research has included formulating psychological profiles of the key decision makers in the organizations. The workshop itself, or series of workshops, will be arranged to last 1–2 days and will probably involve managers who will be responsible for delivering the strategy to be tested. The workshop is set up so that each actor to be examined will be allocated to a separate syndicate room so that all the data in the packs can be spread around the walls and scattered across the tables. The data will include any that may have come from previous 'quick and dirty' role-think exercises, and must include any star diagram data for the actor. Each syndicate room provides a complete 'surround' to the role-thinking of the managers in that room.

In effect, the role-think follows a sequence of strategic moves, or responses, from each actor, and through each round of strategic decision making. Thus, it starts with the strategy making organization delivering their strategic move. The declaration of this move must be formulated to match the expected conduit for knowledge about it as perceived by the actors. Thus if 'rumours in the press' is the most likely conduit, this is what will be the first strategic move, and so, for example, each syndicate room is delivered a newspaper cutting starting the first round of responses. Each actor then responds, or not, according to the data in the syndicate room and the **deep knowledge** of managers undertaking the role-think. *V275*
Any deep knowledge which modifies the response predicted by data available is noted 'on the wall' by the syndicate. It is, of course, possible that a syndicate may decide that the actor concerned does not even notice the strategic move, or that they do not regard it as important, or they decide to wait and see. Each syndicate reports their strategic move to all of the other actors including, (i) the form of the move as it would be promulgated to the other actors, (ii) as it would be delivered internally, and (iii) the reasoning behind it. This stage is the equivalent of the feedback round in 'normal role-think'.

Following the reporting from each syndicate, each actor will be invited to make their next strategic move based upon the new situation. This second set of moves will include a possible response from the strategy making organization. In principle the process continues until the strategic outcomes settle to a stable scenario, or alternatively have indicated that the original strategy must be modified significantly. The scenario which unfolds is likely to be only one of many possible alternative futures – the unfolding dynamics can rarely be forecast with high degrees of accuracy. It is important to remember that the purpose of an extended role-think is that of 'tuning' the proposed strategy so that it is feasible in relation to stakeholder responses (internal or external). It is not designed to be an accurate predictor but rather a strategic thinking device.

Typically, the first 'game' collapses after one or two rounds and the managers involved in the role-think come together to rethink the strategy before trying the role-think for a second time. Gradually, over the two days of such a workshop, the strategy is redesigned, often subtly, in terms of substance, presentation, or timing so that the strategic dynamics generated by stakeholder responses settles to a stable outcome which supports the strategic intent of the strategy making organization.

Working on Alternative Futures – introduction

As with the approach taken to describe stakeholder analysis and management in the above section, we shall explore both manual and computer supported approaches to the analysis of alternative futures. Each of these approaches can be tailored to suit the task, organizational culture, and client. The results of the analysis, which emerge as a series of 'stories' or scenarios, can then be used, not only as a test platform for the strategic options being considered, but also as a means of developing new strategic options.

As we stated at the beginning of the book, we shall not consider here many of the 'standard' forms of environmental analysis. These analyses are well presented in other texts. Here we consider *alternative possible futures* as a basis for:

- developing new strategic options,
- exploring currently proposed strategies,
- creating a strategic journey to ensure that the organization can act opportunistically and flexibly in a strategically appropriate manner,
- creating the circumstances through which opportunities can be utilized faster than by competitors,
- managing uncertainty and turbulence through mental preparedness.

The basis for this part of the journey is that of alternative futures analysis. As with other parts of the book's practical section, we use approaches to developing scenarios that can *involve* managers. This means we consider approaches that can produce clear added value within a half-day or full-day workshop, although often an organization will continue with more substantive analysis and modelling based upon initial workshop based work. There is expected to be added value for managers in terms of individual and organizational learning as well as directly for informing effective strategy making.

The manual technique we present below is effective at generating a number of alternative futures in a fairly 'quick and dirty' fashion, if time is constrained, and allows groups to consider them in a flexible and easy-to-use manner. This means that the analyses can be undertaken by participants able to *influence* the direction of the organization as well as those who will *design* the strategy. The computer supported approach involves the combination of facilitator driven and network computer supported facilities. Here the technology enables the possible futures to be examined in greater depth by allowing easy identification of different categories of data, different forms of relationships between the data, and exploration of feedback loops. The qualitative computer models created in this way – as event based scenarios – can be more easily converted into simulation models facilitating examination of the dynamics of scenarios.

Often the analyses undertaken by a group will be deeper than discussed below and will be informed by exploration of 'expert' knowledge outside the organization (Brightman *et al*, 1997) or by the use of experts directly involved in workshops. As we have argued before, the 'quick and dirty' route allows for a cascading approach where further work can be a continuation if the initial work indicates that further value is likely.

Guidelines for Exploring Alternative Futures – using manual techniques

Before You Do It

1.1   *Choose the participants to be involved in the process.* When using participative methods for developing strategy, the opportunity to be able to capture possible futures as seen by a large number of the organization's staff is attractive. It is often useful to draw upon the different perspectives and knowledge of staff from different parts of the organization and create potentially diverse scenarios, as well as considering the involvement of outside experts or 'remarkable people'.

1.2   *Place 4 pieces of flip-chart paper up on the wall to form a 2 × 2 matrix.* Make sure this is positioned where all of the participants can easily see and access the wall picture, as room design is important.

1.3   *Label the axes 'certainty versus uncertainty' or 'predictable versus unpredictable' and 'important versus unimportant' to form quadrants.* The bottom right quadrant (important and uncertain) indicates the most important area for exploring multiple futures – see figure C8.3. *Determine the time horizon* to be the focus of attention. The appropriate time horizon for considering alternative futures will usually have been determined through other parts of the journey (for example, issue structuring). For some organizations, a 20-year future is appropriate, for others 3–5 years.

1.4   *Provide Post-its and a pen for each participant.* Use the same resources (pens etc.) as suggested in the above material on stakeholder analysis or in the OMT chapter.

How to Do It

Build the importance/uncertainty matrix

The starting point for constructing scenarios of alternative futures is to gain some feel for the sorts of **events** that could significantly **affect the strategic future of the**   *C81 V251 V267*

organization. For them to be significant they must be both important – that is, attack aspirations – and uncertain.

2.1 *Provide a clear explanation of the procedure.* Explain the purpose of the exercise with particular emphasis on the contrast between trend extrapolation forecasting and the idea of alternative futures. One explanation might be that scenarios reflect possible futures within which the organization might have to operate. There are, of course, an infinite number of possible futures to consider; however, the only futures of interest are those which relate to the strategic intent of the organization. Often, futures are considered when intent is very much in draft form; indeed the purpose of considering them is to refine and develop strategic intent. Therefore the group will need to be guided by draft ideas about aspirations, and the draft business model/livelihood scheme. In any event, some guidance for thinking about the future is essential. The group will not be concerned about industry futures, or regional futures, but futures which will have an impact, positive or negative, on the strategic intent of the organization.

C81 V251 V267   2.2 *Ask participants to write key flip-flops/events – one on each Post-it.* Alternative futures analysis commences with participants identifying key *events* or **'flip-flops'** that may occur and *over which the organization has no control.* Flip-flops are those circumstances where the event can result in either one state or another but not be part of a continuum. However, as we discussed in chapter C8, there may be trend based factors that might reach a critical stage and so create a flip-flop event, and these must be included. For example, the market size for a product may diminish to a point where it can no longer sustain all of the products servicing it. In this case the event is that of sustainability, or not, rather than the market size trend having continued. More obvious examples of a flip-flop are: a nuclear accident (there is no half way house, either there is a nuclear accident or not), a European Commission ban on the production of CFCs rather than staying with the status quo, a technological breakthrough, etc. Chapter C8 discusses some of the prompts that can help participants contribute appropriately.

2.3 *Position Post-its on the matrix.* As with the oval mapping technique, ask participants to place their contributions in the position judged to be most appropriate, but without the need for precision. Entries will need to be repositioned during the evaluation. We discuss, in chapter C8, some of the conceptual and practical difficulties associated with the term 'uncertainty'. In particular we note that an event may be predictable, but the timing of the event highly unpredictable. The group must be allowed to interpret the notion of predictability freely.

2.4 *Encourage participants to build off one another.* Seeing the contributions of others results in further elaboration and stimulates additional statements. This process continues until participants are struggling to come up with any further statements. Typically this first stage takes around 15–20 minutes.

2.5 *Ensure other parts of the strategy journey have been used.* The results of a stakeholder power/interest grid will have shown 'strategy context setters'. These must be checked for their contribution to significant future events. If they have been designated as powerful in relation to the strategic future of the organization, then they are likely to be the creators of events that cannot be controlled by the organization. Consider each 'leader' in turn and explore the options open to them. It is also likely that an OMT issue generation workshop will have produced significant events that trigger issues. These should be transferred to the environment analysis.

2.6 *Consider using the PEST categories as prompts.* A common category prompt is that of Political, Environmental/Economic, Social, and Technological (PEST). Such a category may help participants think broadly. However, it can also act as a constraint by taking attention from other possible categories. It is often more appropriate to wait for all events to emerge and then subsequently consider possible categories for the data.

2.7   *Review all entries*, starting from the bottom right quadrant.

2.7.1   *Explore the nature of the event*. Many events suggested during the exercise will be potentially within the strategic control of the organization, or at least amenable to strong strategic influence. These events then move from the analysis to become strategic options (usually marked with an asterisk). Others will be on a boundary between strategic control and environmentally determined, and should be coded as such (usually marked with a cross). The example given above is typical of a **boundary event**, where   *C140* diminishing market size is potentially within the strategic control of a major player in the market. Our experience suggests that as many as one-third of the events noted are within the strategic control of the organization. Consequently, they are marked as strategic options. Converting strategic options to strategies is a *choice* based upon factors such as their salience to attacking aspirations, and the cost–benefit ratio (accounting for the degree of leverage (potency) in relation to the full set of strategies and goals).

2.7.2   *Explore events' positions on the matrix*. For an event to be important it must attack the strategic intent (the draft goal system is often the easiest reference point) in some way: for example, by weakening distinctive competencies and so the business model/livelihood scheme. The debate about positioning is an important part of JOURNEY making for it will reveal new material about aspirations as well as the nature of the event. Typically there is a difficult debate about the **nature of uncertainty** for   *C147* some events. For example, the event of a nuclear accident may be regarded as highly certain, and yet the timing of it may be extremely uncertain. Alternatively, some events may be very certain but the flip-flop nature very significant – for example, in the UK a change in government may be taken as relatively certain and yet be a core flip-flop within at least one scenario. Thus, whilst the bottom right quadrant is the most interesting for scenarios, the top right quadrant will also include key scenario events.

2.7.3   *Explore the nature of the event in relation to actors*. We noted, in the stakeholder section and above, that leaders are often determinants of events. Indeed, there are rarely more than half of the scenario events that are not determined by an actor. Thus, flip-flop events without actors' names attached should be discussed further so that, where possible, the actor can be noted when appropriate. Clearly 'acts of God' and nature are not *usually* regarded as associated with an actor!

2.8   *Check coherence* with goals/aspirations and with stakeholder analyses.

2.8.1   *Examine important events alongside goals*. The notion of importance that emerges from identifying important events must be made to cohere with the goal system or else the goal system must be changed.

2.8.2   *Use actors and events, and stakeholder analysis*. Where events have been identified that are, in essence, triggers for strategic issues, and they are driven by actors, then it is important to ensure that the stakeholder analysis methods are used in relation to them. These methods determine the possibility for strategic control.

Building scenarios

We recommend the use of one of two approaches to building scenarios, dependent on the time available and the creativity of the group. The first approach uses the above matrix of events and seeks to identify scenarios from clusters within this picture. The second approach forces creativity by focusing on the conjunction of two key events. As we shall see, the second approach can follow from the first and encompass most of the work entailed in the first approach.

Stories from clusters of events

3.1 *Build story lines.* Many of the events noted on the matrix will be causally related to each other. For example, in the Northern Ireland peace scenario (figure C8.4) the events 'increased drug trafficking', 'less investment by government', and 'rising unemployment' are each possible scenario events in their own right, but with editing they link together to form a story line for a 'peace scenario'. The causal story line is that a cease-fire may cause less investment and so unemployment, and also lead to involvement from paramilitaries in crime and so drug trafficking. In some cases, as possible story lines develop, a flip-flop will need to be split into two connected events: one side of the flip-flop generating one story line and the other a completely independent, or relatively disconnected, story.

3.2 *Identify clusters of story lines.* Linking events with cause arrows and splitting flip-flops will gradually produce the equivalent of a cause map that is structurally similar to strategy maps. The picture is therefore amenable to some of the cause map analyses – in particular, cluster analysis. Each cluster represents the first draft of a possible scenario story. Typically clusters relate to each other through 'bridge' events and it becomes appropriate to pull clusters together as one alternative future. Analysis can rarely help in this process; judgement is used. Stories need to be different so that they stretch strategic thinking in different ways.

Four stories from two events

4.1 *Select two key events/flip-flops in the high uncertainty/high importance quadrant.* Although it is important to focus attention on those events at the extreme bottom right of the matrix, do not ignore important but certain flip-flops in the top right quadrant. These 'scenario context' variables can be significant drivers for important alternative futures. In making this selection ensure that the key events chosen are flip-flops. Using a key event which is a trend will not result in scenarios that are well enough differentiated. In addition, the approach works best if the two events are not causally related to each other. For example the key events of 'recession rather than boom' and 'oil prices leap rather than oil prices crash' may be seen as related, whereas the key events of 'recession rather than boom' and 'nuclear accident rather than status quo' are not. Finding two unrelated key events will ensure that the scenarios developed are richer and more diverse. It also makes the process more manageable.

4.2 *Use the two key events to form four scenarios.* Construct a 2 × 2 matrix which uses the key event opposites to form the quadrants. Each quadrant represents a scenario. In the example above, this would result in one quadrant comprising the situation of 'boom *and* nuclear accident', another 'boom *and* status quo', the third 'recession *and* nuclear accident', and the fourth 'recession *and* status quo'.

4.3 *Elaborate the stories for the quadrants.* This is achieved by building up the stories that might arise as a result of these two key events occurring together. The events on the uncertainty/importance matrix should be used to inform the building of the stories. Notes about the elaboration are then written into the quadrant to form a 'synopsis' of the scenario.

4.3.1 *Capture the story synopsis in the form of a list.* Here the characteristics are listed as 'bullet' points to form an outline of the story.

4.3.2 *Capture the material in the form of a cause map.* If the first approach has been used as a preface to exploring possible scenarios using this approach, then build on the story lines already established by clusters as a way of elaborating each of the four scenarios. Adopting a 'map like' format often demands more from the facilitator or group leader, but ensures that a more detailed picture than simply a synopsis is developed. For example, developing the story of economic boom and nuclear accident may result in a participant stating that the fear of nuclear energy may lead to plants being closed. This in turn may prompt another participant to add that there would then be unemployment in the short term, but that the demand for energy would result in more oil and coal energy being exploited, which may result in employment in the long term. This process of building from the event shows the knock-on effects of a particular scenario; it also illustrates how two events can interact and consequently increase their impact on the organization.

Polishing and extending the scenarios

5.1 *Agree upon a set of titles for the scenarios.* These **labels** will support the process as they determine what exactly is the situation portrayed in the quadrant. For example recession and a nuclear accident may be entitled 'doom and gloom'. These titles are also catchy ways of remembering the stories and may, as a result, act as quick reminders as strategic options are being evaluated.   *C152*

5.2 *Write up the stories.* The stories constructed so far are the result of causal linkages between events. If the stories are important for the organization then they must include not only the links from and between the events but also the strategic consequences for the aspirations and strategies of the organization. Although we have often presented the stories in the form of a map, it is often helpful to write the stories in the form of a traditional story which is exciting, interesting, and engaging.

5.3 *Repeat the process of story building, if necessary, and if time permits.* By extracting other pairs of key events from the quadrant of high uncertainty/high importance this process can be carried out a number of times. Where *well-differentiated* scenarios can be generated with ease, it is likely that high turbulence is the context of strategy making. Consequently the overall strategy will need to reflect this environmental context. (See below for an extension to this approach when computer support is available.)

5.4 *Building a large number of scenarios.* Participants can be separated into sub-groups to work on alternative stories. By assigning separate key events to each sub-group or asking for different interpretations for the same key events, further elaboration and development can be achieved. In either case, any recurring features can be detected and noted for further consideration.

V270   5.5 *Identify about five* **alternative, and different, strategic futures** for wider circulation. An important purpose of scenario building comes from the JOURNEY making process. Participants will change their view of possible alternative futures, less from the output of the workshops than by the process of generating the scenarios. However, scenarios also play an important role in alerting other managers in the organization to possible strategic futures that might affect their local strategic decision making. Thus, it is usually important to promulgate some selected output from scenario building episodes. As we noted in chapter C8, there

C152 is little theory to inform the choice about the **number of scenarios** to be developed. However, a 'rule-of-thumb' indicates that about five well-differentiated stories will be enough to alert managers to alternative futures and not be too much material to be read. Five stories allow:

1 a story which is not taken as so unlikely as to be ignored, but is, nevertheless, serious in its consequences. This story acts as the 'bait' to draw the reader into other stories;
2 a story which is positive;
3 a bleak story, published to 'keep managers on their toes';
4 an interesting and exciting story;
5 a story which will 'bend the mind' of the reader into considering less likely but very significant possible futures.

5.6 *Identify research projects and scenario triggers.* Each of the scenarios important for strategy making will need to be monitored so that early warning of their occurrence is possible. This demands exploring the events within the story to find

C155 indicators, or **scenario triggers**, that suggest the scenario might be about to unfold. Often these indicators are trend data rather than flip-flops, as the scenario is triggered by the build-up of a portfolio of trends and events arising together.

Rarely will any scenario unfold exactly following the stories created in scenario workshops. The monitoring exercise is seeking to detect an unfolding story which follows the same overall pattern of strategic consequences.

Using the Computer Supported Approach for Exploring Alternative Futures

This technique, whilst requiring more setup time, enables the material to be captured in a form that can be easily recalled and can act as an organizational memory. In addition, it usually results in scenarios being generated in shorter workshops. The computer model, when it follows a cause map, can be the first

C149 stage of constructing a **system dynamics computer simulation model** (see Ackermann *et al*, 1997 for an example of linking cause maps to a system dynamics model). A system dynamics model (Forrester, 1969; Meadows and Meadows, 1972) enables the complexity of events which feed back on themselves to be explored over simulated time. In particular such modelling allows strategic options to be tested. Strategic intervention in feedback loops is non-trivial, and effective options are often counter-intuitive.

The notes below must be taken as a supplement to those above, and they discuss only variances from the manual techniques.

6.1   *Generate key events/flip-flops* and *capture them directly into the computer model.* Unlike the manual technique where the events and trends are written up on Post-its, the facilitator enters them into the system directly. Alternatively, if the networked computer supported system is used, participants enter them into the model. Links may also be entered directly by the participants.

6.2   *Capture possible causal links.* The networked computer system allows participants to link events from their own workstation. In this way each participant reads the events submitted by others and will seek to link material of their own and of others. Analysis of the resulting event cause map can be done in 'real time' with the group and clusters further elaborated into stories. Feedback loops can be found and checked for validity. When significant positive feedback loops are observed they may become, in their own right, the basis of a scenario which is self-sustaining and may possibly be developed into the basic structure for a system dynamics simulation model. In some instances each cluster, or cluster of clusters, may be developed into a full story by sub-groups. Use of the networked computer system can mean that useful scenarios can be developed in 1 hour, but also deeper scenarios can be effectively developed and explored over a 2-day workshop concentrating on alternative futures.

If not constructing scenarios using cause mapping only, then:

6.3   *Analyse the emerging material into categories.* Once participants have exhausted their event entry, then the group begins to examine and analyse the results. The software provides the facility to see the same material presented in different ways concurrently, using multiple views. This is helpful as it means that the group can identify emergent categories of data (using colours and font styles, or 'sets') and explore each category independently and on a different view, without losing the data from the original fuller picture. Using sets means that each entry can be placed in any number of categories (sets). In this manner the data can be 'sliced' many different ways, offering multiple perspectives and so increasing the likelihood of spotting 'counter-intuitive' scenarios.

6.4   *Determine importance and uncertainty.* After categorizing and exploring links within categories the group can return to the full picture, temporarily 'hide' the links so that the picture is less messy, and begin locating events on the screen according to their uncertainty/importance position.

6.5   *Check linkages.* The dual approach to linkages – via the category views, and via the full picture provides an opportunity to see the events in different contexts. It is crucial to focus in on the bundle of events which are important – these are the ones which will have a direct impact on strategic intent. Sometimes very important events may be linked through events which are absolutely unimportant; when this occurs the software enables the descriptor/unimportant events to be hidden and yet the overall link retained. As we have noted elsewhere, it is common for too many linkages to be entered, so that A to B to C to D is also linked as A to C, B to D, and A to D. These multiple links need to be checked. They may be justified as different causality, but typically they are the result of summary thinking, where the link from A to D simply replicates the argumentation linking A to B to C to D. In addition, analysis, such as cluster analysis, and the ability to detect the 'heads' and 'tails', provides the basis for a more thorough check of linkages than can occur with the manual technique.

6.6   *Check for feedback loops.* We noted, above, the significance of feedback loops representing the dynamic consequences of events being linked together in a circular fashion. When these loops are legitimate (not accidental, or the result of bad coding) they may constitute an interesting scenario in their own right.

C154

6.7   *Force creative scenario/stories.* Because groups are attuned to habituated ways of thinking about the future it may be helpful to force 'original thinking' – a substitute for using a **'remarkable person'**. Divide the group into pairs and provide each pair with two key events/flip-flops randomly selected from each category (e.g. political, etc.), and in addition, two events self-selected from the material each member of the pair contributed to the full picture. Aim to allocate about 10–12 events from the full picture to each pair. Where there are well-established linkages between these events and others, these linked events are also assigned to the pair. Thus each pair may be working with about 10 events exclusive to them, and other events which overlap with those addressed by other pairs.

Developing the stories can be undertaken either manually, or with each pair using the software directly. Using the software allows the pairs to be able to enter new events or context which develops a story based on the originally provided events. They are able to do this on their private screen, by making links where appropriate and moving both the events and context around on their own screen. In this way they can examine it from several perspectives. Using the 10–12 core events as prompts it is possible to develop very rich and creative **scenarios which may also contain feedback loops**, etc.

V206

6.8   *Jointly explore and elaborate the stories.* Once each pair have completed their story(ies) the results can be copied into the computer model projecting on to the public screen. Following this, each story is examined and discussed by the group as a whole. Through this discussion possible futures are edited and elaborated so they become clear to all present, and participants have a shared understanding. This process of selecting events and developing scenarios can be repeated until there are no more key events worth considering.

6.9   *Focus on three to five stories.* Depending on the size of the group, and therefore the number of pairs, the group will have generated a minimum of 4–6 possible futures. It is then possible either to develop fully all of the possible futures or select 4–5 for further development. Given the approach used, one way of reducing the number of scenarios is to identify the areas of overlap and for the facilitator to merge two or three together to create a single more detailed scenario.

Yes But . . .

It seems to be difficult to build a story?

Using either the computer supported or manual system a number of events or flip-flops will have been identified. It is then worth asking the participants to say some more by asking questions such as 'are these related in any way?' or 'what are the consequences of these events?'. The elicitation of linkages usually arises as additional explanation and commentary about why and how the link is surfaced. Capture both the explanation (as events/argument) and the linkages. This process usually prompts other participants to add material both in terms of clarification or alternative viewpoints. As with most aspects of JOURNEY making, it is important to avoid promoting a dispute about different interpretations of an event, and more important to be inclusive. By adding the extra material it is likely that the group will find the process of linking becoming easier. If the approach being used is the computer supported mode then using different styles to identify the key events in contrast to the elaborating text helps clarify and categorize the material. In addition to linking the events/themes themselves, encourage participants to link the end points (heads) of the stories to the mandates or goal system of the organization to further build the story and link it to the organization's strategic intent.

How do I get the group away from trend based material and into key events/flip-flops?

Do not worry unduly about the material on first entry. The review process which checks the nature of the material is itself helpful and makes an important contribution to the journey. When facilitating a computer supported workshop it is, therefore, important to enter events on the screen as they are stated rather than policing at that time. Remember not to move too quickly to deleting trend data; rather ask whether it has been noted because the trend is expected to reach a critical point – if so, edit the event description so that it is expressed as a flip-flop.

Further Commentary on Exploring Alternative Futures

As with the computer supported workshops, it is possible to use the network computer supported facility. Once again the 'gather' tool provides a fast and efficient means of generating and capturing, in parallel, the events and links. It will also allow participants to enter their statements anonymously, possibly encouraging wider participation. However, because scenarios are not directly related to strategic action and have less personal implications, anonymity is generally less significant for this part of journey making. The resultant events/themes are then displayed on the main screen and worked on in the manner of guideline 6.3. This ability to switch between the network computer supported mode of operating and a facilitator operated mode resembles that discussed in chapter P3.

On many occasions the management team has been concerned about their ability to identify all of the events which might affect their strategic future. They have, quite properly, been wary of their own blinkered and bounded vision. In these circumstances they have sought out ways in which their own scenarios can be challenged by others outside of the organization. Two common ways of creating this challenge have been (i) to use 'experts' from within the organization – research staff, outlier thinkers, visiting staff; and (ii) to gather together a **group of external experts** and 'remarkable people'. In each case the group become participants working together in exactly the same manner as manager teams and using the same procedures discussed above. However, it will be particularly important to ensure that participants are working with respect to the aspirations of the organization. It is, therefore, most important that a version of the draft strategy, mission statement, and statement of strategic intent is clearly displayed throughout the workshop. Typically, only one senior manager of the organization will be present, to ensure no 'bounding' of the thinking of the experts. Their role is that of host. Often this host will be the Chief Executive who will also act as one of the facilitators of the event. The outcome from the workshop is then used to challenge the work already undertaken by internal managers. It is important that these scenarios are generated after those of the managers so that there is ownership of the process and of one set of scenarios. On several occasions the scenario event for

V267

external experts has invited important stakeholder players to be participants so that the occasion can be used as a part of a stakeholder management strategy.

The final stage is to re-examine the strategic options available to the organization against the scenarios and determine which of the options can perform in all, or nearly all of the possible futures. This process usually generates further development of the options as well as the generation of new options.

MANAGING PROCESS: DESIGNING INTERVENTIONS AND FACILITATING GROUPS

Introduction

Good facilitation of groups is crucial to successful JOURNEY making, regardless of whether the journey is to be facilitated by a manager from within the organization tasked with facilitation, by a senior manager who is also a participant, by a professional internal facilitator, or by an external facilitator consultant. All are possible within the context of the methods introduced in this book. Care in facilitation has to be taken when using the manual or computer based group decision support systems (GDSS) to increase the level of participation (McGoff and Ambrose, 1991; Phillips and Phillips, 1993). Paying attention to process issues is even more important when working on messy, complex qualitative problems/issues relating to strategy making and delivery (Bostrom et al, 1993).

We have argued in this book that it may be desirable to include not only the management team in the strategy development process but also strategic planning specialists, other senior managers, junior managers and experts. This is done for reasons of collecting a richer range of knowledge and wisdom, increasing **creativity**, and seeking greater **ownership and commitment**. If increased partici- *C58 C70: C56* pation is to be successful, rather than debilitating, then providing a means to increase the process gains whilst minimizing the process losses (Huber, 1982) is paramount. Groups initially are composed of individuals who have diverse private views and insights regarding the issues being considered. If the group work goes well, each participant will contribute usefully and feel that they have done so. Participants' contributions will spark off new statements, and through this process powerful new (shared) insights can be created.

The role of the facilitator is often seen as synonymous with that of a consultant or interventionist (Fordyce and Weil, 1971) 'acting in order to help it [the client] to explore its everyday conduct and to assist it in defining how it wishes to change and how it will go about making the change'. Bostrom et al (1993) note that 'facilitation is the dynamic process that involves managing the relationships between people, tasks and technology, as well as structuring tasks and contributing to the effective accomplishment of the meeting's outcome'. Thus, to gain the most from the group it is essential to attend to both process and content issues (Eden, 1990c). There is an intimate relationship between process management – understanding power, politics, and personalities – and content management – capturing, structuring, and analysing.

While there are many guides to facilitation, each providing practical suggestions and tips, this chapter will focus on the issues we consider to be most important when dealing with JOURNEY making. Our interpretation of the role of facilitator/ consultant is clearly informed by our view of the nature of organizations. As we have indicated in the first part of the book, we see organizations as dynamic political enterprises rather than systems. Groups and individuals shape the nature of the enterprise and so strategy is enacted by managers not analysts. Strategy making and delivery is a social activity and requires those with power to undertake a *journey* of strategic change. Therefore facilitation must take into account theory about personal psychology, occupational psychology, group dynamics, social psychology, decision making (particularly strategic decision making), and organizational behaviour. It is informed by, and informs, the capturing and development of wisdom, as well as playing a key role in determining political feasibility. Finally, facilitation also plays an important role in the delivery of strategy.

This section of the chapter focuses on the pre-workshop stage, one that is considered to be as important as the actual workshop itself (Ackermann, 1996; Bostrom *et al*, 1993). Consequently, process management issues including getting started, choosing participants, getting the 'stage management' right, deciding upon the location for a workshop, and working with more than one facilitator will be considered. The following section discusses managing the workshops themselves, and concentrating on getting the balance right between the management of process and the management of content. Most of the material presented in this chapter relates to all of the different methods proposed for capturing and developing assumptions (oval mapping, computer supported workshops, scenario development, and stakeholder analysis and management). Finally, it should be noted that the term client is used for the person initiating, directing, and implementing the strategy journey. This role is one of several in the strategy process (including sponsor, client, key actors, partners, participants, etc. – referred to more fully in chapter P9).

Guidelines for the Management of Process, the Design of Interventions, and the Facilitation of Groups

V212   *Getting started on a JOURNEY*

C55 V224   It is our experience that the first few meetings with the client can be significant for both client and facilitator. Initial meetings demonstrate professionalism, **set expectations, and build trust** and credibility. This section therefore deals with the initial introduction to the strategy process, matching the requirements of the client with the skills of the facilitator, familiarizing the facilitator with the organizational context (if necessary), before moving on to exploring the various design issues surrounding the intervention. The guidelines are based on the assumption that the client is keen on undertaking a strategy development process, and incorporating at least some participative methods for achieving it. However, it should be noted that in many cases, whilst clients are keen on developing the organization's strategy, they are less clear about what it may involve and how it may unfold. As such, the guidelines may act not only as a check list for building relationships but also assist the client when thinking the process through, a process that will act as a continuous learning cycle.

1.1   *Provide the client with a sense of control*

1.1.1 *Manage their role.* Often clients are unsure about what a strategy development process may encompass, what is required of them, and how it might unfold. They may feel uncertain about the direction being suggested and may be concerned that the facilitator will take control away from them. As they may not voice their concerns, finding ways to cue them into the nature of the unfolding process and clarifying that they will remain in control, is important. For example, clients may have only briefly considered issues such as who should participate, and what are the potential dangers and benefits of different levels of involvement. Spending time discussing these issues will help them increase their understanding of the process, and avoid their experiencing too many surprises during any ensuing workshops. Given the nature of some of the techniques to be used, it is worth being clear that some of their meeting skills may be less potent than usual. The facilitator must take the opportunity to demonstrate their worldliness about management.

1.1.2 *Create an agenda together.* Involving the client directly in designing workshop agendas helps them retain a sense of control. They will be able to envisage how the workshop may unfold in advance of the actual event and therefore feel more comfortable about the process.

1.2 *Do not hide potential dangers of participative methods.* Although raising the possibility of dangers appears counterintuitive, addressing them with the client provides him or her with a deeper insight into the process. They can begin to mentally prepare themselves for the event, imagining the types of issues they might encounter. Facilitator and client doing this jointly can help develop trust and bonding between them.

1.2.1 *Encourage the client to be 'human' during the workshop.* When clients feel sufficiently confident, we have found that by encouraging them to confess a lack of knowledge, reveal uncertainty, and so on, other participants are prompted to contribute more easily.

1.2.2 *Accept that past decisions will be criticized.* Defensive behaviour on the part of the client can undermine a good workshop. If the client sets an example by being reflective, rather than defensive, then others are more likely to follow. However, seeking to learn from previous decisions can often be a bruising experience.

1.2.3 *Check the client's intention to implement the resultant actions.* Whilst in many circumstances workshops are clearly billed as a chance to *influence* direction (as part of the ongoing process) rather than make decisions, ensuring that some actions result from the workshop(s) will signal that listening is taking place. Confirming with the client that *something* will happen, helps determine the client's level of commitment as well as avoid later difficulties. In addition, acting on relatively trivial issues and thus providing 'quick wins', can motivate staff and make them feel positive towards the future strategy rather than cynical. Consequently, warning the client that where possible they should watch for issues that can be dealt with straight after a workshop and acknowledged as such during their closing remarks will pay dividends.

1.2.4 *Watch for difficult issues that may emerge.* When using participatory methods which encourage participants to contribute there is a danger that messy, intractable issues may emerge that the client would prefer not to address at all. It is better not to involve participants at all than involve them and ignore obviously important issues. Typically a client is surprised about some of the issues which emerge, and shocked at the emotion behind them. These issues cannot be swept away easily; having once surfaced in a workshop arena they must be dealt with in some way, or else the whole process will fall into disrepute. Ensuring all the elements of **procedural justice** is fundamental to strategic change. *Warn the client.*

C53

1.3 *Provide information about the benefits and losses from increased participation.* Increased participation does not mean only increasing the number of people participating, but also the manner of the participation. Most clients have a fairly clear idea of at least some of the benefits. The shorthand version of benefits include (i) increasing ownership, (ii) increasing the general level of understanding of the organization – organizational learning, and (iii) gaining a wide range of knowledge and expertise to increase the robustness of the strategy.

1.4 *Ensure a match between task, facilitator skill, and the organizational setting.* Careful listening to the client during initial meetings will provide an initial basis for understanding the organization, its culture and the external environment within which it operates. The design of the journey is contingent on these factors, as is the nature of the strategy (see chapter C1). For example, in the NHS the **culture of the organization** meant that the participants were all apprehensive about group working and openly discussing strategy. Consequently, the design necessarily involved individual interviews in order to capture wisdom. Some of the factors to consider in choosing methods are provided below, but further details are provided in the chapters dealing with the methods in detail. In particular we consider, in brief, their relative merits as methods to use when trying to get a strategy journey off the ground.

V213

1.4.1 *Use of interviews and cognitive mapping (chapter P1).* Interviews are useful when the organizational members are not used to being consulted and **may not be open and forthcoming**. They may act as a cathartic experience, helping participants express and understand better their own thinking and views. If there are areas of internal conflict, interviews may be necessary, although the networked computer support system may be an alternative in these circumstances.

V195

Alternatively, when the other members of the management team are hesitant about strategy development, or about an approach which involves them rather than a staff function, it is sometimes possible to get them to agree to brief interviews as an initial commitment. Good interviews, using cognitive maps, most often result in a half-day or 1-day workshop simply to satisfy curiosity about the merged map. This process will help the client gain involvement from the management team.

1.4.2 *Running an oval mapping (OMT) workshop (chapter P2).* This is a fast and cheap way, compared with interviews, of eliciting the views from a number of participants. Other benefits include opportunities for **team building** and organizational learning.

V194

1.4.3 *Using computer supported workshops (chapter P3).* Predominantly used after oval mapping or interviews. The *networked* computer support system can provide an alternative to oval mapping and as a quick 1–2-hour starter workshop with full participant involvement. For example, a half-day strategic intent workshop agreeing distinctive competencies and goal systems is possible as a way of getting started.

1.4.4 *Stakeholder management workshops (chapter P4).* These help by providing an external viewpoint of the organization, and work to build relationships between the organization and some of its stakeholders. This can be aided by involving a selected group of them in a collaborative process which enables them to learn more about the organization itself.

1.4.5 *Developing alternative futures (chapter P4).* Developing a set of possible scenarios against which the strategy and associated strategic programmes are examined can involve participants from both within and without the organization (with selected stakeholders or experts). Typically an exploration of alternative futures suggests new strategic options as well as helping to increase the robustness of the strategy. Nevertheless, it is sometimes difficult for a management team to see the point of scenario development until other parts of the strategy begin to unfold. Like 'brainstorming' workshops, they can go down in the organizational memory as an event which 'was enjoyable, but nothing much came from it'.

1.5 *Negotiate the design for the strategy making process.* Once the facilitator has begun to conceptualize how the organization operates, and to develop an initial understanding of what the client wants, a negotiation process can then take place. The negotiation seeks to agree a process which accounts for client needs but also recognizes the expertise and skills of the facilitator (Eden and Sims, 1979). The proposal is continuously adapted with the client in relation to its applicability to the organization and to the needs of the client – which may not be the same.

1.5.1 *Balance providing a complete overview of the journey with providing a rewarding first stage.* Clients are often uncertain about what the entire process involves and, at the beginning, find it difficult to grasp all the concepts (Yeates, 1996). Given that the overall design of the journey can rarely be established until many of the contingencies begin to surface (see chapter C1), there is a danger of proposing something which is too all-encompassing. Until JOURNEY making is experienced, many managers can find it difficult to appreciate that process outcomes are as important as content outcomes for successful strategic change. Gaining some initial experience of the type of approach presented in this book can make negotiating an overall design both easier and more perceptive.

This requirement for flexibility and gaining experience is counter to the wish of many managers for a clear understanding of the total process (see Bryson, 1995:24–25 for an example of a step-by-step design presented to the client at the beginning of a project). It is therefore most important that early episodes in the journey have a completeness of their own and do not require a **commitment beyond the first workshop**. Each of the early steps must, therefore, provide clear added-value so that the journey can be stopped without these experiences being wasteful. At the same time, the early steps must provide a solid foundation for a continuing process.

V195

1.6 *Gain familiarity with the organization.* Although this is particularly the case for external consultants/facilitators, it is also important for internal facilitators, particularly those from different departments, divisions, or sections. Often internal facilitators make more serious mistakes because of their presumption of knowledge than a 'naive' external facilitator. If a facilitator devotes time to detecting emergent strategizing through an exploration of structures, procedures, informal and formal reward systems, then a degree of familiarity will be gained.

1.6.1 *Become familiar with the jargon.* Acronyms abound in all organizations. Without some basic knowledge of them a strategy workshop can become frustrating for participants where they waste time explaining their own jargon. However, the nature of language and organizational scripts can also give clues to emergent strategizing. Moreover, occasionally attempts by the facilitator to understand local jargon may help participants who are not familiar with the terms but cannot own up to this.

1.6.2 *Understand the management style of the client.* The tension between an autocratic management style and a wish to use participative methods to ensure a better job of strategy making can be difficult for the client and facilitator. Intellectually recognizing the pay-off from JOURNEY making does not mean that the client as a participant can play out the role dictated by the intellectual appreciation. Other participants will be more familiar with the 'everyday' autocracy than the 'new style'. It is important to remember that participative methods are rarely intended to change a 'managerialist' culture to a cooperative or consensus culture. The approaches presented in this book are often used manipulatively, and designed to increase the power of the powerful.

Group issues

C87 2.1 *Establish **membership of workshop groups**.* Choosing who and how many organizational members to involve in any one workshop is an important task to be addressed with the client. It will help in building the client relationship and will

C51 help the client to understand the process. We have argued before that a **minimum level of participation** for strategy making must be the management team. This may be the team of people running the organization, the division, the department, the community pressure group, the collaborative, or whatever entity the strategy is expected to work for. This decision making group of *client and key actors*, is likely to determine the involvement of others as the journey unfolds. As decisions are made about further involvement, it is helpful to use the check list of roles discussed in 2.1.3 below. For the type of strategy workshops proposed in this book, a group size of 5–12 persons is effective. Going beyond 12 participants will usually involve more facilitators and the extensive use of sub-groups.

V245 V249 V268 2.1.1 *Consider **group size** in relation to the type of participants and invisible outcomes.* Size will be dependent on two aspects: the type of group and the type of task. Groups of highly interactive individuals who have worked together previously and are of equal status – peer groups – work well with about 6–8 members. Here team building may be of paramount importance. In these cases the use of computer support increases productivity, enables individuals to contribute fully to the discussion, and make good use of their air-time. In contrast those groups containing members who have little experience of working together before (sometimes they may not have met each other), and which involve different status members, may find it appropriate to work in larger groups where computer support is difficult. Here organizational learning rather than team building may be an important 'invisible' outcome (Friend and Hickling, 1987:103).

2.1.2 *Consider size in relation to the task*. For groups engaged in a decision making activity where participants will be responsible for agreed actions and accountable, involving about 6–8 participants is optimal. Some research suggests that groups working on product/problem solving tasks can involve more participants than those dealing with strategy development (Ackermann, 1991). When using the OMT, groups may be composed of up to 12 participants before the process becomes unwieldy. Computer supported groups may need to be smaller to give clear visibility of the public screen.

2.1.3 *Account for likely **roles of participants***. This is relevant to both group and sub-group composition. One means of achieving this is to work with the client on 'pen portraits' of the participants, providing age, career history, internal 'trading agreements' with other participants, team role profiles (Belbin, 1981) if known, and personality traits. We have found the following role typology helpful in working with clients. The roles are not mutually exclusive:

C35 C47 C57 V224 V233 V275

- *cynics*, who have seen it all before and delight in rubbishing it;
- *saboteurs*, who play the role of the cynic but in a pro-active manner, often deliberately feeding misinformation, subtly 'working to rule';
- *opinion formers*, who can promulgate a view that becomes accepted by others in the organization;
- *anticipated winners*, who believe, rightly or wrongly, that the intervention will work for their personal benefit or the benefit of their department;
- *anticipated losers*, who believe, rightly or wrongly, that the consequences of the intervention will be to their disadvantage; they are also likely to be saboteurs;
- *ideas generators*, similar to the Belbin's 'plant', able to think creatively;
- *wait & sees*, who will watch how things unfold before deciding whether to support, be indifferent, or sabotage;
- *experts*, about stakeholders (where role plays are conceived), or the environment (for scenario planning), or simply internal expertise about procedures, research opportunities, etc. (Ackermann, 1992).

Thinking about these possible roles is important when considering that enthusiastic participants can become irritated with the group design and composition. Where the facilitator appears not to have considered 'ensuring that all participants are comfortable with the process and willing to commit themselves to participating' or 'including participants who are prepared to work hard and change their views when necessary', then frustration may surface to the detriment of the intervention.

Considering sub-group composition is also important. It is usually unhelpful for a manager to be with their own staff. However, it may be useful to create sub-groups to cement coalitions, or ensure they do not form, or to generate organizational learning by combining, for example, headquarters staff with field staff.

2.1.4 *Manage different levels of familiarity.* For participants involved in a series of workshops, ensuring consistent membership is seen as an advantage by participants. This avoids the need to revisit issues to catch up on sessions missed. However, mixing participants may be important for the client, and for content by encouraging a diversity of views.

V219 V223 V226 *Stage management*
V239

Paying attention to the 'stage management' of a workshop is a necessary condition for success. Some aspects of stage management may appear to be 'trivial', but their ability to *increase the probability of success* should not be underestimated. Getting stage management wrong can have a disastrous impact on an otherwise well-designed workshop. Remember Murphy's law: 'if anything can go wrong, it will'!

V219 V244 3.1 *Consider holding the workshop **away from the office** if possible.* In North America this type of workshop is often called a 'retreat' because the event constitutes a retreat from the everyday office routine. Some of the factors that should influence location are:

3.1.1 *Avoid constant interruptions from phone calls, faxes, or messages.* Constant distractions of the daily firefighting do not permit effective work on strategy. In some organizations reminders can become a competition for showing who is the busiest manager. Therefore, try to stop participants from disappearing to make phone calls, sorting out problems (particularly at breaks), or being interrupted by secretaries. Ask for mobile phones to be switched off, or placed in unobtainable mode.

3.1.2 *Provide an obviously different milieu.* This signifies that the task being addressed is different from the day-to-day firefighting of the office, even though it is expected to impact upon it and vice-versa – after all, fire-fighting styles and thinking in action are the basis of emergent strategizing.

3.1.3 *Consider providing breakfast/coffee to open the workshop.* Regardless of whether the meeting is at the office or off site, participants will arrive at different times, including being late. Waiting for others demoralizes and frustrates both the participants who have managed to arrive on time, and the facilitator and client. An effective way of reducing the possibility of too much waiting is to arrange an approximate start time for participants to chat with colleagues, grab a cup of coffee or breakfast, and 'zone' in to the day.

V267 3.2 *Pay attention to **room design** and climate.* Many clients do not appreciate, initially, the importance of this requirement, as it can appear fussy and unnecessary. As the consultant–client relationship develops, this requirement will become less of an issue and the client will begin to understand the rationale behind good design. Ignoring room design can result in unnecessary problems needing to be resolved during the workshop. The guidelines listed below apply in general. Each particular type of workshop, however, will have additional requirements relating to the specific tools/materials.

3.2.1 *Arrange for an appropriate level of illumination.* Sitting in a darkened room, or one using artificial light, can often have an exhausting effect on the group. Use computer projection facilities that can be employed in natural daylight. If these requirements cannot be satisfied then find a breakout room with natural light that will help relax tired eyes and brains.

3.2.2 *Arrange for mental and physical refreshment* (Eden, 1990b). In terms of physical refreshment, if possible provide an unlimited, or regular, supply of coffee, tea, juice, fruit, and water. Schedule regular comfort breaks and keep the quantity of lunch to modest proportions and length. Mental refreshment can be achieved by switching between **different modes of** **working** – for example, moving from manual methods to computer support, from facilitator driven computer support to use of the networked system, and changing facilitators when possible. *C61*

3.2.3 *Ensure sufficient and appropriate wall space is available* Try to ensure that it is not crowded with pictures or other impediments. This is necessary for all of the methods we discuss. Regardless of whether a manual technique or computer support is being adopted, effort to capture material on flip-charts which can be moved around the walls easily will provide a sense of progress. Thus, avoid walls that are panelled, or hotels that do not allow the use of 'Blu-Tack', or have wood chip wallpaper.

3.2.4 *Ensure there is appropriate seating.* This means finding chairs that are comfortable enough to sit in for a whole day but not so comfy that participants are inclined to take a quick nap! When choosing the room, pick a room where there is plenty of space so that people won't be cramped, and that enables all participants to see the screen/wall clearly. To allow the layout of the room to be changed easily and quickly, we rarely use tables. Participants will need to be able to be seated together and standing/mobile together. This also means that the social dynamics can be changed when necessary. An open, and informal, circle of seats is usually best, with primary visual aids at the open end of the circle ensuring ease of readability for everyone. Ensure there can be eye contact among all participants. (Hickling (1990) discusses the architecture of group support, with suggestions about different types of design for different purposes.)

3.2.5 *Plan for technology.* Keep a space for someone to capture (on a computer) the output of the workshop. Set up the equipment in advance and test visibility given the ambient lighting and seating arrangement.

3.2.6 *Take lunch outside the meeting room.* When possible arrange for a separate private lunch room, or a corner of the restaurant to promote continued social bonding.

3.3 *Manage the trivia of facilitation.* This section straddles both the setup of workshops and the workshops themselves.

3.3.1 *Do not write in block capitals.* Use a mixture of upper and lowercase, the 'descendants' (e.g. tail of a 'g' or 'y') and ascendants (e.g. verticals of 'b' or 'h') help fast reading of otherwise illegible writing. It is also faster to write in lower case.

3.3.2 *Use water-based flip-chart pens.* Permanent marker pens leak through flip-chart paper to the wall beneath – expensive charges from the hotel ensue! Also, water-based pens write with fewer scratching noises.

3.3.3 *Write on flip-charts from the elbow and the shoulder rather than the wrist.* This makes it easier to keep writing horizontal and readable.

3.3.4   *Create emergency backup plans*. Particularly when working with technology, having a number of alternative methods/techniques and their associated materials available will reduce facilitator stress levels. Maintain a supply of pens, Post-its, and preferencing self-adhesive 'spots'. It is rare for a workshop to go exactly as planned. Having the necessary equipment to use alternative techniques allows greater flexibility.

V225   3.4   *Carefully construct the content of the 'calling note'*. Given the above issues, it becomes important to construct carefully the memorandum inviting participants to a workshop. This must, obviously, clearly state the purpose, venue, and timing of the event and provide no more than a provisional agenda. However, for many organizations, this is the first time participative methods may have been adopted. Thus, it is helpful to suggest that participants are not required to do much, if any, preparatory work – it is their wisdom which is required. The background to the use of facilitation is sometimes a useful addition. Also, suggesting participants wear informal clothing rather than a business suit will set the scene for a *workshop* rather than formal meeting.

Working with two facilitators

Two facilitators can be employed effectively in any of the techniques suggested in this book. Using two facilitators, cognitive mapping interviews can be expedited by conducting them in parallel and utilizing the gap between interviews to share maps and work on a merged map. Oval mapping workshops can benefit from two facilitators (as noted in chapter P2 and below), especially when larger groups are involved. The picture-on-the-wall can be captured into a computer model by one facilitator while the other works with the group. Computer supported workshops benefit from one facilitator being used for managing the process whilst the other searches the computer model for relevant material, makes the necessary changes, undertakes analysis, and generally manages content. However, there are some difficulties as described below.

V218   4.1   *Keep in step*. Often two facilitators may diverge when there is a need to divert from original plans. Ensuring one facilitator is legitimized as lead facilitator may alleviate this problem. This requirement is often more problematic when the facilitators are both experienced and are used to taking the lead role. The more frequently facilitators work together using the same methods then the more likely it is that a wide repertoire of alternative scripts can be called into play quickly – 'I think we should shift to what we did for xyz at this point . . .' (Andersen and Richardson, 1997).

C46 V194 V210   4.2   *Capitalize on being able to manage both **process** and **content***. Allocating the
V242   roles so that one facilitator focuses predominantly on the process issues and the other on the content issues can increase the workshop's effectiveness. In this manner the facilitator managing process is able to ensure conflict is minimized, participants are able to contribute, and can monitor the client's reaction. Content management is informed by having a detailed knowledge of the computer model and being able to use the content effectively. The content facilitator will focus on capturing and structuring material, and interacting with the group when aspects of the content appear to have direct relevance to the unfolding process. The ability to focus on one role, whilst being aware and occasionally contributing to the other, is

dependent on both facilitators having a good working knowledge of the content and of the processes of facilitation.

4.3 *Work with one external and one **internal facilitator**.* This combination is   V257
particularly powerful when supporting strategy making. Having someone in the organization familiar with the process and resultant computer models, and yet close to the day-to-day discussions in the organization, brings insider knowledge alongside external professional help. Working with an internal participant, often a 'partner', is a valuable means of transferring skills from the consultant to the organization to ensure a greater chance of implementation is achieved.

4.3.1 *Advise the internal facilitator to avoid contributing to content, unless invited.* Internal facilitators often find this very difficult, as the issues being addressed sometimes directly relate to them and they may have strong views. However, if they do start to contribute then their position as a facilitator is undermined and participants will either feel confused as to their role, or no longer treat them as a facilitator.

Yes But . . .

How do I learn facilitation?

Practice and apprenticeship work best. Start with a small low risk project that might be on a small issue within your department or for a charity/community group that you belong to (e.g. drama club). Reading will provide some guidelines but watching others manage workshops will provide better clues. It is worth noting, however, that there are different styles as well as techniques and what will work for one person may not for another. Good introductory reading includes Margerison (1988), Schein (1988) and Schwarz (1994). It is also now possible to talk with other facilitators via the Internet on GRP-FACL (listserv@cnsibm.albany.edu).

What if I am an internal facilitator – how do I manage people senior to me?

It is probably worth talking with the person wishing to embark upon the journey – the client. Explain your concerns and if possible get them, when introducing process to the group, to set clear expectations and ground rules. Try not to treat them any differently from others during the workshop – doing so would not only affect other participants but it might also make them feel uncomfortable. Remember they might also be slightly apprehensive if a new method is being used.

What do I do when I can't manage both process and content at the same time?

Ask the group for help; after all, it is in their best interest. Where a statement is made that you don't manage to capture ask for the proponent to reiterate or if possible write it up. Use a manual technique such as OMT, particularly if you don't feel that you are able to manipulate the software and type fast enough to keep up with the contribution rate. It is worth making sure, however, that you don't just concentrate on one aspect to the detriment of another. If the focus is on content to the detriment of process, the outcome may not be 'owned' by the group or it may be dominated by one or two participants. Concentrating on process may result in the group becoming frustrated with the lack of progress being made. Consider using the review of sections to ensure all is captured and all are happy. Sometimes using the networked computer system can make the demands of process management more structured and can force participants to do more of the content management through their own workstations.

Managing the Intervention

Introduction

This section builds on the above and presumes that adequate preparation has been made for the workshop. However, before discussing managing a workshop, it is worth noting that all facilitators feel some degree of apprehension immediately prior to strategy workshops. Strategy workshops are, by their very nature, unpredictable in many respects. Many facilitators argue that some nervousness is helpful because it enhances performance. A useful method for handling this pre-workshop stage, and building self-confidence, is to visualize the process by considering alternative scenarios of how the workshop might unfold. This process provides a form of 'mental rehearsal' of the event and should encompass emotional as well as descriptive aspects (Sims, 1987). While mentally demanding, this pays off, in particular by teasing out difficulties: for example, trying too much in the time available. Always think through how you would respond to the programme of tasks and to the process if it were to be for you and your own organization and colleagues. Clients are also likely to be anxious, and putting aside time to reassure them will do much in terms of building relationships. Your own efforts at mental rehearsal will help you talk through the events with the client, including what could go awry, and the way such difficulties may be resolved.

Although workshops can be, in principle, of any length, the suggestions made below are based on a 1-day workshop. Other options we have discussed elsewhere in this book include the following.

1   *A half-day workshop*. Typically this provides 4–5 hours of work on site. This length of workshop is best suited to the beginning of strategy making projects.

At the beginning, when the client and other managers are hesitant about the approaches being taken, this length of workshop represents a low risk, low investment, route for gaining some initial experience and credibility. We have often used a **1-day workshop** to do each of: issue surfacing, drafting a goal system, some stakeholder analysis and alternative futures construction, and developing draft strategies. This gives the client group a quick draft strategy, a sense of the methods, and some view on strategy making as JOURNEY making. In half a day this is not possible and so some particular tasks must be identified. Typically, issue surfacing to give a draft goal system and initial set of strategic issues and options is realistic. An alternative, as we describe in chapter P3, is developing a first draft of the strategic intent through the development of a business model or livelihood scheme.

C103 V224 V239

Towards the end of the journey a management team may be meeting regularly, and on site, to develop action programmes, review progress on strategies, and refine existing strategies. When regular workshops become a routine part of the strategic management of the organization, it is not appropriate that they eat into operational tasks and other commitments too much. Gathering a management team together for an on-site half-day workshop is a practical proposition. It minimizes costs and disruption but also ensures that the energy levels remain high.

2   **2-day workshop**. This is a better choice for decision making teams in contrast to   *V210 V223*
a workshop involving 'participants' whose role is to *influence* strategy. At some stages of the journey the management team need to have enough time to absorb the content of the models they are working with. An overnight stay means there is time for the material to be absorbed and be revisited the next day. In addition, when team building and developing **emotional commitment**   *C58*
are important invisible outcomes, 2 days working together on JOURNEY making is effective. Two days allows the group to be able to examine the material in depth before evaluating it and negotiating an agreed strategic intent.

3   *1½-day workshop*. A compromise between a 1-day workshop and the 2-day workshop. Used as a way of getting an evening session by completing one full-day workshop with a following morning session. The evening can be used deliberately as a chance to socialize and discuss progress.

This chapter breaks down the workshops into three stages (Ackermann, 1996; Bostrom *et al*, 1993; Phillips and Phillips, 1993) – scene setting, exploration and development, and closure. The exploration and development stage is further divided into two sections; the first encompasses all types of workshop and the second focuses exclusively on computer supported workshops. A sample design for a 2-day workshop is shown as an appendix to this chapter. The appendix shows the 'official' version which is delivered to participants, but also notes the visible and invisible objectives for each stage of the workshop, and the facilitator notes.

Scene setting

It is important to get off to a good start. Phillips and Phillips (1993) note that the first 10 minutes can have a fundamental effect on the group's performance throughout the remainder of the meeting. The facilitator's apprehensions about the open nature of a workshop are likely to be shared by the team. As we have discussed earlier (chapters P1, P2, P3, and P4), begin by outlining the nature of the process. Explain what the goals are, the agenda and process, what will happen to any outcomes, and the key role expectations for both the facilitator and the participants. This is part of the warming-up and confidence building process. It also invites them to *share the responsibility for the conduct of the event*, rather like a group of mountaineers undertaking a climb together. Where there has been a chance to interview and brief people beforehand, this will have helped reduce misapprehensions before the workshop.

Over-expectation and under-expectation can unbalance a workshop. Giving a feel for the middle ground is a crucial skill in scene setting. One method is to use the interviewing process to uncover expectations and, where necessary, work towards realigning them with what can be realistically achieved in a workshop. The facilitator also must *avoid having misplaced (usually too ambitious) expectations,* and be able to judge how far teamwork, during the workshop, is going to be possible. While participants may initially feel stimulated by high expectations they will realize sooner or later that the expectations are not going to be realized, and consequently are likely to become de-motivated. Alternatively, setting unrealistic expectations could result in participants taking a very cynical view of the proceedings, as they are aware that the expectations are unreachable.

All of the methods discussed in this book may present different ways of working from those normally experienced in an organization, and providing some explanation of them is important. This part of scene setting is even more important when working with computer support. Participants may be threatened by an array of computer equipment, and may suppose that their own computing skills will be displayed in public as less than adequate.

1.1   *Present the day in a calm and relaxed manner.* By introducing the workshop in this manner participants will feel more reassured and an air of confident competence will be assumed.

1.1.1   *Remain seated during the introduction.* This avoids teacher/student role setting. However, ensure participants can maintain easy eye contact with the facilitator.

1.1.2   *Speak at a modulated pace.* Speaking at a moderate speed, and calmly, will relieve, to some extent, the nervous excitement of participants. Avoiding the temptation, when working with a difficult group or a very senior group, to 'get on with the workshop' may also reduce the likelihood of the introduction being hurried and not covering all of the necessary points.

1.1.3   *Incorporate humour.* Humour is a powerful means of relaxing people (both participants and facilitator)! Some consideration of the type of humour used is important. Inappropriate humour is worse than no humour. A joke at the expense of the facilitator is usually safe.

1.1.4   *Develop a script.* Without a written cue-sheet, important points may be missed; however, avoid reading directly from it.

1.2   *Reduce role uncertainty and nervousness.* As noted above, some participants often experience some sense of role ambiguity when attending a workshop, particularly if it is off site.

1.2.1   *Explain what will occur during the day.* Introduce an agenda verbally and subsequently display it on a flip-chart for all to refer to as the workshop unfolds.

1.2.2   *Clarify the role of the equipment.* Explain *the purpose* of the equipment whether it is a wall of flip-chart paper, or a computer plus projection equipment, or an array of computers.

1.2.3   *Describe to participants what will happen to their efforts.* Explain the next steps and the status of the resultant data and suggestions/outcomes that arise from the workshop. Explain how this workshop fits into a total process.

1.3   *Clarify the roles of participants.* It is important to have determined, in advance, participants' familiarity with one another and with the processes to be used. For those who have not worked together before, it will be important to have each participant introduce themselves, stating which department they come from, their job, etc. Groups new to the process will require a thorough introduction, not just to the procedures to be used, but also a brief explanation of the reasons for using them. Sometimes the majority of participants are familiar with the processes, with only one or two new to JOURNEY making. Here a balance must be made, providing enough explanation for the new participants to grasp the concepts whilst not boring or frustrating the others wishing to get on. Experienced participants can start a workshop with a significant advantage over others, which they may deliberately exploit to their advantage and to the detriment of the effectiveness of the workshop. To avoid this it may be necessary to provide special help, in the early stages, to those new to the processes.

1.3.1   *State the **purpose of the workshop***. For example, inform participants about   *V245*
whether the intention of the meeting is to contribute statements in order to *influence* the direction of strategy or to *decide* about strategy.

1.3.2   *Match role to task*. Different tasks may require participants to take on different roles. For example, during an oval mapping workshop, participants are asked to contribute all of *their* views, no matter how tentative or badly expressed, whereas a 'role-think' exercise requires them to visualize themselves as a different person or organizational member.

1.3.3   *Legitimize alternative viewpoints*. Encourage different perspectives on the issues that arise. Note that the participants are from different backgrounds, experience, and departments and so they will each have personal wisdom to contribute that is different from that of others.

1.4   *Establish the ground rules*. These are the 'rules' of conduct that will be expected of participants. Each method has ground rules specific to it: for example, oval mapping relies on participants not removing one another's ovals from the wall picture, placing statements on the wall rather than stockpiling them, and avoiding 'I agree, I don't agree' type comments. Nevertheless, there are some that are common to all of the methods:

1.4.1   *Encourage mutual respect for each other's statements*. This is not a plea for participants to agree. It is a plea for attention to be given to others' experiences and wisdom as valid contributions. One way to explain this is to ask participants to 'use soft words and hard arguments' – to be **constructive** without being too emotional and to contribute arguments   *C69*
rather than evaluations. Encourage the use of 'yes, and . . .' rather than 'yes, but . . .'.

1.4.2   *Use interdependence, and build on it*. Focus on the synergy and creativity of group working.

1.4.3   *Keep an open mind*. Encourage participants to look for new ways of understanding issues, of developing new options rather than fighting over old options. Prompt them into making leaps of understanding. By using the **equivocality** implicit within the mapping technique, prompt   *C50 C67*
participants to work towards negotiating a common view (Fisher and Ury, 1982).

Do not forget to transmit other important information relating to hygiene factors, such as time of breaks, the location of comfort zones, and smoking policies.

This aspect of group work is the one most often addressed in the literature on the use of group decision support systems (Gray, 1985; Huber, 1984; Phillips and Phillips, 1993).

V243 2.1 *Facilitate participants to* **contribute freely**. Relatively equal contributions from all participants is usually important for the success of a workshop. When views are not listened to, and are punished by the rest of the group, the contributor will be inhibited throughout the workshop. Careful consideration of group membership may provide help in ensuring that all who wish to speak get a chance to do so (Collins and Guetzkow, 1964). Although, as mentioned in the scene setting guidelines, participants are asked to respect each other's views and encourage contributions, continuous support from the facilitator is beneficial. Being aware as much as possible of the different political positions around the issue being addressed, and attempting to discover which individuals are seen to be 'powerful', is helpful background information.

2.1.1 *Check participation levels.* By watching participants and examining output, less forthcoming participants can be detected and encouraged. For example, when carrying out an oval mapping workshop, participants who are not writing on ovals may need some initial support from the facilitator. The facilitator may help by listening to their views and writing their statements on to the ovals as examples. Once some are up on the wall they can then encourage the participant to write their own.

2.1.2 *Watch for non-verbals.* Non-verbals such as facial and body expressions and voice tones will signal if participants are uncomfortable with the workshop's progress. Participants may continuously find themselves cut off in mid-flow or unable to 'get a word in edgewise'. Sometimes a 'round-robin' will bring participants back into the flow of the workshop. A round-robin to review progress can sometimes reveal discomfort with an emerging map or computer model, where a participant, and their views, has been left behind. Always watch the non-verbals of the client, particularly when the discussion is moving in a direction earlier identified as problematic. Make sure the client is aware that the facilitator will continually monitor non-verbal messages from them and seek to act accordingly.

2.1.3 *Build in methods to get participants to contribute early in the workshop.* Giving 'the floor' to participants early in the workshop will help those more hesitant. By being invited to use their voice in public less confident participants will gain confidence. 'Round-robin' introductions are sometimes enough to meet this purpose; on other occasions the facilitator deliberately must bring quiet participants into the discussion. Any round-robin usually helps less socially skilled participants because it means they know they will get air-time by invitation and without having to interrupt others. Non-participants have an impact on the behaviour of the rest of the group.

2.2 *Help the group to concentrate on the task.* Because the facilitator is managing both the group (process) and the problem or issue (content) it enables participants to focus on the task. Content management involves providing *structure* to the exploration, evaluation, and resolution of their material, *not providing content*.

Managing the *process* of the group involves time management, keeping the group on track, encouraging members to participate, and alleviating situations of conflict.

2.3 **Ask 'obvious' questions.** Often the facilitator must ask for elaboration when she does not understand the statement being discussed or needs clarification. However, it is also helpful when she believes that there may be more than one interpretation and wants to tease out their nuances. The facilitator also may have a suspicion that not all the participants know about the subject but that they are unable to ask. For example, when we were working for AMCOF there was an issue about technical practice. A lively debate raged, but a number of participants appeared to be confused regarding what was being discussed. When the facilitator asked for a brief explanation she was surprised at how many of the others listened intently. They were grateful for the clarification which they would have been embarrassed to ask for. It is not unusual for a facilitator to ask 'stupid' questions that reveal that none of the participants knows the answer – each had assumed someone else in the group did. *V239*

2.4 *Maintain high levels of energy and enthusiasm.* Productive and effective workshops are tiring both physically and mentally. Maintaining energy levels can be difficult and yet important (Ackermann, 1996; Bostrom *et al*, 1993). A group can only rarely work beyond an 8-hour workshop. On only a few occasions have we been involved with management teams for a longer period and these have always been associated with urgent strategic issues. On these occasions management teams have worked in darkened rooms using computer support for 16-hour stretches, leaving the facilitators absolutely exhausted!

2.4.1 *Make the workshop **fun** as well as productive.* Whilst the objective of the intervention is the development of strategy, providing some enjoyment to the process will stimulate participants into being more creative, enthusiastic, and engaged with the process. We have commented before that a 'role-think' exercise seems to be generally enjoyed. Moving from manual to computer supported working to the networked computer systems tends to increase variety and so enjoyment. It also provides mental refreshment for participants. *C73*

2.4.2 *Draw on the facilitator's own energy.* If the facilitator appears enthusiastic and engaged this can often prompt a mirror reaction in participants.

2.4.3 *Encourage participants to 'play' with data.* Rather than defining the emerging maps or computer models as definitive statements, ensure that the model is seen as something to experiment with.

2.4.4 *Insert, and reward, humour.* Humour, during the workshop, may act as a powerful medium for relieving stress, particularly where it has been induced by conflict. However, some care does have to be taken to ensure that participants are not laughed at; rather the group laughs with them. Watch also for the danger of participants being role cast as 'court jesters' and not taken seriously on substantive issues.

2.4.5 *Design tasks to help with physiological low points.* Using tasks such as 'role-think' helps when dealing with the 'after lunch' slump in energy. Avoiding working with computer projected data after lunch, particularly if the room has to be darkened to allow the material to be easily read, also helps. Where computer usage cannot be avoided, make sure that there are regular breaks and the room lit up. Preventing alcohol and heavy meals being consumed at mid-day will help avoid the worst of the after lunch slumps.

2.4.6 *Create and reinforce an open, positive, and participative environment.* Provide constant rewards for progress and check all participants are able to contribute. Always consider the process and progress from the participant's perspective. **Manage any conflict** that may arise. In some instances, significant conflict can break out. The facilitator must be aware that this may be a problem in the group, not in the facilitator or process (providing the workshop has been well designed and professionally managed). If the reassertion of a chairman role for the facilitator does not work, then a 'cooling off' period might be needed. People may walk out of sessions when cultural protocols have been broken by the design of a process. Not all content management methods are consistent with particular cultural norms. A mismatch between client culture, facilitator personal style, and method used can be disastrous (Cropper, 1990).

V256

2.5 *Make regular reviews of the material.* This will **demonstrate progress** and maintain energy levels. One method is to use the electronic preferencing or the manual equivalent – self-adhesive spots – to check the 'group pulse'. Alternatively, use of the analysis methods, with participants, to check the coverage, the effect of changes on structure, and degree of divergence may provide reassurance and a period of reflection. Often discussions, as they unfold, are being monitored and mapped by the facilitator on a public computer screen. This means participants can keep a watchful eye on the interpretation given by the facilitator. A 20-minute cycle between the start of discussion and the group's attention being drawn to the emerging computer model allows enough time for good debate, and yet a pause for reflection and joint understanding. This form of interactive mapping also enables participants to concentrate on their own contributions rather than being concerned about managing the process or content.

V228 V243

2.5.1 *Show progress by flip-chart reorganization.* When manual techniques are used, flip-charts are never removed from the working walls. Periodically reorganize them to reflect progress from one part of the agenda to others, then this can be explicitly acknowledged.

2.6 *Monitor and control, if necessary, any side conversations.* Side conversations may be disruptive, rather than just a temporary two-person exchange. Before seeking to control them, the facilitator needs to judge content, purpose, and cause. They may occur because of boredom, dissent, and sometimes enthusiasm. Without identifying cause it is difficult to know what should be done. If the conversations are relevant and signify that the participants cannot get air-time then it is up to the facilitator to draw the conversation into the group. One option is to say 'I can hear *valuable* contributions going on that we ought to be capturing and assimilating'. Alternatively, multi-tasking may mean the content can be captured in the computer model alongside the main debate. The conversationalists will be aware their concerns have been captured and will be addressed later.

2.7 *Provide the client with the reassurance of control.* As we have noted (also chapter P9), it is important that facilitator and client act in concert. This means ensuring that breaks are used to review progress, reconfirm the design and timing of the remaining parts of the workshop, and gain help with suggestions of strategies and stakeholders for role-think episodes, etc.

2.8 *Make judicious use of sub-groups.* Designing activities which use sub-groups can help manage dominant participants by, for example, putting them all in the same sub-group. They can be used to encourage the capture of divergent views. Sub-group contributions can then be fed back to the group as whole. Additionally they can be a way of re-energizing participants. It is also possible to cover more ground, by division of labour, where there is insufficient time for the whole group to work through all the material. However, it may not help build a consensus but rather encourage divergence within the group. Time spent on report back times can mean efficiency is no better than working with the whole group.

2.9 *Use language carefully.* Assertive, prescriptive, and evaluative rather than tentative statements from the facilitator can be unhelpful. Take care to allow, at all times, for misunderstanding. Use phrases such as: 'if I understand you correctly . . .' or 'I may be mistaken but . . .'. Whilst the facilitator might be fully aware that a participant has volunteered information on a particular topic and is frustrated when it does not get supported, clearly confronting him or her with this lack of interest will not help.

2.10 *Seek elaboration of potentially cryptic statements.* Some of the skills employed when running a good workshop are similar to running a good interview. The use of, for example, **'laddering'** and the **'oracle question'** can work with a group as well as with an individual. Similarly, the discovery of contrasting poles of concepts, along with additional explanation and context, can help participants reach a consensus about the meaning of concepts. This is especially important when the computer model is to be used by another group who will not have experienced its development.   C91: C92

2.11 *Watch for too much facilitator control.* It is common for facilitators to seek too much control of the group and their ways of working. There is a fine balance between group chemistry and facilitator intervention. 'Active listening' plays an important role in maintaining this balance. Active listening involves the facilitator really paying attention to what people are saying, and communicating non-verbally that careful listening is occurring. This form of listening has the effect of keeping the facilitator in the steering position, but in a sensitive way.

Remember that the role of the facilitator is not to assume responsibility for the client's problems and solve them. Their role is to add value. Therefore, surfacing a crisis may be a very constructive step although disorienting for the group at the time. However, the group may not remember that the role of the facilitator is not to be fully accountable for the event (as is usually the case in, say, a presentation). This means it is possible that participants will treat the facilitator as a scapegoat for the poor performance of the group. When there are tensions about who is in control it is helpful to stay calm, gently remind participants of the 'contract' for facilitating the workshop, and offer help in mapping and modelling the difficulty which has arisen. We have often found that when the group has difficulties, the facilitator is expected to know how to solve them and to be in control. It can help to remind the group that there is a joint responsibility and to ask for their help.

Running a Workshop Using Computer Support

The commentary below is to be read as an addition to that above, rather than as stand-alone material.

3.1 *Explain conventions of the mapping software on the public screen.* This is always best achieved using a simple, and possibly humorous, example. The example should include an explanation of the phrases used as nodes, of contrasting poles, and the shorthand convention of using three dots (an ellipsis) to indicate 'rather than'. It should also encompass the way linking works – causality, influence, implication; the use of colour for signifying categories; the ability to edit and re-edit whenever needed; and the use of numbers against constructs to act as reference points.

3.2 *Ensure there are breaks from looking at the computer screen.* Switching between manual and computer supported modes of working allows mental refreshment.

3.3 *Move between idea generation (through discussion) to review* and confirmation of additions to the computer model (see guideline 2.5 above).

3.4 *Do not move constructs around the screen too quickly.* This can be distracting and puzzling, and even more so when there are more than 15 constructs on view. The software allows 'hot-keys' to be used for all common commands – these should be used at all times – menus popping up on the screen are distracting and obliterate parts of the content.

3.5 *Explain what the software is doing.* Skilled operators can make the manipulation of the software look very slick. However, this can also mean that it is opaque to the participants. Seek a careful balance, making sure participants do not feel alienated by the fast manipulation of the software while avoiding them feeling as though time is wasted through too much explanation.

3.6 *Use an overview to the structure of the computer model.* When participants are working with a model developed from previous workshops, interviews, documents, or oval mapping, it is difficult for them to gain a feel for the overall computer model. An overview produced on flip-chart paper or on one of the views in the software (see chapter P6) can help navigation.

3.7 *Provide a sense of progress.* Unlike manual techniques which clearly show progress, it is not so easy with computer working (Ackermann and Eden, 1994; Eden, 1990b). Ticking off areas on an agenda or a large flip-chart sheet with the overview may help. Also, it is possible for the software to keep a record of material covered or referred to during the workshop.

Closing the Workshop

As with any stage managed event the 'last act' can determine the attitudes of the participants to the whole event. Thus closing a workshop must be done with great care.

4.1 *Finish exactly on time or slightly early.* Successful workshops leave some participants wishing to keep going. It is extremely important to stop at the originally agreed time. Those who have made arrangements to use the time after the workshop must not be punished by missing out on extended work. Only consider extending the workshop when *all* participants are committed to doing so. This means ensuring that some participants do not feel under pressure from others to keep going.

4.2 *Put time aside to review outcomes.* Ensure there is enough time to compare progress made with the workshop objectives and agenda. Go back over the added value from each part of the workshop. In addition agree on the feedback material to be provided and the delivery date for doing so (some feedback may be delivered immediately). Finally decide on the **next steps to be taken**. The client may wish to play an active part in closure, and particularly in decisions about next steps.

4.3   *Produce some instant feedback.* Instant 'minutes' in the form of maps and/or photographs of flip-chart material means participants are reassured that the record of the workshop is valid (see figure P2.3). The use of a small computer printer, 1-hour turnaround photographic services, and readily available photocopying facilities make it possible to provide such instant feedback. It is not necessary that these 'minutes' are all encompassing or neatly laid out, as long as they encapsulate the main points and provide something tangible to take away from the workshop. Emotional and cognitive commitment, and so political feasibility, are reinforced by this process. When using a **photographic record** it is useful to provide copies of   *V234 V268* photographs of the group working together. This will be particularly useful if the group are to come together at a future occasion and quick recall is required – group photographs cue in content records.

4.4   *Re-examine agreed actions.* Check resource needs – energy and time, as well as cash. During the workshop, participants often get caught up in agreeing lots of actions – 'gung ho greening'. Viewing these at the end of the workshop will reintroduce the cold light of reality. Analysis can also check that coding is correct. Moreover, when considering agreeing action programmes, producing instant feedback in the form of small parts of the map illustrating the responsibilities against actions will provide participants with a clear idea of what they have agreed to.

Yes But . . .

What happens if there is a rejection of workshop principles?

Sometimes this can happen explicitly and openly, with open rejection often being easier to deal with. It is likely to happen only when the design process is sloppy and the 'contract' with the client, and with the group, messy. Problems tend to arise when new people have entered into the group unexpectedly. The only way of dealing with the problem is to carefully renegotiate expectations and contract. For example, 'Can I take a "rain check" on how we're doing relative to our original aims. It seems possible that we're shifting our ground. Maybe we need to redesign and adapt to changed circumstances?'.

Sometimes the process is rejected through a hidden agenda, politics, or defensive routines, which makes it difficult to confront the issue directly (Raimond and Eden, 1990). For example, a reluctance to address particular strategic issues may be disguised as rejecting the method. The process becomes the scapegoat.

The use of 'nominal group techniques' (Delbecq *et al*, 1975), particularly using the networked computer system, can often help release hidden agendas and refocus the group on the agreed task.

The group seems unresponsive

It may be that the 'contract' with the group is inadequate and that expectation setting did not reduce task or role ambiguity. As with the covert rejection described above, it may be necessary to switch to an 'issue surfacing' session.

If the group are communicative apart from their lack of response to the task and method, ask participants what is not working for them. Although counter-intuitive, this supports rather than detracts from the facilitator's professionalism (Phillips and Phillips, 1993). For example, consider a group interview (using oval mapping or the networked computer system when possible) on the relevance of the stated purpose and agenda. Try to reshape the purpose and so achieve re-engagement. This re-negotiation should not absorb too much time, it must not become an end in itself. If the group are totally non-communicative, use the nominal group technique and get every participant to write down, or work out, two or three points they would like to get out of the workshop. Eliciting 'hopes and fears' for the outcome of the workshop may act as a good agenda for such an event – it can easily, and naturally, lead to an exploration of emergent aspirations as related to strategic futures (Finn, 1997). Collect them, one at a time, using a 'round-robin', and map them on a flip-chart or by using the public computer display. From this list try to work with participants on the purpose of the workshop and gradually establish a rewritten set of objectives and agenda.

Further Commentary on the Management of Process, the Design of Interventions, and the Facilitation of Groups

The following may act as a brief check list associated with the preparation for, and running of, a workshop. It is not inclusive:

- Negotiate a clear 'contract' with the client. If the client will not be at the workshop then also negotiate with the 'acting client'/sponsor who will be attending.
- Gain agreement from the client on the level of freedom to act contingently.
- Check all of the 'trivialities' before the start – flip-chart paper, pens, refreshments, 'Blu-Tack', ovals, 'Post-its', computer technology, etc.
- Be clear about roles when more than one facilitator is involved.
- Get the group in close to the work area; make it 'cosy' and yourself a member of the group.
- Make the 'Rules of the Game' clear.
- Develop prepared 'scripts' to structure areas where there are likely to be significant process problems.
- Do not become overwhelmed in content management when process management is important, or vice-versa.
- When time is short, ensure there is enough depth for clear added value to show through in each stage, and renegotiate to cut out stages if necessary.
- Use a round-robin when a coalition forms (side conversations) or when one person is becoming dominant or when one or two people are unable to get in.
- Play back the added value summaries to create a sense of progress.
- Watch carefully for non-verbal 'giveaways' about irritation with what's going on or judgements about the style and standard of facilitation.

Working with the networked computer system not only requires consideration of those issues mentioned when using the computer supported mode of working but brings with it a set of unique facilitation requirements.

5.1   *Use the system alongside the 'single user' computer supported mode of working.* Whilst the networked system does provide considerable advantages in terms of speed of contribution and anonymity, these need to be balanced with developing a sense of shared understanding from social interaction.

5.2 *Use the networked system to allow participants to remain silent without penalty.* Although it is worth ensuring that participants are not 'social loafing' (Karau and Williams, 1993), participants may be faced with being forced to contribute to a discussion where they have little or no knowledge. Admitting this in front of the group can be painful – the networked system allows low participation without others being aware of it (other than the facilitator who has data about levels of participation available on their computer screen).

5.3 *Work in 'fit to window' mode when using the 'gather' facility.* The software will usually be set up so that as constructs are contributed they are always visible. This means that constructs will reduce in size as more are added and the display becomes overcrowded. Once the screen has filled to the point where participants are unable to read the text, it is usually a good time to shift from the networked system to the facilitator managing the computer support.

5.4 *Cluster similar material on the screen.* Adopt the same process as the OMT – move concepts to form clusters of material likely to be linked thematically or causally. Use colour ('styles') to signify possible categories of data. It may also be worth bringing on to the screen other statements already captured that are identical or related to the issue being discussed. Attention can then shift, as with the OMT, to linking up the clusters and adding any elaboration necessary.

5.5 *Allocate preferences according to the task and number of alternatives.* When using preferencing to determine which issues are to be followed up, provide participants with a 2:3 ratio of preferences to issues. In this manner each participant is likely to have at least one of their preferences developed and therefore will be more likely to buy into the process. Where actions are being highlighted this ratio might reduce to 1:2 or 1:3. It is worth reminding participants that the preferencing session is to highlight options and is therefore a dialectic.

5.6 *Consider using the rating system.* The rating scale provides a group with a quick way of establishing the relative weight they would give to a range of elements. With preferencing, choices must be made, whereas with rating it is possible for many items to be indistinguishable from each other (rated at the same, or very similar, level) – there is no resource constraint and this can be a significant advantage for some group exercises. However, when using rating scales it is crucial to define unambiguous anchor points for at least two points on the scale.

Appendix – A Sample 2-day Initial JOURNEY Making Workshop Programme with the Client and Key Actors (about 12–16 people)

KEY:
Bold = on programme given to participants
Italics = notes to sponsor, partners, and facilitators only
Bullet and Inset = notes to facilitators only

Aims: [client specific . . . .]

Programme

Rooms: One room with 'concertina wall separator', 20 chairs in each part of room

Prep: 6 × 2 flip-charts on wall, 'triggers' on to Ovals, engineer sub-groups

Kit: 10 Notebook computers (+ 2 spare in case of faults), Master computer, chauffeur computer, network hub and cables, 5× packs of Blu-Tack, 500 Ovals, 20× Oval pens, 5 sets of flip-chart water-based pens (black, blue, red, green, purple), instructions for mapping ×4, instructions for star diagrams, colour printer, SVGA computer projector – at least 400 lumens, camera and 2 × 36 400 ASA colour films.

Wednesday

0900–0915   COFFEE

0915–0930   Welcome and Introduction

From Ken [the client]: 'What I want is . . . . From Colin [the Facilitator]: The programme you have shows what we expect to do. Timing is rough, so that we can exploit opportunities effectively'

0930–1045   Surface policing policy issues and implications (one group)

Process: Oval mapping
Group: all in same room and working together
Visible purpose: surface issues from a blank wall (but with some triggers from the draft 'strategic issues' document, organize them into rough clusters (themes)
Invisible purpose: get the group working together (means standing up, moving around, writing on ovals, etc.)

- ▶ Rough hierarchical clusters
- ▶ Clusters on separate flip-charts when possible
- ▶ Mark up good options
- ▶ Colin at wall
- ▶ Identify labels for each cluster
- ▶ Fran at computer, enter concepts (nn=xxxx) with number on Oval, cluster label as concept (special style) and linked from 'head' of cluster, clusters into sets using shorthand for label

1045–1115   COFFEE (15 mins)

Break expected to be 30 mins
Themes (labels) and sub-themes into one. View ready for linking of themes on public screen

1115–1215   Develop interdependencies, Relative importance and phasing of issues, 'Work up' the priority issues (in sub-groups)

Process: cross link the clusters from 1st session to show interdependency. Material from 1st session will have been input to software. Computers used to vote on relative importance of each issue for the (i) short term, (ii) long term. This gives opportunity for some anonymity (in pairs of relatively like minded people). Then sub-group (4 groups) work, each group working on one s/t and one l/t issue to map it (causality within the issue)
Group: all in same room and working together

Visible purpose: work up a selection of issues beyond 'motherhood'
Invisible purpose: cross link thinking from politicos and the rest at a level of detail which shows the importance of working together

▶ max 25 mins for linking
▶ Fran driving
▶ Colin chauffeur
▶ linking then voting after links and re-clustering (new clusters given the links); red = short term and green = long term
▶ then sub-groups, Fran & Colin walkabout

last 5 mins: Report back after sub-group work – Colin does feedback with some points about 'analysis' of maps produced

1215–1300   Identify the relative power and interest of stakeholders (full group)

Process: using the computers to input names of stakeholders on to a public screen (in pairs) and all the group organize into a grid of power versus interest in policing policy. Get at appropriate level of dis-aggregation (all group).
Group: all in same room and working together to share knowledge
Visible purpose: identify relative power base and interest so as to show KEY stakeholders and explore potential coalitions (if time)
Invisible purpose: gain some group agreement about the mix of key players who need to be thought about.

▶ new model, 'menu off'
▶ pair input (will they all put in the same s/hs?)
▶ dis-aggregation likely to be the important bit
▶ one pair at each computer
▶ Colin driving, Fran at computer
▶ 3 high interest from each pair placed hard left top
▶ then 3 high power (different) placed hard right bottom
▶ move high power up to top right by interest and power relativity
▶ move high interest similarly
▶ dis-aggregate to appropriate level
▶ look for 8–10 'players'
▶ back to normal view to show 8–10 on screen
▶ voting blobs used to denote green = positive, red = negative – all don't have to be used

1300–1400   LIGHT LUNCH

▶ check computer model against clusters and all Ovals
▶ look for choice of options for role play – options that s/hs will react to

1400–1515   Develop the 'perspectives' of key stakeholders identified in the morning session (in sub-groups)

Process: briefing then sub-groups. Each sub-group considering 2 stakeholders and identifying – (i) the basis of power and (ii) the 'spectacles' of interest. Working on flip-charts.

Material recorded in software as it is developed. This material will be used explicitly in the role play exercise below
Group: sub-groups – mixed expertise
Visible purpose: be clear about sanctions and support mechanisms, identify how stakeholders evaluate the issues (what data do they use, what values drive their interpretation of data)
Invisible purpose: keep awake after lunch

- ▶ Fran briefing: basis of star diagram – use Ovals (if any left)
- ▶ basis of power should include conduit
- ▶ both wander to help groups
- ▶ if possible have one of us at each group with a m/c to record?

1515–1545   TEA (15 mins)

1545–1645   Using role play, explore key stakeholder 'game plans' in relation to key issues identified in the morning session (in sub-groups)

Process: having selected some promising 'options', carefully use the output from the sub-group work above to role-play responses of 2 stakeholders (different for each sub-group), and modify it when it does not work. What informal and formal coalitions would the stakeholder form? What 'conduits' would be used?
Group: sub-groups based on a new mix of people compared with that for the above exercise
Visible purpose: refine, in practice, the views about stakeholder behaviour and attitudes and develop and refine options
Invisible purpose: 'a bit of fun', get the participants to think from the others' point of view

- ▶ Colin introduce with example

1645–1830   Sub-group feedback and group discussion, with review of promising options

Process: 10 mins each sub-group, 5 mins general discussion, then 30 mins at end to review the emerging options by computer voting (as a way of gaining closure on progress at end of day)
Group: all together, then in pairs
Visible purpose: share role-play experience and revisit emerging options taking account of role play
Invisible purpose: the 'cabaret' before dinner, something to talk about excitedly over a beer before dinner

- ▶ Fran to chair

1945–   DINNER

Thursday

0900–1045   Review and develop the options for policy development and implementation reflecting, firstly, on strengths and weaknesses

Process: re-evaluate (in the light of maps printed out from the material of yesterday) and prioritize issues in the light of printed material

Group: all in same room and working together using computers to input material in pairs, develop linkages between SWs and issue labels. All together in front of 'big screen'
Visible purpose: identify ways of exploiting strengths and correct weaknesses in relation to policing policy development
Invisible purpose: encourage [xxx – some of the participants] to recognize they have some blind spots

- ▶ Fran drives
- ▶ Colin chauffeur

1045–1115   COFFEE (15 mins)

1115–1230   And, secondly, opportunities available and threats forthcoming in the environment for the implementation of options

Process: same as above – new pairs?
Group: all together in front of 'big screen'
Visible purpose: identify strategies to bring together politicos and others to jointly exploit opportunities and combat threats, particularly as portfolio approach
Invisible purpose: portfolios involve multi-disciplinary and x-organisational groups, and there is synergy in a portfolio approach

- ▶ Colin drives as scenario development and analysis routine
- ▶ Fran chauffeur
- ▶ treat as 'scenario' links

1230–1330   LUNCH

1330–1515   Consider in some detail one possible set, or system, of strategies and actions. This will be undertaken as one example of the many which will need to be considered in the fullness of time.

Process: with computers for each pair, work with the main computer map to sort through one substantial issue. And then explore, in actionable form, what can be done. Final stage prior to wash-up by Ken [the client] – electronic rating of importance/leverage of sub-clusters (tear-drops) and then allocation by electronic voting of resources (energy, cash, time) on the portfolio of actions identified with respect to most highly rated sub-clusters (get at political feasibility – internal – here by inviting veto/blockers as well as energizers through anonymity)
Group: all in same room and working together
Visible purpose: get some example of closure
Invisible purpose: to show that more work on each area must be done and that it can produce action programmes and commitment

- ▶ Colin starts driving, then switch

1515–1545   What next? Confirm, inform, refine, and design strategies and actions to take us forward. Feedback. Consolidation.

Process: Ken [the client] chairing/leading
Group: all in same room and working together

Visible purpose: get some joint agreement about next steps, and a mandate for some actions
Invisible purpose: psychological and emotional commitment to next steps:

Should we take this work forward? What generic (rather than just policing specific) NIO issues have emerged, and how do we work on them further (and, not or, maybe use other existing working groups)? How do we work on the other issues, weaknesses, etc. (beyond the example already worked on today) – staff support? How should we develop the work further? Involving other stakeholders – for example . . .? Issue related workshops involving multiple stakeholders? Sponsored single stakeholder workshops?

Presentation of 'Journeyman' certificate and 'I've made the journey' tee shirts!!!

ANALYSIS: MAPS AND MODELS FOR WORKSHOPS

Introduction

The analysis methods, discussed in this chapter, are separated into two sections (in a manner similar to that of the facilitation chapter P5). In the first section the *analysis of cognitive maps* generated during a round of interviews, or from oval mapping (OMT) workshops, is addressed. The second section focuses specifically on *providing group support through analysis* – supporting decision making group(s) in their exploration and negotiation of the material. Dividing the chapter into two sections does have some difficulties – some of the analyses considered in the second section (particularly those relating to pre-workshop analysis) are similar to those discussed in the first. What is different is their purpose. However, this distinction is not rigid and we recommend that both sections be read before running a workshop using a computer based strategy model.

The analyses aim to support the facilitator, and group, by providing ways of representing the knowledge and wisdom of the individual or group in a format that *helps manage, rather than reduce, complexity*. Analysis of the computer model will surface emergent characteristics and identify important detail. The model will act as a 'transitional object' in negotiating strategy by being a flexible and changing artifact belonging to all and seen by all. The model acts as a vehicle for the *social construction of reality* (Berger and Luckmann, 1966), facilitating the **negotiation of a new order and new social order** (DeSanctis, 1993). As such, the representation – a model – provides a means of jointly reflecting on the deep knowledge, wisdom, and aspirations relating to proposals about strategic direction. As maps are a reflection of individual or group perceptions, they are likely to be both different across individuals and between groups. If good interviews have been conducted, then the maps will show that no two individuals think alike, even though there will be similarity and some alignment of thinking. Determining the extent of the overlap cannot be discovered reliably as interviews unfold and maps are constructed. Difference and similarity are a property of the detail *in* context *and* of the emergent holistic properties. Social negotiation is facilitated by appropriate analysis of maps.

The analysis methods discussed in the first section are likely to be used in the 'backroom', rather than with a group in real time. The second section deals specifically with the analysis for designing and facilitating workshops. As such it begins by noting some of the differences between analysing maps generated by oval mapping workshops, and those created by interviews, before exploring a series of analyses which are common to both. Common analyses are subdivided into sections dealing with (i) tidying up the computer model, (ii) identifying goals and potential key strategy labels, (iii) generating categories through styles, (iv) locating core options, and (v) exploring feedback loops. It is worthwhile noting that

C48

the process of analysing a map is cyclical, rather than linear as implied by the chapter layout. For additional explanation, Eden *et al* (1992) present all of the analysis techniques discussed here from the perspective of cognitive complexity.

Finally, throughout this chapter it will be assumed that the computer software is used to make the process of working with cognitive, or strategic/group, maps easier, but each of the analyses discussed may be done manually. Undoubtedly the process is easier and more reliable when the software is used. Therefore, throughout the chapter the commands used by the software, to undertake the analysis discussed, will be noted in capital letters within single quote marks.

Guidelines for Analysing Interview Maps

How to Do It – *merging individual cognitive maps*

Maps generated during interviews

As noted, in the chapter on cognitive mapping and interviews (Chapter P1), interviews are often structured in a manner where the emergent themes from one interviewee are interjected into those interviews following it. This process not only helps in facilitating the weaving together of maps but also provides a richer perspective on the theme in question. However, we also observed, in that chapter, that in some cases a second interview or feedback interview may be undertaken. This process often requires the cognitive map to be analysed in preparation, or at least entered into the software for 'tidying purposes' before being merged with other interview material. Where this is the case, the processes discussed in the merging of oval mapping workshop models should be adopted.

V210 V215 V216   *Merging maps*

1.1 *Merge topic areas rather than complete individual maps.* By introducing themes and natural overlaps from one interview to the next, cognitive maps produced from a round of interviews will have covered many of the same areas. Entering the material dealing with a particular subject area from all of the maps, will considerably simplify the start of the process of weaving them together.

When it is not possible, or necessary, to create individual computer models for each interview then it is easier to build a merged model directly from notes, and immediately subsequent to each interview. However, the danger in doing it this way is that the early interviews can be too influential on the structure (but not content) and so meaning of the final merged map. However, if the order of interviews has been determined to account for political weighting of views then this will be appropriate. Using the time between the interviews to build the computer models will also indicate new themes to be interjected in following interviews.

On some occasions individual interviews may take place after an oval mapping workshop. On these occasions the interviews are conducted to allow participants to provide their own personal slant on the material produced during the workshop.

V195   Additionally it provides those unable to attend the OMT workshop with the **chance**

to contribute to the overall direction. In these instances, individual material can be added to the computer version of the oval mapping workshop data.

In each of these cases, it is important to use particular ranges of construct numbers, or 'sets', to retain a reference to the person from whom the material was elicited.

1.2   *Always involve all interviewers in the merging process.* The interviews may be carried out by two or more people (depending on the number of interviews to be conducted, the speed with which they must be completed, and the subsequent strategy design process – see chapter P5). In these instances it is *essential* to work together entering the maps. Inevitably each interviewer develops a commitment to their own interviewees and data, and unless the merging is done together then the person doing it will use their own interviews to dominate the model. This may not be done deliberately, but rather represents the consequence of good interviewing where the interviewer really does become empathetic to the views expressed by their own interviewees. We have never known circumstances where this has not happened, so beware. However, there are other reasons:

1.2.1   *Create better understanding of all the material.* If the resultant map is to be used as part of a group process where two facilitators are managing the workshop, ensuring that both facilitators have a good knowledge of the contents of the computer model ensures that the knowledge and wisdom can be used to its fullest capacity.

1.2.2   *Uncover additional information.* Each interviewer will be forced to explain to the other *why* they have made certain links, and what constructs (which have become familiar to them) mean. Through this process they will trigger other information provided during the interview but not captured on the original map. This too can be used to inform either the process or content.

Merging oval mapping workshop models

Where a series of oval mapping workshops has been carried out and their contents captured in computer models (and/or photographically) during the workshop then they will also be amalgamated to allow analysis to be conducted on all of the data. However, unlike individual maps, these oval mapping workshops have already linked the views of many individuals together into a large single structure, and it is the merging of each these group maps which is to take place.

1.3   *Cut and paste the individual models into one group computer model.* Where computer models have already been made (for oval mapping workshops or individual maps) then creating a new model and pasting the information from each of the other models into it is the starting point. This process involves the following steps:

1.3.1   *Create a new group/strategy model.* This new, initially blank, computer model will act as the repository for the amalgamation of all the knowledge and wisdom but will allow the original models to be kept intact.

1.3.2   *Select all the information in the first model and copy it to the new computer model.* Use the 'COPY' and 'PASTE' option to transfer concepts and their links, but not STYLE or SETs.

1.3.3 *Renumber subsequent computer models to avoid overwriting existing material.* It is helpful if each computer model transfer can retain the basic numbering sequence of the original model, as by this stage the facilitator will have become accustomed to the numbers within each original model. Using this process means that concepts can be recalled from memory in the new model, simply by adding the extra digit. Thus, when renumbering ('RENUMBER' from the edit menu), start the new number sequence from, for example, 1001, 2001, etc. The number sequence in the original model of 1–234 will transfer to the new model as 1001-1234. Keeping a record of numbering will also retain a cross link to the original proponent(s) of the concept.

Basic 'Tidying the Map' Analysis

2.1 *Exploring the size of the computer model.* This analysis reveals the number of concepts and the number of linkages that exist in the model. From the results of the analysis on an individual map, some indication can be gained as to the cognitive complexity (number of links between concepts) of the individual interviewed (Eden *et al*, 1992). However, this is highly dependent on the interviewer's agenda and skill. Nevertheless, examining the link-to-concept ratio ('SIZE') will provide clues about the nature of the map. For an individual interview we expect a ratio of approximately 1.15-1.20. Merged maps, or group maps, will have a higher ratio.

2.1.1 *Identify a possible insufficiency of links.* Where the analysis reports that the link-to-concept ratio is less than 1:1 then there are isolated concepts which either require linking up into the body of the text, or are genuinely isolated statements. This outcome may be due to links being missed, or may mean further questions should to be posed to the interviewee to seek further clarification.

2.1.2 *Identify a possible over-abundance of links.* The opposite problem to insufficiency may be an over-abundance of links, where the computer model contains redundant links. For example, there may be a link from A to B to C to D and a link from A to C and B to D, etc. Unless there is a specific and alternate line of argument (usually represented by an inserted concept) then these are summary type links and can be removed.

V217　　2.2 *Detect **orphans**.* Orphans may exist in well-linked computer models, and may be legitimate but must be checked in case they are accidental. The analysis 'ORPHAN' specifically searches through all of the constructs and lists those which are unlinked. This list can then be used in conjunction with a text 'search' routine to find similar or related material and subsequently link the concepts into the map.

2.3 *Conduct a text search.* Searching through the map/computer model for instances of the same word(s) ('FIND') is performed often and not just when tidying up the map. However, it is in this particular stage of analysis that it is used most frequently. The search can be used to identify specific words, or instances where all forms of the word(s) are sought after. For example market, markets, marketing, marketed by using wild cards. It is at this stage that final agreement about jargon and shorthand between facilitators is important. One facilitator/interviewer may have used M-D (for managing director), another Mng Dir, another

Figure P6.1   Different verbal tags (Eden et al, 1983).

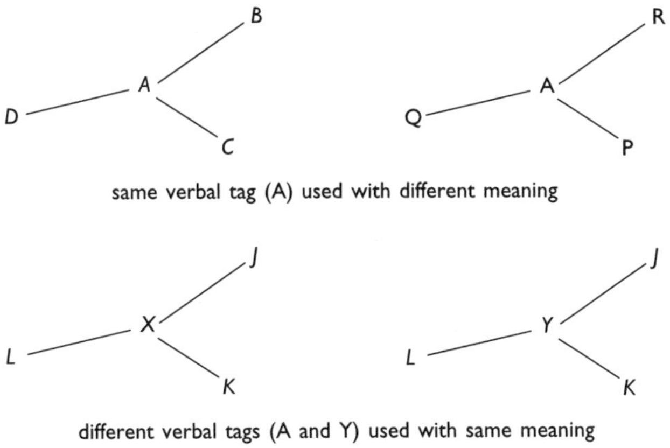

same verbal tag (A) used with different meaning

different verbal tags (A and Y) used with same meaning

CEO, and another the actual name of the managing director! As it is important to identify all concepts which are about the managing director a single expression must be used.

2.4   *Merge concepts*. Often there is a danger or temptation to merge statements   *V217*
which, from their language, appear to be concerned about the same topic, but on further examination demonstrate very different perspectives. It is worthwhile, therefore, to explore the context as well as the content of the statements about to be merged, to determine whether they are indeed about the same subject or not (see figure P6.1). Merging two concepts results in a single concept assuming all of the links of the merged concepts. Thus, two concepts with the same verbal tag and different meanings may be merged allowing new meanings to show through. Alternatively, the same meanings with different concept labels may be merged, retaining a combination of the language used by each proponent.

2.4.1   *Retain the language of both proponents*. Where possible, it is advantageous to retain the language of both contributions. In this manner both participants will continue to 'own' the statement, but with slightly new meaning. This process encourages the possible negotiation of new meanings. The 'MERGE' feature of the software allows the two concepts to be easily joined together and edited.

2.4.2   *Check relationships*. Sometimes, when merging, the links are no longer correct and require revision. This occurs particularly when the concept on one map has a 'positive pole' which is the same as the 'negative pole' of the second map. In this case, some of the positive links may have to be converted to negative links, and vice-versa.

Locating goals and strategic issues   *V217*

3.1   *Locate potential goals*. Goals are those concepts that are 'good in their own   *V218*
right'. Identifying goals in cognitive maps from interviews will be relatively straightforward as they will have been validated by the interviewees. However, while there will be some goals which are synonymous across several interviewees,

Figure P6.2   The map as a hierarchy of 'tear-drops'.

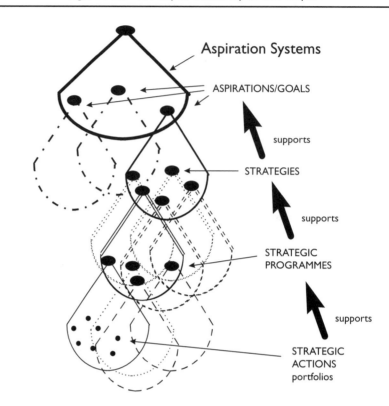

Aspiration Systems

ASPIRATIONS/GOALS

supports

STRATEGIES

supports

STRATEGIC
PROGRAMMES

supports

STRATEGIC
ACTIONS
portfolios

there will be others that are contradictory or opposed. When merging these individual maps, it is appropriate to include in the computer model *all* of the goals so that the negotiation process excludes rather than includes them. All goals will appear at the top part of the hierarchy in a map (see figure P6.2) and will usually comprise a *system* or network of goals.

When building maps (either individually or through oval mapping workshops), and particularly when bringing maps together, concepts may appear at the top of the map (that is, listing 'heads', 'LH') that are not goals. This usually follows incomplete linking and may be dealt with in the same manner as orphans. If the software is being used, then listing heads will produce a catalogue of all of the concepts with no arrows leading from them ('out-degrees'). Orphans will also appear in this list because they are both heads and tails.

After merging is complete, a useful check on goals starts by exploring each head in turn and laddering down the hierarchy, checking each level in turn. Keep moving down the ladder until it is clear that a concept is not a goal *for the group* who are to use the computer model. Then focus in on the goal system ('collapsing' – see 8.1.1 below – on to all goals) and review the whole of the draft, or proposed, goal system.

3.2   *Identify potential strategic issue labels.* Strategic issues, as mentioned in chapter P2, are clusters of material which taken together represent an issue which is long term in nature, often difficult to reverse, and is costly in terms of people, energy, time, and cash. If a strategy was developed to deal with the issue, it would support one or more goals either directly or indirectly. For example 'develop a fundamentally new approach to the xyz market' could be lengthy and costly but designed with a deliberate purpose to reverse the issue of 'decline in market share' and support the goal of 'move to No 1 in the market' to which it is most directly associated. One means of identifying the strategic issue clusters is through a number of analyses, each providing indicative conclusions. The most superordinate construct in the cluster is often chosen as the strategic issue label. As well as formal analysis of the map, it is important to note that a group of constructs that were emotionally significant to individuals, or the group, might also be key strategic issues and should be tagged as such (see the section below on the use of categories and 'styles'). The analyses that are most helpful for identifying strategic issues within a map are:

3.2.1 *Explore the structural 'domain' of each concept.* The 'domain' analysis ('DOMT' or 'DOMAIN' from the analysis menu) calculates the total number of in-arrows and out-arrows (possible explanations and consequences) for each concept – its immediate domain. The analysis can be conducted to reveal the highest number of (i) in-arrows ('DOMI'), (ii) out-arrows ('DOMO'), or (iii) both added together ('DOMT'). Finding the concepts with the highest in *and* out arrows – the most **'busy'** – helps identify the most cognitively central constructs in a cognitive map.　　　　　　　　　　　　　　　　*V218*

This analysis provides a measure of *local complexity* by accounting only for the directly connected constructs. It takes no account of how well connected these close concepts are to other concepts ('reachability' – Nozicka *et al*, 1976).

It is worth noting that the highest scoring constructs may be the result of an interviewee spending unintended time and energy on the topic relative to others. However, in general, busy concepts suggest constructs that are at the core of emergent themes or issues in the map.

3.2.2 *Explore the **centrality** of concepts.* The 'central' analysis ('CENTRAL' from the analysis menu) works alongside the domain analysis in confirming, or　*V218* suggesting, possible themes or strategic issues. This analysis takes account of the wider context of the strategic issue. Instead of focusing only on the first level of elaboration, the analysis expands its search to as many levels of reachability as desired. In order to pay greater attention to concepts whose reach is small (close to the concept being analysed), each subsequent layer is given a weighting which diminishes exponentially. The standard routine available in the software commences with a weighting of 1 for each concept directly related to the concept being evaluated (equivalent to the domain), 0.5 for those two levels out, 0.33 for those three levels out, and so on. See figure P6.3 for a comparison between domain and centrality. Through this analysis it is possible to identify those concepts which are central to the map but may not have extensive elaboration immediately linked to them and vice-versa. Where a concept with high domain score is linked directly to another with high domain, then the two will bolster each other's score.

3.3 *Compare domain and central results.* By detecting similarities and differences between the results of the 'busy' and 'central' analysis a form of triangulation can take place. If an issue appears in both lists, it suggests that it is both locally and globally significant, confirming its position at the core of a potential key issue.

Figure P6.3 Comparing centrality and domain scores.

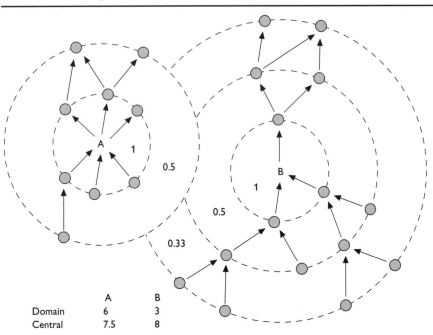

	A	B
Domain	6	3
Central	7.5	8

While a construct which has a high domain score is more likely to have a high central score, sometimes this is not the case. It may be a relatively local phenomenon on the periphery of the map. Alternatively a construct which, on its own, has a low domain score but acts as a bridge between two high domain scoring constructs will score highly on a central analysis. This bridging construct is of interest because without it the map may split into well-separated clusters. These bridging links are likely to be worth further exploration.

Comparison between those constructs scoring high for domain and those scoring high for central analysis may be aided by mapping only high scoring constructs. When using the software, this is best achieved by identifying three styles: one for each of domain high, central high, and high for both analyses (see guideline 4.1 below). When only these three categories are mapped, the high scoring constructs are sometimes seen to be *directly* linked to each other, or very closely related, whereas other constructs are well separated. When they are closely linked then a 'cluster' analysis will place them in the same cluster, and so reveal relatively fewer clusters. In this case the map is of a 'monolithic' structure (see guideline 5.1 below).

Using the software to show how the high domain and central constructs link together by 'collapsing' on to only these constructs, but retaining pathways of linkage between them and through other constructs, provides one type of overview of the complete map. This process of 'collapsing' the map down to a small number of selected constructs of specific interest (for example issue labels and goals) can provide a route map (see guideline 8.1) illustrating the summary linkages between emergent issues, and goals. In particular it enables the analysis to go beyond structural properties and to account for the content relationship between high domain and central constructs.

Figure P6.4 Typical strategy styles.

Goals	**Black, Times Roman, bold 16 point**
Strategies/issues,	*Purple, Arial italic, 14 point*
<u>Strategic programmes</u>	<u>Purple, Arial, underlined, 14 point</u>
Options/assertions	Blue, Arial, 12 point
Agreed actions	*Green, italic, Arial, 12 point*

Creating categories

4.1 *Create styles.* Styles ('CONCEPT STYLE PROPERTIES' from the property menu) are a combination of font type, font size, and colour and are used to distinguish *categories of particular constructs.* Using the software, styles can be created as required and constructs allocated, or re-allocated, to a style as the analysis proceeds. These **style categories** are mutually exclusive, in contrast to 'sets' where constructs can be   *V234* placed in any number of them. Categories may be used to record the results of the analyses discussed above, or simply to identify similar content. For example, in some instances it is worth separating those key issue labels or themes which have been identified through analysis from those that have been identified as related to emotion. Examples of typical styles used for strategy maps are shown in figure P6.4.

4.2 *Use styles to support analysis.* Having developed the styles and attributed them to possible issue labels and goals, then these styles can themselves be used for analysis. Each style is a mutually exclusive 'intrinsic set' and so the content of the style can be listed, mapped and compared with the character of other styles. Each intrinsic set (style) may be added to another so that combinations of styles may be explored.

Groups or Clusters of Constructs – 'Chunking a Map'

One method of exploring the structure and complexity of the maps is to 'slice' the map into 'chunks' or clusters. For interview maps, this analysis allows both the interviewer and interviewee to explore particular parts of a map in detail. For strategy maps it provides the basis for establishing those aspects of strategic thinking that are relatively separate from each other, and so may be candidates for different parts of a workshop(s) agenda. Clustering of constructs is an important part of the process of managing, rather than reducing, complexity. It is an essential part of using the oval mapping technique; however, here the clustering is less formal and is less likely to recognize the linkages between clusters.

5.1 *'Link similarity' clusters.* This analysis ('CLUSTER' from the analysis menu)   *V218* compares pairs of constructs along with their immediate context to determine link similarity (using the Jaccard Coefficient – Gower and Ross, 1969). This is a measure of the similarity of context (and so meaning) of each construct. If the constructs have sufficient common context they are placed in the same cluster; if not, they form the basis of a new cluster. Thus, an attempt is made at creating clusters where each construct within it has a relatively high degree of similarity. Using this approach each cluster is designed to be mutually exclusive – with no construct appearing in more than one cluster. Constructs in each cluster are closely inter-linked and the number of 'bridges' between the different clusters kept to a minimum. The analyst can specify a target size, and minimum size, for a cluster, and also specify a 'seed' set around which clusters will be built. Using these facilities enables the robustness of clusters to be tested – if clusters remain stable given changes in target size and seed set, they are likely to be of particular note.

5.1.1   *Use clusters to detect themes and confirm strategic/key issues.* Clusters provide another useful means of identifying emergent themes, with each cluster potentially representing a theme or emergent issue. Sometimes clusters emerge that do not contain one of the key issue labels, or themes, identified through the domain and central analysis. In these circumstances it is useful to examine the cluster, identify a relatively central construct within the cluster and categorize it as a potential issue label. Clusters that contain several key issues or themes are likely to be particularly 'monolithic' (see below).

5.1.2   *Identify highly interlinked clusters (using list set hierarchy 'LSH').* A cluster analysis seeks to identify groups of constructs that are relatively densely interlinked. To this extent the analysis goes beyond the study of the 'local' structures and identifies whether the structure of the map is monolithic, articulated, or segmented (Norris *et al*, 1970). For example, *monolithic* structures tend to indicate possible rigidity and 'dogmatism' in strategic thinking. Thus, the existence of a small number of clusters that are highly integrated might suggest that the organization is fixed in its view of the strategic future and how to manage it. When this occurs in the cognitive maps of individual managers then they are more likely to be resistant to change, even in the face of large scale dis-confirmation of beliefs (Crockett, 1965). It is also likely, however, that successive or clear dis-confirmation, which might occur during effective JOURNEY making group work, will cause discomfort and result in the need for large scale change. Large scale cognitive change is more possible with psychological negotiation, using social processes which encompass the needs of procedural rationality and justice. Aggregated maps 'oil the wheels' of psychological negotiation through their invitation to construct elaboration (Kelly, 1955) or 'scaffold-ing' (Vygotsky, 1962) rather than dismissal.

Similarly, highly *segmented* structures where several clusters are apparent but there is little linkage between them suggest decisions may be made through a series of jumps across 'bridges' from one cluster to another. The existence of several clusters which are well connected suggests well-*articulated* systems. Here the implication is that these systems of thinking ('recipes') are more readily able to change and re-categorize – essential to the likelihood of 'unfreezing' strategic thinking.

5.1.3   *Compare clusters between maps.* Producing mutually exclusive link similarity clusters enables a number of comparisons to be made. For example, it is possible to compare, across different maps, the emergent 'themes' for each interviewee, or strategy map, produced by this analysis. As a consequence it will be possible to determine the nature of similarities and differences in the themes of cognitive maps from interviews or different oval maps from a series of workshops (Eden and Ackermann, 1998).

5.2 *Identify **hierarchical clusters** or 'tear-drops'*. This analysis explores all of the chains of argument *supporting* each member of a given 'seed set', stopping only when it encounters another member of the 'seed' set ('HIESET' in the analysis menu). The analysis produces 'tear-drop' shaped clusters whose contents are not mutually exclusive (as with link-similarity clusters). Each 'tear-drop' represents an integrated body of argument *supporting* one member of the seed set (see figure P6.2). *V198*

5.2.1 *Choose the 'seed' set.* Typically this set contains both goals and strategic issue labels. It is most usefully conducted after agreement is reached about (i) those constructs which are the best labels used to describe all strategic issues, and (ii) a draft goal system. The constructs chosen as labels for each strategic issue will be based upon the domain, central, and link-similarity cluster analyses and will generally be constructs towards the top of the hierarchy of a cluster. The analysis is designed to explore the detail, or subordinate, constructs in the map by discovering the nature of each hierarchical set ('tear-drop') that supports a strategic issue label or goal. Because the sets are not mutually exclusive, the overlap between the content of each set is of interest. In principle each construct in a set is a *potential option or action* to influence the resolution of a strategic issue or support a goal (see figure P6.5). Hierarchical cluster analysis which seeks to identify 'tear-drops' of strategic issue labels in relation to a seed set of the goals is often used to identify the potential extent of strategic support for each goal.

5.2.2 *Compare hierarchical sets.* Comparisons can focus on the differences in topics of interest either to an interviewee or a group in relation to their strategy map. When apparent synonyms across several maps have been identified, the tear-drops of argument hierarchically supporting these similar verbal tags can be compared. In addition, the size of each hierarchical cluster indicates the extent of detailed elaboration in relation to the issue label or goal. Highly elaborated sets are more likely to contain easily identified strategic options. In comparing hierarchical sets across the maps of several interviewees, the extent to which each individual's hierarchical sets relate to those of another interviewee and to a common goal system is of interest. The extent of overlap between hierarchical sets in the same map suggests the extent to which any strategic options considered are expected to have an impact (positive or negative) on several goals or issue labels.

5.2.3 *Confirm potential strategies/strategic issues.* Hierarchical clusters that contain only two or three constructs *may* suggest that the construct seeding that cluster is not a label for a key issue and that it is elaboration of an alternative key construct or requires further elaboration. Alternatively, those hierarchical sets that are relatively large may contain more than one strategic issue. As with the cluster analysis, it is worth identifying a likely candidate as a key construct, adding it to the seed set and re-running the analysis in order to determine the effect. The process is iterative. As with all analyses, judgement by the facilitator and client is essential – for example, small clusters, or tear-drops, may be of great significance *because they are not able to be well elaborated.*

Figure P6.5   Identifying hierarchical sets.

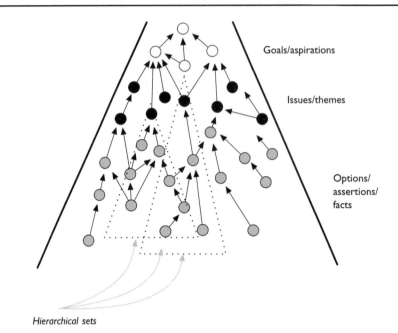

Hierarchical sets

Feedback loops

V218   The occurrence of **feedback loops** within a map is extremely significant ('LOOP' in
the analysis menu). We identified the importance of the role of feedback loops

C103   within the detection and development of **distinctive competencies**. Not only was a
feedback loop a potential distinctive, or even core, competence because of its
uniqueness, it was also important because the distinctive competence was self-
sustaining. However, feedback loops are also important during the process of
identifying strategic issues. Typically a feedback loop will be an important strategic
issue in its own right. A loop represents a description of a chain of consequences
that produces a dynamic outcome by feeding off itself (if positive), or by
controlling itself (negative).

For all of the analyses discussed above, the presence of feedback loops will
affect the results returned (a measure of the significance of loops!). For example,
where a loop of constructs exists, and any 'tear-drops' associated with the loop will
appear in the same hierarchical set. Notwithstanding the significance of loops it is
usually helpful to conduct a loop analysis before undertaking other analyses. It is
also possible for some loops in a map to be the result of incorrect coding rather
than being representative of genuine feedback, because it is often problematic to
determine the direction of causality and so 'accidental' loops appear. Where
feedback loops of this nature appear it is best to discuss with the interviewee, or
group, the direction of the link, to be clear about which of any pair of constructs in
the loop is the option and which is the outcome. This process can be difficult when
one person argues that the link is from A to B and another from B to A. In these

instances it is helpful to get the interviewee or group to verify that the feedback loop itself exists, rather than concentrating on the individual links. In some cases the relationship may be that of a feedback loop in its own right where A influences B and B influences A – creating a nested loop within a loop.

6.1 *Identify the nature of the loops.* The nature of a loop may be representative of positive feedback (virtuous or vicious cycles of behaviour) or negative feedback (self-controlling behaviour). The nature of the loop can be determined by the number of negative links present in the loop. An odd number of negative links depicts negative feedback and so a drive for stability, whereas an even number of negative links (including no negative links) suggests a positive feedback loop where either regenerative or degenerative dynamic behaviour takes place.

6.2 *Explore nested loops.* Often one loop will be a part of another loop so that two or more loops may join together to make large and small loops. For example A→B→C→A and D→B→E→D form three loops because when taken together they form the loop A→B→E→D→B→C→A. When nested loops occur it will be important to ensure they are not dis-aggregated but rather presented together, for the group will need to determine which loops are dominant. Nested loops may involve a combination of positive-vicious, positive-virtuous, and negative controlling loops.

Locating Draft Options and Core Options

While it is important to detect the goal system and associated strategic issues, it is also worth considering those constructs which may provide the means of realizing or changing strategic direction. One means of determining these potential intervention opportunities is to analyse the map to identify which are the most subordinate constructs ('tails' of the map – 'LT'). Where a construct appears at the bottom of the map, it suggests the most detailed potential intervention. The full set of tails becomes a large portfolio of possible options.

However, as maps frequently contain a large proportion of tails (and therefore by implication options), some means of identifying those which represent helpful *summary data* will provide analytical added-value. We discuss two analyses that will help determine 'potent' options and 'composite' tails.

7.1 *Identifying 'potent' options ('POTENT').* To identify the potent options it is *C109 C163 V219* necessary to have first created hierarchical clusters (see guideline 5.2 above). Hierarchical clusters encapsulate *all* of the explanations of each of the strategic issues and goals which are members of the seed set. Consequently, the hierarchical clusters may overlap to a greater or lesser extent. It is this overlap that produces the 'potent' constructs (see figure P6.6). Thus, constructs which support more than one member of the seed set are likely to be more potent than those supporting only one – the more sets any construct appears within then the more potent it is. Potent tails are obviously of particular interest because they represent the most detailed options. Nevertheless, there are a number of issues worth considering:

7.1.1 *Ignore redundant potent options.* The analysis for potent options not only identifies the potent option that is a tail but also any other options which are directly superordinate up to one level beyond any upward branch point. It is therefore more useful to consider, in the analysis of hierarchical sets, only those constructs which are the top of a 'tear-drop' of constructs

Figure P6.6 Potent and composite tail options.

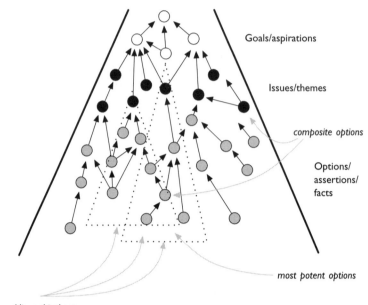

within which there are no subordinate upward branch points. Thus it becomes possible to address only the most superordinate potent options – if these are not attractive then time is not wasted on considering subordinate options which have no alternative consequences. We call these most superordinate branch points 'composite-tails' ('COTAIL') – *all* subordinate constructs have implications *only* for the composite-tail. For a map with no upward branch points the composite tail, and so most superordinate option, will be the only head to the map.

7.1.2 *Determine the significance of the seed set*. Potent options are totally dependent upon the seed set used for creating the hierarchical sets, and so the logic used for identifying the seed set members is crucial.

7.2 *Work first with 'core' potent options*. The core potent options are the most potent of the composite tails. From an examination of the core potent options, it is possible to gain some indication of the complexity of possible action packages which exist within the context of multiple goals set within a goal *system*. Potent options are not necessarily good options, or powerful options – they may represent potent dilemmas where their effect is both positive and negative, or simply options with little leverage on outcomes. Evaluation of options as points of strategic leverage is necessary. Forms of multiple criteria modelling may help with this process. The use of the networked computer system and its 'rating' component can often enable a group to quickly locate promising options from amongst core potent options and potent options. The rating scale can be used to indicate degree of relative leverage on goals and strategic outcomes.

Shape

A map, because it is a hierarchy, may have important characteristics through its shape ('SHAPE'). Here shape means considering the number of nodes at each level of the map in relation to more subordinate and superordinate levels. Thus, the most superordinate level is the number of heads in the map, the second most superordinate level is the number of nodes that relate directly to the heads, and so on. The significance of this form of analysis is problematic. In principle when a shape is flat (lots of short paths between tails and heads) it may indicate little *depth* of strategic thinking, but contrarily it also suggests consideration of a large number and range of alternative views from the group. A thin tall shape (a small number of long paths between tails and heads) may indicate detailed argument without consideration of alternative definitions of the situation.

The shape of a map will be different if it is determined from tails-to-heads rather than the heads-to-tails method outlined above. Which of these two methods of analysis is more appropriate depends upon the coding method used. Most of the maps used in the context of strategy development tend to lay emphasis on the role of heads because they represent desired outcomes, goals, aspirations, or objectives. In these cases an exploration of top-down shape is most appropriate because tails represent an elaboration, rich detail, of the means or options.

The interpretation of a shape analysis can be problematic because it can significantly depend upon the type of model on which the analysis is undertaken. When conducted on a summary, or overview, computer model it will reveal a structure of relative complexity between the categories of nodes (options, central constructs, and goals). Whereas for the detailed and un-categorized computer model the shape will be more indicative of depth of detail (depth versus width) compared with multiplicity of aspects to the issue (width versus depth). Other possibilities include triangular shapes where a pyramid may imply tidiness of goals where each goal supports a summary or superordinate goal, whereas an upside-down pyramid may imply a lack of options coupled with multiplicity of different types of goals. The interpretation of an analysis of shape must be made by the model builder in the context of the strategy making progress.

Yes But . . .

How many analysis iterations should I undertake?

Whilst this is, to some extent, dependent on the amount of time available and the extensiveness of the maps, at least one iteration of all the analysis approaches discussed above is advisable. Many of the analyses provide important alternative perspectives. For example, there is an overlap of purpose between finding busy constructs through domain, through central analyses, and through link clustering. Each iteration provides a chance for new insights, as emergent characteristics are noted and reviewed. Ultimately a map is intended to facilitate a journey – it is not a **precise model**. *The purpose of analysis is exploratory* and expected to be the start of   *V218* the process of preparing for workshops or feedback interviews. The analyses provide assistance to the analyst; they do not replace the analyst's/facilitator's need to use good judgement about the nature of the map and its content.

The process of exploration through analysis helps to provide a better feeling for the stability of the map and for its contents. This is particularly important when merging multiple maps together. It also provides a useful method for becoming familiar with the content of the computer model.

How reliable are the analyses?

As we suggested above, the map is not a precise model. The quality of the map depends upon the listening and coding skills of the facilitator. If the coding is bad – inconsistent or informal – then the analysis will be meaningless. While most of the methods of analysis explore the structural properties of the map and so appear to ignore content, it is important to realize that the map itself is created from analysis of content and so *the analysis of structure is also an analysis of content*. Thus, the reliability of the analysis methods is dependent on judgements made during the creation of the map. Do not ignore judgements made about content beyond any insights that derive from analysis. For example, if constructs are clearly important because emotion, non-verbal behaviour, and general analysis of the situation indicate as much, then they must be classified as such.

Analysing Maps or Computer Models for Managing Workshops – introduction

We noted at the beginning of this chapter that the analysis of interview maps and OMT models is separate from preparing to use the model as a support system for a group. Nevertheless, this section builds on the first – once a draft analysis of the model has been conducted, there are analyses that a decision making group can use to explore and negotiate strategic intent. Thus this stage of the JOURNEY making process commences chronologically from the analysis of maps and encompasses analysing the map *during the workshop(s)* and using analysis for *post-workshop feedback*. This section will adopt a format replicating that used in practice. As seen above, the JOURNEY making process is one of iteration, and there are likely to be a number of workshops where the decision making team review progress, continue to work on the material and then require feedback material to be made available. Therefore processes discussed in this chapter should be treated as cyclical (see Chapter C2, figure C2.7).

Guidelines for Analysing Maps or Computer Models for Managing Workshops

V219   ***Pre-workshop Analysis***

The issues considered when analysing the maps for workshops are closely tied to issues of facilitation – both in terms of getting started (previous section) and managing workshops (current section). The more familiar the facilitator/interviewer is with the map and its contents, the greater the benefit gained by the group. Issues such as how to provide clear 'navigation' through the complexity of a map and how to ensure that all members become involved in the process, need resolving, regardless of whether the map is in an electronic format (i.e. in a computer model) or paper based. Both of these issues and their attendant analysis will be addressed below.

8.1 *Provide clear **navigation** around the computer model.* As we mentioned earlier, if a series of interviews has been undertaken and the resultant cognitive maps merged together, or a number of oval mapping workshops have been carried out, the resultant map is likely to be of considerable size. It is not unusual for strategy maps to contain 800–2000 constructs (see Eden and Ackermann, 1992). Typically such deep knowledge and detail is dealt with by ignoring it – either by not 'hearing it' in the first place or summarizing it. One important characteristic of JOURNEY making is seriously attempting to pay attention to individual wisdom and perspectives by working with subtle detail. If this is important then the complexity of a map must be retained but its potential debilitating effect countered. Consequently, providing ways of navigating around the map or computer model and making the material accessible to participants becomes a matter of critical importance. To manage this complexity, a number of analyses have been developed to support groups working on the maps. These analyses include developing an overview, using emergent categories and using colour and different fonts (styles), and preparing some starting material which recognizes the structure of the material and process management issues.

V219 V242

8.1.1 *Build an **overview**.* An overview can be viewed as a 'road map' of the model where only the goals and key issue labels/themes ('cities') and their relationships ('major highways') are seen. Any route connecting two 'cities' together, regardless of whether it follows several different routes through options or elaborating arguments ('smaller towns'), or goes directly, is displayed. Thus the analysis collapses ('COLLAPSE' on the analysis menu) the map down to just those constructs selected for the overview (see figures P6.7 and P6.8).

V219 V241

This 'collapse' analysis can be undertaken on any 'set' or selection of chosen constructs or on a chosen style. However, typically a collapsed view of all of the goals and key issue labels or themes provides an appropriate overview. In a similar fashion, a map can be simplified by taking out some of the detail in the chains of argumentation. For example, when a construct does not have any branches either up or down the hierarchy, it is possibly serving only the purpose of detailed elaboration and can be temporarily taken out of the map. However, on some occasions the procedure may lose constructs which provide important explanation for linking other, more 'busy', constructs to each other, or provide creative 'options'. Nevertheless, in general, map simplification using this procedure can be helpful. The procedure 'strips' out ('STRIP') the elaboration but does so in a temporary manner preventing links from being lost and allowing the elaboration to be restored when required.

8.1.2 *Use the overview.* The overview can be seen as a summary representation of the organizational knowledge, and its structure, delivered by those staff involved in the production of the strategy map. As such it provides a reasonable representation of the basic emergent strategy of the organization – a sort of **organization recipe** (similar to the notion of an industry recipe – Spender, 1989). In this way participants are easily alerted to the

C27

Figure P6.7   Map before collapse on selected concepts.

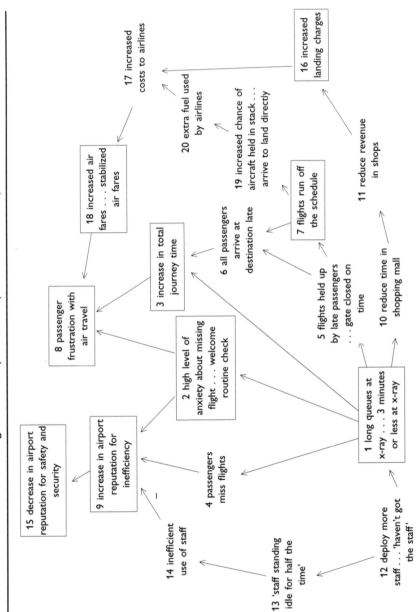

Figure P6.8 Map after collapse on selected concepts.

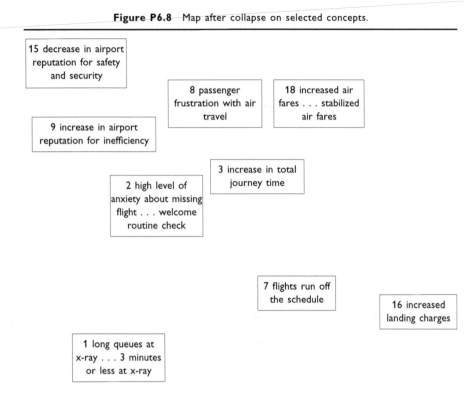

range and extensiveness of the potential strategies or strategic issues and their relationship to the emergent goal system. However, it is worth noting that:

- The resultant map may be very complex (ratio of links to constructs) if the number of routes between constructs collapsed upon is high. This can reduce the benefit of producing the overview, and further steps to simplify the map may have to be taken. Clustering contextually similar goals/key issue labels together as a group is one method for reducing the complexity. Another is further subdividing the overview map into two or more clusters. When goals and issue labels with a high domain are mapped, and the map shows that some of these are linked directly, it is often appropriate to summarize these clusters by merging for the purpose of presentation of the overview only. Merging within the full computer model should occur only when the constructs are truly synonymous and the language of each construct can be retained. In addition the overview map may need to identify primary links and delete secondary links – analysing the number of routes between constructs may be a useful basis for this decision when judgement alone is problematic.

8.1.3 *Produce some maps in advance of a workshop.* As with the overview (or series of overview maps) it may be worth developing a series of maps which provide some elaboration of the key issues and goals. These maps can be produced, saved, and accessed when required. Without some facility to provide deeper elaboration of the meaning (context) of goals and issues many participants will be distressed about a lack of acknowledgement of their own views on the topic. These maps will, of course, become dated very quickly as the group negotiate changes and move towards group ownership. When summary maps are prepared for circulation during a workshop it is crucial to ensure that each member of the group is represented on some maps (see below).

8.1.4   *Use categories (styles) to aid navigation.* Styles, as noted in guideline 4.1, provide a valuable form of navigation. It is helpful for the facilitator to note styles (using colour when appropriate) on flip-chart sheets before-hand, to act as prompts for participants.

8.2   *'Buy in' all of the participants into the process.* JOURNEY making is import-antly a social process, as well as a process of evaluating and deciding about content. As noted in chapter P5 on managing workshops, the early stages of a workshop are crucial to the success of later stages. Attending to social and personal needs is most important at the beginning of a workshop. Maps that are declared during these early stages must account for issues in the process management of the group as much as they should account for the content.

8.2.1   *Ensure that initial views have contributions from all participants.* It is important that every view displayed early in the workshop contains constructs from each participant, as much as is possible. Even when the group map, created through merging, does not reveal a mix of constructs for a particular view, the facilitator must consider adjusting the maps to attend to initial owner-ship of the content. Careful research we have undertaken shows that each participant will look, first, for their own material. Then, after they have reassured themselves that they have been 'heard', they will move on to **being curious about what others have said**, and so by viewing this, absorb the rest of a map and so 'listen' to others. This process is an important part of beginning the 'psychological negotiation' towards new meanings. While merging maps it is, therefore, helpful to retain the numbering sequences for each interviewee (or workshop) so that each individual's contribution can be recognized. After preparing for the workshop the computer model can be renumbered randomly ('RENUMBER' on the edit menu) so as to ensure anonymity. During preparation, it can be very helpful to use styles to colour the contribution of each participant. When doing this, it is impera-tive to retain any previous styles associated with categories of data as sets so that they can replace the colour styles used for participants before the workshop commences!

8.2.2   *Explore participants' awareness of feedback loops.* Feedback loops that emerge from an interview can be identified and discussed with the interviewee. Similarly, loops arising directly out of group discussion during a work-shop can be validated and dealt with during the workshop. However, often feedback loops occur through merging material from several maps, and so no individual participant, or the group as a whole, will be aware of their existence. The loop, as a loop rather than individual beliefs within a loop, will need to be examined and validated by the group. When these circumstances arise, it is useful to explore the material from each parti-cipant's map using word searches to determine whether the topic is

V219

discussed by all participants. On some occasions it is possible that one group, or one interviewee, has referred to the loop by using a loop label (for example, 'the waiting list vicious circle') without elaborating the full content of the loop. In such circumstances eliciting the fuller elaboration is important, given the possible centrality of loops to strategy development. For example, 'housing blight' might have been discussed without the fuller loop elaboration of 'a threat of industrial development is leading to house prices dipping, and so poorer people moving into the area who can't afford to keep houses in good condition and so house prices drop further'. The regular appearance of at least the topic will show how widespread the interest will be in the loop discovered through analysis. Loops which have been identified by one workshop or one participant as 'obvious' will need more careful introduction to the group than those which are new to all participants.

Analysis During the Workshop

Typically, analysis during a workshop is used sparingly, and usually at breaks. However, many of the analyses used for preparing maps can be used in front of the group to great effect. The criterion for their use is the amount of time it takes for the analysis to be completed, which depends mostly upon the computer hardware used, and the interest likely to be generated by the results. As participants become used to working with computer support, they also get to know the different forms of analysis available and often request the facilitator to implement analyses as the computer model changes. When introducing the computer model early in a workshop it is imperative that participants understand fully the process followed by the facilitator in analysing the model prior to the workshop. If this is not done, not only will participants be puzzled about where the styled categories came from, they will not be convinced of, or persuaded by, the **procedural rationality** of the process.   *C55*

9.1   *Provide a clear explanation of the analysis* undertaken on the map's content and structure, possibly introducing simple examples *from their material*.

9.2   *Frequently re-examine the structure of the map*. While prepared views can be used at the beginning of the workshop, once participants begin to refine and add to the map, and explore specific areas, a more contingent approach is necessary. There are a number of simple routines or analyses that can help with the exploration of the map's material. The clustering analyses (both simple linking and hierarchical) are helpful devices to enable participants to establish whether changes they have made fundamentally change the structure of the map.

9.3   *Improve the clarity of constructs' wording*. Whilst not obviously analytical in nature, a number of analytical routines exist that can help with this process. As discussed in the chapter on computer supported visual interactive workshops (chapter P3: 3.4.3), identification and elaboration of cryptic constructs is important.

9.3.1   *Use 'macro edits'*. As participants begin to share statements and develop some sense of shared meaning, agreeing upon universally shared wording becomes important. Participants may initially use different words to describe the same event or issue which during the course of the workshop they decide should be expressed in a single format. Using a macro edit (EDM) enables the group to make these changes throughout the entire map.

9.4   *Search and bring related material on to the main display.* Often participants will raise material located in the computer model, but not shown on the current display, and suggest that it is linked to that being discussed. On other occasions the facilitator will become aware that synonymous, or associated, material exists else-where in the computer model. Using the 'FIND' facility allows the extra material to be found and brought on to the current view as required ('BRING'). The use of a second computer and a content facilitator can help this process.

9.5   *Re-run centrality, clustering, and feedback analysis during breaks.* As new material is being entered into the computer model, new relationships formed, and the structure consequently altered, it is worthwhile reviewing the structure of the model. New key issues may emerge; checking for feedback loops is also important as they not only affect all subsequent analysis but are easy to introduce into the map's structure by mistake.

9.6   *Regularly review progress.* Analyses supporting a review of progress can be undertaken at any point throughout the workshop and form an important part of reviewing progress. This is particularly the case when aiming to achieve closure of stages in the workshop, and when considering 'next steps'.

9.6.1   *List agreed actions/options/strategies.* Giving participants some sense of pro-gress made by listing agreements already reached and material negotiated to a reasonable level of ownership will provide some progress reassurance.

9.6.2   *Carry out set analysis.* The software allows 'set logic' analyses to be carried out as the workshop progresses. Thus, analysing for set similarity, set differences, and set exceptions can provide data about which agreed actions make multiple demands, etc. For example, if a set has been created to collect actions which have financial implications, and another to collect actions which have implications for changes in culture, then it is simple to search for those which have neither implication, or both implications. Sets of categories can be created as the workshop unfolds. Sets may be created to signify responsibilities, implications for resources, stakeholder relation-ships, and full, partial, or no agreement. Because sets are simple 'buckets' into which, or out of which, constructs can be placed, they are an easy way to keep a running set of categories which can then be the subject of set-logic questions.

9.6.3   *Use arrow styles and colours.* As the workshop unfolds, the arrows may become particularly significant for the group, because there is a consensus about the relationship signified by the arrow, or the intensity of the rela-tionship is strong, or the probability of causality is strong, and so on. Similarly, colours on arrows can be introduced to signify different types of relationships: for example, implicative, causal, temporal, possible, uncer-tain, and so on. Note, however, that regardless of style all the arrows will be treated as one when undertaking any of the analyses – none of the analyses differentiates between arrow styles.

V198 V234   **Post-workshop**

Providing participants with feedback reflecting the progress they have made is a critical element of journey 'signposting', and needs to be managed carefully by the facilitator. Providing feedback in a format that is easily interpreted and assimilated may be achieved by including all of the relevant material detailing progress made, but *without overwhelming* participants. As with managing the complexity of the map or computer model during a workshop, it is important to manage the complexity of the feedback maps, otherwise feedback will not be examined and used.

The type of feedback will also depend on the group's stage in the JOURNEY making process – that is, at the beginning of the journey or reaching the point whereby they are moving towards closure. Where the workshop is to be followed by another within a short space of time (for example, a 'psychological week'), then providing a text based summary of progress along with a revised map of the overview may be sufficient. Alternatively, if there is to be a long period of time between the workshops, participants may wish to begin to consider implementing some of the actions. As we noted in chapter C2 managers 'engaged in an active conversation are unable to hold off strategic action until the strategy making is complete' – in these cases provide sufficient detail to ensure a unified direction is taken.

10.1 *Re-analyse the map.* After the workshop, the map will require many of the analyses to be re-run to check whether there has been significant change with respect to the goals, strategies/strategic issues and options (in analytical terms), and whether there are any erroneous 'heads' that are not goals or 'orphans' that should have been linked into the rest of the model.

10.2 *Decide on format of the maps.* Depending on the extensiveness of the map and the number of interviews, or oval mapping workshops, undertaken, the feedback may adopt different forms. Producing a new version of the overview is almost always a useful starting point, as it provides a holistic picture of the structure of the overall map and highlights the key areas – **a 'road map'**. Deciding how the *V198* additional material should be produced is a more contingent matter and may require different options being explored before a final set of maps is produced. Discussing the format of feedback with the client will not only help further good relationships with the client but ensure that the most appropriate form can be produced. Some of the options are as follows.

10.2.1 *Produce hierarchical sets for each of the goals and strategies.* These maps, along with the overview, will provide a comprehensive picture of the material displaying all of the context relating to the goals/key issues. They are useful as they display all of the options and context related to the seed construct. However, there is the danger that some of the hierarchical sets are very large and many constructs appear in many of the sets and so have to be repeated on many of the feedback maps (see guideline 3.3). Depending on the number of strategies and goals, the package produced may be too lengthy and overwhelming. Debilitating complexity is not helpful. To counteract this problem, it may be appropriate to include only the maps that are relevant to each individual. Additionally, where hierarchical sets ('hiesets') are small and related to others, producing several of them on the same map may reduce the overall size of the feedback.

10.2.2 *Produce 'link similarity' clusters.* Because clusters are mutually exclusive, this form of feedback will reduce the number of maps as well as eliminate overlapping material. Size of clusters can be constrained (the parameters of the analysis can be set). However, the interrelationships between the clusters will not be apparent (unlike the hierarchical sets, which are not mutually exclusive) unless the maps are produced with the 'hidden arrows' (additional context) printed on them.

10.2.3 *Use lists.* For some participants the combination of lists and maps is comforting as they have the familiarity of lists but with the richness of the maps. Lists may detail actions, strategies, or goals or may comprise those actions related to specific individuals or subjects. Remember that maps can be meaningless and strange to organizational members not involved in the journey or the specific workshop unless great care is taken to reduce the incidence of cryptic wording.

10.2.4 *Develop 'action' oriented maps.* Action maps exploit the 'collapse' analysis routine as they focus on the actions and strategies in a manner similar to that for producing an overview of the strategies and goals. In this manner it is possible for participants to see *what* it is they have agreed upon, how certain actions relate to other actions, and *why* (what is the purpose) they have been agreed. To produce the maps a hierarchical set analysis can be undertaken with the collapse focusing on the resultant sets. Where the sets appear too small to warrant a map of their own, they can be combined with other related maps (when the strategies are linked together).

10.3 *Fashion effective maps.* Strategy maps or computer models may contain anywhere from four hundred statements upwards, which is too many for a single map both in terms of printing and understanding the contents. While many of the analyses mentioned in this chapter help in slicing the map into more manageable 'chunks' these chunks may still be too large for participants to digest easily.

10.3.1 *Restrict the number of constructs on the map to a maximum of 25.* Getting the size as well as the number of maps right will help participants make use of the maps. This limitation may prove to be difficult especially when using the hierarchical set analysis.

10.3.2 *Print maps in colour.* Not only does this help participants distinguish the categories far faster, but it also adds interest to their composition and allows larger maps to be produced, as the colour coding provides an aid to navigation and slicing. However, if the maps are to be photocopied in black and white, then styles including borders will need to be employed to differentiate between the categories which otherwise would have shown up in colour.

10.4 *Consider ownership of maps.* Ensuring that the maps produced not only reflect the client's interest (and therefore acknowledge the political feasibility of the outcomes) but also take account of each participant, will increase their interest and therefore account of the material. This acknowledgement of individual perspectives and interests will also provide valuable information when considering how much detail and how many maps to produce (see guideline 10.2.1)

Yes But . . .

What if a computer and the software are not available?

Whilst many of the analyses discussed in this chapter are reliant on the additional speed and power of a computer, most of the analysis can be done crudely by hand.

For example, each of the **key issues/goals can be re-written** on a Post-it and moved   *V250*
to a separate wall space or sheet of paper. Using the copies, the interrelationships
can then be explored and developed into a network – an overview. In this manner,
the original can then be kept with the context showing the elaborating text. Ovals/
constructs with a large number of links around them will be immediately obvious,
providing a crude form of domain analysis, and groups with a large number of
bridges to other groups will demonstrate their centrality.

How do I know if the analysis is right?

The analysis of maps is not intended to be anything other than a guide to exploring
the properties of the map. The analyses suggest a range of insights that may be of
use in JOURNEY making, with those undertaking the journey being the judges
of their relevance. As shown in figure P7.3 (in the next chapter) one of the first
tasks for participants is to explore and begin to confirm goals and strategies. If the
analysis has missed areas, for example a strategy appears to be missing, or there is
a superfluous or missing goal, then these can be detected and dealt with. For the
most part, analyses should suggest more goals/issues than are likely to be confirmed by the group – they act as a dialectical device designed to help JOURNEY
making.

By explaining the analytical process, and examining the results with the group,
confirmation, or not, may be gained. The analysis, however, will be insightful only
if the map has properly followed a formal set of mapping guidelines, such as those
discussed in this book. If the map is poor, then the analysis will be poor.

DELIVERING STRATEGY: CLOSURE – STRATEGIC PROGRAMMES AND STRATEGY DELIVERY SUPPORT

Introduction

In chapter C1 we note that the delivery of strategy is dependent on a number of factors and discuss some of the contingencies involved in determining an appropriate form of strategy for an organization. In chapter C8 we argue for closure for symbolic and psychological reasons, amongst others, and in chapter C2 we suggest that strategy making and delivery is inevitably a continuous journey. We argue that organizations will need to move from a joint understanding and reflection stage through to negotiated agreements and finally confirmation and implementation of outcomes. The drive for 'getting on with it' is often strongest in organizations where the process of strategy is a new one. Here, the management team needs to see quickly some outcomes, to convince themselves that strategy making is worthwhile. As the team begins to understand the strategy process and become familiar and therefore confident with it, then it appears that there is less urgency to agree plans. Members become aware that the process itself is creating strategic change, as well as informing and benefiting the group.

Learning, thus, is an important part of the journey. In the context of this chapter, learning can be seen as a means of determining exactly what is meant by a goal, a strategy, what the mission statement should be, etc. Agreeing a goal system with its associated mission/vision statements and attendant strategies goes some way to providing the means for discussing strategy through a common language. In terms of delivery the first section of this chapter deals with the development of *C110 V195* **strategic intent** allowing organizations to clarify a direction while acknowledging their need to be opportunistic and flexible. The second part – that addressing agreeing strategic programmes – builds upon this development, providing a clear sense of the action portfolios necessary for implementation.

C54 C55 During the stage of confirming and (re)designing strategic direction, issues such as the **emotional and cognitive commitment** of both the management team and other managers, is addressed. To increase the likelihood of successful implementation there are a number of key factors. The first is emotional commitment, focusing on the return from applying procedural justice to the process. This form of justice derives from the act of being involved, having a chance to influence and signal areas that are considered to be key. It denotes a sense of fairness, openness, and builds on the benefits gained from participation and open communication. Procedural justice does not advocate equality, but rather a process that gives due consideration to alternative viewpoints before agreeing the strategic direction. Alongside this is the provision of a sense of procedural rationality – the cognitive commitment arising because the process undertaken appears thoughtful, intelligent, and the outcomes robust.

Political feasibility is crucial to closure and implementation – the delivery of strategy. It will have encompassed accounting for the various power bases within the organization. Additionally, addressing the suggested alliances with stakeholders which surfaced during a stakeholder analysis provides a means of making options feasible in a wider political sphere. The agreement to goal systems, mission statements, and strategies will also have taken into account the possible scenarios generated, using techniques for ensuring that what is agreed is viable in many alternative futures. This focus on political feasibility, supported by analysis of the maps and facilitation of groups, significantly informs the process of strategy delivery.

In addition, the process of learning which is a part of agreeing strategic direction will also result in helping participants see things differently (evidenced by a cognitive change) and from this position start moving towards a greater degree of **cooperation and coordination** (see figure C10.1). Through the process of *C48* agreeing the goals and strategies of the organization, a better understanding of different departmental roles and duties become evident. This may be likened to some extent to the notion of Business Process Re-engineering where processes are examined to determine their best fit (Davenport, 1993). Yeates (1996), when discussing the strategic process undertaken by his organization, noted

> 'a subtle but significant shift in approach has been promoted, for example, rather than question how can the Education & Training department improve the skills bases, we are now guided by a goal expressing the aspiration to create a learning community and the strategies we agreed to put in place to meet this aspiration'.

It will not be appropriate for all organizations to develop strategic programmes with associated action portfolios. However, regardless of the type of organization, developing and agreeing a goal system, a set of associated strategies, examining the organization's distinctive competencies to ensure that they support the **business** *C79* **model or livelihood scheme,** and agreeing a mission or vision statement – all of which represents a strategic intent – is likely.

Guidelines for Delivering Strategy – agreeing strategic intent and strategic programmes

Agreeing the Aspirations/Goals System

Agreement to the **goals system** and business model or livelihood scheme is an *C95 V257* appropriate place to start the whole process of closure. This is because it is pivotal to all other analyses and agreements. Stakeholder and alternative futures analysis cannot be undertaken effectively without, at least a draft, goals system. It is the goal system that informs the relevancy of any analysis. Strategies are usually considered in the light of the goals they are aiming to achieve and thus are considered after the agreement of the draft goal system. Nevertheless, as with the entire strategy process, it is necessary to cycle around the various steps to ensure coherence, and so the goals will inevitably change to a greater or lesser degree. This chapter will start by explaining the process of agreeing a goal system, before discussing the production of the mission statement, the prioritization of the strategies, and finally the development of action programmes.

Creating the goal system can be achieved using one of a number of the techniques mentioned earlier (and often a combination of them). The oval mapping technique (OMT), or cognitive mapping interviews followed by a workshop, are the most typical processes. From these processes, emergent potential goals and key issues or themes (some of which later become prioritized as strategies) can be identified. With both processes it is important to start with the detection of **emergent goal**s – those that appear currently to drive the creation of a strategic future. Both processes start by eliciting the key issues and potential strategic options. As such, effort has to be directed specifically towards asking the 'so what' question of the material, to '**ladder**' up to goals *and negative-goals*. As the goals begin to emerge, some effort may be expended in trying to determine how much the goals are organizationally driven through embedded procedures and how much they are driven by the preferences and beliefs of specific individuals (see figure C10.2). This distinction is more difficult to make when using the OMT as the process invloves a group negotiating the goal system. In the case of interviews, each of the maps that contribute to the group map will have been constructed in the light of an opportunity to observe non-verbal cues about the nature of desired outcomes – whether they are emotionally or procedurally driven.

V248

C91

1.1 *Use the analysis to provide an initial draft of the goal system.* It is often useful to create a first draft from a routine analysis of the hierarchy and then subsequently correct for judgement. This process can be undertaken in preparation for a workshop or alternatively by the group. Time available will probably determine which approach is appropriate. As with all JOURNEY making it is usually better for the group to be involved in all parts of the journey, if possible.

Every 'head' in the group map should, in principle, be a goal/negative-goal, value, or aspiration. It is also likely that goals and negative-goals will also appear in a hierarchically subordinate position to the heads. Thus, start at the top of the map and check whether each head seems a *likely candidate* as a goal/negative-goal. Then work down the hierarchy one level at a time, and establish further candidates for goals. Keep working down each path of the hierarchy until the construct considered is a clear *means to an end rather than an end in itself.* This is the first draft of the goal system. Following this routine, the group or analyst should scan the rest of the map, noting any other constructs that are goals because they are outcomes that are good or bad in their own right, and not seen as 'up for grabs' as means to other ends. Often this first draft will produce 50–70 goals. This is partly because it is important to be inclusive, and partly because it is important to *include some goal statements from every participant.* In any event the major task for the group will be agreeing a more manageable goal system of 15–20 goals. The process will typically result in the group agreeing that some draft goals are potential strategies, and others should be merged to create inclusive goal statements.

This process provides two benefits: (i) it produces a goal *system* demonstrating the extent to which goals are interrelated, where each goal in turn is supported by or supports other goals, and (ii) it enables all participants to gain a sense of the diversity of goals, and yet interconnection between them – how goals relating to different parts of the organization support each other, and work togther *as a system.*

1.1.1 *Show the relationship of goals to potential strategic issues or themes.* It is important that the process of negotiating agreement about goals is done within the context of strategic issues and emergent themes. The meaning of a goal arises from its context – the context of other goals that support it, and the possible strategies required to make it happen, or strategic issues that give rise to its presence.

1.2   *Check whether there are missing goals.* The draft goal system is emergent and so will not encompass new aspirations or those that seem so obvious they will not have appeared during OMT workshops or interviews. However, as these are added, it is helpful to tag them as 'new'/proposed goals so that they can be distinguished as '**espoused**' goals rather than emergent goals representing '**theories-in-action**'.   *C37*
Checking goals in relation to the distinctive competencies and so the business model/livelihood scheme will ultimately be the most important validation of the goal system.

1.3   *Establish, when relevant, whether the **goals are facilitative** or core.* Core goals   *V218 V250 V257*
are those directly relating to the business model. Facilitative goals reflect the ways in which these core goals will be achieved but are nevertheless such important statements about the nature of the organization that they are ends in their own right. Facilitative goals are, of course, of no consequence unless they are an integral part of supporting core goals, since they cannot be sustained without the servicing of core goals. It is sometimes useful to categorize goals in this way because often, when reviewing the potential goal system of an organization, it turns out to be focused too much on one area rather than the other. A good mission statement, or statement of strategic intent, usually needs to include statements about what the organization values about the way it runs itself as well as core business goals.

For example, Scottish Natural Heritage (see vignette) discovered that their focus was very much on the internal nature of the organization, pivoting around a central goal of 'build an effective and credible organization'. This strong focus on facilitative goals suggested that the core purpose of the organization – that of managing and protecting the natural heritage – was, at that time, being subordinated to that of managing the organization. This was an important statement about the strategic issues facing the organization at that time – a statement that played a key role in jointly understanding and reflecting on the emergent strategic situation faced by the organization. Further negotiation adjusted the balance and encompassed other goals which had, to some extent, been taken for granted. The focus on effective management was still adopted as a realistic stance towards the next five years of strategic development for the organization (producing the goal system presented as a map shown in figure P8.2). In contrast, other organizations, for example Govan Initiative (see vignette), initially found themselves focusing almost solely on core goals and ignoring facilitative goals.

1.4   *Confirm that draft goals 'truly' are goals rather than potential strategies.* This task is different from considering the relationship between one goal and another – the nature of the goals as a *system* (see guideline 1.1 above). It is the first step in reducing the number of draft goals by exploring the boundary between the goal/ aspirations part of the map and the strategies part of the map.

1.4.1   *Check whether the potential goal is a good outcome or aspiration 'in its own right'.* An appropriate question to ask is: 'is the organization concentrating on pursuing the candidate goal because it would wish to achieve it regardless of its role in supporting other goals?'. Typically this task may take some effort to debate and result in further goals being suggested before the number of candidate goals reduces. However, the task is an important part of the journey and should not be skimped. Participants will begin to gain a common understanding of the potential goals and of their meaning through the process of checking each goal individually and within its context of other goals and strategies.

1.4.2   *Consider the time horizon*. Throughout this book we have discussed aspirations, goals/negative-goals, and values. Values are taken to be personal and will, of course, influence goals and aspirations but will rarely form a direct part of a goal system. Aspirations are typically unattainable in any absolute sense, rather the organization will continually make progress towards their achievement (Ackoff and Emery (1972) call these 'ideals'). Goals, however, tend to be more concrete and attainable, even if in the longer term. Although we find it practically useful to differentiate these terms conceptually we do not usually use all of these terms with management teams; rather we use whichever label suits their own organizational language and culture. Indeed, in this book we have deliberately used the terms interchangeably, for strategy development goals need to relate to a time horizon appropriate to the overall strategy making of the organization. Where a draft goal is attainable over a relatively short time horizon, it may be useful to identify it as a potential strategy.

1.5   *Decide upon the number of goals*. While there are no clear rules concerning the appropriate number of goals, having 'too many' will give rise to problems when considering promulgation. As noted in chapter C5 the goal system will usually be an important part of stakeholder management. In our experience, organizations typically use 5–12 goals as a primary focus, although some organizations have worked with up to 25 goals. When many goals are used, in order to simplify the goal system it is helpful to prioritize them, for example with 1, 2, or 3 star ratings.

V250   One method for reducing the number of goals is to determine whether any goal constructs can be merged. *It is important that **goals are not merged** too early during strategy making, for each merge changes the shape of the goal system.* Therefore, before merging takes place the system must be addressed in detail and as a whole (that is, complete the above steps first). Then, if the software is being used, the 'STRIP' analysis can be carried out. This analysis is helpful as it hides all the goals that appear as linking argument between central goals (those with more relationships to other goals). Thus, goals having only one in-arrow and one out-arrow are temporarily stripped out of the system. The result is a smaller, more highly linked, goal system. If this new system looks sensible then the full goal system should be restored and the elaborating argument gradually merged into the other, more central, goals so that the new wording reflects all of the elaboration. The stripped out material is usually merged into the subordinate goal so that the extended goal becomes the 'story' upwards to the next goal in the hierarchy. This process can be undertaken without the software.

V197   1.6   *Review **mandates*** (if a public sector organization). Most public sector organizations have their activities mandated by another 'sponsoring' body such as government. Sometimes there are clear mandates established through legislation. These mandates must play an important role in influencing a goal system. Mandates may be treated as the most superordinate goals, but they may also be seen as constraints, when they do not meet the 'definition' of a goal and so be subordinate context to the goal system.

In Scottish Natural Heritage's case (figure P8.2), the goal system demonstrates their *choice* of how the mandate set by government was to be achieved – it was treated as the ultimate goal. Scottish Natural Heritage's mandate was complex and contained potentially conflicting goals. Often, working on the goal system reveals the inadequacy of mandates and may lead to their renegotiation with the sponsor. Typically, public sector organizations need to demonstrate to their sponsors – often various funding stakeholder bodies – a commitment to the organization's mandated purpose.

1.7 *Examine the wording of the goals.* At some stage it will be important to ensure that the wording of each goal, *within the context of other goals* and supporting strategies, is clear to those outside of the management team. More than any other part of the strategy map the goal statements need to be understood by many others, have action oriented meaning, and be more than 'motherhood' statements. Make sure the language is clear and not cryptic, and that each goal is written in an aspirational language, rather than being a statement of 'what is'. Think carefully about the impact of the wording on the 'players' identified by the stakeholder analysis. A goal system will be continuously open to change as coherence checks are carried out with respect to each part of the journey. Thus, the precise copy-writing of the goals will be a task to be undertaken at the end of the journey.

1.8 *Do not ignore '**negative-goals**'.* Focusing on goals alone often contrives   *C90* towards an overtly optimistic view of the world without acknowledging the need avoid disasters. Negative-goals are those potentially hazardous ramifications whose outcomes are to be avoided. In addition they inform the agreement of a goal system. However, the opposite aspect of a negative-goal does not always signify a goal. For example a negative-value may be 'I experience stress and burnout' where the opposite would not necessarily imply a value. In some cases negative-goals may suggest stronger clues about the emergent strategic direction of the organization than the goals themselves (see chapter C5).

1.9 *Validate the goal system through the business model/livelihood scheme.*

Producing a Mission Statement   *C161*

A mission statement is a statement of the aims and values of an organization. Most large companies, and many public organizations, have drawn up such statements, although their importance varies – in some cases it is only a statement demanded by powerful stakeholders. Many have a poor reputation, and are seen as meaningless and unrealistic. This reputation makes the process of developing a good mission statement very difficult. They can be fairly elaborate statements of where the company wants to go and how it wants to get there (strategic intent); alternatively they can be brief catch phrases intended to inspire staff. One well-known example of the latter is Star Trek's split infinitive – 'to boldly go where no one has gone before'! Of all of the strategy literature produced by the organization, it is the mission statement that is most likely to be seen by the public and evaluated accordingly. As we noted in chapter C8, we do not find it theoretically helpful or pragmatically useful to debate the definition of a mission statement. It can be called a statement of strategic intent, a vision statement, or anything which fits the organization's needs. Chapter C6 discusses the nature of the statement and presents some of the important characteristics which ought to be included in the statement (figure C6.1).

2.1 *Use the first version of the goal system to produce an **initial draft of the***   *V196 V257* ***mission statement***. This draft will miss many aspects but it will contain many of the words that need to be encompassed within it. The goal system should be translated, without any additions, from a map into a standard piece of text. The text should seek to communicate the structure of the goals as a system, as much as is possible.

2.2   *Review the draft mission statement (as goals) in relation to the organization's business.* Ask questions such as 'Does it address the shared beliefs and values of the organization?' and 'Does it define the business in terms of needs being satisfied, the markets chosen, and means of reaching market?'. This will provide some useful indication about how the mission of the organization can be aligned with its business/livelihood. As noted above, given the public nature of the mission statement, another key question that may be worth asking is, 'Is it something the organization can live with – as it is interpreted by others?' For public sector organizations the mandates, including those treated as constraints, will also inform the mission statement.

2.3   *Ensure that the mission statement focuses on a new level of performance or area of activity.* This focuses the organization on what is truly important with respect to its future. As such it will not only provide a sense of the organization and its aspirations but also provide valuable clues about the culture of the organization – its ethos. A good mission statement commits the organization to the business model/livelihood scheme which differentiates it then, strategically, from other organizations, and so will act as a constraint as well as an incentive towards particular behaviour. A private company should avoid a mission statement which commits it to 'making a reasonable profit' or 'maintaining market share', as these do not differentiate the organization from other organizations in the same field.

C161   2.4   *Consider the **length of the mission statement**.* Mission statements work best if they can be stated on one sheet of paper. This means that they should not be more than about 250 words, allowing for appropriate graphic design. While many organizations have produced mission statements that are no more than 10–12 words, it is our view that these rarely differentiate the organization from others in a clear enough manner. They most certainly cannot communicate the important factors which Campbell (1989) determined were important influences on strategic behaviour.

2.5   *Test stakeholder reactions to the mission statement.* A mission statement should, ideally, have a bearing on everyone with whom the organization is concerned, both internal and external – the 'players'. It is worth considering whether it takes into account legitimate claims of core 'players' as stakeholders. For example, within the National Health Service, a Trust hospital may want to ensure that it has acknowledged the claims made on it by patients as stakeholders. They should do this only if the strategies to be delivered seek to move patients from being 'subjects' with little power to 'players' with substantial power. If this is not the case then they are not important stakeholders to that organization. The mission statement must be a realistic call to action, not simply a public relations statement. Of course the

C129   mission statement may be used as a part of **stakeholder management**.
V257   An important and socially justifiable **mission statement** can also be a source of inspiration to key stakeholders, in particular the organization's employees. For Govan Initiative (see vignette), their mission *'Govan Initiative Limited shall ensure that the Greater Govan area will establish itself as one of the best performing inner areas of any city in the United Kingdom. The company shall focus all of its employees upon the pursuit of excellence'* demonstrates a socially justified mission and one fitting with their role in the community. However, the statement suffers from being short – it does not easily communicate a sense of mission likely to be very different from

those of other similar organizations, although it does clearly reflect a core *and* facilitative goal in a short statement.

2.6   *Get at the 'hearts and minds'.* Use inspirational language that taps emotional commitment as well as providing guidance. Careful use of language encompassing **drama** and rhetoric can turn a dry statement of goals into an attractive vision of a future worth working for.   *C110 C161*

This process of producing a mission statement is iterative, as it cycles between identifying and agreeing upon a goal system that clearly encompasses key values, checking the goal system with the distinctive competencies, reworking the business model or livelihood scheme, and determining a mission statement.

Identifying, Negotiating, and Agreeing Strategies

The last stage for determining a basic strategic intent for an organization is that of agreeing *and prioritizing* a portfolio of strategies. Organizations normally are unable to support an extensive range of strategies in terms of either staff time, energy, or costs. There is a danger that the effort becomes diluted. As we discuss early in this book, there is always a tension between **continuity and change**. It is important for   *C34* organizations to ensure that current activity continues to operate while strategic change occurs.

The agreement to strategies involves undertaking a similar set of tasks to that of agreeing the goal system. Issues such as getting the language right, determining the appropriate level of detail of strategic programmes are addressed, but here they are developed in the context of the goal system itself. Strategies are the means of achieving the goals. They usually stem from discriminating between the multiple key issues, or themes, that have surfaced using any of the above techniques. In many cases, the number of *potential* strategies may be high (sometimes as many as 30 to 60).

Some strategies are usually related to resolving selected key strategic issues that appear to have the greatest priority in terms of the organization's emphasis for the strategy period. Other strategies are new and address future concerns, new aspirations, the development of new distinctive competencies, the management of stakeholders, and the management of the environment. Although the guidelines below are presented in a step by step manner, cyclic iteration between them is essential, especially as each guideline offers the possibility of gaining new insights with implications for previous steps.

3.1   *Review all potential strategies within the context of the goal system.* In some instances, participants may have already viewed the key issues when considering the elements for the goal system. One of the first guidelines suggested for agreeing the goal system (1.1.1) was to explore an 'overview' of the captured material, in most circumstances incorporating both goals and key strategic issue labels. From this position a number of further distinctions are possible.

3.1.1   *Examine the number of key issues impacting each goal.* Where a goal appears to be superordinate to relatively few key potential strategies, it is helpful to consider why this might be. For example, is it because the goal is: easy to attain, is of little substance, and so on. Similarly it is valuable to explore the basis of a goal's being impacted by many potential strategies. Are the potential strategies fundamentally different aspects of a complete portfolio, where losing any one of them would destroy the possibility of delivery of the goal? Where this is so, the portfolio will need to be linked in the map so that the multiple potential strategies, in effect, represent one strategy.

3.1.2   *Identify those potential strategies that appear to be 'potent' with respect to goals.* These are potential strategies that support a large number of goals. The strategic issues from which some of these strategies arise must be addressed by participants. They are a good starting point, even though they may turn out not to yield extensive leverage – the potent analysis can be misleading – and it is important to evaluate them, for they may be critical strategies with multiple pay-offs.

3.2   *Explore the emotionally charged strategic issues.* Throughout the process of capturing the assumptions and wisdom some of the key issues will have frequently occurred as emotionally charged and probably driving organizational behaviour. For some of the participation workshops (even though they were only providing participants with the opportunity to influence) a process of rough prioritization will have been undertaken. The issues raised in these fora will need to be carefully addressed in order to sustain procedural justice. To ignore issues which participants have identified as important to them will discredit much of the rest of the strategy making.

3.3   *Use analyses to help inform the prioritization process.* This process of analytically examining the key issues will also help decision makers when agreeing the strategies. The analysis will help ensure that each goal is properly supported by at least one strategy regardless of the wealth or not of possible strategies. For example, when working with Govan Initiative (see vignette), the number of strategic issues was over 30 and some means of managing the complexity of the relationships between the key issues and goals was necessary. Using the analysis techniques it was possible to subdivide the key issues and attendant goals into four subsections and address each subsection (see figure P7.1). Following this process it was then possible to examine the entire overview as a map with 17 strategy candidates and 5 goals. A further round of prioritization could then take place but this time taking into account all of the goals and all of the strategies, thus being more holistic. The resultant goal and strategy map showed 5 goals and 11 strategies.

More formal analysis processes can be helpful. The use of the rating system within the networked computer system can be the first step to formally evaluating the relative leverage of each strategy on the goal system. If this process does not establish clear priorities then it is relatively easy to move on to an evaluation using multiple criteria (the goal system) decision modelling methods (Belton *et al*, 1997) and other Group Decision Support software packages such as HiView and Equity.

C48   3.4   *Check potential strategies cover both **core and facilitative dimensions**.* There is a danger that starting strategy development from the situation of an organization in crisis can focus overly on internal strategic issues – 'what and who went wrong?'. It is useful to check for the core goals being attained directly through clear strategies for change in products/services (exploitation of competencies), rather than just through facilitative goals. This danger is exacerbated because there is a temptation to start (and so finish) with developing strategies for goals at the bottom of the goal hierarchy (those normally facilitative).

3.5   *Examine and test candidate strategies in relation to stakeholder and alternative futures analyses.* While we presume that JOURNEY making will have included some stakeholder and alternative future analysis, there is a risk that this part of the

Figure P7.1 Subdividing key issues into manageable sections. Key issues are in italic, goals in bold.

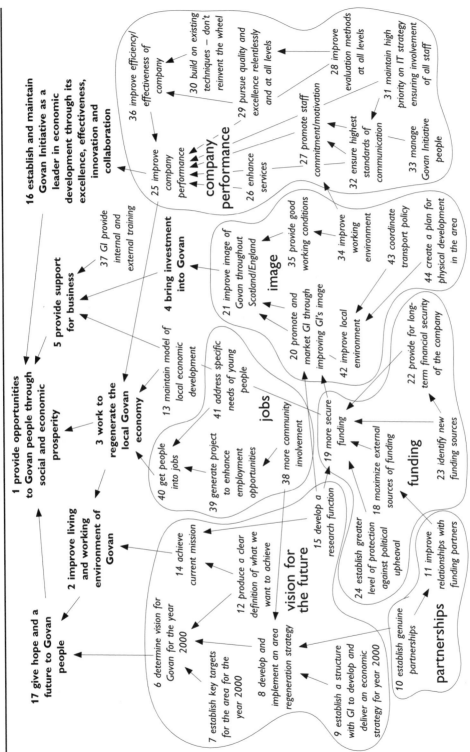

journey will ignore the insights gained. In particular, where the organization has conducted a workshop with selected stakeholders as participants, reviewing those strategies the stakeholders considered paramount will ensure more successful **stakeholder management**. For example, when working with AMCOF (see vignette), the strategy process involved the participation of two key members from one of their key client organizations. This was to ensure that the outcomes would be in enough alignment with those desired by the clients. While AMCOF was keen to avoid simply accepting all of the client organization's requirements in a subservient manner, they did want to ensure that there were no serious conflicts of interest. They wanted to demonstrate that they had paid attention and acknowledged those areas that were of crucial importance to the client. During the workshop, it was noted that two key issues previously not considered critical were fundamental to the client, thus changing the emphasis and status of those key issues.

V244 V254

It is important to remember that the analysis of stakeholders and alternative futures will, in their own right, have generated potential strategies that must now be prioritized against those demanding attention from an issues management perspective.

3.6   *Cut out redundancy and repetition.* Often a number of the key strategic issues, once examined thoroughly, may address very similar portfolios of ends/goals, and so some form of 'merging' is possible.

3.7   *Check that candidate strategies are indeed of strategic significance.* During the joint understanding and reflection stages of negotiating strategies, participants will become unsure about what makes a strategy different from a strategic option. A number of important characteristics of a strategy can be established as follows.

> 3.7.1   *Check that the proposed strategy encompasses developments across a range of strategic options.* A strategy will not be easy to attain and is likely to involve strategic action across a number of aspects of the organization. Thus, it will depend upon a *portfolio* of options/actions – a 'tear-drop' of interlinked actions making a strategic programme. Production of a strategic intent may not involve the development of strategic programmes; nevertheless strategies should be thought of as if they needed a portfolio of action even if not explicated.
>
> 3.7.2   *Test whether the proposed strategy has a long term pay-off.* Identify whether it is possible to deliver it in a short period of time or rather whether, in order to get any benefit, a period of sustained effort is required.
>
> 3.7.3   *Identify whether the outcomes from implementing the proposed strategy are (relatively) irreversible.* In many cases the results of delivering the strategy (regardless of whether it is successful or not) may be difficult to undo. A strategy often puts in place new emergent behaviour which cannot be shifted around to suit managers' whims.

Yes But . . .

What if the goals suggested by my stakeholders, who are 'players', are different from those considered important by managers within the organization?

It may be worth seeking to explore the basis for the differences. For example, is it differences in goals or differences in beliefs or perspective? Alternatively, determine whether many stakeholders hold the same view. Where the players are key (in the top right quadrant of the power/interest grid) then the dynamics that may follow from introducing the strategy need to be discovered in some detail so that creative options leading to stable and positive dynamic outcomes can be developed. Here the serious and **extended use of 'role-think'**, and possibly formal **game analysis** may provide help. In all organizations there will be some strategies that are out of line with the interests of some stakeholders, for the organization will be deliberately differentiating itself from them. The stakeholder management trick is to design strategies exploiting the knowledge gained from the power/interest star diagram.

V273 C133

What is the easiest way of being able to work with all of the material at once in an iterative fashion?

This depends on whether you are using manual or computer supported methods. In either case, having all of the material displayed in overviews and summaries, where everyone is able to see it and refer to it, will help integration. As noted above, starting with the goal system displayed either using computer projection or on flip-chart sheets (but using 'ovals' and acetate so that they can be moved and arrows changed) will allow participants to concentrate on the goals and explore proposed changes as they arise by editing and re-editing. Once an initial agreement has been made about the goal system it can replace the messy first draft models – so symbolizing some degree of closure. When computer projection is used, it is still important to produce a large wall chart copy when the first draft has been negotiated, so that this can be continuously and always referred to as other issues are discussed.

How do I ensure that the mission statement is 'bullet-proof' – and not a 'hostage to fortune'?

Mission statements by their nature tend to be broad (being influenced by the goals) and therefore sometimes open to wide interpretation – both a danger and an advantage. It is a danger because it may be misinterpreted, and it may communicate nothing of strategic intent and so not influence attitudes and behaviour in any significant way. It may be an advantage because the ambiguity allows for interpretation to shift over time. Where there is some concern a role-think exercise may provide some clues as to stakeholder responses, as will testing the statement out on key stakeholders to elicit their views.

How do I manage the group when facilitating?

Given that the group working on agreeing the goals, mission statement, and strategies of the organization tends to be the management team, it will be around 6–8 persons. Many of the techniques used by other processes for managing groups therefore apply. However, it is worth noting that this process has greater consequences for the organization and so enough time and review must be built into the process to allow all involved to design and confirm the outcomes (Ackermann and Eden, 1998). It is also worth ensuring that 'the sponsor' (see chapter P9) joins the group to ensure that they feel able to defend the outcome.

Does it matter if we are not sure what we mean by goal, a mission statement, strategy – do we have to use this language?

No. Identifying the differences between the conceptual categories of goal, aspiration, strategy, strategic programme, and so on will be helpful in almost any circumstance. However, it is very important to use labels for the categories that are those in the common parlance of, or developed by, the organization. Often an organization will gently grow into new terminology as the journey itself introduces the need for categories and structure.

Whilst this learning process is important, the exact language used is less important than using it consistently and with a meaning common to the participants.

Further Commentary on Delivery Strategy

Although the above discussion refers to manual and computer supported means of agreeing goal systems and prioritizing strategies, the networked computer system has also been used with great effect. An example is the use of preferencing as a means of prioritizing. Here participants are presented with the overview map (or a subsection) and assigned a number of electronic 'sticky spots'. As noted in chapter P3, these electronic preferences can be categorized according to a number of criteria. In particular the prioritization of goals and strategies can be aided by paying particular attention to the political feasibility of those chosen. Capitalizing on the benefits of anonymity, it is possible to use electronic 'preferencing' to allow participants to express not only support for, but also indicate a veto or admission of potential sabotage of, goals or strategies. Additionally, the same system allows participants to prioritize strategies not only in terms of their importance (both in the short and the long term future) but also in relation to their impact on stakeholders, attendant resource implications, or in relation to the goals they support.

When agreeing the goal system, the above prioritization process can be used. Likewise, the networked system allows participants to enter directly into the computer model any goals they feel they have missed. Although this process often results in a large number being generated, they can be merged together or relegated to potential key issues when reviewing the results.

C40 C159 C176
V206 V242 V247
Developing Strategic Programmes, Actions, and a Strategy Delivery Support System

Introduction

This second section of this chapter focuses upon the creation of action programmes and the beginning of a Strategy Delivery Support System (SDSS). This process of agreeing action programmes presumes that the organization has decided that the appropriate strategy for them tends towards a deliberate and planned approach with detailed actions, responsibilities, delivery dates, and budgets. Our experience suggests that many of the organizations that develop action programmes and an SDSS have similar overlapping characteristics. Firstly, these organizations have been accustomed to action planning as a part of their culture. Secondly, they are often bureaucracies operating in the public sector. Finally, because of their need for accountability, and the context of multiple stakeholders who are 'players', they must be prepared for continuous audits. Most of our work with public organizations has led to the development of an SDSS, whereas work within the private sector has more often led to a halfway stage of producing a fairly detailed statement of strategic intent that guides detailed budgeting (see figure V1 which describes the vignettes on this dimension). Organizations dependent upon the extensive use of capital rather than people skills also tend towards more detailed action planning, whereas organizations operating in turbulent environments often need to utilize the multiple and changing perspectives of their professional workforce and so regard strategy only as a framework within which to be opportunistic.

As a consequence it is not always appropriate to develop a detailed SDSS, and so the relevance of this section depends upon the contingencies of the strategic setting of the organization. However, often an SDSS provides a system that guides strategy delivery, and can be changed easily to reflect new circumstances, and so can facilitate more rather than less flexibility. By locking strategy delivery into other procedures, such as **reward systems**, annual performance review, and linking   V222
strategy with operations, real strategic change is more likely to occur. The SDSS can act as a powerful vehicle for doing this. Organizations are able to act opportunistically but with the means of identifying not only what the actions might be, but ensuring that the strategic rationale is made explicit by forcing linkage between actions, strategies, and goals. The journey which has led to agreements will have produced, as a matter of course, an **organizational memory**. This memory can now   C41
be used to manage both continuity and strategic change.

This section presumes the use of the computer support system allowing the SDSS to be on a manager's desk as a Decision Support System (DSS) as well as providing group support. For the individual manager the system can act as a decision support system to aid **personal performance reviews**, and as a part of   C165
regular action reviews with individual staff. With the system networked across different parts of the organization in different parts of the world it becomes possible to develop strategic thinking through continuous updating of the SDSS computer model. However, while slower and more clumsy, the principles have been replicated using manual systems. In particular the process of developing the SDSS can be managed using oval mapping techniques and flip-charts.

Agreeing action packages is a process that demands checks across a wide range of criteria, thus requiring a cyclical process. The first set of guidelines, therefore, are designed to prepare a strategy map for workshops aiming to agree strategic programmes and strategic action portfolios. Following this are the steps to be undertaken during workshops where actions will be agreed, taking account of resource demands and responsibilities for the delivery of programmes and actions.

A 'strategic programme' is a *portfolio* of 'strategic actions' which, when carried out, support one or more 'strategies'. The programmes are usually relatively concrete, in the sense that the statements of requirement are sufficiently comprehensive for managers to know what to do and why it is being done. The organization should also be able to detect whether it is making progress in their attainment. Some parts of a programme may support more than one strategy, as strategies are usually achieved through the delivery of a number of strategic programmes. Similarly, some strategic actions may support more than one strategic programme. Indeed, a part of the prioritization process will consider the 'potency' of options. The typical structure of the SDSS, following this convention, will take the form presented in figure P7.2, with goals supported by strategies which are in turn supported by strategic programmes, supported by strategic actions. The processes of agreeing strategy will usually categorize these hierarchical levels using an intuitively recognizable set of colours – the colours we have found to be most effective are: goals in black (solid/immovable), strategies in purple (rich/royal), programme labels in blue, and actions in green (go). (As we noted in the analysis chapter, when using the software it is also helpful to use fonts which will signify each of these categories when printed in monochrome.)

Guidelines for Developing Strategic Programmes, Actions, and a Strategy Delivery Support System

Identifying Potential Programmes and Option Portfolios

4.1   *Identify potential action programmes and portfolios through analysis.* In order to prompt productive discussion about actions the analysis of maps provides essential guidance. The analysis can reveal promising hierarchies of options that could become programmes, and may suggest potent options which serve several programmes and strategies. These analyses do not replace judgement, nor critical evaluation. Other analysis techniques such as multiple criteria decision analysis (Bana e Costa *et al*, 1997), System Dynamics (Eden 1994; Ackermann *et al*, 1997), and, of course, spreadsheet analysis also provide useful alternative approaches which build naturally from maps. As a result of these analyses, new potential actions will emerge and can be discussed. The analysis procedure presented below is suggested as a *standard routine* always worth undertaking and which provides the first set of ideas for discussion.

4.1.1   *'Ladder' down from strategies to identify potential programme labels.* Each strategy will be supported by a number of option paths. These paths will be more or less separable from each other and may represent a 'tear-drop' of material that is shallow and wide or deep and narrow (the 'tear-drops' can be identified easily using the HIESET analysis – request 'HIESET nn' where nn is the construct reference number). The first step is to ladder down from the strategy to constructs having more than one in-arrow or out-arrow. If they have more than one out-arrow then this path up the map may lead through another construct within the tear-drop to the same strategy, or may lead to supporting other strategies. When the construct has more than one in-arrow then there is a potential *portfolio of actions* supporting it. In either case the construct represents a label for a possible strategic programme. Repeat this process for all strategies and tag all potential programmes by attributing them to a suitable 'style' or 'set'.

4.1.2   *Execute a potent analysis on all the potential programmes.* This analysis (see chapter P6) will reveal the 'potency' of each potential programme for strategies, where those more potent have an impact (not necessarily positive) on a number of strategies. These potent programmes are likely to be of greater interest.

Figure P7.2   The strategy map as part of the strategy making process.

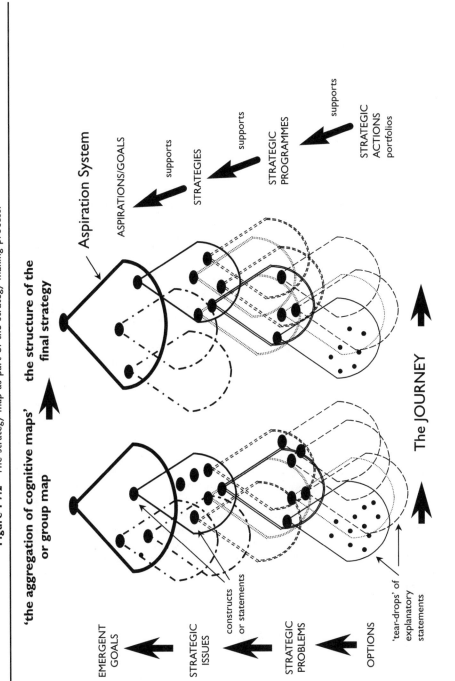

4.1.3   *Check the proposed 'strategic programme' size and the overlap of other potential programmes.* Each potential programme represents a tear-drop of options. Where the tear-drop is large it may be necessary to move further down the hierarchy to create new sub-programmes which are then split off from the initial programme proposed. As the software identifies the content of each tear-drop it allows this process to be iterated with guideline 4.1.2 until sensible potential programmes are established. However, it is possible that two or more potential programmes are very similar in content – the tear-drops considerably overlap. When this occurs it is helpful to combine the tear-drops to form one programme, and so merge the programme labels.

4.1.4   *Establish the potency of potential programmes occurring through potent options.* The analyses for discovering potent options that are also constructs with more than one out-arrow ('cotails') is discussed in chapter P6. Here we are interested in the extent to which any programme tear-drop has within it options that not only support the specific programme being considered but also impact upon other programmes and so strategies. The programmes containing the high scoring potent options are important to consider in the process of agreeing programmes and actions. Once again, a judicious use of sets and styles to tag each of these categories will help participants work with the computer model.

4.1.5   *Acknowledge the prioritization process of previous groups.* If participatory workshops have been used, then paying attention to the options these groups saw as the most important or persuasive will be important for procedural justice. Firstly, the judgements made by these groups may inform debate and agreements. Secondly, unless they are at least 'listened to' then the advantages of procedural justice to aid strategy delivery will fail.

4.2   *Check that each strategy is supported by at least one strategic programme with its associated strategic actions.* Once the above analyses have been carried out it is useful to make a final check that each strategy has at least one programme supporting it. Where there appears to be a deficiency it is worth noting this and considering addressing the deficiency in the action planning workshop. The above process will have ensured that all the programmes are at least sensible from a structural viewpoint. Programmes that are supported by small tear-drops need to be carefully judged, as they may be very important and warrant inclusion. Finally, the potent and composite tail analysis will have located the most potent options from a structural stance and these options will have been tagged (we often call these 'poptions') so that the group can start their work with those constructs which appear most relevant.

V257   **Running Action Planning Workshops**

The set of steps above completes the preparation for a workshop focusing on agreeing strategic programmes and action portfolios. Typically several such workshops are required, with the facilitator/analyst repeating the above analyses in the 'back-room' between each workshop. Consequently each workshop will start with a review of the results of the analysis – suggested programmes, and potent 'cotail' options. Providing an overview map showing the relationship between potent options, programmes, and strategies is important for the same reasons as agreeing strategies in relation to goals. We believe the steps below are also worth integrating into the action planning workshops. As each may be relevant at any time, the order in which they are presented below is not significant.

5.1   *Examine each strategy to identify programmes, and each programme to identify actions*. Whilst the analysis suggested above has identified potential programmes and actions, it is essential to examine these with participants. Each strategy or programme is explored along with its context, any new material allowing participants to negotiate towards an agreed set of programmes for each strategy, and actions for each programme.

5.2   **Check resource implications**. Each conceptual level (goal, strategy, strategic programme) of the computer model can be seen as a 'resource gate' through which all subordinate actions and the resources required to deliver them must go (Eden and Cropper, 1992). This means that a hierarchical set analysis can enable participants to make a rough estimate of resource requirements for each 'resource gate'. Potent programmes and actions are included in each tear-drop calculation and so the 'gate' shows the total cost for either particular programmes or strategies depending on which has been used as the seed set. However, this also means that while costs between, for example, strategies, can be compared, total costs for all strategies will be misleading, with some actions counting several times. *C159 C165*

For the purpose of strategy delivery it is important to account for different types of resource. For example, energy and effort requirements, opportunity costs against continuity demands, cash, and time of in-house staff. The hierarchical structure of resource gates (tear-drop data) can, if necessary, be transferred to a spreadsheet for detailed arithmetic analysis. We find that groups are able to make sensible judgements about the whole of a tear-drop without continuously referring to detailed data.

However, one form of resource expenditure analysis required is the demand on the time *and energy* of specific staff. Thus resource demand checks will occur at different stages in the negotiation of action, where demands on specific staff will need to be computed after 'Agreeing Responsibilities and Time-scales' (step 5.4 below).

5.2.1   *Map options on a time/cost grid*. By drawing up a large 2 × 2 grid with the axis being short term vs long term, very costly versus less costly, options can be placed according to their position on the matrix. From this, participants are able to choose programmes in a discriminatory fashion, ensuring that a balance of options is selected. This process can either be carried out manually – using a flip-chart sheet and 'Post-its' – or using the computer to simulate the grid (as for the power/interest grid).

5.3   *Identify some 'quick wins'*. The rationale behind deliberately selecting some 'quick wins' is to demonstrate to the organization, as a whole and particularly to those who have participated in strategy making workshops, that the management team is committed to implementation. This can provide a renewed burst of enthusiasm and energy from staff as they recognize that things are changing and will change, and that management is serious about the strategy. 'Quick wins' may be actions that have earlier been actioned by the management team and are close to delivery, although not currently publicly known about. *C168 V222*

5.4   *Agree **responsibilities and time-scales**. Once a range of actions has been agreed it is important to assign responsibility for delivery to individuals (not *C165* departments or divisions or teams). This is because during the process of agreeing actions, participants experience a sense of progress, and get caught up in their own enthusiasm. They therefore begin to agree more actions than can be supported by the organization – 'gung-ho greening'. By allocating actions to specific individuals an air of reality tends to assert itself. We find that the process of editing constructs, so that the name (or initials) of the person are recorded at the end of the construct wording, *in front of the group* is important in this negotiation – the record as an artifact prompts the realism. Consequently the action will show firstly the person responsible for delivering the action. Next to this is the manager responsible for overseeing the task in the light of the needs of the programme or strategy, *and* the management team member responsible for reporting to the management team on progress (see figure P7.3).

5.4.1   *Balance continuity with change.* As the process of allocating actions to individuals can take place over a number of workshops, it is worth carrying out a check on each individual's loading. This check can be undertaken by the software during a workshop to aid the negotiation process. The check must not only consider the new actions that are being allocated but also the ongoing operational tasks and responsibilities of managers. It is necessary to balance the continuity (existing tasks) with change (moving the organizations towards the future).

5.4.2   *Acknowledge that some tasks will be on-going.* During the process of agreeing roles and responsibilities, also consider time-scales – expected dates for the completion of the actions. The map is a form of project management network and so a tear-drop needs to be consistent in delivery expectations. Providing a date by which the action has to be completed begins to prime the SDSS with a means for monitoring progress. As these are being agreed, it is worth noting whether the task can be completed as a 'one-off' – not to be repeated – or whether the task is likely to be 'on-going'. For example, a 'one-off' might involve 'establish a library of research/development literature', whereas an on-going one could be 'provide appropriate training for staff in line with strategic goals'. While each organization develops its own system for recording progress, a framework we have found to be particularly useful distinguishes (using styles) whether an action has 'not yet been started', is 'progressing', or is 'completed' (some actions are always progressing). The construct would also record the date when its progress would next be reviewed. Searches on dates within styles provide the basic monitoring tool.

5.4.3   *Agree upon a colour coding structure to denote progress.* During the process of agreeing actions it is worth creating and attributing styles to indicate progress. As with agreeing styles for categorizing goals, actions, programmes, and options, colours and fonts also can effectively highlight achievement. However, these new styles should not be implemented until all programmes and actions have been agreed, so that the existing styles can continue to be used. By using sets labelled to match the categories, it becomes possible to switch from one use of style to another. The use of colour for progress means that as particular parts of the strategy are displayed in context, the overall colour of the constructs on the display will quickly communicate overall progress.

A colour scheme that moves from red to depict not-started, to dark blue indicating started, through to light blue illustrating substantial progress,

Figure P7.3   An example of an SDSS – Govan Initiative.

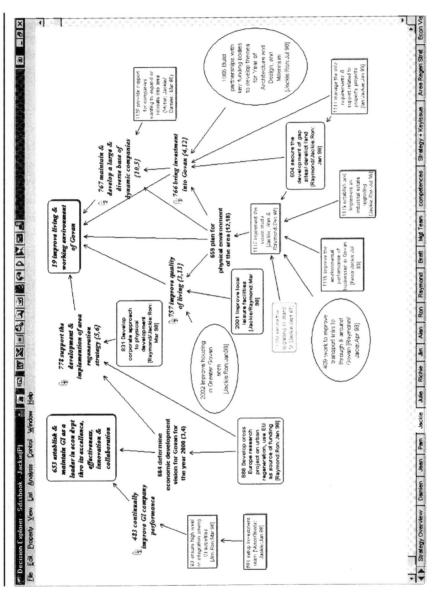

and finally light grey to indicate completion, works well. This colour range shows progress as a lighter colour on a white display, and so actions with less progress stand out more fully. These approaches to delivery management are discussed in greater detail in chapter P8.

V201 V260   5.5   ***Involve staff.*** Although the agreement to the strategies, goals, and mission statement is likely to be carried out by the management team, others can make a valuable contribution to action planning workshops. There have been a number of organizations who have found that by involving participants further down the organization in discussing specific programmes they have been able to gain greater commitment and use valuable expertise. In particular the process of agreeing programmes and actions is an ideal opportunity for involving potential saboteurs and using the opportunity to try to 'buy' them into the strategy. On some occasions the management team will set up a 'task-force' with specific responsibility for working up the strategic programme *within the context of the strategy.* In this way many of the important lessons from successful Total Quality Management programmes can be transferred to strategy delivery.

5.6   *Design a workable strategy computer model – the SDSS.* During the action planning workshops the strategy computer model will usually grow (often doubling in size as actions are added in order to make a programme practicable and specific). Having thinned a model down through merging goals and issues during the issue-based workshops and interviews, and consequently 'got a grip' on the basis of a strategy, a management team can become disillusioned at the increase in complexity as action plans are fleshed out. Strategy computer models can often contain more than a thousand constructs, which makes navigation problematic. Analytical routines can assist with this problem by extracting unnecessary data – data which repeats or provides unnecessary elaboration retained only to facilitate new social order. Although this process of reduction could be undertaken at any time, it is worth making as much material as possible available to the participants during the process of agreement. This means that the emphasis should be on managing the complexity rather than reducing it. However, once agreements have been negotiated, producing a computer model that is useful to the managers is more important. By this time ownership and commitment issues should have been resolved by the JOURNEY making.

V222   5.6.1   *Produce an **abbreviated computer model** for general use.* Use the principles of the 'strip' analysis to *merge* all constructs with only one in-arrow, one out-arrow, or one in- and one out-arrow (see chapter P6). Additionally, simplify the model using the 'collapse' analysis so that only the goals, strategies, action programmes, and actions are visible. Care has to be taken, however, as this analysis will often produce a model with a substantial number of links since each path between those selected is displayed. Thus, while the number of constructs displayed is reduced, the link-to-construct ratio often becomes unworkable. Consequently there is a temptation to delete a number of these links. Before doing so it is worth checking the full chain of argument. If links are deleted for the abbreviated computer model, these deleted links *must* be those considered as secondary and not the major strategic purpose of actions or programmes. However, often a number of the links in the collapsed model reflect a secondary payoff rather than the primary reason for the action. When the link-to-construct ratio is not too high it may be possible to use the facility of varying thickness of arrows to reflect the primary and secondary links. Beware of producing an abbreviated computer model without keeping a copy of the original model.

5.6.2   *Design a quick reference guide.* If there is an expectation of the action planning computer model being used as an SDSS by just the client group or other managers, then ensuring they are able to navigate around the model will facilitate and encourage its use. A laminated sheet showing, (i) the conceptual categories – styles, colours and fonts, (ii) small overview maps in colour – for example, the goal system, and (iii) the most often used software commands, can act as a simple guide.

Performance Indicators

C174 C176 V207

Performance indicators help monitor progress being achieved at a macro rather than micro level. Using the SDSS as a Decision Support System (chapter P8), the completion of actions can be monitored and assessed on a micro level illustrating the performance of discrete events. However, in order to ensure that the linkages between the actions and strategies are appropriate, some check at a more macro level is necessary. Govan Initiative (see vignette), when creating their measurement system, designed it to take account of the requirements of various funding stakeholders – significant 'players'. They needed to be able to measure progress at both a macro and micro level. Therefore, at the top level – that of the Mission/ Vision of the organization – they produced what they called Tracking Indicators. These acknowledged that their organization was only one component of success in attainment of their mission – to achieve their mission (that of regional economic regeneration) other stakeholders (for example, the police) were necessary (see figure P7.4). Additionally they were aware that they could not accurately determine how much they had contributed to their mission's attainment. Given that the SDSS provided the means for tracking performance at the micro level, they then needed performance indicators (PIs) for indicating progress in strategy delivery.

The process of agreeing performance indicators is typically seen as something to do towards the end of strategy making. Often it is carried out either during the strategic action planning process, or when considering project management. However, we have found thinking about good performance indicators is a good way of surfacing new and creative strategic options. Therefore, beginning the process of developing performance indicators earlier ensures that agreeing action programmes is more effective. Regardless of when it is carried out, we consider it to be a very important step:

> 'A major systematic difficulty that many firms today confront is the inability to develop sensible criteria for assessing the long term performance of individual business elements' (Lorange and Murphy, 1983:130).

When considering performance indicators for a particular strategy it is essential that the particular meaning of the strategy is understood. This can be done only when the construct describing the strategy is seen in the context of what it is intended to achieve and what is required to achieve it. Thus a 'domain' map depicts meaning rather than just the words in the construct. The context of a strategy construct usually suggests a range of possible performance indicators.

Suggestions always include indicators to which the response is: 'well, why don't we actually do that if we think it is an important measure of success?', and so new options are generated. Qualitative indicators should be seen as being as important as more easily measured quantitative indicators. As we argued in chapter C8, there is a great tendency for organizations to search for performance indicators that are essentially quantitative in nature. This then forces strategic action which fits only those measures – so distorting, sometimes out of all recognition, the purpose and intent of the strategy.

V261   6.1 **Capture and agree performance indicators** *for strategies.* As we have noted above, discussing how the performance of each strategy may be measured may generate a large number of practical strategic options. Typically about a third to one half of the statements that come forward as possible indicators are better thought of as options. For example, 'customer product awareness as measured by customer survey' may be suggested as a performance indicator for a strategy about 'increased market share'. Increasing customer awareness is a strategic option which may not have been expressed before.

Capturing performance indicators can be achieved either through the use of Post-its being written up (manual support) and mapped around the strategy and its context or entered into the software which displays the strategy statement and its context on the public screen (computer supported).

   6.1.1 *Capture performance indicators manually.* Using Post-its attached to a large wall display allows participants to work on a range of strategies at once, generating performance indicators and attaching them to the most appropriate strategies. Participants are able to write down their statements simultaneously and work on those areas with which they are most familiar. As with the oval mapping workshops the results can then be prioritized through the use of 'sticky dots' as preferences.

   6.1.2 *Use computer support.* Because of the restrictions of screen size participants are less able to generate indicators for several strategies simultaneously. However, it is relatively easy to copy potential indicators so that they are a part of subsequent strategies considered. All possible indicators are captured immediately within the software and are available for editing, linking, moving, clustering, etc. During this process, issues relating to the type of data required for assessing them, as well as their meaning, can be raised. If, during this examination, they suggest possible options rather than progress measures they can be categorized accordingly and linked into relevant sections of the computer model.

   6.1.3 *Cluster and merge indicators.* The exercise usually produces a wide range of possible indicators – far too many to use, even after those which are best seen as options are extracted. Clustering and mapping will give order to the material and produce a series of tear-drops where each tear-drop may be considered as one performance indicator. The most superordinate construct in the tear-drop is designated as the indicator for the tear-drop cluster and reworded by some judicious merging. The final wording of indicators is very important; they will drive organizational behaviour. What remains of the cluster works to give contextual meaning to the indicator.

   6.2 *Assess current level of performance against the agreed strategy performance indicators.* There are two aims for this stage in establishing performance indicators:

Figure P7.4 Results of evaluating a strategy's indicators.

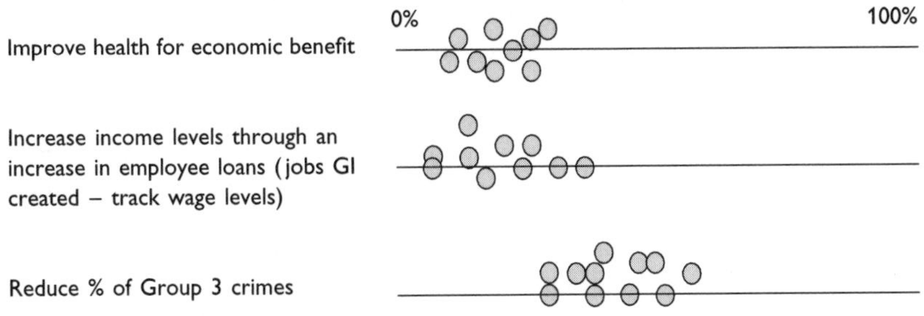

(i) test their practicability – if they do not work in a year's time, it is too late to change them, and often they look workable until they are tried out; (ii) establish present-day reference points/bench-marks against which future reviews can work. Prepare flip-chart sheets with the strategy label as a heading and each of the indicators tagging a progress scale of 0–100% achievement. Determine the meaning of each of the anchor points (0% and 100%). 100% is best established as that expectation of performance over a given time-scale – for example, by the end of 5 years from now. The meaning of 0% is more difficult to determine. It is often helpful to go back to a point in history which was a critical incident for the organization – for example, the appointment of a new chief executive or the start of the strategy making process. It is important to go back in time, rather than use the present day, because it will provide a much better test of whether the indicator can work in practice. For quantitative indicators each of the anchor points can be established relatively easily, and the quantitative expectations written at the 0% and 100% ends of the scale. However, in practice, quantitative indicators are often very difficult and/or very expensive to measure.

Participants are then provided with self-adhesive spots which they position at the current performance level of the organization (see figure P7.4). Resulting clusters of spots should be at the lower end of the scale – if not, then the anchor points are incorrect and the 100% point is not aspirational enough, or the strategy is redundant! The process will determine whether the indicator is appropriate and workable. If participants are unable to easily assess current performance (because, for example, they are unsure of how to access the necessary information), a review of the nature of the indicator might be necessary. Where there is considerable spread across the scale, then a debate about the reasons for disagreement will usually result in a 'tuning-up' of the wording of the indicator and associated constructs in the cluster from which it was derived. Sometimes disagreement is genuine and not the result of misunderstanding.

Exploiting Planned and Emergent Opportunities

We suggested above, that once the action programmes have been agreed and the responsibilities and time-scales added to the actions, the computer model is collapsed on to goals, strategies, and strategic programme labels. Even so, it is important to retain the full, un-abbreviated, computer model. This is because it is unlikely that all of the actions agreed will turn out to be practicable, and so reference to other possible alternatives will be helpful. Unexpected changes in both the internal and, more frequently, external environment may also render a subset of actions no longer viable or appropriate – alternatives therefore have to be found. They must not only replace the actions but do so in a manner that properly maintains and supports the associated agreed strategic programmes and strategies. It is *essential* to avoid managers replacing actions without considering the original purpose of the action – the out-arrows. An action is only meaningful, as a part of strategy delivery, if it meets its aims. Often managers will deliver an action in a manner which literally 'ticks it off' but makes no contribution to strategy. The organizational memory contained in the full computer model becomes invaluable, as it not only provides alternatives ('options as assets') but also reveals why actions were chosen.

In addition, as the organization succeeds in creating strategic change it will become involved in the substantial and deliberate organizational learning entailed in delivering strategy. This learning is the basis for moving itself to a new 'strategic platform' where the organization then becomes capable of levering even more strategic performance that could not even be envisaged during the original strategy making – 'Strategy as Stretch and Leverage' (Hamel and Prahalad, 1993). However good the exploration of alternative futures has been, unanticipated environmental changes will release new strategic opportunities – providing the strategy making has prepared the organization to exploit them. The analysis of alternative futures will help to inform the exploitation of these opportunities, but so too will using the SDSS as a source of reference with details of existing plans and their rationale. In this way it is possible for the organization not only to act faster, but also more flexibly, exploiting both planned and emergent opportunities within a strategic framework which is consistent and coherent. The original computer model can be used as a reservoir, maintaining remaining options as assets – options, which might, given different circumstances, become more significant and powerful.

Yes But . . .

Who should have access to the SDSS?

We have found that this may range from the senior decision maker or chief executive using it for themselves, to each member of the management team and senior line managers having access on their own desk – see chapter P8. It is interesting to note that many 'computer illiterate' managers have wanted to gain access to the computer model as a DSS after they have been involved in a number of computer supported workshops. These managers have purchased computers (insisting on exactly the same model as those we use!) in order to be able to access the system. In some cases these managers have been converted to the use of computers and computer networks through their involvement in strategy making. We have found that managers with absolutely no experience of using a computer keyboard and mouse have become enthusiasts after 30 minutes of training in the use of the SDSS software (with 15 minutes of this training devoted to the use of a mouse!). When managers make individual use of the computer model, they will often add their own notes to the model, particularly when reviewing progress with other managers responsible for implementation. This will mean that numerous different models will appear around the organization. When managers make changes, it may be important to request that no changes are made to a 'master' computer model except through group sessions, or that additions may be made using unique styles.

Should we assign responsibilities to people not at the workshop?

This question frequently arises, as it is usually the management team who decides which actions are to be pursued and who is responsible for them. The approach we recommend is that while other staff are allocated responsibilities in the usual manner, one of the management team present at the workshop also must be allocated responsibility for communicating the responsibility and for reporting on progress. Often the allocation of responsibilities does not follow the existing reporting structures in the organization. Strategic change will usually cross department and division, and often involve multidisciplinary teams. Thus, reference to the organizational chart will rarely help in the allocation of tasks. Once the actions have been agreed, it is essential to communicate responsibilities through the mapping notation. Unless responsibilities are set in their full strategic context, actions will be taken which meet the requirements of the wording of the action but do not meet the strategic purpose. The out-arrows are a crucial, and minimum, representation of the *meaning* of the action. Our own research suggests that *many strategic change episodes fail because actions are taken based upon lists of what to do, and lose the emphasis on why it must be done.* The strategy map, in summary and full form, is the ideal way to ensure that tasks are completed according to its purpose. Working with the computer model will ensure that both the action and its rationale are understood and that the individuals are able to determine where their responsibilities fit within the overall strategy. Some senior managers of multinational companies use computer projection of the final computer model from their notebook computer as the way of communicating with teams in different parts of the world.

What if a strategy doesn't have any actions associated with it?

This would indicate that the guidelines we outline above have not been followed! Often strategies may have had no options associated with them prior to action planning workshops. In these circumstances option surfacing stages within the workshop will be essential. As well as the use of performance indicator generation (see 6.1 above), if the network computer system is available then option surfacing can be very efficient. In some instances specific workshops may need to be designed that have the sole purpose of addressing a given strategy (see 4.2 above).

How do I show categories when I am unable to use the computer software?

When creating styles it is important to use different fonts (size and typeface) to distinguish between them when working in monochrome. Similarly when a manual technique is being used it will be helpful to use different coloured marking pens, capital letters as well as lower case, or symbols associated with different categories – asterisks, blobs, triangles, etc. Determining the styles to be used in advance of the workshop, so that a flip-chart can be prepared showing a key to the meaning of the styles or symbols, will help.

How do we accelerate politically feasible agreements about action programmes?

V258   When producing action packages, allow participants to **enter alternative actions and links directly into the networked computer system**. However, only those actions that directly support the strategy and programmes are considered legitimate; any actions found unrelated are removed. The process of prioritizing the actions not only involves identifying the top five options but ranking them in order of their importance. Thus, a greater degree of discrimination is possible. Electronic preferencing using the networked system provides groups with initial sorting based on 'veto' and 'support' preferences that are anonymous.

Further Commentary on Developing Strategic Programmes, Actions, and a Strategy Delivery Support System

Using the networked computer system is a powerful alternative method for considering performance indicators. Here the software helps: (i) identifying indicators (using the 'gather' tool), (ii) linking them into clusters (participants send proposed links to the public screen), (iii) merging proposed indicators to 'tidy' clusters/tear-drops, and (iv) prioritizing them (using the anonymous 'preferencing' tool). As is usually the case, the networked system not only increases the speed through which the process can be undertaken but also increases the content which can be addressed (and concomitant complexity) and allows anonymity should it be desirable. The gathering stage often generates options as well as potential indicators, and, because these are captured in the software, they can be easily linked to other parts of the strategy model – to those strategies or programmes that they may support.

In addition, the rating tool is ideal for assessing the level of progress. When working with performance indicators, the rating tool may be used to identify the current position using a scale from 0% to 100%, as participants can replicate the manual process (see step 6.2). This position may act as a benchmark when focusing on review but it also helps test out whether the performance indicators identified are measurable, as participants concentrate on determining how they can assess performance.

The second use of the rating tool is that of evaluating the leverage from strategies and options. For example, when determining which strategies are the most important in order to achieve a goal(s), each strategy can be examined in relation to its relative contribution (leverage) towards the goal's attainment. The strategies that yield the greatest leverage are therefore potent candidates. This process may also be used to assess the actions chosen for each strategy.

Finally, the software permits mem(ory) cards (yellow 'Post- it' like entities) to be attributed to strategies so that each strategy's performance indicators are tagged to the strategy. Another use for the memo cards is to attach sourcing data to individual constructs. This may be particularly useful when incorporating outside expertise or documentary evidence into the strategy computer model.

During the process of developing action plans and a strategic delivery support system, substantial organizational learning should occur. Do not ignore the significance of this, often invisible, outcome. Participants will begin to: appreciate systemic properties of organizational activities and behaviour; pay attention to, and appreciate, multiple perspectives and wisdom as the direction forward is negotiated; and gain a holistic sense of direction. Managers will gain a deeper level of knowledge influencing their ways of thinking and behaviour and going well beyond any decisions acknowledged in the computer model. The model is a 'transitional object' used to facilitate a journey towards a strategy which is politically feasible.

The implementation of the strategy depends more upon the process outcomes from JOURNEY making than it does on the artifact of the strategy statements. However, the implementation of strategic change also depends upon the strategy being coherent, where operations and strategy knit together, and where strategic problem solving is implicitly, as well as explicitly, informed by strategic intent. These are the aims of the method we are discussing in this book, and are shown by the diagrams displayed in chapter C2. These diagrams describe the conceptual and theoretical basis for developing strategy using the guidelines we have presented above, but they also act as an important check list for a facilitator who is designing action planning workshops. The design will always be contingent on the specific organization as well as the personal competencies of the facilitator, but the diagrams act as a check list of features to be designed into the workshops in all instances.

DELIVERING STRATEGY: COMMUNICATION, MANAGEMENT, AND REVIEW

Introduction

This chapter encompasses that part of the journey from promulgating the agreed strategy throughout the organization to exploring methods for its implementation, monitoring, and review. The chapter begins with an exploration of the different methods we have found useful for communicating strategy, as well as discussing a few of the pitfalls and concerns. Following on from promulgation, the chapter then considers how the SDSS can be used as part of a project management instrument, and how the operational aspects of the organization can be integrated with the strategy. Finally attention is focused on techniques for monitoring and reviewing progress. Although organizational learning takes place throughout each stage of the JOURNEY making process, its impact on delivering the strategic intent of the organization is considered more fully in this chapter. The chapter is in three parts: communicating the strategy, project management, and strategy review.

V221 V235 V263 **Communicating strategy**
V263

Communicating the agreed strategy across an organization is a critical part of successful strategic change. Staff members will be curious about the results of a process they believe has implications for their own future. In addition, if they have been involved, they will be keen to see whether their own input has influenced the outcome. We have argued elsewhere that once a strategy making process becomes a serious exercise, rather than a 'rain dance', then managers will begin to see themselves as potential winners or losers. As the journey unfolds, the design of JOURNEY making itself should have influenced these attitudes. Indeed, some managers will have anticipated changes and may have left the organization, so influencing the process of change in a new strategic direction. However, some managers will be preparing to 'knock' the strategy. It is never possible to avoid completely having some anticipated losers and potential saboteurs. More than anything else, if the strategy does not seem to be grounded in the organizational reality, or is incoherent, competent and committed managers will be prepared to disown it. 'Ordinary' organizational staff have an uncanny knack of detecting incoherence in strategy. They may not be able to articulate exactly why it does not make sense but they will usually be correct in their judgement. Too often senior managers believe they can dupe staff into a commitment to something which is not coherent.

Most staff have a cynical attitude to strategy, having seen previous strategies come and go without having any impact upon the organization. Convincing staff that strategy will have real consequences for the organization both in the short and long term is never easy. Some staff will be keen to demonstrate, once again, that strategy development has failed. The other side of this coin is that many staff will be genuinely keen to understand how they fit into a future that they hope will be successful. They want their organization to succeed and want the management team to have undertaken some good and sensible strategy making. Chapter C1 considered some of the outcomes of strategy making, and before communicating strategy it is helpful to revisit some of these demands of strategy.

Bowman and Asch (1987) observe that 'an effective communication network is an invaluable tool in enabling strategy implementation to take place in an efficient manner'. Effective communication of the strategy can enhance understanding, ownership, and therefore commitment. In addition, providing some form of dissemination of the resultant strategy is also important because it demonstrates management's commitment to the staff. It can show that the management team are: (i) able to provide staff with a clear idea of the strategy, demonstrating that senior 'managers understand their own strategy', and (ii) that they take staff seriously and are prepared to expend effort in explaining the strategy to staff.

How the communication is achieved varies. The style of communicating the strategy should be representative of the strategy itself. If a part of the strategy demands a culture shift then the style of communication should be coherent with this aspiration. Thus, it will depend on the nature of the strategy, the organization, its business, its size, the style of the management team, and the resources available. In some organizations it may be appropriate to use the relatively formal method of a published strategy document, with lists of procedures or policies. Other organizations may prefer a more informal process involving small groups and discussion. The larger the organization, then the more likely it is that the organization will need to adopt at least some formal method as a means of informing all of their staff. Perhaps the greatest difficulty in communicating strategy is not communicating its content, but rather providing a sense of what the organization will look like after the strategic change has occurred. We discuss below some of the approaches used in the organizations we have been involved with.

Timing is important. 'Feedback' to staff who have been involved in strategy workshops must be made within 4–5 weeks of their involvement if it is to build on their energy and enthusiasm. Given that strategy making will often take much longer than this, it means that feedback about progress and the role of staff contributions must be made on a regular basis. Thus, when the final presentation is made, staff will be familiar with the content *and process*. Gaining emotional commitment and ensuring procedural justice and rationality depends on thinking about, and acting upon, decisions about communicating strategy *before* the end of the journey arises. Waiting too long may result in the cynics and saboteurs being able to say 'I told you so – nothing was going to change'. The general climate of the strategy delivery then changes to one of disillusionment rather than excitement and enthusiasm.

Although untypical, we have managed to complete the entire strategy making process within a 1.5-week cycle for an organization of 120 staff, incorporating the direct involvement of 30 staff from all levels. This strategy was then immediately promulgated to all those involved (including staff based overseas). The impact on the emotional as well as cognitive commitment was immensely positive. While the strategy making did not result in a fully costed and detailed set of action programmes it did involve the organization in a significant strategic change of culture, markets, and worldwide office location. Fast turnaround is possible and can be highly successful in managing strategic change.

Guidelines for Delivering Strategy – communication

Producing the Material – working in the backroom

Once the strategy has been agreed, whether it is a statement of strategic intent, or a full set of action programmes, it is important to devote time to checking for internal coherence. The mapping process followed during strategy making will have increased the probability of coherence, but the final stages of agreement and abbreviation can produce apparent incoherence because of the summarizing procedures followed. It is tempting to regard this task as routine, involving the facilitator/analyst only. However, coherence and logic belong to the organization not the facilitator. It is imperative that at least one management team member is involved in this checking process. If possible, also use a more junior member of staff who has been involved at some stage in the JOURNEY making as this can provide a perspective from 'down the organization'. Delegating some parts of this process may further 'buy in' staff as well as providing a useful group of people 'qualified' to update and maintain the computer model. Including the facilitator is the least important consideration; their role can only be advisory and technical.

    1.1 *Check the coherence of the computer model in relation to external forces.* Before publishing and/or presenting the strategy some attention to the external coherence of the material is important. It is almost impossible to be assured that a strategy document is not leaked to the outside world. In the public sector there is usually a requirement that it be made public. Checking the coherence may take the form of ensuring that the resultant actions will not elicit any negative response from stakeholders, and that potential coalitions are not triggered or capitalized upon. In addition, reviewing the material alongside the results of the stakeholder analysis will further advance the possibilities for stakeholder management, as potential collaborations may be developed. Actions also may profit from being scrutinized in connection with the results of the scenario analysis to test their robustness against possible different futures. Those actions that operate under the greatest number of possible futures are the most robust.

    1.2 *Check the coherence of the computer model itself.* In addition to checking how the action programmes, strategies, and goals perform in relation to the external world, exploring the internal consistency/coherence of the computer model is important. Checks ensuring that action programmes designed for one strategy don't conflict with those chosen for another strategy are vital. They also ensure that maximum use can be derived from the action programmes. Finally, testing whether the action programmes can be supported financially is important.

    1.2.1 *Analyse the computer model for negative links.* As negative links suggest that there exists a potential conflict between two statements in the model then identifying these statements and the link will allow examination and resolution. Negative links can be rapidly identified through listing links and identifying any represented by a '–' sign. These relationships can then be further explored through the e'X'plore command displaying the relationship in a map form. Changes, for example rewording the action, can then be instigated. The aim is not only to simplify the resultant presentation but also to provide a more positive frame.

1.2.2 *Review the computer model for possible synergies.* One of the methods mentioned in the previous chapter (chapter P7) for developing action programmes suggested involving line managers. These managers would then take responsibility for the implementation of any actions they suggested. Whilst this method undoubtedly gains a greater degree of understanding and commitment to the strategy, it does, however, not exploit the full potential of the action programmes, as each task force usually deals with one strategy only. Therefore it is worth examining each action programme to determine whether the entire programme or elements within it can also support one of the other strategies. This process can be achieved by producing an overview and examining each action programme against other parts of the overview.

1.2.3 *Test the resource demands of the strategy alongside organizational availability.* Making a final check to ensure that the organization is able to implement the actions in terms of manpower, energy, and cash will avoid actions being discontinued due to lack of resources. This reality check is necessary so as to avoid staff becoming disappointed and disillusioned with the strategy. Matching actions to resources, through acknowledging the need to continue carrying out the business whilst changing the organization, is examined in further detail in chapter C9.

1.3 ***Get the language right.*** During the process of developing the strategy, *V222* many of the statements captured are expressed in a cryptic manner. A form of shorthand or jargon will have been used, and understood only by those participants privy to the strategy making process. Paying attention to wording the actions, strategic programmes, and strategies in such a manner as to make their meaning unambiguous will further increase the chances of implementation through enhanced understanding, although it is the context of what a construct will achieve (out-arrows) and what is needed to support it (in-arrows) which gives it action oriented meaning. In addition to this process of clarification, ensuring that each action and programme is phrased in a positive manner will also be helpful. As strategy is about inspiring the organization towards change, avoiding incorporating negative elements will facilitate this process. Normally, there is more incentive towards the execution of positive actions than active avoidance of negative ones. However, during the process of rewording the actions and programmes it is worth paying attention to encapsulating, as much as possible, the original wording so as to retain as much ownership as possible from participants. Staff involved in the workshops will remember the outcomes of their efforts, and so retaining their language will increase the chance of recognition and therefore 'buy in'.

1.4 *Choose the format of the presentation.* As noted above, there are a large number of different methods for presenting the strategy, each with its own benefits and rationale. One consistent theme, however, appears to be the publication of a document – an artifact that organizational members can continue to read and remind themselves of the strategic direction.

1.4.1 ***Agree what to publish.*** Regardless of the type of organization, i.e. public, not-for-profit, or private, deciding what to publish is important. This consideration can be seen as a further form of stakeholder management –

as stakeholders gain access to the strategy either deliberately or inadvertently. For example, given the nature of the Northern Ireland Prison Service (see vignette) it was necessary to consider how much of the strategy could be published, given the possibility of negating any of the benefits accrued from developing it. The management team believed that if various stakeholders gained access to the strategy then the advantages gained could be diminished (this is also true for private sector organizations). In addition they were concerned that if certain strategies or actions were made known to the public then, if for any reason the organization was unable to implement them, they could be used against them – the organization would be a **hostage to fortune**. One solution to this dilemma is to publish two strategy documents, one for external consideration and a second for internal consumption. In the case of the Northern Ireland Prison Service they decided to publish only one document for internal and external consumption. Finally, alongside this discussion of what to publish, is the question of how much to publish without overwhelming or confusing the audiences.

C176 V221

1.4.2   *Agree intended audiences.* In a similar vein to the above guideline, there is also a question relating to 'exactly who is going to be the recipient'. In the authors' experience organizations want to extract the maximum benefit from undertaking a strategy journey. One means of doing this is to use the resultant strategy as a demonstrator for good practice. For example, a private sector organization might wish to present itself in a positive light to a significant customer through harnessing the strategy as an illustration of their serious consideration to creating a robust and coherent future. Alternatively, public sector companies who are financed by a number of funding bodies have numerous stakeholder demands to meet. Govan Initiative (see vignette), when assessing audiences, decided to publish three documents. One was a comprehensive document for internal and some external use. The second was a short three-page summary for Board Members (see figure P8.1), with the third being a promotional document for the various funding stakeholders. All three documents were internally consistent and built from the same material. The difference was the emphasis taken.

V263

1.4.3   *Continually provide feedback.* An alternative means of communicating the strategy is to provide regular progress reports. Not only does this involve providing feedback from the workshops (see chapter P5) but also informing staff of progress made by the management team. For example, Scottish Natural Heritage, having reached the stage of agreeing the organization's goals, then produced the **goal system as a map** and published it in the company newsletter (see figure P8.2). Staff members were then able to appreciate that whilst they were currently not being actively involved, progress was being made.

V277

1.4.4   *Decide upon the publication mechanisms.* As noted earlier, providing some artifact that can readily be referred to, and acts as a reminder, is a powerful way of promulgating what has been agreed. Some of the other traditional formats include printing the mission statement on the back of staff members' ID cards (as a continuous reminder), and producing **brochures** or desk gimmicks, including inserts with the mission and goal system to be pinned up in the office for constant review. Whilst glossy brochures might not be within the resource means of all organizations,

V277

Figure P8.1   Two pages from Govan Initiative's three-page summary brochure.

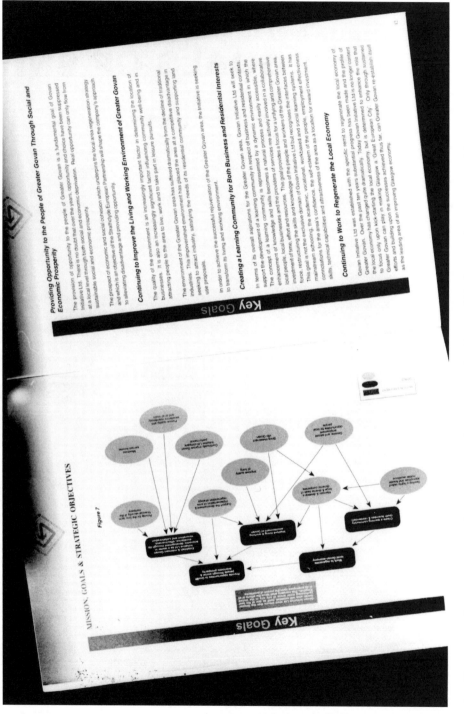

Note: The purpose of this diagram, taken from actual material, is not that it should be readable, but provide an indication of form rather than content.

Figure P8.2   Page from Scottish Natural Heritage's newsletter, showing the goal system.

Chief Executive's Column
THE GOALS OF SNH

When we are so busy it is all too easy for us to forget why SNH exists, what our key goals are and the strategies we must adopt to achieve them. The diagram sets these goals and strategies out.

It must be our primary task to ensure that we deliver our five key statutory tasks: these are our driving force and hence our key goal. You have been provided with guidance on our interpretation of these tasks. We shall also be providing guidance on the limits of our remit.

The two supporting goals are the two corporate aims set out in our Corporate and Operational Plans. Both recognise that we cannot achieve our responsibilities on our own: operating in partnership is essential. We seek to influence others through our policies, for instance on agriculture, on red deer, and on the marine environment, through our analysis of changes to the state of the natural heritage and by providing advice and guidance in manuals, booklets and demonstrations and in many other ways. We seek to take a practical approach to the management of the natural heritage. We shall continue to put a great deal of effort into designated sites and areas. This will include improving our approach to NSAs, establishing new monitoring schemes for SSSIs and the very substantial and important work of securing Scotland's contribution to European species and habitat protection through Natura 2000. In addition, we shall contribute very significantly to the Cairngorms Partnership Board and to the work in the Loch Lomond and Trossachs area. This will continue to be complemented by our wider countryside work delivered through advice and guidance, capital and revenue support to projects and activities, management agreements, and locally-based special initiatives.

We cannot achieve any of these goals unless we build an effective and credible organisation in the

wholly funded by the Secretary of State. At the same time we should be prepared, in the light of our statutory remit and the Government's own environment policy, to make our views and proposals known to Government. How we become more influential and effective requires careful judgement as is clear in the case of the second Forth crossing proposals.

Combine objectivity with advocacy: we wish to advocate new policies, programmes and practices in a way which influences others. This is best achieved by using our knowledge

and expertise objectively: the rhetoric must be based on sound information and careful interpretation. Our work on translating the ethics and principles of sustainability

our broader remit. Guidance has been produced and more in preparation. And our training programme and recruitment policies have reflected the need to broaden our skill base to fully address our remit.

Engender staff morale and develop corporate pride: you are immensely committed to our remit. All managers within SNH share in the vital tasks of managing and motivating staff. Training them in this role is an important element of our Training Strategy. Our commitment to staff as our greatest asset will be taken forward through our Staff

Development Programme and our wider Human Resources Strategy which we will be developing over the coming months. Our review and streamlining of Natural Standards for its re-launch early in the New Year is another

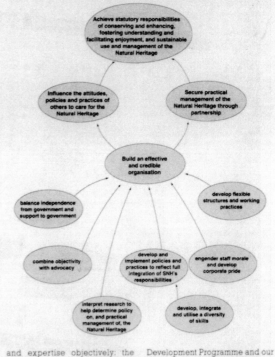

Note: The purpose of this diagram, taken from actual material, is not that it should be readable, but provide an indication of form rather than content.

many have found that investment in a good quality publication symbolizes its importance and permanence. Finally, displaying the actions publicly and noting their progress also serves as a useful communication device albeit one that is only suitable for a small number of actions (for example, departmental strategy – see Ackermann, 1992).

1.5 **Present the strategy 'live'.** In addition to providing some form of documentation, presenting the strategy through a live presentation helps to renew enthusiasm. Importantly, an interactive presentation enables staff to ask questions – matters of clarification or misunderstanding can be resolved. When staff have been engaged in the strategy making, and procedural justice has been achieved, a live presentation provides a wonderful opportunity for staff to congratulate themselves and the management team. Presentations often incorporate slide shows combining maps of the goals, strategies, and action programmes with text explaining how the process has unfolded. In addition, some organizations have made the computer model of all the strategy material available so that any participant who wishes to explore the model to check whether their team's contribution was captured may do so. *V221*

1.5.1 *Present the strategy to all the staff at once.* For divisions or small organizations, presenting the strategy to all staff together can minimize the effort (and avoid repeated questions). It can also build a sense of togetherness – a team. Another useful stratagem is to have the chief executive present some of the material along with other members of the management team and other staff. Not only will it demonstrate their commitment to the process but also add variety through the different presentation styles. **Humour** can be used to great effect – including comedy sketches depicting current practice in contrast to future practice. *V277*

1.5.2 *Consider using a series of 'road shows'.* This method has been used by organizations unable to present to the entire organization at one time. However, running road shows has other benefits. For example, the Northern Ireland Prison Service (see vignette) deliberately involved two directors, one from headquarters and the other from the field. They also ensured that the audience comprised a similar mix. This was designed to further reduce the tension between the two parties which had arisen as a strategic issue during workshops. Each director had an active part in presenting the strategy along with answering any questions raised. The National Health Service Unit also used this format. However, in this case, those presenting the strategy presented it twice (with a different partner – as 'rolling pairs') allowing each member to be involved while maintaining a degree of consistency. *V222 V236*

Yes But . . .

How do I know how many people to involve in the live presentations?

This is difficult. Obviously as many as possible so as to ensure that they feel part of the process. Nevertheless, due to resources and the size of the organization this might not be possible. Providing each organizational member with a copy of the published material will give them some insight about what has been agreed. Another consideration is to choose carefully the staff attending the presentation(s) so as to incorporate the cynics and opinion leaders. Alternatively ensure that line managers are involved in the presentations and then mandated to re-present the strategy to their staff and demonstrate how it relates to them. This process can become a repeated cascade down the organization.

What if I don't have the resources to produce a glossy brochure?

V221   Don't worry. The National Health Service Unit produced their **document** using simple word processed text, and maps drawn using the mapping software. They then placed the material in a ring bound folder with the logo on the front. The document was very cheap to produce and yet was extemely successful because great care had gone into selecting the material and designing an appropriate format for the culture of their organization. Key strategic actions were also listed at the back for easy reference.

How much explanation should I put in the document about the process and form of the output in the document?

In our experience providing managers with assistance when reading maps (if these are incorporated in the brochures/presentation) does help, as the map format used in documents is often different from that to which they are accustomed. Although some participants will have attended workshops, it is still better to revisit the process than rely on their memory. Including information about the process of prioritization, and monitoring progress will also contribute to increasing participants' sense of procedural justice and rationality. Many organizations forget to put a simple fold-out key to the colour coding and style used throughout the document.

How can I know how the strategy will be received, and how do I know I have got the presentation format right?

Try it out on a small group of staff and gauge their reactions. It is also helpful to get feedback from those outside of the process to check on the clarity of the layout and content and to assess the document's reception. In addition, it may be possible to capitalize on the pilot exercise by deliberately using opinion formers and potential saboteurs who may then become 'privileged advocates'.

Further Commentary on Delivering Strategy – communication of strategy

Taking care to communicate the strategy may seem costly and time consuming; however, if done properly, it does increase significantly the likelihood for implementation. Ensuring that as many of the organization's members as possible are able to listen to the process of how the strategy was created and to view the results not only elicits a greater understanding of the results (the strategic actions) but also demonstrates commitment by management. Both road shows and attendant brochures provide a means to see the results of the process – a process that a number of them may have been involved in. They are therefore able to see the results of their work, and this offers **closure**. It also provides the opportunity to ask   *C158* questions, learn more about the various components of the organization, and, if a brochure is provided, have reference to an artifact.

Project Management – gaining organizational learning through assessing performance

By incorporating performance assessment and organizational learning together the likelihood of successful implementation is increased. The very process of using the SDSS to determine the progress towards the strategic direction will help managers begin to understand not only the direction that is being aspired towards, but also how it is impacting upon the environment, and how the environment is reacting to, and dictating changes upon, the strategy. Illustrating this symbiotic relation, Yeates (1996) notes that:

> 'the nature of the Govan Initiative strategy model is such that it overtly recognizes that strategy development and planning is not a static process but one that moves and changes according to life experiences. It allows for the continual addition of new experiences, arguments and occurrences to inform and shape the model. Through the implementation of a performance management system the experiences of managers can be entered into the strategy model and gradually the original model can be shaped by future events'.

This perspective is echoed and extended in chapter C8:

> '. . . we need to acknowledge the real need for closure and stability with the equally real need for continuous organizational learning and strategic change. Thus, we must devise processes for monitoring, review, and strategic control that in themselves promote organizational learning, do not stultify strategy, and yet provide respect for a carefully developed strategy. That enables operational effectiveness and efficiency to develop'.

Both these comments demonstrate the integral link between monitoring performance and organizational learning. By providing staff with a sense of progress and understanding, it is possible to move them towards the achievement of their efforts. Incorporating the different techniques/methods we have introduced for discussing the organization's strategic future promotes organizational learning. Learning is continuous (as is the strategy process) and can be viewed as yet another form of journey, one that parallels the journey of strategy development. Through the strategy journey staff learn more about what is possible – identifying potential synergies, powerful stakeholder management options, etc. which in turn inform the strategy journey. The need for staff to grasp the concepts of strategy in order to design a strategic direction is illustrated by Yeates's (1996) observation:

> 'A good example of achieving a high level of shared understanding was provided by the management team . . . the meaning and understanding of concepts such as vision and

mission statements, goals, strategies and actions represented an ongoing issue among members of the management team. Through our own working experiences we had developed individual interpretations of the concepts yet at a group level there was no shared understanding. It is difficult to move forward in terms of strategy development when there is no shared understanding of what that means. Through ongoing discussion, debate and practical examples a shared understanding has evolved. This did not necessarily represent the views of any one individual but emerged from the actual process of group learning. Individual managers are now much more "comfortable" with their understanding of the concepts and accordingly are less defensive and more open to debating what strategy means' (Yeates, 1996).

C77 Carefully designing a strategic direction and then reviewing its success in terms of implementation allows staff to complete the **learning cycle**. In this manner reflection (upon observed characteristics) leads to designed action packages that are put into place (plunging into action) and subsequently reviewed (to determine their success). From this, both cognitive and behavioural aspects of learning are addressed. It is worth mentioning that project management provides one form of review – usually at the micro level – and that formal review procedures (as noted later in this chapter) also contribute to the learning process – at a more macro level.

C71 Guidelines for Using the Computer Model as an Organizational Memory

The relationship between performance assessment and organizational learning is corroborated through the use of the SDSS model as a form of organizational memory as well as a project management tool. Developing an organizational memory (as opposed to organizational learning), suggests creating an artifact that can be left behind in the organization – a living artifact of strategy making that can be used by the chief executive only, some or all of the management team, and line managers, depending on the organization and objectives. Choosing who or how many managers have access will, to some extent, be informed by the intended purpose.

2.1 *Capitalize on the computer model as a transitional object.* One of the most basic ways to use the model and to capitalize on the richness of the information and its attendant rationale, is to use it as a reminder of what was agreed. It can also be used to brief staff not involved in the strategy process, including induction of new managers (see below, and Eden and Sims (1981)).

2.1.1 *Use the computer model as a memory refresher.* Many clients find the computer model a powerful means of keeping themselves aware of what was agreed during the design and confirmation of the strategy. Several senior managers use the model as a means of reviewing the direction, actions, and objectives before attending meetings. In this way they ensure that what ensues from the meeting matches the strategic intent. One aim is to ensure that a tighter match between operational and strategic objectives follows.

2.1.2 *Use the computer model as a briefing tool to explain the rationale of the strategy to staff.* A managing director, who had just completed a strategy exercise, used the organizational memory model when presenting the strategy to staff who, due to geographical location, were unable to contribute to the process (showing not only what had been agreed but why and how it fitted together). He updated his own version with additional commentary after each visit by noting arguments about expected difficulties in implementation and ways managers expected to resolve these difficulties.

2.2 *Manage 'options as assets'*. Strategic actions and programmes, chosen during the strategy process, often become untenable due to environmental changes, or new opportunities emerge. If opportunties can be spotted earlier and acted upon quickly then they can yield significant benefits to the organization. By exploring both the reduced computer model and the complete computer model (see chapter P7), alternative paths of action can be identified, considered, and the most appropriate selected, resulting in faster decisions. Not only can organizations act opportunistically but can do so in accordance with the strategic direction. One chief executive, working in a particularly turbulent environment, referred to his strategy model as 'having a warm coat' – he felt comfortable about making rapid strategic decisions knowing that they fitted in with the overall strategic intent, and would be seen as obvious strategic moves by his colleagues.

2.3 *Help with the induction of new staff*. As noted earlier, the environment does not remain static, but also changes occur within the organization – staff leave and new staff are appointed. If new staff are to function in accordance with the strategy then they need to have an understanding of what has been agreed. By providing them with a copy of the model (either electronically or a set of maps) they can *explore* what has been agreed by following their own interests and role – accessing parts of the strategy as a DSS when required. For one chief executive this process was explicitly part of the recruitment process – **implementing parts of the** *V247* **strategy, as it was reflected in the computer model, was the job description**.

Using the Computer Model as a Project Management Tool

By using the computer model as a form of **Decision Support System (DSS) for** *C172* **project management**, it is possible to continue to manage better the balance between continuity and change. This is achieved by continually reviewing current tasks and objectives against organizational resources. Moreover, not only can the system support regular reviews of progress – a useful mechanism when reporting to key stakeholders – but as noted above it may act as an organizational memory – a memory that facilitates a holistic view. The project management DSS (or rather SDSS) enables the strategy to remain *dynamic*, allowing managers to balance alignment to the strategic direction with opportunism. Although some senior managers resist using computers, in our experience the value of the material and experiencing its use in workshops reduces such disinclination.

Getting started

3.1 *Start slowly to gain confidence* Given that many senior managers are still relatively unfamiliar with computers, it is appropriate to start at a relatively simple but effective level. This will allow them to gain confidence before gradually using more of the software facilities available.

3.1.1   *Build on learning gained through experience.* One of the most powerful means of helping anyone interrogate the computer model is seeing others using it, and this will, in part, have been achieved by their having seen its use by facilitators during workshops. For many managers the process of strategy making is new, as is the mode of capturing and manipulating the strategic assumptions. Unlike spreadsheets that have been around for decades and are well understood, strategy software has no commonly experienced manual replica to fall back on. Experiencing the structuring processes and becoming familiar with the JOURNEY making methodology will go some way to providing managers with this information. Managers have 'learnt mainly from observation and then finding ways to do it' (Ackermann *et al*, 1992).

3.1.2   *Produce a single sheet of instructions.* Where a number of staff are going to be using the computer model then providing them with a sheet of the most common and useful instructions appropriate to *their* model (styles, categories, strategy concepts, etc.) has been very powerful. To increase its durability, laminate the sheet in plastic coating.

3.1.3   *Develop a set of procedures for using the model.* If a number of staff intend or are required to use the computer model, then producing a clear set of rules about editing material is useful. Access can be set to 'view only', or specific areas delegated and any alterations restricted to those areas. Alternatively the 'bulletin board' facility provides a useful place to enter queries and additional material without altering the structure of the computer model.

3.2   *Delegate to others.* For some organizations, having a single staff member responsible for the maintenance of the computer model has been helpful. This, however, may be only a temporary measure until other staff members become more familiar with the process and it becomes embedded across the organization. For example, one organization had a member of staff responsible for regularly interviewing individual senior managers to determine progress. This was followed by reporting back overall progress made and apparent blockages at monthly strategy meetings. As staff became familiar with noting the progress made, updating the model and reviewing overall progress, each member of the management team was provided with access to the model and made responsible for the implementation of his/her own section of the model.

3.3   *Carry out regular updates on strategic progress.* As mentioned in the previous chapter, an effective form of progress monitoring uses colour coding moving from red (not started) to dark blue (1–50% progress) to light blue (over 50% progress) to finally light grey (complete). The computer model will start off predominantly red; the regular updating should reveal significant shifts in the overall colour of the model.

C165 V214   3.4   *Provide more meaningful **means of measurement** of progress and staff loading.*

3.4.1   *Explore not just which actions are not being completed but why.* By examining
C173   the **strategic actions in context**, the review process can determine whether the person responsible was at fault or whether lack of progress was due to a more subordinate action (the responsibility of another organizational member).

3.4.2   *Check the work loads of staff.* Use the computer model to examine work loads to ensure that any new emergent actions are assigned to appropriate staff.

Figure P8.3 Different forms of set analysis.

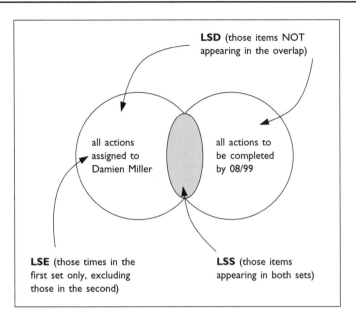

LSD (those items NOT appearing in the overlap)

all actions assigned to Damien Miller

all actions to be completed by 08/99

LSE (those times in the first set only, excluding those in the second)

LSS (those items appearing in both sets)

3.4.3 *Ensure that at all times new actions are chosen in relation to the strategic direction.* This increases the chance of the actions being implemented in accordance with their original intention.

3.5 *Analyse performance.* In addition to keeping the computer model up to date, the different analyses extend the SDSS's use as a project management tool. For example, patterns can be detected, programmes not performing noted and chased, and completed actions identified and published to 'boast' about progress. There are a number of useful analyses (see also chapter P6):

3.5.1 *List the different progress styles.* Lists of strategy actions not started, in progress, or completed can be displayed on the screen in the context of their supporting actions and purpose and can be assessed.

3.5.2 *Search on names and dates.* By using the 'FIND' command (in the list menu) any instance of either a staff member's name or particular date can be identified. By scrutinizing individual lists it is possible to determine the level of performance of the staff member responsible (useful if an annual performance review is about to occur). Searching on dates or names is useful; however, further benefit can be gained from identifying over-lapping lists (see figure P8.3 which shows the different types of analysis). For example, identify all of the actions that have to be reviewed by the end of August 1999 (*08/99*) by Damien Miller (*DM*): search for all of the instances of DM and place these in a *set* followed by a search for actions bearing the information 08/99 (also placed in a set); various forms of set analysis can be undertaken – the conjunction ('LSS') of the two sets shows which of DM actions should be reviewed at 08/99.

3.6   *Use the SDSS or strategic intent computer model as an organizational memory.* Not only can the model aid with project management, it is able to keep a record of what has been achieved each year and allow comparisons across years.

3.7   *Reward progress.* One method for tapping and renewing the energy and enthusiasm, is through regularly disseminating the levels of progress made. Not only will this help the organization as a whole gain a sense of progress – that something is really happening – but also individual members as their efforts are publicly praised.

C171 V263   3.8   **Integrate the strategic intent and strategic action programmes with operational tasks.** Some staff will not have strategic actions assigned to them, nor perhaps experience the communication of the strategy. Nevertheless, these members are responsible for important operational tasks. Expending effort in linking operational tasks to the strategic actions will help ensure these staff feel that they are contributing towards the overall effort and are valued. It will also ensure that the balance between continuity and change is maintained. One of the benefits of high levels of participation in JOURNEY making can be the move away from departmental concerns to focus on a shared set of organizational goals. Nevertheless it is crucial to maintain a means of *demonstrating the achievement* of operational tasks and how they *contribute to the overall picture.*

3.8.1   *Link operational tasks to strategy actions.* For example, the method employed by Govan Initiative (see vignette) started by examining operational tasks (whose progress was monitored by various funding bodies) and exploring how they contributed to the strategic action programmes. The organization found weaving the two together helped develop a better understanding of the strategic direction, as well as increasing overall coherence. Where a strategic action programme appeared to have no associated operational tasks they explored the impact of this on resources – this would be a new development. Conversely, where it was difficult to link operational tasks to a strategic action it prompted reassessment. Not only did this ensure a tighter and more synergistic fit between the two systems of action programmes but also it brought the two systems together so as to cut down the amount of work to be done.

3.8.2   *Capitalize on familiarity of existing systems.* For many organizations, systems for monitoring operational tasks already exist. Finding methods for explicitly illustrating the link between these tasks and the strategic actions will reduce the amount of learning necessary. Govan Initiative decided not to include the operational tasks in the project management model. Instead, the revised version of their Quarterly Monitoring System was extended to encompass the strategy actions. In this manner they could easily identify how each operational task supported the actions that in turn supported the strategies and so on (figure P8.4).

3.8.3   *Track progress at all levels.* By linking the two task systems, progress can be measured both at the very detailed micro level and at the more macro level of strategic actions and strategies. For Govan Initiative, staff familiar with their operational system were able to measure their progress, knowing how their efforts were supporting the strategic actions. Thus, very discrete tasks were seen as foundations for the overall strategy. Both the strategy and its associated measurement scheme could be easily understood and checked for coherence.

Figure P8.4   Linking operational tasks to the strategy.

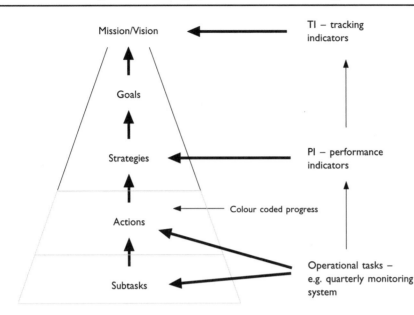

Further Commentary on Using the Computer Model as an Organizational Memory

Some organizations develop systems that combine the use of the computer model as a project management device with an **increase in delegation**. By placing the computer model on the world-wide computer network all departmental heads are given access to the model. Each has a clearly defined area of responsibility within the strategies, and is able to actively take part in monitoring their progress along-side that of their colleagues. In addition to assessing their level of performance they can also enter new actions when appropriate and in a way that must be seen to support the efforts of the other managers rather than acting in isolation. As a consequence a great deal more synergy can be gained.

V247

Cascading the strategy down the organization by the deliberate creation of linked sub-strategies for departments and divisions or operating companies also helps extend effective project management. For example, the General Manager of the National Health Service Unit succeeded in buying many departmental heads further into the overall strategy by developing strategies for each department. The General Manager's idea was to take the strategy a level down the organization and create a sub-strategy. He started with a Training Strategy. To achieve this, staff involved in training and development processes were interviewed using the normal JOURNEY making approach and then later involved in computer sup-ported workshops. The only constraint the group had in developing their training strategy was guaranteeing that goals of the training strategy supported the overall strategy. Many of the goals and a number of the strategies were directly translated from one computer model to another, ensuring the consistency between them whilst elaborating specific areas in considerable depth.

C175 **Reviewing Strategy Performance**

Although the use of the computer model as a project management tool allows managers to monitor progress, it tends to focus on micro rather than the macro performance – focusing on achieving actions rather than assessing realization of strategies and goals. In many instances this concentration on specific actions and their level of progress tends to result in the examination addressing specific strategies or action programmes rather than taking a broad, holistic view. Taking time to deliberately review the strategy at a more 'superordinate' level provides a chance both to revisit the overall strategic intentions of the organization and to determine the extent of progress towards the goals.

The strategy's progress must be regularly checked against the performance indicators identified – regardless of whether the organization has agreed only its strategic intent or developed a detailed set of action programmes. Linking each senior manager's performance objectives to specific strategies and associated actions maintains strategy implementation as a continual focus. This process is reinforced by specifying that all requests for resources be made in connection with the strategy.

Review of strategy acts as a form of strategic 'control' by deliberately designing processes for assessing the overall impact of the actions upon the strategies, and the strategies upon the organizational goals. This conscious focusing of attention towards examining not only the impact of the actions, but the effect the strategies have had on organizational success, is rarely accomplished. Horovitz (1979:5) suggests that:

> 'an analysis of current practices has shown that long range and in some cases strategic planning exist. However, when one looks at chief executive control, empirical evidence suggests that there is no control system to match such planning'.

Nevertheless, concentrating on performance is only one aspect of reviewing strategy. As illustrated in the early part of the book (chapter C2), the journey of strategy making is ongoing. Reviewing the effect of the deliberated strategy and its relationship with newly emergent strategies completes the cycle of strategy *making*.

Guidelines for Reviewing the Performance of Strategies

4.1 *Regularly set aside time to review progress.* By explicitly putting aside time it is possible to weave it into organizational life and therefore allow those organizational members involved to plan accordingly. Formalizing the procedure will not only ensure that the dates for meeting are in relevant diaries but also reinforce the serious intent of making the strategy work.

4.1.1 *Carry out a review every 3 or 6 months.* Determining the frequency of the reviews will depend on the nature of the organization; however, our experience suggests that once every six months is a reasonable guide. Six months is chosen for two reasons: (i) enough progress will have been made towards the achievement of the strategies to assess their level of effectiveness, and (ii) there will be time to re-energize or re-emphasize strategies not performing as well as anticipated. However, it is important to consider the type of activity being undertaken – see guidelines 4.2, 4.5, and 5.1

4.1.2   *Allocate between half a day and a day for the review.* This will allow sufficient time to be spent doing a satisfactorily thorough job, any less and the review will turn out to be seen as a 'waste of time'. When allocating an entire day, strategies can be assessed against the performance indicators **(achievement) along with a check on the level of commitment** and understanding attained. However, it is appreciated that spending an entire day may be problematic given the pressures of organizational everyday life and that two half-days (each focusing on one of the above tasks) may be the only practical response to other operational pressures.   C175

4.1.3   *Make reviews a routine part of other regular reviews/meetings.* Coupling a number of reviewing activities together will allow staff to begin to better appreciate how operational tasks can impact upon the strategy and vice-versa. For example, Govan Initiative's management team has deliberately built in time to carry out their strategic reviews during their quarterly monitoring meetings, so that operational and strategic tasks are seen as integrally linked.

4.2   *Focus on horizontal and vertical reviews.* As the strategy model often contains between one hundred to three hundred goals, strategies, and actions, reviewing the entire model is a complex and often exhausting task. A common way of managing review is to examine the level of progress being realized for one entire strategy at a time – a vertical slice. This involves staff responsible for the implementation of the actions along with one or two management team members coming together to evaluate the success of this strategy. The process involves assessing each action's level of progress (not started, in progress or complete), and examining whether each action is contributing towards the achievement of the strategy (examining the arrow). However, this type of review does not get at the holistic aspect of the strategy model. It is therefore useful to carry out an overall review of all of the strategies' performance with reference to the goals – a horizontal slice. Here the entire management team is involved, allowing the insights gained from vertical reviews to inform the horizontal review.

4.3   *Review the strategy in relation to performance indicators.* Each strategy will be measured against a number of performance indicators. The results can then be used when examining the strategies with respect to assumptions about levels of dissemination and implementation.

4.3.1   *Write each strategy, along with its attendant performance indicators, on separate flip-chart sheets.* Place the content of the strategy at the top of the sheet (landscape) and list each of the performance indicators underneath (see figure P7.4). Alongside each of the performance indicators draw in a line to denote the extent of progress made (for example 0% to 100%). Sometimes it is useful to provide participants with the ability to flag possible backwards or negative progress. We often start the achievement continuum at –30%.

4.3.2   *Provide each participant with self-adhesive spots.* Participants allocate one spot for each performance indicator. Ask participants to position the spots on the scale where they believe the strategy's level of progress currently stands. Use the same anchor points that were agreed and tested during the development of performance indicators. While the measures can be relatively crude, particularly for qualitative indicators, the results will nevertheless be indicative and a good basis for jointly understanding and reflecting on progress. This process of assessment can be carried out in two ways. Review is best achieved by taking each strategy in turn and rating performance and then discussing. However, when doing it this way, time management becomes a problem and it is likely that a review of all strategies will not be made in the planned time. If an overrun cannot be dealt with then, an alternative method requires attaching all of the strategy flip-charts to the walls around the room and asking participants in their own time to wander around and assess progress for all strategies. This latter approach allows participants to see the entire panoply and so gain a holistic sense of progress before debate. Following an overall evaluation, discussion can focus on those areas which are a problem or where there is disagreement.

4.3.3 *Use the results as a dialectic process and encourage reflection.* In our experience, participants often find that on many of the indicators there is little agreement (spots stretch from one end of the continuum to the other). In these instances it is important to ask participants to reflect upon why they had chosen that particular point on the scale, so that others can understand their point of view. As the explanations surface, participants gain a greater understanding of exactly what is being measured and how each of them interprets the results. The process may also reveal that in some parts of the organization the strategy is performing well whereas in others it is struggling. Consequently examples of good practice can be exchanged, and any danger points highlighted along with methods to settle them. In the manner of the Delphi approach (Dalkey and Helmer, 1963), it may be useful to allow participants to re-rate following the discussion and test whether more consensus about performance is emerging. The act of actually assessing performance and subsequently reviewing the performance acts as a test of the implementation of the strategy. In turn it may lead to establishing a degree of consensus and possibly rewording or revising the performance indicators.

4.3.4 *Compare the results against those generated at inception, or other reviews.* If, when creating the performance indicators, there was the opportunity to assess the current position of the organization against the attainment of the strategy, then this information can be used to measure progress. Additionally where other review episodes have been undertaken, their results can inform progress assessment.

4.4 *Include staff from all parts of the organization, wherever possible.* This will contribute towards maintaining the enthusiasm and ownership generated earlier in the process. Vertical reviews provide the best opportunity for involving staff not in the management team, as this type of review calls for a range of expertise and evaluation when considering the progress of the strategy's actions.

4.5 *Assess the strategy in relation to the degree of commitment judged to be embedded in the organization.* Using the 2 × 2 grids shown in chapter C8 it is possible to explore each strategy's performance against two dimensions. The first dimension determines the degree to which a particular strategy is embedded in the organization – the axis of understanding and commitment. The second dimension is the degree to which that particular strategy has succeeded in relation to expectations of attainment over the time period – the axis of implementation. This second axis is informed through the performance indicators results (see guideline 4.3). Once the strategies have been placed on the grid, it is possible to identify courses of action.

Those in the bottom left quadrant (incorporating incoherent programmes, and mixed messages) suggest further resources and attention, whereas those in the top left quadrant (appearing 'magical' and driven by emergent strategizing) require further examination and promotion. Finally, strategies in the bottom right (encountering practical difficulties, and possibly wrong reward systems) suggest that alternative actions should be considered since the organization knows what it wants to achieve but current actions are not having the desired effect.

4.6   *Publish the results*. As not every organizational member is able to be involved in the review process, it may, depending on the results, be worth publishing them.

Reviewing the appropriateness of the strategy

This form of strategy focuses on a more long term view. Rather than assessing progress it concentrates on the appropriateness of the different strategies and scrutinizing the assumptions about making strategy happen – the relationships (arrows) rather than the statements themselves.

5.1   *Examine core assumptions*. The guidelines below help participants determine whether the *system* of strategies and strategic programmes is turning out to be the most effective when seeking to achieve the goals (and so may consider the goal system itself).

5.1.1   *Review the relationships between strategies and between strategic programmes and strategies*. Starting with the most superordinate strategy, examine the means by which it is attained. Ask whether the relationship is still valid. Links that are no longer valid in the context of the strategy, i.e. they are no longer an effective means towards achieving the outcome of the pair of constructs, are removed and the strategy map examined to determine the effect. One possible effect may be that a strategic programme or strategy is no longer potent in relation to the goal system. In these instances focus on a review of the nature of the programme or strategy (using data from discussion about performance). Where the relationship does still support the achievement of the outcome, then the analysis moves to the next level down. In this way each strategy tear-drop of supporting strategies and programmes is reviewed.

5.1.2   *Examine the remaining strategic intent to determine missing areas*. Once the relationships have been inspected, take time to re-evaluate the overall strategic intent to determine whether any new strategies should be considered. We commented above that, as time passes, the original strategy will have succeeded in moving the organization to a new strategic 'platform', thus realizing strategic opportunities that would not have been politically or logically feasible when the strategy making was first undertaken. Reviewing strategy provides an opportunity to consider this possibility and perhaps explore the benefits of a major overhaul of strategy.

5.2   *Assess performance against benchmarks*. By determining the current state of the market or sector overall, it may be appropriate to determine how the organization is performing in relation to others at the goal level. In the public sector, where organizational goals and distinctive competencies (livelihood scheme) are expected to be similar, benchmarking is wholly appropriate. For the private sector, goals and the business model may be highly differentiated and benchmarking can, imperceptibly, destroy such strategic differentiation. For example, when Govan Initiative (see vignette) were addressing measurement systems, they were very keen to measure not only their own impact on the geographical area of their responsibility but also the contributions from other organizations such as the police service, welfare, etc. They developed what they called 'tracking indicators'. For example, the goal 'improve the living and working conditions of Govan' was assessed through the tracking indicators of 'more owner occupied homes', 'see £500m invested in the area before 2001', and 'reduce the percentage of group 1 crimes'. Govan Initiative could not achieve complete success against the indicators on their own, nor could they assess to what extent their work contributed towards their attainment. However, using the measures, they were able to explore how the Govan area was performing in relation to other areas. For example, had unemployment suddenly risen all across Glasgow/Scotland or was it just their area? This not only helped them assess their performance at a macro level but also clearly demonstrated that they recognized that the stakeholders' contributions were vital.

Reinforce 'buy in'

Here we discuss a couple of often used methods for making strategy a part of 'everyday' managerial life.

6.1   *Build strategy review into manager performance review procedures.* Designing strategic objectives into senior managers' performance measures will further reinforce the link between their operational responsibilities and strategic aims and reinforce their commitment to the strategy. Doing so legitimizes time spent in pursuing the strategic objectives and reminds them of the overall strategic intent. In addition it should enable senior managers to gain an increased understanding of how one another's contribution supports the overall whole. For example, in the National Health Service Unit (see vignette) each senior manager's **annual performance objectives** were constructed in terms of personal aspirations, operational considerations, and contribution to the realization of strategy. Using the SDSS each manager was able to see how his or her contribution supported, or was dependent upon another.

V222

6.2   *Ensure all major resource requests are made in relation to strategy.* This can be a way of ensuring that staff read and become familiar with the strategy. Not only do managers get to know the strategy intimately but also so does the chief executive, who needs to know the strategy, and every angle on it, to check the validity of the resource demands. The process, if well done, forces out double-messages that derive from resource allocation procedures.

Yes But . . .

V237   *What if my* **client moves on** *or there is a significant shift in key organizational actors?*

There is no easy answer to this question; however, it may be more or less problematic depending on how embedded the strategy is within the organization (that is, how successful has the journey making been as a journey) and how determined the new players are to make their own mark on the organization's direction. In some circumstances, the client may move on to a more senior position in the organization and may adopt the same approach at a more macro level. This in turn may support the strategy they were originally involved with, particularly if the replacement is a member of the team that created it. However, where the client moves to another organization – a common occurrence in the public sector with senior civil servants, and in multinational organizations – then the strategy's success relies on the group pressures from those who have completed the journey.

There are huge amounts of disagreement about levels of performance – what do I do?

Encourage managers to explain why they have chosen positions at alternate ends of the scale. To do this, explicitly build in time to explore the outcome in an atmosphere of enquiry rather than defensiveness (which may result otherwise). As noted in guideline 4.3.3, participants often have different interpretations of the indicator and thus measure its performance differently. Another explanation may be that in parts of the organization success has been achieved but that other parts have not been able to make progress for particular reasons. Therefore, alternative actions may be required, as may different means of assessing performance or different indicators.

What if we are making no progress towards a strategy?

Find out why progress is not being achieved. This may be due to staff not being aware of the strategy, not understanding its purpose, or not having sufficient resources to act upon it. Some clues to the explanation may be gained through trying to place it on the implementation versus commitment and understanding grid. Discussions with those who are responsible for implementation may also highlight problems. This is best done in an atmosphere of discovery rather than blame. It may also be worth considering whether the particular strategy is still valid in relation to the other strategies and goals – it could be that managers have already questioned the links in the strategy map and acted accordingly.

How can I encourage managers to focus on the strategy rather than just the day-to-day firefighting?

One method is through attaching strategic actions or programmes to managers' performance objectives (see guideline 6.1); however, there are others. Consider rewarding those teams or managers who are making particularly good progress against difficult circumstances. This reward does not necessarily have to be financial; other forms of reward such as public recognition can have equally motivating affects.

Further Commentary on Reviewing Strategy

As we noted in chapter C2, one of the measures of success of the journey is that the resultant strategy becomes embedded in the culture ('the way we do things around here') and in the thinking of managers as they take action in relation to their 'world-taken-for-granted'.

A further check on examining performance comes from attempts at triangulation. For example, if the strategic actions are being achieved (using the SDSS) then it should be possible to see this progress reflected in the accomplishment of the strategies (evidenced by the performance indicators). Likewise, if the performance indicators show progress, then the team should see this reflected by increased actions-in-progress. Where this is not the case, an explanation is that either the actions or indicators are not the right ones, or something else is influencing the progress. The third leg of the triangle is that of bench marking.

THE INTERVENTION: THE FACILITATOR AND THE CLIENT

Strategy making, as practised following the theory, concepts, and practice outlined in this book, is a client oriented activity. We have consistently used the term 'client', not organization, as the centre of attention for the facilitator. Here we discuss what we mean by the term 'client'. Although not a specific step in the JOURNEY making process, building and maintaining client relationships can have a significant effect on the success or otherwise of the process. This chapter focuses on a number of issues about client management of the facilitator and vice-versa. These include: considering different participant categories, determining who the client is, and who are the other internal key 'actors' in relation to the client, as well as the processes of building trust and commitment. In some senses the chapter could be treated as an appendix to be read alongside the chapter on facilitation (chapter P5). A good client–facilitator relationship encourages the client to say more about their personal as well as organizational aspirations and concerns. A close working relationship, based on mutual trust, will assist in understanding the organization, its culture, and the personalities of key actors. These insights will influence significantly the design of the JOURNEY.

Client, Sponsor, Key Actors, Other Participants

The client, sponsor, and key actors are the internal stakeholders who are the users of JOURNEY making. While everyone involved in JOURNEY making is in some way a participant we find it helpful to distinguish three categories of stakeholder who are particularly significant – the client, the sponsor, and key actors.

The *client* we take to be a person who has commissioned JOURNEY making, is $V196$ responsible for approving its design, signs off or requests resource usage, calls participants to events, and acts as the focus of attention for the facilitator. The client will usually be a single person, but sometimes may be a small group. The client is not the organization, division, or department. It must be somebody or a small group who can be related to as if in normal conversation. The facilitator must be able to develop a trusting and trusted relationship with the client. If the client is taken to be a small group then, for this relationship to work, one implication might be that the facilitator thinks of the group as if they were one person. Thus, the facilitator will need to make a judgement about the extent to which each client group member has similar views about the journey's purpose. Rarely will this be the case; after all, the basis of JOURNEY making assumes that each management team member will have a different stake in the outcome of the journey as well as a different perspective on strategy. Most members of the management team will see themselves as winners or losers – whereas the client will see themselves as always the winner, and it will be the job of the facilitator to ensure that this is always the case. In addition, as well as the public objectives of strategy making, a client will usually have secondary objectives that are not intended to be visible. One example is bringing the thinking of one management team member into greater alignment with others.

On many occasions there may be more than one client during the course of an intervention, and distinguishing between them is important. For example, the client that initiates JOURNEY making may not necessarily be the one that is the focus for the process as it unfolds. It is the management of all purported clients that is important to the adoption of both the process and outcomes. As we noted in chapter C1, it is rare for any major strategic change to be initiated without its being prompted by some sort of strategic crisis. The position of the client, key actors, and sponsor within the politics of the crisis arising can be one of the most important aspects that the facilitator must understand. It will also prescribe much of the client's invisible agenda. Without the client's 'buy in' to the design of the intervention, the likelihood of strategic change becomes problematic, as the resources require authorization and energy has to be maintained. The facilitator thus needs to build a lasting relationship with the client based on mutual trust.

Furthermore, the client is often not the most senior person in the organization – the strategy may be for a divisional manager, operating company president, or departmental manager. He or she may be required to demonstrate the use of JOURNEY making to others – for example, selling the outcome up the line, justifying resource usage, etc. In these circumstances it becomes important for the facilitator to work out who may be the **sponsor** for the work. The sponsor, for us, is that person who has agreed that the client may pursue the project. They will have some ownership of the project and wish to protect it even though they may have no direct involvement. For example, for all of the projects reported in the vignettes the client needed to gain the support of a sponsor who would protect the project during the inevitable problem periods (Bryson, 1988).

V267

The sponsor also will have an interest in evaluating the performance of the JOURNEY making process. They are likely to be interested in whether the use of the approach disrupts the corporate culture beyond that of the client's area of responsibility. In particular, the introduction of participative approaches in one part of the organization can raise expectations elsewhere. This introduction will often put at risk an autocratic power culture and provide participants with changed expectations about the process of decision making across the whole organization. Clearly we may also expect the sponsor to be particularly interested in 'value for money' as compared with other corporate demands. There is a danger that, because the sponsor is not a participant, and therefore unable to evaluate process outcomes (particularly against objectives that are designed to be 'invisible' to anyone other than the client) or decision quality, the evaluation of value for money is likely to be crude compared with that made by the client – for example, seeing absolute costs (including staff time) as more important than outcomes.

Evaluation also focuses upon the client's confidence in the process. For the client, the overall credibility of the approach may be as crucial a criterion as the reputation of the facilitator. After all, the credibility of the facilitator may lie as much with the extent of professional symbolism associated with the approach to be used as with the professionalism of the facilitator. Alongside this assessment of the approach's validity are the important anticipated outcomes, as these too influence the evaluation made by the client. The relatively hard-nosed considerations of value for money in relation to person-days of facilitator time and expected outcomes are but one component. Typically, other softer issues are considered: for example, can the client understand the approach (in our case JOURNEY making) to be employed? If the approach seems too opaque, or potentially 'magic', then the client is likely to be uneasy and, more importantly, feel as though he or she is unable to retain control of the process. In this case they are concerned that control is transferred from them to the method, to the facilitator, or to both. Moreover, if the method transfers power in such a way that it risks loss of ultimate control then many clients will evaluate a proposed intervention negatively. Another issue to consider is where other participants may see an increase in their power, which cannot be experienced as a loss of power by the client. For some clients any increase in others' power is seen within the context of a zero-sum game and rejected accordingly. Clients are also interested in the extent to which the intervention method provides opportunities for disassociation from the method if needed. For example, the ability to transfer blame for failed outcomes, or lack of implementation of conclusions, may need to be attributed to the method and facilitator in order to lower risk to acceptable levels for the client. Some methods or approaches, and they way in which they are used, allow for ambiguity of failure or success and others do not.

Key actors are those participating in JOURNEY making but having significant power in relation to the political feasibility of delivering strategy. They are *internal* stakeholders with high power to influence outcomes and process and a high interest in the process and its possible outcomes. When there is uncertainty about who is the client, then the facilitator may treat the group of key actors as if they were the client, hoping that the client will gradually emerge from within their number. They may be those participants who are seen by the client as potential saboteurs, opinion leaders/formers, those seeing themselves as potential winners or losers, and those who are likely to carry some individual implementation responsibility. To some extent key actors will be the group who can most easily influence the client about whether JOURNEY making was a success. They are the group who can 'vote with their feet' if they don't like the way in which the journey is unfolding. Sometimes they are those who have enough autonomy to decide **not to attend strategy workshops even though invited**. For this group their evaluation of the method and the facilitator will be influenced by the power advantage or disadvantage to them that follows from their being a participant. *V214 V243 V249*

V226

Finally, other *participants* are those whose presence is requested because their opinions, experience, and/or knowledge is needed. Alternatively they need to be given the impression that they have had a chance to offer their views (so being 'bought in'). Thus, they are participants who do not have the status of client or key actors. As this group of stakeholders are also participants in JOURNEY making events, they too will evaluate the method and facilitator along a number of dimensions that are important to the client and key actors. These participants may be encouraged to see themselves as offering 'expert' views that might influence importantly the strategy development outcomes. Therefore, one of their evaluation criteria will be the extent to which the method succeeds in allowing them 'to be taken seriously' and treated as having a useful role compared with alternatives. This attention promotes a sense of **procedural justice** and **procedural rationality**. *C53: C55*

This group also are more likely to be influenced by 'the feel good' factor than the other stakeholders. The uniqueness, novelty, and fun associated with JOURNEY making workshops may provide the base for a 'good social event'. Some approaches to strategy making do a good job at collecting data from the 'other participants' but do not attend to the social needs of the group of people from whom the data was derived. Consequently they risk creating events where

1.1.3 *Be prepared for changes in the client.* Where JOURNEY making appears to be successful, managers further up the organizational hierarchy take note. In some cases these managers then seek to broaden the scope of the journey by embracing it within their own sphere of influence. Although this outcome can be pleasing for the facilitator, as the remit widens the issue of 'who is the client' surfaces once more. Clear demarcations may need to be drawn, as loyalties between the original client and the new, organizationally superordinate, client may conflict.

1.2 *Separate key actors from other participants.* In practice the number of key actors who can be attended to within any intervention is relatively small. As the key actors and client are likely to be the decision making team the boundary between key actors and participants is likely to arise after about 9–11 key actors have been identified. Clearly the key actors group should exist as a cluster which separates itself from others if an internal power/interest grid were constructed. Therefore the final group size will vary around about 7–11 people. It is important to remember that, while the client will probably not change over the project (with the exception of the above guideline), the key actors are likely to change as some become winners and others losers.

1.3 *Locate **partners** as champions within the organization.* These are the people   *V214 V224* within the organization who take on responsibility for much of the routine preparation and information exchange activities. Their importance flows from their ability to know what is going on day by day through their informal networks. In addition, they understand the politics of the organization and so can advise the facilitator as to what is politically feasible and what is not. As a result they may act as the main link with the facilitator regardless of whether the facilitator is internal or external. However, they must not take on the role of the client or sponsor in either their or the facilitator's mind, regardless of the fact that they may often be the easiest conduit to work through. A final consideration is that they must be committed to the process and choice of method and facilitator.

1.3.1 *Use partners.* Because of their interest in the process and knowledge of the organization in many circumstances these individuals become co-facilitators. This is one way of ensuring that the organization is able to work with the SDSS computer model, carry out reviews, and consider strategy redesign on their own rather than be reliant on the original facilitator. In a number of interventions this training has been an explicit requirement from the organization. However, using internal facilitators on projects that the facilitator is interested in may cause serious conflicts of interest and undermine the success of the workshops (see chapter P5, guideline 4.3.1). Furthermore, their position and influence in the company may also limit their success as a facilitator. Other participants will not see them as unbiased parties and therefore will seek to censor their contributions. Further complications may occur where the partner is a senior member in the organization (and possibly the client) as their power gets in the way of important characteristics of the JOURNEY making approach.

2.1 ***Work with the client.*** These guidelines are closely linked with those   *V238* relating to facilitation in chapter P5 and should be read in conjunction with that chapter.

V216 V224 V249   2.1.1   *Set clear expectations with the client about the nature of the **facilitator–client relationship**.* This focuses upon clarifying the client–facilitator expectations about ways of working rather than the expectations of group working. In particular it implies ensuring that the client understands you will treat them as the client in all respects. This can be achieved partly by respecting their need to feel in control of the process, respecting their views about the key actors, and exploring invisible objectives.

2.1.2   *Acknowledge client prerogatives.* One of the main concerns clients may have when working in a participative environment is the impact that it will have upon their own managerial prerogatives. The guidelines suggested in P5 (guideline 1.1) provide some suggestions.

2.1.3   *Ensure the client understands fully the possible behaviours of participants in workshops and some of the possible (even if unlikely) outcomes.* Providing examples of previous workshops (it may be helpful to use extracts from the vignettes provided in this book) may assist. While each client will want to see their organization and strategy as unique (which they indeed are), some reassurance of where the process has been used before and what outcomes are reasonable is beneficial. This is particularly the case if the strategy being developed is for a department or division (rather than the entire company). In these situations the client/manager may be asked to defend his decision to undertake JOURNEY making to a more senior member.

2.1.4   *Undersell rather than oversell the process.* It is often tempting to promise more than can be delivered and therefore disappoint the client. By doing the opposite, within reason, the client and management team will be pleased with their own performance as well as that of the facilitator. It may also contribute towards increasing credibility, as the client appreciates being presented with a realistic process.

V223   3.1   *Build **trust and develop a personal relationship** with the client.* This is probably the most important guideline of all, as it will influence the extent and flavour of the JOURNEY making process. Where a high degree of trust is established, a greater degree of freedom to be jointly flexible and creative is possible, with recognition that some innovations may not succeed.

3.1.1   *Carefully manage the initial meeting.* At this meeting determine whether there is an overlap between the client's needs and the facilitator's skills (Eden and Sims, 1979). During this process of discovery and negotiation, the client is then able to make judgements about the facilitator, and vice-versa. Exploring possible hidden agenda items usually reassures the client that the process will address the realistic political setting within which any change will have to occur. Senior managers are suspicious of processes and analysis that will logically lead to recommended action which is not politically feasible. Finally, it is worth examining the extent to which participative methods of working are appropriate. Although JOURNEY making can be highly participative or simply involve the management team, it is not appropriate to compare it with the standard strategy analysis methods in terms of its impact on the organization. One consequence of exploring this issue along with the others, is that the meeting acts as the first step in a gradual building up of the relationship between the facilitator and client.

3.1.2   *Gain an appreciation of the client's local situation.* One option open to the facilitator is to acknowledge openly the client's competing pressures. Although the intervention is central to the facilitator's life it is usually less central for the client. Workshops may be postponed due to emergencies, individuals being unable to be involved, and the client being unable to attend to the process as much as they would wish.

4.1   *Stay in regular contact with the client.* Ensuring continuous contact takes place throughout the journey, before workshops, during them, and after, helps build trust. Although more exacerbated when working with external facilitators, lack of regular communication may leave clients feeling isolated and uncertain. Remembering that clients are accountable for the JOURNEY making project means they will often want reassurance about progress. Frequent informal meetings will surface concerns and help build on opportunities.

4.1.1   *Call or meet the client before each workshop.* By **involving clients in both the process and content design**, questions can be raised, and problems relating to difficult participants and potentially emotive issues resolved.   *V228*

4.1.2   ***Actively seek time for review** after the workshop.* This can be difficult because the energy levels of both facilitator and the client are low after workshops. When a workshop has gone well, and the client is on a 'high', she or he will be enthusiastic about wanting to review the day and discuss next steps often extending the process. However, 'bad' workshops deserve at least as much attention. Here plans for damage limitation and learning points can be discussed.   *V244 V260*

4.1.3   *Avoid long time gaps occurring between communication.* Clients are continuously balancing operational concerns with that of developing a strategic direction. As a result, firefighting may take over and the motivation and understanding for the journey will diminish. Regular discussions can help prevent this. As the relationship develops, clients often want to talk over other issues, not necessarily directly related to the journey but impinging upon it. These are good opportunities to develop trust and build joint confidence.

5.1   *Design the intervention to match client needs rather than those of the facilitator.* Facilitators as external consultants are inevitably tempted to sell a lengthy intervention, which in many situations is neither appropriate nor desired. Indeed, facilitator/analysts are also inclined to demand more analysis and process than the client wants. Clients are more likely to seek a reasonable level of satisfaction ('satisficing'). Moreover, it is important to recognize that clients are often not very sure about what is involved in a major project for strategy making. Neither are they sure whether they can work with the process or the facilitator. A 'quick and dirty' strategy workshop can be an important introduction. There are a number of reasons for doing this:

5.1.1   *Establish credibility.* By designing a 'quick and dirty' workshop the client group will be able to determine whether the JOURNEY making process is appropriate for them. It is unfortunate that the expression 'quick and dirty' has such a negative connotation, as this type of intervention does not indicate a lack of value. Instead, it aims to produce an efficient use of time and resources, particularly where there is any uncertainty. One example of a quick and dirty journey might be a half-day workshop focusing on the surfacing of strategic issues and exploration of emergent aspirations. Alternatively, it could involve a whole day, where the morning is spent working with the oval mapping technique to surface strategic issues and the afternoon spent exploring distinctive competencies to produce a draft statement of strategic intent. This process of **commencing with a 'taster'** was undertaken by Govan Initiative (see vignette) and reflected upon by a member of that team who, when reviewing the process that his organization had undertaken – which had deliberately been designed as a step by step approach – reflected that it had been important 'to allow the Management Team to determine whether the process was appropriate for the organization and ensure that any work undertaken was not wasted. The process was designed so that each phase would build and expand upon the previous, producing a strategy model that would be owned by the organization and also would be capable of reflecting the dynamic nature of the organization and its environment'.

V223 V254

5.1.2 *Strike a balance between incrementalism and a fully designed project in advance of the intervention starting.* For some organizations, gaining approval for a lengthy intervention can prove difficult, if not impossible. A client will usually want some understanding of the extent of a total commitment while at the same time wanting to pursue only some parts of the journey. These parts must be designed in a manner that ensures immediate rewards without a commitment to a full strategy making process. This means that the client must be offered not only a 'quick and dirty' workshop but one that can contribute to a longer journey. We believe that all of the parts of JOURNEY making enable an organization to build a launch platform that facilitates strategic change and organizational achievement. The approach to starting the journey, therefore, should be contingent on the particular context of the client and organization. In some cases a complete journey will be specified, in others incrementalism suggested, and in others a balance through incremental journey episodes.

Yes But . . .

What if I don't get on with the client?

This matters; a client and facilitator need to establish mutual trust if the journey is to be successful. Common reasons may be the client's personality in relation to that of the facilitator, and the client's intended use of the process (for example, is it to coerce members into a set agenda, or refusal to acknowledge specific process issues?). Clearly it should be possible to avoid working with the client, by either finding a colleague who can, or walking away from the project. Careful negotiation and discussion of the difficulties may overcome some types of difficulties.

Regardless of the action taken, it is worth remembering that staying with the project may in the long term result in a worse outcome: for example, outcomes where either the process fails (because of the client not appreciating the difficulties) or the facilitator is blamed.

What if the client is resistant to some of the JOURNEY making theory, method, or technique?

Find out why. It may be that she or he doesn't understand the reasons behind the actions and further explanation may help. Because we have sought to ensure that theory and practice are related, then it is always possible to have recourse to a coherent body of theory (which must usually, of course, be explained in non-academic language) to support proposals. More often, it is due to particular organizational cultural circumstances that need to be planned around. The method is intended to be customized – that's what the theory says! So it is possible that the proposal being made has not taken due account of the particular contingencies of the organization and of client needs. Case examples are usually helpful in enabling a client to understand the basis for suggestions.

What if the client moves on during a JOURNEY making project – what happens?

Firstly determine how well established the JOURNEY making process is within the organization. If there are many champions then transfer will be relatively painless. However, the choice of client from among the many champions needs to take account of power as well as interest. Building trust between the new client and facilitator can often be forgotten when the facilitator already feels comfortable with the key actors and the organization. Facilitators have often, by this stage, presumed that they have developed their own power base, and it is likely that their power is partly dependent on their relationship with the previous client and not the new client. Be careful.

The client wants to be a sponsor and partner as well!?

While some clients are able to act as sponsors (particularly those in very senior positions), having them presume the partner role may cause problems. It is in the client's interest to have a sponsor who will protect the process during the downs as well as ups in the journey. Having a senior manager acting as a partner, and so assisting with the facilitation of the workshop, will cause participants to be more careful with their contributions. Remember that an important role for a partner is for them to be the 'eyes and ears' of the facilitator at the level of key actors who are not a part of the management team and at the level of other participants. It is unlikely that the client can gain reliable data from these people. When there are two facilitators it is often useful to set up one facilitator as the 'everyday' link with client and key actors, and the other as the link to other participants.

REFERENCES

Ackermann, F. (1990) 'The Role of Computers in Group Decision Support', in C. Eden and J. Radford (eds), *Tackling Strategic Problems: the role of group decision support.* London: Sage. pp. 132–141.

Ackermann, F. (1991) *Consideration of a specific group decision support methodology in the light of the group decision support systems literature.* University of Strathclyde: PhD Thesis.

Ackermann, F. (1992) 'Strategic Direction Through Burning Issues – using SODA as a strategic decision support system', *OR Insight,* 5: 24–28.

Ackermann, F. (1996) 'Participants' Perceptions on the Role of Facilitators using Group Decision Support Systems', *Group Decision and Negotiation,* 5: 93–112.

Ackermann, F. (1996) 'Working with Groups using Groupware: Electronic Problem Structuring and Project Management support for face to face and dispersed organisational groups', in B. Glasson, D. Vogel, P. Bots, and J. Nunamaker (eds), *The International Office of the Future: Design Options and Solution Strategies.* London: Chapman and Hall. pp. 13–27.

Ackermann, F., Cropper, S. and Eden, C. (1990) 'Cognitive Mapping – A User's Guide'. Working Paper, Department of Management Science, University of Strathclyde, 90/02.

Ackermann, F., Cropper, S. and Eden, C. (1992) 'Getting Started with Cognitive Mapping', in *7th Young OR Conference Tutorial Papers.* Birmingham: O.R. Society.

Ackermann, F., Cropper, S. and Eden, C. (1992) 'Moving between Groups and Individuals using a DSS', *Journal of Decision Sciences,* 1: 17–34.

Ackermann, F., Cropper, S. and Eden, C. (1993) 'The Role of Decision Support in Individual Performance Review', in P. W. G. Bots, H. G. Sol, and R. Traunmuller (eds), *Decision Support in Public Administration.* Amsterdam: Elsevier Science Publishers BV. pp. 43–55.

Ackermann, F. and Eden, C. (1994) 'Issues in Computer and Non-Computer Supported GDSSs', *International Journal of Decision Support Systems,* 12: 381–390.

Ackermann, F. and Eden, C. (1998) 'Contrasting GDSSs and GSSs in the context of Strategic Change – implications for facilitation', *Journal of Decision Systems,* 6: 221–250.

Ackermann, F., Eden, C. and Williams, T. (1997) 'Modeling for Litigation: Mixing Qualitative and Quantitative Approaches', *Interfaces,* 27: 48–65.

Ackoff, R. (1974) *Redesigning the Future: a systems approach to societal problems.* New York: Wiley.

Ackoff, R. and Emery, F. (1972) *On Purposeful Systems.* London: Tavistock.

Adams, J.L. (1979) *Conceptual Blockbusting.* New York: Norton.

Agor, W.H. (ed.) (1989) *Intuition in Organizations.* Newbury Park, CA: Sage.

Allison, G.T. (1971) *Essence of Decision: explaining the Cuban missile crisis.* Boston: Little Brown.

Andersen, D.F. and Richardson, G.P. (1997) 'Scripts for Group Model Building', *System Dynamics Review,* 13: 107–130.

Andrews, K.R. (1980) *The Concept of Corporate Strategy.* New York: McGraw-Hill.

Ansoff, I. (1965) *Corporate Strategy.* New York: McGraw-Hill.

Ansoff, I. (1991) 'Critique of Henry Mintzbert's "The design school: reconsidering the basic premises of strategic management"', *Strategic Management Journal,* 1: 449–461.

Argyle, M. (1984) 'Social Behaviour', in C. Cooper and P. Makin (eds), *Psychology for Managers*. London: British Psychological Society. pp. 161–181.

Argyle, M. (1988) *Bodily Communication (2nd Edition)*. London: Methuen.

Argyris, C. (1982) *Reasoning, Learning, and Action*. San Francisco: Jossey-Bass.

Argyris, C. and Schon, D.A. (1974) *Theories in Practice*. San Francisco: Jossey-Bass.

Argyris, C. and Schon, D. (1978) *Organizational Learning: a theory of action perspective*. Reading, MA: Addison-Wesley.

Axelrod, R. (1976) *Structure of Decision*. Princeton, NJ: Princeton University Press.

Backoff, R.W. and Nutt, P.C. (1988) 'A Process for Strategic Management with Specific Application for the Nonprofit Organization', in J.M. Bryson and R.C. Einsweiler (eds), *Strategic Planning: threats and opportunities for planners*. Chicago: Planners Press. pp. 120–144.

Bana e Costa, C.A., Enslinn, L., Correa, E.C. and Vansnick, J.-C. (1997) 'Decision Support Systems in Action: integration application in a multicriteria decision aid process', Presented at the EURO Conference, Barcelona.

Barnard, C. (1938) *The Functions of the Executive*. Cambridge, MA: Harvard University Press.

Barney, J.B. (1991) 'Firm Resources and Sustained Competitive Advantage', *Journal of Management*, 17: 99–120.

Barr, P.S., Stimpert, J.L. and Huff, A.S. (1992) 'Cognitive Change, Strategic Action, and Organizational Renewal', *Strategic Management Journal*, 13: 15–36.

Bartunek, J. (1984) 'Changing Interpretive Schemes and Organizational Restructuring: the example of a religious order', *Administrative Science Quarterly*, 29: 355–372.

Bartunek, J. and Moch, M. (1987) 'First-Order, Second-Order, and Third-Order Change and Organizational Development Interventions: a cognitive approach', *Journal of Applied Behavioral Science*, 23: 483–500.

Beer, M., Eienstat, R. and Spector, B. (1990) 'Why Change Programs Don't Produce Change', *Harvard Business Review*, 68: 158–166.

Beer, S. (1966) *Decision and Control*. London: Wiley.

Belbin, R.M. (1981) *Management Teams: why they succeed or fail*. Oxford: Heinemann.

Belton, V., Ackermann, F. and Shepherd, I. (1997) 'Integrated Support from Problem Structuring through to Alternative Evaluation Using COPE and V.I.S.A.', *Journal of Multi-Criteria Decision Analysis*, 6: 115–130.

Bennett, P. (1995) 'Modelling Decisions in International Relations: game theory and beyond', *International Studies Review*, 39: 19–52.

Bennett, P.G. (1980) 'Hypergames: developing a model of conflict', *Futures*, 12: 489–507.

Bennett, P.G. (1990) 'Mixing Methods: combining conflict analysis, SODA, and strategic choice', in C. Eden and J. Radford (eds), *Tackling Strategic Problems: the role of group decision support*. London: Sage. pp. 99–109.

Bennett, P.G., Dando, M.R. and Sharp, R.G. (1980) 'Using Hypergames to Model Difficult Social Issues: an approach to the case of soccer hooliganism', *Journal of the Operational Research Society*, 31: 621–635.

Bennett, P.G. and Huxham, C.S. (1982) 'Hypergames and What They Do: a "Soft OR" approach', *Journal of the Operational Research Society*, 33: 41–50.

Bennett, P.G., Huxham, C.S. and Dando, M.R. (1981) 'Shipping in Crisis: a trial run for live application of the hypergame approach', *Omega*, 9: 579–594.

Bennett, P.G., Tait, A. and Macdonath, K. (1994) 'INTERACT: developing software for interactive decisions', *Group Decision and Negotiation*, 3: 351–372.

Bennis, W. (1968) 'Future of the Social Sciences', *Antioch Review*, 28: 227.

Berger, P.L. and Luckmann, T. (1966) *The Social Construction of Reality*. New York: Doubleday.

Boal, K.B. and Bryson, J.M. (1987) 'Charismatic Leadership: a phenomenological and structural approach', in J.G. Hunt, B.R. Balinga, H.P. Dachler and C.A. Schriescheim (eds), *Emerging Leadership Vistas*. New York: Pergamon. pp. 11–28.

Bogner, W.C. and Thomas, H. (1994) 'Core Competence and Competitor Advantage: a model and illustrative evidence from the pharmaceutical industry', in G. Hamel and A. Heene (eds), *Competence Based Competition*. Chichester: Wiley. pp. 111–143.

Boland, R.J., Greenberg, R.H., Park, S.H. and Han, I. (1990) 'Mapping the Process of Problem Reformulation: implications for understanding strategic thought', in A.S. Huff (ed.), *Mapping Strategic Thought*. New York: Wiley. pp. 195–226.

Bossel, H. (ed.) (1977) *Concepts and Tools of Computer Assisted Policy Analysis*. Basel: Birkhauser.

Bostrom, R.P., Anson, R. and Clawson, V.K. (1993) 'Group Facilitation and Group Support Systems', in L.M. Jessup and J.S. Valacich (eds), *Group Support Systems: New Perspectives*. New York: Macmillan. pp. 146–168.

Bouchard, T.J., Drauden, G. and Barsaloux, J. (1974) 'Brainstorming Procedure, Group Size and Sex as Determinants of the Problem Solving Effectiveness of Groups and Individuals', *Journal of Applied Psychology*, 59: 135–138.

Bouchard, T.J. and Hare, M. (1970) 'Size, Performance and Potential in Brainstorming Groups', *Journal of Applied Psychology*, 54: 51–55.

Bougon, M., Weick, K. and Binkhorst, D. (1977) 'Cognition in Organizations: analysis of the Utrecht Jazz Orchestra', *Administrative Science Quarterly*, 22: 609–632.

Bowman, C. and Asch, D. (1987) *Strategic Management*. Basingstoke: Macmillan.

Braumhart, R. (1968) *An Honest Profit: what businessmen say about ethics in business*. New York: Holt, Rinehart, and Winston.

Bridges, W. (1980) *Transitions: making sense of life's changes*. Reading, MA: Addison-Wesley.

Brightman, J., Eden, C., Langford, D. and van der Heijden, K. (1997) *CAFE: Construction Alternative Futures Explorer*. Glasgow, Scotland: University of Strathclyde.

Brindle, D. (1991) 'Meetings cost the NHS too much', *Guardian, 15 April*, report on study by Leicester Polytechnic.

Brown, S. (1992) 'Cognitive Mapping and Repertory Grids for Qualitative Survey Research: some comparative observations', *Journal of Management Studies*, 29: 287–308.

Bryson, J.M. (1988) 'Strategic Planning and the Nature of Big Wins and Small Wins', *Public Money and Management*, Autumn: 11–15.

Bryson, J.M. (1995) *Strategic Planning for Public and Nonprofit Organizations*. San Francisco: Jossey-Bass.

Bryson, J.M., Ackermann, F., Eden, C. and Finn, C. (1995) 'Using the Oval Mapping Process to Identify Strategic issues and Formulate Effective Strategies', in J. Bryson (ed.), *Strategic Planning for Public and Nonprofit Organizations*. San Francisco: Jossey-Bass. pp. 257–275.

Bryson, J.M., Ackermann, F., Eden, C. and Finn, C. (1996) 'Critical Incidents and Emergent Issues in the Management of Large Scale Change Effects', in D. Kettl and H. Brinton (eds), *The State of Public Management*. Baltimore, MD: Johns Hopkins Press. pp. 267–285.

Burgelman, R.A. (1983) 'A Model of the Interaction of Strategic Behaviour, Corporate Context, and the Concept of Strategy', *Academy of Management Review*, 8: 61–70.

Burke, K. (1969) *A Grammar of Motives*. Berkeley: University of California Press.

Calori, R., Lubatkin, M. and Very, P. (1998) 'The Development of National Collective Knowledge in Management', in C. Eden and J.-C. Spender (eds), *Managerial and Organizational Cognition*. London: Sage. pp. 147–167.

Cameron, K., Sutton, R. and Whetten, D. (1988) *Readings in Organizational Decline*. Cambridge, MA: Ballinger.

Campbell, A. (1989, 11 January) 'Mission accomplished or ignored?', *Financial Times*.

Campbell, A. and Tawadey, K. (1990) *Mission and Business Philosophy*. Oxford: Heinemann.

Campbell, J., Dunnette, M., Lawler, E. and Weick, K. (1970) *Managerial Behaviour, Performance, and Effectiveness*. New York: McGraw-Hill.

Campbell, R. (1996) *Making Strategy Work in Police Organisations*. Glasgow: PhD Thesis, University of Strathclyde.

Campion, M.A., Campion, J.E. and Hudson, J.P. (1994) 'Structured Interviewing – a note on incremental validity and alternative question types', *Journal of Applied Psychology*, 79: 998–1002.

Cannel, C.F. and Kahn, R.K. (1968) 'Interviewing', in G. Lindzey and E. Aronson (eds), *Handbook of Social Psychology*. Reading, MA: Addison-Wesley. p. 229.

Chakravarthy, B. (1982) 'Adaptation: a promising metaphor for strategic management', *Academy of Management Review*, 7: 33–44.

Checkland, P. (1981) *Systems Thinking, Systems Practice*. London: Wiley.

Churchill, J. (1990) 'Complexity and Strategic Decision Making', in C. Eden and J. Radford (eds), *Tackling Strategic Problems: the role of group decision support*. London: Sage. pp. 11–17.

Clarkson, M.B.E. (1991) 'Defining, Evaluating, and Managing Corporate Social Performance: a stakeholder management model', in J.E. Post (ed.), *Research in Corporate Social Performance and Policy*. Greenwich, CT: JAI Press. pp. 331–358.

Clawson, V. (1992) *The Role of the Facilitator in Computer-Assisted Environments: a critical incidents study*. Walden University: Unpublished Ph.D. dissertation.

Collins, B. and Guetzkow, H. (1964) *A Social Psychology of Processes for Decision Making*. New York: Wiley.

Connolly, T., Jessup, L.M. and Valacich, J.S. (1990) 'Effects of Anonymity and Evaluative Tone on Idea Generation in Computer-mediated Groups', *Management Science*, 36: 689–703.

Crockett, W.H. (1965) 'Cognitive complexity and impression formation', in B.A. Maher (ed.), *Progress in Experimental Personality Research, Vol 2*. New York: Academic Press. p. 47.

Cropper, S. (1990) 'The Complexity of Decision Support Practice', in C. Eden and J. Radford (eds), *Tackling Strategic Problems: the role of group decision support*. London: Sage. pp. 29–39.

Cropper, S., Eden, C. and Ackermann, F. (1990) 'Keeping Sense of Accounts Using Computer-based Cognitive Maps', *Social Science Computer Review*, 8: 345–366.

Dalkey, N. and Helmer, O. (1963) 'An Experimental Application of the Delphi Method to the Use of Experts', *Management Science*, 9: 458–467.

Davenport, T.H. (1993) *Process Innovation: reengineering work through information technology*. Boston, MA: Harvard Business School Press.

Deal, T. and Kennedy, A. (1982) *Corporate Cultures: the rites and rituals of corporate life*. Reading, MA: Addison-Wesley.

Dearborn, D.C. and Simon, H.A. (1958) 'Selective Perception: a note on the department identifications of executives', *Sociometry*, 21: 140–144.

de Bono, E. (1982) *de Bono's Thinking Course*. London: BBC.

Degeling, P. and Colebatch, H. (1994) 'Structure and Action as Constructs in the Practice of Public Administration', in M. Hill (ed.), *A Policy Reader*. London: Harvester.

de Geus, A. (1988) 'Planning as Learning', *Harvard Business Review*, March–April: 70–74.

Delbecq, A.L., Van de Ven, A.H. and Gustafson, D.H. (1975) *Group Techniques for Program Planning*. Glenview, IL: Scott Foresman.

DeSanctis, G. (1993) 'Shifting Foundations in Group Support System Research', in L.M. Jessup and J.S. Valacich (eds), *Group Support Systems: new perspectives*. New York: Macmillan. pp. 97–111.

DeSanctis, G. and Gallupe, R.B. (1987) 'A Foundation for Group Decision Support System Design', *Management Science*, 33: 589–609.

Donnellon, A. (1986) 'Language and Communication in Organizations: bridging cognition and behaviour', in H. Sims and D. Gioia (eds), *The Thinking Organization*. San Francisco: Jossey-Bass. pp. 136–164.

Downs, A. (1967) *Inside Bureaucracy*. Boston: Little, Brown.

Dutton, J. and Ashford, S. (1993) 'Selling Issues to Top Management', *Academy of Management Review*, 18: 397–428.

Eden, C. (1977) 'Modelling the Influence of Decision Makers on the Future', *Futures*, 9: 272–284.

Eden, C. (1978) 'Computer Assisted Policy Analysis: contributions from Germany', *Policy Sciences*, 9: 345–360.

Eden, C. (1983) 'Review of "Creative Thinking and Brainstorming"', *Journal of Management Studies*, 20: 277–279.

Eden, C. (1985) 'Perish the Thought', *Journal of the Operational Research Society*, 36: 809–819.

Eden, C. (1986) 'Competitive Awareness Through Role Play Gaming', Working Paper, Centre for the Study of Organizational Change and Development, University of Bath.

Eden, C. (1987) 'Problem Solving or Problem Finishing?', in M.C. Keys and P. Johnson (eds), *New Directions in Management Science*. Aldershot, Hants: Gower. pp. 97–108.

Eden, C. (1988) 'Cognitive Mapping: a review', *European Journal of Operational Research*, 36: 1–13.

Eden, C. (1989) 'Strategic Options Development and Analysis – SODA', in J. Rosenhead (ed.), *Rational Analysis in a Problematic World*. London: Wiley. pp. 21–42.

Eden, C. (1990a) 'Strategic Thinking with Computers', *International Journal of Strategic Management*, 23: 35–43.

Eden, C. (1990b) 'Managing the Environment as a Means to Managing Complexity', in C. Eden and J. Radford (eds), *Tackling Strategic Problems: the role of group decision support*. London: Sage. pp. 154–161.

Eden, C. (1990c) 'The Unfolding Nature of Group Decision Support', in C. Eden and J. Radford (eds), *Tackling Strategic Problems: the role of group decision support*. London: Sage. pp. 48–52.

Eden, C. (1992a) 'On the Nature of Cognitive Maps', *Journal of Management Studies*, 29: 261–265.

Eden, C. (1992b) 'Strategic Management as a Social Process', *Journal of Management Studies*, 29: 799–811.

Eden, C. (1993) 'From the Playpen to the Bombsite: the changing nature of management science', *Omega*, 21: 139–154.

Eden, C. (1994) 'Cognitive Mapping and Problem Structuring for System Dynamics Model Building', *System Dynamics Review*, 10: 257–276.

Eden, C. (1995) 'On the Evaluation of "Wide-Band" GDSS's', *European Journal of Operational Research*, 81: 302–311.

Eden, C. (1996) 'The Stakeholder/Collaborator Strategic Workshop – the Northern Ireland case', in C. Huxham (ed.), *Creating Collaborative Advantage*. London: Sage. pp. 44–56.

Eden, C. and Ackermann, F. (1992) 'Strategic Development and Implementation – the role of a Group Decision Support System', in S. Kinney, R. Bostrom and R. Watson (eds), *Computer Augmented Teamwork: a guided tour*. New York: Van Nostrand and Reinhold. pp. 325–343.

Eden, C. and Ackermann, F. (1993) 'Evaluating Strategy: its role within the context of strategic control', *Journal of the Operational Research Society*, 44: 853–865.

Eden, C. and Ackermann, F. (1998) 'Analysing and Comparing Idiographic Causal Maps', in C. Eden and J.-C. Spender (eds), *Managerial and Organizational Cognition*. London: Sage. pp. 192–209.

Eden, C., Ackermann, F. and Cropper, S. (1992) 'The Analysis of Cause Maps', *Journal of Management Studies*, 29: 309–324.

Eden, C., Bennett, P.G., Clark, P. and Stringer, J. (1993) 'Problem Formulation and Negotiation in Multi-Organisational Contexts', *Journal of the Operational Research Society*, 44: 625–628.

Eden, C. and Cropper, S. (1992) 'Coherence and Balance in Strategies for the Management of Public Services: two confidence tests for strategy development, review and renewal', *Public Money and Management*, 12: 43–52.

Eden, C. and Fineman, S. (1986) 'Problem Centred Role Play: the challenge of open ended simulation', *Simulation/Games for Learning*, 16: 3–11.

Eden, C. and Harris, J. (1976) *Management Decision and Decision Analysis*. London: Macmillan.

Eden, C. and Huxham, C. (1988) 'Action Oriented Strategic Management', *Journal of the Operational Research Society*, 39: 889–899.

Eden, C. and Huxham, C. (1996) 'Action Research for the Study of Organizations', in S. Clegg, C. Hardy and W. Nord (eds), *Handbook of Organization Studies*. Beverley Hills, CA: Sage. pp. 526–542.

Eden, C., Huxham, C. and Vangen, S. (1996) 'The Dynamics of Negotiating Purpose in Multi-organizational Collaborative Groups: achieving collaborative advantage for social development', Academy of Management Conference, Cincinnati.

Eden, C. and Jones, S. (1980) 'Publish or Perish – a case study', *Journal of the Operational Research Society*, 31: 131–139.

Eden, C. and Jones, S. (1984) 'Using Repertory Grids for Problem Construction', *Journal of the Operational Research Society*, 35: 779–790.

Eden, C., Jones, S. and Sims, D. (1979) *Thinking in Organisations*. London: Macmillan.

Eden, C., Jones, S. and Sims, D. (1983) *Messing About in Problems*. Oxford: Pergamon.

Eden, C., Jones, S., Sims, D. and Smithin, T. (1981) 'The intersubjectivity of issues and issues of intersubjectivity', *Journal of Management Studies*, 18: 37–47.

Eden, C. and Sims, D. (1979) 'On the nature of problems in consulting practice', *Omega*, 7: 119–127.

Eden, C. and Sims, D. (1981) 'Computerized Vicarious Experience: the future of management induction?', *Personnel Review*, 10: 22–25.

Eden, C., Vangen, S. and Huxham, C. (1994) 'The Language of Collaboration', International Workshop on Multi-Organizational Partnerships: working together across organizational boundaries, EIASM: 19–20 September, Brussels.

Eden, C. and van der Heijden, K. (1995) 'Detecting Emergent Strategy', in H. Thomas, D. O'Neal and J. Kelly (eds), *Strategic Renaissance and Business Transformation*. Chichester: Wiley.

Eden, C., Williams, H. and Smithin, T. (1986) 'Synthetic Wisdom: the design of a mixed mode modelling system for organizational decision making', *Journal of the Operational Research Society*, 37: 233–241.

Eisenberg, E.M. (1984) 'Ambiguity as strategy in organisational communication', *Communication Monographs*, 51: 231.

Eisenhardt, K.M. (1989) 'Making fast decisions in high velocity environments', *Academy of Management Journal*, 32: 543–576.

Eisenhardt, K.M. and Zbaracki, M.J. (1992) 'Strategic decision making', *Strategic Management Journal*, 13: 17–37.

Evan, W.M. and Freeman, R.E. (1988) 'A Stakeholder Theory of the Modern Corporation: Kantian capitalism', in T. Beauchamp and N. Bowie (eds), *Ethical Theory and Business*. Englewood Cliffs, NJ: Prentice-Hall.

Finn, C. (1996) 'Utilizing Stakeholder Strategies for Positive Collaboration', in C. Huxham (ed.), *Creating Collaborative Advantage*. London: Sage. pp. 152–164.

Finn, C. (1997) *Stakeholder Analysis*. Glasgow, Scotland: PhD Thesis, University of Strathclyde.

Fisher, R. and Brown, C. (1988) *Getting Together: building a relationship that gets to yes*. Boston, MA: Houghton-Mifflin.

Fisher, R. and Ury, W. (1982) *Getting to Yes*. London: Hutchinson.

Flanagan, J. (1954) 'The Critical Incident Technique', *Psychological Bulletin*, 51: 327–358.

Floyd, S.W. and Wooldridge, B. (1992) 'Managing Strategic Consensus: the foundation of effective implementation', *Academy of Management Review*, 6: 27–39.

Folger, R. and Konovsky, M.K. (1989) 'Effects of Procedural and Distributive Justice on Reactions to Pay Decisions', *Academy of Management Journal*, 32: 115–130.

Ford, J.D. and Ford, L.W. (1995) 'The Role of Conversations in Producing Intentional Change in Organizations', *Academy of Management Review*, 20: 541–570.

Fordyce, J.K.W. and Weil, R. (1971) *Managing with People: a manager's handbook of organizational methods*. New York: Addison-Wesley.

Forrester, J. (1961) *Industrial Dynamics*. Cambridge, MA: MIT Press.

Forrester, J. (1969) *Urban Dynamics*. Cambridge, MA: MIT Press.

Fransella, F. and Bannister, D. (1977) *A Manual for Repertory Grid Technique*. London: Academic Press.

Freeman, R.E. (1984) *Strategic Management: a stakeholder approach*. Marshfield, MA: Pitman Publishing.

Friend, J. and Hickling, A. (1987) *Planning Under Pressure: the strategic choice approach*. Oxford: Pergamon.

Frost, P. (1987) 'Power, Politics, and Influence', in F. Jablin, L.L. Putnam, K. Roberts and L. Porter (eds), *Handbook of Organizational Conversation: an interdisciplinary perspective*. Newbury Park, CA: Sage. pp. 503–548.

Galer, G. and van der Heijden, K. (1992) 'The Learning Organisation: how planners create organisational learning', *Marketing Intelligence and Planning*, 10: 512.

Garrett, B. (1990) *Creating a Learning Organization: a guide to leadership, learning, and development*. Cambridge: Simon & Schuster.

Garvin, D.A. (1993) 'Building a Learning Organization', *Harvard Business Review*, July–August: 78–91.

Geertz, C. (1974) *The Interpretation of Cultures*. New York: Basic Books.

Gilmore and Camillas (1996) 'Do Your Planning Processes Meet the Reality Test?', *Long Range Planning*, 29: 869–879.

Gioia, D. and Sims, H. (1986) 'Social Cognition in Organizations', in D. Gioia and H. Sims (eds), *The Thinking Organization*. San Francisco: Jossey-Bass. pp. 1–19.

Godet, M. (1987) *Scenarios and Strategic Management*. London: Butterworth.

Goold, M. and Quinn, J.J. (1990) 'The Paradox of Strategic Controls', *Strategic Management Journal*, 11: 43–57.

Gower, J.C. and Ross, G.J.S. (1969) 'Minimum Spanning Trees and Single Linkage Cluster Analysis', *Applied Statistics*, 18: 56–64.

Gray, P. (1985) 'Group Decision Support Systems', *Decision Support Systems*, 3: 233–242.

Guth, W.D. and MacMillan, I.C. (1986) 'Strategy Implementation versus Middle Management Self Interest', *Strategic Management Journal*, 7: 313–327.

Hage, J. and Dewar, R. (1973) 'Elite Values versus Organizational Structure in Predicting Innovation', *Administrative Science Quarterly*, 18: 279–290.

Halal, W.E. (1990) 'The New Management: business and social institutions in the information age', *Business in the Contemporary World*, 2: 41–54.

Hambrick, D. and d'Aveni, R. (1988) 'Large Corporate Failures as Downward Spirals', *Administrative Science Quarterly*, 33: 1–23.

Hamel, G. (1994) 'The Concept of Core Competence', in G. Hamel and A. Heene (eds), *Competence Based Competition*. Chichester: Wiley. pp. 11–13.

Hamel, G. and Prahalad, C.K. (1993) 'Strategy as Stretch and Leverage', *Harvard Business Review*, March–April: 75–84.

Hampden-Turner, C.M. (1993) 'Dilemmas of Strategic Learning Loops', in J. Hendry, G. Johnson and J. Newton (eds), *Strategic Thinking: leadership and the management of change*. London: Wiley. pp. 327–346.

Hannan, M. and Freeman, J. (1984) 'Structural Inertia and Organizational Change', *American Sociological Review*, 49: 149–164.

Harmon, J. and Rohrbaugh, J. (1990) 'Social Judgement Analysis and Small Group Decision Making: cognitive feedback effects on individual and collective performance', *Organizational Behaviour and Human Decision Processes*, 46: 34–54.

Harvey, J. (1988) 'The Abilene Paradox: the management of agreement', *Organizational Dynamics*, Summer: 17–34.

Harvey-Jones, J. (1988) *Making It Happen*. London: Collins.

Haveman, H. (1992) 'Between a Rock and a Hard Place: organizational change and performance under conditions of fundamental transformation', *Administrative Science Quarterly*, 37: 48–75.

Hayes, R.H., Wheelwright, S.C. and Clark, K.B. (1988) *Dynamic Manufacturing: creating the learning organization*. New York: Free Press.

Healey, M.J. and Rawlinson, M.B. (1993) 'Interviewing Business Owners and Managers: a review of methods and techniques', *Geoforum*, 24: 339–355.

Helmer, O. (1981) 'Reassessment of Cross Impact Analysis', *Future*, 3.

Helmer, O. (1983) *Looking Forward: a guide to futures research*. London: Sage.

Hickling, A. (1990) '"Decision Spaces": a scenario about designing appropriate rooms for group decision management', in C. Eden and J. Radford (eds), *Tackling Strategic Problems: the role of group decision support*. London: Sage. pp. 169–177.

Hickson, D.J., Butler, R.J., Cray, D., Mallory, G.R. and Wilson, D.C. (1986) *Top Decisions: strategic decision making in organizations*. San Francisco, CA: Jossey-Bass.

Hill, G.W. (1982) 'Group versus Individual Performance: are N+1 heads better than one?', *Psychological Bulletin*, 91: 517–539.

Hoffman, L.R. (1965) 'Group Problem Solving', in L. Berkowitz (ed.), *Advances in Experimental Psychology (Vol. 2)*. New York: Academic Press. pp. 99–132.

Hofstede, G. (1980) *Cultures Consequences*. London: Sage.

Hogarth, R.M. (1987) *Judgment and Choice: the psychology of decision*. New York: Wiley.

Hopwood, A. and Miller, P. (1996) *Accounting as Social and Institutional Practice*. Cambridge: Cambridge University Press.

Horovitz, J.H. (1979) 'Strategic Control: a new task for top management', *International Journal of Strategic Management*, 12: 2–7.

Huber, G. (1982) 'Group Decision Support Systems as Aid in the Use of Structured Group Management Techniques', in G. Dickson (ed.), *Transactions in the Second International Conference on Decision Support Systems*. San Francisco, CA: 96–108.

Huber, G. (1984) 'Issues in the Design of Group Decision Support Systems', *Management Information Systems Quarterly*, 8: 195–204.

Huff, A. (ed.) (1990) *Mapping Strategic Thought*. New York: Wiley.

Huff, A.S. (1982) 'Industry Influence on Strategy Formulation', *Strategic Management Journal*, 3: 119–131.

Huxham, C. (ed.) (1996) *Creating Collaborative Advantage*. London: Sage.

Ichheiser, G. (1949) 'Misunderstandings in Human Relations', *American Journal of Sociology*, 55: 1–10.

Ikle, F.C. (1967) 'Can Social Predictions be Evaluated', *Daedalus*, Summer: 747.

Isenberg, D.J. (1987) 'The Tactics of Strategic Opportunism', *Harvard Business Review*, 65: 92–97.

Janis, I.L. (1972) *Victims of Group Think*. Boston: Houghton-Mifflin.

Janis, I.L. (1989) *Crucial Decisions*. New York: Free Press.

Janis, I.L. and Mann, L. (1977) *Decision Making: a psychological analysis of conflict, choice and commitment*. New York: Free Press.

Jessup, L.M. and Tansik, D.A. (1991) 'Decision Making in an Automated Environment: the effects of anonymity and proximity with a group decision support system', *Decision Science*, 22: 266–279.

Johnson, G. and Scholes, K. (1993) *Exploring Corporate Strategy*. Hemel Hempstead: Prentice-Hall.

Karau, S.J. and Williams, K.D. (1993) 'Social Loafing: a meta-analytic review and theoretical integration', *Journal of Personality and Social Psychology*, 65: 681–706.

Kelly, G.A. (1955) *The Psychology of Personal Constructs*. New York: Norton.

Kepner, C.H. and Tregoe, B.B. (1965) *The Rational Manager: a systematic approach to problem solving and decision making*. New York: McGraw-Hill.

Kerr, S. (1995) 'On the Folly of Rewarding A, while Hoping for B', *Academy of Management Executive*, 9: 7–16.

Khalifa, A. (1996) *Conflict Based Models for Scenario Analysis*. Glasgow: University of Strathclyde, DBA Thesis.

Kim, W.C. and Mauborgne, R.A. (1991) 'Implementing Global Strategies: the role of procedural justice', *Strategic Management Journal*, 12: 125–143.

Kim, W.C. and Mauborgne, R.A. (1993) 'Procedural Justice, Attitudes, and Subsidiary Top Management Compliance with Multinationals' Corporate Strategic Decisions', *Academy of Management Journal*, June: 502–526.

Kim, W.C. and Mauborgne, R.A. (1995) 'A Procedural Justice Model of Strategic Decision Making', *Organization Science*, 6: 44–61.

Kolb, D.A. (1984) *Experiential Learning*. Englewood Cliffs, NJ: Prentice-Hall.

Kolb, D. and Rubin, I.M. (1991) *Organizational Behavior, An Experimental Approach*. Englewood Cliffs, NJ: Prentice-Hall.

Korsgaard, M.A., Schweiger, D.M. and Sapienza, H.J. (1995) 'Building Commitment, Attachment, and Trust in Strategic Decision Making Teams: the role of procedural justice', *Academy of Management Journal*, 38: 60–84.

Laing, R.D. (1971) *Knots*. London: Tavistock.

Leung, K. and Li, W. (1990) 'Psychological Mechanisms of Process-control Effects', *Journal of Applied Psychology*, 75: 613–620.

Lewin, K. (1951) *Field Theory in Social Science*. New York: Harper and Row.

Lind, E.A., Kanfer, R. and Earley, P.C. (1990) 'Voice, control, and procedural justice: instrumental and noninstrumental concerns in fairness judgments', *Journal of Personality and Social Psychology*, 59: 952–959.

Lindblom, C.E. (1959) 'The Science of Muddling Through', *Public Administration Review*, 19: 79–88.

Lindblom, C.E. (1980) *The Policy Making Process (2nd Edition)*. Englewood Cliffs, NJ: Prentice-Hall.

Lofland, J. (1976) *Doing Social Life*. New York: Wiley.

Lorange, P. and Murphy, D.C. (1983) 'Strategic and Human Resources: concepts and practice', *Human Resource Management*, XXII: 111–133.

Lorange, P., Scott Morton, M.F. and Goshal, S. (1986) *Strategic Control*. St Paul, MN: West Publishing.

Mangham, I.L. (1978) *Interactions and Interventions in Organizations*. London: Wiley.

Mangham, I.L. and Overington, M.A. (1987) *Organizations as Theatre: a social psychology of dramatic appearances*. New York: Wiley.

March, J.G. (1991) 'Exploration and Exploitation in Organizational Learning', *Organization Science*, 2: 71–87.

Margerison, C.J. (1988) *Managerial Consulting Skills: a practical guide*. Aldershot, Hants: Gower.

McFarlin, D.B. and Sweeney, P.D. (1992) 'Distributive and Procedural Justice as Predictors of Satisfaction with Personal and Organizational Outcomes', *Academy of Management Journal*, 35: 626–637.

McGill, M.E., Slocum, J.W. and Lei, D. (1992) 'Management Practices in Learning Organizations', *Organizational Dynamics*, 21: 5–17.

McGoff, C. and Ambrose, L. (1991) 'Empirical Information from the Field: a practitioner's view of using GDSS in business', in *Proceedings of the 24th Annual Hawaii International Conference on Systems Sciences*. Los Alamitos, CA: Society Press. pp. 805–811.

McGrath, J. (1984) *Groups: Interaction and Performance*. Englewood Cliffs, NJ: Prentice-Hall.

Meadows, D. and Meadows, D. (1972) *The Limits to Growth*. London: Earth Island.

Michael, D. (1973) *On Learning to Plan – and Planning to Learn*. San Francisco: Jossey-Bass.

Miles, R.R. and Snow, C.C. (1978) *Organizational Strategy, Structure and Process*. Englewood Cliffs, NJ: Prentice-Hall.

Miller, C.C. and Cardinal, L.B. (1994) 'Strategic Planning and Firm Performance: a synthesis of more than two decades of research', *Academy of Management Journal*, 37: 1649–1665.

Mintzberg, H. (1987) 'Crafting Strategy', *Harvard Business Review*, July–August: 66–75.

Mintzberg, H. (1990a) 'The Design School: reconsidering the basic premises of strategic management', *Strategic Management Journal*, 11: 171–195.

Mintzberg, H. (1990b) 'Strategy Formation: schools of thought', in J. Frederickson (ed.), *Perspectives on Strategic Management*. New York: Harper & Row. pp. 105–235.

Mintzberg, H. (1994) 'The Fall and Rise of Strategic Planning', *Harvard Business Review*, Jan–Feb: 107–114.

Mintzberg, H., Raisinghani, H. and Theoret, A. (1976) 'The Structure of "Unstructured" Decision Processes', *Administrative Science Quarterly*, 21: 246–275.

Mintzberg, H. and Waters, J.A. (1985) 'Of Strategies, Deliberate and Emergent', *Strategic Management Journal*, 6: 257–272.

Monteverde, K. and Teece, D. (1982) 'Supplier Switching Costs and Vertical Integration in the Automobile Industry', *Bell Journal of Economics*, 20: 207–213.

Nisbett, R. and Wilson, T. (1977) 'Telling More Than We Can Know: verbal reports on mental processes', *Psychological Review*, 84: 231–259.

Normann, R. (1985) 'Developing Capabilities for Organizational Learning', in J. Pennings and Associates (eds), *Organizational Strategy and Change*. San Francisco: Jossey-Bass.

Norris, F.M., Jones, H.G. and Norris, H. (1970) 'Articulation of the Conceptual Structure in Obsessional Neurosis', *British Journal of Social and Clinical Psychology*, 9: 264–274.

Nozicka, G., Bonham, G.M. and Shapiro, M.J. (1976) 'Simulation Techniques', in R. Axelrod (ed.), *Structure of Decision*. Princeton, NJ: Princeton University Press. pp. 349–359.

Nunamaker, J.F., Dennis, A.R., Valacich, J.S. and Vogel, D.R. (1991) 'Electronic Meeting Systems to Support Group Work', *Communications of the ACM*, 34: 40–61.

Nutt, P.C. (1984) 'Types of Organizational Decision Processes', *Administrative Science Quarterly*, 29: 414–450.

Nutt, P.C. and Backoff, R. (1992) *Strategic Management of Public and Third Sector Organizations*. San Francisco: Jossey-Bass.

Orts, E.W. (1992) 'Beyond Shareholders: interpreting corporate constituency statutes', *The George Washington Law Review*, 61: 14–15.

Ouchi, W. (1981) *Theory Z*. Reading, MA: Addison-Wesley.

Ozbekhan, H. (1974) 'Thoughts on the Emerging Methodology of Planning', *Fields within Fields*, 10.

Pedler, M., Boydell, T. and Burgoyne, J. (1989) 'Towards a Learning Company', *Management Education and Development*, 20: 1–8.

Perrow, C. (1986) *Complex Organizations (3rd Edition)*. New York: Random House.

Peters, T.J. and Waterman, R.H. (1982) *In Search of Excellence: lessons from America's best-run companies*. New York: HarperCollins.

Pettigrew, A.M. (1977) 'Strategy Formulation as a Political Process', *International Studies in Management and Organization*, 7: 78–87.

Pettigrew, A.M. (1985) *The Awakening Giant: Continuity and Change in ICI*. Oxford: Basil Blackwell.

Pettigrew, A., Ferlie, E. and Mckee, L. (1992) *Shaping Strategic Change: making change in large organizations*. London: Sage.

Pettigrew, A.M. and Whipp, R. (1992) *Managing Change for Competitive Success*. Oxford: Blackwell.

Phillips, L. and Phillips, M.C. (1993) 'Facilitated Work Groups: theory and practice', *Journal of the Operational Research Society*, 44: 533–549.

Phillips, L.D. (1984) 'A Theory of Requisite Decision Models', *Acta Psychologica*, 56: 29–48.

Piaget, J. (1971) *Structuralism*. London: Routledge.

Piaget, J. (1972) 'Intellectual Evolution from Adolescence to Adulthood', *Human Development*, 15: 1–12.

Porter, M. (1985) *Competitive Advantage*. New York: Free Press.

Porter, M.E. (1980) *Competitive Strategy: techniques for analysing industries and competitors*. New York: Free Press.

Prahalad, C.K. and Bettis, R. (1986) 'The Dominant Logic: a new linkage between diversity and performance', *Strategic Management Journal*, 7: 485–501.

Prahalad, C.K. and Hamel, G. (1990) 'The Core Competences of the Corporation', *Harvard Business Review*, May–June: 79–91.

Quinn, J.B. (1980) *Strategies for Change: logical incrementalism*. Homewood, IL: Irwin.

Radford, K.J. (1984) 'Stimulating Involvement in Complex Decision Situations', *Omega*, 12: 125–130.

Raimond, P. and Eden, C. (1990) 'Making Strategy Work', *International Journal of Strategic Management*, 23: 97–105.

Rawlinson, G. (1981) *Creating Thinking and Brainstorming*. Farnborough, Hants: Gower.

Richardson, G. (1991) *Feedback Thought in Social Science and Systems Theory*. Philadelphia: University of Pennsylvania Press.

Rosenhead, J. (1980) 'Planning Under Uncertainty: II. A Methodology for Robustness Analysis', *Journal of the Operational Research Society*, 31: 331–342.

Rosenhead, J. (1989) 'Diversity Unity: the principles and prospects for problem structuring methods', in J. Rosenhead (ed.), *Rational Analysis for a Problematic World*. London: Wiley. pp. 341–358.

Sabatier, P.A. (1991) 'Toward Better Theories of the Policy Process', *Political Science and Politics*, 24: 144–156.

Salaman, G. (1979) *Work, Organisations: Resistance and Control*. London: Longman.

Schein, E.H. (1988) *Process Consultant (Vols 1 & 2)*. Reading, MA: Addison-Wesley.

Schnaars, S.P. (1986) 'How to develop business strategies from multiple scenarios', in W.D. Guth (ed.), *Handbook of Business Strategy*. Boston, MA: Warren, Gosham and Lamont.

Schnelle, E. (1979) *The Metaplan-Method: communication tools for planning and learning groups*. Hamburg: Quickborn.

Schoemaker, P.J.H. (1992) 'How to Link Strategic Vision to Core Capabilities', *Sloan Management Review*, 34: 67–81.

Schreyogg, G. and Steinmann, H. (1987) 'Strategic Control: a new perspective', *Academy of Management Review*, 12: 91–103.

Schumacher, E.F. (1973) *Small is Beautiful*. Abacus.

Schwartz, P. (1991) *The Art of the Long View*. New York: Doubleday.

Schwarz, R.M. (1994) *The Skilled Facilitator: practical wisdom for developing effective groups*. San Francisco: Jossey-Bass.

Selznick, P. (1957) *Leadership in Administration: a sociological interpretation*. Evanston, IL: Row Peterson.

Senge, P. (1992) *The Fifth Discipline*. New York: Doubleday.

Shepherd, C.R. (1964) *Small Groups: some sociological perspectives*. San Francisco: Chandler Publishing.

Silverman, D. (1970) *The Theory of Organizations*. London: Heinemann.

Simon, H.A. (1957) *Models of Man*. New York: Wiley.

Simon, H.A. (1958) *Organizations*. New York: Wiley.

Simon, H.A. (1976) 'From Substantive to Procedural Rationality', in S.J. Latsis (ed.), *Method and Appraisal in Economics*. Cambridge: Cambridge University Press.

Simons, R. (1995) *Levers of Control*. Harvard, MA: Harvard Business School Press.

Sims, D. (1987) 'Mental Simulation: an effective technique for adult learning', *International Journal of Innovative Higher Education*, 3: 33–35.

Sims, D. and Eden, C. (1984) 'Futures Research – working with management teams', *Long Range Planning*, 17: 51–59.

Smith, K. and Grimm, C. (1987) 'Environmental Variation, Strategic Change, and Firm Performance: a study of railroad deregulation', *Strategic Management Journal*, 8: 363–376.

Smithin, T. and Eden, C. (1986) 'Computer Decision Support for Senior Managers: encouraging exploitation', *International Journal of Man–Machine Studies*, 25: 139–152.

Spencer, L. (1989) *Winning Through Participation*. Dubuque, IA: Kendall/Hunt.

Spender, J.C. (1989) *Industry Recipes: an enquiry into the nature and sources of managerial judgment*. Oxford: Blackwell.

Spender, J.C. (1998) 'The Dynamics of Individual and Organizational Knowledge', in C. Eden and J.C. Spender (eds), *Managerial and Organizational Cognition: Theory, Methods and Research*. London: Sage. pp. 13–39.

Starbuck, W. and Milliken, F. (1988) 'Executive Perceptual Filters: what they notice and how they make sense', in D. Hambrick (ed.), *The Executive Effect: concepts and methods for studying top managers*. Greenwich, CT: JAI Press.

Steiner, G.A. (1979) *Strategic Planning: what every manager needs to know*. New York: Free Press.

Sterman, J.D. (1989) 'Modelling of managerial behavior: misperceptions of feedback in a dynamic decision making experiment', *Management Science*, 35: 321–339.

Strauss, A. and Schatzman, L. (1963) 'The Hospital and its Negotiated Order', in E. Friedson (ed.), *The Hospital in Modern Society*. New York: Macmillan. pp. 147–169.

Taylor, D.W., Berry, P.C. and Block, C.H. (1958) 'Does Group Participation when Using Brainstorming Facilitate or Inhibit Creative Thinking?', *Administrative Science Quarterly*, 3: 23–47.

Thibaut, J. and Walker, J. (1975) *Procedural Justice: a psychological analysis*. Hillsdale, NJ: Erlbaum.

Thomas, W.I. and Thomas, D.S. (1928) *The Child in America: behavior problems and programs*. New York: Knopf.

Tregoe, B.B. and Zimmerman, J.W. (1980) *Top Management Survey*. New York: Simon and Schuster.

Trompenaars, F. (1994) *Riding the Waves of Culture*. Chicago: Irwin.

Valacich, J., Jessup, L., Dennis, A. and Nunamaker, J. (1992) 'A Conceptual Framework of Anonymity in Group Support Systems', *Group Decision and Negotiation*, 1: 219–242.

van der Heijden, K. (1991) 'Business Appraisal Processes in Organizations Views in Context', in K. van der Heijden and C. Eden (eds), *General and Strategic Management – strategic interventions issues reader*. Glasgow: SGBS, University of Strathclyde. pp. 265–271.

van der Heijden, K. (1996) *Scenarios: the art of strategic conversation*. Chichester: Wiley.

Vickers, G. (1983) *The Art of Judgement*. London: Harper and Row.

von Krogh, G., Roos, J. and Slocum, K. (1994) 'An Essay on Corporate Epistemology', *Strategic Management Journal*, 15: 53–71.

von Oech, R. (1982) *A Whack on the Side of the Head*. Menlo Park, CA: Creative Think.

Vygotsky, L.S. (1962 (first published 1934)) *Thought and Language*. Cambridge, MA: MIT Press.

Vygotsky, L.S. (1981) 'The Genesis of Higher Mental Functions', in J.V. Wertsch (ed.), *The Concept of Activity in Soviet Psychology*. Armonk, NY: Sharpe. pp. 144–188.

Wack, P. (1985) 'Scenarios, Uncharted Waters Ahead', *Harvard Business Review*, September–October: 73–89.

Wack, P. (1987) 'Scenarios, Shooting the Rapids', *Harvard Business Review*, July–August: 139–150.

Waller, M.J., Huber, G.P. and Glick, W.H. (1995) 'Functional Background as a Determinant of Executives' Selective Perception', *Academy of Management Journal*, 38: 943–974.

Walsh, J.P. (1988) 'Selectivity and Selective Perception: an investigation of managers' belief structures and information processing', *Academy of Management Journal*, 31: 873–896.

Walsh, J.P., Henderson, C.M. and Deighton, J. (1988) 'Negotiated Belief Structures and Decision Performance: an empirical investigation', *Organization Behavior and Human Decision Processes*, 42: 194–216.

Ward, C. (1990) *The Child in the City*. London: Bedford Square Press.

Ward, M.J. (1992) *Strategic Options Development and Analysis: as experienced in a National Health Service Unit*. Aston, Birmingham: MSc Dissertation, Aston University.

Weick, K. (1976) 'Educational Organizations as Loosely Coupled Systems', *Administrative Science Quarterly*, 21: 1–19.

Weick, K.E. (1979) *The Social Psychology of Organizing*. Reading, MA: Addison-Wesley.

Weick, K.E. (1983) 'Management Thought in the Context of Action', in S. Srivastava (ed.), *The Executive Mind*. San Francisco: Jossey-Bass. pp. 221–242.

Weick, K.E. (1985) 'The Significance of Corporate Culture', in P. Frost, L.F. Moore, M.R. Louis, C.C. Lundberg and J. Martin (eds), *Organizational Culture*. Beverley Hills: Sage. pp. 381–389.

Weick, K.E. (1995) *Sensemaking in Organizations*. Thousand Oaks, CA: Sage.

Wernerfelt, B. (1989) 'From Critical Resources to Corporate Strategy', *Journal of General Management*, 14: 4–12.

Whittington, R. (1993) *What is Strategy and Does it Matter?* London: Routledge.

Whyte, W.F. (1957) 'On Asking Indirect Questions', *Human Organizations*, 15: 21–23.

Williamson, O.E. (1985) *The Economic Institutions of Capitalism*. New York: Free Press.

Winograd, T. and Flores, F. (1986) *Understanding Computers and Cognition*. Norwood, NJ: Ablex.

Wooldridge, S.W. and Floyd, B. (1990) 'The Strategy Process, Middle Management Involvement, and Organizational Performance', *Strategic Management Journal*, 11: 231–241.

Yeates, D.F. (1996) *Strategy Development Programme – Govan Initiative Ltd.* Glasgow: MBA Project Report, Strathclyde Graduate Business School.

Zajac, E. and Shortell, S. (1989) 'Changing Generic Strategies: likelihood, direction, and performance implications', *Strategic Management Journal*, 10: 413–430.

NAME INDEX

Ackermann, F., 43, 61, 90, 97, 165, 302, 304, 321, 323, 337, 366, 372, 377, 383, 387, 390, 409, 415, 435, 438, 459, 464
Ackoff, R., 66, 91, 118, 136, 155, 428
Adams, J. L., 70
Agor, W. H., 67
Allison, G. T., 25, 27
Ambrose, L., 371
Anderson, D. F., 336, 380
Andrews, K. R., 25, 32
Ansoff, I., 13, 26, 32, 57
Argyle, M., 290
Argyris, C., 25, 31, 89, 298
Asch, D., 453
Ashford, S., 64
Axelrod, R., 89

Backoff, R. W., 3, 100, 130
Baird, E., 87
Bana e Costa, C. A., 335, 438
Bannister, D., 94
Barnard, C., 41
Barney, J. B., 103
Barr, P. S., 26
Bartunek, J., 26, 101
Beer, S., 155, 159
Belton, V., 335, 432
Bennett, P. G., 125, 148
Bennis, W., 137
Berger, P. L., 25, 399
Bettis, R., 34
Boal, K. B., 169
Bogner, W. C., 102
Boland, R. J., 169
Bossel, H., 148, 149
Bostrom, R. P., 302, 323, 383, 387
Bouchard, T. J., 70
Bougon, M., 34
Bowman, C., 453
Braumhart, R., 114
Bridges, W., 159
Brightman, J., 145, 155, 361
Brindle, D., 58
Brown, C., 49
Brown, S., 285
Browning, G., 59

Bryson, J. M., 17, 21, 51, 55, 65, 91, 100, 117, 169, 476
Burgelman, R. A., 88
Burke, K., 149

Calori, R., 4
Cameron, K., 138
Camillas, 43
Campbell, A., 57, 91, 110, 162, 430
Campion, M. A., 284
Cannel, C. F., 284
Cardinal, L. B., 12
Chakravarthy, B., 168
Checkland, P., 91, 114
Churchill, J., 69
Clarkson, M. B. E., 114
Clawson, V., 91
Colebatch, H., 32
Collins, B., 52, 386
Connolly, T., 61
Crockett, W. H., 408
Cropper, S., 101, 165, 166, 388, 441

Dahrendorf, R., 121
Dalkey, N., 139, 470
d'Aveni, R., 56, 138
Davenport, T. H., 425
De Bono, E., 70
De Geus, A., 67, 69, 74, 165
De Sanctis, G., 60, 337, 399
Deal, T., 57
Dearborn, D. C., 81
Degeling, P., 32
Delbecq, A. L., 100, 391
Dewar, R., 57
Donnellon, A., 63
Downs, A., 103
Drucker, P., 104
Dutton, J., 64

Eden, C., 21, 25, 27, 43, 47, 55, 61, 65, 68, 70, 74, 87, 89, 90, 91, 92, 94, 100, 101, 125, 129, 132, 134, 148, 149, 165, 166, 285, 301, 304, 321, 322, 336, 350, 355, 371, 375, 390, 400, 402, 409, 415, 435, 438, 441, 462, 480
Eisenberg, E. M., 162

Eisenhardt, K. M., 16, 53
Emery, F., 66, 428
Evan, W. M., 118

Finn, C., 129, 392, 478
Fisher, R., 49, 51, 56, 68, 69, 70, 300
Flanagan, J., 91
Flores, F., 64
Floyd, S. W., 53
Folger, R., 53
Ford, J. D., 159
Ford, L. W., 159
Fordyce, J. K. W., 371
Forrester, J., 30, 139, 366
Fransella, F., 94
Freeman, J., 171
Freeman, R. E., 114, 116, 117, 118, 125
Friend, J., 377
Frost, P., 47

Galer, G., 75
Gallupe, R. B., 60
Garrett, B., 75
Garvin, D. A., 75
Geertz, C., 167
Gilmore, 43
Gioia, D., 34
Godet, M., 142, 144, 150, 155
Goold, M., 171
Gower, J. C., 407
Gray, P., 386
Grimm, C., 137
Guetzkow, H., 52, 386
Guth, W. D., 53, 57

Hague, J., 57
Halal, W. E., 114
Hambrick, D., 56, 138
Hamel, G., 3, 102, 448
Hampden-Turner, C. M., 24, 33
Hannan, M., 171
Hare, M., 70
Harman, J., 60
Harris, J., 149
Harvey, J., 50
Harvey-Jones, J., 57
Haveman, H., 137
Hayes, R. H., 75
Healey, M. J., 284
Helmer, O., 139, 151, 470
Hickling, A., 377, 379
Hickson, C., 65
Hill, G. W., 58
Hoffman, L. R., 60
Hogarth, R. M., 30
Hopwood, A., 84

Horovitz, J. H., 468
Huber, G., 371, 386
Huff, A., 34, 89
Huxham, C., 89, 90, 125, 132, 133, 148, 350, 355

Ichheiser, G., 88
Ikle, F. C., 136
Isenberg, D. J., 28

Janis, I. L., 49, 50, 51, 60, 61, 175
Jessup, L. M., 61
Johnson, G., 25, 26, 27, 125
Jones, S., 90, 94

Kahn, R. K., 284
Karau, S., 393
Kelly, G. A., 31, 64, 70, 73, 89, 97, 285, 408
Kennedy, A., 57
Kepner, C. H., 91
Kerr, S., 172
Khalifa, A., 148
Kim, W. C., 54, 55
King, M. L., 15
Kolb, D. A., 31, 77
Konovsky, M. K., 53
Korsgaard, M. A., 54

Laing, R. D., 172
Laker, F., 117
Leung, K., 54
Lewin, K., 63
Li, W., 54
Lind, E. A., 54
Lindblom, C. E., 4, 21, 25, 26, 31
Lofland, J., 284
Lorange, P., 179, 445
Luckman, T., 25, 399

MacMillan, I. C., 53, 57
Mangham, I. L., 47, 49, 64
Mann, L., 49, 60, 61
March, J. G., 25, 34
Margerison, C. J., 381
Marx, K., 169
Mauborgne, R. A., 54, 55
McFarlin, D. B., 53
McGill, M. E., 75
McGoff, C., 371
McGrath, J., 300
Meacham, 76
Meadows, D., 149, 366
Michael, D., 74
Miles, R. R., 103
Miller, C. C., 12

Miller, D., 465
Miller, P., 84
Milliken, F., 81
Mintzberg, H., 4, 16, 21, 24, 26, 63, 65
Moch, M., 101
Monteverde, K., 168
Murphy, D. C., 445

Nisbett, R., 91
Normann, R., 75
Norris, F. M., 408
Nozicka, G. 405
Nunamaker, J. F., 61
Nutt, P. C., 3, 49, 65, 100, 130

Orts, E. W., 115
Ouchi, W., 57
Overington, M. A., 49, 64
Ozbekhan, H., 91

Pascale, R., 21
Pedler, M., 75
Perrow, C., 17, 25, 47
Peters, T. J., 12, 48
Pettigrew, A. H., 25, 26, 27, 64, 165, 166, 168, 177
Phillips, L., 73, 150, 302, 319, 371, 383, 386, 392
Phillips, M. C., 302, 319, 371, 383, 386, 392
Piaget, J., 31
Porter, M., 25, 26, 104, 117, 127, 139
Prahalad, C. K., 3, 34, 102, 448

Quinn, J. B., 21, 25, 31, 57, 171

Radford, K. J., 134
Raimond, P., 25, 27, 47, 55, 391
Rawlinson, G., 70
Rawlinson, M. B., 284
Richardson, G., 31, 336, 380
Rohrbaugh, J., 60
Rosenhead, J., 59, 156, 163
Ross, G. J. S., 407
Rubin, I. M., 77

Sabatier, P. A., 57
Salaman, G., 27
Schatzman, L., 48
Schein, E. H., 381
Schnaars, S. P., 156
Schoemaker, P. J. H., 102
Scholes, K., 25, 26, 27, 125
Schon, D., 25, 31, 74, 89, 298
Schreyogg, G., 179
Schwartz, P., 142, 152

Schwarz, R. M., 156, 381
Selznick, P., 25, 32, 102
Senge, P., 75
Shepherd, C. R., 60
Shortell, S., 180
Silverman, D., 25, 27
Simon, H. A., 25, 28, 45, 55, 66, 81
Simons, R., 159
Sims, D., 321, 375, 382, 462, 480
Sims, H., 34
Smith, K., 137
Smithin, T., 74
Snow, C. C., 103
Spencer, L., 304
Spender, J. C., 4, 88, 127
Starbuck, W., 81
Steiner, G. A., 55
Steinmann, H., 179
Sterman, J. D., 31
Strauss, A., 48
Sweeney, P. D., 53

Tausik, D. A., 61
Tawadey, K., 162
Taylor, D. W., 70
Teece, D., 168
Thibaut, J., 53
Thomas, D. S., 47, 299
Thomas, H., 102
Thomas, W. I., 47, 299
Tregoe, B. B., 32, 91
Trompenaars, F., 89

Ury, W., 49, 51, 56, 68, 69, 70, 300

Valacich, J., 61
Van der Heijden, K., 21, 75, 89, 92, 142, 145, 151, 154, 171, 175
Vickers, G., 49
Von Krogh, G., 34
Von Oech, R., 70
Vygotsky, L. S., 70, 97, 408

Wack, P., 139, 142
Walker, J., 53
Waller, M. J., 81
Walsh, J. P., 52, 81
Ward, C., 74
Waterman, R. H., 12, 48
Waters, J. A., 21, 26
Weick, K. E., 4, 16, 25, 26, 27, 28, 82, 88, 91
Weil, R., 371
Wernerfelt, B., 22
Whipp, R., 165, 166
Whittington, R., 24
Whyte, W. F., 284

Williams, K. D., 393
Williamson, O. E., 114
Wilson, T., 91
Winograd, T., 64
Wooldridge, B., 53

Yeates, D. F. 425, 461

Zajac, E., 180
Zbaracki, M. J., 16
Zimmerman, J. W., 32

SUBJECT INDEX

Alternative futures, scenario planning, C139, V251, V266
  choice about the number of scenarios, C152, P366
  deciding that part of the environment to be considered, C140, P363
  distinct scenarios, C149, V270, P366
  driver events, C151, C155, V267, V270, V271
  event-based focus for scenario building, V267, P361
  external experts, V267, P369
  identifying Key Scenario Events, C143, V206
    flip-flop events, C145, V206, V267, P362
  nature of uncertainty, C147, P363
  outsiders to bring an alternative view of the future, C154, V205, V267
  possible futures, within the context of the mandate, V206
  practical variables to monitor, C155, V271, P366
  'remarkable people', C14, C154, V271, P368
  scenario titles, C152, P365
  structural properties and their role in determining, C81, P361
  system dynamics simulation models, C149, V206, P366
Analysis of maps
  categories, V234, P407
  centrality, V218, P405
  clusters, V218, P407
  feedback loops, V218, P410
  hierarchical clusters, V198, P409
  merging, C72, V196, V217, P403
  orphans, V217, P402
  overview, V219, V241, V242, P415
  potent, C109, C163, V219, V270, P411
  pre-workshop analysis, V219, P414
  simplification, V222, P444
Anonymity, C61, C68, V202, V244, P298, P337
  'Oval Mapping Techniques', the networked computer system and anonymity, C154, P337

Aspirations, or goals, system, C5, C95, V214, V248, V251, V277, P289, P314, P425, P456
  core goals compared with facilitative goals, C48, P432
  draft of the aspirations or goal system, C98, V197, V248, V250, V257, P329, P423
  elicitation of an emergent goal system, C92, V229, P288
  emergent goals, V248, P426
  facilitative goals, C48, V218, V250, V257, P427, P432
  'hostage to fortune', C180, V221
  mandates, V197, P428
  merging goals, V250, P428
  meta-goals, C132, V250
  'negative-goals', C90, P314, P429
Assessing progress of strategy, C175, V213, P469

Business model, livelihood scheme, C76, C79, V257, V266, P332, P425

Changing your mind, C91, P286
Coalitions, C120, V232
Cognitive mapping
  call for action, C160, P290
  contrast, or opposite pole, C94, P290
  curiosity of spider-diagram approach, V214, P299
  embedded, deep knowledge, C133, V275, P359
  keeping up with mapping, V196, P293
  'laddering', C91, C94, P310, P389, P426
  process of managerial cognition, C149
  reasons for using interviews and cognitive maps, V242, P298
  recording meaning, V215, P293
  scheduling interviews, V210, P293
Coherence of strategy, C134, P358
  coherence with the goal system, V251
Collaborative advantage, C106, V248
Communicating strategy and dissemination
  across the whole organization, C54, V221, V263, V277, P452, P456
  publication of the strategy, V221, V222, V235, V263, V277, P456, P460
  road shows, V222, V236, P459

Competencies, distinctive, C103, V266, P304, P330, P410
 pattern of competencies, C107, P330
 potency of a competence, C109, P411
 self sustaining feedback loops, C80, P330
Computer support
 2-day computer supported workshop, V210, P383
 capture in 'real time', V242, P325
 follow on from an oval mapping workshop, V241, P327
Consultant–client relationship, V216, V249, P480
 commitment beyond the first workshop, V195, P375
 key actors, V214, V243, V249, P477
 negotiating the design, V238, P479, P481
 partners, V214, V224, P479
 seek time for review, V244, V260, P481
Continuity and strategic change, C34, P431
Coordinated and coherent thinking, C34, V213
Coordination and cooperation, C48, P425
Creativity, C58, C70, V256, P371
Critical incidents and 'Laddering', C91, P288, P389, P426
Culture of an organization, C27, V203, V213, P374
Cyclical nature of strategy making, C22, C30, V228, V262, P311, P341

Delivery of strategy
 action planning workshops, V257, P440
 check resource implications, C159, P441
 computer model to monitor progress (Strategy Delivery Support System), V242, P436
 'fine tuning' the strategy, V276, P352
 'quick wins', C168, V222, P441
 responsibilities and time-scales, C165, P441
 restructuring the organization, C171, V247, P463
 strategic actions in context, C173, P464
 strategic intent and strategic action programmes with operational tasks, C171, P466
 strategy becomes a 'hostage to fortune', C180, P456
Distinctive competencies, C103, V266, P304, P330, P410
 pattern of competencies, C107, P330
 potency of a competence, C109, P411
 self-sustaining feedback loops, C80, P330

Emergent strategizing, C4, C21, C81, V201, V209, V216, P289

 detect key assumptions and 'taken-for-granteds', C77, V202
 emergent goals, V248, P426
 emergent strategic issues, C91, P298, P329
 honour the past, C21, V257
Emotional, cognitive, commitment, C52, C54, C58, P304, P383, P424
Equivocality, C50, C67, P328, P385
Expectations setting, building trust, C55, V214, V215, V224, V225, V244, V255, P302, P307, P323, P372, P390

Facilitation
 calling note, V225, P380
 conflict, V256, P388
 contributions, V195, V239, V243, P386, P387, P400
 group feedback photographs, V234, V268, P391
 group size, V245, V249, V268, P376
 internal facilitator, V257, P381
 negotiated social relationships, C49, V227
 process and content, V194, P380
 progress, V228, V243, P388
 work of the rational analyst and the work of the social process facilitator, C46, P380
Fast strategy development, C103, P382
 deliverable strategy within the space of two days, C2, C103, V224, P329
 developing a strategy within nine days, C59, V210
Feedback properties, 'stable' dynamics, C30, C80, V218, P292, P330, P333, P354, P410
Fun, play, C73, P321, P387

Getting started, V212, P372
Goals system, C5, C95, V214, V248, V251, V277, P289, P314, P425, P456
 core goals compared with facilitative goals, C48, P432
 draft of the aspirations or goal system, C98, V197, V248, V250, V257, P329, P423
 elicitation of an emergent goal system, C92, V229, P288
 emergent goals, V248, P426
 facilitative goals, C48, V218, V250, V257, P427, P432
 'hostage to fortune', C180, V221
 mandates, V197, P428
 merging goals, V250, P428
 meta-goals, C132, V250
 'negative-goals', C90, P314, P429

Group maps, strategy maps, C67, C72, V254
  call for action, C160, P290
  challenging or 'obvious' questions, V239, P308
  label the emergent theme, V250, P311
  'laddering', P310
  merging maps, V196
  prompting group members to record their views, C101, P309
  vehicle for negotiation in groups as maps, P286
Group think, C50, P298

Interviews, C90, V242, P284
  begin with the more powerful participants, V213, P301
  cathartic device, V215, P298
  considering the language, V217, P291
  embedded assumptions and wisdom, C89, C90, P284
  'laddering', C91, C94, P310, P389, P426
  monitoring non verbals, C97, P290
  nervousness of interviewees, V213, P299
  'Oracle' question, C92, P389
  'psychological week', V210, P196, P302
  second interview, V196, V216, P297

'Laddering', C91, C94, P310, P389, P426
Learning cycle, C77, P462
Learning organization and organizational learning, C74, V213, P305

Mandates, V197, P428
Mapping, cognitive
  call for action, C160, P290
  contrast, or opposite pole, C94, P290
  curiosity of spider-diagram approach, V214, P299
  embedded, deep knowledge, C133, V275, P359
  keeping up with mapping, V196, P293
  'laddering', C91, C94, P310, P389, P426
  process of managerial cognition, C149
  reasons for using interviews and cognitive maps, V242, P298
  recording meaning, V215, P293
  scheduling interviews, V210, P293
Mapping, oval, C100, V195, V210, V227, V238, V248, V254, V267, P303, P310
  call for action, C160, P290
  challenging or 'obvious' questions, V239, P308
  cluster ovals, C101, V227, V269, P308
  group maps, strategy maps, C67, C72, V254
  label the emergent theme, V250, P311

'laddering', P310
merging maps, V196
prompting group members to record their views, C101, P309
vehicle for negotiation in groups as maps, P286
Maps, analysis of
  categories, V234, P407
  centrality, V218, P405
  clusters, V218, P407
  feedback loops, V218, P410
  hierarchical clusters, V198, P409
  merging, C72, V196, V217, P403
  orphans, V217, P402
  overview, V219, V241, V242, P415
  pre-workshop analysis, V219, P414
  potent, C109, C163, V219, V270, P411
  simplification, V222, P444
Mission statement, C110, C161, V196, V197, V277, V257, V263, P332, P429, P430, P431
Multi-organizational setting, C119, V248
Multiple perspectives, C73, C76, V202, V227, V266

'Negative-goals', C90, P289, P314, P429
Negotiated order, C48, P284, P305, P328, P399, P478
Negotiation, C11, C60, V248, P321
Networked computer support system, C60, V202, V228, V258, P336, P338, P450

'Oracle Question', C92, P288, P389
Order, negotiated, C48, P284, P305, P328, P399, P478
Organizational learning, C74, P305
Organizational memory, C41, C71, V198, V273, P321, P437, P462
Organizational politics, C46, V226
Outcomes from Strategic Management, C13, V213
Oval mapping, C100, V195, V210, V227, V238, V248, V254, V267, P303, P310
  call for action, C160, P290
  challenging or 'obvious' questions, V239, P308
  cluster ovals, C101, V227, V269, P308
  group maps, strategy maps, C67, C72, V254
  label the emergent theme, V250, P311
  'laddering', P310
  merging maps, V196
  prompting group members to record their views, C101, P309
  vehicle for negotiation in groups as maps, P286

Ownership, C15, C56, V223, V235, P320, P371

Participation in strategy making, C54, C56, C59, V201, V202, V227, V233, V238, V257, V260, P284, P376, P444
  bilateral communication, C54, V237
  duping staff, cynics, C58, V225, V227, V234
  experts, opinion formers, power brokers, saboteurs, etc., C35, C57, P377
  membership of workshop groups, C87, P376
Performance, success, indicators, C174, C175, C176, V207, V261, P445, P446, P464, P468
  assessing progress of strategy, C175, V213, P469
  qualitative indicators, C176, V261
Personal aspirations system in an occupational role-setting, C92, P288
Personal performance reviews, C165, P437, P464
Politics, organizational, C46, C47, V195, V226, P374, P477
Power, shifts in, C68, C121, P344
  social power, V256
Preferencing, V198, V228, V241, V243, V251, V258, V271, P313, P338
Procedural Justice, C53, V196, V244, P286, P374, P477
Procedural Rationality, C55, V244, V255, P329, P419, P477
Productivity of meetings, C58, V202
'Psychological week', V210, P196, P302

Recipes,
  'industry recipe', C127, V274, P356
  organizational, C27, P415
Restructuring the organization, C171, V247, P463
Review of strategy, C175, P468, P469
  computer model to monitor progress (Strategy Delivery Support System), V242, P436
  listening for the changes in the scripts used, C160, V278
  performance indicators, C174, C175, C176, V207, V261, P445, P446, P464, P468
Robustness of strategy, C134, V276

Scenario planning, alternative futures, C139, V251, V266
  choice about the number of scenarios, C152, P366
  deciding that part the environment to be considered, C140, P363

distinct scenarios, C149, V270, P366
driver events, C151, C155, V267, V270, V271
event-based focus for scenario building, V267, P361
external experts, V267, P369
identifying Key Scenario Events, C143, V206
  flip-flop events, C145, V206, V267, P362
nature of uncertainty, C147, P363
outsiders to bring an alternative view of the future, C154, V205, V267
possible futures, within the context of the mandate, V206
practical variables to monitor, C155, V271, P366
'remarkable people', C14, C154, V271, P368
scenario titles, C152, P365
structural properties and their role in determining, C81, P361
system dynamics simulation models, C149, V206, P366
Shared understanding, C50, P304, P321
Social order, C49, P305, P328, P478
Special purpose software, V215, P298
Stage management, V219, V225, V226, V239, V267, V249, P378
Staged process, V195, V223, V254, P375, P482
Stakeholder analysis, C119, V198, V261, V273
  actor influence network maps, C128, V200, V230, P342, P349
  coalitions and collaboratives, C129, V230
  categories of stakeholders, C125, P356
  'Power/Interest' star diagram, C126, V200, V231, P341, P345
  Stakeholder grid, C121, V255, P314
    appropriate level of dis-aggregation, C124, C125, V199, V230, P345, P356
    disposition of potential stakeholders, C124, V200, P345
    players, C122, C124, C126, C131, V201, V230, V273, P345
Stakeholder management, C129, V198, V236, V262, V274, P355
  game theory analysis, C133., P435
  role-think, C133, V231, V273, P342, P350
    extended 'role-think', V273, V276, P354, P435
    managerial thinking of competitors, V274
  stakeholder workshops, V205, V244, V254, P355, P434

Strategic intent, C39, C110, V195, V247, P424

Strategic issues, C90, V197, V218, V223, P329, P403
  cluster or theme, V214, P289
  elaborate the issues, C101, P309
  hierarchical map, V227, V239, P311
  measuring the level of agreement, V244, P338
  nature of the strategic issues, C91, V198, P290, P298

Strategic programmes
  evaluating strategic programmes and strategic options, C159, V206, V260, P441
  resource implications, C164, P441

Strategy delivery
  action planning workshops, V257, P440
  check resource implications, C159, P441
  computer model to monitor progress (Strategy Delivery Support System), V242, P436
  'fine tuning' the strategy, V276, P352
  'quick wins', C168, V222, P441
  responsibilities and time-scales, C165, P441
  restructuring the organization, C171, V247, P463
  strategic actions in context, C173, P464

  strategic intent and strategic action programmes with operational tasks, C171, P466
  strategy becomes a 'hostage to fortune', C180, P456

Strategy delivery support system (SDSS), C40, C159, C165, C172, V222, V242, P334, P436, P463
  responsibilities are assigned and delivery dates agreed, C165, V260, P441

Strategy maps, C98, P285, P329, P325

System dynamics modelling, C149, V206, P366

System of strategies, C5, V258

Team development, building, C17, C60, V194, V213, V225, V231, P374

Theories in use, theories-in-action, espoused theories, C37, C81, C89, P284, P286, P303, P353, P427

Transitional object, C67, P286

Trust, V215, V223, P293, P480

Winners and losers, saboteurs, C23, V275

Workshops
  purpose of, V245, P385
  standard one-day, V239, P382
  two-day workshop, V223, P383